THE IRAN-IRAQ WAR

THE GREATEST LAND WAR OF THE LATE TWENTIETH CENTURY

E. R. Hooton, Tom Cooper and
Farzin Nadimi with Bob Mackenzie

Helion & Company

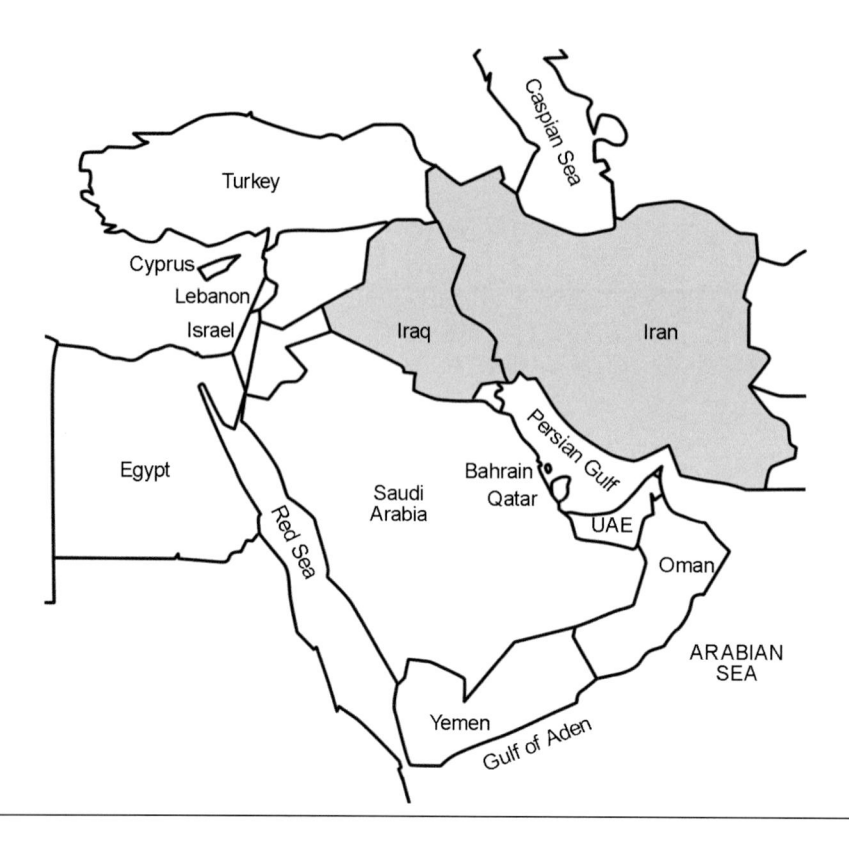

Helion & Company Limited
Unit 8 Amherst Business Centre
Budbrooke Road
Warwick CV34 5WE
England
Tel. 01926 499 619
Email: info@helion.co.uk
Website: www.helion.co.uk
Twitter: @helionbooks
Blog: blog.helion.co.uk

Published by Helion & Company 2022
Designed and typeset by Farr out Publications, Wokingham, Berkshire
Cover designed by Paul Hewitt, Battlefield Design (www.battlefield-design.co.uk)

Text © E. R. Hooton, Tom Cooper and Farzin Nadimi with Bob Mackenzie 2022
Colour artwork © Tom Cooper, Radek Panchartek, Peter Penev and Renato Dalmaso 2022
Maps drawn by George Anderson © Helion & Company 2022

Every reasonable effort has been made to trace copyright holders and to obtain their permission for the use of copyright material. The author and publisher apologize for any errors or omissions in this work, and would be grateful if notified of any corrections that should be incorporated in future reprints or editions of this book.

ISBN 978-1-80451-156-5

British Library Cataloguing-in-Publication Data.
A catalogue record for this book is available from the British Library.

All rights reserved. No part of this publication may be reproduced, stored in a retrieval system, or transmitted, in any form, or by any means, electronic, mechanical, photocopying, recording or otherwise, without the express written consent of Helion & Company Limited.

For details of other military history titles published by Helion & Company Limited contact the above address, or visit our website: http://www.helion.co.uk.

We always welcome receiving book proposals from prospective authors.

CONTENTS

Glossary and abbreviations	v
Introduction to the special edition	vii

PART I

1	Background to a Bloody War	8
2	Two Armies	14
3	From Border War to Invasion	30
4	The Invasion of Khuzestan	37
5	The Iranians Strike Back	56
6	The Writing on the Wall	67
7	Disaster for Iraq	77
	Colour Section 1	94
8	An Unholy Bloodbath	100
9	Battles in the Marshes	117
10	The Slough of Despond	134
11	The Thriving Armourers	146
12	The Brilliant Blow	155
	Colour Section 2	178
13	Iran's Last Chance	184
14	Two Armies	209
15	Saddam's First Blow	222
16	Iranian Burnout	233
17	End Game	243
	Colour Section 3	252

PART II: THE FORGOTTEN FRONTS

18	The Opening Operations	257
19	Private Wars	270
20	The Central Front 1982–1987	277
21	The Northern Front 1982–1987	294
22	Iran's Last Chance	301
23	The Kurdish Front 1980–1988	308
24	The Last Battles 1988	319
	Colour Section 4	329

Appendices

I	Arms Acquisitions and Ground Forces Equipment of Iran	335
II	Organisation of the Iranian Army	344
III	Organisation of the Islamic Revolutionary Guards Corps (IRGC)	356
IV	Iraqi Weapons Deliveries	359
V	Iraqi Organisation	372

Colour Section 5	382
Bibliography	390
Notes	395

GLOSSARY AND ABBREVIATIONS

AEW	airborne early warning	**HE**	high explosive
AFGC	Armed Forces General Command (Iraq)	**IFF**	identification friend or foe
AFV	armoured fighting vehicle	**IFV**	infantry fighting vehicle
AK/AKM	*Automat Kalashnikova* (general designation for a class of Soviet or former Eastern Bloc-manufactured assault rifles)	**IrAAC**	Iraqi Army Aviation Corps
		IrAF	Iraqi Air Force
		IRI	Islamic Republic of Iran
An	Antonov (the design bureau led by Oleg Antonov, USSR)	**IRIA**	Islamic Republic of Iran Army
		IRIAA	Islamic Republic of Iran Army Aviation
APC	armoured personnel carrier	**IRIAF**	Islamic Republic of Iran Air Force
AS-7 Kyle	ASCC/NATO-codename for Soviet-made Kh-28 ASM	**IRIN**	Islamic Republic of Iran Navy
		IrN	Iraqi Navy
AS-14 Kedge	ASCC/NATO-codename for Soviet-made Kh-29 or 9M721 ASM	**LSM**	landing ship medium
		MANPADS	man-portable air defence system
ASM	air-to-surface missile	**MBT**	main battle tank
ASCC	Air Standardisation Coordinating Committee (USA, Great Britain, Australia, New Zealand)	**MHz**	Megahertz, millions of cycles per second
		MiG	Mikoyan i Gurevich (the design bureau led by Artyom Ivanovich Mikoyan and Mikhail Iosifovich Gurevich, also known as OKB-155 or MMZ 'Zenit', USSR)
AT-2A Swatter	ASCC/NATO-codename for Soviet-made 3M11 Falanga ATGM		
AT-2B Swatter	ASCC/NATO-codename for Soviet-made 9K17 Skorpion ATGM		
		MLR	main line of resistance
AT-3 Sagger	ASCC/NATO-codename for Soviet-made 9K11 Malyutka ATGM	**MRLS**	multiple rocket launch system
		NATO	North Atlantic Treaty Organisation
AT-4 Spigot	ASCC/NATO-codename for Soviet-made 9K111 Fagot ATGM	**NFOHQ**	Northern Forward Operational Headquarters (Iran)
AT-5 Spandrel	ASCC/NATO-codename for Soviet-made 9M113 Konkurs ATGM	**OKB**	*Opytno-Konstrooktorskoye Byuro* (design bureau, USSR)
ATGM	anti-tank guided missile	**OPEC**	Organization of the Petroleum Exporting Countries
AVLB	armoured vehicle launched bridge		
AWACS	airborne early warning and control system	**ORBAT**	Order of Battle
BRDM	*Boyevaya Razvedyvatelnaya Dozornaya Mashina* (combat reconnaissance patrol vehicle, Soviet reconnaissance car)	**RCC**	Revolutionary Command Council (Iraq)
		RGWHQ	Ramadan Guerrilla Warfare Headquarters (Iran)
C3	command, control and communication	**RPG**	rocket propelled grenade
CAS	close air support	**SA-2 Guideline**	ASCC/NATO-codename for Soviet-made S-75 family of SAMs
CAP	combat air patrol		
CIA	Central Intelligence Agency (USA)	**SA-3 Goa**	ASCC/NATO-codename for Soviet-made S-125 family of SAMs
COIN	counterinsurgency		
COMINT	communications intelligence	**SA-6 Gainful**	ASCC/NATO-codename for Soviet-made 2K12 Kub SAM
CSG/GSG	Combat Support/General Support Group (IRIAA formations)		
		SA-7 Grail	ASCC/NATO-codename for Soviet-made 9K32 Strela-2 MANPAD
DIA	Defence Intelligence Agency (USA)		
ECM	electronic countermeasures	**SA-8 Gecko**	ASCC/NATO-codename for Soviet-made 9K33M Osa SAM
ESM	electronic support measures		
ELINT	electronic intelligence	**SA-9 Gaskin**	ASCC/NATO-codename for Soviet-made 9K31 Strela-1 SAM
FAC	forward air controller		
FAC	fast attack craft (warship)	**SA-13 Gopher**	ASCC/NATO-codename for Soviet-made 9K35 Strela-10 SAM
FEBA	forward edge of battle area		
GCC	Gulf Cooperation Council	**SAM**	surface to air missile
GMID	General Military Intelligence Directorate (Iraq)	**SFOH**	Southern Front Operations Headquarters (Iraq)

SEAL	Sea, Air, Land (Naval Commandos)
S-Hour	Arabic for Zero (*Sifr*) Hour
SIGINT	signals intelligence
SS-N-2 Styx	ASCC/NATO-codename for Soviet-made P-15 Termit anti-ship SSM
Silkworm	ASCC/NATO-codename for Chinese-made HY-2/C.601 Hai Ying anti-ship SSM
SSM	surface-to-surface missile
Su	Sukhoi (the design bureau led by Pavel Ossipovich Sukhoi, also known as OKB-51, USSR)
TAOR	Tactical Area of Responsibility
TOW	Tube-launched, Opticall tracked, Wire-guided (US-made BGM-71 ATGM)
UAV	unmanned aerial vehicle
USSR	Union of Soviet Socialist Republics
Y-Day	Arabic for D-Day (from Yom/Day)

INTRODUCTION TO THE SPECIAL EDITION

The Iran-Iraq War, fought from 1980 to 1988, was the longest conventional war of the twentieth century. It was one of the most bitterly contested wars and remains one of the most fateful conflicts in the Middle East, strongly influencing the fate of both belligerents to the present day. Regardless of how much of its history has been published, it remains hard to summarise. Essentially, in September 1980, Iraq decided to invade Iran at a time when the latter was in a state of civil war, unrest, and chaos and was thus massively weakened, despite its immense military build-up of the 1970s. Iraq did so without much of a plan, and things rapidly went wrong. The invasion turned into a costly failure that nearly bankrupted the government in Baghdad, leaving it overdependent on extensive sponsorship by the oil-rich states of the Persian Gulf. By 1982, Iran had not only recovered most of the terrain lost but was in possession of the strategic initiative. For the next five years, the Iranians launched ever more powerful attempts to invade Iraq and break the back of its armed forces. Ultimately, Iran failed, buying time for Iraq to recover and then deliver a series of devastating blows against both the Iranian economy and armed forces that, in 1988, destroyed Iran's ability to continue fighting.

There are plenty of reasons why the Iran–Iraq War remains one of the most intriguing modern armed conflicts – for both professionals and enthusiasts alike. Early on, Iran was almost exclusively equipped with some of the best weapon systems that the USA and Great Britain could offer. Its armed forces were built-up, trained, and organised based on US experience from the Vietnam War, and Israeli experience from the Arab–Israeli Wars. On the contrary, Iraq was foremost equipped with weapon systems imported from the USSR and widely considered by Western observers to be fighting in the Soviet style. Therefore, many foreign observers expected that by monitoring the experiences of this war one could deduct useful conclusions about the possible outcome of a major showdown between the US-led forces of NATO and Soviet-led forces of the Warsaw Pact in central Europe.

Actually, this was just one of the illusions about this war. Not only did the Iraqis actually operate on the basis of a mixture of British military doctrine (as many of their officers had been trained by the British) and their own experiences from wars with Israel and the Kurds, but the longer the conflict went on the more the nature of the combat changed. After the first two years of the war, the regular Iranian armed forces were worn out to a degree where they ceased playing a dominant role on the battlefield. Henceforth, it was the Islamic Revolutionary Guards Corps that took over the command of the battlefield on the Iranian side. Initially, its commanders were convinced that the religious zeal of their combatants alone was sufficient to grant them a victory over Iraq. Combat experience taught them better, and thus they began expanding their organisation and improving their armament and tactics. However, they never managed to improve their doctrine nor their strategy – and the mass of their offensive operations proved little more than costly blunders. On the other side, the longer the war went on, the more dependent Iraq became upon ever more sophisticated weapon systems – foremost from France but, later on, from the USSR too.

Ultimately, the Iran-Iraq War ended in a draw, with both sides exhausted to a degree where long-term effects remain strongly felt until today. Neither the economy of Iran or Iraq, nor the Iranian or Iraqi armed forces have ever recovered from all of the blows that they suffered, and the Iraqi government hurriedly involved the country and its armed forces in the next adventure, thus threading the path to the ultimate downfall of the country of the last 20 years.

In the wake of the success of the four volumes about the Iran–Iraq War published in the Middle East@War book series, we have decided to republish these in the form of one hardback volume, with added appendices detailing the equipment and structure of the two armies, and thus offer our readers the opportunity to read what is widely considered as the most authoritative, most comprehensive, most detailed, and best-illustrated military history of the ground warfare in this conflict in one volume. Packed with information drawn primarily from Iranian and Iraqi sources, and heavily illustrated – mostly in colour – this volume provides an exclusive and uniquely precise insight into an affair certain to continue influencing the future of both of involved countries for decades to come.

PART I
1
BACKGROUND TO A BLOODY WAR

For 94 months between 1980 and 1988, Iran and Iraq fought the longest, uninterrupted, conventional conflict of the twentieth century, which cost hundreds of thousands of lives. It was called The Imposed War by the Iranians, the Great Qadisiyya or Qadisiyyat Saddam by the Iraqis, or simply the Gulf War, until that term was pressganged to describe Iraq's 1990–1991 and 2003 conflicts with the American-led Coalition.[1]

The conflict may be the last conventional war which involved masses of men and equipment in a direct struggle, and the cost was huge. Western post-war studies usually calculate Iraqi casualties as varying widely between 190,000–1,040,000, including 150,000–340,000 killed, with another 70,000 POWs, and Iranian casualties at 1,050,000–1,930,000, including 450,000–730,000 killed, while 45,000 were taken prisoner.[2] Such figures are much inflated, for official Iranian publications cite 1,133,000 casualties, including 188,000 dead and 945,000 wounded, with 73,000 missing military personnel. Not usually included in such reports are around 90,000 civilian casualties, including 11,000 dead. In comparison, no official data on Iraqi casualties was ever released.[3] Furthermore, the conflict caused about 2.5 million refugees and cost $2.28 billion, of which $2.4 billion was spent on weapons.[4]

The region is one of the Middle East's cockpits because the Tigris-Euphrates plain, which forms the heartland of Iraq, has long been a cultural watershed. It marked the fiercely contested eastern boundary of the Roman, Arab and Ottoman Empires against the Parthians and Persians, as well as the fault line in the Islamic schism between Sunni and Shi'a. Modern Iran and Iraq were born as monarchies after the First World War, with growing oil wealth, but both were occupied by the Allied Powers during the Second World War. In the post-war world, each sought to buttress its independence from external pressure, but followed very different routes which laid the foundations for this war.[5]

Centuries of the Ottoman Empire and decades of quasi-colonial rule of the British and French over territories predominantly populated by Arabs and Moslems in the Middle East, and the

Abadan refinery – at the time one of largest in the world – seen in the 1940s, with the Shatt al-Arab in foreground, right. (Mark Lepko collection)

The first indication of new relations between Iran and the USA occurred in 1967, when Tehran was granted permission to place an order for 32 McDonnell Douglas F-4D Phantom II interceptors. Ten years later, nearly 230 Phantom IIs of three major variants formed the backbone of the Iranian Air Force. (Tom Cooper collection)

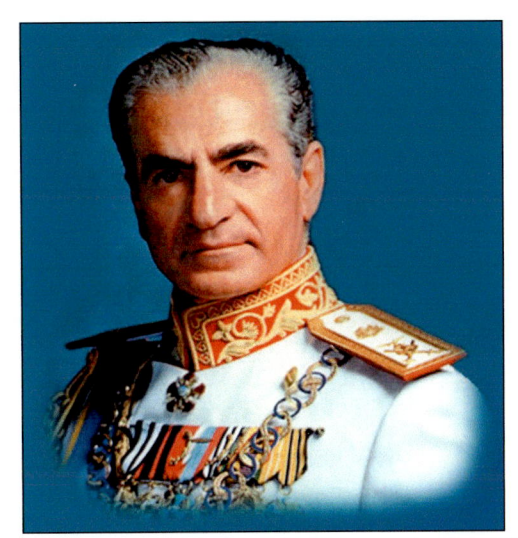

PART I: BACKGROUND TO A BLOODY WAR

Shah Mohammad Reza Pahlavi, Emperor of Iran, and a close US ally for nearly 30 years, played an influential role in pushing through a number of spectacular arms deals that brought the latest US technology to his country in the 1970s. (Mark Lepko collection)

Saddam Hussein Abd al-Majid at-Tikriti played a key role in the 1968 coup (also known as the '17th July Revolution') that brought the Ba'ath Party to power in Iraq and installed himself as the fifth President of the country in July 1979. (Mark Lepko collection)

After spending more than 15 years in exile for his opposition to the Shah, Grand Ayatollah Seyed Ruhollah Musavi Khomeini (known in the West as Ayatollah Khomeini) became the Supreme Leader of the Islamic Republic of Iran – the new highest-ranking political and religious authority of the nation. (Mark Lepko collection)

creation of a number of artificial nations (including Lebanon, Syria, Iraq, Jordan and Palestine) with arbitrary borders instead of a unified Arab state widely demanded by the local population, resulted in the spread of pan-Arab nationalism and anti-imperialism during the 1950s. However, the rule of the major protagonist of such ideas, Egyptian President Gamal Abdel Nasser, disappointed many and created plenty of unrest, especially in Iraq and Syria. Amid latent political instability that spread through the Middle East during the early 1960s, and in the light of the creation of Israel in 1947–1949, a number of newly emerging Arab leaders usurped the ideology of radical change along the ideals of the Arab Socialist Renaissance Party (al-Ba'ath al-Arabi al-Ishtiraki, colloquially the Ba'ath Party). Ba'ath regimes established their control over Iraq and Syria: while stabilising the political situation and resulting in a period of unprecedented economic growth, they maintained themselves in power with the help of police states.

Mohammed Reza Shah Pahlavi, ruler of Iran from 1943, regarded Moscow as the prime threat to his regime and placed himself firmly on the Western side during the Cold War. He exploited Iran's geopolitical location to strengthen its position both within the Persian Gulf (called the Arabian Gulf by his Arab neighbours) and Southwest Asia, while also seeking to modernise the country's economy and social structure. Neighbouring Iraq was his closest rival; their relations were marred by economic rivalry and religious friction, because most Iranian Moslems are Shi'a, and because of the Shah's unofficial support for Israel. With the decline of British power in the early 1970s, and emboldened by the administration of US President Richard B. Nixon, the Shah of Iran sought to become the dominant military and political power in the Middle East. Sending a clear signal to all neighbours, in November 1971, only a day after the official British withdrawal from the Persian Gulf, the Iranian military seized Abu Mussa and Tunb Islands in the Hormuz Straits. Although held by the Persians for most of the last few thousand years, these strategically positioned islands were meanwhile claimed by the United Arab Emirates (UAE), another British artificial creation, combining six minor sheikhdoms into a federation that was developed into a major financial powerhouse in the area.

Exploiting military links between Baghdad and Moscow for his purposes, the Shah then sought to undermine the Ba'ath regime in Iraq by supporting Kurdish tribesmen in the north of that country. At odds with successive Iraqi governments since the country's creation, the Kurds launched a major uprising that sucked 160,000 of the Iraqi Army's 200,000 men into a campaign waged through most of 1974 and into early 1975. The then Foreign Minister of the Iraqi government, but already the actual strongman in Baghdad, Saddam Hussein al-Takriti (usually known as Saddam) would later claim this war cost Iraq up to 17,000 casualties and most of the national military's ammunition stocks.[6]

Eventually, the governments in Baghdad and Tehran accepted an Algerian-brokered agreement on 6 March 1975. Like many Iraqis, Saddam regarded it as a personal humiliation, for the terms were dictated by Tehran – meanwhile further emboldened by immense purchases of arms from the USA. Iran ceased military support for the Kurds but would now share in control of the Shatt al-Arab (the Shatt), the waterway between the two states (called the River Arvand by the Iranians). Baghdad had always claimed exclusive authority over the Shatt, which leads to Iraq's main port of Basra and the major Iranian ports of Khorramshahr and Abadan. The agreement also called upon both countries to formally define their

The Iranian order for 80 Grumman F-14A Tomcat interceptors and associated AIM-54A Phoenix long-range air-to-air missiles, placed in 1973–1974, was another high point of US-Iranian relations of that time. (Tom Cooper collection)

land frontier, which Iraq interpreted as Tehran's willingness to cede some 240km² of disputed border territory around Qasr-e Shirin and Mehran.

The Iranians sent a delegation to Baghdad, which led to the Treaty on International Borders and Good Neighbourly Relations on 13 June 1975. Known as the Algiers Treaty, as it was brokered by the Algerians and signed in their capital, yet within three days Iraq sought to improve its terms at bayonet point. The army threw a pontoon bridge across the Shatt and used it to establish a bridgehead in Khuzestan, but the Iranians crushed the incursion within two days after 88 Iraqis and three Iranians were killed.[7] While railing against the new 'imperialists', Baghdad could do little as Tehran now dominated the region, boosted by its economic and demographic power. Iran produced 5.2 million barrels of oil per day in 1978, compared with Iraq's 2.6 million, and had more than 39 million people, of whom 5.1 million men could serve in the armed forces; this compared with an Iraqi population of 13.5 million, of whom only 1.7 million could be called to the colours.[8]

In the uneasy peace which followed the Algiers Treaty, the Shah used the vast wealth created by the 1973–1974 oil crisis to further strengthen and modernise his military forces and industry, spending about $15.5 billion on equipment between 1975 and 1979 (compared with Iraq's $8.1 billion).[9] The Ba'ath Party regime in Baghdad also faced a problem with the Shi'a, who made up 50–65 percent of the population and were increasingly restive under Sunni rule. Many Iraqi Ba'athists feared that Tehran might encourage an uprising of the Shi'a. Saddam's cousin and mentor, President Ahmad Hassan al-Bakr, reportedly sought a conciliatory approach, but hardliners led by Saddam engineered his overthrow in July 1979: they replaced him as president and began to persecute both the Shi'a and communists.[10]

A regime change with tremendous consequences for the entire Middle East then took place in Iran. The Shah's efforts to modernise the country and its military were compromised by the end of the oil boom and declining oil prices. This further exacerbated already high social divisions in the country, and resulted in large-scale protests through 1978. Already facing massive criticism for often brutal methods of ruling his country, Mohammed Reza Shah Pahlavi was surprised by the protests and determined to use troops to suppress the unrest. But the armed forces, although personally dominated by the Shah, were reluctant to confront civilian unrest and lacked the training for this role. A few lukewarm attempts to quash protests were made, the most notorious of which resulted in 'Black Friday' on 8 September 1978. Before long however, elements of the military began joining the masses, making the country essentially ungovernable.

In times of trouble, the people tended to turn to God. While much of this mass protest movement was organised and run by very different political parties, religion began to play an ever more important role. Always strongly influenced by their religious leaders (ayatollahs, imams and mullahs), the urban and rural poor joined the calls for the replacement of the Shah's secular regime with one based upon Islamic spiritual values. On 16 January 1979, Mohammed Reza Shah Pahlavi felt forced to leave the country: he went into exile in the USA and then Egypt, where he would die in July 1980.[11]

Meanwhile, on 1 February 1979, the spiritual leader of the Iranian Shi'a, Ayatollah Ruhollah al-Musavi al-Khomeini, returned from years of exile to a tumultuous reception of over a million people in Tehran. In the course of a fierce power struggle during the following months of this Islamic Revolution – some of which included firefights between members of different Iranian political parties – Khomeni established himself in power over the theocratic Islamic Republic of Iran (IRI), aiming to create 'God's Kingdom on Earth' in the form of an 'Islamic imamate'.[12]

For any opponents of the new rule – whether active, or even only suspected – the newly declared IRI became a literal 'hell on earth'. Those seeking greater secular power or demanding regional autonomy faced widespread arrests, endless brutalities and summary executions. Unsurprisingly, some – especially Kurds in north-western Iran – responded by launching insurgencies, while others reacted with terrorism.

Inevitably, the revolutionary fervour crossed the border to Iraq, which soon harboured many opponents of the clerics. While within Iraq's Shi'a community a militant organisation, the al Daawa al-Ismaliya (Islamic Call or Daawa) Party, began a terror campaign. Their spiritual leader, Ayatollah Muhammad Baqer al-Sadr, was a personal friend of Khomeini and pointedly noted that 'other tyrants' would see their day of reckoning. Pro-Khomeini Shi'a demonstrations in June 1979 led to a crackdown with numerous arrests including al-Sadr. On 30 March 1980, Baghdad made membership of Daawa a capital offence. The following day, the Daawa Party tried unsuccessfully to assassinate Iraq's Foreign

PART I: BACKGROUND TO A BLOODY WAR

Colloquially known as the 'Islamic Revolution', public unrest in Iran in 1978–1979 was originally organised by a number of diverse groups, including not only Islamists but also several leftist political parties. (Albert Grandolini collection)

October 1979, Saddam set out his stall when he publicly demanded the abrogation of the Algiers Treaty, the restoration of 'Iraqi rights' over the Shatt, the evacuation of Abu Musa and the Tunbs, as well as full autonomy both for Iran's Kurds of the Kordestan Province and the Sunni Arabs of Khuzestan Province which borders the Shatt. Tehran naturally rejected these demands and tensions rose steadily. Then on 6 November 1979, two days after the US Embassy in Tehran was occupied and its staff taken hostage, Iraqi consulate offices in Kermanshah and Khorramshahr were seized. In March 1980, Iraq and Iran expelled each other's ambassadors and the diplomatic war escalated, although they did not formally break off diplomatic relations until June that year. This followed Iraq's first elections since the monarchy was overthrown in 1958, which led to a Ba'athist majority and strengthened Saddam's control over the country while providing a veneer of popular support.

Minister and Deputy Premier Tariq Aziz, which led Saddam in retaliation to execute al-Sadr.[13]

Opponents of the Iraqi and Iranian regimes traditionally found sanctuary across the respective border. Indeed, Khomeini had been expelled from Iraq following the Algiers Treaty, so naturally each side accused the other of supporting their opponents. Saddam hoped the new regime in Tehran would be more flexible on the land-border provisions of the Algiers Treaty, but the revolutionary regime focused upon internal threats, despite small-scale border clashes which began even as Saddam assumed power. On 31

Although some Western observers recently concluded that Saddam's decision to invade Iran was essentially a 'snap-shot' reaction, taken in a matter of only two days, it was actually a well-thought-out action. Beginning to regard himself as a new Salahaddin (the

A view of downtown Baghdad, the capital of the Republic of Iraq, showing the Jamahiriya Bridge, seen in the mid-1970s when the city was the epicentre of a rapidly developing nation. (Mark Lepko collection)

11

In an attempt to match the US-Iranian partnership, Iraq signed several treaties of friendship and trade with Moscow during the 1970s. Amongst others, these resulted in the delivery of Mikoyan i Gurevich MiG-23MS interceptors to the IrAF. Iraqi expectations for this type were greatly disappointed as it proved no match for US-made F-14As acquired by Iran. (Farzin Nadimi collection)

Tikrit-born An-Nasir Salah ad-Din Yusuf iby Ayyub, better known in the West as Saladin), Saddam intended to exploit his country's economic and military power to lead a renaissance in which he would restore the Arabs to a leading role on the world stage.[14] By the early summer of 1980, Egypt's political accommodation with Israel had undermined that country's prestige in the Arab world, Jordan was Iraq's traditional friend, while negotiations for a union with Syria failed. This left Iran, Baghdad's traditional foe, as an obstacle to Saddam's ambitions and one which now sought to undermine his regime. With this arch enemy – and especially its military – in a state of chaos, there was a unique opportunity for Iraq to exploit the situation. This becomes obvious when studying such Iraqi documents as a report from the General Military Intelligence Directorate (Mudiriyyat al-Istikhabarat al-Askariyya al-Amma, GMID) on the state of Iran during the first half of 1980, issued in July of that year.[15] This noted the country was racked by internecine fighting as the economy collapsed, aggravated by Khomeini's ill health and imminent 'departure', which was envisaged within the next two years. The report played into Saddam's hands, 'confirming' it was time for the Iraqi military to make a show of force along the border and draw in the remaining meagre Iranian military resources, thus accelerating regime change in Tehran.

This decision was communicated at a joint meeting of the Ba'ath Party and State Command on 6 July at Abu Ghraib, 32km west of Baghdad, although Saddam, together with Iraqi Air Force (IrAF), Air Defence and Navy commanders were absent.[16] Attending this meeting were Defence Minister General Adnan Khairallah Talfah (usually referred to as Khairallah), Army Chief-of-Staff General Jabbah al-Shanshal and Operations chief Lieutenant General Abdul al-Jabar al-Asadi.[17] The following day, corps and divisional commanders were informed that Saddam intended to invade Iran to pre-empt an Iranian attack, which would encourage Shi'a rebel activity. According to Lieutenant General Ra'ad Majid Rashid al-Hamdani, many of these military leaders were convinced war was inevitable due to 'Iran's continuous attacks'. It was later claimed that while all the corps and divisional commanders regarded war as inevitable, none were enthusiastic, but, according to Major General Aladdin Hussein Makki Khamas, only the 7th Infantry Division commander, Brigadier Nayar al-Kharyranyi (al-Khazraji), raised serious concerns about the operation's prospects. He noted the army had focused upon counterinsurgency for the best part of a decade and would take two years to regain proficiency in conventional operations. The others, fearing Saddam's wrath, reprimanded him for openly expressing such pessimism, although it is likely that most shared these very justified concerns.

Shanshal was assigned the task of planning operations, but although described as a good staff officer and instructor he was also said to be a bad military leader with a '1940s mentality', while the British Defence Attaché to Baghdad noted in 1981 that he had served for 10 years and 'he is getting older and fatter'.[18] He sensibly delegated the task to Asadi, a British Staff School graduate regarded as 'an excellent officer'.[19]

Asadi did not, as some claimed, simply rewrite a British staff exercise in the Baghdad War College or the 1941 Anglo-Indian Army invasion of Persia.[20] The Iraqis had long prepared cross-border contingency plans, which focused upon seizing the main communications hubs in western Iran together with the Bytaq and Dezful passes in the Zagros Mountains.[21] The growing strength of the Iranian Army forced major revisions of these plans during Bakr's presidency. The objective now was simply to occupy Khuzestan, which had a large ethnic Arab population and was more accessible to mechanised forces, while its oil wealth made it a valuable strategic asset.

Asadi retained this element for Operation Qadisiyya II, but adjusted it to meet Saddam's political aims, which resembled those of Egypt's President Gamal Abdel Nasser when he ordered his military to deploy in the Sinai in May 1967: as a game of political chess. Saddam aimed to force Tehran to renegotiate the Algiers Treaty in Iraq's favour by seizing territory as a bargaining counter. Asadi's plan reflected this and envisaged a four-to-six-week operation in which light forces would first cross the border and penetrate some 5km to detect, locate and reduce enemy reserves. The heavy mechanised

Hardened by years of war against the Kurds and the October 1973 War with Israel, and equipped with reasonably advanced fighter-bombers of Soviet origin, IrAF pilots considered themselves the elite of the Iraqi military. This group of fliers from No. 5 or No. 44 Squadron are in front of a Sukhoi Su-20M (serial number 2077) in summer 1980. (Tom Cooper collection)

forces would then advance 10–20km into Iran in what have been described as 'tank raids', with each division given a city or major town as an objective. Saddam anticipated the Iranians would strip troops from the interior to stop the invaders; this would weaken resistance to popular uprisings, which would establish a secular government more compliant to Iraqi demands. The plan's great flaw was the assumption the new government would be more compliant; it ignored profound Iranian nationalism.[22]

Saddam's timing of the offensive would have ominous echoes of Operation Barbarossa, Hitler's invasion of Russia in 1941, where the Wehrmacht's initial success was followed by stubborn and bitter resistance which caused it to be stopped by the harsh Russian winter. Saddam's timing was undoubtedly driven by meteorological conditions, for summer temperatures in Khuzestan, the prime theatre, can reach 45–50°C.[23] However, during the winter, the major rivers are swollen by rain and water from the mountains, while in the north, the troops would also face ice and snow. Iraqi planners may have foreseen the weather as an ally to hamstring the Iranian response, but only if Baghdad's troops achieved all their objectives before the weather turned, rather like Hitler and Moscow in October 1941. From late September, the temperature drops to around 35–40°C, but there is only a narrow window of opportunity before the winter rains turn desert into marshland and confine all movement to roads on embankments. Between June and September, there is virtually no rain in western Khuzestan, but the monthly total in the Ahwaz-Abadan area, in which Ahwaz receives approximately 33 percent of the rainfall, shows 5.7mm in October, 26.15mm in November, 41.65mm in December and 43.8mm in January. The rainfall gradually eases into March.[24]

2
TWO ARMIES

While nominally an instrument of national foreign policy, the Iraqi military was primarily an internal security force.[1] During the Arab-Israeli Wars of 1948–1949, in June 1967 and in October 1973, the Iraqi Republic despatched its military forces against Israel, but Israeli and most Western reporting usually rates their performance as the 'worst of all Arab forces'.[2] However, official and unofficial Iraqi sources stress the Iraqi Air Force (IrAF) fared much better than usually assessed.

The losses the Iraqi Army suffered during the October 1973 war were quickly replaced by rapid purchases from Czechoslovakia and the Soviet Union, which included about 800 T-54/55, 1,300 T-62 and 155 T-72 main battle tanks (MBT), 1,600 BTR-60/BTR-152 wheeled and 200 BTR-50 tracked armoured personnel carriers (APC), as well as 620 BMP tracked infantry fighting vehicles (IFV), by 1980. Substantial quantities of artillery were also supplied to give Iraq 900 guns, including 126 D-30 122mm howitzers, 60 D-74 122mm guns, 400 M-46 130mm guns, 96 ML-20, 75 D-20 and 36 D-1 152mm howitzers, and nine S-23 180mm guns, supported by 90 multiple launch rocket systems (MLRS); 36 BM-21s and 54 BM-13s.[3]

Impressed by US-made M109 and M110 self-propelled howitzers imported by Iran, Baghdad sought similar equipment and in 1978 placed orders for 50 2S1 Gvozdika (Carnation) 122mm self-propelled howitzers and 50 2S3 Akatsiya (Acacia) 152mm self-propelled guns.

Only two batteries of these were in service with the 6th Armoured Division by 1980, but none saw service before 1982.[4] Other equipment was purchased from Czechoslovakia, including 395 OT-62 Topas tracked APCs (with 70 ambulance versions), and 386 OT-64 SKOT wheeled APCs, most of which were delivered, but negotiations for 100 T-54A tanks (T-55M) apparently failed.[5] Overall, Ba'athist relations with the Soviet Union and its allies were always stormy, and thus Soviet advisors were never permitted to work with Iraqi military units.

Baghdad also sought to find alternative sources of arms. Following lengthy negotiations with Paris, in 1968 Iraq contracted Panhard for 185 AML-60/90 reconnaissance vehicles, 205 M-3 light wheeled APCs and 100 ERC-TH anti-armour missile vehicles. In the mid-1970s, orders were also placed for French aircraft and missiles.[6] The Iraqi Army also purchased 200 Engesa EE-9 Cascavel reconnaissance vehicles from Brazil, with deliveries beginning in 1979.[7] The strategic movement of heavy armour would be aided by the expansion of the tank transporter fleet from 205 West German Fauns in 1973 to about 1,000 in 1986.[8]

This equipment meant that by 1980, Baghdad had momentarily achieved military equality, if not superiority, with Iran, fielding an army of some 200,000 men plus 256,000 reservists, supported by about 2,600 tanks, a similar number of APCs and IFVs, and 800 artillery pieces.[9] This equipment was operated by 12 divisions controlled by three corps headquarters, with a further six independent manoeuvre brigades. Another independent brigade was assigned to the Navy, while two missile brigades operated Soviet-made 9K52 Luna-M (ASCC/NATO codename 'FROG-7') and R-17E (ASCC/NATO codename 'SS-1' 'Scud') surface-to-surface missiles.

The three corps commands and their divisions were distributed as follows:

> I Corps with headquarters in Kirkuk, in control of 2nd, 4th and 7th Mountain Divisions, the 8th and reinforced 11th Infantry Divisions, 12th Armoured Division and 31st and 32nd

Some of the first modern armoured vehicles of the Imperial Iranian Army were US-made M24 Chafee light tanks, one of which is seen in this photograph from the early 1970s. By 1980, they had been replaced by the British-made Scorpions and the M24s were instead used as static pillboxes along the border with Iraq. (Albert Grandolini collection)

PART I: TWO ARMIES

The Chieftain was the backbone of the Iranian armoured formations, especially six battalions assigned to the 92nd Armoured Division deployed in Khuzestan, close to the Iraqi border. Other units equipped with the type included the 16th and the 81st Armoured Divisions, and the 37th Armoured Brigade. The 88th Brigade was in the process of preparing to convert to the much more advanced Shir Iran MBT when the Shah was toppled. (Tom Cooper collection)

Special Forces Brigades. The corps had a total of 21 manoeuvre brigades, which were smaller than their IRIA equivalents.

II Corps controlled the strategic reserve and was headquartered in Baghdad. It controlled the 3rd, 6th and 10th Armoured Divisions with a total of 11 manoeuvre brigades; the 10th Armoured Brigade and the 17th SF Brigade. The 10th Armoured Brigade supported the Republican Guards Brigade (Al-Haris al-Jamhuri), which consisted of four manoeuvre battalions, and was further augmented by elements of 31st SF Brigade.

III Corps was headquartered in Nassiriyah. It controlled the 1st and 5th Mechanised Divisions and 9th Armoured Division, including a total of 10 manoeuvre brigades.[10]

The Iraqi Army exercised control over the Border Guard Force with a nominal 24 brigades, which was transferred to the Defence Ministry on 4 February 1980 to support the army in counterinsurgency operations, although it would also augment the regular army on the southern front.[11]

A reserve was created from 1974 onwards based upon 10 regional administrative brigades, each with six battalions, loosely supported by regular infantry divisions.[12] There was also the Ba'ath Party's paramilitary organisation to counterbalance the army, the Popular Army (Al-Jaysh Al-Shabi), which had 75,000 men under Taha Yasin Ramadan al-Jazrawi, and whose Chief-of-Staff was Brigadier General Ghazi Mahmud al-Omar Saddam. It was created on 8 February 1970, under the Revolutionary Command Council (RCC) as the successor of the National Guard, to give Party members military training and provided an excuse for them to dress like soldiers. All Ba'ath Party members aged 18–45 were given compulsory training, nominally for six hours a week, to handle small arms, while units attended an annual camp during the summer to receive some rudimentary combat training. It was steadily expanded from 50,000 in 1975, and by 1980 the leadership sought Cuban assistance to triple its size.[13]

The focus of Iraqi training was on conventional operations

In the early 1970s, Iran acquired 460 M60A1s. The type was assigned to the mechanised battalions of infantry divisions, and to eight tank battalions of the 81st Armoured Division (deployed in north-western Iran). (Albert Grandolini collection)

The oldest main battle tank type still in active service with the Iranian Army as of 1980 were survivors of 400 M47 tanks acquired in late 1960s, and then locally upgraded (primarily through installation of new engines) to M47M standard. Each Iranian division boasted two battalions equipped with M47Ms. (Albert Grandolini collection)

One of the Shah's final decisions before he was forced to leave the country, was to deploy his army against protesters. This Chieftain broke down and was then abandoned by its crew. (Albert Grandolini collection)

against Israel or Iran. The Iraqi military drew many important lessons from its involvement in the June 1967 and October 1973 Arab-Israeli Wars, and during the 1970s undertook serious attempts to improve professional standards within the officer corps and made a great effort to provide realistic combined-arms tactical training for conventional warfare.[14] To some degree, training was hindered by overdependence on conscripts, many of whom were illiterate. Overall, while the Army managed to run several combined-arms exercises, most of the training of its various elements was undertaken in isolation.[15]

This issue proved a handicap during counterinsurgency (COIN) operations against the Kurds which had involved I Corps, Special Forces and brigades rotated or drafted into Kurdistan. The guerrilla war against the Kurds diluted Iraqi Army training in conventional warfare, despite clashes with the Imperial Iranian Army (Artesh Rahaibakhshe Iran). Even five years later, lack of expertise had not been overcome: in late 1980, a staff officer was forced to inform Saddam that an entire brigade had never received any kind of training on a weapons system as simple as the Soviet-made RPG-7, which was in widespread use.[16]

The Iraqi Air Force was a proud service and theoretically a significant asset, with at least 330 combat aircraft. It could look back to a long history and rich heritage, as well as a number of battles against Israel. However, it was primarily equipped for air defence purposes and COIN warfare against the Kurds, and its offensive capabilities were minimal.

Another major problem was the politicisation of senior command. In July 1979, Saddam removed all the corps and division commanders, many of whom were well-regarded professionally, and replaced them with men loyal to him. Many were junior officers, few of whom had commanded even a brigade, while fewer were qualified staff officers. The nominal supreme decision-making body, the RCC, had no professional military leaders. Saddam himself received an honorary degree from Iraq's military college in 1976 and was given the rank of lieutenant general, and three years later as president and commander-in-chief he was 'promoted' to field marshal. His brother-in-law, Khairallah, was a junior officer rapidly promoted first to colonel and then to general in October 1977, before becoming Defence Minister. To control the Army throughout the war, Saddam would rule through a 'carrot and stick' (in Arabic targhib/tarhib) policy. The former meant promotions, pay rises and generous fringe benefits, while the latter involved constant monitoring of the Army by the security apparatus, which could arrest or rotate anyone at Saddam's will.[17] Ultimate decision making was in Saddam's hands and he allowed his subordinates little initiative, so they would respond to crises by seeking his orders.

PART I: TWO ARMIES

As of 1979–1980, remaining Iranian M47Ms were largely replaced by M48s and M60s, and frequently operated on internal security duties. This example was photographed on the streets of Tehran in January 1979. (Albert Grandolini collection)

Although the Shah's military did open fire on several occasions, most of its troops eventually sided with the protesters – as did the crew of this Scorpion reconnaissance tank and several other soldiers. (Albert Grandolini collection)

history of modern warfare. Other problems reported by American advisors included a tendency to rely upon firepower rather than manoeuvre, as well as shortages of NCOs, training and storage facilities. Finally, the Shah's constant reshuffles of commanders – aimed to thwart the prospects of any kind of military coups – also caused many problems.[19]

With up to 30 percent of national revenues spent upon the armed forces, the Army was lavishly equipped, especially by the United States, which sold it $16 billion worth of equipment between 1972 and 1977, ostensibly to balance Iraqi acquisitions, but actually to ensure that a reliable US ally dominated the Gulf.[20] Here it is worth mentioning that while the Imperial Iranian Army was purchasing much equipment, many of these sophisticated acquisitions proved difficult to assimilate, as the Army spent most of the 1970s trying to reorganise and modernise itself based upon US experience in South-East Asia and Israeli lessons from the 1973 Arab-Israeli war. Furthermore, a combination of large-scale acquisitions of the most modern equipment and rapid expansion of the force resulted in lack of qualified and experienced personnel, leaving Tehran heavily dependent upon large numbers of foreign advisors and even technical support, despite immense investment into support infrastructure and large-scale development of the domestic defence sector.

At the time of the Shah's fall, the Imperial Iranian Army, soon renamed the Islamic Republic of Iran Army (IRIA), was nominally the most powerful in the Middle East, capable of meeting and at least delaying even a Soviet mechanised threat. Many of its officers and non-commissioned officers (NCOs) had fresh combat experience from Oman, where six brigades with air support had been rotated on three-month tours since the early 1970s to help the Sultan against Communist-motivated insurgents active in Dhofar Province. A British general who served with them noted the leadership still seemed to be feudally based, with an emphasis upon obedience to authority rather than initiative.[18] However, there is meanwhile little doubt that Iranian involvement in this conflict proved instrumental for one of only a few completely successful COIN efforts in the

During the 1960s and through the 1970s, Iran acquired 400 M47s (of which 160 were modified to M47M standard in Iran), 260 M48A1s and 460 M60A1s for tank battalions assigned to infantry divisions. Mechanised and reconnaissance battalions were equipped with 400 M113A1 tracked APCs. Artillery of the Iranian Army was equipped with a total of 40 M107 (175mm), 38 M110 (203mm), 50 M109A1 and 440 M109A/A1B (155mm) self-propelled artillery pieces; while towed artillery included 330 M101 (105mm), 112 M114A1 (155mm), and 50 M115 (203mm) pieces. Generally, the towed artillery was assigned to infantry formations, while self-propelled artillery was organised into independent artillery groups – each of which included between four and five tube-battalions, and one

17

Although a staunch US ally, the Shah and the Iranian military also ordered Soviet-made arms whenever Washington showed reluctance to deliver whatever the Iranians thought necessary. One such contract with Moscow from 1969 resulted in the delivery of BTR-60 armoured personnel carriers. This example was photographed while guarding an official building in Tehran in early 1979. (Albert Grandolini collection)

During the 1970s, the Iranian Army experimented with various items of heavy equipment and the organization of its large units and was thus relatively slow in purchasing self-propelled artillery. Correspondingly, only about 430 M109A1 155mm self-propelled howitzers were acquired. (Albert Grandolini collection)

battalion equipped with MLRS (see Table 1 for details). Moreover, during the 1970s the Iranian Army acquired 23,824 BGM-71 TOW and 10,350 FGM-77 Dragon guided anti-tank missiles.[21]

During the Shah's rule, the government in Tehran also sought other sources for equipment, notably the United Kingdom, which supplied Scorpion tracked reconnaissance vehicles. More importantly, in December 1971, London and Tehran signed a contract worth £654 million for nearly 800 Chieftain AFVs, including 750 FV 4201 MBTs, 73 FV 4204 Armoured Recovery Vehicles (ARVs) and 14 FV 4205 armoured bridge layers (AVLBs). Three years later, the British received a £1.2 billion contract for development and procurement of 1,475 MBTs under the three-phase FV 4030 programme: this included deliveries of 150 improved Chieftains (FV 4030/1), 125 redesigned Chieftains (FV 4030/2) designated Shir or Shir Iran 1, and 1,200 redesigned Chieftains with Chobham armour (FV 4030/3) as Shir or Shir Iran 2. This contract was modified, with the last 43 MBTs of the original order being added to the FV 4030/1 contract.[22]

Between 1973 and 1978, Iran purchased 707 MBTs (73 Mk 3/3P and 624 Mk 5/3P), 14 AVLBs (1975–1976) and 41 ARVs (1978–1979). From the FV 4030 programme, Iran received only 185 MBTs (Mk 5/5P): two MBTs were retained in Britain for trials and demonstrations while six were in the process of being re-engined when Tehran cancelled this order, plus that for 77 further Chieftains (including eight FV 4030/1 and 32 ARVs), in February 1979.[23] The Chieftains equipped 15 tank battalions in the 16th and 92nd Armoured Divisions. Although equipped with excellent armour and a powerful gun, the Chieftain was underpowered, with an unreliable power pack, and, despite improved TN37 transmission, the Shir Iran 1 – planned to enter service with three to-be-established armoured divisions – suffered the same problem, with the Armoured Trials and Development Unit having to replace the power pack every 39 miles.[24]

The Shah also purchased Soviet equipment worth $110 million in January 1967, including BTR-50 and BTR-152 APCs, between 100 and 170 122mm calibre D-30 howitzers, 72 BM-21 MLRS and around 200 ZSU-23-4 and ZSU-57-2 self-propelled anti-aircraft guns.[25] However, potentially one of the most important Iranian purchases from the Soviet Union took place only in 1977, when Iran placed an order for 18 9P117 transporter-erector-launchers (TELs) and 36 R-17E Elbrus (ASCC/NATO codename 'SS-1c' 'Scud B') surface-to-surface missiles for an entirely new unit that was in the process of being established at a newly constructed, underground base north of

In addition to M109s, Iran also acquired 38 M110 self-propelled 203mm howitzers. With their range of 32 kilometres, they could out-gun any artillery piece in the Iraqi arsenal. Iranian self-propelled artillery was assigned to mechanised and reconnaissance battalions and proved undoubtedly superior to its Iraqi opponents. (Albert Grandolini collection)

18

PART I: TWO ARMIES

Another Iranian order for Soviet arms from 1969 resulted in the delivery of 100 ZSU-23-4 Shilka quadruple-barrel, radar-directed, self-propelled anti-aircraft guns. (Albert Grandolini collection)

After studying US experience from the Vietnam War, the Iranian Army began developing its own version of 'air cavalry' and placed huge orders for helicopters of US origin. The centrepiece of the new service became 202 Bell AH-1J Cobra attack helicopters. (Tom Cooper collection)

most of the equipment ordered in the USA and UK, and began to expel Western instructors and technicians. Failing to recognise the importance of the military as a shield against foreign aggression and a prime COIN asset, the revolutionaries watched as thousands of officers and NCOs were demobilised or arrested during the following months. Never trusting even those units that proved loyal to his regime, Khomeini was anxious to retain only about a third of the total force once it was 'reformed'.

In the summer of 1980, the acting commander-in-chief of the military was President Abol Hassan Bani-Sadr, who had supported Khomeini during his exile in France and was a clergyman's son. The armed forces were now led by nine officers who had been former prisoners of the Shah, while a retired Special Forces officer, Colonel Nasrollah Tavakkoli, advised Khomeini. He suggested which officers were more supportive of the new regime, while clerical officers were assigned to all headquarters to act like Soviet commissars. The Islamic Revolution was generally supported by the rank and file and many junior officers, especially technicians. Senior officers were either more ambivalent or hostile, and it was these who bore the brunt of a series of purges, in the course of which between 10,000 and 12,000 military personnel were removed, mostly from the Army, by mid-1980. These included up to 40 percent of the 36,480-strong officer corps. Contrary to reports about widespread executions, 'only' 77 Army officers were executed, 42 were jailed and 215 were retired, although others fled abroad. The executed included 26 of 180 generals, mostly closely linked with the old regime and including members of the paramilitary or security forces.[27] Some 500 senior officers, including every division and brigade commander, were dismissed, but only 0.05 percent of the Army's medium-level officers suffered and almost none of the junior officers.[28]

Khorramabad. The unit and base were about 80 percent complete, but only eight TELs and a few missiles were delivered by the time of the revolution in 1979. Further development of this capability was suspended and the Khorramabad base – and all the weapons stored inside bunkers there – practically abandoned: indeed, the new Islamic government subsequently banned the procurement of ballistic missiles.[26]

The IRIA did possess one advantage over the Iraqis in a substantial, well balanced and well-trained army air corps (Islamic Republic of Iran Army Aviation, IRIAA). This huge force operated over 1,000 helicopters and was originally planned to become the core of three air cavalry divisions and then five air groups.

On 6 March 1979, the new government in Tehran renounced Iran's role as 'policeman of the Gulf', slashed the military budget, cancelled all major related contracts, refused to accept delivery of

Irrespective of statistics, the atmosphere of suspicion caused thousands of junior officers and skilled technicians to leave voluntarily: one estimate suggests that up to half of the medium-level officers (majors and colonels) left because suspicious clerics questioned their orders and repeatedly disrupted their command.

19

MIDDLE EAST@WAR SERIES SPECIAL #1: THE IRAN-IRAQ WAR

The major medium transport helicopter type of the newly established Imperial Iranian Army Aviation (later Islamic Republic of Iran Army Aviation) became 287 Bell 214A Esfahans. The Iranians originally planned to launch domestic production of further, much improved variants of this type in the 1980s. (Tom Cooper collection)

The IIAA and the IIAF ordered a total of 86 Boeing-Meridionali CH-47C Chinook helicopters in the late 1970s, about 67 of which were eventually delivered (some of them as late as 1981). (Albert Grandolini collection)

In addition to nearly 1,000 helicopters, the Iranian Army Aviation operated a miscellany of nearly 100 light and medium-sized transport aircraft, including the Fokker F.27. As with the rest of the service, they saw intensive deployment during the war with Iraq. (Tom Cooper collection)

The purges and enforced retirements meant that divisions, brigades and battalions were led by inexperienced officers and operated with limited capability. Some 30 percent of IRIA equipment was non-operational, as well as 60 percent of IRIA and IRIAA helicopters, while, despite the acquisition of 10 years' worth of spares during the 1970s, the entire support infrastructure collapsed during the chaos of revolution, and there were

Table 1: Order of Battle for the Islamic Republic of Iran Army (IRIA), September 1980		
Operational Zone	Division & HQ	Brigades & Notes
Azerbaijan Province	64th Infantry Division, Urmia	1st Brigade (Urmia), 2nd Brigade (Salmas), 3rd Brigade (Naqdeh); total of 43 MBTs and 69 artillery pieces available
Kurdistan Province	28th Infantry Division, Sanandaj	1st Brigade (Sanandaj), 2nd Brigade (Saqqez), 3rd Brigade (Marivan); total of 27 MBTs and 27 artillery pieces available
Kermanshah Province	81st Armoured Division, Kermanshah	1st Brigade (Kermanshah, 53 MBTs, 136 APCs), 2nd Brigade (Hashabad, 92 MBTs, 28 APCs), 3rd Brigade (Sar-e Pol-e Zahab, 79 MBTs, 60 APCs); equipped with Chieftain MBTs; 5 artillery battalions (42 M109A1, 10 105mm field guns)
Khuzestan Province	92nd Armoured Division, Ahwaz	1st Brigade (Ahwaz, 96 MBTs, 53 APCs), 2nd Brigade (Dezful, 82 MBTs, 30 APCs), 3rd Brigade (Hamidiyeh, 92 MBTs, 98 APCs); equipped with Chieftain MBTs; 151st Fortress Battalion (Shalamcheh) equipped with M4s; 4 artillery battalions (73 M109A1)
	22nd (Independent) Artillery Group, Ahwaz	
Oresian Province	84th Infantry Brigade, Khoramabad	total of 48 MBTs and 14 artillery pieces available
Qazvin Province	16th Armoured Division, Qazvin	1st Brigade (Qazvin, 82 MBTs, 64 APCs), 2nd Brigade (Zanjan, 66 MBTs, 92 APCs), 3rd Brigade (Hamedan, 36 MBTs, 40 APCs); equipped with Chieftain MBTs; 3 artillery battalions (44 M109A1)
Tehran Province	21st Infantry Division, Tehran	1st, 2nd, 3rd Brigades (Tehran), 4th (Armoured) Brigade (Tehran); total of 134 MBTs, 70 APCs and 69 artillery pieces available
	23rd Special Forces Brigade, Nowhed	5 special forces battalions
	33rd Artillery Group, Tehran	3 artillery & 1 MLRS battalion; 33 artillery pieces and 12 BM-21s
Sharqi Province	40th Infantry Brigade, Sarab	
	11th Artillery Group, Maragheh	5 artillery & 1 MLRS battalions; 60 artillery pieces, 12 BM-21
Fars Province	37th Armoured Brigade, Shiraz	89 M60A1 & 71 M113s (but only 52 and 39 operational, respectively)
	55th Airborne Brigade, Shiraz	5 airborne infantry battalions
Esfahan Province	22nd Artillery Group, Esfahan	4 artillery & 1 MLRS battalion; 59 artillery pieces and 12 BM-21s
	44th Artillery Group, Esfahan	2 artillery & 1 MLRS battalion; 26 artillery pieces and 12 BM-21s
	55th Artillery Group, Esfahan	2 artillery & 1 MLRS battalion; 26 artillery pieces and 12 BM-21s
	Training Regiment	3 artillery battalions, 42 artillery pieces
Andapan Province	30th Infantry Brigade, Gorgan	
Khorasan Province	77th Infantry Division, Mashhad	1st Brigade (Bojnurd), 2nd Brigade (Quchan), 3rd Brigade (Mashhad); total of 99 MBTs and 51 artillery pieces available
Sistan-Va-Baluchistan Province	88th Armoured Division, Zahedan	in the process of expansion from 88th Armoured Brigade and conversion to Shir Iran MBTs; equipped with only 29 MBTs, 20 APCs, and 10 M109A1; in garrison until late 1980

already shortages of these, as well as ammunition, communications equipment, transport vehicles and even food.

Khomeini demanded the restoration of discipline, but this proved very difficult and slow to implement under prevalent circumstances. Clerical fears of a coup and personnel unrest meant that not only training using live ammunition ceased, but so did all sorts of periodic maintenance, while armoured units were largely confined to simulators or classrooms as clerical demands for religious instruction and political indoctrination undermined even basic training. Furthermore, there remained within the IRIA sufficient loyalists to plot coups.

The last major attempt was the 'Nojeh Coup'. This was thwarted (apparently with some help from Soviet intelligence agencies) in July 1980 and involved 280 officers – primarily from the 92nd Armoured Division and 55th Airborne Brigade – who were arrested, with many executed.

IRIA formations thus became little more than shells: the Army shrank from 190,000-strong to 100,000 by mid-1980, as troops quit their barracks with small arms and ammunition to join various militia groups. Yet the IRIA remained the foundation of the new regime's security against a variety of threats, including revolutionary groups who had formerly been Khomeini's allies, such as the People's Struggle (Mojahedin e-Khalq or Mojahedin), the People's Guerrillas (Cherikha-ye Faday e-Khalq or Fadaeeyan) and the Masses Party

One of the 20 Agusta-Sikorsky AS-61A-4 Sea King helicopters of the Iranian Navy, seen shortly prior to delivery in the 1970s. Although configured for anti-submarine and anti-surface warfare, they saw frequent deployment in the operations of Iranian special forces, especially the Special Boat Service. (Albert Grandolini collection)

The creation of the Iraqi military was strongly influenced by the British, and British-made equipment was dominant even as of the late 1960s. This double column of Churchill tanks (with a few Centurions in the background) was photographed during a military parade in 1954. (Albert Grandolini collection)

(Tudeh), which was a pseudo-Communist organisation. There were also rebellions by ethnic minorities living near the borders; the Kurdish one being the largest, which was suppressed only in 1988 with the IRIA alone suffering 3,000 casualties, in addition to revolts among the Baluchs in the east and, briefly, the Arabs in the west.[29]

With the merging of the two Imperial Guard divisions around Tehran into the 21st Infantry Division, the IRIA was left with a total of 30 manoeuvre brigades, mostly organic to seven divisions (which usually had the equivalent of an extra manoeuvre brigade in division troops), five artillery and three engineer groups (see Table 1). It remained distributed as it had been under the Shah, with most units facing Iraq, but while these were formerly under the I Corps headquarters at Khermanshah, this and the other corps were dissolved during the revolution. From north to south, this corps had commanded the 64th Infantry Division (at Urmia, also written Orumiyeh), 28th Infantry Division (Sanandaj), 81st Armoured Division (Kermanshah) and 92nd Armoured Division (Ahwaz), as well as the 40th (Sarab) and 84th (Khorramabad) Independent Infantry Brigades. Each armoured division had six tank and five mechanised infantry battalions organised into three brigades, but by 1980 they were each able to deploy only one understrength brigade along the border with Iraq.[30] As a strategic reserve, the Tehran-based II Corps had had the 16th Armoured Division (Qazvin), 21st Infantry Division and 23rd SF Brigade (Nohed), while to the south had been III Corps at Shiraz, with 37th Armoured Brigade and 55th Airborne Brigade. Watching Afghanistan was the task of the Mashhad-based 77th Infantry Division and 30th Infantry Brigade (Gorgan), while the 88th Armoured Brigade (later expanded into a division) was created at Zahedan as the cadre for a planned fourth corps at Chahbahar. The Navy had two Marine battalions.

There was also a paramilitary force, the IIG, formerly the Imperial Iranian Gendarmerie, about 75,000 strong (half of them conscripts) as of early 1979. Subject to the Ministry of Interior, the IIG was responsible for rural law enforcement and border security. It was organised into 16 districts, each of which had two to five 'regiments' for a total of some 250 companies. The IIG units

PART I: TWO ARMIES

Table 2: Order of Battle for the Islamic Republic of Iran Army Aviation (IRIAA), September 1980		
Operational Zone	Nominal Strength	Notes
1st Direct Combat Support Group/1st Combat Support Base, Kermanshah	3 Attack Battalions (AH-1Js)	1 battalion operational (12 AH-1Js)
	3 Assault Battalions (Bell 214As)	1 battalion operational (12 Bell 214As)
	2 Reconnaissance Battalions (Bell 206)	1 company operational (4–6 Bell 206)
	1 Transport Battalion (CH-47C)	1 company operational (4–6 CH-47Cs)
		detachment at Qassr-e-Shirin from 23 September incl. 6 AH-1Js, 8 Bell 214As, 2 AB.206s
2nd Direct Combat Support Group/2nd Combat Support Base, Masjed Soleiman	2 Attack Battalions (AH-1Js)	1 company operational
	2 Assault Battalions (Bell 214As)	1 company operational
	1 Reconnaissance Battalion (AB.206)	1 company operational
	1 Transport Company (CH-47C)	few helicopters operational
3rd Direct Combat Support Group/3rd Combat Support Base, Kerman	1 Attack Battalion (AH-1Js)	1 company operational
	1 Assault Battalion (Bell 214As)	1 company operational
	1 Reconnaissance Company (AB.206)	1 company operational
	1 Transport Company (CH-47C)	few helicopters operational
		detachment at TFB.4 from 26 September including 8 AH-1Js and 6 Bell 214As
4th General Support Group/4th Combat & Logistics Base, Esfahan	4 Attack Battalions (AH-1Js)	1 battalion operational (12 AH-1Js)
	5 Assault Battalions (Bell 214As)	1 battalion operational (12 Bell 214As)
	3 Reconnaissance Battalions (Bell 206s)	1 company operational (4–6 Bell 206s)
	1 Transport Battalion (CH-47C)	1 company operational (4–8 CH-47C)
	1 Transport Battalion (Turbo Commander)	1 company operational (1–2 aircraft)
	1 Transport Battalion (F.27)	1 company operational (1–2 aircraft)
		detachment at TFB.4 from 25 September including 8 AH-1Js and 6 Bell 214As
5th Operational Communications Company/5th General Support Base, Qaleh Morgi (Tehran)	miscellaneous detachments and aircraft	

were equipped with BTR-60 APCs, light anti-tank weapons such as bazookas and RPG-7s, and 60–81mm mortars and operated an excellent communications system. While its strength dropped to about 40,000 men in mid-1980, it still operated a number of posts along the border with Iraq, each with up to 20 men, supported by 'strike' companies and 81mm mortars, all linked by VHF radio: they were to play an important role in the early battles against invaders.[31]

Khomeini's regime perceived the United States as the prime enemy, and its clerics were virulently opposed to the 'corrupt' West. Iran's anti-US policy led Washington to withdraw some 6,500

Starting in 1956, the USA began donating armament to the Iraqi military. Included was a batch of M24 Chafee light tanks, several of which can be seen in this photograph – together with half a dozen British-made Ferret Scout Cars. US-Iraqi military cooperation was rudely interrupted by the February 1958 Revolution. (Albert Grandolini collection)

23

Table 3: Order of Battle for the Iraqi Army (IrA), September 1980		
Corps	Division & HQ	Brigades & Notes
I Corps	Kirkuk	
	2nd Infantry Division ('Khalid Force'), Kirkuk	2nd, 4th, 36th (Mountain) Infantry Brigades
	4th (Mountain) Infantry Division ('Qaqaa Force'), Mosul	5th, 18th and 29th Infantry Brigades
	7th Infantry Division, Suleimaniyah	19th, 38th and 39th Infantry Brigades
	8th Infantry Division, Erbil	3rd, 22nd, 23rd Infantry Brigades
	11th Infantry Division ('Miqdad Force'), Erbil	44th, 45th and 48th Infantry Brigades
	12th Armoured Division ('Nauman Force'), Sinjar	37th and 50th Armoured, 46th Mechanised Brigades
	31st Special Forces Brigade	
	32nd Special Forces Brigade	redeployed from the II Corps
	95th and 97th Reserved Brigades	cadre only
II Corps	Diyala	
	3rd Armoured Division ('Saladin Force'), Tikrit	6th and 12th Armoured, 8th Mechanised Brigades; equipped with T-62s and BMP-1s
	6th Armoured Division, Baqubah	16th and 30th Armoured, 25th Mechanised Brigades; equipped with T-62s and BMP-1s
	10th Armoured Division, Baghdad & al-Kut	17th and 42nd Armoured, 24th Mechanised Brigades; 17th Armoured Brigade equipped with T-72s and BMP-1s, others with T-62s and BMP-1s
	Republican Guards Brigade, Baghdad	1 Armoured Battalion (T-72), 1 SF-Regiment, 1 SP-artillery battalion, 1 BM-21 battalion
	10th Armoured Brigade	
	17th Special Forces Brigade	
	90th, 93rd, 94th, 96th Reserve Brigades	cadre only
III Corps	Basra	
	1st Mechanised Infantry Division, Diwaniyah	1st and 27th Mechanised, 34th Armoured Brigades (51st Armoured Brigade added in 1981); equipped with T-55s & OT-64s
	5th Mechanised Infantry Division ('Muhammad Qassim Force'), Zubayr	15th and 20th Mechanised, 26th Armoured Brigades; equipped with T-55s & OT-64s
	9th Armoured Division ('Osama Force'), Samarah	35th and 43rd Armoured, 14th Mechanised Brigades
	33rd Special Forces Brigade	
	91st, 92nd, 98th Reserve Brigades	cadre only
Balance of Forces	30th Infantry Division (also 'Border Guards Division', and including Iraqi National Guard/Popular Army forces)	est. early 1980 along patterns of the British Army to control numerous task forces of the Border Guards and the Iraqi National Guard, including such as the 90th, 91st, 92nd, 93rd, 94th, 95th, 96th, 97th, 98th and 99th Brigades/Task Forces of the Border Guards, and – later on – 101st, 102nd, 103rd, 104th, 105th, 106th, 107th, 108th, 109th, 110th, 111th, 112th, 113th, 114th, 115th, 116th and 117th Task Forces of the National Guard/Popular Army. Provided the core for the 441st Task Force, expanded into the Naval Infantry Brigade, and Task Force 12 (or 'al-Badaah Force') including the 412th Infantry Brigade.
	223rd Missile Brigade, Baghdad	2 SCUD battalions (10 TELs)
	224th Missile Brigade, Khan al-Mahawil	2 SCUD battalions (10 TELs)
	Unid. Missile Brigade, Khan al-Mahawil	5 FROG battalions (7 TELs)

PART I: TWO ARMIES

Table 4: Known Units of the Iraqi Army Aviation Corps, September 1980	
Unit	Helicopter Type
No. 2 Squadron	Mi-8/17
No. 4 Squadron	Mi-8/17
No. 12 Squadron	Mi-8/17
No. 15 Squadron	Mi-8/17
No. 21 Squadron	SA.342 Gazelle
No. 22 Squadron	SA.342 Gazelle
No. 25 Squadron	Mi-25
No. 30 Squadron	SE.316B
No. 31 Squadron	SA.342
No. 55 Squadron	Mi-8/17
No. 61 Squadron	Mi-25
No. 66 Squadron	Mi-25
No. 84 Squadron	SA.342 Gazelle
No. 88 Squadron	SA.342 Gazelle

advisors and technical experts vital to the running of the armed forces, who took with them most of the computerised records of the Shah's logistical system. The administration of US President Jimmy Carter did seek an accommodation with new government in Tehran, which in August 1979 cancelled military equipment orders worth $8 billion. However, in November of the same year, the American Embassy was occupied by demonstrators, who took hostage most of the staff.[32]

Unable to achieve a diplomatic solution, Washington, which had frozen $6 billion worth of Iranian assets (including $900 million of military spares), tried a covert military rescue operation in April 1980, but this turned into a bloody and embarrassing farce which heightened Tehran's fear of what the clergy called 'The Great Satan'. The hostages were eventually freed in January 1981, on the same day a new US president, Ronald Reagan, was inaugurated.

The shortages of both technicians and spare parts especially plagued the Islamic Republic of Iran Air Force (IRIAF), which had 15 combat squadrons in the west, nine along the coast and seven acting as a strategic reserve, with a total nominal strength of 445 combat aircraft. While the Iraqis expected Iranian serviceability rates of 30–40 percent for fighters and 50 percent for helicopters, the condition of the air force was actually slightly better, although by August 1980 all the personnel were in urgent need of refresher training. The situation was similar in the case of the IRIA, which had about 500 tanks, of which 300 were operational, but the Iranians could man only a fraction of them because of personnel shortages. Much more damaging were massive purges of top officers, which caused disrupted chains of command in all services, making inexperienced novice commanders heavily dependent on pre-1978 planning in the case of a war, much of which was either obsolete or betrayed to the Iraqis.[33]

Clerical suspicion of the IRIA led the new regime to create

The most powerful main battle tanks of the Iraqi Army as of the late 1950s, and for much of the 1960s, were British-made Centurions. Replaced by T-55s, most seem to have eventually been donated to Jordan in the late 1960s. (Albert Grandolini collection)

As well as tanks and armoured cars, the mainstay of the Iraqi Army's artillery for much of the mid-twentieth century was also British-made. This photograph from the mid-1950s shows a battery of the famous 25-pounders. (Albert Grandolini collection)

Starting in 1958, but especially following the June 1967 Arab-Israeli War, Iraq began importing about 800 T-54 and T-55 main battle tanks from the USSR and Czechoslovakia. This example was photographed somewhere on the frontlines east of Basra, early during the war with Iran. (Albert Grandolini collection)

The most modern MBT of the Iraqi Army as of September 1980 was the T-72, about 155 of which were in service – exclusively with the much-dreaded 10th Armoured Brigade. Moscow were so annoyed by Saddam's decision to invade Iran without bothering to inform them that another shipment of 139 T-72s underway to Iraq was promptly ordered back to the Soviet Union. Soviet-built tanks exported to the Middle East usually arrived with most of their crucial equipment separate from the vehicle: instructions in English applied within the vehicle usually marked where the equipment was to be installed. (Albert Grandolini collection)

ideological mission of holy war in the way of God and fighting to expand the rule of God's law in the world.' Paragraph 150 noted the Pasdaran would 'continue its role in guarding the revolution and its offshoots', or, as one writer observed, that the Pasdaran's 'military, religious, and revolutionary mandates are intertwined'.[35]

The Pasdaran had a triumvirate leadership: Mohsen Rezai was the military leader, Mohsen Rafiq-Dust the Pasdaran Minister in the government, with Ali Riza Afshar responsible for the 'staff'. By the summer of 1980, they commanded some 30,000 men organised into 10 provincial areas and deployed in combat or protection units, each of two 10-man teams or squads.[36] They were augmented by the National Mobilisation Organisation (Sazman-e Basij-e Milli), more commonly called the Mobilisation of the Oppressed (Basij-e Mustazafin, or Basiji), created in November 1979 as a 75,000-strong popular force to defend the revolution. Basiji primarily consisted of young, uneducated and usually rural poor who volunteered for the role.[37] Despite the national framework, both militias remained at local level extremely autonomous, under the control of individual clerics who were often jockeying for power, and enforced their views, accepting or ignoring central control as they wished. The units in Khorasan, for example, ignored mobilisation orders from Tehran, as did others if they were signed by an official of whom they did not approve.[38]

The Pasdaran and IRIA leaders cooperated in counterinsurgency operations, especially in Kurdistan, but mutual suspicions remained. In many respects, the IRIA had an advantage, for it retained specialists such as tank and artillery crews, few of whom appear to have wished to join the Pasdaran. Some senior IRIA leaders desired closer cooperation bordering on integration, but Defence Minister Mostofa Ali Chamran was more interested in converting the armed forces into supporters of the revolution.

its own forces, both to meet internal threats and to counterbalance the Army. In April 1979, the Islamic Army of the Guardians of the Islamic Revolution (Sepah-e Pasdaran-e Enghelab-e Eslami or Pasdaran) – officially reorganised as the Islamic Revolutionary Guards Corps (IRGC) in January 1981 – was founded.[34] The new constitution, ratified in December 1979, stated: 'The Army of the Islamic Republic and the Guards Corps of the Revolution will be responsible not only for defending the borders, but also for the

The primary armoured personnel carrier in Iraqi mechanised infantry formations of the 1970s and early 1980s was the OT-62 – a Czechoslovak-manufactured variant of the BTR-50 – 395 of which were acquired in the early 1970s. The vehicle used the same chassis as the PT-76 reconnaissance tank and could carry up to 20 troops. (Albert Grandolini collection)

The primary APC of the Iraqi infantry in the early 1980s was the BTR-60. This wheeled vehicle was amphibious and could carry 16 troops. (Albert Grandolini collection)

MIDDLE EAST@WAR SERIES SPECIAL #1: THE IRAN-IRAQ WAR

The BMP-1 infantry fighting vehicle was still relatively new to the Iraqi Army, although up to 620 were acquired before September 1980. Equipped with a 73mm gun and 9K11/9M14 Malyutka (AT-3 Sagger) anti-tank missile, the type became the primary vehicle of the Iraqi mechanised infantry during the war with Iran. (Albert Grandolini collection)

In order to attempt to match the Iranian advantage in mobile artillery, the Iraqis purchased a total of 85 AUF1 155mm self-propelled howitzers from France, starting in 1983. The system proved reliable and was still in use as of 1991, when this example was captured by the US Army. (Albert Grandolini collection)

PART I: TWO ARMIES

Another attempt at equalising the Iranian advantage in mobile artillery resulted in the Iraqis adapting various artillery pieces to the surplus chassis of Soviet-made tanks. This former T-54/55 received what appears to be a 100mm T-12 anti-tank gun with shield. (Albert Grandolini collection)

During the summer of 1980, the newly established Iraqi Army Aviation Corps received the first batch of 12 Mil Mi-25 helicopter gunships. This heavily armed, armoured, and fast type saw intensive service during the war with Iran. (Ali Tobchi collection)

Between 1977 and 1984 Iraq acquired a total of 35 SA.342M, 56 SA.342K and 20 SA.342H Gazelle helicopters from France, and they formed the backbone of light attack units assigned to all three wings of the IrAAC early during the war. (Ali Tobchi collection)

29

3
FROM BORDER WAR TO INVASION

When the IRIAF was put on the lowest level of alert, on 8 April 1980, the threat to Iran from the west was growing, but the country's leaders were obsessed with the internal struggle. The Iraqis were very aware that the IRIA was a giant with feet of clay. The GMID's 'Report Assessing Political, Military and Economic Conditions in Iran' concluded that the Army was poorly led and had no more than 60 percent of its established strength, discipline was weak, morale was low, there was little training and the general deterioration was likely to continue.[1]

Led by Brigadier General Abdul Jawad Dhannoun, the GMID had obtained strength returns for the 55th Artillery Group and noted a shortage of privates in technically based organisations. For example, the 394th Artillery Battalion had only 58 specialists, although a total of 19 officers and 72 NCOs. This pattern was repeated to a greater or lesser extent throughout the IRIA after all the above-mentioned purges.[2] Furthermore, the GMID noted that the Kurds had inflicted heavy losses on the 28th and 64th Infantry Division and 16th Armoured Division. It rated the 92nd Armoured Division as the best Iranian unit, although badly understrength and running no training at all. The same report concluded that 'Iran has no power to launch wide offensive operations against Iraq, or to defend itself on a large scale'.[3]

The GMID was a slender reed to lean on for intelligence on Iran. Founded in 1932, it was responsible directly to the president and was responsible for tactical and strategic reconnaissance, as well as monitoring the armed forces' loyalty. In September 1980, its Iran desk had just three officers, of whom only one had studied Farsi. Indeed, there were only three Farsi-speaking officers in the entire Iraqi Army.[4] The GMID had few agents in Iran, and their number further decreased once Khomeini came to power. It lacked accurate maps of the country and was in no condition to decipher enemy communications.[5]

To the US intelligence agencies, the Iraqi 'invasion' of Iran seemed more an increase in intensity of border operations, for tensions between the two countries grew soon after the Shah was deposed.[6] From April 1979, shells and mortar bombs were fired across the border, sparking a series of tit-for-tat raids and bombardments, sometimes involving air strikes which cost both sides aircraft.[7]

Although formal preparations for an invasion of Iran did not begin until July, when units were filled out and put in supply requests, there was increased activity in Iraqi maintenance facilities and ammunition dumps from March as training was intensified. By the time Iraqi mobilisation began on 4 September, there were clashes and artillery duels along the frontier almost on a daily basis. Some Iranian cities near the border, including Qasr-e Shirin and Mehran, were shelled, while both sides increasingly deployed fixed and rotary-wing aircraft. The Superpowers observed this with their satellites but remained unsure what was happening; the Americans thought the preparations were for a major exercise (Nassour 4) in the training grounds near the Jordanian border, until it became clear during the summer that the flow of Iraqi traffic was eastward. Moscow had experts with the Iraqi Army but was also in the dark, despite increasing demands for military equipment from Baghdad.

The scale of fighting slowly increased when the Iraqis began flying air strikes into Iranian Kurdistan, and during the summer there were frequent clashes between border patrols. The Iranians marked the frontier with a line of IIG outposts: 29 on the sector south of the Hawizah Marshes (Hawr al Hawizah), underpinned with strongpoints some 3km to the east, sometimes augmented by elements of the IRIA. Each outpost south of the marshes was reinforced by two dug-in tanks acting as pillboxes and manned by the 92nd Armoured Division's 151st Fortress Battalion. The IIG strongpoints were undermanned and ill-equipped; the position covering Shalamcheh had a mechanised infantry unit but was short of food, fuel, ammunition and radios, leaving the men demoralised.[8] In the face of an increasing number of cross-

A Chieftain of the Imperial Guards Division (later 21st Infantry Division) drives up to support the police guarding an official building in Tehran, during the unrest that led to the Shah's overthrow. (Albert Grandolini collection)

PART I: FROM BORDER WAR TO INVASION

when this was ignored they seized them on 7 September. The absence of Iranian efforts to recover them encouraged Saddam to nibble away at the frontier. By 10 September, Iraqi troops had taken six border posts and Saddam claimed to have 'recovered' almost all the 240km² of territory, including 130km² in northern Khuzestan on the border with Maysan Province, which he claimed as owed to his country. The same day, the Iraqis also took a forward communications intelligence (COMINT) base, prompting local Iranian commanders to call the IRIAF to bomb and destroy this facility.

Iran's political leaders remained focused on the internecine conflict and the frontier troubles were, in theatrical terms, 'noises off stage'.[9] US intelligence noted the Iranians in general – with the exception of the IRIA and IRIAF – seemed unwilling, or unable, to grasp the seriousness of the threat. Accompanied by Army leaders, Bani-Sadr toured the Qassr-e-Shirin area on 15 August to discuss the frontier conflict with forward commanders. Together with his entourage, he had a lucky escape when their helicopter suffered an electrical failure and crash-landed. On 9 September, Iran's acting Chief-of-Staff, General Valiollah Fallahi (deputy chairman of the Joint Chiefs of Staff), with Ground Forces commander General Qasem Ali Zahirnejhad and IRIAF commander Colonel Javad Fakuri, visited Kermanshah Province and discussed the situation with the commander of the 81st Division.[10] This formation, together with elements of the 82nd and 92nd Armoured Division, 28th Infantry Division and 84th Infantry Brigade, was responsible for defence of the border with Iraq. But it was able to deploy only seriously understrength brigades, most of which were battalion-sized task forces. In Khuzestan, these were supported by the 22nd and 55th Artillery Groups.

From early September, Tehran made half-hearted attempts to strengthen the border, deploying elements of the 16th IRIA Armoured Division, 37th Armoured Brigade (as Task Force 37), augmented by 13 detachments of the 23rd SF Brigade and a part of 55th Airborne Brigade. A battalion-sized task force based on some of these units deployed in the Sardasht area, while individual companies went to Sanandaj and Dezful. Meanwhile, the majority of troops remained either deployed on counterinsurgency operations or restricted to barracks, watched closely by their spiritual advisors.[11]

On 13 September, Khuzestan's Governor, Seyed Mohamad Gharazi, closed the border and the following afternoon, Bani-Sadr, Premier Mohamad Ali-Rajaie, Fallahi, Zahirnejhad and Javad Fakuri made another tour of inspection near Ilam (capital of Ilam Province) in helicopters, escorted by two Cobras, but their pilots had to make evasive manoeuvres to avoid Iraqi aircraft.[12] Tehran promptly announced that it would no longer abide by the Algiers Treaty, but a day later deployed a large IRIA contingent not to the Iraq border but to Kordistan, which demonstrated Tehran's

The crew of this Guards Division Chieftain dispatched to suppress protests clearly changed sides and at some stage fraternised with civilians – resulting in their vehicle being decorated with a large photograph of Ayatollah Khomeini. (Albert Grandolini collection)

border raids aimed at 'recovering' disputed border territory, the outgunned and outnumbered Iranians often gave way.

Countdown to Invasion

On 4 September 1980, as Iraqi mobilisation began, Baghdad accused Tehran of shelling the vicinity of two villages, Zain al Qaws and Saif Saad, which Iraq was supposed to receive under the Algiers Treaty. The Iraqis now demanded they be handed over, and

Quite early during the Revolution, the Iranian clergy began establishing its own security force. Colloquially known as 'Pasdaran', these frequently paraded in the streets of Tehran – sometimes armed with G3 rifles, as seen here. Before long, they were to become involved in combat operations against various insurgents inside Iran, and then the invading Iraqis. (Albert Grandolini collection)

Often consisting of various local units, the Iranian Gendarmerie was responsible for law and order in rural areas and the defence of borders. The latter were usually controlled from 'Dezh' (fortress) border posts manned by squadrons of up to 20 troops equipped with light infantry weapons, bazookas, RPG-7s, and some 60mm and 81mm mortars. Iranian Gendarmes suffered heavy losses early during the war with Iraq. (Albert Grandolini collection)

continued preoccupation with its internal enemies. It was only after the Iraqi invasion that Bani-Sadr ordered a ceasefire in Kordistan so he could concentrate meagre Army resources in the west.[13]

Just after midnight on 16 September, Saddam presented his plans to both the RCC and the National Command, and revealed he now wanted total control of the Shatt, a decision apparently made a few nights before.[14] The alleged failure of Tehran to implement the Algiers Treaty was Saddam's justification for military action to control the waterway: 'We have to stick Iran's head in the mud and force them to say yes so we can get done quickly with this matter.' Saddam was asked to clarify Iraq's position with regard to Khuzestan, unofficially called Arabistan because of its substantial Arab population, which had never been part of Iraq. Saddam replied that he would strike into the region only if Tehran contested his claim to the Shatt, and he dismissed questions about the implications for Soviet support, especially regarding the supply of artillery ammunition, if the situation escalated.[15] Contrary to some contemporary claims, it is virtually certain that it was not until November 1980 that he began planning to establish Arabistan as an 'autonomous region closely linked with Iraq'.[16]

On 17 September, Saddam formally abrogated the Algiers Treaty and demanded that Tehran cede control of the Shatt, adding: 'We in no way intend to launch war against Iran.' While denying any territorial ambitions upon Iranian territory, he did demand adjustments to the land frontier and, to strengthen his pan-Arab credentials, the transfer of Abu Musa and the Tunb Islands to the UAE, but he remained silent about Kurdish or Khuzestan Arab autonomy. Bani-Sadr promptly ordered all available IRIA units westwards and summoned the National Security Council to discuss the situation, and after 12 hours it agreed upon a stiff response to the Iraqi attacks. The same day, the Iranian Joint Staff issued its first communiqué rejecting Saddam's demands, although it admitted a full-scale invasion was possible but claimed that Iraq, with US support, had imposed a war upon Iran since the beginning of September. Bani-Sadr also claimed that the Iraqis planned a counterrevolution led by émigré former Iranian Premier Shapour Bakhtiar.

Only a day later, Iraqi forces began attacking Iranian frontier posts in Khuzestan, with the 4th Infantry Division advancing on Bostan and 7th Infantry Division on Fakkeh.[17] The following day, Iranian naval units in Abadan and Khorramshahr were alerted and naval reservists mobilised.[18]

Nevertheless, the 92nd IRIA Armoured Division, the backbone of Khuzestan's defence, had been disrupted by the loss of personnel arrested in July, lack of training and lapsed maintenance, so it took several days to deploy company-sized units.[19]

Meanwhile, Iraqi forces began deploying eastward, into the area of responsibility of II Corps. The 6th Armoured Division was the first to leave its barracks, followed by the 10th Armoured Division on 20 September. Within III Corps' area of responsibility, the 1st Mechanised Division arrived on 5 September, followed by 5th Mechanised Division about a week later. The 9th Armoured Division began deploying along the frontier on 20 September and was followed, two days later, by 3rd Armoured Division.[20] I Corps' activity is uncertain, but it probably began deploying elements of its divisions eastwards from early September.

By comparison, the Iranians never managed to build up coherent defences for their frontier, either because the information was not taken seriously or because internal rivalry prevented Bani-Sadr acting quickly. Only on 20 September did he order the mobilisation of the country's almost non-existent reserves, whose organisation had collapsed during the revolution.[21] However, Iran did begin evacuating civilians from the frontier region as fighting intensified, the Iraqis seizing more border posts as, from 18 September, the II (al-Yarmouk Force) and III (al-Qadissya Force) Iraqi Corps secured their assembly points (in US terminology, line of departure) from enemy artillery, using 17th SF Brigade from the 6th Armoured Division and 1st Mechanised Division to establish positions.[22]

On 21 September, as Tehran ordered conscript soldiers discharged the previous year to return to the colours, the IrAF received orders to strike at eight IRIAF air bases and two major bases of the IRIA within the range of available aircraft. A day later, 192 Iraqi bombers and fighter-bombers pressed home their attack, opening the war.

Opening Blows

The opening strike of the Iraqi Air Force was not, as so often claimed, intended to emulate the crushing success of the Israeli Air Force offensive at the beginning of the June 1967 Arab-Israeli War. Instead, it was primarily intended to crater runways on Iranian air bases and thus render them inoperative for the first 48 hours of the Iraqi offensive, and increase already widespread chaos in the Iranian armed forces.[23] Correspondingly, only three IRIAF aircraft were destroyed on the ground.[24]

PART I: FROM BORDER WAR TO INVASION

The main units of the Iraqi and Iranian ground forces on the southern frontlines during the first few days of the war. (Map by George Anderson)

Even so, these raids cost the Iraqis not only one Tu-16 (ASCC/NATO codename 'Badger') bomber and three fighter-bombers, but had no significant effect upon the IRIAF: acting according to long-established plans in case of a war with Iraq (further updated on 18 August), the Iranians returned the favour by launching about 70 combat sorties – including several raids on Iraqi air bases – within only two hours of the first Iraqi attack. Furthermore, on the following morning, the IRIAF launched Operation Kaman-99, deploying 129 F-4 Phantoms and F-5 Tigers in a major air strike on 15 Iraqi air bases, oil installations and other facilities. While losing nine aircraft in the process (at least four of these to mechanical malfunctions), the Iranians claimed the destruction of 20 IrAF aircraft on the ground (the Iraqis confirmed only two of these).[25]

This was the main effect of the opening Iraqi air strike, and for the first 48 hours of the war, large Iraqi mechanised forces were able to roam the flat terrain of south-western Khuzestan largely unmolested by the IRIAF. Overall, the Iraqis committed all or parts of eight divisions, totalling about 98,000 men, 1,500 tanks and 520 artillery pieces.[26] By November 1980, this force was reinforced through three additional divisions (35,000 men) of the Army and 40,000 troops of the Popular Army (the latter primarily deployed to guard lines of communication).[27]

Because Iraqi corps and division commanders never received clear instructions from Saddam, the invasion was made on six uncoordinated axes, whose general objective was the line connecting Musian–Susangerd–Ahwaz–Khorramshahr to create a bridgehead which they would fortify and hold. The planners ignored the highways which ran parallel with the frontier just beyond this line, which would be the backbone for their operational level supply system and springboards for further offensives, and also failed to seize the mountain passes, through which men and materiel flowed to Khuzestan from Tehran.[28]

The Iraqi operation was a land grab rather than a properly run military invasion. It eventually did penetrate as deep as 65km into Iran, but in most places it remained rather shallow, with an average depth of 20–40km. Even so, the Iraqis eventually found themselves in possession of about 10,686km² of Iranian territory.[29] Although the Iraqis possessed the advantage in COMINT during the early months of the war, because Iranians communicated *en clair*, they failed to exploit this factor.[30] One reason for the shallow advance was a logistics system based upon that of the Soviet Army: the so-called 'supply push' philosophy, in which materiel was automatically sent forward to meet anticipated demand, rather than the 'demand pull' system, which responds to the units' actual requirements. This emptied Iraqi Army supply depots within a week, although much materiel was simply held by the forward units.[31]

Helicopter Support

Despite the many shortcomings of their military, sheer numerical superiority usually resulted in the Iraqis overpowering their opponents. True enough, the Iraqi planning and execution of military operations improved considerably through the 1970s – also at a tactical level – and the Iranians still suffered terribly due to revolutionary chaos. However, many Iraqi brigade, division and even corps COs proved inadequate and outright incompetent at operational and strategic levels. Worse still, Saddam insisted on painstakingly monitoring all battlefield activity and repeatedly meddled in command decisions with entirely useless suggestions and orders. This resulted in his subordinates finding themselves forced to ignore the realities of the battlefield and produce wildly exaggerated estimates of enemy strength to explain their sluggish advance.[32] Already by November 1980, it was noticeable that Iraqi troops would break under pressure; 'the Iraqi spirit I always feared', as Saddam put it. The head of the presidential secretariat, Tariq Hamed al-Abdullah, commented: 'That is why our mobile defence fails … we always (abandon) land.'[33]

Helicopters would play a major role supporting the armies during the next eight years. The IRAA operated 740 helicopter gunships, scout and transport helicopters and other combat support types in 31 battalions, dwarfing the 260 of the Iraqi Army Air Corps' (IrAAC) eight squadrons. Types in service ranged from the light (under 5 tonnes take-off weight) observation models such as the Augusta Bell 206A Jet Ranger in Iran and Aerospatiale SA 316C Alouette and SA 342 Gazelle in Iraq; to medium weight (5–12 tonnes take-off weight) utility transport aircraft such as the Agusta Bell 205A Iroquois and Bell 214 A/C Esfahan in Iran, and Mil Mi-8 (ASCC/NATO codename 'Hip C') in Iraq; and heavy (12 tonnes and above)

Ironically, the first combat missions of the Iranian Army Aviation were operations against Kurdish insurgents in north-western Iran in late 1979. This photograph shows Lieutenant Ahmed Keshavari and his colleagues with an AH-1J during pre-revolutionary training in Esfahan. (via N.R.)

PART I: FROM BORDER WAR TO INVASION

The Iranian Kurds proved to be good marksmen and they managed to shoot down a number of IRIAA helicopters. Interestingly enough, the Iranian military recovered every piece of wreckage it could get its hands upon, and most of the wrecked Cobras and Esfahans visible in this photograph were subsequently repaired and returned to service or recycled for spares. (via N.R.)

transports such as the Meridionali-Vertol CH-47C Chinook in Iran and Aerospatiale SA 321 Super Frelon in Iraq.

Both sides began deploying large numbers of armed helicopter gunships, though tactics employed were entirely different. Around 200 purpose-built, armoured Bell AH-1J Cobras of the IRIAA usually made low-level, terrain-following approaches to the battlefield, detected targets with the aid of M65 electro-optical sights, then climbed to launch BGM-71 TOW wire-guided anti-tank missiles (ATGMs) with a maximum range of 4.2km. Additionally, they had a 20mm three-barrel gun for attacks on soft targets and light armour, and 68mm calibre unguided rockets.[34] The combat radius of the AH-1J was about 290km.

The Iraqis had nothing comparable to the AH-1J. The most similar in terms of anti-tank capability and armour were about 20 of the much bigger and heavier Mil Mi-25 Hind helicopter gunships. However, their 9K17 Skorpion (Scorpion) (ASCC/NATO codename 'AT-2B' 'Swatter B') ATGMs were obsolete and these heavy helicopters were unable to hover in hot and high conditions, so their crews flew them as fighter-bombers. About 40 Gazelles, originally purchased by the IrAF but in service with the IrAAC by August 1980, were fast and nimble. Some were equipped with the SFIM APX-Bézu 334 or APX-397 gyrostabilised sights and could be armed with up to four French-made HOT ATGMs with a maximum range of 4.3km. When deploying such weapons, they operated in similar fashion to IRIAA Cobras. However, they lacked armour and their 'glasshouse' type cockpit proved very vulnerable, even to small arms fire. Nevertheless, for operations in 'low threat' areas, Gazelles were regularly armed with 20mm cannons installed inside the cabin and firing through the left door. Both sides' daylight operations benefited from television-based sighting systems and laser rangefinders, but night-time operations were severely restricted by the absence of thermal imagers and the shortage of image intensifiers, especially night vision goggles.[35]

Early Battles

On 28 September, after concluding he had achieved most of his territorial objectives, Saddam said he would accept a ceasefire, provided Tehran accepted Iraq's total rights over the Shatt and 'usurped Iraqi territories', and withdrew from the disputed islands in the Gulf. Actually, by this time the Iraqi military began to feel the power of the IRIAF, which was now not only unleashing regular strikes against the Iraqi oil industry, but also launched an all-out effort against enemy mechanised forces in Khuzestan. That day, the UN Security Council called for an end to hostilities and mediation on the dispute, while several organisations also offered to mediate. On 4 October, the Iraqi Army was ordered to destroy the captured border posts and tear up the frontier markers, and the following day Saddam announced a unilateral ceasefire, designed both to give the enemy time to seek terms and his own forces to rest and regroup.[36] However, this was little else but a propaganda effort: the fact was that by this time a few scattered task forces of the IRIA and three wings of the IRIAF were so effectively fighting the Iraqis in Khuzestan Province that the invasion was de facto brought to a standstill.

Unsurprisingly considering this, Tehran rejected both the ceasefire and all offers of mediation, then set its own price for peace as an immediate and rapid Iraqi withdrawal from the occupied territories, Saddam's resignation, $130 billion reparations (with Basra placed in Iranian hands as security) and autonomy for Iraqi Kurds. Nationalist emotion in response to the invasion boosted the Iranian regime: not only that, even Khuzestan's Sunni Arabs remained loyal to Iran (indeed one of them, Ali Shamkhani would later become Iranian Defence Minister), and their armed forces were soon bitterly fighting the Iraqis at every opportunity. If Tehran was serious with these demands, then it – just like Saddam before – badly overestimated its position. The diplomatic impasse continued for a month, during which it has been suggested that the clerics rejected

Saddam's terms because the war provided a useful instrument with which to beat their 'unpatriotic' secular enemies.[37]

When Saddam finally recognised there would be no immediate negotiated solution, he ordered his forces to renew their advance in November 1980. Progress was again slow and ended with the onset of the rainy season, which continued until early March and converted much of the battlefield into a swamp.[38] Within six weeks of the invasion, Saddam appears to have become concerned that he had the tiger by the tail. Not only had the IRIAF knocked out most of the Iraqi oil industry, forcing the country to stop exports and start importing fuel, but the Army also proved unable to maintain its momentum. Nevertheless, on 30 October he assured his cronies that the enemy was on the verge of defeat, although warning that it might take another six to 12 months. In typical fashion of a contradictive dictator, during a speech to the National Assembly on 4 November 1980, he admitted he now knew 'it would have been better if we did not go to war. But we had no other choice'.[39]

The Americans noted the advance appeared to meet little resistance at first, for the Iranians were stunned by Saddam's actions and only 25,000 members of the IRIA and IIG were deployed along the frontier.[40] Initially, resistance was sporadic and uncoordinated, with gendarmerie, border police, volunteers and Pasdaran setting up roadblocks or ambushes, then retreating or changing position without any apparent order or purpose. This led to the loss of much equipment, often after only token resistance.[41] There were a few exceptions to this rule, one of these being Task Force 37. Deployed to the frontline as the first Iranian armoured formation, it found itself equipped with only six M47Ms (two were unserviceable) and five M60A1s (one unserviceable) on the afternoon of 22 September. Nevertheless, it knocked out 18 Iraqi tanks during the fighting near the Fakkeh border post that day. By the next morning, the task force was down to three runners (two M60A1s and one M47M), but it not only knocked out another 15 Iraqi tanks but also successfully evacuated all eight tanks damaged the previous day. The task force continued in this fashion for several weeks thanks to plentiful provision of close air support (CAS) by the IRIAF and IRIAA, skilful manoeuvring, repeated counterattacks into Iraqi flanks and sporadic reinforcements in the form of small groups of Chieftains from the 92nd Armoured Division, together with hundreds of CAS sorties by Dezful-based F-5Es. Ultimately, it stopped the Iraqi advance upon Dezful in October.

Overall, the Iraqis claimed to have taken 10,000 prisoners of war (POWs), of which about 15 percent were junior officers and NCOs, some being paramilitary troops, although many of these were shot out of hand.[42] Actually, Iranian losses in manpower and materiel were minimal because – despite many claims to the contrary – they had very few military units deployed along the border with Iraq.

Curiously, US intelligence organisations such as the Defense Intelligence Agency largely ignored the presence of Iranian paramilitary forces, probably because they were no match for the Iraqis in open country where the Iranians, before the revolution, had planned to rely upon IRIA armoured units. Immediately after the invasion, the Iranian armoured brigades were reinforced by elements of 21st and 77th IRIA Infantry Divisions and the 84th Infantry Brigade. Most of the divisional artilleries were also deployed, some before the invasion and their skilful use began to be another important factor encouraging Iraqi caution. As the Iranians recovered, they began making more effective use of their US-supplied heavy weapons, especially gunships and artillery, augmented by the Soviet MLRS, despite frequent problems with ammunition supply.

The crew of an Iraqi T-55 – probably from the 5th Mechanised Division – seen west of Khorramshahr, waiting for orders to invade Iran in September 1980. Contrary to their expectations, the undertaking proved a major challenge for the Iraqi armoured juggernaut. (Albert Grandolini collection)

Ironically, despite the success of the IRIA, Iran's political leaders appear to have preferred to encourage the Pasdaran and Basij volunteers to provide the backbone of the defence, and significant elements of the IRIA, including the 88th Armoured Division, and 28th and 64th Infantry Divisions, remained in barracks during most of October and even later.[43]

4
THE INVASION OF KHUZESTAN

Khuzestan is Iran's prime source of hydrocarbons, with the Abadan refinery providing much of the country's refining capacity at 630,000 barrels a day. With these resources Saddam could rival Saudi Arabia, and he hoped for local support because a third of the province's 3.1 million population are Arabs. In April 1979, they had staged demonstrations in Khorramshahr for greater autonomy, but the Pasdaran and marines soon crushed this movement, losing a dozen Pasdaran and killing 100 Arabs.[1]

Saddam was indifferent to their fate; his prime objective was to control the Shatt. Lieutenant General Isma'ail Tayeh Ni'ami's III Corps was to take the northern bank by mid-September, then capture Abadan, both to deprive Iran of its largest refinery and to threaten the oil fields. The campaign saw a noticeable lack of support from Khuzestan's Arabs because of the brutal repression by the Iraqi Army, notably 9th Armoured Division's commander, Brigadier General Talia Khalil Al-Duri, who was praised by Saddam for executing 56 members of one tribe.[2] As a result, resistance within the province would be the fiercest and most effective encountered by the Iraqis.

Saddam's strategy also ignored the terrain. Khuzestan is bounded in the north-east by the Zagros Mountains (Kuhha-ye Zagros), which are more than 3,000 metres high and run north-west to south-east across the north-eastern third of the province. The north-western approaches to Khuzestan are through the neighbouring province of Ilam, with a main road running parallel with the international border from Mehran through Dehloran and Musian (also Daskt Mishan), where one fork leads eastward to Dezful down to Fakkeh, all in Ilam Province, with the latter being the gateway to Khuzestan. From there, one road leads north-eastwards to link with the Musian-Dezful road, with a side road from Chananeh (or Cheananeh) to Shush (also called Susa), which lies on the River Karkheh (Rudklianeh-ye Karkheh or Kharkhe Rud).

Between the frontier and the Karkheh is a region of sand dunes rising some 500–800 metres above the desert and running roughly east to west. This divided operations from the very beginning of the Iran-Iraq War: correspondingly, those north and south of the region will be dealt with in one of subsequent chapters.

The Karkheh and the Karun (Rud-e Karun) are the major rivers of Khuzestan. From the mountains, the Karkheh winds southwards through sandy desert, passing Dezful to the west, leaving a marshy trail like a snail. East of Bostan, the waters feed numerous fields crisscrossed with irrigation ditches, then the river passes north of Susangerd (called Khafajiyah by the Arabs). The river is also fed from the west by tributaries from the Hawizah (or Howeizah) Marshes, of which the most important is the River Karkheh Kur in the south, which runs roughly parallel south of the Karkheh before turning sharply north to join it at Hamidiyeh. At Hamidiyeh, the Karkheh also makes a 90° turn north-east to enter the Karun some 35km north of Ahwaz, an oil management and administrative centre, which also controls the main road and rail links to the south. The terrain in the western approaches from al-Amarah to Ahwaz make mechanised movement difficult and confine most traffic to the highway, which skirts the northern edge of the Hawizah Marshes and the northern bank of the Karkheh, which it crosses at Bostan and then runs along the southern bank of the river through Susangerd to Ahwaz.

The Karun, which runs through Ahwaz, is the principal river in south-west Khuzestan and Iran's only navigable inland waterway. South of Ahwaz, it meanders south-south-west, usually through irrigated fields, to empty into the Shatt just south of Khorramshahr

A platoon of T-62Ms – probably from the 3rd Armoured Division – advancing line abreast through the desert of western Khuzestan on 22 September 1980, the first day of the Iraqi invasion. Most Soviet-made vehicles showed a tendency to overheat in the hot environment because they were designed for operations in entirely different climatic conditions. (Tom Cooper collection)

A company of Iraqi T-55s seen lined-up for inspection before moving out. (Albert Grandolini collection)

The crew of an Iraqi Army OT-62 APC seen going into laager at the end of the day, near several T-55s. The soldier to the right is bringing a can of fresh water for a brew-up. (Albert Grandolini collection)

The 92nd Armoured Division, IRIAA, included the 151st Fortress Battalion, which operated a number of static M4 Shermans, armed with 105mm howitzers, positioned as pillboxes along the border. All such posts – including the one defended by this vehicle – were quickly overrun by the Iraqis, sometimes without a shot being fired. (Albert Grandolini collection)

(called Muhammarah by the Arabs). Between the river and the Hawizah Marshes is desert, which can become marshy during the winter rains, but in summer, according to British Army maps of 1943, is firm, allowing 1.5-tonne trucks to drive at speeds 'up to 40 mph' (74 km/h). There are some ancient stream beds across this region, where most transport is by minor roads, many of them on embankments, with a junction south-west of Susangerd at Hoveyzeh (also known as Huzgan). On either side of the river are two major metalled hard top highways which lead from Ahwaz in the west to Khorramshahr and to the east to Abadan.

Khorramshahr is a key communications hub, with a railway running alongside the Ahwaz highway and another highway running westwards along the northern bank of the Shatt through the border town of Shalamcheh (in Arabic, Shalmaja) to Basra. This highway ran past numerous palm plantations, which could not be penetrated by armoured vehicles and which could provide cover for infantry movement. Abadan is 8km from Khorramshahr and lies between the Shatt and the salt flats of the Musa Marshes (Khowr-e Musa), which are boggy in the winter but dry out in the summer and can often support the weight of a tank. There are numerous oil and gas fields in these marshes, with highways running eastward to the ports of Bandar-e Emam Khomeini (formerly Bandar-e Shahpur, and for convenience written as Bandar-e Khomeini) and Bandar-e Mashur (also Bande-e Mushahr or Bandar-e Mahshahr).

Ni'ami had retired from the Army in 1978 to become ambassador to Venezuela, then rejoined the colours in 1980 as Deputy Chief of the General Staff, but was given III Corps because he had helped to create it and was familiar both with its mission and leaders.[3] Because the plan assumed there would be no significant opposition from the weakened Iranian Army, Ni'ami allowed the offensive axes to diverge, but with only 20 battalions he faced a chronic shortage of infantry, which would make it difficult to consolidate his gains.

PART I: THE INVASION OF KHUZESTAN

A pair of Iraqi T-55s – probably from the 5th Mechanised Division – assembling outside Khorramshahr while their commander examines the terrain ahead of him. This division lost five such tanks on 3 October 1980 alone. (Albert Grandolini collection)

Members of the Iranian Gendarmerie posing with their small arms and MG1 machine guns, sometime in mid-September 1980. Most likely, the frontier post in question was overrun by the Iraqis only a few days later. (Albert Grandolini collection)

An Iranian volunteer soldier poses with a US-made M47 Dragon. This small and relatively light anti-tank system fired a missile with a diameter of only 140mm and had a maximum range of 1,000 metres. While its relatively short range made it quite unpopular among US troops, the Iranians made extensive use of Dragon, especially early during the war. Indeed, the effectiveness of the system was such that it prompted the Iraqis to start shopping for it too. (Albert Grandolini collection)

The northern prong consisted of part of the 10th Armoured Division and 1st Mechanised Division, which advanced upon Dezful, north of the dune region (the former reinforced by 10th Armoured Brigade on 26 September), while to the south, 9th Armoured Division drove towards Ahwaz.[4] These moves were intended to prevent reinforcements coming south to Ahwaz and allow 9th Armoured Division to link up with the 5th Mechanised Division, which spearheaded the southern axis. The latter had the most important strategic role in the campaign, to seize Khorramshahr and Abadan, then secure the northern bank of the Shatt al-Arab. Ni'ami had to control two diverging thrusts and, as insurance, he retained 3rd Armoured Division in second echelon, but would use its 6th Armoured Brigade and 8th Mechanised Brigade to isolate Khorramshahr from the north, storm across the River Karun and advance to Abadan.

Learning by Experience

Holding the 200km Khuzestan frontier were the IIG, assorted militia and the IRIA's half-strength 92nd Armoured Division, augmented by an armoured battalion of 88th Armoured Division and an infantry battalion each of 21st and 77th Infantry Divisions. The 92nd Division was deployed (north to south) with 2nd Brigade west of Dezful, 3rd Brigade west of Ahwaz and 1st Brigade between Ahwaz and Khorramshahr. Iraqi raids left the border forces nervous and near panic when they heard the growing roar of armoured vehicles approaching along the main roads on the morning of 22 September. Some border guards fled, often with civilians from border villages, while others made a brief, heroic but ultimately futile stand against the invaders' heavy weapons and superior numbers.

The first regular Iranian Army unit to offer serious resistance to the Iraqi 1st Mechanised and 10th Armoured Division as these advanced across the border was a small group of vehicles and troops from the 283rd Armoured Cavalry Battalion of the 92nd Armoured Division. The unit in question consisted of three M113 APCs and a few M38A1 jeeps toting launchers for BGM-71 TOW ATGMs, and four Scorpion light tanks, all commanded by Captain Tahami. Its baptism of fire on the afternoon of 22 September 1980 was as uneven as horrific a match: badly demoralised by the post-revolutionary chaos and purges of the preceding months, not to mention the sight of a massive formation of Iraqi armour moving in their direction, the Iranians were desperate and lacked confidence. Reluctantly, they fired the first missile: when this scored a hit, causing an Iraqi tank to explode, a salvo of TOWs followed, and the Iranians then continued with every weapon at their disposal as the range continued decreasing. Although losing numerous vehicles, the Iraqis fired back with everything they had, almost surrounding Tahami's unit before being forced to stop. After 24 hours of – in the words of one of the Iranian NCOs – 'fierce fireworks', this unit received the order to withdraw behind the Karoun River. The survivors did manage to extract themselves despite massive volumes of Iraqi artillery fire.1

While no Iraqi accounts of this clash are available, there is little doubt that the firepower of even this small Iranian unit left

An Iranian M60 providing cover for infantry during one of many local counterattacks launched to keep the invaders off balance. (Albert Grandolini collection)

Iranian naval commandos with a jeep mounting an M40 106mm recoilless gun, inside Khorramshahr in October 1980. The Iranian Navy's SBS unit and marines played a major, yet under-recognised role in defending Khorramshahr for 35 days in October and November 1980. In addition to fighting, they often also ran training courses for the local population and Pasdaran. (Farzin Nadimi collection)

Despite their cautious advance, the Iraqi Army suffered a steady toll of casualties from Iranian snipers and ATGM teams. This photograph shows the evacuation of several wounded crewmembers of a BMP-1. (Albert Grandolini collection)

the invaders impressed: henceforth, they would continue their advance with painful slowness, beginning each day with a bombardment – often onto empty ground. Their subsequent progress was cautious and led by tanks whose turrets were swinging backwards and forwards like sniffing dogs, constantly alert to resistance. Whenever reaching their daily objective, they would 'circle the wagons', vehicles and troops occupying defensive positions hastily constructed by bulldozers – which also formed the next day's jump-off point. Artillery was the weapon of choice to overcome resistance, and certainly leaving the Iranians deeply impressed already at this stage of the war.

Regrouping east of Karoun, Tahami was informed that the Iraqis were intent on quickly capturing TFB.4 outside Dezful. Therefore, he ordered his surviving six TOW-equipped vehicles into positions carved out by the bulldozers of the combat engineers along the eastern side of the river, on either side of the bridge carrying the expressway connecting Shoush with Dezful. The unit barely reached the area on the morning of 26 September, when IRIAF F-5Es from the nearby air base opened the battle with a fierce air strike upon the approaching Iraqis. Moments later, the nearest Iraqi tanks started firing at the Iranians: recognising that their position was identified by the enemy, but well-hidden behind earthen berms, the latter loaded their missiles and returned fire. In a matter of a few minutes, each M113 unleashed at least five TOWs, reportedly scoring 'hits on something of value each time': each hit caused the Iraqis to stop and debus to seek shelter in trenches and behind dirt mounds. For the following 24 hours, the small group of Iranian survivors held up the attack of an entire Iraqi division, losing one M113 and its crew in the process despite massive volumes of tank and artillery fire poured into its position. By the time it was reinforced by another group of TOW-equipped M113s and M38 jeeps on 28 September, nobody had slept or eaten, and their ammunition was almost exhausted. The Iraqis did attempt to reattack that day, launching a fierce onslaught. However, understanding the utmost importance of the bridge for the fate of not only Dezful and TFB.4, but the entirety of Khuzestan too, the Iranians offered fanatic resistance and held them off once again. About a dozen TOW-equipped M113s and M38 jeeps, a handful of Scorpion light tanks, and IRIAF air strikes thus managed to block the main Iraqi advance on Dezful for the crucial first week of the war.[5], [6]

Advance on Bostan and Susangerd

General Talia ad-Duri's 9th Armoured Division had mixed fortunes after it crossed the border supported by 12th Armoured Brigade/3rd Armoured Division and 31st SF Brigade. The 12th Armoured Brigade cleared the way through a 30km sweep which isolated a fortified IRIAF command and control facility, then ad-Duri's two

PART I: THE INVASION OF KHUZESTAN

Survivors from Task Force 37, posing in front of one of their M47Ms. The unit deployed six of these obsolete tanks and five M60s to counter the major Iraqi armoured thrust into northern Khuzestan. Exhaustion and heavy wear are clearly visible not only on their mount, but also on the faces and uniforms of the men. (Tom Cooper collection)

later commented, 'When this war was imposed on us, we moved from stage to stage with lots of hardship.'[9]

The Iraqis had only hours to enjoy their success, for at dawn on 17 November the Iranian counterattack struck along the southern bank of the Karkheh to retake Susangerd by the end of the day, supported by some 25 tactical fighter sorties. Not only did the Iranians regain Susangerd, but they also drove a wedge between the two Iraqi brigades to take Hoveyzeh and cut 9th Armoured Division's direct communications to the west. The Iraqis tried desperately to retake the village, but by 21 November it was firmly in Iranian hands.

armoured brigades drove along the Karkheh to take both Bostan and Susangerd without a fight on 28 September. Susangerd, a small provincial town 40km north-west of Ahwaz, had a population of some 20,000 and lay in rolling territory, but was a minor prize whose only value was that it controlled a bridge over a tributary of the River Karkheh. Ad-Duri lacked infantry to hold the town, which he then abandoned but covered with a chain of observation posts in an arc to the west and south while he renewed his advance upon Ahwaz. By 5 October, the Iraqis finally managed to cross the Karkheh Kur at three locations and secure a 10km-wide bridgehead, but progress eastwards was slow as Iranian resistance increased and 9th Armoured Division's supply lines were not only stretched, but were also heavily struck by the IRIAF. By mid-October, the advance was held some 40km south-west of Ahwaz by defenders who consisted largely of Pasdaran augmented by two understrength companies (one tank and one mechanised) and two self-propelled batteries (M109, M107) from the 92nd IRIA Armoured Division's 3rd Brigade, whose main body was concentrated around Ahwaz. By mid-November, the Iranians had established a firm line on the southern bank of the Karkheh anchored on Susangerd, which lay like a boil near the Iraqi supply lines and which Talia Al-Duri now sought to lance. He sent 35th and 43rd Armoured Brigades to retake the town, defended by 400 IIG and Pasdaran, leaving 14th Mech Brigade to mask Ahwaz. The attack began on 13 November but took three days to take the town and several Iraqi tanks were lost.

Meanwhile, IRIA engineers helped the local power company to flood first the Karkheh and later Karkheh Kur valleys by breaking the banks and opening sluices.[7] Later, the Iranians flew visitors over the site, where some 150 armoured vehicles were reported still covered by water with their turrets sticking out.[8] Meanwhile, Iranian ground forces, helicopter gunships and IRIAF intensively interdicted enemy supply columns and Tehran assembled some 2,000 Pasdaran and IRIA troops, including an armoured battalion of 92nd IRIA Division, at Hamidiyeh to recapture Susangerd. Many of the Pasdaran had previously been fighting a counterinsurgency campaign in the northern mountains of Kurdistan and found it hard to adjust to conventional warfare in open terrain. Some found themselves under shellfire for the first time, and one commander

Battle of Shalamcheh

By late November, 9th Armoured Division controlled an arc south-west of Ahwaz and Operations Chief Asadi was considering a new assault upon Ahwaz with Talia ad-Duri's division reinforced by 20th Mech Brigade/5th Mechanised Division and 3rd Armoured Division's 8th Mech Brigade. Flooding caused a shortage of drinking water, and while 20th Brigade drew some from the Karkheh, much of it had to be brought in from Basra as work began on boring artesian wells. IRIA gunners maintained sustained and accurate fire, which further encouraged Saddam's troops to dig in and became such a problem that Asadi asked the 5th Mechanised Division commander, Brigadier General Salah Al-Qadhi, to consider a helicopter assault upon enemy batteries.[10]

On III Corps' right flank, Qadhi's 5th Mechanised Division had the key role of the campaign, which was to secure the Shatt's northern bank, then extend Iraqi control up the Karun to Ahwaz, where it would link with 9th Armoured Division. His forces here advanced on two narrow axes split by a flooded anti-armour feature dubbed the Fish Lake (Buhayrat Al-Asmak), with 15th Mech Brigade advancing from al-Qurnah between the Hawizah Marshes and the lake. It crossed the frontier and easily reached the Khorramshahr–Ahwaz highway despite light resistance from an understrength tank company, two mechanised companies of 3rd Brigade/92nd IRIA Armoured Division supported by a battalion of 22 M109s and two batteries of 10 M107s. It took three days to advance some 50km to Hamid, from where it made contact with 9th Armoured Division while still 30km from Ahwaz.[11]

In Basra, Qadhi concentrated 26 AB and 20 MB from 9 September, as engineers threw a 390-metre Soviet-built PMP pontoon bridge (with a carrying capacity of 60 tonnes) across the Tigris with what US intelligence described as 'considerable skill'. Iraqi river crossing equipment inventory included the GSP ferry system (carrying capacity 52 tonnes), the 40-metre TMM truck-launched bridge system (capacity 60 tonnes), the TPP heavy pontoon bridge which could carry up to 70 tonnes in the 185-metre version and PTS tracked amphibious trucks with 10 tonnes capacity.[12]

Thought to have been grounded by the majority of Western observers, the IRIAA rushed its AH-1 Cobras into combat right from the start of the war. Together with Northrop F-5 Tiger II fighter-bombers from Tactical Fighter Base 4, Iranian helicopter gunships played a crucial role in the defence of Dezful. (Tom Cooper collection)

An F-5E Tiger II from TFB.4, underway at low altitude. Flying up to 60 close air support sorties a day, the three squadrons based at Vahdati AB near Dezful smashed the Iraqi advance toward that town. (Farzin Nadimi collection)

Fire support came from artillery and MLRS batteries east of Basra, while on the south bank of the Shatt, opposite Khorramshahr and Abadan, was an 18-gun artillery battalion and 160mm mortar batteries. They were augmented by 140mm MLRS on two of the Iraqi Navy's Polish-built Polnocny-D (Project 773) class medium landing ships which were being refitted in Basra when the war broke out, and each ship's pair of launchers could easily reach the north bank of the Shatt.[13] The batteries were protected by air defence assets ranging from ZSU-23-4 self-propelled quad 23mm guns to 2K12 Kub (Cube) (ASCC/NATO codename 'SA-6' 'Gainful') self-propelled triple-missile launchers organised into brigades, with 3rd, 6th and 10th Armoured Divisions supported by the 155th, 162nd and 175th Missile Brigades respectively.[14]

By 15 September, the Iranians could see enemy armour assembling at the border near Shalamcheh, and as word filtered eastwards the border guards were augmented by a ragtag group of individuals including marines, some Pasdaran and a few people calling themselves Fadaeiyan-e Islam (Devotees of Islam). Most were killed fighting 26th Armoured Brigade as it advanced upon Shalamcheh, where the advance was briefly held as Pasdaran, with little ammunition, defended a demolished bridge before being overwhelmed. Most survivors, short of food which they scavenged from abandoned shops, sometimes leaving payment, retreated to Khorramshahr, although some fought as guerrillas in Shalamcheh until they were killed.[15] Militia reinforcements arrived to a very confused and fluid battlefield. An Iranian history notes that a force of Isfahan Basij arriving on the

PART I: THE INVASION OF KHUZESTAN

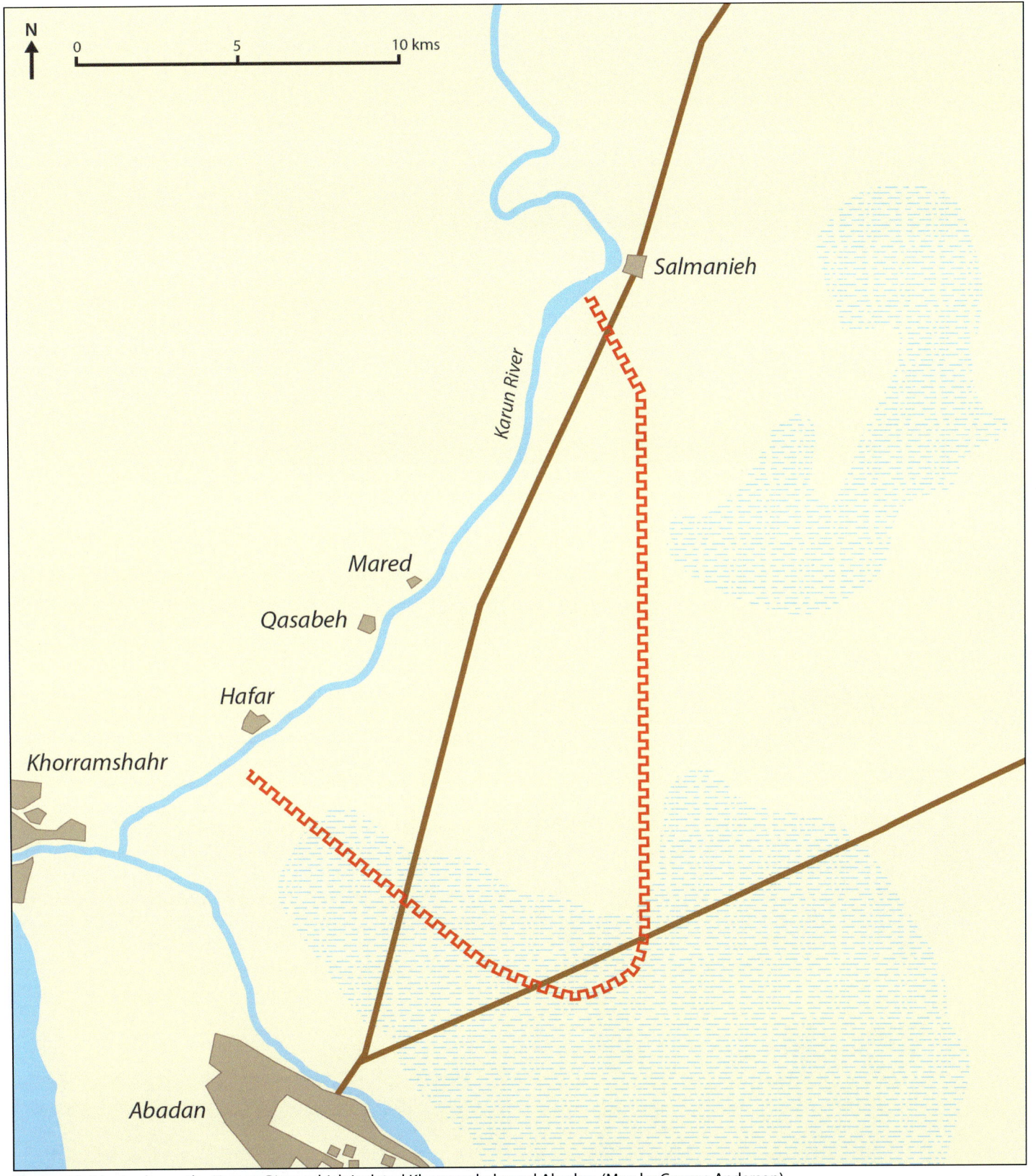

The Iraqi bridgehead over the Karoun River, which isolated Khorramshahr and Abadan. (Map by George Anderson)

battlefield by bus did not realise they had reached the Forward Edge of Battle Area (FEBA) until they came under fire and later came across the remnants of another convoy which had been destroyed.[16]

The hardworking Iraqi engineer corps quickly replaced the Shalamcheh bridge and the advance continued, joined by 3rd Armoured Division (Brigadier General Kaddoori Jabiar Al-Duri), which would isolate Khorramshahr from the north. The division's 12th Armoured Brigade was with 9th Armoured Division, while three artillery battalions were in the corps reserve. Recognising the severity of the threat, the IRIAF directed considerable effort against the enemy advance and helped to restrict progress, so it took the Iraqis three or four days to advance the 15km from the border, cut the main road north to Ahwaz and reach the northern outskirts of Khorramshahr. Iraqi Gazelle helicopter gunships with HOT anti-armour missiles were also active on the Khuzestan front and claimed 17 Chieftains during 1980.[17] With the Iranian

Troops of the Iraqi 6th Armoured Brigade seen on the morning of 11 October 1980, waiting for the order to advance using two PMP pontoon bridges constructed over the Karoun River, near Mared. This operation was intended to become a springboard for capturing Abadan. (Tom Cooper collection)

government still suspicious of the IRIA, Tehran was forced to transfer operational command in the south to the IIG, with headquarters at Arvand Kenar, although the Gendermerie commanders were unsuitable for conventional military operations.

Battles of Khorramshahr and Abadan

Khorramshahr was once Khuzestan's capital and was now the southern terminus of the north-south rail line. Under the Shah, from 1965 it became a city of 270,000 people, although most of the women, children and elderly were evacuated on 25 September. The city is 7km long and 5km wide and sits at the confluence of the Karun and the Shatt, with part on the Karun's south bank linked by the Basra–Abadan highway bridge some 2.5km upstream.[18] The highway runs west-north-west to east-south-east, with most of the modern city, including the Grand Mosque and police station, to the north, and some 500 metres south of these two buildings there is a roundabout, from which the highway runs straight to the bridge.

Between the highway, the Shatt and the Karun, lies of the heart of the city with the rail station in the north-west and palm groves along the Shatt. Where the waterways meet are the port and oil terminal, with rows of jetties, wharves, quays, a maze of oil pipelines, as well as the customs area with warehouses and storage yards. To the east, sprawling along the Karun's northern bank, was the old town, up to 2km long and 1.5km deep, a maze of twisting streets and alleyways. The north and west was a substantial suburban sprawl following the expansion of the population in the previous decade, while across the bridge the city gradually merged with Abadan to create a single urban area. The outskirts consisted of single-storey brick or mud-brick buildings, often with small gardens, while the centre was dominated by modern, multi-storey buildings.

Having crossed the Karoun, Iraqi infantry tried in vain to fight their way into Abadan. These troops are shown while taking cover behind an embankment, supported by an RPG gunner and a machine-gunner. (Albert Grandolini collection)

Infantry from either the 3rd Armoured or the 5th Mechanised Division cautiously combing tall grass along the bank of the Karoun, while moving towards Khorramshahr. (Albert Grandolini collection)

PART I: THE INVASION OF KHUZESTAN

A dug-in T-62M of the 3rd Armoured Division seen against the backdrop of a palm grove, near the Shatt al-Arab, while preparing to support another push on Khorramshahr. (Albert Grandolini collection)

The fierce resistance of Iranian Army regulars and various local militias infuriated the invading Iraqis. This is clearly shown by the ill treatment of both military and civilian prisoners by the crew of this OT-62. (Albert Grandolini collection)

The IRIA garrison from 92nd Division consisted of only 500 men from the 151st Fortress Battalion and elements of 3rd Brigade, for the Army realised the city was too exposed and could not be held for long. The only other regular troops present were an understrength Marine battalion reinforced by cadets from the naval base. However, volunteers had rushed to the city's defence and there would be 3,000 fighters, Pasdaran, police, customs officials, Basij and ordinary civilians directed by Pasdaran commander Mohamad Ali Jahanara from the Grand Mosque. The twisting streets of the old town were blocked with barricades, while trenches were dug elsewhere and the handful of mortars were carefully emplaced. Although ammunition might have been a problem in the long run, the defenders had a plentiful supply of both food and water.[19]

The western approaches to the town were shielded by two berms, earth or sand walls created from the earth of a ditch in front of it. With modern earthmoving equipment, they were easy to construct, especially in deserts, to provide an obstacle to vehicle movement. They were thick enough to shelter infantry in foxholes and slit trenches just beyond the crest or immediately behind. The first berm was reportedly held largely by IRIA troops, while the second, some 5km behind it, had militias, together with heavy weapons and some Chieftain tanks, allegedly with orders to shoot the regulars if they attempted to withdraw.

With Saddam's attention focused upon Abadan and Ahwaz, the Iraqis wished to avoid a prolonged urban battle for Khorramshahr. Indeed, on 1 October, Saddam said he wanted to 'take over the land not the city', which was to be destroyed.[20] Qadhi was to push into the city from the west with 26th Armoured Brigade, while 3rd Armoured Division (Jabiar Al-Duri) isolated it, then push 6th Armoured Brigade through its northern suburbs to take the highway bridge. He would then advance to Abadan while Qadhi covered his left as Khorramshahr was mopped up and occupied by Special Forces and Popular Army troops. A fast-moving mechanised force might have achieved this, but Jabiar Al-Duri was too slow, and as he entered the city's northern and eastern suburbs resistance was stiffening. He was soon under fire from all sides, but desperately decided to press on as the battle for Khorramshahr, like Topsy in Uncle Tom's Cabin, 'just growed'.

The Iraqis' first task was to take the berms, and from 26 September Khorramshahr endured two days of artillery, rocket and mortar fire from the west and across the Shatt. The berms were then assaulted after a separate bombardment and quickly fell, most of the IRIA defenders being lost, and by the night of 29/30 September Jabiar Al-Duri had isolated Khorramshahr. But as he and Qadhi pushed into the suburbs, they suffered losses in a string of ambushes which cost them men and vehicles. The urban environment was ideal for the untrained defenders, for AFVs are vulnerable to short-range anti-armour weapons, which included RPG-7s and US M40 106mm recoilless rifles with their tracer-equipped spotting rifles, as well as Molotov cocktails. The defenders' few Chieftain MBTs acted as mobile anti-tank guns to dominate open areas and pick off enemy armour.

The intensity of the resistance was an unpleasant surprise for the Iraqis and underlined a significant weakness, for while 3rd Armoured Division had plenty of AFVs and artillery support, it lacked infantry, with no more than 2,500–3,000 men available. As the invaders paused to take stock, the IRIA appeared to change its mind about defending the town for, on 1 October, troops from

45

Artillery support proved a major problem for the Iraqis. A shortage of airburst fuses for 130mm guns led Shanshal to order Field Artillery Director Major General Salim Bakr to transfer a battery of retired British 87mm gun-howitzers (25-pdrs) from the artillery school to the Khorramshahr front. The BM-21 MLRS provided some compensation and the front had priority for these rockets.[22]

Firepower gradually pushed back the defenders and allowed the Iraqis to establish a command post, protected by T-62 and T-55 tanks, in a fertiliser factory and free part of 5th Mechanised Division. By 3 October, they controlled most of the customs areas in the west, but not the port and were probing the old town, where conditions were ideal for the lightly armed defenders. The battlefield became covered with dense and acrid clouds of black smoke from the blazing oil storage tanks on Abadan, retaliatory bombardments of Iraqi facilities and ships in the Shatt deliberately shelled or caught in the crossfire. Iranian bombardment of the refinery on the Faw Peninsula forced the Iraqis to evacuate the 70,000 civilian population from Faw town, while many of Abadan's 300,000 civilians fled northwards.

During 3 October, the Iraqis tried to advance from the northern part of the customs area to the main road, and from there to the bridge, but encountered the usual fierce resistance, which left 15 AFVs destroyed, including five tanks. Whenever an Iraqi advance was held, the invaders were given no respite and faced frequent counterattacks, sometimes supported by armour, while police units used tear gas and irritant agents.[23] Artillery fire usually broke up these attacks, but exploiting the success was difficult, especially in the old town, where the narrow streets, often barricaded, restricted AFV movement, while sniper fire took its toll of the infantry.

The ruins of Khorramshahr made ideal defensive terrain for the Iranians – whether regulars from the IRIA, surviving gendarmes, the police, or the Pasdaran. One of the latter is seen in this photograph, crouching in the road with his G3 rifle ready. (Albert Grandolini collection)

55th Airborne Brigade were brought in by helicopter, while Iranian artillery fire increased in intensity in the enemy rear.

Despite the earlier setback, Qadhi began pushing into the western edges of the city, relying upon artillery to clear the way, but the rubble restricted AFV movement and provided concealment and shelter for the defenders. Reinforced by two mechanised rifle battalions and elements of the 33rd SF Brigade (initially only 8th Battalion), but still relying upon their tanks and IFVs, Iraqi spearheads, preceded by rolling barrages, reached the rail station. Some troops may have benefited from hasty training in an unconventional warfare training complex being built at Salam Pak, some 25km south-east of Baghdad, although it was not completed until February 1981.[21]

When commandos, armour and artillery proved insufficient, the Iraqis rushed some of 100 ERC-TH armoured cars armed with HOT (*Haut subsonique Otpiquement Teleguide tire d'un tube*) ATGMs to the frontlines around Abadan. This vehicle was photographed while crossing the Karoun River. (Albert Grandolini collection)

The apparent lack of support from IRIA forces, notably the headquarters of 1st Brigade/92nd Armoured Division, reinforced Pasdaran paranoia as the defenders ran short of heavy weapons, ammunition and even men. The brigade had only its 165th Mechanised Infantry Battalion, augmented from the divisional reserve by an artillery battalion (M109) and the Chieftains of 232nd Armoured Battalion, all of these units at half-strength, scattered over a 110km front between Ahwaz and Abadan and in no condition to stage a counteroffensive.[24] The IRIAF began striking supply dumps, gun positions and communications, but on 6 October the Iraqis, now with 12 Armoured Brigade and reinforced the next day by nine batteries (32 guns), secured the northern suburbs and the western part of the port. The port's eastern part remained firmly in the defenders' hands, together with the old town and bridge, but Iraqi tanks along the waterfront enfiladed streets which ran parallel to the river.

Ni'ami belatedly realised he was no nearer taking Abadan and would need a new approach at Khorramshahr. He was sent reinforcements, augmented from 2 October by new engineer units, as he prepared to go around Khorramshahr, while three days later his artillery began to interdict the east bank highway to Ahwaz. Pressure upon Khorramshahr continued, and from 7 October, as Ni'ami appears to have taken tactical control of storming the city, the Iraqis pushed into both the eastern docks and the old town, remorselessly advancing block by block in three days of bloody fighting. They benefited from special forces reinforcements, so there were now four battalions (2,000 men) from the 33rd SF Brigade, as well as the 3rd Republican Guards Battalion (500 men), who were better trained than the average conscript and both self-reliant and flexible in their approach. But there had also been hasty retraining of the infantry in combined-arms and urban warfare tactics, as well as night operations.

On 11 October, the 3rd Armoured Division by now reinforced by up to six infantry battalions, including from II Corps 49th Brigade/11th Infantry Division and 23rd Brigade/8th Infantry Division, as well as two Popular Army battalions with a total strength of some 5,000 men was ready to complete the capture of Khorramshahr, having established a bridgehead across the Karun some hours earlier (see below). Within the city there was a drive southwards into the old town, which a mechanised battalion tried to roll up from the east by pushing along the bank as commandos advanced upon the highway bridge. This took Jahanara by surprise, but he reacted quickly, aided by the Iraqis' usual caution, and the advance was quickly stopped.

On 12 October, Iraqi special forces took the bridge, but another four days were required to eliminate the defenders around the structure and its northern approaches. With the old town now isolated, the Iraqis began to crush the remaining resistance with increased fire support from across the Shatt, where Ni'ami had added another artillery battalion and mortar batteries. By 24 October, he had taken the whole of Khorramshahr north of the river and established a bridgehead south of the bridge, but the Iranians stopped every Iraqi attempt to break out.

Two Pasdaran seen inside a wrecked building in Khorramshahr. With their excellent knowledge of the local buildings and streets, the Iranians were in possession of a significant advantage even when fighting Iraqi commando units. (Albert Grandolini collection)

After a brief pause, the Iraqis began a last effort to take the remainder of the city with a new bombardment from 24 October which was so heavy the Iranians complained they could not evacuate their wounded in ambulances.[25] The remaining Iranian Chieftain tanks were unable to contribute much to the defence because the narrow streets limited their fields of fire. During the next two days, the Iraqis tightened their grip and on the night of 25/26 October, most of the defenders, including Jahanara, slipped away to join the defence of Abadan, leaving a wrecked city. The Iranians only acknowledged the loss on 4 November, when batteries on Abadan Island began laying down bombardments on its battered streets. The victors looted the city and sometimes fought among themselves for the spoils, a reaction to their heavy losses estimated at between 4,000 (1,000 dead) to 12,000 (4,000 dead) and up to 100 AFVs; little wonder both sides later referred to the city as Khooninshahr, Khuninistan or 'City of Blood'.[26]

Even as the bloody battle for Khorramshahr raged on, Ni'ami prepared to advance upon Abadan to secure the north bank of the Shatt. But this seemed likely to be as great a hazard as Khorramshahr. Abadan is effectively a 155km² island, with the Shatt curling round to the west and south, the Karun to the north and the Bahmanshir (also written as Bahamshehr) in the east. The Musa Marshes to the north and east extend some 5km north of Abadan's suburbs, while to the north is a dusty plain which is subject to flooding during the rainy season. It is a modern city with a huge oil refinery with a storage 'tank farm' at its heart, with most of the homes being to the east.

Abadan faced a heavy bombardment, which included FROG missiles, directed from an observation post across the Shatt near the tiny Iraqi port of Siba. The bombardment was a trial for the defenders, and Iraqi COMINT intercepted a stream of complaints demanding action to relieve their suffering. The garrison was a mechanised battalion, a tank battalion (probably with only 25 tanks), the local IIG regiment, a naval battle group based upon

Two Iranian SBS commandos that helped defend Khorramshahr, seen during a lull in the fighting on 19 October 1980. (Farzin Nadimi collection)

the two Marine battalions and Pasdaran; indeed half the 7,000 defenders were the Islamic Revolution's bearded warriors.[27] They were placed under 2nd Brigade/77th IRIA Infantry Division, which was gradually transferred from Mashad over a six-week period from late September with some of its component units.[28]

Unable to take the highway bridge in Khorramshahr, Ni'ami decided to launch an amphibious assault north of the city. On 5 October, he received pontoon and ferry companies as political pressure grew, Defence Minister Khairrallah bombarded his headquarters for nearly a fortnight urging him to hurry, while a visit from Shanshal added pressure. Khairrallah proposed using Mil Mi-6 (ASCC/NATO codename 'Hook') heavy helicopters to carry vehicles across the Karun and the reinforcement of 3rd Armoured Division with Popular Army units.[29]

With most of 3rd Armoured Division in Khorramshahr and the remainder of III Corps fully committed, Saddam decided to leave Jabiar Al-Duri in overall command of crossing the Karun, but augmented his forces with elements of 5th Mechanised Division and II Corps. Shanshal had planned to use Khazraji's 7th Mountain Division, which began practising river crossings, but this was replaced by 8th Infantry Division's 23rd Brigade, together with 5th Mechanised Division's 26th Armoured Brigade which would provide flank cover.[30]

The crossing point was to be near Mared, some 15km north-east of Khorramshahr, where there was firm ground for armour. Jabiar Al-Duri's plan called for 23rd Brigade, led by special forces, to storm the opposite bank and establish a bridgehead using GSP ferries, then his engineers would deploy two PMP bridges for 6th Armoured Brigade. Because the Musa Marshes restricted exploitation eastward, with only the highways north to Ahwaz and east to Bandar-e Khomeini/Bandar-e Mashur being suitable for armour, these meeting just north of Abadan, 6th Armoured Brigade would seize this junction and advance along the highways as far as possible to isolate Abadan from the north. The defence was weak and was further undermined when 92nd IRIA Division's 232nd Armoured Battalion simply provided a screen of tank platoons along the bank of the Karun.

The crossing began on the night 10/11 October when there was limited visibility, but it was aided by a 1.5-metre drop in water level during the previous two days. However, a 20-metre band of soft mud on either side meant a considerable amount of preparation work before bridging the river. First, infantry crossed in assault boats to clear the riverbank and captured 10 Chieftain MBTs, virtually annihilating the armoured detachment. This was the Iraqi Army's first forced river crossing and the 23rd Brigade's heart was not in the mission, with the men unhappy fighting in swampy terrain against aggressive enemy infantry. When enemy pressure forced one battalion commander to adjust his lines by pulling back his lead company, this panicked the rest, who believed it was withdrawing, and while the panic was eventually stopped, it meant the bridgehead was smaller than planned. Meanwhile, Iraqi engineers began assembling the PMPs, but 6th Armoured Brigade failed to arrive on time, so at dawn work ceased while both equipment and vehicles were camouflaged to avoid IRIAF detection. Iraqi errors actually helped their operation, for they convinced the defenders it was either just a raid or a reconnaissance.

During the day, 6th Armoured Brigade arrived, and from dusk the PMPs were assembled and most of the armour crossed to assemble upon the eastern bank on 14 October, as 26th Brigade moved in behind it to cover its flank. The defenders were unaware of the scale of the threat until the afternoon, when a tank battalion of 6th Armoured Brigade drove up the Ahwaz road and ambushed a convoy coming the other way. Chieftain tanks escorting the convoy covered its hasty retreat, exploiting their superior guns and armour, but both sides were hamstrung by the off-road mud which mired many tanks. The Iranians were driven back and lost a number of AFVs, including at least 20 tanks, as the road came under Iraqi artillery fire, yet it remained a major Iranian artery despite the danger and difficulty. The IRIAF and IRIAA interdicted the bridges, but even when they hit them the modular nature of the PMP made them easy to repair.

Meanwhile, 6th Armoured Brigade approached Abadan along the eastern bank of the River Bahmanshir. Although harassed by Iranian gunships and leaving a trail of destroyed vehicles, by 16 October it had cut both of the highways to Ahwaz and Bandar-e Khomeini and Bandar-e Mashur to create a bridgehead some 20km deep and 15km wide. But the Iraqis remained within the marsh line and were unable to cut the junction of the two highways to the east, and these became the Abadan garrison's prime supply route. The

PART I: THE INVASION OF KHUZESTAN

southern tip of Abadan 'island' was not covered by Iraqi artillery fire, which allowed the Iranians to use small boats, hovercraft and helicopters to ferry reinforcements and supplies, mostly at night, then evacuate the wounded. Some vessels continued to sail into Abadan's naval base, Muhammara, and one was shelled by the newly arrived 49th Infantry Brigade/11th Infantry Division in early October, but when the Iraqi Navy tried to interdict maritime traffic into Abadan it suffered serious losses. The lifelines helped to reinforce the garrison, bringing the defenders to some 10,000 men, including 5,000 Pasdaran, who were grimly confident of holding the wrecked city, yet they would not be tested too greatly.

The Iraqis sought to tighten their hold on Abadan, and on the night of 31 October/1 November used assault boats to cross the Bahmanshir to the south of Abadan and established a pontoon bridge to support a bridgehead. This bridgehead was slowly expanded in the face of stiff resistance, with numerous counterattacks, while fixed-wing and rotary-wing aircraft pounded the Iraqi rear, but, ultimately, it was the Iraqis' lack of infantry which hamstrung their attempt to take Abadan. The front remained extremely open, and early in November, Iranian Oil Minister Muhammad Jawad Baqir and several aides were captured while making an unescorted tour of inspection of the oil fields. He would tell his captors that even ministers were not informed about events on the battlefield.[31]

For 10 days the struggle continued, then the Iranians launched an attack using the 77th IRIA Division's 153rd Infantry Battalion (Lieutenant Colonel Manuchehr Kehtari), marines and Pasdaran, with helicopter and some fixed-wing air support, and this drove the

Chieftains – probably from the 232nd Armoured Battalion – line up before engaging the Iraqi forces that crossed the Karoun. (Albert Grandolini collection)

One of several Iranian Chieftains knocked out by the Iraqis during the advances on Abadan and Khorramshahr. (Tom Cooper collection)

enemy back across the river by 19 November, their pontoon bridge being destroyed. By now Abadan was under constant tank and artillery bombardment, and to create a jump-off point for a new attack into the town during November, the Iraqis tried to throw another PMP across the Shatt directly into Khorramshahr but were thwarted by accurate Iranian artillery fire. Nevertheless, the Iraqis were able to strengthen their bridgehead across the Karun and to take more of the road to Bander-e Mahshur and Bandar-e Khomeini, but exhaustion and the weather combined to bring operations against Abadan to a halt by mid-November.[32] US intelligence commented that the two urban battles deprived the Iraqis of 'the psychological, logistical and strategic initiative'.[33] One side effect of the two battles was that the Iranian marines suffered some 90 percent casualties and Tehran disbanded the corps.[34]

The Armies Take Stock

Baghdad had hoped to take Abadan and Khorramshahr by the Islamic festival of Eid al-Adha (Festival of the Sacrifice) on 20 October. But on 19 October, Saddam appeared on television to state that victory had eluded his forces because of 'geographical injustice' and the enemy's technological superiority. During this speech, he referred to the conflict as a 'Jihad' (holy war) which would be second only to the Battle of Qadisiyya. During the third week of November, the rainy season began and lasted until the end of February 1981, washing out the fighting. The rivers flooded and the plains became marshes, effectively isolating many Iraqi formations, but the problem was anticipated and Iraqi engineers had begun to build a network of all-weather roads from Basra towards Ahwaz, and these were used to distribute arms, ammunition and supplies to forward depots.

With fighting reduced to skirmishes and artillery duels, both sides took stock. The Iraqi Army had barely achieved its minimum objectives and failed to take most key urban areas due to excessive caution of specific commanders. Blind firepower replaced well-timed manoeuvre, there was an overreliance upon armoured/mechanised forces and little attempt at combined-arms operations or even of integrating them with air power. Indeed, in stark contrast to the IRIAA, the first time the IrAAC planned and used its helicopter force, according to General Hamdani, was only on 27 October.[35]

As one commentator noted: 'Operationally, the offensive was marred by excessively centralised command and control, poorly chosen objectives, faulty tailoring of forces, ineffective combined-arms and lack of joint co-ordination'.[36]

Saddam demanded his commanders learn the lessons from their experiences, yet he was responsible for many of the problems, either directly (through centralised command) or indirectly (through his choice of subordinates). With every month, Iran's numerical superiority became a growing threat, with the force ratio dropping from 6:1 in Saddam's favour to 2:1 by November, and soon it would be reversed. This made him acutely aware of casualties, yet while he demanded reductions in casualties, he informed 10th Armoured Division commander Major General Hesham Sahah to avoid heavy losses and later complained to his cronies that Sahah needed to be 'educated'. On 7 December 1980, Saddam announced Iraq would confine itself to ambushes, raids and patrols and that ambushes were to be well-planned, avoid excessive losses and seek a 1:5 casualty rate in Iraq's favour.[37]

Saddam recognised he was in a strategic impasse; his gamble that a swift seizure of terrain would encourage regime change in Tehran had failed, leaving him unable either to advance or retreat. The Iranian regime was in no mood to negotiate, and while unready

Iraqi troops atop a captured Chieftain near Susangerd in late September 1980. The vehicle might have been lost to mechanical failure or because it ran out of fuel. (Albert Grandolini collection)

to launch its own offensives, it certainly would not allow Saddam simply to fold his tent and withdraw. Even if he did, the loss of prestige would probably encourage Shi'a unrest within his own borders, so all he could do was to strengthen his bridgeheads and hope for an opportunity to negotiate control of the Shatt.

In Tehran, the political situation was unsettled, with a struggle for control of the revolution between the secular liberals and leftists on one side and the clerics on the other. For the clerics, the war created a situation beyond their comprehension. They conceived of combat in heroic terms, led by the Pasdaran fighting and dying until they had killed all the hated invaders. IRIA attempts to introduce reality in terms of combined-arms tactics and logistics were regarded, if at all, with suspicion. Yet the situation was not without hope, for the country had a huge numerical advantage in terms of manpower; indeed, so many Iranians volunteered to fight that neither the IRIA nor the Pasdaran could absorb them, and many were sent to eastern Iran on policing and counterinsurgency duties. Many unarmed Pasdaran (and Basij) recruits went to the front to continue the fight with weapons from those killed or wounded, while some IRIA armoured and mechanised units had twice as many men to man their vehicles than they needed and began rotating their personnel so they spent only one week in four at the front. The IRIA and the regular armed forces were further boosted with the reintroduction of tax privileges for their personnel, both to attract their return to the colours and to boost their morale.[38]

However, there was a shortage of qualified junior leaders, while command and control was further hamstrung, both by a lack of radios and the presence of suspicious clerical 'advisors' acting like Soviet Army commissars, ready to meddle in military matters. There remained great tensions between the IRIA and the Pasdaran, whose brave and stubborn defence of urban areas had enhanced their prestige, although their performance in mobile operations was untested. Bani-Sadr's support for the IRIA was a major source of friction between himself and the clerics, which overshadowed the Iranian response to the invasion.

The IRIA's artillery won the clerics' grudging respect because it proved more than a match for their opponents in terms of accuracy and firepower. Because much Iranian ordnance consisted of self-propelled mountings, they could, in the contemporary jargon, 'shoot and scoot', and were especially effective in a counterbattery role against the less mobile and more exposed Iraqi towed artillery. Saddam's 130mm guns were also running short of ammunition and were increasingly augmented by 122mm M-30 howitzers from the mountain divisions, but by late October 1980 the Iraqis had also fired 40,000 of its 83,000 rounds of 122mm howitzer ammunition.[39]

The 'Achilles heel' of the Iranian forces was logistics, a weakness inherited from the Shah's army. The sophisticated American-developed computer-based inventory system for all the services' logistical organisations was not operational when the revolution broke out, and then 'the Great Satan' took many of the electronic records. It took much time, amid the chaos of revolution and war, to get the system back online, often using manual methods to locate material and then update computer inventories, and the Iranians discovered that poor storage and maintenance techniques had left some material useless.

The loss of many experienced maintenance personnel from the armed forces during the revolution had reduced serviceability rates, especially vehicles and aircraft. While many returned after the invasion, a year's neglect meant much equipment required extensive maintenance and repair, which consumed huge amounts of spares. Abandoned vehicles now had to be recovered for repair, which created backlogs at maintenance centres which were hundreds of kilometres behind the front. This forced the Iranians to cannibalise for spares on a large scale, which provided another hurdle to offensive operations.[40]

Tehran had the advantage of five production facilities, developed by the Shah and producing infantry weapons such as the 7.62mm German-designed G3 rifle, MG 1 machine gun and RPG-7, 105mm and 155mm shells, 81mm and 120mm mortar bombs, ammunition, propellants, explosives and some communications equipment. There was also a tank repair facility at Masjed-e Soleyman, but this had relied upon foreign supervision, mostly West German and American, and their departure saw production and maintenance capabilities decline.[41]

While the Iraqis also faced logistical problems, their organisation remained one of the Army's most efficient elements. US intelligence would note about 1984 that their logistic and support preparations were 'reasonably competent'.[42] The Iraqis displayed an 'inventive use' of their tank transporter fleet, while the engineer organisation was especially effective in building roads and providing bridging.

But unlike Iran, Iraq had made no effort to ease its dependence upon imported defence equipment. It even lacked a small arms ammunition plant, and although it would create small arms and shell production facilities, initially it depended upon pre-war stocks.[43]

The failure of Saddam's 'smash-and-grab' strategy exposed this weakness,

Every evening, Iraqi units went into a laager behind earthen berms dug by their engineers. In this photograph, T-55s move out to their laager while passing a bulldozer that had spent the afternoon erecting such a protective position. (Albert Grandolini collection)

Time and again, Iraqi laagers were exposed to local Iranian counterattacks. These two T-55s were photographed shortly after repelling such a counterattack (note the spent shell casings on and around these two tanks). Note the turret markings in the form of small fields in black or blue-green, with the word 'Jaysh' and turret number in white. (Albert Grandolini collection)

which within four months caused serious shortages of all materials, but especially spares and ammunition. The country was dependent upon imports even of fuel, for the IRIAF methodically bombed Petrol Oil and Lubricants (POL) targets to create fuel shortages, overcome only through imports from Kuwait and Saudi Arabia.

Saddam's failure either to consult with, or to warn, the Soviet Union of his intentions provoked fury in Moscow, which was hoping to win influence in Tehran. Indeed, in October 1980, Soviet Minister Vladimir Vinogradov met Iran's Premier, Mohammad Ali Rajai, and Speaker, Hojatolislam Ali Akbar Rafsanjani, to discuss improved relations between the two countries. Between January and September 1980, Iraq received $1.9 billion worth of military equipment, mostly from the Soviet Union, including 300 T-54/55s, 700 T-62s, 50 T-72s, 250 BTR-50s, 250 BTR-60PBs and 200 BMP-1s. An angry Moscow now refused to replace military materiel consumed during the invasion, and some ships were ordered to return to the Soviet Union, including a consignment of 139 T-72 MBTs scheduled to re-equip an armoured brigade which reached the Jordanian port of Aqaba immediately after the invasion.[44] In November 1980, Soviet Communist Party General Secretary Leonid Brezhnev ordered an end to all weapons transfers. While two visits to Moscow by Foreign Minister Tariq Aziz in September and November to secure additional arms shipments were rebuffed, Poland and East Germany were more venal and received orders for T-54/55 tanks.[45] Only during the spring of 1981, when it was obvious the Iranian theocracy intended to keep the atheist communists at arm's length, did Moscow change its mind. Yet the Soviets would keep their options open, and by 1987 they would supply an estimated $11.8 billion of military equipment to Iran, compared with $43.2 billion to Iraq.[46]

But absorbing equipment proved more difficult for the Iraqi Army than acquiring it, because a shortage of trained manpower forced it to rely upon semi-skilled or even unskilled men, even in armoured units. Neglect and inadequate training was reflected in serious and widespread problems keeping vehicles, and even artillery, working, even though each division had vehicle repair facilities, while there were depots in the rear to repair vehicles, including APCs and two major repair facilities at Baghdad and Khan al-Mahawil for tanks and other equipment.[47] There was much training to overcome the problem, yet units still returned sophisticated equipment, especially electronics and electro-optics, to depots because they were unable to repair them. Much of this depot work was carried out by foreign technicians, and it appears that a Soviet team was largely responsible for maintaining the power packs of the T-72s.[48]

Saddam had to recognise his army was weaker than the enemy in several significant areas. The IRIAF's Phantoms were striking all over Iraq, hitting carefully selected targets. By November 1980, they

A T-62M from the 3rd Armoured Division cautiously manoeuvring down a street inside Khorramshahr. With the Iranians turning the entire city into a giant minefield, covered by snipers and tank-hunting teams, the Iraqis quickly learned the lessons of urban warfare. (Albert Grandolini collection)

effectively destroyed the Iraqi oil industry and fuel stocks, causing severe shortages of fuel which forced Baghdad to start importing via Jordan and Kuwait. IRIAA helicopters proved not only superior to those of the IrAAC, but also capable of – in cooperation with a few scattered task forces of the Iranian Army – holding off assaults by entire Iraqi Army corps. In Khuzestan, there was an added problem when the shield against Iranian air attacks was weakened with the withdrawal, in October, of 155th Missile Brigade with its Gainful SAMs from the sector under the control of the 3rd Armoured Division, because these were necessary for defence of the construction site of Iraq's nuclear reactor at Tuwaitha. Iranian artillery was also superior: it not only proved more mobile than that of the Iraqi Army, but longer-ranged too: 18km for the M109A1's 155mm howitzer and 40km for the M107's 175mm gun, allowing them to strike Iraqi rear areas with impunity. By contrast, the Iraqi 122mm M-30 and D-30 howitzers had a range of 11.8 and 15.4km, and the 152mm ML-20 and D-20 gun-howitzers could reach just over 17km, although the 130mm gun had a range of 27.5km.

Anticipating this problem, the Iraqi Army wanted each corps to have an artillery brigade with a battery of 30.4km-range Soviet S-23 180mm towed guns. The Soviets themselves had produced only a small number of these guns and were reluctant to export them; they even tried to cancel the original Iraqi order for one battery.[49]

The Iraqis began to seek their own heavy artillery for counterbattery fire, as well as self-propelled platforms, but this weakness would take a couple of years to overcome. Iraqi artillery support was also undermined by a tendency to break down batteries into two-gun sections, which prevented massed fire, while batteries were stationed too far in the rear to bring down fire on enemy forces. Close air support could not compensate for these weaknesses because there was no direct communication between the units of the two services. The Americans claimed the IrAF leadership was reluctant to commit aircraft for fear of losses, and this was reflected by their pilots, who tended to deliver ordnance prematurely or inaccurately.[50]

PART I: THE INVASION OF KHUZESTAN

A famous photograph of another T-62M from the 3rd Armoured Division, taken in front of the city's Grand Mosque. Notable is the turret number (12) applied in white, and the crew's sleeping bags and other kit attached behind the hatches. (Albert Grandolini collection)

The end of the year saw both sides reorganising in Khuzestan. The Iraqis began building defences, which marked the high tide of their advance and left their forces in positions like flotsam. They built berms behind barbed wire entanglements and minefields and buttressed them with triangular company positions as the main line of resistance (MLR) with a screen of outposts some 350 metres ahead, and a second berm up to 2km behind, with infantry positions and revetments for AFVs to shelter reserves.[51] A shortage of infantry meant the MLR was very lightly held at first, although flooded areas restricted enemy access in the north. The Iraqis had a mechanised brigade in Khorramshahr, one in the north facing Ahwaz and a third along the Karun. An armoured brigade was south-east of Khorramshahr and a second had moved south-west of Basra, while the Karun bridgehead, supported by a third PMP bridge, had an armoured and a mechanised brigade. III Corps was extending the road network around, and to, Basra, while more pontoon bridges were brought in for major waterways.[52]

The Iranians also improved their communications, and in December threw a pontoon bridge across the Bahmanshir some 5km south-east of Abadan to improve the flow of supplies into the town. This was aided by mobilising a fleet of trucks, tractor-trailers, vehicle- and barge-mounted cranes as well as enrolling naval helicopters and BH-7 hovercraft. The Iranians also made no attempt to defend in depth, with positions dug on the FEBA to ensure not an inch more of territory was lost and to help their forces reorganise for a riposte, for which they began to launch numerous small raids and made extensive use of their attack helicopters.

Around the enemy Karun bridgehead, and south-east of Abadan, the IRIA augmented the Pasdaran with two tank battalions (66 tanks), a mechanised battalion and an artillery battalion of 92nd Armoured Division, together with air defence batteries of ZSU-23-4, although there were also MIM-23 HAWK surface-to-air missile emplacements near Bandar-e Mahshur. Pasdaran forces flooded into the province, but so did the IRIA, which despatched brigades of the 21st and 37th Infantry Divisions to support the 92nd Division's 1st and 3rd Brigades, while the 55th Airborne Brigade moved down from the Dezful front and on 11 November, the Gendarmerie Khuzestan Command was ordered to relieve Abadan.[53]

It was obvious that the Iranian response could not reply upon a myriad local uncoordinated organisations, and Ground Forces Headquarters established four forward operations headquarters, including the east at Torbat-e Heydariyeh, the north-west at Urmia (also written Urumiyeh) and the west at Kermanshah. The Southern Forward Operations Headquarters (SFOH), also known as Karbala, was at Ahwaz, split into the Dezful and Khuzestan sectors, and supported by the 22nd and 33rd Artillery Groups, as well as the 2nd and 3rd Area Support Commands for logistics and elements of Transportation and Engineering Commands, the last also responsible for signal groups.[54] The Iranians benefited from the excellent strategic communications system created by the Shah and based at Lavisan.[55]

Bani-Sadr's grip of military affairs was always uncertain and it was clear that direction of the war effort needed greater coordination between the armed forces and the government. Neither Khomeini nor the clerics had any real understanding of military matters and he would later condemn those 'who interfere with the armed forces, while being ignorant of military affairs like myself'. To improve direction of the war effort, Bani-Sadr visited Khomeini in early October to sanction the revival of the Supreme Defence Council (SDC), established by the Shah and dissolved with his fall. The SDC was created on 13 October 1980 with the president at its head, and had six more members, of whom half were from the armed forces and half were senior clerics, for Khomeini insisted no one side could dominate decision making.[56]

A major problem which would affect Iran throughout the war was the weakness of the national communications system along the whole front, but especially in Khuzestan. The system ran mostly north to south rather than east to west, partly because it was designed to support resistance to a Soviet invasion from the north, and this made it difficult to supply the front. The system inevitably came under attack and a Soviet source estimated the damage to the Iranian transport network from 1980 to 1985 was worth $4 billion.[57]

Iran had 4,525km of single-track, standard gauge (1.435 metre) rail line, often with weak beds and most of the main lines ran westwards from Tehran.[58] One ran north-westwards to Van in Turkey and another ran from Qasvin through Qom, Ademeshk (west of Dezful) to Ahwaz and Abadan in Khuzestan through the mountainous terrain, which slowed movement, which could be made only in one direction at a time. The network lacked locomotives and rolling stock, with only 344 of the former and 13,872 freight wagons with a total capacity of 6,347 tonnes, the freight trains being capable

53

An Iraqi T-55 on the streets of Khorramshahr, with a soldier from a commando unit passing by. Soviet-built tanks like this T-55 were particularly cramped and crews tended to carry all of their personal gear, food, water and ammunition on fittings around the turret. (Albert Grandolini collection)

of a maximum speed of 55km/h (28mph).[59] The average capacity of the trains was 849 tonnes, of which 365–725 tonnes could be moved into Khuzestan.

The Shah augmented this system with an excellent road network consisting of 85,000km of highway, of which 19,000km was hard top bituminous surface, 36,000km was crushed stone/gravel and the remainder was simple beaten earth.[60] The metalled roads were largely found in the west and south of the country and had two lanes, but the roads were vulnerable to the weather, and both they and the railways in the Zagros Mountains could be blocked by snow, while the winter floods swamped many roads in Khuzestan, although the major routes were usually on embankments.

Although the IRIA was estimated to have some 22,500 US and Soviet trucks and 900 MAZ-537 and Faun tank transporters, many of these were unserviceable.[61] This caused a serious shortage of vehicles, which forced Tehran to mobilise civil vehicles, including double-decker buses, but this disrupted the economy, a logistical problem similar to that experienced by the Wehrmacht during Operation Barbarossa, the invasion of Russia. During the war, about half the military supplies were carried in foreign-made civilian vehicles, for which it was difficult to obtain spares, the difficulty made greater by the wide variety of models.[62] Individual transport owners quickly found ways to make large profits from moving war materiel, while some government officials siphoned off goods for personal gain.[63] Fuel and lubricants for all the forces was also a problem for a country which had lost considerable refining capability; indeed, even in the early twenty-first century it suffered shortages of vehicle fuel, leading to rationing. Because of this inadequate road network, transport aircraft of the IRIAF and IRIAA were heavily utilised and in December 1980 moved all the personnel of 88th Armoured Brigade from Chahbahar to Khuzestan.

While supplies could be shipped to Khuzestan through Bandar-e Khomeini, Bandar-e Mahshur, Bushehr and Bandar Abbas, the ports were severely congested. US intelligence estimated Bandar-e Khomeini (probably including Bandar-e Mashur) had a capacity of 15,000 tonnes per day, but it was so close to the war zone that few merchantmen were willing to sail there. Bandar Abbas had a military capacity of 9,300 tonnes per day, and its civilian port was not yet operational. However, it was 1,600km from Tehran and 950km from the front line. Bushehr was closer to the front but had a capacity of only 3,200 tonnes, and also had a poor transport infrastructure. Increased activity and inadequate loading/unloading facilities meant lengthy delays for ships using the ports, and with only Bandar-e Khomeini having a rail link, all other traffic was by truck.[64]

The Iraqis also had transport problems, beginning with their ports. In normal times, the port of Basra could handle 11,800 tonnes daily, while Um Qasr could unload 4,400 tonnes, but access to Basra was blocked by dozens of derelict foreign merchant ships, which would remain until the end of the war, while fire from each bank of the Shatt further prevented shipping movements.[65]

Consequently, supplies had to come overland. Baghdad's relations with Kuwait and Saudi Arabia to the south were good, but Iranian control of the Straits of Hormuz meant few military supplies could be brought in through the Gulf. Syria had long been a rival

An Iraqi ZU-23-2 twin barrel 23mm anti-aircraft gun covering the Shatt al-Arab from Iranian air strikes. Visible in the background are some of the 80 ships from 20 different countries that were trapped in this vital waterway by the Iraqi invasion. (Albert Grandolini collection)

of Iraq, and therefore a friend of Iran, despite President Asad's Ba'athist and secular policies, so it not only closed the border but also the oil pipeline from Iraq. Turkey was friendly to both countries and had a common foe in the Kurds, but there were few roads into Iraq through the mountainous frontier and this prevented any substantial movement of military equipment. Fortunately for Saddam, Jordan was a traditional friend of Baghdad, which meant the Red Sea port of Aqaba would become the main conduit of Iraqi military (and civilian) supplies. However, according to a 1985 US Defense Intelligence Agency report, Iraq's primary source for Soviet supplies was Thuwal, near Jeddah, in Saudi Arabia, some 1,800km from Baghdad. The DIA claimed that in 1981 a million tonnes of military supplies were delivered through the Saudi port, which it calls Tuwwal.[66]

Distribution of the supplies was aided by Iraq's two rail lines; one with standard (1.435 metre) gauge and the other with a narrow (1 metre) gauge. The 1,000km standard gauge line was a single-track running from Syria down to Basra and Um Qasr, and had 308 diesel locomotives and 8,040 items of rolling stock, including 4,480 freight platforms, of which 400 were flat bed and 457 were for liquids. The 500km narrow gauge line ran north-east from Baghdad to Irbil, and had 77 steam locomotives and a rolling stock inventory of 2,260.[67]

Far more reliance was placed on the road system, which was especially well developed in the east and also across the Jordanian border. The country had 9,000km of hardtop road, with two routes crossing the border into Iran, and 12,000km of gravel or beaten earth road. The Army vehicle fleet could be augmented by some 80,000 civilian trucks and buses, including plenty of heavy trucks and tractor-trailers, to bring supplies up from Aqaba, augmented by Jordanian vehicles. Baghdad also had sufficient storage facilities for 300,000 tonnes of ammunition but suffered periodic shortages due to its dependency upon imports.[68] While Baghdad faced greater problems importing war materiel than Iran, it had the advantage of interior lines, which made it easier to distribute supplies and equipment at all levels.

5
THE IRANIANS STRIKE BACK

The need to expel the Iraqi invaders was an issue of personal survival for President Bani-Sadr. Spearheaded by Ayatollah Seyyed Mohammad Hosseini Beheshti's Islamic Republic Party (IRP), the clerics began to isolate him and berated his failure to liberate the occupied territory. This aggravated their paranoia and many suspected him of 'Bonapartist tendencies', fearing he wished to use the IRIA against Khomeini, their fears fed when he temporarily placed the Pasdaran under its command. Khomeini was more tolerant because he and Bani-Sadr had developed a close relationship while sharing their Parisian exile, and continued to urge his followers not to criticise the regular armed forces so vehemently.

The IRP demanded seats on the SDC to control the armed forces, and Bani-Sadr urgently needed a battlefield victory to regain prestige. His allies in the IRIA agreed but wished to wait until the spring when the ground had dried, for they were aware that much of the IRIA remained committed against the Kurds, there was a shortage of trained staff officers and artillery ammunition, while much of the IRIAA fleet was undergoing maintenance. Yet they had little choice but to begin planning Operation Hoveyzeh (also written as Howeizeh and Hoveize) and supporting operations from 18/20 December.[1]

As diversionary attacks were launched upon the central front around Qasr-e Shirin and Mehran, the Ahwaz-based SFOH would launch three offensives, whose prime objective was to eliminate the Iraqi salient pointing at the city like a dagger. These attacks would be channelled by extensive inundations created by the Iranians to shield the western approaches to Ahwaz, which, together with the seasonal rains, had left much of the battlefield muddy. Operation Hoveyzeh would be launched in the Karkheh and Karkheh Kur valleys to roll up the northern face of the salient. The 3rd Brigade/16th IRIA Armoured Division would strike eastwards from the narrow Hoveyzeh Salient with two Chieftain MBT battalions and a BMP-equipped mechanised battalion, followed by 2nd Brigade with one Chieftain battalion and two BTR-50/60 mechanised battalions. They would drive along the south bank of the Karkheh Kur and roll up the defences, while 1st Brigade/16th Division, organised like 2nd Brigade, together with elements of the 21st IRIA Infantry Division, would pin down the defenders from the north by attacking across the dry 'land bridge', south-west of the village of Tarrah.

This would distract the enemy while Operation Nasr was launched south of Ahwaz. Here, a task force based upon 2nd Brigade/92nd IRIA Armoured Division would cross the Karun and penetrate the inundations from the east to take the eastern anchor of the Iraqi defences at Dub-e Said. The two arms would then combine and drive down the Ahwaz–Khorramshahr highway while a third offensive, Operation Tavakkol (Trust in God, also written Tavakole), would strike the enemy bridgehead across the Karun north of Abadan with elements of 77th IRIA Infantry Division supported by 37th IRIA Armoured Brigade, to pave the way for the relief of Abadan. The operations around Ahwaz involved some 200 MBTs, and to support Hoveyzeh/Tavakkol there were six self-propelled artillery battalions (M109 and one with M107) and a MLRS battery, while to support Nasr there were three battalions of M109s and three towed batteries, a total of some 155 guns.[2] However, air support was confined to 16 Cobra gunships and four understrength squadrons of Tigers and Phantoms, some manned by pilots who had only recently been released from prison.[3]

The Iraqi defences exploited the swamps west of Ahwaz, which were some 20km long and 10km wide, to lap against both sides of the Ahwaz–Khorramshahr highway, augmented by anti-tank ditches across the 'land bridge'. Covering the northern defences was the 9th Armoured Division (Talia Al-Duri), which held a 40km line mostly shielded by the Karkheh Kur from Hoveyzeh through Achmedabad (the centre of the Iraqi line) to Dub-e Said, where the line ran south along the highway. Duri's 35th Armoured Brigade invested Susangerd in the west, and (west to east) he had 43rd Armoured and 14th Mechanised Brigades, the latter in the tip of the salient, augmented by battalions of 31st SF Brigade, while on his right was 3rd Armoured Division's 15th Mechanised Brigade, a force whose total strength was estimated by US intelligence at 556 tanks and 141 guns.[4] With III Corps' 3rd Armoured Division and 5th Mechanised Division fully committed south of Ahwaz, although the arrival of 11th Infantry Division was easing their burden, Ni'ami's only tactical/operational level reserve was Colonel Mahmood Shukur Shaheen's 10th Armoured Brigade, which was on his extreme left flank at Fakkeh, some 80km north of Hoveyzeh, but Baghdad had not anticipated enemy action until March, when the ground had dried.

It was forewarned by COMINT, which, with Soviet technical assistance, exploited poor Iranian communications discipline. Scouting parties, and possibly spies, may have added some details, and Duri had sufficient warning to evacuate his outposts before the blow fell. The IRIA also had a COMINT service under Military Intelligence, the IRIA Sigint Services Communications (ISSC) network, which was based in Tehran, with most sites in south-west Iran monitoring battlefield communications. But all intercepted signals were forwarded to Tehran, although during intense ground fighting the interceptions provided direct support to frontline units.[5]

Operations Howeizeh, Nassr and Tawakkol

The Iranians knew their enemies fought poorly at night and decided to exploit this with probing attacks before dawn on 5 January to discover weaknesses in the enemy line. It was raining on 3 January and foggy the following day, but from 5 January onwards the rains

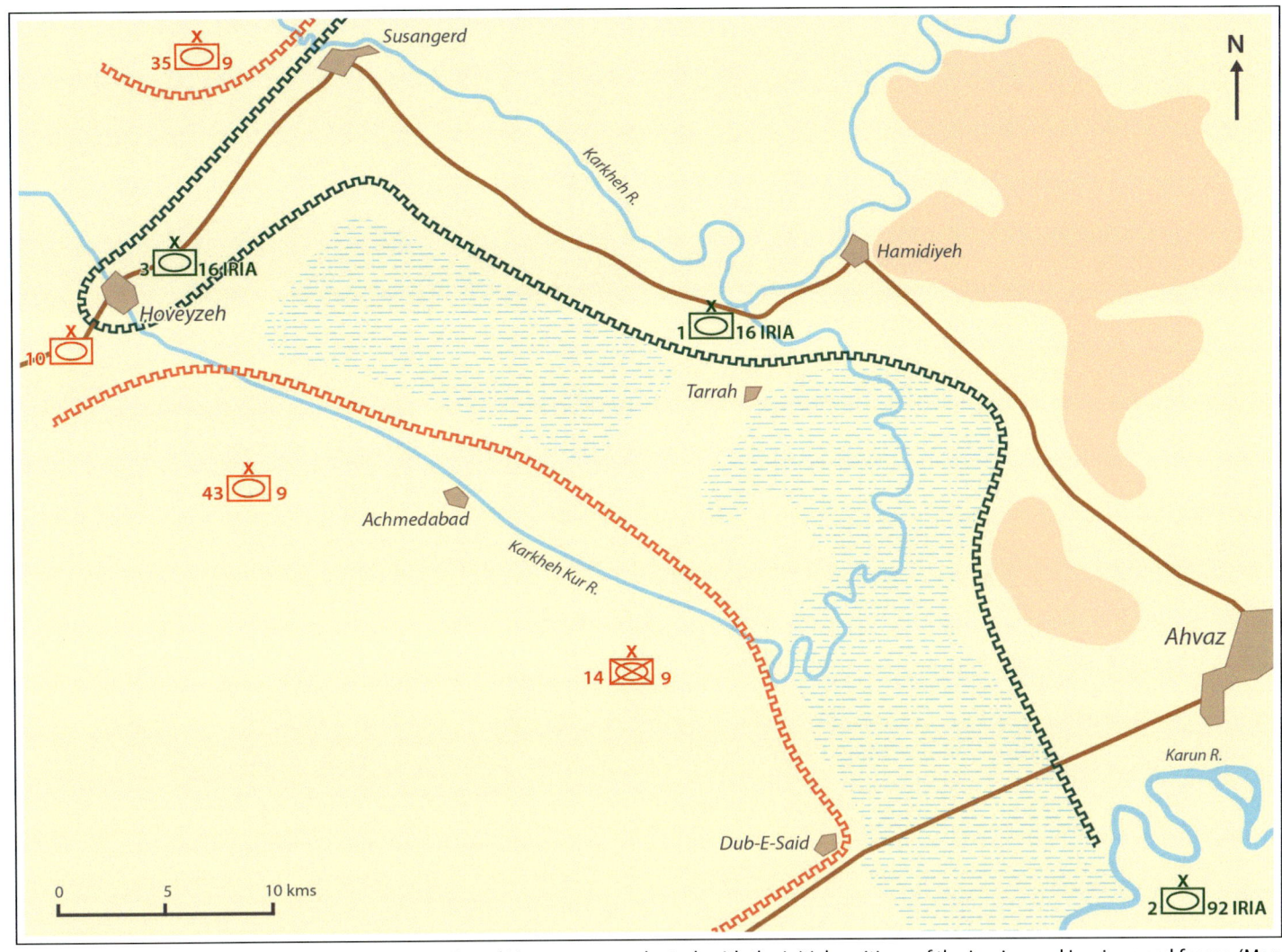

A map of the territory on which Operation Hoveyzeh and Nassr were conducted, with the initial positions of the Iranian and Iraqi ground forces. (Map by George Anderson)

ceased for four days, although the muddy ground meant the 16th IRIA Division spearhead could deploy its MBT battalions only on a narrow front. Deployment was further hampered because the ground between the Karkheh in the north and the Karkheh Kur in the south was crisscrossed with irrigation channels. The Iranians threw bridges across the Karkheh to ensure supplies for their armoured spearhead and the 21st Division's attack.

Despite the advanced warning, the incompetent Talia Al-Duri bungled the defence, allowing the Iranian armoured brigade to drive out of Hoveyzeh while the northern attack penetrated his MLR to take Achmedabad, driving back 43rd Armoured Brigade, overrunning 9th Armoured Division's gun line and threatening the whole Karkheh Kur line. Ni'ami's scout helicopters monitored the advance as he sent up a tank battalion each of 12th Armoured Brigade/3rd Armoured Division and 30th Armoured Brigade/6th Armoured Division to buttress the line, but to stabilise the front he needed Shukur. During the afternoon, he despatched tank transporters for two tank battalions and ordered Shukur to Susangerd (or Khafajiyah as the Iraqis called it), while the mechanised battalion would travel on its tracks, although it did not arrive until 7 January.[6] The corps chief-of-staff briefed Shukur and ordered him to restore the 43rd Armoured Brigade front, and as there were only sufficient tank transporters for half of 10th Brigade's tanks, he reinforced him with a battalion of T-55s, the reinforced brigade assembling between Susangerd and Hoveyzeh about dawn of 6 January. Meanwhile, Iraqi fighters dispersed Iranian helicopter gunships as the IRIAF made the mistake of using its limited resources for battlefield interdiction rather than close air support, which weakened air support for the Iranian advance.[7]

As Shukur deployed on 6 January, the Iranians continued to exploit their success by building a bridge near Achmedabad and committing a new tank battalion, although this too could advance only along a narrow front. Talia Al-Duri's command post was threatened and he ordered a withdrawal into the second position, but his incompetent handling of the situation caused chaos. By contrast, Ni'ami reacted promptly, aided by the ever-reliable COMINT service, to exploit the road systems on each side of the breakthrough to bring up reserves. Talia Al-Duri's 43rd Armoured Brigade deployed a tank battalion to block the enemy advance, while 14th Mechanised Brigade's tanks enfiladed the enemy armour from the reserve position as 31st SF Brigade was brought in to stiffen the defences. The IrAF was extremely active and largely neutralised enemy artillery fire as well as disrupting gunship support for the Chieftains.

During the day, the 12th Armoured Brigade's tank battalion came up from the south to support 14th Brigade and helped to contain the threat from Achmedabad. In the west, Shukur began his counterattack from south-west of Susangerd, punching eastward through the Hoveyzeh Salient to secure the dry ground between the Karkheh and the flooded areas to the south. He then planned to strike south to Hoveyzeh, cross the Karkheh Kur and retake 43rd Armoured Brigade's positions. He had only 80 MBTs and deployed them in a single wave at 100-metre intervals between vehicles, with orders to drive at top cross-country speed of 20km/h, firing rapidly at three rds/min when engaging the enemy.[8] An Iranian intelligence officer warned the Ahwaz headquarters the Iraqis might be luring 16th Division into a deadly trap, but his superiors believed they faced only screening forces, a view encouraged by Iraqi tactical withdrawals. During the day, the trap was finally sprung as Shukur pushed from the west, while T-55s and T-62s struck from the south, in a close-range battle which trapped the Iranians against the flooded zone.

The Iranians tried to deploy off the road, but their heavy (55 tonne) Chieftain tanks often became stuck in the mud, unlike the lighter (36–40 tonne) enemy tanks. However, the Chieftain's marksmanship was better and they had superior fire control, based upon the Marconi FV/GCE Mk 4 fire control system, which used a ranging machine gun and Barr and Stroud LF2 laser rangefinder, while the T-54 and T-62 had only optical sights. The Iranian tanks also had the 120mm L11A5 gun (range 3km with APDS and 8km with HESH), which could fire a sustained rate of six rounds a minute compared with four to five in the T-54/55, whose 100mm D-10T gun fired BK-17 AP and HEAT rounds with a range of up to a kilometre.[9] But the T-72s were a match for the Chieftains, aided by their TPD-K1 laser rangefinder and 2A46 125mm L/48 smoothbore gun with its APFSDS rounds, which, US intelligence concluded, could outrange by up to a kilometre the rifled guns of the Iranian tanks, while the front glacis armour of the T-72 was virtually impervious to anti-armour fire.[10] By the afternoon, Shukur had secured a bridgehead south of the Karkheh, but was low on ammunition as the Iranians fled the Hoveyzeh Salient, running the gauntlet of Iraqi MBTs and IRIAF friendly fire, which led local commanders to shoot at any aircraft they saw. Among those who reportedly suffered was a Pasdaran company, which included 70 of the 'students' who had seized the American Embassy in Tehran.[11]

The isolation of Hoveyzeh and the Iranian 3rd Brigade left the latter running short of fuel and ammunition. In a desperate attempt to relieve them, 16th Division used 2nd Brigade to strike from the north with gunship support on 7 January, but the ground here also bogged down vehicles. At the same time, the ZSU-57-2 self-propelled air defence guns inhibited Iranian helicopter operations and allowed the Iraqi gunships to intervene, while the IrAF was also extremely active, using large numbers of cluster bombs. Both sides became intertwined as the IrAF struck targets both on the battlefield and the bridges across the Karkheh and Karkheh Kur around the Hoveyzeh Salient, the Iranians reportedly losing half their vehicles. This air support played a major role in Shukur's survival, for he spent most of the day replenishing fuel and ammunition as well as bringing up the rest of the brigade.

On 8 January, Shukur pushed south to Hoveyzeh and then along the Karkheh Kur to restore the line and recapture 9th Armoured Division's lost guns. For their part, the Iranians abandoned the relief operation the following day as the survivors of 3rd Brigade picked their way through the flooded zones to safety, having abandoned their vehicles. The Iraqis claimed to have captured some 120 tanks and 65 AFVs, some allegedly with their engines still running, and to have destroyed another 114, while foreign journalists observed about 140 AFVs in the mud.[12]

The biggest single tank action of the Iran Iraq War involved 450 MBTs from eight Iraqi and three Iranian tank battalions. It is

IRIAA troops celebrating their initial success during Operation Nassr – also known as Operation Hoveyzeh in the West. Soon enough, an Iraqi counterattack was to drive them back with heavy losses. (Albert Grandolini collection)

A crewmember of an Iranian Chieftain during a morning prayer: the vehicle is dug-in behind an earthen berm, with the rest of the crew on watch. Chieftains played a prominent role in Operation Hoveyzeh but suffered heavy losses – especially to Malyutka ATGMs and 125mm APFSDS fired from Iraqi T-72s. Tankers of the 10th Armoured Brigade were specially advised by their Soviet instructors to use that type of ammunition against Iranian tanks. (Albert Grandolini collection)

estimated Iraqi losses were between 80 and 130 AFVs, including 60–100 MBTs, although Shukur's brigade lost only three T-72s, all to Iranian Cobra gunships with TOW heavy anti-armour missiles, which proved a potent combination during the battle and would continue to do so in the coming months. However, the Cobras lost

PART I: THE IRANIANS STRIKE BACK

A crew from the 10th Armoured Brigade seen with one of their mounts in early 1981. The T-72 was cleared for export only in 1978, and due to Moscow's disagreement with the Iraqi invasion of Iran, no further vehicles of this type were sold to Baghdad again until July 1982. Nevertheless, the Soviets continued providing spares and ammunition for the type, and their instructors remained in Iraq. Indeed, according to Iraqi reports they played an important advisory role during Operation Hoveyzeh. (Albert Grandolini collection)

half their strength, mostly to ground fire.[13] Shukur's brigade was given the credit for the success and was named 'al Qa'qaa' after al Qa'qaa ibn Amr at Tamimi, who played a key role in the Arab victory over the Persians at Qadisiyya. Colonel Shukur was promoted to brigadier general on 15 May to command 6th Armoured Division, and from August 1983 he headed GMID but was dismissed in 1986 following the loss of the Faw Peninsula, which was partly blamed upon poor intelligence, but he would later become 1st Special Corps' chief-of-staff.[14]

Ni'ami appears to have probed around Susangerd shortly afterwards, but the defenders (reinforced by part of 55th IRIA Airborne Brigade brought in by helicopter) were supported by the remnants of 16th Division. The Iraqi probes were largely based upon artillery bombardments and were abandoned having achieved little while suffering heavy losses from AGM-65A Maverick guided air-to-surface missiles launched by IRIAF Phantoms.[15]

Meanwhile, the other element of the Iranian offensive, Operation Nasr, was also launched on 5 January, using the 2nd Brigade/92nd IRIA Armoured Division reinforced by an M47 tank battalion of 77th IRIA Division and a mixture of a Pasdaran battalion and guerrilla force under Dr Mustafa Ali Chamran. A Pasdaran battalion crossed the inundations some 15km south-west of Ahwaz and struck positions around Dub-e Said but was thrown back by a counterattack within three days.

Despite these failures, two days after this defeat, and a day after the IRIA abandoned its meagre gains from Hoveyzeh, the IRIA launched the forlorn hope which was Operation Tavakkol. The Iraqi 3rd Armoured Division headquarters (Jabar al-Duri) had 6th Armoured Brigade, whose organic units were augmented battalions of 3rd and 44th Infantry Brigades and 26th Armoured Brigade. On the far side of the Karun, 5th Mechanised Division had 20th Mechanised Brigade to bolster the salient's northern shoulder, while 49th Infantry Brigade/11th Division was at Khorramshahr.

The plan called for the 37th IRIA Armoured Brigade, reinforced by a tank battalion of 77th Division and a Pasdaran battalion, to strike down the Bandar-e-Khomeini highway while 2nd Brigade/77th IRIA Infantry Division broke out of the Abadan bridgehead up the highway. They were to link, then strike northwards to clear the bridgehead, and there were even dreams of crossing the Karun and retaking Khorramshahr. With only nine combat (armour and infantry) battalions against 17 defending battalions, there was never any prospect of success and the attackers were mowed down, the only consolation being that the IRIA did receive a more realistic understanding of Iraqi defences.[16]

Driven by political rather than military considerations, Bani-Sadr's plan was too ambitious and launched at the wrong time of the year. The IRIA performed poorly, with notable failures in tactical intelligence as well as command and control which slowed its reaction, while there was an overreliance, like the Iraqis four months earlier, upon armour. The Iraqi performance was uneven, still over-reliant upon armour and short of infantry, yet Saddam was encouraged and believed the victory showed the enemy they could not defeat the Iraqi Army.

The offensive seriously eroded IRIA armoured strength and prestige, while making Ban-Sadr's fall from grace inevitable, and on 11 March, the parliament restricted his powers. The clerics also persuaded Khomeini that the IRIA lacked the political commitment to prosecute the war successfully. As a man who had spent his life surrounded by spiritual texts, Khomeini was naturally attracted to the idea of belief overcoming physical obstacles, and increasingly he supported the Pasdaran as the key to military success. IRIA strength would continue to rise during the year and would reach 170,000 men, while the Pasdaran expanded to at least 50,000 men, increasingly organised into battalions which could be augmented by the Basiji, who were placed under Pasdaran command on New Year's Day 1981.[17]

Yet the Iranians benefited from a serious Iraqi security breach when Saddam's press secretary accidentally revealed the Iraqis were intercepting enemy communications. The Iraqis quickly acquired Crypto C-52 mechanical enciphering machines and tried to impose better communications discipline upon the IRIA, and these moves provided a degree of security for the remainder of the year.[18]

The Gathering Storm

As the temperature rose from 20°C to 30°C and the ground dried, Susangerd now became the focus for both sides. On 19 March, 35th Armoured Brigade attacked the town with strong artillery support but made little progress, and the following day, with casualties mounting, Saddam closed down this operation. It was an ominous failure, for the Iraqis had been unable to take their objectives while the Iranians had demonstrated defensive skill.[19]

The Iraqi failure reinforced Iranian determination to remove the threat to Susangerd. They targeted the Allah Akbar Heights, low dunes (42–44 metres) some 25km north-west of Susangerd between the town and the main dune region, which was both the enemy's northern anchor and a base for Gainful missile batteries, which were a constant threat to the IRIAF. Operation Imam Ali was to eliminate the threat, and the task was assigned to of the 8th Najaf Ashraf Pasdaran Brigade, supported by two battalions of 3rd Brigade/92nd IRIA Armoured Division; the M60-equipped 231st Tank and BMP-equipped 145th Mechanised.[20] The attack, launched during the night of 21/22 May, was a simple frontal assault, but the Iraqi defenders were a tank battalion of 35th Armoured Brigade, a unit totally unsuitable for holding ground, who were rapidly overwhelmed, losing 30 tanks and it was claimed only nine soldiers returned to allege that they never saw their officers.[21]

A counterattack was launched the following day, but the Pasdaran stood their ground and beat them off with the aid of M47 Dragon and TOW anti-armour missiles transferred from IRIA supply depots. Nine IRIA self-propelled artillery batteries, mostly M109 but including two with M107, now began to pound the Iraqi positions. To prevent an armoured riposte, the Iranians again flooded the low ground around Susangerd, while Pasdaran forces infiltrated across the Karkheh Kur to harass enemy positions and communications. This pressure eventually forced a further Iraqi retreat westwards of 58km on 26 May, nearer the supply base of Bostan.

This minor victory demonstrated to the Pasdaran and their supporters what it could achieve with IRIA support. But there would be a tragic post-script, for on 2 June the new Iranian regime's first Defence Minister, the US-educated scientist turned guerrilla leader Mostafa Ali Chamran, was killed. He was the Pasdaran's first commander in April 1979 before becoming Defence Minister five months later. He always led from the front and his death was reported as due either to a sniper or a mortar bomb. He was succeeded as Pasdaran commander by their intelligence chief, Mohzen Rezai (or Resai), who would hold this position until 1997, although on poor terms with Pasdaran Minister Mohsen Rafiq-Dust. Rezai's father supported Khomeini and was jailed, which led to Rezai Junior being dismissed from military school to become a revolutionary. He would repeatedly fail in his attempts to command all of Iran's ground forces.[22]

To follow on the success, there was a new attack on the Karun bridgehead, Operation Farmande Kole Ghova, Khomeni Rooh Khoda (Khomeini is our Supreme Commander), involving the Najaf Ashraf Brigade augmented by Basij, part of 55th IRIA Airborne

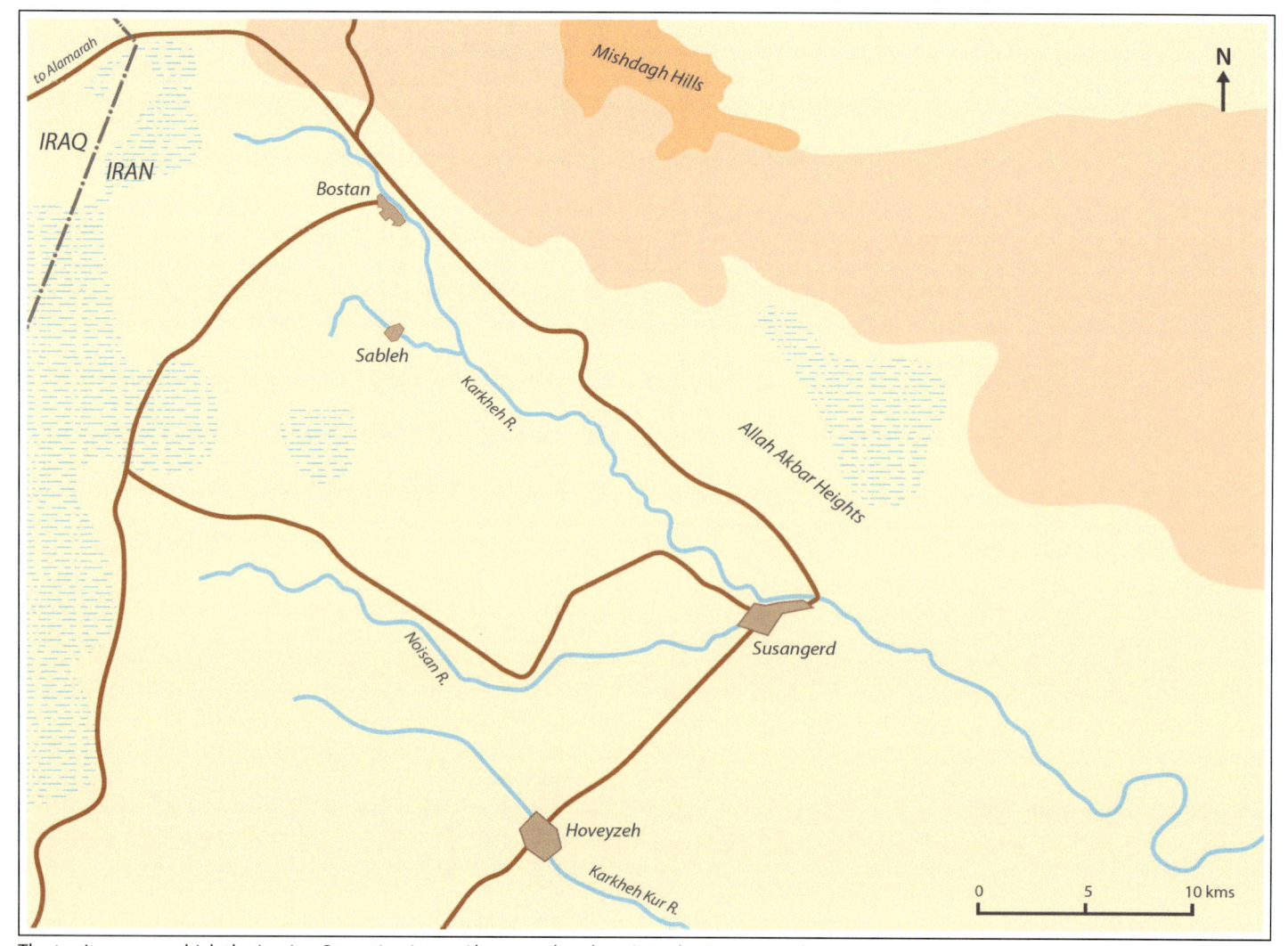

The territory over which the Iranian Operation Imam Ali was undertaken. (Map by George Anderson)

PART I: THE IRANIANS STRIKE BACK

Brigade, a tank battalion of 77th IRIA Division and Cobra gunships. The attack began on 11 June and aimed to take the northernmost pontoon bridge at Mared, and while this was not achieved, the defenders, 6th Armoured Brigade/3rd Armoured Division, whose right was close to Salmanieh, were driven back some 5km, which brought the bridge within easy artillery range. It was no longer tenable and was dismantled shortly afterwards, although in revenge the Iraqis increased pressure upon Abadan, now defended by 10,000–15,000 men, including 2nd Brigade/77th IRIA Infantry Division, with some 60 M47 MBTs.

An Iraqi T-55 crew preparing for a mission early in the morning. Like the Iranians, the Iraqis made extensive use of earth berms to improve the protection of their equipment and personnel. These were necessary because of the generally featureless and flat desert of western Khuzestan. (Albert Grandolini collection)

As the offensive was launched, Khomeini dismissed Bani-Sadr as Commander-in-Chief and replaced him with Fallahi. Then, on 20 June, parliament impeached Bani-Sadr for incompetence and ordered his arrest, although it was not until 24 July that his successor, the radical cleric Mohammad Ali Rajai, was appointed. Bani-Sadr went into hiding, then escaped to France in a defecting IRIAF KC-707 tanker, but the departure of someone whom the clerics regarded as a champion of the Old Guard marked a watershed in IRIA-Pasdaran relations. The clerics could now begin to appreciate the IRIA's sacrifices, which set the stage for better cooperation between the two as they recognised, despite mutual suspicions, they had no option except working together.[23]

It was helped by the fact the IRIA was gaining a new generation of junior leaders who were more in tune with the regime and who had fought alongside the Pasders against the Kurds, yet the clerics continued to restrict the authority of senior officers 'to reduce abuse of power and corruption'.[24] Khomeini waited until 2 September before appointing Colonel (then Brigadier General) Sayad Musa Namjoo as Defence Minister for his work developing IRIA-Pasdaran cooperation. Pasdaran Deputy Commander Ali Yousef Kolahduz was to command the frontline Pasdaran, while IRIAF commander Colonel Javad Fakuri authorised additional close air support for the ground forces.

Khomeini also continued to condemn both the friction between the regular armed forces and the Pasdaran, and also the commissars, noting: 'Experts should be allowed to perform

The crew of an Iranian Chieftain monitoring a road in Khuzestan. Gauging by their clearly relaxed posture, no threat was imminent when this photograph was taken. Notable is extensive storage of kit around the rear top of the turret. Chieftains were generally considered as poor tanks by Iranian crews: although they report receiving excellent technical support, the type was underpowered, and not only the engine and transmission, but even the gun stabilisation malfunctioned frequently. (Tom Cooper collection)

Wreckage of an IrAAC Mi-8 helicopter inspected by Iranian troops. Iranian and Iraqi Helicopters saw intensive deployment during Operation Hoveyzeh, and each side lost about half a dozen of various models; at least four of these in air combat or to enemy interceptors. (Albert Grandolini collection)

their tasks unencumbered by meddling from those who have no knowledge of the subject.' Yet the clerical commissars continued to roam formations, headquarters and bases, seeking out those who held 'incorrect' political or religious views, despite Shirazi and Resai's attempts to clip their wings. This was another hurdle facing Iranian offensive plans, already hamstrung by factors including a shortage of qualified staff officers, as well as continued maintenance and logistical problems.[25]

Another reason why the Pasdaran suspicions of the IRIA were eroded was the militia's growing military professionalism created by the harsh realities of war, although ranks would not be introduced until May 1990.[26] Until the summer of 1981, many Pasdaran were sent to the front without training; indeed early in the year, SFOH had to organise a three-day training course for newly arrived militia.[27]

By the summer, the Pasdaran had begun organising their own military training centres as the 20–30-man platoons, with which they started the war, were expanded into rifle companies with three platoons, while three companies and a heavy weapons company were combined into battalions of some 300–325 men. The battalions were increasingly combined into brigades of three or four battalions, many of which would soon be expanded into divisions of 4,000–4,500 men.[28]

Officially, this process began February 1982 with the creation of 27th Mohamad Rasoolallah Brigade, which became a division in September 1982, but many Pasdaran regions demonstrated their autonomy by redesignating their formations unofficially before this, from June 1981 in the case of brigades, and by late 1981 with divisions. While the Pasdaran Ministry disapproved, domestic politics forced them to accept the fait accompli, then officially roll out the upgrading process. On 26 July, the Pasdaran, supported by two IRIA tank battalions, tried to regain Hoveyzeh, but this attack ended in disaster. The Iraqi 14th Mechanised Brigade first withdrew under pressure, but three days later staged a successful counterattack which drove back the Pasders. Undaunted, the Iranians immediately struck west of Susangerd, using elements of 16th and 92nd IRIA Armoured Divisions, together with Pasdaran/Basij forces, to gain some ground and allow their combat engineers to spend most of the month examining the enemy defences in the region.[29]

By now both sides were exhausted, and during the heat of August they licked their wounds, restricting themselves to bombardments and raids designed to take key terrain as jump-off points for major offensives. Ominously, the Iranians, on 12 August, accused the enemy of using poison gas, which may have been true on a small scale. For their part, the Iranians began to reinforce their fronts significantly by doubling the size of their forces, while the Iraqis built fortifications and sometimes levelled villages to provide fields of fire.[30]

Iranian planning during the summer was hindered by a ferocious terrorist campaign by the People's Mujahideen (or Mojahedin) which killed many leading members of the government and parliament, including Beheshti on 28 June, while the bombing of the SDC on 30 August killed President Rajai. Yet Khomeini continued to demand an operation to end the siege of Abadan, and this would reflect the improved relations between the IRIA and Pasdaran.

Both recognised that the Iraqi superiority in mechanised warfare could be overcome only by exploiting Iranian superiority in manpower and artillery. The architect of the new strategy was the new Chief of the Joint Staff, Major General Qasem Ali Zahirnejhad, who sought to combine the primal force of the Pasdaran with the IRIA's technical expertise, although this was undermined by the shortage of armour, helicopters and artillery ammunition. The SFOH at Ahwaz retained responsibility for operational level planning but no longer had a monopoly on tactical level operations, which would be coordinated by ad hoc tactical headquarters. There would now be infantry assaults spearheaded by the Pasdaran, which would exploit terrain and be supported by the IRIA with artillery and engineers.

The key was reconnaissance, where both the Pasdaran and IRIA Special Forces would infiltrate enemy positions to conduct covert scouting. This allowed the Iranians to detect weak points and plan to exploit those weaknesses. Diversions, probes and artillery bombardments would pin down the better Iraqi units, while massed infantry assaults with artillery and armoured support would isolate the weak points, which would be stormed at leisure, while the gaps created would be exploited by Pasdaran infantry and IRIA mechanised forces.[31] A US intelligence history noted: 'Iraq was

Early in 1981, Iraqi Mi-25 helicopter gunships saw their first deployment in large numbers over a relatively limited sector of the frontlines. They deployed about 50 3M11 Falanga (AT-2 Swatter) anti-tank missiles with some success, but primarily used unguided 68mm rockets. At least one was shot down in an air combat with Iranian interceptors. (Tom Cooper collection)

fighting a limited war while Iran was fighting a total one, at least within its capabilities.'[32]

As the storm clouds gathered, Iraq faced the price of failing to assign military objectives in its poorly planned invasion. Iraqi units had been dumped like flotsam by the high tide of invasion on a long, meandering line from which Saddam would accept neither adjustment nor withdrawal. He was convinced that by defending every inch of captured territory and inflicting unacceptable losses, he would force Tehran to the negotiating table. There was no other strategy; Iraq lacked the resources to stage a war-winning offensive, and prestige precluded the abandonment of Iranian territory without compensation.[33]

Years later, General Makki, who was attached to the Iraqi III Corps in 1981 and became its chief-of-staff later in the year, illustrated the problem. During an inspection of the front in May 1981, he noticed gaps and suggested expanding the minefields, regrouping forces and bringing up reserves. Corps commander Ni'ami and his chief-of-staff (General Na'ima al-Mihyawi) disagreed, and asked: 'Why should we relinquish ground that we have gained through blood?' When Makki pointed out that at staff college the general had advocated defence in depth, he was told: 'Not only do I not agree, the chief-of-staff does not agree, and Saddam does not agree.'[34] Ni'ami had, in fact, wished to abandon exposed positions, but when he suggested that Shanshal propose this to Saddam, he was told: 'I will not tell him. You tell him, you are the corps commander.'[35]

The problem with this strategy was that Iraq faced a demoralising war of attrition which it ultimately could not win. Artillery bombardments and raids by the increasingly aggressive Iranians inflicted a steady stream of casualties, although, like Pétain at Verdun, the Iraqis tried to spread the pain by rotating units after 40-day tours. Unfortunately, this merely added to problems because units neglected frontline maintenance in anticipation that this would be performed in the rear when they were rotated. Many generals interpreted Saddam's demands that casualties be kept to a minimum by strengthening their defences and avoiding any provocative action such as patrolling beyond the minefields. This was welcome to the troops, who were growing more exhausted and demoralised, for, although they were well fed, they faced the strain of constant vigilance both day and night. Little wonder there was a serious desertion problem, with US intelligence calculating that in the 150,000–200,000-man Iraqi Army there were 6,000–8,000 deserters.[36]

The chronic shortage of infantry led to the decision to rename police COIN formations as infantry brigades, while regular and reserve brigades were augmented with support troops who were often from the Popular Army. It was estimated that by early 1982, about 10 percent of the Popular Army was in the front line, serving three-month frontline tours.[37] It is doubtful whether the Army commanders really welcomed this 'reinforcement', and Saddam would later regret the decision. He would describe the Popular Army as a 'burden to the regular army.'[38] Yet the Iraqi Army was unprepared for static defence. The DIA noted: 'Simple procedures, such as co-ordination of unit boundaries and fire co-ordination planning, were apparently beyond the ability of unit commanders.' Commanders were often unable to determine the enemy's main axes, which made them reluctant to commit their reserves for fear they would be held responsible for defeat.[39]

Operation Imam Ali had demonstrated the futility of mechanised units in static defence, and as an interim measure Ni'ami augmented them with battalions from 31st and 32nd SF Brigades, which should have been withdrawn for the training they needed to maintain their edge.[40]

Ni'ami had received 11th Infantry Division, which was partly deployed around the mouth of the Karun and on the Faw Peninsula to invest Abadan, while 3rd Armoured Division concentrated upon the Karun bridgehead.

Saddam was certainly warned about the problems by GMID Director General Dhannoun during the first half of 1981. He pointed out that the Iraqis were not mounting continuous surveillance and that during bombardments the troops would remain in their dugouts. Units failed to deploy screening forces, while their defences lacked wire and minefields. He warned that the Iranian attrition strategy might be capable of 'limited success', eroding Iraqi strength and boosting Iranian morale.[41] Despite this, on 25 August, Saddam met the General Command of the Armed Forces and laid out his two-pronged strategy, which was to bleed to death the Iranian Army on the battlefield, and their economy through attacks on their oil industry and electricity generation facilities.[42]

Operation Samene-Al-Aeme

To meet Khomeini's demand for the relief of Abadan, the Iranians began to plan Operation Samene-al-Aeme from late August, and planning intensified from then although D-Day was not set until 24 September.[43]

The immediate objective was to destroy the Karun bridgehead and relieve Abadan, but it was regarded as the first step in the strategy to liberate all of Khuzestan.

Logistics were a major problem because supplies could come only along the highways to Abadan from Ahwaz and Bandar-e-Khomeini, the former within range of long-range Iraqi artillery, while the latter's maritime approaches were interdicted by the IrAF and Iraqi Navy. Fortunately for the Iranians, personnel could be fed in through an air-bridge to major cities using Boeing 707, Boeing 747, C-130 Hercules and F.27 Troopship transports.[44] In addition, 77th IRIA Division engineers built a road, the Unity Road, into the town from the east, while other engineers built a 60km canal from the Karun River to prevent the enemy flooding the battlefield.[45]

The Iranians aimed to squeeze out the salient, but first there would be a diversion in the north to draw off reserves. Supported by elements of 16th IRIA Armoured Division and 55th IRIA Airborne Brigade, plus nine batteries (54 guns, including 18 towed tubes), some 3,000–4,000 Pasdaran struck on the night of 1/2 September, and for three weeks mixed company-sized units conducted a hit-and-run campaign along the northern face of the Ahwaz Salient against 9th Armoured Division (14th Mechanised and 43rd Armoured Brigades). Many broke through the berms, and the attacks intensified from 18 September as Ni'ami weakened the defences of Abadan by moving 6th Armoured Brigade/3rd Armoured Division northwards to contain the threat, upon which the Iraqis claimed to have inflicted 7,700 casualties, although they hinted their own casualties were similar. The IRIAF was extremely active in this diversion, and from 21 August to mid-September dropped nearly 170 tonnes of bombs.

Meanwhile, some 20,000 men were assembled for the main offensive, supported by another 15,000 in Abadan. The operation was directed by the 77th IRIA Infantry Division's commander, Colonel Shahab-Al-Din Javadi, who set up his headquarters at Bander-e Mashur, and its main axes were predictably along the two highways into Abadan. The northern axis (along the Ahwaz highway) had Javadi's 3rd Brigade and the southern axis 37th IRIA Armoured Brigade (three armoured and mechanised battalions), while Javadi's remaining brigades faced the southern (1st Brigade) and eastern (2nd Brigade, with a mechanised battalion) faces of the salient. Dispersed among the IRIA were some 8,000 Pasdaran of the 8th Najaf Ashraf and 14th Imam Hossein Brigades, reinforced by Basij, and the offensive would be supported by six self-propelled (M109) and five towed batteries. Heavy weapons were at a premium, and US intelligence calculated the Iranians had only 66 tanks, 67 guns and 64 APCs in the area.

The Iraqi bridgehead was some 20km long and 15km deep between a dry flood plain south of Mared, the River Bahmanshir and the Musa Marshes. It was supplied by two PMP bridges at Qasabeh and Hafar on the western bank of the Karun, covered by scattered tank and mechanised platoons of 12th Armoured Brigade augmented by Popular Army units and 31st SF Brigade. The 7,000-man garrison, which was supported by 11 batteries augmented by a dozen more on the opposite bank of the Shatt, consisted in the north of 8th Mechanised Brigade, reinforced by two battalions of the 31st SF Brigade and Popular Army units, and in the south by 44th Infantry Brigade, mostly distributed in company or platoon strongpoints. Having lost 6th Armoured Brigade, 3rd Armoured Division was reduced to two brigades, but was joined near the mouth of the Karun by 44th and 49th Infantry Brigades/11th Infantry Division.

Ni'ami had retained 10th Armoured Brigade as his tactical/operational level reserve, but the Iraqis were anxious to conserve their precious T-72s and operated them jointly with T-55/62 tank units, which acted as 'missile catchers'.[46] The brigade was near Basra and the Iraqis clearly received some warning of the wrath to come, because Shukur began to move part of his brigade eastwards. Its presence would help to give the Iraqis, according to US intelligence, 300 tanks and 62 guns, with 175 IFV/APCs, and they also had strong air defences, including seven batteries of Gainful. The Iranians were fully informed about the state of the enemy defences because the Iraqis had not cleared civilians from the villages and also failed to conduct patrols.

On the night of 26/27 September, small teams of Pasdaran troops and IRIA commandos struck along the whole length of the Karun bridgehead, often infiltrating along company and battalion boundaries. They isolated some positions, which the Pasdaran units would then storm from all sides to overwhelm the defenders, tactics especially successful against Popular Army troops. Even if they were unable to storm the positions, the Iranians inflicted heavy casualties to bewilder the defenders and cause panic at all levels, including the higher echelons.

As dawn broke, the Iranians launched conventional attacks, with strong fixed- and rotary-wing air support, down the highways from Darkhovin in the north and Bandar-e Mashur in the east, the latter including a subsidiary thrust along the soft-topped embanked road from the highway to Mared as temperatures rose to around 40°C. Iranian tactics emphasised massed infantry attack, often behind a rolling artillery barrage and with tank support, but this was limited in distance and the infantry tended to move in 'bounds' of up to 3km.[47]

Inflexible fire control arrangements meant the Iraqi artillery appears to have played little part in the defence. The Mared defenders were ordered to withdraw to avoid encirclement, but no preparations were made.[48] As news of this withdrawal flashed along the line, it caused panic, especially among Popular Army units, and during the morning men began to stream westward towards the two bridges, which were now under air attack. As the northern defences collapsed, those in the south also came under pressure and a further withdrawal began here. At this point, IRIAF attacks cut both the Qasabeh and Hafar bridges, and increasingly panicky men desperately sought to escape the oncoming Iranians; some seized small boats or built makeshift rafts to cross the Karun to safety. Meanwhile, with little opposition, the Iranian tide lapped ever closer to the Karun.

To stabilise the situation, 10th Armoured Brigade was committed but confined itself to firing across the Karun, enfilading the Iranian advance to cover the eastern approaches to the bridge, which engineers prepared to demolish. It lost some AFVs to the deadly Cobra/TOW combination, but the Iranians would lose nine gunships in this operation.[49]

Ni'ami's efforts, and those of the gunners, gave the Iraqis time to evacuate possibly half of their troops, but little equipment, before the bridge was blown up on 28 September, leaving them with only an enclave in southern Khorramshahr. The Iranians mopped up and completed the relief of Abadan the following day, and their success

PART I: THE IRANIANS STRIKE BACK

The crew of this T-72 from the 10th Armoured Brigade was photographed while monitoring helicopter activity over the frontline ahead of them. Their tank was well dug-in behind a berm but its 125mm 2A46 main gun could be depressed by only six degrees, which meant that in the event of a major battle, the vehicle usually had to leave the safety of its foxhole. (Albert Grandolini collection)

compelled a major reorganisation of the Iraqi III Corps' forces to face the potential new threat from the east: 9th Armoured Division was transferred from the northern face of the Ahwaz Salient to the Karun front north of 3rd Armoured Division, and its sector was taken over by 6th Armoured Division.

The Iranians had achieved a spectacular victory, which removed a major incursion, but their claims of capturing 200 AFVs, including 40–100 tanks, and to have inflicted 34,000 casualties (more than eight times the strength of the bridgehead garrison), were grossly exaggerated. US intelligence put the number of captured AFVs at 30–40 (based upon satellite images) and the total casualties of both sides at 5,000. It seems the Iraqis suffered some 1,800 casualties and lost 1,500 prisoners, a high proportion from the Popular Army, and 300 vehicles, as well as five 155mm guns, while the Iranians may have been left with a casualty list twice that of the defenders. The IRIAA also suffered severely, losing 14 helicopters, but IRIAF losses were lighter, and their operations more effective, thanks to the skilled use of aerial reconnaissance. The victory was due to the Iranians successfully harnessing the strengths of the IRIA and Pasdaran into a winning team, as confidence grew that Iraqi positions could not withstand Iranian infantry attack. The joy was mixed with sadness, for the C-130 carrying almost all the recently appointed Iranian military leadership (Namjoo, Fallahi, Kolahduz and Fakuri) crashed in the Kharizak Mountains some 10km from Tehran on 30 September and all were killed, depriving Iran of an experienced and proven command team.

The new Defence Minister was Major General Mohamad Salimi, who joined the Imperial Iranian Army in 1950 and rose through hard work and dedication. His opposition to the Shah, which led to imprisonment, together with his piety and loyalty to the new regime, made this thoroughly professional soldier acceptable to everyone. On 2 October, Brigadier General Qasem Ali Zahirnejhad

The Iranians lost dozens of armoured vehicles during Operation Nassr/Hoveyzeh, and over 1,000 by 1987. Few were actually destroyed: most were abandoned due to various technical failures – and collected by the triumphant Iraqis. This collection includes a few M47Ms, M48s, M60s, at least one Chieftain and two Scorpions. (Albert Grandolini collection)

replaced Fallahi, while Major General Ali Sayad Shirazi (also written Seyyed-Shirhani) became Commander of IRIA Ground Forces, the latter also known for his piety, which led the Americans to call him 'The Man of God.'[50]

Shirazi shared Khomeini's views on the Islamification of the IRIA, and as liaison officer in Kurdistan with the Pasdaran was dismissed by Bani-Sadr for his support for brutal repression. Clerical influence ensured he was reinstated as 28th Infantry Division commander in Kordistan Province and, following Bani-Sadr's dismissal, he became commander of the North West Forward Operations Headquarters (NWFOH). Shirazi's background ensured that he and Pasdaran commander Mohsen Rezai developed a good working relationship, the general integrating the Pasdaran with the NWFOH.[51]

The loss of the bridgehead also led to major changes in the Iraqi command. Ni'ami's position had been undermined and he was replaced in III Corps by 5th Mechanised Division commander General Al-Qadhi, who would need to focus upon keeping the enemy east of the Karun. With II Corps under mounting pressure, communications into northern Khuzestan needed to be secured, and on 22 October IV Corps was established under Major General Hisham Sabah Al-Fakhry to cover this supply route from threats which might emerge from the sand dune region or up the Karkheh valley. The corps was carved from the right of II Corps (1st Mechanised and 10th Armoured Divisions), together with the newly formed 14th Infantry Division under Brigadier General Suhail Ismael Al-Adhami, a competent but outspoken commander.[52]

6
THE WRITING ON THE WALL

Replacing the Iranian high command delayed Khomeini's hopes of clearing Khuzestan, but another step to this goal was being prepared during October and November. The Iraqis had two major supply lines into southern Khuzestan, from the south through Salamcheh and Khorramshahr and from the north through Bostan, and they had extended the road network in between.[1]

From the summer, the Iranians had exploited the terrain and gaps in the enemy defences to harass the northern supply routes and tightened their control of the sand dunes north of the Karkheh. To the south, the Iraqi lines followed the Amarah-Ahwaz highway before turning south at the Allah Akbar Heights and running south to Hoveyzeh after crossing the Rivers Sableh, Al Abbas and Noisan (also Neisan or Meysan), which would restrict a counterattack from the Karkheh defences which were still augmented by inundations.

By late 1980, Iranian President Bani Sadr was facing growing opposition from the clerics. He and the military were also under pressure to launch the first offensive against the occupying Iraqis as soon as possible. In an effort to restore his prestige, he authorised Operation Nassr/Hoveyzeh, in January 1981. This photograph shows him during one of his many visits to the frontlines, surrounded by IRIA personnel – and a watchful cleric. (Albert Grandolini collection)

Operation Tarigh Al-Qods, November–December 1981
An Iranian planning team led by Colonel Aqbal Mohammad Zadeh and including Colonels Masood Bakhtiari and Houshang Navabi, began to draft a plan, Tarigh al-Qods (The Way to Jerusalem), to cut the northern supply line during the rainy season by taking Bostan.[2]

Not only would this end the threat to Susangerd, but it would also pave the way for destroying the Ahwaz Salient; the Iranians intended to envelop the enemy with a surprise attack from the sand dune region, that was held only by light screening forces, as well as along the south bank of the Karkheh, with the arms linking at Bostan.[3]

A significant feature would reflect the growing professionalism of the Pasdaran. During the second half of 1981, some Pasdaran brigades were expanded into light infantry divisions, usually in three brigades. One was the 14th Imam Hossein Brigade, now a division, which used guns captured in the Karun bridgehead to establish its own artillery department, although generally the Pasdaran remained dependent upon the IRIA for armour, artillery and engineering support.

Two Iranian soldiers seen waiting behind a corner, ready to attack an enemy position inside Susangerd as soon as their leader has thrown his grenade. (Albert Grandolini collection)

The attackers were organised into two task forces. The northern force, with some 9,000 men, led by the 14th Imam Hossein Pasdaran Division, would sweep through the sand ridge area, and was supported by the 1st Brigade/77th IRIA Infantry Division (Colonel Aminian) with an M47 battalion, and a Chieftain battalion of Colonel Bahrami's 3rd Brigade/92nd IRIA Armoured Division. The southern one, with some 11,500 men, under 31st Ashura Pasdaran Division, would advance along the north bank of the Karkheh and would consist of the division's three brigades, supported by another three Pasdaran brigades, of which the 15th Imam Hassan and 25th Karbala would be on the north bank of the Karkheh, while the 34th Sijjad Brigade would be on the southern bank, supported by Colonel Zamanfar's 2nd Brigade of 16th IRIA Armoured Division with Chieftains. The offensive would be supported by five battalions of 33rd Artillery Group, 57 IRIAF aircraft and the IRIAA, which had received a new shipment of TOW missiles.

Zadeh planned to pin down the defenders in the Karkheh valley by a combination of traditional artillery preparation and Pasdaran assault supported by 16th Armoured Division, while Imam Hossein worked its way around the enemy's open northern flank to emerge deep in the rear around Bostan. The latter moved out on the night of 28/29 November, as airborne troops landed by helicopter and took the key passes in the Mishdagh or Mushtaq Hills (Kuh-e Mish-Dagh) east of Bostan to ease their advance.

An increase in radio traffic and aerial reconnaissance alerted Iraqi intelligence that something was in the wind, but little more. On 14 November, the GMID concluded that while the enemy would renew their attack at some point, until then they would hold the front with lightly armed troops and recommended limited offensives all along the front to throw the enemy off balance. Another assessment concluded the destruction of Iranian armour during Operation Hoveyzeh meant the enemy would now rely upon artillery and massed infantry assaults.[4]

The Iraqi line east of Hoveyzeh was held by 5th Mechanised Division (minus 26th Armoured Brigade), while the 100km front west of Hoveyzeh to the border was held by 14th Infantry Division with four brigades (11,000 men), supported by four artillery battalions (70 guns). The Iraqi formations were, from south to north, 48th Infantry and 93rd Reserve Brigades holding the 55km line from Hoveyzeh to the Karkheh, while north of the river were 31st SF Brigade and 26th Armoured Brigade, neither of which was suitable for holding the 30km stretch of line. In reserve was 14th Division's 422nd Infantry Brigade.

At 12:30 a.m. on 29 November, SFOH ordered the offensive to begin, but at dawn revolutionary fervour overcame military precision. Anxious to attack the enemy, the Pasdaran ignored the IRIA fire schedule and charged through the rain in the first of what would be quickly dubbed 'human wave' assaults. Most swarmed past the company strongpoints, exploiting ravines to press on to the rear, for, as US intelligence noted: 'The Iranians used 'human wave' tactics but carefully orchestrated them against exposed or isolated Iraqi positions.'[5] The 93rd Brigade bore the brunt of the assault and appears to have disintegrated, and by capturing the bridge over the Sableh at 10:00 a.m. the Pasdaran isolated Bostan from the south.

An Iranian MG 3 gunner inside a fortified position in Susangerd. (Albert Grandolini collection)

Exhausted Army and Pasdaran troops wondering through Susangerd after securing it from the Iraqis in January 1981. (Albert Grandolini collection)

PART I: THE WRITING ON THE WALL

As the battle raged for the town, Imam Hossein had been steadily advancing through the sand dunes, supported by IRIA armour.[6] During the night of 29/30 November, it began to emerge behind 26th Armoured Brigade, which fell back in confusion, exposing the rear of the lightly armed 31st SF Brigade, which was overwhelmed as the Iranians, making increased use of combined-arms tactics with air support, threatened the 14th Division gun line. IV Corps sent 10th Armoured Division's 17th Armoured and 24th Mechanised Brigades, 6th Armoured Division's 30th Armoured Brigade, the new 51st Armoured Brigade and 422nd Brigade, together with a Republican Guard battalion, all under Shukur's command, to stabilise the situation. Initially they covered the 15km Iraqi retreat northwards to a more defendable point on the frontier between the dunes and marshes, which they retained after a bitterly fought night battle.

In the south, during the evening of 30 November, the Pasdaran stormed Bostan (renamed Tarigh al-Qods by the Ayatollah on 6 December), while Sijjad marched westwards towards the Marshes along the minor river valleys which sheltered them from enemy mechanised counterattacks. The Iraqi 9th Armoured Division sent 35th Armoured Brigade to reinforce the battered 48th Brigade, and together they established a new line some 30km south of Bostan. From their new positions, the Iraqis launched counterattacks which lasted until 6 December and regained 7km to the River Noisan before both sides broke off the battle.

The Iranians claimed to have captured 1,300 troops, together with 100 MBTs, 70 APCs and 19 guns, and while this is an exaggeration, the Iraqis certainly suffered heavy material losses. The 31st SF Brigade was destroyed, and probably the 93rd Res Brigade, which would suggest some 3,000 casualties, while an Iranian source claims they suffered 6,000 casualties, which, if true, amounted to a third of the attackers.[7] After the attack, a furious Saddam Hussein reportedly dismissed senior officers involved in the defeat and demoted others.[8]

The Pasdaran analysed their experiences during a January seminar in Tehran and concluded that they should swamp the enemy with infantry while the IRIA provided support and technical services. The Pasdaran now decided upon a major expansion and began to raise at least a brigade in every province of the country. They also demanded tanks and artillery, but the IRIA declined, arguing that there was no time to train the crews.[9]

The Sinews of War

At the outbreak of war both sides faced embargoes. Moscow's would have had less effect upon Iraq if Saddam's plans had worked, but the effects increased as the war became protracted. When Saddam revealed his plans on 6 July, he airily dismissed fears that the Soviets would not replace munitions, especially shells and bombs, yet within a week of the invasion his generals were reporting 15 percent of the

An Iranian infantryman prays in front of his dugout. The Iranians rarely dug deep trenches and this one – barely waist deep – is a good example for their usual practice. (Albert Grandolini collection)

Operation Tarigh al-Qods (The Path to Jerusalem), conducted in November and December 1981, was one of the first major Iranian successes. It not only regained the town of Bostan, but also captured a large number of vehicles left behind by the Iraqis. Amongst these was this BTR-60, possibly knocked out by an RPG operator like the one in the foreground. (Albert Grandolini collection)

A dug-in Iraqi T-62. The 115mm 2A20 smoothbore gun of this tank could also be depressed by only six degrees, severely restricting its value in defensive battles. (Albert Grandolini collection)

Iraqi mechanised infantry posing with a large picture of Saddam Hussein, atop a T-55 dug-in somewhere along the Karoun River in 1981. (Albert Grandolini collection)

130mm ammunition consumed, together with up to four percent of some tank ammunition.[10] Greece and Turkey offered to provide Saddam with 155mm and 175mm ammunition for captured Iranian guns but too few were captured to make deliveries viable, although Baghdad later diversified its artillery inventory with towed 155mm ordnance from Yugoslavia, which he praised on 22 November 1980 for supplying everything requested.[11] Towards the end of 1980, Greece and India began to supply 130mm and 155mm artillery ammunition under threat of the loss of Iraqi oil.

The spares problem was acute in an AFV fleet dominated by Soviet vehicles and the Soviet philosophy shaped to meet the needs of armed forces with few technically-qualified personnel. Spares were replaced after a specific time, rather than when they were failing, as with Western vehicles, so that consumption was high, while Soviet spares were not designed for prolonged lives. Soviet vehicles were also designed for cold weather and tended to overheat in the desert, a major problem for troop carriers and the T-72.

Yet Baghdad was not totally dependent upon the Warsaw Pact, and the pre-war diversification programme was accelerated. Brazil received a new $1 billion contract for light armour, including Cascavel, EE-11 Urutu wheeled APCs, together with EE-15 4x4, EE-25 and EE-50 6x6 trucks and ammunition. Under a pre-war contract, France would, from 1981, supply 1,000 HOT long-range anti-armour missiles, while Thomson-CSF began to build a radio transceiver factory and won contracts for field telephone equipment.[12] Contracts were also placed with South Korea for commercial soft skin vehicles such as trucks and 4x4 light all-terrain vehicles, while Italy also won a contract for Campagnola Fiat 4x4 light all-terrain vehicles.[13]

Cairo was an enthusiastic supporter of Baghdad, and in March 1981 supplied 4,000 tonnes of materiel, most from army inventories, including T-55s, Walid 4x4 wheeled APCs and artillery. During the war, Egypt was estimated to have supplied $500 million worth of equipment and munitions, although the quality of this aid was uneven. The armour and artillery would have seen extensive service in Egyptian hands and have limited life, while the Walid, which was similar to the BTR-40, was essentially a reconnaissance or counterinsurgency vehicle, but the ammunition would undoubtedly have been valuable. Iraq's other significant Arab friend was Jordan, which ostensibly ordered GHN-45 155mm gun-howitzers from Noricum in Austria and then secretly transferred them across the border into Iraq.

PART I: THE WRITING ON THE WALL

Iran had some friends in the Arab world, notably Syria and Libya, who channelled Soviet origin equipment, spares and ammunition to Tehran, but this would remain a trickle and Iran remained almost as dependent upon the United States as Iraq was upon the Soviet Union.[14]

The confrontation with Washington doomed any chance that the IRIA might regain direct access to US stocks of equipment, spares and ammunition, the Iranians having bitten the hand that fed them. Yet just as Moscow's allies were willing to ignore Soviet embargoes, so were Washington's, who were eager to meet Iranian requirements for oil or cash. Taiwan and South Korea might not be willing to supply equipment, but they could provide spares; indeed, Iranian F-5 fighter-bombers depended upon these sources. For new equipment, Iran had to

A T-55 drives through the ruins of Khorramshahr in 1981. Battles there cost the Iraqis heavy casualties both in men and machines. (Albert Grandolini collection)

A T-62 seen while approaching one of the pontoon bridges across the Karoun. These bridges were vital for support of the Iraqi bridgehead investing Abadan. Both came under threat during the summer of 1981, and eventually had to be blown up during the Iranian Operation Samene-al-Aeme. (Albert Grandolini collection)

turn to the Soviet Union and China, the latter receiving a contract for Type 63 107mm MLRS, while Brazil, a major supplier to Iraq, would deliver light armour and munitions, especially for aircraft, to Iran through Libya.

As a prolonged war became inevitable, from 1981 both sides found it difficult to pay for the growing amounts of equipment and munitions they needed. In the aftermath of the 1973 Arab-Israeli War Arab oil blockade, the price of oil more than tripled to around $13 a barrel, with OPEC setting the price and production quotas to fuel a boom for oil producers. But demand then eased as the world used oil more efficiently to force down the price from $36.71 per barrel in 1980 to $31.71 in 1981. A desperate Tehran decided to undercut the OPEC price and almost double production, and by 1982 was selling at $30.20 a barrel and producing 2.3 million barrels a day against the OPEC quota of 1.2 million.[15] Iran had the advantage of unrestricted access to the sea, which eased exports through the Straits of Hormuz. Iraq was dependent upon overland pipelines through Turkey and Syria; the former vulnerable to Kurdish guerrilla attacks and the latter running through the territory of Iraq's arch-rival and Tehran's friend.

International Support

By early 1981, Moscow recognised its bid for rapprochement with Tehran had failed and began to mend fences with Baghdad, with arms shipments resuming in May. A new agreement, reportedly worth $1 billion, was signed on 19 September, which included T-72B/G and T-62 MBTs, BMD-1 IFVs and artillery, with deliveries accelerated in 1983 and 1984.[16] An order for T-55s was also placed in Moscow, but was sub-contracted to Czechoslovak and Polish factories because Soviet production had ceased, and they also provided some T-72s and BMP-1s.

French arms exports to Iraq increased. During 1981, GIAT won a $600 million contract for GIAT Grande Cadence de Tir (GCT) 155mm self-propelled howitzers on the AMX chassis, reflecting Baghdad's need for self-propelled ordnance. The same year saw orders for the Euromissile Roland mobile surface-to-air missile system, with 13 truck-mounted and 100 static launchers, which were delivered between 1982 and 1985, as well as 2,260 missiles. Panhard also shipped 100 ERC-TH anti-armour vehicles with Euromissile HOT UTM-800 turrets under an order placed in 1976. Renault provided TRM-10000 and TRM-900 trucks, while during 1981, the British company Scammell received a £40 million order from Iraq for 200 trucks. Brazil continued to sell to Iraq and in 1981 won a $250 million contract for more Cascaval and Urutu, together with EE-3 Jararaca reconnaissance vehicles and ASTROS 2 MLRS systems. In his desire to expand his forces, Saddam also turned to a new source, and in 1981 placed an order in China for Type 59 MBT, a derivative of the T-54/55.

Officially, the United Kingdom was neutral in the Iran-Iraq War and imposed an arms embargo, which excluded non-lethal materiel, of which £321.9 million was sold in 1980. During 1981, Britain's Racal supplied £750,000 worth of radios to Iraq, which was seeking Jaguar V frequency-hopping transceivers but would receive only Syncal 30 or obsolete BCC-349 sets. In 1981, the Defence Export Sales Organisation (DESO) sought to sell Chieftain MBT and armoured recovery vehicles (ARV) to Iraq via Jordan, which signed a £1.17 million contract for 15 ARV on March 14. The Foreign Office

Table 5: Major Orders by Iraq

Order placed	Country	Equipment			Deliveries
		Type	Model	No	
1980	Brazil	Recon	EE-9	35	1980–1981
		APC	EE-11	148	1982–1984
	East Germany	MBT	T-54/55	50	1981–1982
	Poland	MBT	T-54/55	400	1981–1982
	Yugoslavia	Towed Arty	76, 155mm	100	1980–1981
1981	Austria	Towed Arty	GHN-45	200	1981–1986
	Brazil	Recon	EE-9	200	1982–1985
		APC	E-11	100	1982–1984
		Recon	EE-3	280	1984–1985
		MLRS	Astros 2	67	1984
	China	MBT	Type 59	300	1982–1984
	Czechoslovakia	MBT	T-55	200	1982–1985
		ICV	BMP-1	750	1981–1987
	Egypt	MBT	T-55	250	1981–1983
		APC	Walid	100	1981
		Towed Arty	130mm	100	1981–1982
	France	SP Arty	GCT	83	1983–1985
	Poland	MBT	T-55	200	1982–1985
	USSR	MBT	T-72	500	1982–1990
		MBT	T-62	2,150	1982–1989
		ICV	BMD	10	1981
		Towed Arty	130mm	580	1982–1987
		SP Arty	Gvozdika	50	1982–1984
		SP Arty	Akatsiya	50	1982–1984
		MLRS	BM-21	200	1983–1984

PART I: THE WRITING ON THE WALL

Table 6: Major Orders by Iran					
Order placed	Country	Equipment			Deliveries
		Type	Model	No	
1980	China	MLRS	Type 63	300	1981–1987
1981	China	MBT	Type 59	300	1982–1984
		Towed Arty	130mm	300	1982–1984
	North Korea	MBT	T-62	150	1982–1985
		Towed Arty	130mm	400	1982–1985
	Libya	Recon	EE-9	130	1981
		MBT	T-54/55	125	1981
		MBT	T-62	65	1981
	Syria	ICV	BMP-1	200	1981–1984

and DESO sought ways to get Chieftain MBTs to Iraq via Jordan, but then Baghdad secured Soviet supplies.[17]

Ammunition expenditure for both sides was higher than anticipated, and a document relating to the relatively quiet week of 19–25 April 1981 showed some 182 tonnes was consumed every day![18] Daily consumption of artillery ammunition for both sides amounted to 6,235 artillery rounds (75–155mm), or more than 150 tonnes, together with 204 missiles (13.5 tonnes) from multiple launch rocket systems. The situation became acute in January 1981 when stocks fell dangerously low as divisions were firing up to 1,000 rounds per day. Some ammunition for Soviet guns was no longer manufactured by the Warsaw Pact, while alternative sources had either limited manufacturing capability or limited stocks. Yugoslavia received a contract for 3,000 130mm and 5,000 152mm shells, Greece agreed to supply 20,000 shells, while Somalia provided ammunition it had received from Egypt. A major potential source was China, but this was initially unreliable and on 31 January, Shanshal informed Saddam that their promised shipment of shells was delayed for at least four months. Meanwhile, friendly Middle Eastern states including Jordan, Kuwait, Saudi Arabia and Yemen provided Soviet, French and even US artillery.[19]

In all, Iraq was estimated to have received $3.74 billion worth of military equipment during 1981, while Iran received some $800 million.[20] The figures are academic, for it is unclear whether these are actual expenditure or merely the face value of the materiel supplied.

By contrast, Iran suffered a general shortage of equipment, ammunition and spares due to her self-created diplomatic isolation. This dammed the flow of supplies not only from the United States but also from the United Kingdom, and meant few frontline artillery battalions were able to deploy their authorised 18 tubes. The average was 15, but as few as 15 percent of these would be serviceable, while air defence units were lucky to have half their weapons serviceable, leading to frequent complaints from brigades about their exposure to enemy airpower.[21] European and Asian black market sources of spares and ammunition for Anglo-American equipment were unreliable in terms of quantity and quality, with some dealers providing obsolete or inoperable equipment, while corrupt officials sometimes skimmed money.[22] Moscow slammed the door to Soviet aid following the persecution of Iranian communists, a rare example of the Superpowers being in agreement.

US intelligence noted Tehran was seeking new sources of supply for tank spares and artillery ammunition (especially 155mm and 175mm) in Eastern Europe, North Korea and even Israel, while friendly Libya and Syria did what they could. Tripoli provided T-54/55 and T-62 MBTs from its inventories, together with some ammunition, while Syria supplied BMP-1, Sagger anti-armour missiles and 150 launchers for Grail surface-to-air missiles, with three missiles per launcher. Libya placed an order in North Korea on Iran's behalf for its version of the T-62 (Ch'onma-ho), as well as artillery, but Pyongyang's northern neighbour, China, would prove Iran's biggest supplier and won a $2 billion contract for Type 59 tanks, Type 59-I towed 130mm guns

An Iraqi S-23 180mm towed gun firing on the Khuzestan front in 1981. This weapon had a range of 30.4 kilometres, which was less than the 175mm M107 deployed by Iranians. The Soviets proved quite reluctant to deliver larger numbers of S-23s, and Iraq received only one battery of them. (Albert Grandolini collection)

and, reportedly, Shenyang F-6 fighters.

Only in small arms was the Iranian situation adequate, and throughout the war there were no reports of Iranian infantry lacking such equipment. Iranian operations, therefore, were based largely upon their infantry, although their superior artillery would also play a key role throughout the year, the superiority in self-propelled ordnance allowing them to concentrate fire rapidly and force the Iraqi batteries to disperse along a broad front, leaving them short of firepower at critical moments.[23]

A good study of an IRIA trench in Khuzestan (with a shell exploding in the background). As usual, the trench is rather shallow, but quite wide. (Albert Grandolini collection)

An interesting view of an IRGC-operated observation post and an RPG-team in western Khuzestan in 1981. (Albert Grandolini collection)

PART I: THE WRITING ON THE WALL

Crews of the 92nd Armoured Division posing with their Chieftains during a graduation ceremony, prior to being sent to the frontlines. Notable is that most of the vehicles in the background show very fresh colours, indicating they had been taken out of storage very recently. (Albert Grandolini collection)

A rear view of a Chieftain Mk.3 from the 92nd Armoured Division. This version was powered by 650hp Leyland L60 engine. As with the uprated 720hp version that powered Iranian Chieftain Mk.5s, this proved too weak for the task. (Tom Cooper collection)

A TOW-armed AH-1J Cobra (serial 3-4572) passing low over the battlefield, heavily scarred by the tracks of dozens of vehicles. The Iranians made extensive use of TOW and knocked out thousands of Iraqi armoured vehicles and bunkers during the war, countering their weakness in armour. (Farzin Nadimi collection)

A famous photo of an Iraqi Mi-25 thundering low over BMP-1s of an armoured unit in western Khuzestan, sometime early during the Iran-Iraq War. The Mi-25 was a fast, well-armed and protected helicopter, but could not hover in the hot local conditions and had to be flown like a fighter aircraft. In the words of a former Iraqi pilot flying the type against Iran, 'it felt like being the biggest target over the battlefield'. (Albert Grandolini collection)

7
DISASTER FOR IRAQ

Despite shortages of equipment, the confidence of Iran's military leaders grew during 1981 as they found solutions to their operational and logistical problems and became more capable at both the tactical and operational levels. The Pasdaran and their clerical supporters were now more willing to cooperate with the IRIA, which itself was willing to bend before the wind, although mutual trust remained skin deep. Inevitably there remained personal and corporate rivalries, yet patriotism meant that the IRIA professionals, regulars and conscripts, together with the Pasdaran and Basij 'amateurs', were now reluctantly willing to work towards the joint goal of driving out the invader.[1] It was a measure of the regime's confidence in the IRIA that it was allowed to create, from late 1981, short-term reservist Qods (Jerusalem) infantry battalions of 500 men, beginning with the 1901st. They were usually assigned to understrength divisions, especially on the Northern and Central Fronts, which trained them for up to six weeks and retained them for a maximum of 18 months before they were disbanded, then reformed with new personnel.[2]

Yet there remained formidable problems in exploiting the country's huge reserves of manpower. Command and control was hindered by a continued shortage of experienced staff officers, while at brigade level and above, many formations were led by officers propelled beyond their experience or abilities. There was also a shortage of experienced non-commissioned officers (NCOs), the oil in all armed forces, while the revolution continued to undermine military discipline for, despite Khomeini's strictures, many clerical commissars continued to question and even countermand officers' orders.[3]

Communications were hamstrung by a severe shortage of radios and field telephones. Before the revolution, each division had 2,000 radio sets, but the expansion of the Pasdaran and the perennial shortage of spares reduced availability as the regime trawled the world's markets for replacements. There was always considerable HF traffic, especially for logistics and movements, as well as between the front and higher commands. Even if the enemy could not decrypt the signals, the level of traffic alerted them that an offensive was imminent. As the Iranians became aware of their communications security problem, they made greater use of multi-channel radios as well as landline communications, while couriers were also used extensively.[4]

As the winter rains eased, the Iranians prepared to drive out the invader and launched their first blow in March 1982 around Dezful in Operation Fath-ol Mobin, which proved a devastating success and even sucked in Iraq's 3rd Armoured Division from the Karun front.[5] To pre-empt this attack, divert enemy reserves and boost his prestige, Saddam demanded an offensive towards Bostan.[6] As the 14th Infantry Division had lost Bostan, it was now given the opportunity to regain its honour by retaking the town using the 10th Armoured Division's 17th Armoured and 24th Mechanised Brigades, 3rd Armoured Division's 12th Armoured Brigade, 18th and 108th Infantry Brigades, as well as the 1st and 8th Popular Army Special Missions (PASM) Brigades. A frontal assault supported by 12 artillery battalions (200 guns) was launched by 24th Mechanised Brigade/10th Armoured Division at dawn on 6 February in rain which turned the battlefield into a swamp. The defenders, Pasdaran supported by the reinforced 3rd Brigade/92nd IRIA Armoured Division, and four self-propelled artillery battalions augmented by a towed battery (80 guns), resisted fiercely, using a berm outside Bostan as the MLR.

On his own initiative, the 6th Armoured Division commander (General Mahmood Shukur, the former 10th Armoured Brigade commander) sent his 25th Mechanised Brigade northward towards Sableh on a raid which captured six Chieftain MBT but did not cause the defenders much trouble.[7]

Reinforcements were rushed from Dezful to Bostan, but the Iraqi attack was never a serious threat and ended three days later after gaining little ground, although the Popular Army formations were reported to have distinguished themselves. The operation did, however, force the Iranians to consume much of the artillery ammunition assembled for the Dezful offensive and allowed the Iraqis to strengthen the defences east of al-Amarah.

Iraqi morale was boosted, but Saddam was unhappy and demoted some officers while augmenting the artillery train to renew battle on 13–14 February, then again on 20 March. But the continued muddy conditions prevented any progress, and hopes of renewing the operation when the ground dried were dashed two days later when the Iranians launched their own offensive.

The success of Tarigh al-Qods, followed by Fath-ol Mobin, saw new dissensions within the Iranian leadership. The rift was within the IRIA, but also between it and the Pasdaran, with old wounds reopened by the Ghotbzadeh Plot. Former Foreign Minister Sadiq Ghotbzadeh was arrested on 9 April, accused of planning Khomeini's assassination, and would publicly admit his guilt. He also implicated the IRIA, which led to a new purge and by mid-August 70 officers had been shot.[8]

Against this background, Rezai and the Pasdaran argued in the SDC in simplistic terms against the IRIA's set-piece combined-arms operation, which required substantial materiel support, whose assembly took time. They downplayed the role of the IRIA and emphasised how the Pasders' fervour had carried them through the enemy defences and deep into their rear. They wished to strike the moment the ground was dry enough in southern Khuzestan, removing the external threat to the regime, which could then focus upon the internal one and complete the Islamic Revolution. Shirazi and Zahirnejad urged delay so the offensive would have adequate

77

MIDDLE EAST@WAR SERIES SPECIAL #1: THE IRAN-IRAQ WAR

The positions of the Iranian and Iraqi ground forces at the start of Operation Beit-ol-Moghaddas. (Map by George Anderson)

An interesting study of an Iranian Chieftain, the crew of which increased its protection by adding sandbags to the top of the turret and the front of the hull. Such measures became necessary when the type proved vulnerable to APFSDS hits from Iraqi T-72s, and HOT anti-tank missiles fired by Iraqi helicopters. Sandbags also gave additional protection against Iraqi artillery. (Tom Cooper collection)

support, but Defence Minister Salimi, excited by the success at Dezful, overruled them.

Planning for Operation Beit-ol-Mogaddas (Sacred House, a Koranic name for Jerusalem) began in late February or March but intensified during April under the direction of General Rahim Safavi.[9] There was an intense reconnaissance effort conducted by the Pasdaran and much of 23rd SF Brigade, reinforced by a naval commando and four IIG companies, to detect weaknesses in the enemy defences. In these missions, the scouts exploited their superior night-fighting equipment acquired by the Shah.[10] They received local help, notably exploring the Darkhovin Salient, where they were aided by the local Arab Bani-Kar tribe, a telling indictment of Iraqi political failure. COMINT helped to fill out the intelligence picture, while the IRIAF deployed photographic reconnaissance and SIGINT squadrons, and twice used Unmanned Aerial Vehicles.[11]

The Iraqi enclave in Khuzestan was bounded by the Karkheh Kur in the north, the Shatt al-Arab in the south, the Hawizah Marshes in the west and the Karun in the east. The Iraqis had again blocked irrigation ditches during the winter rains to flood large areas in front of their defences, notably between the Karkheh and the Karkheh Kur, east of the Susangerd-Hoveyzeh line, as well as along 55km of the Karun's western bank a few kilometres north of Darkhovin, this inundation lapping along on the Ahwaz–Khorramshahr highway.

The 65km northern face was anchored west of Hoveyzeh on the River Noisan and in the west by Dub-e Said. East of Hoveyzeh it overlooked flooded land, apart from the land bridge south-west of Tarrah, while the northern part of the 105km eastern defences, which followed the Ahwaz–Khorramshahr highway, also covered inundations, with major strongpoints at Hamid and Ahu. South-east of Ahu, and the southern edge of the flooded area, the river meanders eastward, twisting and turning for some 20km before straightening out near Darkhovin and running south-west to the Shatt.

The Iraqi line here bulged outwards to form the Darkhovin Salient, which encompassed a small stream, shown on Soviet maps as Nakhr Peyen, which ran from near Hoseyniyeh (also written Hoseinieh or Hosseinieh) north-east through an area of prehistoric settlements, of which only earthen mounds (tels) remained. Behind was the desert, with numerous natural obstacles to aid the defence, along with minor roads and tracks, often on embankments, while west to east obstacles to movement in the southern part of the salient included abandoned irrigation canals and river channels.[12]

To overcome these obstacles, Tehran assembled some 135,000 troops, half of them Pasdaran and Basij, with some 350 tanks, 100 self-propelled and towed guns, 40 MLRS and 26 Cobra gunships, as the revolution's sword was raised to cut off the invader's hand.

Safavi envisaged enveloping the enclave, and on 20 April assembled three task forces (Gharargah): Qods opposite the northern face, Fath on the upper Karun and Nasr on the lower Karun, together with an IRIAF forward headquarters at Vahdati AFB under Colonel Bahram Houshyar. In addition to their own troops, the task forces could count upon the 22nd and 55th Artillery Groups, with some 20 artillery battalions and seven MLRS batteries.

Task Force Qods would pin down the forces on the northern face along three axes. West of Hoveyzeh, 1st Brigade/16th IRIA Armoured Division (minus a tank battalion but with three Pasdaran

From 1982 the IrAAC began combining its Mi-25s and SA.342 Gazelles into 'hunter-killer' teams: Mi-25s would saturate the target zone with unguided rockets and machine gun fire, after which the more vulnerable Gazelles would try to target Iranian armour or fortifications with HOT anti-tank guided missiles. (Albert Grandolini collection)

T-62s and T-55s of an Iraqi armoured company seen somewhere in the Dezful area, shortly before the Iranians launched their Operation Beit-ol-Mogaddas. The standard armoured company of an Iraqi armoured division had 11 MBTs (it seems that by early 1982 some Iraqi units were so short on T-62s that they had to also use T-55s), a BTR-60 for the command team, and at least one BTS-3 armoured recovery vehicle attached (one of the latter is visible in the foreground, left). (Albert Grandolini collection)

battalions and two IIG companies) would demonstrate as 2nd Brigade advanced upon Hoveyzeh. Meanwhile, the 58th Malek-e Ashtar Pasdaran Brigade, which was boosted to double strength like the other Pasdaran units, would make a separate thrust across the Tarrah land bridge to storm the enemy defences, supported by a special forces battalion and 3rd Brigade/16th Armoured Division.

Simultaneously, the main blow would be launched around Darkhovin, the boundary between Task Forces Fath and Nasr, at the enemy salient on the opposite bank. Fath would would cross in the north at Halub (also Jish Haloub) with 55th IRIA Airborne Brigade, with the Pasdaran 19th Fajr Sar-Allah and 30th Beit-ol-Mogaddas Divisions and 59th Zolfaqhar Brigade. It would strike up the Nakhr Peyen valley, with the airborne troops covering the right flank, to establish a bridgehead into which would be fed first the IRIA's 92nd Armoured Division, then the 37th Armoured Brigade. These would spearhead a breakout to the west and north-west to cut the Ahwaz–Khorramshahr highway and isolate the Ahwaz Salient. Meanwhile, the infantry-heavy Task Force Nasr would exploit little islands near Mesian to establish a

PART I: DISASTER FOR IRAQ

Sudanese volunteers on parade before being sent to the frontlines. Several contingents of foreign workers were coerced to serve with the Iraqi Army during the war with Iran, but there were volunteers too. Amongst these were about 3,000 members of the al-Yarmouk Force, the battalions of which were assigned to the 7th and 15th Infantry Divisions. They proved of poor quality and some even mutinied. All Jordanians were withdrawn by 1983. (Albert Grandolini collection)

IRGC troops approaching an olive grove near Khorramshahr. Poorly trained and equipped, but highly motivated and zealous, they eventually developed into the force that the Iraqi generals feared the most. (Farzin Nadimi collection)

In order to counter the threat of the Iraqi armour, the Pasdaran formed motorcycle-mounted teams, with the pillion passenger carrying an RPG-7. Motorcycles also saw widespread use in resupply missions for forward-deployed units. (Albert Grandolini collection)

bridgehead with the IRIA 21st Infantry Division and the Pasdaran 5th Nasr and 31st Ashura Divisions, as well as the 40th IRIA Infantry Brigade, to shield Fath from relief attempts from the south.

Once Safavi sprung the trap, the two armoured divisions would then isolate and destroy the Ahwaz Salient and up to three enemy divisions, but what if the Iraqis exploited the road network between the Hawizah Marshes and the Karun to escape across the border? Khomeini opposed any crossing of the frontier, even in 'hot pursuit', and while pressure was mounting on him to change his mind, this remained official policy, which meant the enemy would have a sanctuary. If Qods could not pin down the northern face, then Safavi's prime objective might not be achieved. He was more confident of achieving the second part, for while part of Nasr put pressure on the Khorramshahr bridgehead, the remainder, with Fath, would drive south to take the border town of Shalamcheh and isolate Khorramshahr.

The IRIAF had achieved air superiority in the two previous offensives and Safavi hoped it would repeat this feat, despite being severely understrength, with only 20 strike aircraft (F-4 and F-5) available for what it dubbed Operation Shahbah 3 (Phantom 3), plus reconnaissance and transport units. However, three fighter squadrons (F-14) were available to shield the Iranian rear, together with surface-to-air missiles, three HAWK batteries (two in the Abadan area) and a Rapier battery, while the troops had a significant number of Libyan and Syrian-supplied Grail man-portable weapons, which they first used in April.

From 7 April, the Iraqis noticed enemy preparations, including 21st Division training with boats, the assembly of bridging equipment as well as the arrival of 22 field hospitals and, 10 days later, the transfer of forces south from the Dezful front (including a tank battalion of 64th Division) and recognised the implications. These were confirmed by an increase in Iranian probes, with a steady rise in raids, artillery bombardments and reconnaissance flights. Baghdad realised that an offensive was imminent and where it would fall, but lacked the power to disrupt it; indeed, the recent Iranian successes left the more thoughtful Iraqi officers contemplating the coming year with growing concern, although its leaders loudly proclaimed confidence.

The new Iranian tactics bewildered even the best Iraqi officers, as General Hamdani later commented to the Americans:

> Each phase of a military operation is supposed to happen at a certain time (for fire support etc.), but these Iranians had neither phases nor organisation. They did not care if they had fire support or anything; they had no concept of command and control, timing etc. They just kept moving, they swarmed through our artillery zones, which wrecked our plans and calculations.[13]

This echoed comments by conservative British and French officers on the Western Front in 1918 about German *Schwerpunkt Taktik*, and possibly of their successors in France in May 1940.

Massed infantry assaults, which most armies would have handled with a combination of firepower and mechanised manoeuvre, left the Iraqis bewildered. They were unsure when, or where, to launch the necessary ripostes, and tended to hit the enemy centre rather than striking the flanks, which caused heavy losses to artillery and anti-armour missiles. Iraqi artillery fire arrangements, which should have been based upon flexible plans at brigade level, were too rigid and often dictated by the divisional commander, who had little knowledge of the fluid tactical situation.[14] The Iraqis would begin to discuss the problem only in April 1982, and only a year later did the first doctrinal manuals appear.[15]

MIDDLE EAST@WAR SERIES SPECIAL #1: THE IRAN-IRAQ WAR

Both sides made extensive use of Soviet-made BM-21 multiple rocket launcher systems, ammunition supplies permitting. The 40-tube system could fire 70kg rockets to a range of about 20 kilometres. This was one of dozens of examples operated by the Iranians. (Tom Cooper collection)

M113s of an Iranian reconnaissance battalion – probably that of the 21st Infantry Division – waiting for the order to advance during Operation Beit-ol-Mogaddas. (Tom Cooper collection)

This Iraqi mechanised company was quickly overrun during Operation Beit-ol-Mogaddas, and most of its vehicles – including at least four BMP-1s and three OT-62s – were captured intact. (Tom Cooper collection)

In the meantime, the only practical defence was to strengthen the fortifications during the rainy season, which topped up the flooded areas north of the Karkheh Kur and on the western bank of the Karun. Behind them was usually a strong screen of rifle companies, which would be withdrawn to the MLR in the face of a major assault. These positions were behind barbed wire entanglements and deep minefields, 5th Mechanised Division alone laying 38,329 mines, of which 11.5 percent were anti-armour versions.[16] The MLR was a kilometre behind and remained upon a buttressed berm, often built with materials from demolished villages, sheltered by more wire entanglements and minefields.

As autonomous company strongpoints had proved too weak, the berms were now buttressed with battalion strongpoints, each holding a 2km section of the line, with two company positions on the MLR and a third, linked by more berms, some 2km behind. Brigade headquarters would have two battalions up and one in reserve 58km from the FEBA, while divisional mechanised reserves were in fortified positions 1,520km behind them. The continued shortage of infantry meant that up to half the MLR berm was unmanned and covered only with fire from the battalion strongpoints. For this reason, the Iraqi mechanised forces created company-sized reaction forces, armoured brigades deploying up to 40 tanks and 10 APC, while mechanised brigades had 10 tanks and 40 APCs. US intelligence described Iraqi defensive concepts as 'ill-conceived', with open division and brigade flanks (unmanned berms), and armoured units in fixed defences with little infantry support.

The mechanised reaction forces were especially important

PART I: DISASTER FOR IRAQ

A blazing Iraqi T-54/55 knocked out by an AH-1J Cobra helicopter with a TOW missile, while attempting to run away from a position about to be overrun by Iranians. Note the 120mm mortar in the foreground. (Tom Cooper collection)

The Iraqis also lost hundreds of MBTs, and even more other vehicles and precious equipment during Operation Beit-ol-Mogaddas. This group of T-54/55s was knocked out and captured while attempting to shelter inside a palm grove. (Tom Cooper collection)

1973, would now act to channel any major assault into a killing zone around the Nakhr Peyen valley, which held a gun line, sometimes with fortified fire bases, many around the tels that acted as observation posts.[17]

Considerable effort was expended fortifying the Khorramshahr area, where the southern bridgehead had berms studded with bunkers, observation points and fire posts covering fire zones created by levelling up to a third of the surviving buildings and vegetation. For the first time, the northern part of the town was fortified, with bulldozers and earthmovers levelling buildings and trees to create good fields of fire, then build a 2.5-metre berm which arced across the city, with the Shatt al-Arab at its back, this being nicknamed by some 'The Wall of Persia'.[18] The emphasis, however, was upon repelling attacks from across the river, not along its banks from the north and the significant weak point in the defences where the Karun meandered south-east.

Intelligence was vital to the Iraqi plans, but units were reluctant to send out reconnaissance patrols, while higher level collection and analysis remained major problems until the summer of 1982, partly due to a continued shortage of Farsi-speaking officers. Baghdad pleaded with Jordan and Saudi Arabia for intelligence support, but even

along the eastern part of the front facing the Karun, where the area east of the Ahwaz–Khorramshahr highway was to be a killing zone for any enemy crossing. The highway embankment had been fortified to act as the MLR, while a screen of fortified observation posts was established along the riverbank, with the gaps between them covered by teams of mobile scouts. In most places this killing zone was 1,000m deep, but there was a significant weakness near the middle, opposite the Darkhovin Salient, where the killing zone was twice this depth.

With only three infantry brigades to cover this sector, the fortified observation posts would play a significant role in the defence, although some five-metre berms were built to restrict enemy movement after the Karun bridgehead, which had acted as a breakwater to shelter this salient, was lost in September. The observation points, like those in the Bar Lev Line on the Suez Canal in

then the system was over-centralised; data was first sent to Baghdad for evaluation by the General Headquarters and the GMID. Vital information often did not reach the front line in time, while IrAF reconnaissance photographs often took 48 hours to reach units.[19]

The cloud had a silver lining, for during the autumn of 1981 an Iranian officer defected and brought with him a Crypto C-52 electro-mechanical enciphering machine. With it, the GMID, backed by Soviet KGB technical assistance, began to crack enemy codes and confirmed the enemy build-up in Khuzestan and its support by bridging and ferry units, together with North Korean technical experts.[20]

Yet the Iraqis were probably unaware of either the timing or its ambitious objectives. In March, 3rd Armoured Division (now under Kurdish infantry officer Brigadier General Juwad Assad Shetna) was withdrawn from the western bank of the Karun in response to

MIDDLE EAST@WAR SERIES SPECIAL #1: THE IRAN-IRAQ WAR

This knocked-out T-72 burned completely after a direct hit set on fire the fuel cells installed above its right fender. Notable is that the vehicle was still wearing the original olive-green colour applied in the USSR before delivery. It is possible that this was 'enhanced' by the addition of some mud, resulting in what looks like a stripe of grey colour on the gun tube. (Tom Cooper collection)

The extent of the Iraqi defeat during Operation Beit-ol-Mogaddas was immense. The heavy equipment left behind by retreating or destroyed Iraqi units was sufficient to equip several new armoured and mechanised brigades of the IRGC. (Tom Cooper collection)

operational level reserve was 10th Armoured Brigade, which remained in the Basra area.

The 3rd Armoured Division returned to the Darkhovin Salient and had 6th, 12th and 30th Armoured, 8th Mechanised and 19th, 418th and 606th Infantry Brigades, the infantry units augmented by battalions of 33rd SF Brigade. The 9th Armoured Division (Brigadier General Kamil Mishri) shuffled northward opposite the flooded areas of the upper Karun with 14th Mechanised, 35th and 43rd Armoured and 104th Infantry Brigades. The northern face of the Ahwaz Salient was held by two divisions: 6th Armoured Division in the west, still under Shukur, with 16th and 56th Armoured, 25th Mechanised and 45th, 49th and 90th Infantry Brigades; and 5th Mechanised Division in the east with 15th and 20th Mechanised, 26th Armoured 109th, 419th and 504th Infantry Brigades, and battalions of 31st SF Brigade. Holding the lower Karun around Khorramshahr was 11th Infantry Division (Brigadier General Said Mohammed Fethi) with 22nd, 28th 48th 102nd, 113th, 117th and 502nd Infantry Brigades, augmented by a tank battalion and 2nd PASM Brigade, as well as the equivalent of a brigade of Border Guards.[22]

By 27 April, the Iraqis had a good idea of both enemy forces and intentions, and at 6:30 p.m. on 28 April the GMID correctly warned the enemy would attack

Fath-ol Mobin, but it returned in April in response to the emerging threat, having suffered relatively light losses because it had been used sparingly at Dezful.[21] Its return brought Qadhi's III Corps to five divisions, each swollen to twice the usual size with a total of some 30 brigades, together with 15th Infantry Division (Major General Mohammad Abdul Qader) on the Faw Peninsula with 420th and 501st Infantry Brigades, 1st PASM Brigade and a brigade-size battle group. North of the Shatt, the corps had 90,000 men holding the 215km line in the Hoyehzeh–Ahwaz–Khorramshahr triangle, but it remained AFV-heavy, with the regular infantry severely diluted by reserve, police and Popular Army units. Qadhi had 750–1,000 tanks, mostly deployed as tactical level reserves, and the only

around midnight on 29/30 April and as also anticipated, the attack would be on all three fronts. The Qods attack west of Hoveyzeh, supported by seven bridges, established a bridgehead over the Noisan with 2nd Brigade/16th Division, but made little progress because the bridges were struck by the IrAF. The Iraqi 6th Armoured Division had contained the situation and the news from the neighbouring 5th Mechanised Division was also encouraging, although neither was aware that within a day the Iranian 1st Brigade/16th Division had been quietly withdrawn and sent south.

The 5th Mechanised Division planned first to contain the Iranian attackers, then drive them back with mechanised reserves which were moving up even as the bombardment began. Yet the superior Iranian artillery pounded its positions with its usual accuracy, and this was

PART I: DISASTER FOR IRAQ

exploited by the Pasdaran and Basij with their customary élan. Within two-and-a-half hours, they had made several dangerous penetrations in 109th and 419th Infantry Brigade's front, but the arrival of the mechanised brigades restored the line by 9:00 a.m. The Iranians desperately called for reinforcements and artillery support, but by late afternoon had been driven back to their start line.

Undaunted, the attacks were renewed with dwindling intensity over the next three days, but even when they forced their way through artillery fire and the obstacle belt, the Iranians were swiftly driven back by counterattacks. The Iraqi 5th Mechanised Division claimed to have inflicted 10,000 dead, destroyed five tanks and taken 151 prisoners, while suffering 1,028 casualties, including 176 dead and 357 missing, with losses of 12 tanks, eight APC and six howitzers.[23] Task Force Quds failed to achieve its objective of pinning down the enemy because it had to strike on three independent axes, which would ultimately allow the Iraqis to salvage something from the wreck.

Meanwhile, to the south, a cancer was growing in the weakest point in the Iraqi defences. The main Iranian blow was launched across the 200-metre-wide Karun some 60km south of Ahwaz on both sides of the Darkhovin Salient. The sector was under General Assad of 3rd Armoured Division, who had earned a high reputation against the Israelis in Syria and then against his own people in 1974.[24] With only three infantry brigades (9,000 men), he had to plan a defence in depth in killing fields far from the Karun, where he would exploit his superior tank strength, some 300 tanks against 200 Iranian.

Supported by battalions of 23rd SF Brigade, the main Iranian crossings were north and south of Darkhovin; Task Force Fath led by Fajr Sar-Allah and 55th Airborne Brigade, while Ashura spearheaded Task Force Nasr. The Iranians exploited the gaps to infiltrate the observation posts and storm those threatening the bridging sites, airborne troops striking those in the north and the Pasdaran those in the south. Engineers then began work throwing three bridges into the Fath bridgehead and two into the Nasr one.[25] The IrAF, which

In attempt to suppress the activity of the IRIAA's AH-1 Cobra attack helicopters, the Iraqis began deploying large numbers of ZSU-57-2s along their frontlines in 1982. The system was handicapped by a lack of radar control, but its range proved superior to that of the ZU-23, and it was also effective against exposed infantry formations. (Tom Cooper collection)

An Iraqi OT-64 SKOT APC knocked out during Operation Beit-ol-Mogaddas. Iraq imported 386 such vehicles from Czechoslovakia in the 1970s, but they seem to have seen active service only during the first two years of the war with Iran. (Tom Cooper collection)

flew 218 fixed-wing sorties that day compared with 20 by the IRIAF, vainly attempted to destroy the bridges, across which Fath began to send 1st and 2nd Brigades of 92nd Division, some 20,000 men, 500 AFVs, 5,000 vehicles and 200 tonnes of ammunition on the first day alone, while Nasr sent two brigades of 21st Division.

Meanwhile, the IRIA and Pasdaran, with good gunship and light armoured support, pushed the shoulders of the bridgehead along the Karun, while the Fath spearhead drove southwest through the fortified tels, many Pasdaran fighting on foot but led by others in light trucks or even on motorcycles! The Nasr troops had to fight their way westwards across irrigated fields, and despite enemy helicopter attacks they claimed to have cut the highway south of Hoseyniyeh by 11:00 a.m., although they were probably held short of the road. By the end of the day, the Iranians had established a

85

A view of an Iraqi bivouac overrun by Iranian infantry during Operation Beit-ol-Mogaddas. In foreground is a BRDM-2, behind it a ZPU-4 anti-aircraft machine-gun, while two BTR-60s and a T-62 can be made out in the background. (Albert Grandolini collection)

A Brigadier General of the Iraqi Army, together with dozens of his troops, most apparently from the Popular Army (al-Jaysh ash-Shabi). Up to 15,000 Iraqi troops were captured during Operation Beit-ol-Moqaddas. (Tom Cooper collection)

bridgehead some 25km deep and up to 30km wide, the Americans noting: 'The Iranians were able consistently to out-maneuver their opponent during the initial attack.'[26]

The speed of the Fath advance was an unwelcome surprise for Assad, disrupting his tactical plan because most of his armour was too far in the rear to aid the battered infantry, who could rely only upon Sagger missiles and RPGs against AFVs. The closest Iraqi formation was 12th Armoured Brigade, which began a series of desperate and unsupported counterattacks, but every Iraqi attempt to stand was compromised as the Iranians sliced through Popular Army units like a hot knife through butter. This allowed the Iranians to expand the bridgehead on 1 May, with Fath receiving 37th Armoured Brigade while the rest of 21st Division joined the Nasr spearhead. Iraqi aircraft ran the gauntlet of Grail missiles and ZSU-23-4s, which together claimed 16 aircraft, forcing Saddam to order an end to the attacks.

During the afternoon and early evening, 9th Armoured Division sent its mechanised reserves south to meet the Iranian threat as Fath regrouped. On the morning of 2 May, the Iranian 92nd Armoured Division began pushing northwards in dense fog, which allowed it to infiltrate the three defending brigades but also confused the attackers, who gained ground but were unable to exploit their success.[27] The IrAF sought to establish air superiority and to interdict the battlefield, but IRIAF fighters and missiles would claim some 44–50 of their aircraft.[28] Piecemeal Iraqi counterattacks against the northern part of the bridgehead continued as Assad brought up his 8th Mechanised Brigade to support 606th Infantry Brigade, while 9th Armoured Division committed 14th Mechanised Brigade, but the Iraqis were steadily pushed back, allowing the enemy to cut the Ahwaz–Khorramshahr highway as Assad tried desperately to organise a coordinated response while appealing for reinforcements. By the end of the day, Iraqi intelligence identified eight divisions and a dozen brigades (most of the latter Pasdaran) west of the Karun.

He finally coordinated a riposte with 9th Armoured Division, and on 3 May, despite fog followed by rain, which obscured vision and put a film of mud on the desert tracks, the two counterattacked

PART I: DISASTER FOR IRAQ

with gunship support. But the attack was poorly executed and conducted on too narrow a front to face tenacious defence, especially from the Pasdaran, who ignored their casualties until 92nd Division parried the Iraqis, who allegedly lost 100 tanks and regained little ground. More ominously, as the battle raged, 1st Brigade/16th Armoured Division began to enter the Iranian Karun bridgehead and with its aid the attackers regained more territory in the fog and drizzle, and by 4 May were pushing ever closer to the Ahwaz–Khorramshahr highway.

Meanwhile, the Iranians had focused upon the enemy choke point around Shalamcheh and the highway to Ahvez, with the IRIAF interdicting enemy movements, expending 64 tonnes of ordnance in 40 sorties from 27 May. The disruption of enemy communications increased on 3 May when the Iranian 55th Airborne Brigade despatched a company-strong force which landed by helicopter north of Shalamcheh to harass the Ahwaz–Khorramshahr highway.[29]

Iranian Brigadier General Qasem-Ali Zahrinejad giving his presentation on Iranian military successes during Operation Beit-ol-Moqaddas to the representatives of the international media in March 1982. Zahrinejad was the Chief of the Joint Staff and Khomeini's representative at the Supreme Defence Council at the time. Before that, he served as the Commander of the Iranian Ground Forces. (Albert Grandolini collection)

On 5 May, the 92nd Division broke through on a 25km front, overran Assad's gun line and ended the day in control of the highway between Hamid and Ahu, despite fierce Iraqi air attacks. The threat to the Ahwaz Salient was growing with every hour; the options were to remain like sheep for slaughter or to evacuate it and use the saved forces for a counteroffensive. Qadhi vacillated, aware that Saddam would never forgive him for abandoning such prestigious territory. A solution to his dilemma seemed on offer on 5 May, when his mentor Shanshal arrived at his headquarters. But when Qadhi asked him to select the option of either abandoning the salient or regrouping the forces there for a counterattack, Shanshal was non-committal. His proximity to Saddam made him even more aware that a decision would be a hot potato, and he only replied: 'You are the corps commander, you decide.'[30]

With Shukur's 6th Armoured Division having contained the situation around Hoveyzeh, Qadhi could have switched it south to join the attack around the Darkhovin Salient, leaving 5th Mechanised Division to exploit the extensive fortifications to hold the northern face. It would have been a gamble but with good odds, yet Qadhi was in an agony of indecision and did nothing except to leave Shukur and 5th Mechanised Divisions holding the northern face of the salient. Mishiri and Assad continued their counterattacks on 6 May, attempting to drive through the prevailing fog and rain to destroy the bridges supporting Task Force Fath. The conditions for the Iranian defenders were especially favourable, allowing the Pasdaran, with their anti-armour missiles and RPGs, to get close to enemy AFVs and take a steady toll of them, especially, Mishiri whose progress slowed to a snail's pace. This exposed Assad's left to a counterattack by 92nd Division, which pushed it back. As the Iraqis began to withdraw amid much confusion, the retreat turned into a rout, forcing Mishiri to break off his attack and retreat, although he found it difficult to break contact.

With the Iraqis reeling, the Iranians exploited the situation and during the late evening began the second phase of the offensive. Fath assembled for a breakout during the night in an attempt to isolate 3rd and 6th Armoured Divisions, and in the morning thrust westwards to Taialyeh and Kushk, spearheaded by 1st Brigade/16th Division and 37th Armoured Brigade, while Nasr made the main drive southwards. The Pasdaran tore a great gap through the collapsing defences, which allowed 1st and 3rd Brigades/92nd Division to advance 17km down the Ahwaz–Khorramshahr highway.[31] Saddam's 'fire brigade', 10th Armoured Brigade, began counterattacks but in poor visibility lost a steady trickle of AFVs to Iranian RPGs.

As the weather improved on 7 May, the Iranian juggernaut drove on and four Iraqi brigades were routed. The GMID warned this exposed 6th Armoured and 5th Mechanised Divisions and forced Qadhi to bite the bullet and order them to withdraw to the south-west, covered by 9th Armoured Division. The divisions retreated 30km on the first day, and in announcing the decision on 8 May, Baghdad claimed it was 'to reinforce forces to the south'. Saddam finally recognised the danger and ordered the retreating troops into Khorramshahr, where they were joined by 15th Infantry Division's 420nd Brigade in what the Iraqi leader ominously announced would be a new Stalingrad. Yet the Iraqi Army was falling apart and the defence increasingly relied upon air power; on this day alone, Saddam's Falcons flew 155 fixed-wing and 98 rotary-wing sorties, causing the IRIAF to move a HAWK battery close to the Darkhovin bridgehead on 8 May.

Two IRIA M113s in a laager during the summer of 1982. The type was primarily used by the reconnaissance battalions assigned to each Iranian Army division. To keep the troops cool, they brought their vehicles together and then draped a canvas over the two rear doors. (Tom Cooper collection)

Task Force Qods stepped up the pressure, and 2nd Brigade/16th Division isolated Hoveyzeh on 9 May, although the latter village reportedly held out until 18 May, but it was too late and the Iranians had to recognise the enemy were escaping the trap. Although Fath sent troops north to take Hamid and the abandoned Iraqi supply base at Jeghir (also Jofeyr), the thrust westward was too slow, probably because the bulk of supplies were funnelled southward, and during the day, 6th Armoured, 9th Armoured and 5th Mechanised Divisions retreated through Taialyeh (also Shabhabi) and Kushk into Iraq, the two villages falling the next day.

Meanwhile, the Iranian 92nd Division advanced south, pushing back the infantry elements of 6th Armoured Division (45th and 49th Infantry Brigades), destroying Assad's 6th Armoured Brigade and outflanking the left of 11th Infantry Division (48th Brigade), as well as relieving the heliborne troops of 55th Brigade. Throughout the night, 10th Armoured, 48th and 90th Infantry Brigades fought desperate rear-guard actions, although the last may have been destroyed in the process, while infantry formations were ordered into Khorramshahr. The Iranians also needed more infantry, and 6,000 men of 1st and 2nd Brigades/77th Division were flown from Mashad to Omidiyeh air base near Ahwaz during the night 9/10 May in Boeing 747s (in doing so, they broke a world record for the number flown in a single aircraft with 1,430 troops).[32]

At midnight on 9/10 May, the Iranians began to pin down 11th Infantry Division with an attack on southern Khorramshahr. By 10 May, the Iranians were approaching Shalamcheh, which fell at 10:00 a.m. as artillery and mortar fire set the riverside palm groves ablaze. The 2nd Brigade/92nd Division and 55th Airborne Brigade

Iranian artillery played an important role in Operation Beit-ol-Mogaddas; primarily through destroying enemy positions, but with counterbattery work too. Here an M109 is in the process of conducting a fire-support mission. (Tom Cooper collection)

PART I: DISASTER FOR IRAQ

augmented the Pasdaran units to secure the town, while Assad tried desperately to retrieve the situation with another armoured counterattack north of Khorramshahr. But despite strong air support, this had little success and 92nd Division, now reinforced by Fath armoured units, continued to bulldoze the wreckage of the Iraqi Army southwards and the GMID warned the enemy might push into Iraq.

Both sides suffered major logistics problems, which forced the Iraqis to abandon much equipment, the Iranians later claiming to have captured some 100 MBTs, 150 other AFVs and up to 100 guns. But the Iranians in turn began to run out of fuel or ammunition, halting many units; the Iranians would later admit they had not advanced as quickly as they had hoped.[33] Saddam briefly contemplated a counteroffensive using 3rd Armoured Division, elements of 9th Armoured Division and the newly arrived 7th Infantry Division, but the battered armoured division was too weak, and while there was some probing, the Iraqi leader was ultimately understandably reluctant to weaken the shield to defend Basra.[34] Perhaps he was also encouraged by the slowing of the enemy advance, and after he cancelled this plan the Iraqis cobbled together a line covering the Basra–Abadan highway as the Iranians deliberately remained on their side of the frontier.

Several Chieftains lining-up before another attack during Operation Beit-ol-Mogaddas. The IRIA's success in getting these hefty vehicles across the Karoun River was crucial for the victory, although Iranian officials give all the credit to the IRGC. (Tom Cooper collection)

With commendable foresight, Saddam had begun in April to strengthen defences east of Basra. The water barrier of the Fish Lake had shielded the city since President Bakr's time, but now work began on developing strongpoints across the Basra–Abadan highway, using army engineers and civilians mobilised by the Basra Council. In addition, work began on strengthening the frontier defences, but to gain time and retain the only substantial gain of the 1980 campaign, Saddam was determined to hold Khorramshahr. He was also alarmed at the collapse of Iraqi morale and ordered any

The primary Iranian light reconnaissance vehicle was the British-made Scorpion light tank, a squadron of which was assigned to the reconnaissance battalion of each division. Their crews prided themselves on very fast driving of this 8-tonne vehicle over almost any terrain – including marshes – and especially for rapid advances into the flanks of Iraqi armoured units. The weak spot of the Scorpion was its gasoline fuel, which was rather rare around the frontlines of this war. (Tom Cooper collection)

A dense column of IRIA and IRGC vehicles about to cross a pontoon bridge on the way to Abadan in spring 1982. (Albert Grandolini collection)

Members of an IRIA TOW-team posing in front of their M151 MUTT jeep, after surviving a sharp clash with the withdrawing Iraqis, east of Basra, in the summer of 1982. (Tom Cooper collection)

Division south of Jeghir (later reinforced by 37th Armoured Brigade) and the 92nd Division shielding the Hoseyniyeh area. The 21st Division was around Shalamcheh with up to five Pasdaran brigades, and was joined by 40th IRIA Infantry Brigade.

That day, GMID warned Saddam that the defences of Khorramshahr facing the new threat lacked both minefields and wire, and those which had been built were not covered by fire. While the Pasdaran were willing to rush the Khorramshahr defences, even they recognised the need for supplies and replacements, and assembling them took a fortnight. This gave the IRIA a fortnight to prepare support for the assault upon the city, which was held by 40,000 men under Fethi's 11th Infantry Division. The division had a tank and a reconnaissance battalion, but command and control was impossible for the divisional headquarters was in Iraq and had to control a reported 15 brigades, a figure which may include Border Guard units, within the city.[36]

The defences in the southern arc, facing Abadan, were strong, while those in the northern and western arc were weak, although 11th Infantry Division vigorously acted to improve them while also laying carpets of giant caltrops and cars upended vertically in open areas to prevent any heliborne assault. But as Cordesman observed in The Lessons of Modern War, 'Khorramshahr had become more of a trap for Iraq than a fortress', resembling Hitler's *Festungs* in which so much of the German Army was sacrificed.[37] A pontoon bridge across the Shatt into the south-west corner linked the city with the outside world, but this soon came under artillery fire and little in the way of reinforcement or sustenance could be expected over it.

Fath began the task of crushing the last pocket of enemy-held territory, and during a thunderstorm on the night of 20/21 May, struck from the west to cut the link with the pontoon bridge and push the enemy tighter into their tomb. This set the scene for a full-scale assault upon the city two nights later, Nasr striking down the Karun and from Abadan while Fath pushed from the west, both attacks spearheaded by Pasdaran with IRIA artillery and armour.

soldier fleeing from the battlefield to be shot, a counterproductive action which may actually have encouraged his troops to surrender.

On 13 May, the SDC sought Khomeini's permission to cross the border, but Zahirnejhad told a reporter the Ayatollah vetoed it.[35] Yet the issue was clearly not going away, and on 19 May President Khamenei chaired a night-time meeting of the SDC in which the pleas for cross-border operations were underlined by Iraqi counterattacks earlier in the day by 46th Mechanised and 38th Armoured Brigades/12th Armoured Division and 14th Armoured Brigade/9th Armoured Division, joined by 37th Armoured Brigade/12th Armoured Division the following day. To hold the ground, IRIA engineers dug berms which the attackers were unable to overcome, and the defenders' tank-hunting groups claimed 58 AFVs. Underpinning the Iranian border defences were 16th Armoured

PART I: DISASTER FOR IRAQ

Whenever the Iranians or Iraqis reached a new position, their engineers would rapidly erect berms of sand or earth up to 3-metres high, often combined with anti-armour ditches in front. These Iranian troops have further modified their berm with several shallow foxholes, dug out just behind its top. (Albert Grandolini collection)

The GMID warned of the imminent attack involving 77th Division on 22 May, and it was launched through the rain during the night of 22/23 May, with the Pasders and Basij trading corpses for metres in a human wave assault. By dawn, the bridge across the Karun linking northern and southern Khorramshahr was in Iranian hands and Nasr was mopping up, Popular Army and Border Guard units readily surrendering. Meanwhile, Fath made steady progress through the weaker western defences, driving the increasingly demoralised defenders into the old town, while Iraqi batteries had great difficulty locating targets amid the ruins. Fethi tried to arrange an evacuation, but it was impossible and many defenders sought to escape across the Shatt in boats, small craft and even rafts, while others tried to swim to safety, only to drown. In despair, thousands surrendered on the morning of 24 May. By the end of the day, the city was in Iranian hands, together with 12,000–13,000 prisoners and 56 AFVs.[38] Some 2,000 Iraqis were allegedly executed for rape.[39]

The offensive had recovered 5,480km² of Iranian territory and taken 25,400 prisoners, as well as 200 tanks, 250 other AFVs (250 AFVs were destroyed) and 300 guns. As one commentator noted: 'It was the greatest feat of Iranian arms since the eighteenth century.'[40] But it was costly, with some 30,000 casualties (22 percent), including at least 4,500 dead, although one source has suggested, with considerable exaggeration, a figure of 110,000, including 60,000 dead.[41] The booty did permit the Pasdaran to begin creating artillery batteries, and there were sufficient tanks for them to create two armoured brigades.[42]

The Iranians achieved a spectacular victory by making virtue out of necessity, and US intelligence considered that, with better logistics and especially transport, the Iranians might have reached Basra, although this was never Tehran's intention. It noted: 'Iran's main asset was the dedicated, fearless Pasdaran prepared to suffer incredible hardships and losses.'[43] Many commentators have emphasised this point and assumed the Iranian victory was due purely to them burying the enemy in bodies through human wave assaults. But while the Pasdar were notoriously careless with their lives, they were not reckless, and massed infantry assaults were usually directed at night with great precision at positions which had been infiltrated and isolated.[44] The Iranians also had excellent heavy-weapon support despite problems with the resupply of ammunition. Their artillery continued to be superior, with the self-propelled artillery unmatched in the Iraqi Army through its ability to be rapidly concentrated at crucial points.

Iranian air power also proved important, with US intelligence noting the Iranians also became adept at using heliborne forces to insert units to capture key positions in advance of their offensives. They also used TOW-equipped Cobra helicopters in close air support missions to compensate for their lack of armour. This strategy was effective against the Iraqis, and vice versa, because both lacked or did not employ effectively, air defence resources to suppress helicopters or other forms of close air support.[45]

Despite being numerically inferior to the IrAF, the IRIAF played a small, but important, role in the victory, mostly by achieving air superiority. Of the 1,083 combat sorties, nearly 86 percent were combat air patrol, but they claimed 55 victories to aircraft and missiles. Only 12 percent of sorties (130) were close air support or battlefield interdiction, but total losses were only four aircraft. The IRIAF also flew 315 air refuelling and 847 transport sorties in support of the offensive.[46] The IrAF is reported to have flown more than 1,200 sorties between 30 April and 12 May, while the IrAAC flew half that number, but flew some 80 sorties a day up to mid-May.

The greatest Iraqi defeat of the war saw heavy losses in the air matched by those on the ground. US intelligence estimated the Iraqis had suffered 15,000 casualties, while others suggest 30,000–50,000. The Iraqi Army strength certainly fell from 210,000 to 150,000, but this was also the result of the Dezful defeat.[47] The complacent belief in the Iraqi Army's technical superiority was a major factor in shaping the defeat, for it restricted its ability to adapt to a changing battlefield situation. Instead of rigidly defending every metre of the 500km line, it should have sought to exploit its numerical superiority in armour to fight deep defensive battles at the operational level. But few of its corps and divisional commanders possessed the confidence to seek this strategy, especially in the face of Saddam's blind obstinacy to hold all the captured terrain. Most were selected for their political reliability rather than military capability and were in a straitjacket of a rigidly hierarchical command structure, answerable to Saddam himself. Iraqi air support was also inferior to Iran's, although there had been improvements in air-ground cooperation, notably with helicopters, yet problems remained with coordination.[48]

Saddam was shocked and angry at the defeat in Khorramshahr. The first to feel the weight of Saddam's wrath were III Corps commander Qadhi, the Kurdish commander of 3rd Armoured Division, Assad and his subordinate Colonel Masa Abd-al-Jalil, the 12th Armoured Brigade commander.[49] Their court martial was held in July 1982 in Basra, in front of Defence Minister Khairrallah, Deputy Defence Minister Izzat Ibrahim al-Duri, Saddam's political deputy, party leaders and several senior generals, all of whom were desperate to distance themselves from the catastrophe and demonstrate their loyalty to Saddam. The result resembled a Soviet show trial, one Iraqi general noting: 'It was not a regular trial; it was tense with a lot

The Iranians quickly rushed into service a number of ZSU-57-2s captured from the Iraqis, and these provided good service against Iraqi attack helicopters. (Tom Cooper collection)

A column of T-55s – only recently captured from Iraqis and then rushed to service by the IRGC – seen advancing in the direction of Basra in summer 1982. (Albert Grandolini collection)

of screaming, yelling and hurling of insults.' The result was never in doubt, and all three were shot, possibly followed by another dozen officers, while up to 300 were demoted or dismissed.[50]

In the aftermath, Saddam further restricted the individual initiative of divisional commanders so that only corps commanders could authorise reconnaissance missions.[51] In a further ominous parallel with the Soviet Union, Saddam created Punishment Corps (Fayaliq al-Iqab) which were stationed behind units, ready to execute deserters and those commanders who performed poorly.[52]

Events elsewhere offered the Iraqi leader the opportunity for a face-saving gesture. On 3 June, the Israeli ambassador in London was gunned down by a Palestinian and the incensed Israelis decided to smash the Palestinian Liberation Organization in Lebanon, which they invaded three days later. On 10 June, the RCC offered a unilateral ceasefire which would allow Iraqi and Iranian troops to join forces and fight in Lebanon. Shirazi was willing, and a small force was sent, but the radicals regarded the whole affair as an American conspiracy to save Saddam. On 21 June, Khomeini publicly announced the war would continue, and even ignored Saddam's claim on 29 June to have withdrawn from all Iranian territory so that all Moslem troops could 'assist the Palestinians', because he still retained bridgeheads in Iran.

The recapture of Khorramshahr had emboldened Iran, and the euphoria which followed encouraged hardliners, led by Parliament's Speaker, Akbar Hashemi-Rafsanjani, but including Shirazi and Rezai, to argue for the expansion of Iranian war operations into Iraq. Rafsanjari set out Iran's terms for a ceasefire, including Baghdad's admission that it had started the war, the payment of a $100 billion indemnity, reaffirmation of the Algiers Agreement as well as the removal of Saddam and his trial for war crimes. Predictably it was rejected, as the pragmatic Rafsanjani probably expected.

Saddam's gamble had gone horribly wrong, for far from leading to a collapse of the theocracy in Tehran, the invasion had strengthened its authority and now his own regime was under threat. Within six weeks of the loss of Khorramshahr, the Iranians took the war to their enemy with a massive assault towards Basra. The war would continue for another eight years, and when it ended the lines were almost the same as when the Iraqis invaded.

PART I: DISASTER FOR IRAQ

Pasdaran taking cover from the simmering heat in the little shadow provided by a recently captured BMP-1, somewhere east of Basra in the summer of 1982. See the colour section for details about this vehicle. (Tom Cooper collection)

A Bell AH-1 Cobra of the IRIAA in its natrual environment: hovering only metres above the tops of the nearest palms, searching for a suitable target. Its combination with TOW ATGMs proved highly effective during the Iran-Iraq War. (Tom Cooper collection)

An Iraqi MT-LB APC knocked out by a TOW fired from an AH-1 in May 1982. (Albert Grandolini collection)

COLOUR SECTION 1

One of the 624 Chieftain Mk. 5/3P MBTs purchased by Iran from the United Kingdom in the 1970s. All Iranian Ground Forces vehicles of the 1970s and early 1980s were painted in the same light olive-green colour, similar to that used by the Israeli Defence Force. National markings consisted of small roundels, usually applied on the storage boxes around the turret. The vehicle number (usually consisting of four digits, but in this case limited to '146') was applied in black on turret sides and the front and the rear of the hull. The so-called 'Onion' – the stylised word 'Allah', the official crest of the Islamic Republic of Iran – was frequently added on the sideskirts, sometimes in the form of a stencil and in red, as shown here, but at least as often applied rather crudely with a brush. (Artwork by Radek Panchartek)

One of 460 M60A1s acquired by Iran from the US during the 1960s. They wore the same standardised colours and national markings as applied on all other Iranian Army vehicles of that time, though apparently without any hull numbers. Nearly all had a Shi'a call for the 12th Imam painted on their turrets too: this was the Arabic inscription 'Ya Qaem-e al-e Mohammad' (meaning 'I call up you the [still alive] hidden member of the Mohammad's family'). (Artwork by Radek Panchartek)

The Iranian Army acquired about 300 M113A1 and M113A2 APCs for its armoured divisions in the 1970s, but for most of the war with Iraq these served instead with the reconnaissance battalions of the various divisions. All were painted in standardised colours, and most received various kinds of inscriptions on their hull sides (and different forms of storage baskets, usually on their hull-fronts). In this case, the inscriptions included hull number '29' in red and 'Allah o-Akbar' ('God is great') in white. (Artwork by Radek Panchartek)

COLOUR SECTION 1

Iraq had only 155 T-72s at the start of the war, all of them assigned to the 10th Armoured Brigade. Most were built in 1975. Although severely cramped, tending to overheat and equipped with a poor fire-control system, they proved much more reliable and capable of outclassing the Chieftain on the battlefield. While some of these early Iraqi T-72s were left in the olive-green colour applied before delivery, at least some received the standardised Iraqi Army camouflage pattern consisting of yellow sand and blue-green, shown here. Most also received turret-numbers (shown here is the example '12'), usually applied in white. (Artwork by Radek Panchartek)

About 1,300 T-62s formed the primary armament of Iraqi armoured divisions at the start of the war. The type proved not only cramped, but also very vulnerable to any kind of combat damage (even a glancing hit on the front hull could cause internally stored ammunition to detonate), and rapidly overheated the crew during any kind of engagement. Most of the Iraqi T-62s were painted in a standardised camouflage pattern consisting of yellow sand, with wide stripes of blue-green applied down their sides. Identifcation insignia (in this case a square of orange, with a vertical blue line) were usually applied on the turret sides (next to the turret number, '127' in this case) and often also on the fume extractor. (Artwork by Radek Panchartek)

The general appearance of Iraqi Army T-54/-55s early in the war was similar to that of all other vehicles operated by the service: a camouflage pattern consisting of yellow sand, with wide stripes of blue-green applied almost vertically down the front and sides. Turret insignia was applied in a number of ways, apparently depending on the unit in question. In this case, it consists of the letter 'J' (standing for 'Jaysh', or 'Army') and the digits '24'. Turret top and sides, and the rear deck, were often crammed with the crew's personal belongings, water cans and machine-gun ammunition. (Artwork by Radek Panchartek)

MIDDLE EAST@WAR SERIES SPECIAL #1: THE IRAN-IRAQ WAR

The principal APC of the Iraqi armoured and mechanised formations early in the war with Iran was the OT-62, a Czechoslovak-manufactured BTR-50 variant. Although seldom armed, the type proved reliable and quite popular in service. It could carry up to 20 fully armed troops and had amphibious capabilities. While a few examples were left in the olive-green colour applied before delivery, most were camouflaged in standard colours consisting of yellow sand and blue-green. (Artwork by Radek Panchartek)

Intensive service use and weathering conspired to literally disintegrate the camouflage pattern of most Iraqi vehicles within weeks of the start of the war with Iran. This OT-62 survived long enough to receive a small splotch of blue-green on which the hull number ('122') was applied. The rear deck was usually crammed with the personal belongings of the crew – though sometimes, as illustrated here, it was used to carry additional fuel cells taken from T-54 or T-55 MBTs. (Artwork by Radek Panchartek)

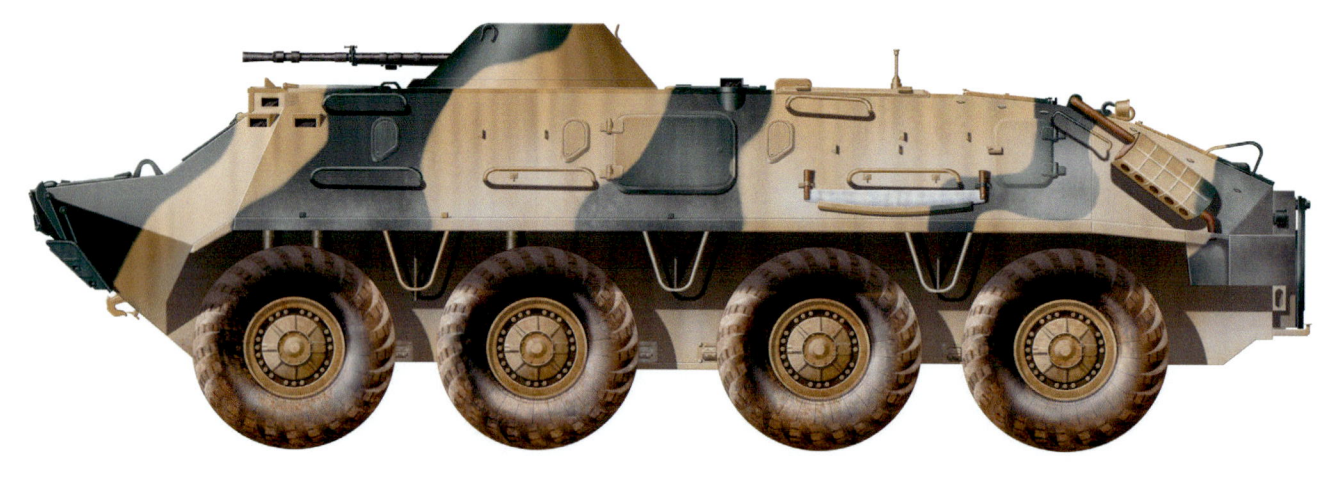

Although armed with a 14.5mm KPVT machine gun and capable of carrying up to 16 fully armed troops, BTR-60s of the Iraqi Army were at least as often used to transport unit staff instead. Their usual camouflage consisted of yellow sand and blue-green, often applied in near-vertical stripes down the hull, but sometimes in irregular splotches instead. (Artwork by Radek Panchartek)

COLOUR SECTION 1

Although Iraq imported 620 BMP-1s during the 1970s, the type was still relatively rare and usually reserved for crack armoured units, like the 10th Armoured Brigade or 3rd Armoured Division. Most vehicles were camouflaged as shown here: in yellow sand overall, with near-vertical stripes of blue-green. Many carried various unit insignia or codes on their hull, or turret-sides as shown here, but exact details of the system remain unknown. (Artwork by Radek Panchartek)

A reconstruction of another Iraqi Army BMP-1 sighted early during the war with Iran, somewhere in the Khorramshahr area. As usual, the vehicle is camouflaged in yellow sand and blue-green, covered by quite a thick layer of sand. The inscription on the turret reads 'J43', with 'J' usually standing for 'Jaysh' ('Army'). (Artwork by Radek Panchartek)

Short-range air defence of all mobile formations of the Iraqi Army was the job of the *Zenitnaya Samokhodnaya Ustanovka* (ZSU) -23-4 Shilka: a vehicle with four 23mm 2A7 cannons capable of firing up to 4,000 rounds per minute. Fire-control was provided by an RPK-2 (1RL33) radar working in the J-band, at a frequency between 10 and 20 GHz. This could detect aircraft and helicopters out to a range of 20km, but its performance was generally degraded by ground clutter. While some Iraqi Shilkas were left in the olive-green colour applied before delivery, at least a few received the standard camouflage pattern consisting of yellow sand and blue-green. None are known to have worn any kind of national or unit insignia. (Artwork by Radek Panchartek)

MIDDLE EAST@WAR SERIES SPECIAL #1: THE IRAN-IRAQ WAR

Iran acquired 214 Bell 206As and Bell 206A-1s in three large batches during the 1970s, at least 12 of which went to the air force, a few to the navy, while the rest served with the IIAA – and then the IRIAA. Painted in dark yellow sand and dark earth over, and pale grey under, they received serials in the range 2-4101 up to 2-4284. Bell 206A-1s could be armed with a General Electric GAU-2B/A 7.62mm Minigun, mounted on a pylon protruding through the side of the rear cabin, where ammunition was also stored. Inset is the official patch of the Imperial Iranian Army Aviation, applied on all of its helicopters in the 1970s: although largely removed by 1980, some IRIAA aircraft went into the war against Iraq still wearing this patch on their sides. The last two or three digits of the serial number were often repeated on the nose. (Artwork by Tom Cooper)

No fewer than 296 Bell 214As – a variant specially developed and built for Iran – were acquired by the IIAA during the 1970s, and locally designated Esfahan. All were painted in dark yellow sand and dark earth over, and pale grey under. The first batch received serial numbers 6-4651 through to 3-4937, the second 2-6003 to 2-6008. The IIAA patch was usually worn on cockpit doors during the 1970s, but generally replaced by the 'Onion' after the revolution of 1979. The service title – originally IIAA, but extended to IRIAA after 1979 – was usually applied on cabin doors, often in white. As illustrated here, Iranian Bell 214As could be armed – usually with LAU-3/A or similar launchers for 3.75in unguided rockets – but are not known to have used this confguration during the war with Iraq. (Artwork by Tom Cooper)

The IIAA received a total of 202 AH-1Js, about 190 of which were available when Iraq invaded Iran. The first 140 of these were delivered with standard armament consisting of the 20mm gun and standard wing stores. But three of these, and subsequently another 62 examples, were modifed to the full confguration compatible with BGM-71 TOW ATGMs. All were painted in dark yellow sand and dark earth over, and pale grey under. With much of the Iranian military demobilised and then mauled by purges of commanding officers, the IRIAA struggled to mobilise in response to the Iraqi invasion. Many of its helicopters were rushed into combat with incomplete service titles: the first 'I' – standing for 'Imperial' – and the IIAA patch were crudely removed, and only 'IAA' left in its place. (Artwork by Tom Cooper)

COLOUR SECTION 1

The first armed helicopters in Iraqi service were about 50 Aerospatiale SE.316C Alouette IIIs, acquired in several irregular batches during the 1970s. Most went to the Iraqi Army Aviation Corps when this was established in 1980, and they saw intensive service early during the war with Iran – often armed with AS.12 ATGMs or launchers for unguided rockets. All wore a standardised camouflage pattern consisting of sand, mauve and dark green over, and light blue under, and had a large Iraqi national flag on the fuselage. Serials – known examples are 1076 (shown here), 1214 and 1298 – were applied on the boom with a brush. (Artwork by Tom Cooper)

The IrAAC inherited a large feet of about 200 Mi-8Ts and Mi-17s from the IrAF in 1980. Most Mi-8Ts were acquired in the early 1970s and left in olive-green over and light admiralty grey (BS381C/697 or FS35622) on undersides. Serials (here the example serialled as 1268) were left over from the time of their service with the IrAF, applied in order of delivery, and thus anywhere within the range 1200–2100. Applied in black, often with the help of stencils, these were worn on the boom. Nearly all wore large national flags applied on the rear cabin sides; some also had two sets of national insignia. (Artwork by Tom Cooper)

Later during the war with Iran, surviving Mi-8Ts of the IrAAC were overhauled and received a new, standardised camouflage pattern shown here, consisting of sand, dark brown, and dark green on upper surfaces and sides, and light admiralty grey (BS381C/697 or FS35622) on undersides. Their serials were reapplied in European digits, in black, on the boom. Although primarily used for transport and liaison, Iraqi Mi-8Ts were often armed, usually with two or four UB-16-57 or UB-32-57 (shown here) pods for 68mm unguided rockets. (Artwork by Tom Cooper)

8
AN UNHOLY BLOODBATH

By the summer of 1982 the government of Saddam Hussein at-Tikriti in Baghdad had seen a tremendous change in fortunes, barely 18 months after invading Iran. Back in September 1980, Saddam tried to exploit the post-revolution chaos in Iran both to strengthen Iraq's frontiers and to gain control of the Shatt al-Arab, the waterway leading to the great port of Basra (also Basrah). His objective was to seize a long strip of Iranian territory along the frontier, together with a major bridgehead in Khuzestan, to encourage a revolt against the theocratic government of Ayatollah Ruhollah al-Musavi al-Khomeini (Ayatollah Khomeini). Saddam hoped a new government would be more amenable to a diplomatic solution which would give Baghdad control of both disputed border territory and the Shatt al-Arab.

But poor planning, and the absence of any strategic military goals, left the Iraqi Army impaled on the frontier by the end of 1980. Far from encouraging Khomeini's enemies, the invasion helped the clerics to consolidate their power until in 1982 they inflicted two major defeats upon the Iraqi Army – which had to abandon most of the conquered territory, apart from a few toeholds in the extreme north-west of Khuzestan and to the north. With the Israeli invasion of Lebanon in the summer of 1982, Saddam offered Tehran a ceasefire, nominally so they could both fight the Israelis, but the Iranians rejected the offer.

With the expulsion of the invader, Iran's Supreme Defence Council (SDC) considered the next move. The ultimate arbiter of Iranian strategy was Khomeini, who wished to rein-in his troops on the Iranian side of the frontier and consolidate the revolution. Strategy may be driven by passion rather than reason, especially with revolutionary regimes, and the twin desires for revenge and the expansion of God's Kingdom on Earth were too heady a mixture for the mullahs to resist.[1]

The idea of quitting while ahead was supported by many of the senior members of government, notably President Ali Hosseini Khamenei (Khameneh), Premier Seyyed Mir-Hossein Mousavi and even hard-line Foreign Minister Ali Akbar Velayati. They argued that Iran would be regarded as an aggressor if it crossed the frontier and lose its few Arab friends, including Saudi Arabia which had indicated a willingness to fund Iraqi war reparations to help restore the war-wrecked economy.

They also emphasised that Iran lacked the resources to pursue an offensive strategy at a time when the army faced a major insurgency problem in Kordestan. The Islamic Republic of Iran

Operation Beit-ol-Mogaddas resulted in the destruction of one Iraqi division and the mauling of several others, with up to 200 Iraqi tanks – including these five T-55s – being captured by the Iranians. Thus began a new phase of the Iran-Iraq War, during which Tehran staged ever bigger offensives. (Tom Cooper collection)

PART I: AN UNHOLY BLOODBATH

Army (IRIA) Commander-in-Chief, Brigadier General Qasem Ali Zahirnejhad, echoed the latter concern and noted the armed forces' lack of experience in projecting power when there was a shortage of firepower, mobility and air support, together with significant logistical problems. Compared to Iraq's 3,000 MBTs and 1,800 guns, Iran had only 900 of each, and many of these were unserviceable due to the growing spares shortage. For Zahirnejhad this was a U-turn, for he would later claim that soon after his appointment in 1981, Khomeini had vetoed his plan to drive into Iraq once Abadan had been relieved.

Yet the generals were undermined by the deeply devout and optimistic Commander of the IRIA Ground Forces, Major General Ali Sayad Shirazi, who felt like, Mohsen Rezai, leader of the Islamic Army of the Guardians of the Islamic Revolution (Sepah-e Pasdaran-e Enghelab-e Eslami) – or Pasdaran – that the enemy was on the point of collapse and that the zeal of Islam's devoted soldiers would overcome all obstacles. They were joined by the Parliament's highly influential Speaker, and 'voice' of the Iranian Parliament, Akbar Hashemi-Rafsanjani, to persuade Khomeini to sanction a cross-border offensive.

Shirazi stated: 'We will continue the war until Saddam Hussein is overthrown so that we can pray at Karbala and Jerusalem', while Rafsanjani claimed: 'We are not going to attack any territory. We only want our rights (including the overthrow of Saddam).' They argued that the massed Iraqi Army on the frontier could strike again, indeed artillery bombardments upon of Khorramshahr and Abadan were already taking Iranian lives. These could be shielded only by establishing a buffer zone in enemy territory which would be a valuable bargaining chip to force Saddam to the negotiating table. With unconscious irony, Tehran's radicals were echoing almost the same arguments which Saddam had made in justifying his invasion two years earlier. The radicals also feared that the end of the war would destroy a national unifying factor in the face of continued revolutionary turmoil.

Iraqi prisoners of war stream out of Khorramshahr after one of their defeats in early 1982. Between 12,000 and 13,000 Iraqi troops were captured forcing Baghdad to rebuild a number of battered divisions. Of those captured the Iranians summarily executed about 2,000. Many of the captured Iraqis were Shi'a, some of whom were eventually persuaded by the Iranians to change sides. (Tom Cooper collection)

Mohsen Rezai (centre left, with cap), a leading Iranian war planner and battlefield commander during the mid-1980s. (Tom Cooper collection)

On the morning of 27 May, the SDC – including Khamenei, Rafsanjani, Defence Minister Major General Mohamad Salimi, Zahirnejhad, Shirazi and Rezai – went to Khomeini's home and it was later announced that 'certain decisions' had been made. In fact Khomeini at first backed the conservatives but then Rafsanjani and Rezai began to meet him separately, bringing with them exiled Iraqi Shias, including Hojatolislam Mohammad Bakir al-Hakim who led the Supreme Council of the Islamic Revolution in Iraq (SCIRI).

Hakim had created the guerrilla Badr Brigades which had struck army supply centres in Iraq during the May 1982 offensive.[2] Hakim claimed the Shia were waiting to rise the moment Iranian forces crossed the frontier and would clear the way for the

A group of officers from the 92nd Armoured Division IRIA clustering around an M577 armoured command post. Such vehicles played an important role as mobile communication centres and in directing artillery fire. (Tom Cooper collection)

An Iranian armoured battalion equipped with M47Ms, probably from the 77th Infantry Division, while moving out at the start of Operation Ramadan Mubarak. (Mark Lepko collection)

A rifle platoon of Pasdaran squatting on the ground while being briefed for their next mission. Most are armed with AK-47 assault rifles, either captured from the Iraqis or purchased from China. (Albert Grandolini collection)

invaders. The radicals also reminded Khomeini that if left unchallenged, the enemy could rebuild their forces and again threaten Iran. To prevent this Iran had to carry the war to the enemy until the secular Ba'athist regime was defeated and overthrown.

Mulling these arguments, Khomeini began to waver and decided in favour of the offensive, probably on 20 June, for the next day he announced: 'We shall get to Lebanon, and to Jerusalem, through Iraq, but first we have to defeat the sinister Ba'ath party', while a popular revolutionary refrain claimed: 'The road to Jerusalem passes through Karbala'. Ominously for Saddam, Iraqi Shiites began rioting in Baghdad and despite the expulsion of 100,000 their resistance organisation, Daawa, attempted to assassinate the Iraqi leader at Dujayal on 11 July.

Two days earlier Rafsanjani listed Tehran's terms for ending the war; acceptance of the Algiers Agreement of 1975, repatriation of 100,000 expelled Iraqi Shias, acceptance by Iraq of responsibility for the war, US$100 billion in reparations and Saddam to be tried as a war criminal. The terms were clearly unacceptable and, fearing a continuation of the conflict, the UN Security Council on 12 July passed a resolution calling for a ceasefire and a withdrawal of forces to their borders, but by then the Iranians were completing their final preparations.[3] However, Khomeini's insistence that the SDC avoid heavily populated areas to avoid heavy casualties among the Iraqi Shia limited their options. Hakim would accompany the Iranian forces to encourage a rising and help the Pasdaran win them over. But this Fifth Column never emerged, for as with the Sunni Arabs of Khuzestan, the inhabitants generally regarded themselves as Iraqis first and Shias second.

The 1,700-kilometre-long front offered few weak points which might prove lethal to Saddam's regime. Mountains barred progress to the northern oil fields, but Kurdish desire for autonomy could be exploited to harass exports through Turkey and force the dictator to maintain large numbers of troops in the region. In the centre, Iran's poor road network saw general logistics issues restrain any drive into the Sunni heartland of Iraq by restricting the assembly of troops, which left the southern front as the best strategic level option. The prize was Basra, the capital of a Shia region which

PART I: AN UNHOLY BLOODBATH

A volley of rockets fired from an Iraqi BM-21 Grad MLRS. Both sides used this Soviet-made, truck-mounted system in large numbers for area attacks. The BM-21 proved devastating against exposed infantry and quite valuable in destroying defences in counter-battery work. (Tom Cooper collection)

Two AH-1 Cobras, with a Bell 214A Esfahan (background), of the IRIAA in the process of taking off from a forward operating location. Iranian Army Aviation deployed one tactical group with 34 attack and transport helicopters in support of Operation Ramadan Mubarak. (Tom Cooper collection)

held much of Iran's hydrocarbon wealth, but it was also a region which held a major concentration of Iranian forces with the best communications network in the country.

The first campaigns here would be fought south of the Hawizah Marshes (Hawr al Hawizah) in a knife-shaped stretch of land some 55 kilometres long and 45 kilometres at its widest point. The straight edge was the international border in the east while the Shatt al-Arab, known to the Iranians as the River Arvand, was the edge of the 'blade' which curved gently eastward on its way to the Gulf. Within the 'blade' and south of the Ghuzail, an area of desolate salt flats and sand just south of the marshes, the ground rose imperceptibly to act as a land bridge between the marshes and the coastal salt flats.

Much of this ground consisted of desert, crisscrossed with earth roads on embankments or berms but the high water table, up to three metres, meant they could become marshy during the winter rains, although in summer, according to British Army maps of 1943, the ground was firm enough to allow 1.5-tonne trucks to drive at speeds 'up to 40 mph' (74 km/h). Earth roads crisscrossed the desert to provide a degree of all-weather communications while along the northern bank of the Shatt lay a major metalled (hard top) highway linking Basra to Khorramshahr. To the south, the banks of the Shatt up to four kilometres wide are extensively cultivated, dotted with palm groves and crisscrossed by irrigation ditches. Within the Shatt itself lay numerous small islands which would play a greater role in later operations.

The dominating feature was the so-called Fish Lake (Buhayrat al-Asmak, called Kanal Mahi by the Iranians) some 15 kilometres northeast of Basra. This was a 30 kilometre-long flooded anti-armour ditch, built in the late 1970s to split an Iranian offensive, and it was 1.25 kilometres wide, up to 3 metres deep, with water pumped in from the Shatt through irrigation channels and dedicated pumps.[4] On the west bank of the lake was a berm 1.5 metres high and 10 metres wide, from which defenders could cover the waters and the two causeways which crossed them to launch counterattacks. Across the lake there was an embankment with an earth road running from near the Shatt to Hoseyniyeh on the Ahwaz–Khorramshahr highway and railway in Iran. From the northern end of the lake there was a potential obstacle or switch line in the River Kamuban (Katiban or Kutayban) which ran westward to the Shatt which it enters 14 kilometres north of Basra.

As the Iraqi occupation began to crumble, around April 1982, work began upon defences around the Fish Lake to shield Basra. The

Iraqi tanks suffered losses from Iranian attack helicopters: this T-62 was bogged down in the mud and then hit by a BGM-71 TOW, which caused an explosion that flipped the turret on its side. (Tom Cooper collection)

work was directed and planned by the corps engineer commander, Brigadier Adnan Hussein Makki, and executed as a state engineering or State Central Effort (Jahd ad-Dawla al-Markzi), by his battalions, civilian contractors and labour, together with drafted civilians provided by the Mayor of Basra – who was responsible for the State Central Effort. The plans were drawn up by the corps then sent for approval to the Defence Ministry's Planning Directorate. Once approved, the army would build the field fortifications while the civilians would produce the communications and rear fortifications.

The first task was to build a berm-based defensive line from the southern edge of the Fish Lake across the Basra–Khorramshahr highway, because the high water table made trenches deeper than waist or shoulder height impractical. Three battalion-strongpoints were built, and by mid-July work had begun upon a second and a third berm line behind the first, the third acting as a switch position west of the lake. To divide an advance, lake water was allowed to spill out opposite its central section to flood terrain several kilometres wide to the east up to, and beyond, the border.

Yet the Iraqi defences were mostly along the frontier for, like most politicians and dictators, Saddam was loathed to surrender territory because it eroded his personal prestige. On each side of the flooded area an anti-armour ditch some 90 kilometres long was dug along the border, and the excavated earth and sand was used to construct a 2.25–4-metre-high berm which would be the forward element of the defences. This berm was the basis for triangular battalion-strongpoints with triangular company-strongpoints sited for all-round defence in each angle, two in the forward wall some two kilometres apart, with a third a kilometre behind, all linked by berms about 1.9–2 metres high.[5] Some of these positions were built upon the sites of former Border Guard installations.

At each corner of the fortification would be a fire position with reinforced-concrete walls and overhead cover, linked by trenches along the berm tops; the men living in trenches or dugouts. The walls of the berm were an easily-scalable 45 degree angle, but were studded with wire and mines and covered with fire positions within the berm wall and outside it. The berm fire positions had excellent fields of fire over deep and dense obstacle fields; with anti-armour and anti-personnel mines as well as barbed wire and razor wire entanglements between the berm and the anti-armour ditch. Along the ditch was a screening force both to prevent raids and provide early warning of imminent assault; with each brigade deploying a platoon, while in front of this were company-size guard forces, although along the northern face of the defences the 6th Armoured Division reconnaissance regiment provided the equivalent of a battalion. The Iraqis also decided upon a tactical experiment in which the screening forces were augmented by an Offensive Delaying Force (Quwat at-Taweek at-Taaruthia) consisting of platoon or company strongpoints on the flanks of potential axes of advance in order to disrupt the advance before withdrawing, with the screening force, to the main line of resistance (MLR).

The Iraqi Army staff had finally persuaded Saddam of the value of defence in depth, so their forces were deployed in echelon. The battle interrupted work on a berm which was to be the basis of a new backstop defensive system covering the north-eastern segment of the Fish Lake, up to 10 kilometres from the northern border and 25 kilometres from the eastern, which was used largely to shelter artillery and armoured reserves. Separate positions covered by berms were used to shelter batteries and reserve armoured/mechanised forces while work began on a road network to the Basra railhead.

Although IRIAF RF-4Es are known to have flown up to a dozen reconnaissance sorties over the operational zone, and although it is known that two of the IRIAF's C-130E Khofaash SIGINT-gatherers were reading Iraqi military communications in real time, it is unclear how much the IRIA knew of these defences when outline planning for what became Operation Ramadan Mubarak (Blessed Ramadan) began in June, but it appears to have been limited. At least one Pasdaran source indicates the reconnaissance was found wanting.[6] The work probably began as a contingency plan which the inexperienced IRIA staff officers no doubt hoped – given the condition of their forces – would not have to be executed. Their hopes probably began to fade from mid-June when it became obvious the SDC was slowly swinging towards an offensive. Detailed planning probably did not begin until late June or early July as the IRIAF's reconnaissance aircraft flew more sorties over the potential battlefield.

Once again General Rahim Safavi, the mastermind of the Beit-ol-Moqaddas triumph, would plan the operation, although the IRIA remained under a cloud following the Ghotbzadeh Plot described earlier. US intelligence calculated that Safavi had 150,000 men and intended to strike north of the Fish Lake; punch a hole through the MLR and then push an armoured spearhead around the north of the lake through Harithah to a distance of 30 kilometres; cross

PART I: AN UNHOLY BLOODBATH

Ramadan Mubarak was often fought in fierce sandstorms, which explains why these two Iraqi T-62s came to be bogged down and trapped in what appears to be an Iraqi anti-armour ditch. (Tom Cooper collection)

the River Kamuban and then circle behind the lake to link up at Tanumah opposite Basra.[7] There it would link up with a secondary thrust which would advance 15 kilometres along the Abadan–Basra highway and together they would swarm into the city.[8]

Essentially the Iranians intended to bulldoze their way through the defences with a frontal assault westwards and would not try to split the defenders through an assault from the north. This may reflect a lack of intelligence at a time when the Iranians wrongly assumed that the Iraqi forces were still in turmoil after the recent defeats in Khuzestan. A major problem for the Iranians was that they launched their offensive only 50 days after taking Khorramshahr, leaving little time for the Pasdaran to replace losses in men and equipment, although the IRIA had the advantage of a well-established replacement organisation which could provide ad hoc Qods (Jerusalem) battalions. There were also problems with supplies as the Ahwaz–Khorramshahr rail line had been badly damaged during the Iraqi occupation, with much of the rail bed and rails removed to create fortifications, and the line was still being repaired when 'Ramadan' was launched.

The operation would be directed by the Ahwaz-based Southern Forward Operations Headquarters (SFOH) – also known as Karbala – but following their success in Beit-ol-Mogaddas, tactical control was assigned to the task forces (Gharargah); once temporary command groupings but now permanent professional organisations. Operations north of the flooded area were conducted by Task Force Fath, under Colonel Niaki, while those south of the area would be conducted by Task Force Nasr; a total of some 76,000 men, including 37,000 Pasdaran and Basiji. Niaki had a mechanised brigade of the 16th Armoured Division (IRIA, but reinforced by the 40th Sarab Infantry Brigade, IRGC), the 77th Infantry Division (IRIA) teamed with the 1st Qods and 7th Vali Asr Infantry Divisions of the IRGC, and two brigades (1st Mechanised and 4th Armoured) of 92nd Armoured Division teamed with the 3rd Saheb ol-Zamen Infantry Division (IRGC). Nasr's offensive would be launched by the 21st Infantry Division (IRIA, but reinforced by a tank battalion and a special forces battalion) and 5th Nasr Infantry Division reinforced by elements of the 30th Beit-ol-Moghaddas Armoured Division (both

IRGC). However, Ramadan Mubarak was hamstrung by a shortage of material; between them the armoured formations had only 200 tanks, the lion's share with the 92nd Division.

This was the first offensive in which the Pasdaran used armour, concentrated within the 30th 'Beit-ol-Moghaddas' Division, which began to receive captured T-55 MBTs, together with BMP-1 infantry fighting vehicles (IFVs), and Chinese Type-63 armoured personnel carriers (APCs), although its operational armour consisted only of one or two battalions of second-hand IRIA M47 Pattons. In fact none of the army divisions was complete, apparently deploying no more than two brigades each, while the 22nd and 33rd Artillery Groups had six battalions of M109 self-propelled 155mm howitzers, three batteries of M107 175mm self-propelled guns, nine battalions of towed guns and two batteries (about a dozen) of Multiple Launch Rocket Systems (MLRS) – in total some 270 tubes. Yet during Operation Beit-ol-Mogaddas, barely two months earlier, the Iranians had deployed some 20 artillery battalions with more than 300 guns and 40 MLRS, as well as 350 MBTs, an ominous drop in the level of support. Further support was provided by the Islamic Republic Iran Army Aviation (IRIAA), the army air corps had assembled 34 Bell AH-1J Cobra attack helicopters augmented by Bell 204s, Bell 206s, Bell 214s and Boeing CH-47 Chinooks in the support role. The Islamic Republic of Iran Air Force (IRIAF) had lost some 120 aircraft in the past 18 months but still had some 250 combat aircraft. Much of the fleet was undergoing overhauls, badly needed after massive battles for the liberation of Khuzestan, and there was some lack of ammunition too, but even more serious was the lack of experienced crews caused by losses early during the war. Correspondingly, the IRIAF was forced to husband its resources and limit involvement in offensive operations.[9]

Pasdaran operations with the IRIA were coordinated by their deputy military commander, Yahya Rahim Safavi, repeating the successful arrangements during Beit-ol-Moqaddas, and they would play a major role in the offensive together with the National Mobilisation Organisation (Sazman-e Basij-e Milli) or Basij. By now many Pasdaran leaders were battle-scarred veterans, yet there remained a hard core of leaders who were brave but functionally illiterate and who saw little point in intricately prepared plans.

Further hurdles for the Iranian troops were meteorological and spiritual. In April the clerics pressed for the early liberation of Khuzestan and argued that it would be impossible during the blazing summer months, yet they were now so anxious to take the war to Iraq that they demanded an attack during July. This would mean fighting in open desert under cloudless skies in temperatures normally reaching up to 120° F or 49° C.[10] Worse, the fighting would take place during the holy month of Ramadan al-Mubarak (23 June–22 July), which gave its name to the offensive, during which

105

In July 1982, the Soviet Union began selling arms to Iraq again. One of the first orders Baghdad placed was for additional T-72s. Several of these can be seen while in the process of deploying east of Basra, about a year later. (Tom Cooper collection)

Still from a video taken in summer 1982, showing an Iraqi Mi-25 in the process of launching an AT-2 Swatter ATGM. (Iraqi National TV capture)

Moslems are expected to fast and avoid water during the daylight hours. Followers may receive exemption in severe physical or meteorological conditions but it is unclear whether or not the clerics gave the assault troops dispensation, without it the Iranians would rapidly face exhaustion.

Across the frontier, the defending III Corps had been in a state of frantic, almost chaotic, activity in the aftermath of Beit-ol-Mogaddas. The former commander, General Salah al-Qadhi was arrested in June, court-martialled the following month for the loss of Khuzestan and Khorramshahr, and executed. He was replaced by Major General Sa'adi Tumma al-Juburi whose chief-of-staff was Brigadier Aladdin Hussein Makki Khamas (who stood in no relation to the corps' engineer chief). Unlike so many senior officers in the Iraqi Army, these were extremely capable and experienced staff officers who would play key roles in reforming the army.[11] Immediately they conducted a personal reconnaissance of the front, familiarising themselves with the divisions' conditions, following which Makki drew up an operational plan incorporating the latest intelligence in which the divisional commanders were briefed to fight a defence in depth with the frontier berm line as the main line of resistance (MLR). Prompt counterattacks were to squeeze out any penetrations of the MLR and an armoured reaction force would prevent any major break through by a coordinated counterattack with heavy artillery and air support.[12]

However, the Iraqi Army was still recovering from the battering it had received in the spring when it was reduced to 150,000 men and two armoured divisions were reduced to brigade strength.[13] The army was being rapidly rebuilt and expanded by combing out those previously excluded from conscription and by drafting in more Popular Army (al-Jaysh ah-Shabi) Ba'ath Party militia and transferring more paramilitary forces from the Police and Border Guards. It was easier to replace the large amounts of equipment lost in Iran through the renewal of Soviet arms sales in 1981, augmented by Egyptian Army surplus equipment of East European origin, the newly opened supply line from China, and deliveries from non-Communist countries, especially Brazil and France.

In the aftermath of the disaster at Khorramshahr there were significant changes in the Iraqi Army. Saddam is reported to have dismissed 200–300 officers, and executed some, replacing them with those who had demonstrated ability. The crisis meant that ability temporarily became the criterion, with less of the rotation of division and corps commanders intended to prevent them from challenging the regime. However, personal ties with Saddam, such as marriage, coming from his birthplace of Tikrit, or having

PART I: AN UNHOLY BLOODBATH

Table 7: IRIA/IRGC, Southern Forward Operations HQ (Karbala HQ), July 1982		
Corps	Division & HQ	Brigades & Notes
	Direct Combat Support Group (IRIAA)	1 Attack Battalion (AH-1Js), 1 Assault Battalion (Bell 214As), 1 Reconnaissance Battalion (Bell 206), 1 Transport Battalion (CH-47C)
	22nd Artillery Group (Esfahan)	3 battalions of M109; 2 batteries of M107; 3 battalions of towed artillery pieces; 1 MLRS battalion (total of about 100 artillery pieces and 12 BM-21s)
	33rd Artillery Group (Tehran)	3 battalions of M109; 1 battery of M107; 4 battalions of towed artillery pieces; 1 MLRS battalion (total of about 100 artillery pieces and 12 BM-21s)
Task Force Fath	16th Armoured Division (IRIA)	1 armoured brigade only; reinforced by 40th Sarab Brigade (IRGC)
	77th Infantry Division (IRIA)	
	92nd Armoured Division	1st Mechanised and 4th Armoured Brigades only
	1st Qods Division (IRGC)	
	3rd Saheb al-Zamen Division (IRGC)	
	7th Vali Asr Division (IRGC)	
Task Force Nasr	21st Infantry Division (IRIA)	reinforced by 1 tank battalion and 1 SF battalion
	30th Beit-ol-Moghaddas Armoured Division (IRGC)	

Table 8: III Corps Iraqi Army, 1982	
Division	Brigades and Notes
3rd Armoured Division	6th Armoured Brigade; 8th Mechanised Brigade; 418th and 504th Infantry Brigades; 12 artillery batteries
5th Mechanised Division	26th and 55th Armoured Brigades; 15th and 20th Mechanised Brigades; 419th Infantry Brigade; 18 artillery and MLRS batteries
6th Armoured Division	11th Border Guard Brigade; 16th, 30th and 56th Armoured Brigades; 25th Mechanised Brigade; 94th Infantry Brigade
9th Armoured Division	35th and 43rd Armoured Brigades; 14th Mechanised and 104th Infantry Brigades; 9 artillery and MLRS batteries
11th Infantry Division	22nd, 38th, 45th, 47th, 48th, 49th, 109th, 502nd Infantry Brigades; 12th Armoured Brigade; battalion from 6th Armoured Brigade; 18 artillery batteries
reserve forces	10th Armoured Brigade
reserve forces	33rd SF Brigade

close tribal affiliations also helped. By the end of the war, senior officers including Generals Maher, Rashid, Shaban and Director of State Intelligence (Mukhabarat) al-Barrak, were all members of Saddam's Albu Nasr clan.[14] This growing professionalism led to a reappraisal of Iraqi Army doctrine, which led to a greater reliance upon defence in depth and the use of mobile reserves of mechanised and special forces, together with more patrolling and probing of enemy positions; a US intelligence report later noting that Iraqi commanders displayed 'greater skill and imagination in the conduct of the defence' aided by improved air and artillery support.[15]

The backbone of the defence remained the same formations which had failed to hold Khuzestan; 3rd, 6th and 9th Armoured Divisions, 5th Mechanised Division and 11th Infantry Division – all of which had been battered to a greater or lesser extent in the debacle – augmented by 10th Armoured Guards based in Basra and 33rd Special Forces Brigade. These were stationed behind the Fish Lake beside the HQ of the 3rd Armoured Division. Generous leave arrangements meant the defenders had some 85,000 men, 1,300 MBTs, 490 guns (81 batteries), three mortar units with 240mm tubes, and an MLRS regiment with 60 122mm BM-21 Grad (Hail) weapon systems, possibly augmented by launchers aboard the Project 771-class (ASCC/NATO codename 'Polnocny-B') landing ships rusting in the Basra naval base. Six artillery batteries remained

Table 9: Known Units of the Iraqi Army Aviation Corps (IrAAC), 1982–1984	
Unit	Helicopter Type
No. 2 Squadron	Mi-8/17
No. 4 Squadron	Mi-8/17
No. 12 Squadron	Mi-8/17
No. 15 Squadron	Mi-8/17
No. 21 Squadron	SA.342 Gazelle
No. 22 Squadron	SA.342 Gazelle
No. 25 Squadron	Mi-25
No. 30 Squadron	SE.316B
No. 31 Squadron	SA.342 Gazelle
No. 55 Squadron	Mi-8/17
No. 61 Squadron	Mi-25
No. 66 Squadron	Mi-25
No. 84 Squadron	SA.342 Gazelle
No. 88 Squadron	SA.342 Gazelle

under corps command, while another six were assigned to III Corps' 15th Infantry Division on the south bank of the Shatt and the Faw Peninsula to interdict the enemy on the other side of the waterway.[16]

Some of the divisions were under new commanders, such as 11th Infantry Division (nominally in command of Khorramshahr as of May 1982), although Brigadier Said Mohammad Fethi's headquarters were in Iraq at the time. Fethi, a competent although plodding officer, was not held accountable for its loss and in late June was transferred to command a Border Guards division, being replaced by Major General Mohammad Abdul Qadir. This former 15th Infantry Division commander was a clever, dynamic and brilliant leader who quickly reorganised his forces and turned their fortifications into model defensive positions to block the Basra–Khorramshahr highway. He had eight infantry brigades, positioned – from north to south – as follows: 109th, 49th, 45th, 22nd, 47th, 48th, 38th and 502nd. The 12th Armoured Brigade reinforced by a tank battalion from the 6th Armoured Brigade, 18 artillery batteries with 78 guns and some MLRS completed his order of battle (ORBAT). On the northern side was 6th Armoured Division under Major General Mahmood Shukur Shahin who had demonstrated competence under fire in Iran. Shukur had (west to east), 11th Border Guard, 56th Armoured, 16th Armoured, 25th Mechanised and 94th Infantry Brigades and in reserve 30th Armoured Brigade, although this could be reinforced by III Corps' 10th Armoured Brigade – equipped with T-72 main battle tanks (MBTs). For fire support he had 12 batteries with 72 tubes (including nine self-propelled 2S1 Gvozdika 122mm howitzers).

The eastern face of the defences, which would face the brunt of the attacks, consisted of Brigadier Maher Abdul Rashid's 5th Mechanised Division, Brigadier Khudaier Abbas Al-Khathban's 9th Armoured Division and Brigadier Hussein Rashid's 3rd Armoured

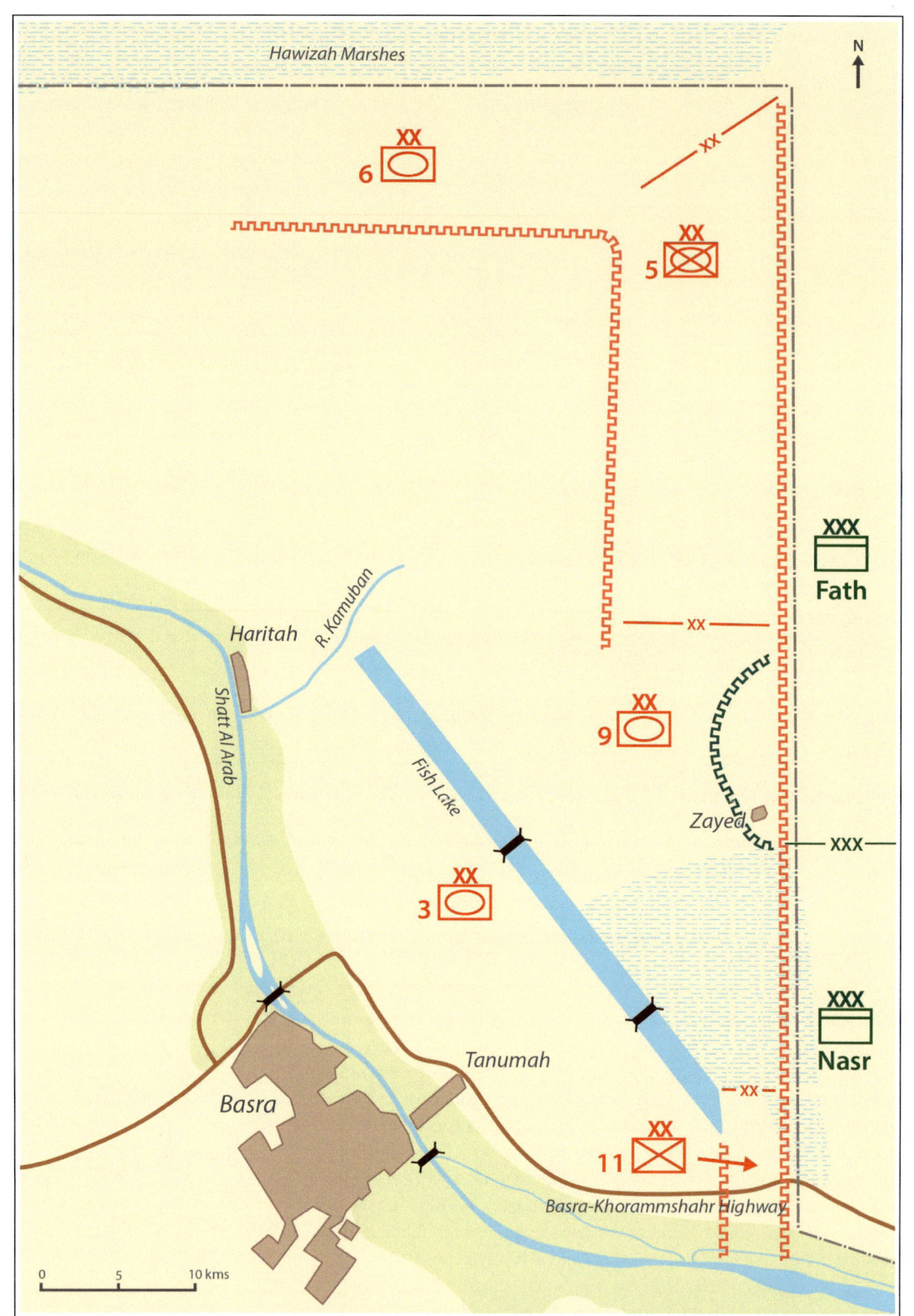

Iranian and Iraqi positions at the start of Operation Ramadan Mubarak. (Map by George Anderson)

Division, the last straddling the Fish Lake. Both Abdul Rashid and Hussein Rashid were from Saddam's hometown of Tikrit, while Khathban was a Shi'a commander who owed much to his Ba'athist credentials. Maher Rashid had 26th and 55th Armoured, 15th and 20th Mechanised as well as 419th Infantry Brigades, with 18 batteries and more than 100 guns, a few batteries of MLRS and a dozen 120mm mortars. Khathban had 35th and 43rd Armoured, 14th Mechanised and 104th Infantry Brigades, supported by nine batteries (36 guns) and MLRS, while Hussein Rashid's 3rd Armoured

Division controlled the 6th Armoured, 8th Mechanised, 418th and 504th Infantry Brigades and a dozen batteries with 54 guns.

The Iraqis had been reading enemy radio communications since the spring of 1982 which provided a good idea of their intentions, although because the Pasdaran lacked radios and communicated largely by landline or messenger, Baghdad was unsure of overall enemy strength. Sa'adi's men were certainly on the alert from early July as enemy artillery preparation increased especially from 12 July, while Iraqi Communications Intelligence (COMINT) monitored the airways for the enemy signal which would begin the offensive. These signals tended to be words or phrases from the Koran, a practise called in Farsi 'estekhareh' and in English 'bibliomancy', although references to Shia saints were also included.[17]

On the evening of 13 July the Iranians broadcast the code-phrase 'Thou absent Imam! Thou absent Imam!' (Ya Saheb ez-Zaman! Ya Saheb ez-Zaman!) – and at 2210 hrs the Iranians began to move out as III Corps alerted its formations and decided to bring the T-72s of the 10th Armoured Brigade across the Shatt during the evening. Saddam was also informed and sent as his representative Izzat Ibrahim ad-Duri, vice chairman of the Revolutionary Command Council (RCC), the Ba'ath Party equivalent of the Soviet Politburo, to Sa'adi's headquarters 'to raise morale' and also to act as Saddam's unwelcome eyes.

First Offensive 13–14 July
The Iranians advanced along much of the front, with Task Force Nasr hitting the 11th Infantry Division on the Iraqi right. This diversion appears to have inflicted heavy casualties on Qadir's 49th Infantry Brigade, although this brigade still prevented them from reaching the eastern bank of the Fish Lake and eliminated the Iranian presence in the morning. The main assault was made by Task Force Fath on a 10 kilometre front opposite the northern Fish Lake, extending from 5th Mechanised Division's 20th Mechanised Brigade to 3rd Armoured Division's 418th Infantry Brigade; but, the main blow – by 92nd Armoured Division reinforced by Saheb al-Zaman and Vali Asr – exploited a small bridgehead previously established along the frontier around the Iraqi frontier post at Zayed (also Said, Seid, Zaid or Zeid) opposite 9th Armoured Division's sector, to strike its two forward units: the 104th Infantry and 14th Mechanised Brigades.

The Iranian bridgehead allowed IRIA engineers to secretly clear paths through the obstacle fields. When the attack began this eased the passage of the infantry led by the Basiji, who sometimes accidentally strayed off the paths to inadvertently act as human minesweepers. They and the Pasdaran moved forward, with armoured units up to a kilometre behind them, and quickly pushed back the screening forces as the bombardment fell. When it lifted they were able to swarm up the berms and claimed they took many strongpoints within 90 minutes, although Tehran later stated it had only 600 prisoners. IRIA engineers bulldozed gaps in the berms to allow armour and motorised troops, the latter including Pasdaran in Toyota pick-up trucks, automobiles and even motorcycles, to sweep westwards supported by 92nd Division's Chieftains and mechanised infantry battalions. Part of this force reached the Fish Lake, but they lacked the means to cross it and some units were isolated by counterattacks and had a hard time fighting their way back to friendly territory.

Soon after midnight they encountered 9th Armoured Division's reserve (35th and 43rd Armoured Brigades), still largely in their fortified laagers, which the Iranians infiltrated in order to reach and to overrun Khathban's headquarters and capture his Mercedes-Benz limousine, which was a gift from Saddam. The two armoured brigades made a hasty withdrawal, with 43rd Brigade moving west to the newly constructed berm around the gap between its southern edge and the Fish Lake, while the 35th Brigade retreated southwards to one of the Fish Lake crossing points from where it desperately resisted.

To the north 77th and Qods Divisions had struck Abdul Rashid's 5th Mechanised Division some 15 minutes before the main blow. They emulated the early success of their southern neighbours and pushed through 20th Mechanised and 419th Infantry Brigades, but Abdul Rashid's counterattacks by the well-placed 26th and 55th Armoured Brigades prevented them striking northwards. Niaki's spearheads did advance some 25 kilometres to the west but fierce resistance from Rashid's armour and Khathban's surviving brigades prevented them circling around the northern Fish Lake. Nevertheless, the success was sufficient to attract part of 21st Division northwards to help exploit it.

As dawn approached, the Pasdaran and Basiji began to consolidate their hold, but the IRIA were already suffering major supply problems which might have been exacerbated if Iraqi air power had not been largely grounded by a sandstorm. The Pasdaran and Basiji depots were receiving food from the regions or mosques, while ammunition from the Pasdaran Ministry was received in fits and starts.[18] The militias were soon running out of essentials, while the rudimentary command and control system meant spearheads were stuck on their first objective unless one of the more dynamic leaders personally led them beyond. Worse still, while they might dig foxholes for personal safety, they rarely created a defensive system with obstacles, interlocking fields of fire and access to artillery or even air support, features which were abundant in the Iraqi defences.

The situation by morning was critical but neither Sa'adi nor Makki panicked, despite losing touch with Khathban, while the other divisional commanders also kept their heads and fed III Corps headquarters a steady stream of reports. Within five hours they had built up an accurate picture of the situation and were determined to launch an armoured riposte under Shukur, whose 30th Armoured Brigade was reinforced by the newly arrived 10th and 16th Armoured Brigades, withdrawn from the forward defences.

At dawn on 14 July, Sa'adi and Makki left the operations officer at divisional headquarters and set out from III Corps headquarters, with a small command team, for 6th Armoured Division headquarters. As they drove eastwards there was a scare when small arms fire was heard from the Fish Lake where elements of 21st Division had established a presence on its banks. Makki quickly organised troops to contain this threat – the newly arrived 5th Mountain Brigade was diverted to meet it by Qadir's headquarters – while Sa'adi drove on to meet Shukur.

Iranian aircraft observed the Iraqi concentration but could do little more than warn of the impending threat as the sandstorm denied each side air support by reducing visibility to a few metres. The attack by 350 tanks began at 0945 hrs, after a short bombardment possibly including CS (O-Chlororbenzyl-malononitrile) tear gas.[19] The Iranians lacked gas masks and suffered streaming eyes and raucous coughs which undermined the resolve of men who would normally and enthusiastically charge through sheets of bullets and showers of shells. Meanwhile, Shukur's two brigades drove out from the gap between the new berm and the Fish Lake, with their right secured by the Fish Lake, while 10th Brigade advanced from the eastern side of the new berm, its left secured by 5th Mechanised Division, as fierce fighting developed.

In good visibility the outnumbered Iranian Chieftain tank-killers would have given a better account of themselves because they were superior to everything except the T-72, but swirling dust clouds imposed a double penalty. The tank's fire control system, which was superior to anything in a Soviet-designed MBT, was neutralised as both sides pounded each other at point-blank range, while the dust aggravated the British tank's weak point, its notoriously unreliable L60 engine which tended to overheat, especially when the filters were clogged with fine dust. The gun stabilisation system was so unreliable that the crews had stopped repairing them and preferred to hang a heavy stone under the breach to keep the gun in a horizontal position.[20]

Because they proved vulnerable to small-arms fire, SA.342 Gazelles usually followed Mi-25s into attack and fired their HOT anti-tank missiles from stand-off ranges. (Tom Cooper collection)

Many vehicles broke down and had to be abandoned, while many crews owed their lives to the 'wet stowage' of the bagged combustible charges (which were in cells surrounded by pressurised water and glycol). If the cells were penetrated, the charges would be saturated, to make a distinctive sizzling sound and emit white smoke, giving the crew several minutes to bale-out, often with wounded men.[21] The Iranians still accounted for many MBTs, many of which fought private battles, before the survivors were gradually pushed westwards and, ultimately, across the border. The RPG teams, who were often on motorcycles, were hindered by a shortage of ammunition, each member of the two- or three-man teams carrying only three rounds, and their commanders had demanded they be used economically. They were to use them only when they were certain they would hit an AFV, which meant approaching to as little as 200 metres, a task which required a great deal of skill and luck. When their RPGs were expended, some men tried to board the tanks to throw a grenade inside, but few succeeded and losses were high. The Iranians would claim 85 AFVs, but the infantry – especially the Pasdaran and Basiji, already reeling from gas – was caught in the open desert and slaughtered with one Iranian tank commander later claiming that 70 percent of the volunteers attached to his unit were dead by midday.[22]

The divisions of the regular Iranian Army retired in good order to the former Iraqi forward defences, which they still held and there followed a pause during the night, but the Iraqis renewed their assault on the frontier defences during the morning and by the end of the day regained the lost positions. Defence Minister and Deputy Commander-in-Chief, Major General Adnan Khairallah Talfah, who was flying over the battlefield, brought some of the first reports of an enemy retreat. His actions were extremely brave but foolhardy, for his helicopter was frequently fired upon by his own troops, leading Sa'adi to admonish his men not to fire upon friendly aircraft. Helicopters were later used to fly crews forward to recover enemy vehicles.[23]

A feature of this offensive was Iraq's use on the battlefield of the Soviet Mi-25 (ASCC/NATO codename 'Hind') armoured helicopters, with a combat radius of some 225 kilometres.[24] At the start of the war the IrAAC had only seven, and five were lost in the next four months, and with Afghanistan given priority for these aircraft by Moscow, replacements were slow to arrive, so that by August 1982 only 20 were operational. Until the summer of 1982 they were used to carry reaction forces to counter commando raids on important installations such as radar stations, being described by the Iraqis as 'combat transports.' With East German assistance during the summer, they were integrated into conventional operations, working as teams with the Gazelles, five such teams being organised. The Hinds would lead the anti-armour aircraft and suppress air defences with unguided rockets and a 12.7mm Gatling gun, allowing the Gazelles to exploit the enemy's confusion and use HOT anti-tank guided missiles (ATGM) to pick off individual AFVs. The Hind was built to carry up to four 9K17 Skorpion (ASCC/NATO codename 'AT-2B Swatter') radio-guided missiles, with a 2.5 kilometre range, and 1,000 were delivered with the aircraft. Although expended in considerable numbers they proved ineffective against Chieftains. Curiously, Soviet advisors noted these formidable helicopters rarely carried these weapons, while US Army Intelligence noted the Hinds were still being used 'to move both men and equipment to critical spots'.[25]

The Iranian attack had been held, but it was a very close thing and the Iraqis had suffered heavy casualties, with about half of 9th Armoured Division destroyed together with 5th Mechanised Division's 20th Mechanised Brigade. The Iraqis had been forced to commit almost all their armoured reserve, much of which now had to hold the forward defences. The need to replace units saw I Corps ordered to transfer 8th Infantry Division and most of 12th Armoured Division (37th Armoured and 46th Mechanised Brigades) as well as 4th Mountain, 5th Mountain and 18th Infantry Brigades, while II Corps' 10th Armoured Division lost its 24th Mechanised Brigade, and the 1st Mechanised Division lost the 34th Armoured Brigade.

PART I: AN UNHOLY BLOODBATH

Iraqi attack helicopters caused heavy losses to inexperienced tankers of the IRGC, in summer 1982. This BMP-1 was knocked out by an ATGM-hit and had its turret blown away. The open hatch at the rear might indicate that some of the crew managed to escape. (Tom Cooper collection)

The Iranian 77th Infantry Division assaulted the northern end of the Iraqi border defences during Operation Ramadan Mubarak. Casualties were heavy and included this BMP-1 and two MBTs (type unrecognizable), which became trapped in the anti-armour ditch and were then knocked out. (Tom Cooper collection)

Also sent south were 53rd Armoured, 427th and 602nd Infantry Brigades. The Iranians had also suffered badly, with 92nd Division losing some 100 AFVs, but they had the manpower to continue.

Second Offensive July 16

On the morning of 16 July, Makki debriefed the divisional commanders and in a meeting lasting until noon they refined their plans while engineers feverishly worked to turn the second berm line into a succession of strongpoints. Yet the situation remained critical, for Sa'adi had been forced to commit his whole mechanised reserve and until reinforcements arrived there remained a hole in the former 9th Armoured Division sector. Abdul Rashid's badly battered 15th Mechanised Brigade had had to be withdrawn for rest and reorganisation, leaving Shurkur's 30th Armoured Brigade and GHQ's 10th Armoured Brigade now in the line on each side of the 5th Mechanised/9th Armoured Division boundary, Shukur's 20th Mechanised Brigade was next in line, while Khathban's surviving 43rd and 35th Armoured Brigades held 9th Armoured Division's right. With Shukur's 26th Armoured Brigade pressed to hold his line, the only armoured reserve uncommitted was his 16th and 55th Armoured Brigades.

Niaki recognised he had come close to success and after an intensive IRIAF reconnaissance effort which undoubtedly revealed the enemy's lack of reserves, he decided to exploit his previous success with a renewed assault upon 9th Armoured Division's sector. He struck on the night of 16–17 July, again spearheaded by 77th Division supported by the battered Pasdaran formations and a brigade of 92nd Division. The defenders lacked infantry to hold the weakened and battered strongpoints, there were only half-a-dozen infantry battalions to hold the whole 9th Armoured Division sector, so once again the forward positions were quickly lost. But when the Iranians reached the open ground they were slowed by heavy artillery fire and stopped by the mechanised formations. Inevitably, the Iranians' greatest successes were against Khathban's two brigades, but luckily Hussein Rashid's 3rd Armoured Division was not seriously engaged and in the morning staged a counterattack into the enemy's southern flank using 6th Armoured and 8th Mechanised Brigades, while Sa'adi committed 33rd Special Forces Brigade from the west. The Iranians lacked sufficient armour to contain the threat, and under heavy air attack fell back, again screened by the IRIA, losing only 500 prisoners.

This failure, on top of what the Iraqi dictator described as the 'mother of all disasters', was too great to save Khathban, who was relieved on 17 July. It is possible that 9th Armoured Division's troubles were a combination of Khathban's bungling and a flow of inexperienced commanders following the heavy losses during the last battles in Iran. On the night 17/18 July, Sa'adi visited 5th

Mechanised Division headquarters and they agreed substantial reinforcements were needed and that 9th Armoured Division should be withdrawn as soon as possible.

It was clear Sa'adi lacked infantry to hold the forward line until the reinforcements arrived and, as Shukur's 6th Armoured Division had not been significantly engaged, the III Corps commander used its headquarters for a reaction force with 16th and 30th Armoured and 25th Mechanised Brigades, and 10th Independent Armoured Brigade, with the ultimate objective of retaking 9th Armoured Division's forward strongpoints. In the meantime Sa'adi successfully gambled that that 5th Mechanised Division could hold the line until he completed preparations for a set-piece counterattack from 18 until 21 July with 3rd Armoured Division, adjusting its positions ready to launch another riposte northwards. Sa'adi and Makki then toured the divisions on 19–20 July completing their plans so that everything was ready by 21 July.

Third Offensive 21–22 July

It was just in time for that night, from 2030 hrs, the Iranians tried again to seize the initiative with 77th Division and the Pasdaran joined by part of 16th IRIA Division. Inevitably they quickly overran the forward defences and penetrated up to 10 kilometres on a 15-kilometre front, but within six hours they were again blocked by the Iraqi mechanised reserves, with heavy artillery support directed personally by the III Corps artillery chief, Major General Abdul Wahid Saeed. With dawn came the inevitable Iraqi riposte, spearheaded by 3rd Armoured Division, which slowly drove them back and claimed to have captured 39 tanks as well as 22 APCs, while Iranian dead lay scattered across the battlefield, black and bloated under the merciless sun, amid a landscape of blazing armour and installations.

Fourth Offensive 23–24 July

Their failure prompted the Iranians to make the first major revision in their plan, which meant temporarily abandoning efforts to outflank the Fish Lake north of the flooded area. To suck in the enemy reserves, and especially 3rd Armoured Division, Task Force Nasr was now ordered to break through south of the flooded area. There all of Qadir's infantry brigades were deployed along the frontier, but he had reinforced each strongpoint with a detachment of three tanks which used ramps to help cover the obstacle zone. However, his defences followed the frontier, then swung eastwards to expose half the division to envelopment from the north.

Yet Task Force Nasr on the night of 23 to 24 July made no attempt to exploit this tactical weakness, and simply launched a frontal assault upon the four brigades (north to south: 109th, 49th, 45th, and 22nd) on Qadir's left. This was the most strongly fortified part of III Corps' defences, yet despite the weight of artillery fire the attackers managed to struggle through the obstacle zone and up the forward slopes of the berms leading to fierce battles in the forward positions. The 45th Brigade was pushed back, exposing a bridge which carried the Basra–Khorramshahr highway, but this had been prepared for demolition and was dropped as the Pasdaran swarmed across. Then a counterattack from the south by 22nd Infantry Brigade, together with Qadir's own armoured brigade, pushed back the Iranians who returned to their start lines having suffered heavy losses. Much of the credit for Qadir's defence was his artillery fire plan carefully prepared with General Wahid Saeed.

Fifth Offensive 28–29 July

From 25 until 27 July there was a brief lull during which the Iranian cabinet was briefed on the situation by Defence Minister Salami. Fighting was confined to artillery exchanges as well as probing in the southern sector, while roving Iraqi helicopters picked off vehicles. The brief lull gave Sa'adi time to relieve 9th Armoured Division on 27 July with 8th Infantry Division (23rd, 27th, 28th, Infantry- and 42nd Armoured Brigades) under Brigadier Diea Tawfik Ibraheem, which brought with it 12 new batteries (72 guns) and more MLRS.[26]

The losses of the 9th Armoured Division were so heavy (possibly up to 60 percent) that Saddam disbanded it: the salvageable elements were used to create the 17th Armoured Division in II Corps as compensation for the armour redeployed south. By contrast both Hussein Rashid and Maher Abdul Rashid were promoted to Major General, the former during the battle for his excellent command.[27]

Even as Tawfik's troops began to occupy their new positions, Sa'adi brought him the unwelcome news that COMINT had intercepted signals indicating there would be a renewed assault on his sector and 5th Mechanised Division within 24 hours. By now the Iranians were frequently radioing *en clair* due either to a shortage of encryption machines or to the pace of the assaults meaning that encrypted communications were taking too long. Tawfik had time to insert only 42nd Armoured and 27th Infantry Brigades and assume command of 5th Mountain Brigade, before Task Force Fath began a probing attack on the night from 27 to 28 July – which alerted both the corps and its two northern divisions.

The main blow came the following night and struck the whole 5th Mechanised Division front, which had 10th and 16th Armoured Brigades holding the strongpoints on the division's right, but it was a forlorn hope as the assault was by the exhausted survivors of earlier attacks. For once there was an element of imagination in Iranian tactics with Abdul Rashid's left flank unit, 419th Brigade, struck both from the east and the north. Abdul Rashid's troops were also tired and the new assault gained ground in bitter close-quarter combat. The attack on the southern brigades, having penetrated 5 kilometres into the defences, now turned northwards in a bid to isolate all of the four forward brigades. Abdul Rashid committed his rested 15th Mechanised Brigade, joined by the newly arrived 37th Armoured and 46th Mechanised Brigades, which stabilised the situation because the 92nd Division was unable to intervene with any effect. To the south, despite having little time to prepare, the fresh 8th Division held off the enemy who made few inroads into its positions as the attacks broke down under intense artillery fire.

On the banks of the Shatt, Qadir faced a new challenge as Task Force Nasr tried in vain to reach the Fish Lake. The Pasdaran made a little progress during the night, but heavy fire restricted movement and with the dawn they hastily withdrew, and this was repeated the following evening.

On the main front, with reinforcements now arriving in strength, Sa'adi Tumma was determined to resolve the situation with a coordinated counterattack again using 6th Armoured Division, which joined Abdul Rashid's armoured reserves to sweep from west to east. The attacks ground forward but paused for the night and were resumed on 31 July, by which time almost all the lost ground had been regained with the Iranians suffering further serious losses in men and material. Zahirnejhad must always have known this was a forlorn hope and as early as 29 July he visited Khomeini to give him the news that the assault had failed, and with it all hopes of a breakthrough.

PART I: AN UNHOLY BLOODBATH

Yet there was one last desperate attempt: after dusk of 1 August, using three widely spaced divisions reinforced with every militiaman the IRGC could find. The Iranians struck from a sliver of Iraqi territory around Zayed against 8th Infantry Division, but the attack followed the previous pattern, made few gains and was abandoned at dawn on 3 August, with Islamic fervour being sapped by the heat, humidity, exhaustion and shortage of supplies, although bloody bickering continued for a couple of days more.

The Iranians had secured an 80 square kilometre salient inside Iraq around Zayed, some five kilometres deep and 15 kilometres long, opposite the Fish Lake, from which they claimed they could see the lights of Basra some 25 kilometres away. This was small reward for an enterprise which had begun with such high hopes and at one time had occupied up to 300 square kilometres of Iraqi territory at high cost. US intelligence estimated the Iranians suffered 14,000 casualties (or up to 14 percent of the involved troops); Tehran admitted 7,000 killed, while US intelligence estimated the Iranians had also lost 250–260 AFVs.[28] They captured some 1,700 prisoners and claimed to have taken about 100 AFVs, including four T-72s, but Iraqi casualties were much lower and they had sharply reduced Iranian equipment with an estimated 20–25 percent loss. By 27 July the Iraqis, who dubbed the offensive 'The First Battle East of Basra', were claiming to have destroyed 339 AFVs and to have captured 59 MBTs with 22 APCs and IFVs – even though they might have lost up to 370 of their own AFVs. One commentator observed: 'Operation Ramadan was, by any standard, a criminal failure of leadership and strategy', while another observed: 'The failed offensive against al-Basrah shone a spotlight on Iran's most significant military shortcomings. Iran's basic strategy was roughly equivalent to trying to use a hammer to destroy an anvil'.[29] Sayyad Shirazi would later

The crew of an Iraqi OT-62 stretching their legs during a break in fighting. Losses in 1982, and the reopening of supply-lines to Moscow, resulted in the early demise of this venerable and reliable mount, and its replacement with BMP-1s. (Albert Grandolini collection)

The crew of an Iraqi T-72 from the 10th Armoured Brigade posing at the rear of their vehicle. This unit played a key role in spearheading counterattacks against Ramadan Mubarak and generally acting as a fire-brigade. (Albert Grandolini collection)

blame 'over-confidence' following the spring successes and the Iranians certainly underestimated enemy resilience, but poor preparation and inadequate use of reconnaissance, also contributed to the failure.

The IRIA was content to allow the militia-dominated infantry to break through the defences in the hope that its mechanised forces could exploit the success, but these forces rarely seemed to seek the enemy flank or rear to envelop them. The IRIA armour was also hamstrung by inferior supply arrangements, indeed the logistical system appears to have reached near breakdown. Coordination between the militias and the IRIA's mechanised forces and artillery was poor, making it difficult to change fires or to exploit sudden successes. Yet the IRIA had still to master the art of logistical support for offensive operations and it lacked the flexibility to respond to major changes or crises.

The shortcomings of the IRIA were not the most serious problem for, as the IRIA leaders had tried to hint, the Pasdaran and Basiji lacked the command-and-control infrastructure and the heavy weapons for successful conventional operations. Their commanders often operated autonomously with little attempt to coordinate operations with either neighbours or support units, which led to a propensity for frontal attacks without fire support. Like many generals on the Western Front in 1915–1917, the Pasdaran commanders would prefer to reinforce forces which had been stopped or bogged down. They lacked the mobility to match the enemy mechanised reserves, as well as the training and equipment, while the shortage of radios made it difficult for commanders to recall or redirect their units, especially when they were fully engaged with enemy defences. Many Pasdaran commanders failed to time their attacks to exploit artillery support and often ignored pre-planned operational timing to rush enemy positions before artillery preparation.[30]

Here, for the first time in 18 months, the IRIA artillery was unable to dominate the battlefield. The cumulative effects of 22 months fighting were now undermining the Iranian gunners with their largely Shah-purchased US inventory of mostly self-propelled weapons such as the M109 155mm howitzer and the M107 175mm gun. Despite the diligence of Iranian purchasing commissions, supplies of ammunition and spares were running short and even before Operation Ramadan began batteries were operating at less than full strength, while compounding this problem was the fact that the irreplaceable gun barrels were literally being worn-out, steadily reducing the IRIA's artillery inventory.

The offensive also proved a setback for relations between the IRIA and the Pasdaran. Combat experience from 1981 to the successful spring offensive of 1982 had seen a grudging mutual regard develop and the Pasdaran reluctantly accepted the IRIA's advice to mutual benefit. The Ghotbzadeh Plot seemed to show the regulars still harboured anti-government views, which led to more vocal criticism of the IRIA's commitment both to the war and the Islamic Revolution. The situation became so bad that during Operation Ramadan Mubarak, Zahirnejhad threatened to resign 'if unqualified people continue to meddle with the conduct of the war' and Khomeini had to order the clerics and Pasdaran to cooperate with the IRIA. The IRIA resented the fact that the Pasdaran had official favour and exerted a disproportionate weight in terms of military decision making, although they were forced to recognise that there was a growing professionalism. This meant that in response to Pasdaran complaints about shortages of heavy weapons they were allowed to seek armour and artillery as well as creating staffs to plan, supply and administer the battle.[31]

While the Iranian SDC publicly proclaimed the offensive a success because it demonstrated the country's resolve, in reality it was profoundly disappointed not only by the defeat but also by the failure of the Iraqi Shias to rise in revolt. It was also unpleasantly surprised by the determined and tenacious resistance offered by the Iraqis who were now fighting a foreign invader themselves. Even the

Both sides acquired hundreds of tank transporters before the war: the Iraqis ended the war against Iran possessing more than 1,000 such vehicles, which enabled them to move an entire armoured division from one portion of the front line in as little as a day. This US-made Mack is hauling an IRGC T-55 to the front. (Albert Grandolini collection)

PART I: AN UNHOLY BLOODBATH

An Iranian Army TOW-team, mounted on a M151 MUTT jeep, approaching a sector of front line held by the IRGC, along the highway connecting Khorramshahr with Basra. (Tom Cooper collection)

clerics were appalled by the scale of the Pasdaran losses and when men in the cities learned of them by word-of-mouth the numbers of volunteers were reduced to a trickle and the Pasdaran had to advertise for more. Such was their shortage of equipment that on 15 July they made a public plea for khaki uniforms, army boots and webbing. There would certainly be no swift return to the southern battlefield after so chastening an experience. The IRIA and Pasdaran were both exhausted and Zahirnejhad argued successfully for a pause to allow battered formations to receive and to train replacements as well as meditate upon the causes of their failures. Time was also needed to replace the lost armour and to expand the artillery, with the result that a lull fell on the Basra front and the Iranians spent the next 20 months licking their wounds and confining offensive activity to the northern theatres.[32]

> Now it became Iran's turn to apply dogmatically a strategy that had worked well under different circumstance, only to find that it could not compensate for real disadvantages and new Iraqi resolve. Time and again the Iranians hurled themselves onto Iraqi positions with all the vigour of the past, only to shatter against well-prepared defences. The war had entered a new phase.[33]

For Saddam the thwarting of Iranian ambitions proved a huge relief which strengthened his position, boosted Iraqi morale and led the Soviet Union to abandon neutrality and rearm the Iraqis. Some sources indicate that it was in the middle of the battle that the Iraqis began to receive maps from the United States, based upon satellite images, to identify enemy concentrations and intentions, but Iraqi sources say this was untrue. Although this and COMINT provided much useful information, intelligence collection and analysis remained a serious problem for Iraq, although there was certainly an improvement in Iraqi tactical intelligence from July 1982.[34]

US intelligence concluded that while Iraq had successfully solved the problem of defending all but the periphery of its territory through fortifications, which absorbed the enemy assault which then became vulnerable to mechanised counterattacks, the Iranians' logistical weakness and shortage of armour prevented them driving deep into Iraq. This was probably the last time in this conflict in which ATGMs were used in large numbers for their designed role. From now onwards, at least half their targets would be static armour and strongpoints, while for every aimed missile or RPG, three or four were merely fired to harass the enemy. There also remained problems with co-ordinating the various services; the IrAAF lost a number of helicopters to the Iraqi army's own SA-7s. Henceforth, the air defence system would be closed down when they operated over the battlefield.[35]

However, the Iraqi success in Ramadan was not easily achieved, and despite the crowing statements from Baghdad Radio it was – as the Duke of Wellington said of Waterloo – 'a damn close-run thing.' The Iraqis had taken heavy losses, with at least two brigades destroyed, and the enemy retained a toehold, the Zayed Salient, along the border which could act as a springboard for future assaults. This salient also compromised Saddam's desired strategy of defending the frontier and, no doubt to the relief of the more professional Iraqi officers, he was forced to accept defence in depth and abandon the old strongpoint line apart from screening forces. The berm covering the north-eastern approaches to the Fish Lake became the basis of a double strongpoint line, more strongpoints were added along the lake's western bank while within the waters was created a satanic combination of concertina wire entanglements. The Basra–Khorramshahr highway defences were strengthened, especially south of the lake, with only a screening force left along the frontier.[36]

Manning these defences would remain a problem for the Iraqi Army almost until the end of the war. The country had a smaller pool of manpower than its enemy, indeed on 22 July the Defence Ministry called up reservists born in 1953, or who were conscripted in 1972, and they were ordered to report by 3 August. The best educated or most technically skilled men were skimmed off by the air force or mechanised forces leaving few to fill the infantry battalions, and the Iraqis would begin to conscript small numbers of Arab foreigners, especially Egyptians and Sudanese, for use in support units. In April 1982, as a gesture of Arab solidarity, King Hussein of Jordan sent the 2,000–3,000 man al-Yamouk Force to join the Iraqi Army, with battalions joining 7th and 15th Infantry Divisions. Unfortunately, some of these battalions were made up of criminals who were promised a pardon in return for volunteering. Some units mutinied and while they were suppressed, the Jordanians tended to be used in secondary sectors and were withdrawn some time in 1983.[37]

Meanwhile, the Iraqis increased the inundations east of the lake until they largely covered the southern approaches. To counter this the Iranians dug a canal to drain these inundations, but its capacity to dry out the land was more than matched by the Iraqis' ability to increase the flow of water by adding a feeder channel from the Shatt. In the meantime the Fish Lake front rumbled along, with Basra now under artillery fire, despite Khomeini's injunction to avoid civilian casualties, in retaliation for Iraqi shelling of cities such as Khorramshahr and Abadan.

Operation Ramadan had aimed to knock Iraq out of the war and had failed, and both sides now faced the grim prospect of a prolonged conflict.

9
BATTLES IN THE MARSHES

Despite the twin disappointments of the Operation Ramadan defeat and the absence of an Iraqi Shia rising, the SDC remained mesmerised by Basra while recognising it would be a long time before there would be sufficient armour and artillery to assault the Fish Lake Line. Publicly the Iranian strategic position was explained by IRIA Commander-in-Chief General Shirazi: 'Our strategy is designed to liberate not only the occupied Iranian territories but also Jerusalem and all Islamic countries where people feel the need to vanquish tyranny. Ours is a war that we are waging for God and he will guide us to victory'.[1]

The frontier between Ahwaz and Khorramshahr became a huge staging area with camps, supply dumps and training grounds as the Iranians tried to exploit operational experience in improved training. While Basra remained beyond Tehran's reach the leadership had no intention of relinquishing the strategic level (army group and above) initiative so they sought a decision on the Northern and Central Fronts with the Val Fajr (or Wal Fajr) series of offensives. These gained a little ground at great cost, but at the tactical level (operations within army corps) they improved the lightly armed Pasdarans' professional capabilities especially within rough terrain. In fact the Kurdish-dominated northern front with its mountain chains made a breakthrough impossible, while the deserts west of Khuzestan remained a death-trap, but as activity on the Kurdish front declined during late 1983 there was increased interest in resuming an offensive against Basra – possibly to draw reserves away from that front.[2]

The Val Fajr series of operations suggested to Rezai and Safavi that it might be possible to cross the Hawizah Marshes and take Basra from the north. They began to canvas support for this idea during 1983, with the bonus from the clerics' viewpoint, that the terrain favoured Pasdaran troops rather than the IRIA. The marsh was largely impassable for AFVs, it was lightly held and the defences around it were weak so Tehran could conceal the assembly of a Pasdaran-based assault force intended to strike southwards to outflank the northern Fish Lake defences, and then push down to Basra. To reduce the threat from the IrAF and IrAAC it was decided to launch the offensive during the tail end of the rainy season when an average of 28.5mm of rain falls in January and drops to 15.2 mm in February. The low clouds would restrict enemy air power but the water levels within the marsh would be high enough to permit rapid movement by boat.

The Iranians, who had now learned the virtue of planning and preparation, created a network of roads along the border, and especially in the south, during the summer of 1983 which they used to fill supply dumps. To prevent the enemy inundating the marshes from the Tigris, during 1983 the Iranians began to dig a 58-kilometre-long canal from the River Karun to drain away flood waters and this was completed by early 1984. In response Iraq created a new set of large embankments which ran parallel to the front. Meanwhile, the Iranian forces began to train and to equip their forces for assaults across rivers and obstacles as well as positioning forces to bypass them. The region was selected because the defenders' weakness was shown by the lack of military activity, apart from the occasional clash of patrols, and an attack on several axes would force the enemy to scatter his forces and prevent them from using large numbers of AFVs. The mosquito-ridden Hawizah Marshes would be the focus of bitter fighting over the next 12 months, and at the time of the Iran-Iraq War they were a formidable obstacle to conventional armies especially during the rainy season. Inhabited by the so-called Marsh Arabs (Ma'dan), the Hawizah Marshes were fed from the Tigris (Nahr Dijlah) by the Rivers Musharah and al-Zahla from the north and while their boundaries are fluid, they are generally about 50 kilometres from north to south and 65–105 kilometres from east to west, and cover an area of some 3,000 square kilometres, although this can expand during the rainy season to 60 and 115 kilometres respectively.[3]

The northern and central parts were permanently flooded to a depth of up to 6 metres, with open stretches of water bounded by dense reed beds up to 7 metres above the water level, and which can conceal movement. There were three small lakes in this part, the largest being the Hawr al Hawizah and Hawr Limar Sawan, and there were two areas of firm land. Most of the Ma'dan lived in this region in tiny villages of houses made of reeds on a reed-woven base, anchored to the sand and the silt beneath the water, or on tiny islets which were little more than muddy embankments. Some villages were linked by narrow (5-metre) embankments or 'bunds', a few metres above the water level, or by a few narrow, navigable channels, but most of the channels were clogged with reeds or weeds.

West of the marshes lay the meandering Tigris which is 75–250 metres wide and can flood the surrounding plain to a depth of 3 metres. At what would be the northern end of the battlefield was a broad strip of land some 10 kilometres wide between the river and the marshes, just north of al-Uzayr (also al-Azair, as-Sulayb and Ozair). From here a finger of land some 4–5 kilometres broad and five kilometres long pointed north-east into the marshes, with the village of al-Harrah at its tip. From Harrah a narrow road ran along a bund through the villages al-Beida (also al-Bayda, El Bauda and Beizeh) and Madina back to Uzayr where there was a bridge across the Tigris to the Baghdad–Basra highway which came south from al-Amarah. This highway, with the Baghdad–Basra railway some 15 kilometres to the west, ran for 40 kilometres alongside the western bank of the Tigris to al-Qurnah, where the two rivers meet to form the Shatt, while from the river's eastern bank was a narrow strip of raised land averaging 5–6 kilometres wide to the marsh edge.

The southern part of the marshes was more seasonal in nature, with the deepest channels only 3 metres deep, and here significant

Cheerful Pasdaran forming up at one of the embarkation points from which they were deployed into attack on board a miscellany of speedboats at the beginning of Khaiber. IRGC troops sent into the battles of 1984 were better equipped than ever before, all wearing uniforms and even steel helmets. (Tom Cooper collection)

A group of youthful Pasdaran waiting for their turn to attack through the Hoveyzeh Marshes in February 1983. (Tom Cooper collection)

the Majnoon (Crazy) Islands (Jazaer-e Majmun also written Majnun), dotted with oil rigs and with a small administrative centre in the south-western corner of South Majnoon.

By the time Iraq invaded Iran, Petrobras had reached the engineering phase for production facilities and had 14 drilling rigs at both Majnoon and at the nearby Nahr Umr field, while there were more than 20 exploration wells in Majnoon, one of which had penetrated 14 oil-bearing zones. When the war broke out Petrobras' foreign oil workers fled after capping the wells.[5]

West of the Majnoons, between the marshes and the Tigris, lay a five to seven-kilometre-wide strip of intensely cultivated farmland which ran 15 kilometres down to Tuyrabah and featured numerous irrigation channels and palm groves. The key Baghdad–Basra highway runs west of the Tigris and the meanderings of the river mean it often runs along its bank before reaching Qurnah, which is bounded in the east by the Tigris and in the south by Euphrates (al-Furat). The highway crosses the latter river on two bridges before running to Basra but, in this battlefield, it is linked to the west by only two bridges, at Uzayr and Nashwah (Nashveh in Farsi), the latter 25 kilometres north of Basra. On the opposite bank a smaller, gravelled, road ran along an embankment which ran parallel to the highway to Basra.

attempts began to drain the marsh. In the 1970s, the British oil company BP led a boycott of Iraq after it nationalised foreign oil producers, but in June 1972 the Latin American producer Petrobras Braspetro of Brazil (Petrobras or Braspetro) broke the embargo. A grateful Baghdad gave Petrobras concessions to discover and to exploit oil on behalf of the Iraqi National Oil Corporation, and during the 1970s Brazilian prospectors discovered that an extension of the Great Rumaila Triangle oil field lay under the marshes, with a potential 7 billion barrels of heavy-to-medium oil.[4]

To exploit this wealth Petrobras began draining water from the south-eastern corner of the marshes and excavating sand and mud to create causeways, dykes and canals, together with an embankment bounded island totalling 170 square kilometres. Split by a 2-kilometre lateral drainage channel into two areas dubbed

The Majnoons lay only two kilometres from where the international frontier turned north from the 31st Parallel, which meant they were within easy reach if the Iranians wanted a base to strike south and this was the basis on which Operation Khyber was prepared from early in 1984. The decision to change offensive activity away from conventional trials of strength allowed the SDC to slowly build up the Islamic Republic's forces so that the IRIA had some 300,000 men while the Pasdaran had a similar figure which could be augmented temporarily by up to 100,000 Basiji. An artillery park of some 600–1,000 guns had been assembled although, compared with the start of the war, its battlefield mobility was restricted because it was easier to acquire towed rather than self-propelled ordnance. The armoured force had also been expanded through a combination

PART I: BATTLES IN THE MARSHES

Members of at least two of the many IRGC RPG-7 teams embarking an assault launch in preparation for crossing the Hoveyzeh Marshes. Note the characteristic rucksacks with pouches for spare rounds carried by nearly all of them. (Tom Cooper collection)

While most of the 500 or so assault boats used by the IRGC for crossing the Hoveyzeh Marshes were unarmed, some had a heavy machine gun installed for air defence purposes. This one has a 14.5mm KPV-1. (Tom Cooper collection)

of 'heroic' maintenance and cannibalisation work on American and British vehicles augmented by the acquisition of Chinese and former Iraqi vehicles to give the IRIA 500 MBTs and the Pasdaran 250, most distributed to independent tank battalions.[6]

The Spearhead

This campaign would mark a stage in the war when operations would be dominated by the clerics' forces; the Pasdaran and the Basiji. The Pasdaran had grown from a fervent, but untrained, police-force-cum-militia into a counterinsurgency force and then into a semi-conventional army which was becoming increasingly professional, with uniforms and saluting, although leaders were given no formal rank and everyone was addressed as 'Brother'. The provincial platoons had gradually coalesced into battalions, the battalions grouped into brigades, whose support was strengthened, and the brigades into divisions. The Pasdaran had now also created artillery, armoured and mechanised units manned by the more experienced, or better educated, troops, although it was not until September 1985 that it would be formally divided into specialist branches.[7]

Each brigade had four infantry battalions of 300–325 men, now augmented by a reconnaissance company and a support company with heavy machine guns, 81mm mortars and recoilless artillery, together with a logistics unit to total some 1,400 men. There were three brigades in a division which also had a support battalion with 107mm MLRS, 81–120mm mortars, recoilless artillery and air defence weapons, together with reconnaissance and engineer battalions, while increasingly they received an artillery battalion with 105mm–130mm guns and some 122mm MLRS, to give them up to 6,500 men.

While the Pasdaran had learned from working alongside the IRIA, the small command teams had little experience of staff work, while the logistical organisation remained rudimentary. With each of the 11 Pasdaran regions jealously guarding its independence from

As well as hundreds of minor boats, the IRGC made use of larger barges for crossing the Hoveyzeh Marshes. This one is hauling a load of water or petrol to the front lines. (Tom Cooper collection)

Despite many reports to the contrary (especially in the West), the Iranians paid great attention to CASEVAC and MEDEVAC. This boat was evacuating at least two injured Pasdaran. Usually, they would be brought to one of the many field hospitals positioned close to the embarkation points. (Tom Cooper collection)

An Iranian tank-transporter carrying a British-made, 55-tonne BH.7 Wellington air-cushion landing craft towards the Hoveyzeh Marshes in preparation for Operation Kheiber. (Tom Cooper collection)

The Pasdaran were usually 18–26-year-old volunteers, unmarried, and largely drawn from the urban poor with selection often based upon the family, or personal, relationships with the clerics. This relationship spurred recruitment together with the desire for social change and patriotism to give the Pasdaran a sense of purpose reinforced by good pay and benefits. Officially all were committed to the ideals of the Islamic Revolution but while most were fiercely patriotic the degree to which they imbibed the Shia fascination for martyrdom varied from man to man. The Pasdaran were certainly run by zealous commanders who led from the front and expected revolutionary fervour to achieve victory. The downside upon unit cohesion was heavy casualties due to command-and-control weaknesses. These heavy casualties meant experienced men were replaced by raw recruits who diluted unit effectiveness. Even the Pasdaran were not immune to the demoralising psychological effects of heavy casualties and gradually the flow of volunteers slowed to a trickle forcing the provinces increasingly to despatch conscripts, many of whom were less driven by religious rhetoric.[8]

Increasingly the Pasdaran faced a nominally fixed period of service of 24 months, contrasting with 30 months for the IRIA, but in both services the men could re-enlist. Units were normally kept in camps and deployed for short, intense, periods of combat before being withdrawn to unwind; chatting, pursuing hobbies and playing sport such as volleyball and soccer. This certainly helped reduce the toll from battle fatigue and after unwinding they could return to training, but the heavy losses of veterans meant many units returned to action with a growing ratio of raw recruits who, in turn, suffered heavy losses to steadily erode unit combat effectiveness. However, a major health problem, especially for troops who were not native to the western desert region, was Sand Fly Fever, a debilitating disease whose symptoms included not only severe fever but also headaches, aching limbs and light-sensitivity. Both the Naples and Sicilian strains of the virus were encountered by Iranian medical staff, although almost all the troops

the Pasdaran Ministry in Tehran, it was impossible to coordinate a constant flow of supplies and replacements to the front, although the ministry controlled the supply of weapons and ammunition. Formations appear to have organised the distribution of supplies to frontline units using daring drivers in civilian pick-up trucks or even motorcyclists whose forays around the Forward Edge of Battle (FEBA) exposed them to enemy fire. The Iranians' perennial lack of radios meant the IRIA received the lion's share of communication equipment and this severely restricted Pasdaran command and control which often depended upon vulnerable land lines or even more vulnerable messengers. This would be a serious problem when the tiny divisional staffs were 'double-hatted' to become task force commands.

PART I: BATTLES IN THE MARSHES

The Islamic Republic of Iran Navy (IRIN) deployed six of its Wellington hovercraft for Kheiber. Powered by a Rolls-Royce Proteus Gnome gas turbine, these could carry up to 60 men or 18 tonnes at speeds up to 60 knots. (Tom Cooper collection)

Prior to Operation Kheiber, the IRGC took over a number of stored BTR-50s from the IRIA, re-engined them with US-made diesels and deployed them in combat – because of their amphibious capabilities – as Kashayar. Two of these are shown towing a section of a pontoon bridge through the Hoveyzeh Marshes. (Tom Cooper collection)

For moving troops, supplies and heavier equipment through the Hoveyzeh Marshes, the Iranians acquired pressurised Styrofoam floats from South Korea, which were then used as the basis for pontoon bridges. The longest of these bridges was over 30km long. (Tom Cooper collection)

had the latter strain which needed treatment with bed rest, pain medication and fluids for a problem also encountered by Iraqi Army doctors.[9]

The Basiji, by contrast, were the poorly-trained cannon-fodder of the Islamic Revolution grouped into company-sized, mosque-based, units of up to 200 men designated 'battalions', two or three of which would be attached to each Pasdaran brigade. They tended to be older than the Pasdaran, generally aged 20–30 although their ages ranged from 13–70, often married, uneducated and usually they came from the rural poor. Khomeini opened the Iranian New Year in 1982 (20 March) by allowing boys of 12–18 to join the Basij, their enlistment documents being dubbed 'Passports to Paradise'. After Khyber the Pasdaran Ministry would claim that 57 percent of the assault force (i.e. some 80,000 troops) were 'school children,' but the term probably ranges from schoolboy Basiji to teenage Pasdaran. Like the Pasdaran the ideals of the Islamic Revolution motivated Basiji recruitment. The sense of community provided unit cohesion, like the British Pals Battalions of the First World War, but it also meant that heavy casualties would have a devastating impact upon their home villages and towns.[10]

Their rural background meant that Basiji mobilisation was restricted to the periods between sowing and harvest and they rarely served for more than three months. They would be transported from their mosques piecemeal to assembly camps, usually sleeping on the bare earth because no tents were provided, which made it difficult for any intelligence agency to monitor build ups. Often they took their own food and water, which mosques would replenish when possible, and at the front they would receive a weapon and a little

To protect their troops from Iraqi aircraft and helicopters during Operation Kheiber, the Iranians organised an air defence system consisting of early warning radars, MIM-23B I-HAWK SAMs, various anti-aircraft artillery guns and 9K32 Strela-2 (or SA-7 Grail) man-portable missile systems (MANPADS). This Pasdaran is posing with his Strela launcher: the weapon fired a 9.8kg, infrared homing missile, with a 1.15kg warhead, out to a range of 3,700 metres. (Tom Cooper collection)

ammunition, often a single magazine, then a fortnight's military training. Their fervour would be sustained by fiery speeches, readings from the Koran, hymns and prayers from their religious leaders before they attacked.

The Basiji, like most militias, were little more than a wild mob with little or no command and control, who would simply charge forward, sometimes accidentally clearing minefields with their own bodies because they were unaware of the mines' presence, then kept going out of sheer terror. Contrary to numerous accounts during and after the war of Pasdaran 'human wave' attacks, their tactics were far more sophisticated. The Pasdaran would carefully reconnoitre enemy defences to determine their weaknesses and use the Basiji to help clear the approaches. They would then infiltrate the defences, overwhelming positions where possible and isolating the strongest positions whose defenders would then be subdued by small arms fire before they were stormed.

Planning for Operation Khyber

The operation was reportedly planned by Major General Hassan Abshenasan and although it was to be commanded by Deputy

An abandoned Iraqi artillery position, originally constructed to cover the marshes. Like so many forward positions, it proved vulnerable to infiltration and attacks by IRGC infantry using speedboats. (Tom Cooper collection)

Every piece of dry land in the Hoveyzeh Marshes was used for the deployment of heavier equipment. This islet was occupied by a 23mm ZU-23 anti-aircraft cannon operated by the IRGC. This weapon had a high rate of fire and a range of about 2,000 metres. As such, it proved too short-ranged for effective use, even against Iraqi helicopter gunships. Nevertheless, it proved effective against infantry and even lightly armoured vehicles. (Tom Cooper collection)

PART I: BATTLES IN THE MARSHES

As well as nearly 100 lighter helicopters, the IRIAA and IRIAF deployed their CH-47C Chinooks for hauling light artillery pieces and vehicles to the front lines. This example is carrying a jeep with 106mm recoilless gun. At least one of the Chinooks survived a hit from an Iraqi interceptor that disabled the rear engine. (Tom Cooper collection)

Ground Forces Commander General Ali Jalali. For the first time SFOH (Karbala Command) was not in sole control as the spearhead was exclusively under the Pasdaran Najaf Command. Contrary to many reports, efforts of interservice cooperation and mutually-supporting joint operations were at the heart of this operation, for while the Pasdaran would provide most of the spearhead, all the traditional services provided support in terms of firepower, logistics, air and even maritime power. The militias had nine divisions and seven infantry brigades, together with an armoured brigade, a total of some 95,000 Pasdaran and Basiji, but only one artillery battalion per division, totalling some 115 guns (except for the Task Force Honain division which commanded no batteries). By contrast the 35,000 IRIA personnel, in five brigades, were supported by some 200 guns, although many batteries would also support the Pasdaran.[11]

Khybers' objective was to isolate the Iraqi forces around Basra to pave the way for their destruction and the city's capture, but Operation Ramadan Mubarak clearly demonstrated this could not be achieved in one move. Instead it would be conducted in two phases; the first to secure what the US Army describes as 'the line of departure' or 'jump-off point' from which the isolation of the enemy could then be achieved.[12]

Najaf Command was to secure bridgeheads on the western and southern edges of the marshes with Pasdaran forces augmented by 1st Battalion of the 23rd Special Forces Brigade and a battalion of the 55th Airborne Brigade. Two task forces with some 15,000 men would secure the right flank; Nasr in the north would take the firm ground north of Uzayr with 5th Nasr Division and 15th Imam Hassan Brigades, then take the bridge across the Tigris at Uzayr to cut the Baghdad–Basra highway; while to the south Task Force Hadid with 21st Imam Reza and 44th Qamar Bani Hashem Brigades would secure the eastern Tigris including the cultivated area to threaten Qurnah in the southwest.

The main strike forces were Task Forces Honain and Badr which would enter the marshes from the east then swing southwards. The former, with the 27th Mohamad Rasoolallah Division together with 18th Al-Ghadir and 33rd Al-Mahdi Brigades (11,000 men) would first take North Majnoon Island then reinforce Badr, which had 17th Ali Ibn Abu Talib and 41st Sarallah Divisions, with 10th

A Bell 214A of the IRIAA disembarking commandos of the 23rd Special Forces Brigade during a mission behind enemy lines in Hoveyzeh. (Tom Cooper collection)

A Bell 214A Esfahan of the IRIAA navigating low over the Hoveyzeh Marshes. Some Iranian assaults involved up to 40 such helicopters. (Tom Cooper collection)

Table 10: IRIA/IRGC, Southern Forward Operations HQ (Karbala HQ), February 1984		
Corps	Division & HQ	Brigades & Notes
	Direct Combat Support Group (IRIAA)	2 attack battalions (AH-1Js), 3 assault battalions (Bell 214As), 2 reconnaissance battalions (Bell 206), 2 transport battalions (CH-47C)
Task Force Najaf		23rd SF Brigade (1st Battalion only)
		55th Airborne Brigade (1 battalion only)
Task Force Nasr	5th Nasr Infantry Division (IRGC)	
		15th Imam Hassan Infantry Brigade (IRGC)
Task Force Hadid		21st Imam Reza Infantry Brigade (IRGC)
		44th Qamar Bani Hashem Infantry Brigade (IRGC)
Task Force Honain	27th Mohammad Rasoolallah Infantry Division (IRGC)	including 18th al-Ghadir and 33rd al-Mahdi Infantry Brigades
Task Force Badr	17th Ali Ibn Abu Talib Infantry Division (IRGC)	
	41st Sarallah Infantry Division (IRGC)	
		10th Seyed ol-Shohada Infantry Brigade (IRGC)
Task Force Fath	8th Najaf Ashraf Infantry Division (IRGC)	
	19th Fajr Infantry Division (IRGC)	
	31st Ashura Infantry Division (IRGC)	
Task Force Zeid	16th Armoured Division	1 brigade only
	92nd Armoured Division	1 brigade only
	21st Infantry Division (IRIA)	1 brigade only
	28th Infantry Division (IRIA)	1 brigade only
	77th Infantry Division (IRIA)	1 brigade only
		20th Ramadan Armoured Brigade (IRGC)
		72nd Moharram Armoured Brigade (IRGC)
	7th Valli Assr Infantry Division (IRGC)	
	14th Imam Hussein Infantry Division (IRGC)	
		28th Zafar Infantry Brigade (IRGC)

Seyed ol-Shohada Brigade (19,000 men). They were to first take South Majnoon, then push past Qurnah to take Nashwah. Once the Majnoons were taken then the IRIA 1st Area Support Command would establish a reliable supply route eastwards to their main supply base of Talaiyeh (also Taialyeh).

When these forces were in place two more task forces would drive some 60 kilometres westwards to Nashwah under separate commands; Najaf and the Army's Karbala Command. Najaf's Task Force Fath, with 21,000 men, was to strike from Talaiyeh towards Nashwah with 8th Najaf Ashraf, 19th Fajr and 31st Ashura Divisions, but it needed the expertise of the IRIA's Task Force Zeid with 31,000 men and some 250 MBTs to punch a hole through the northern defensive belt to reach Nashwah. Supported by the 33rd and 55th Artillery Groups, it was based upon a brigade each of the 16th and 92nd IRIA Armoured Divisions, and the 21st, 28th and 77th Infantry Divisions reinforced by the Pasdaran's 20th Ramadan and 72nd Moharram Armoured Brigades, the 7th Vali Asr and 14th Imam Hossein Divisions as well as the 28th Zafar Brigade. The IRIA had a secondary role in this offensive, but it continued to provide considerable expertise in planning and logistics as well as providing artillery and engineering support. Much of the 1st Area Support Command was assembled, with bulldozers ready to push roads from Talaiyeh into the marshes and augment these roads with pontoon and other bridging equipment, while light pontoon bridges were made from Korean-supplied Styrofoam floats with planking laid down on them to augment bunds and help move infantry and light supplies through the wetlands. The IRIAA would provide some 130 aircraft under the personal command of Lieutenant Colonel Mohamad-Hossein Jajali, who would fly the first night mission of the offensive. Forward resupply points were established so the IRIAA could bring ammunition to the task forces moving through the marshes with a dozen helicopters, half of them large Chinook transports each capable of carrying 33 men or 8.5 tonnes of cargo, assigned to Task Force Badr.[13]

The Islamic Republic of Iran Navy (IRIN) would also play an important role and established a command to support the seizure of the Majnoon Islands. This included the Hovercraft Brigade whose six BH-7 could each move 60 men or 18 tonnes and a base with some 500 boats and barges which varied 'from large aluminium ones, capable of carrying up to 100 men, to small craft with outboard motors, able only to take half-a-dozen or so'. There were also barges capable of carrying APCs and the watercraft would also be used to evacuate the wounded.[14]

PART I: BATTLES IN THE MARSHES

Table 11: III and IV Corps Iraqi Army, February 1984		
Corps	Division	Brigades & Notes
III Corps	Corps Troops	8th Border Brigade; 33rd SF Brigade; 65th Commando Brigade; III Corps Artillery Brigade (10 artillery and 5 MLRS batteries)
	4th Mountain Division	5th Mountain Brigade; 18th and 29th Infantry Brigades
	5th Mechanised Division	26th and 55th Armoured Brigades; 15th and 20th Mechanised Brigades; 19th and 419th Infantry Brigades
	8th Infantry Division	22nd, 23rd, 28th, 425th Infantry Brigades
IV Corps	Corps Troops	66th and 68th Commando Brigades; IV Corps Artillery Brigade
	10th Armoured Division	17th and 42nd Armoured Brigades; 24th Mechanised Brigade
	14th Infantry Division	18th and 422nd Infantry Brigades
	19th Infantry Division	108th, 113th, 419th Infantry Brigades
Reserve Forces	3rd Armoured Division	6th and 12th Armoured Brigades; 8th Mechanised Brigade
	6th Armoured Division	16th, 30th and 56th Armoured Brigades; 25th Mechanised Brigade

Unlike Operation Ramadan Mubarak, the operation would be fought in relatively cooler times, the temperature averaging 68–76°F (20–24°C) and there was certainly no threat from heat exhaustion or dehydration. There was, however, extensive reconnaissance by the IRIAF, Iranian Special Forces from 23rd Brigade and Pasdaran scouting units, aided by Marsh Arab sympathisers, some of them members of Hakim's Badr Brigades. These helped to identify weak points in the defence and the fact that much of it was in the hands of the Popular Army, the Ba'ath Party militia.

Iraqi Preparations

In early February the Iraqis reviewed contingency plans to meet anticipated threats. Within each corps sector at least three infantry or special forces (Alwiyat al-Quwat al-Khassah)/commando (Alwiyat al-Maqhaweer) brigades were allocated a reaction role, together with armoured/mechanised divisions. The IV Corps (Major General Thabit Sultan) defending Maysan Province in the north and III Corps defending Basra Province in the south were no exceptions. Both corps were under new commanders; Sultan had relieved Major General Husham Sabbah al-Fakhri at the beginning of the year when Fakhri became Deputy Chief-of-Staff for Operations. In January 1984 Lieutenant General Maher Abdul Rashid assumed command of III Corps after previously leading I Corps and 5th Mechanised Division. He came from Tikrit, was a relative of Saddam, and his daughter would later marry Uday Hussein. While generally regarded as a competent commander he was foul-mouthed and regarded as 'a very nasty person.'[15]

The Iranian offensive would strike along the corps' mutual boundary at a time when Sultan and Rashid were focused upon threats from the east to Amarah and Basra respectively and their forces were spread thinly to cover the 150 kilometres between them. Sultan had 14th Infantry Division on his right with 18th and 422nd Infantry Brigades holding the sector from Uzayr northwards but was deployed to cover the Baghdad–Basra highway with some 6,000 men. To screen the marshes, where there seemed only a minor threat from raiders and infiltrators supporting Shia insurgents, the Iraqis deployed 8th Border Guard Brigade and some sailors. As early as May 1981 the Iraqis had considered draining the marshes and planned a 12-metre-wide levee some 3.5 metres above the water linked to similar levees built around Basra, but the plan

An Iranian M47M drives over the Kheiber Bridge to North Majnoon Islet. Note the few branches placed on each pontoon in the vain attempt to camouflage them from air attacks: they were certainly more effective in concealing this huge construction from views from the ground. (Tom Cooper collection)

three battalions, probably augmented by Border Guards, who were responsible for the security of the Majnoon Islands, and some naval personnel operating patrol boats; and these brought the number of III Corps defenders to about 15,000 men.[17]

The bulk of III Corps remained in, or behind, the Fish Lake defences which had been substantially expanded since Operation Ramadan had demonstrated the futility of trying to make the frontier the main line of resistance (MLR), and on 16 February the importance of the new defences was again stressed. The angle of battalion strongpoints covering the north-eastern approaches to the Fish Lake had been strengthened to provide both security and greater economy of forces. Holding these defences were the 4th Mountain Infantry Division in the north and 8th Infantry Division and the 5th Mechanised Division in the east. In reserve were 3rd and 6th Armoured Divisions, 33rd Special Forces and 65th Commando Brigades, and they would be supported by III Corps artillery with 10 tube batteries and five MLRS batteries; a grand total of some 90,000 men with 675 MBTs. In addition, Basra Command had 95th Infantry Brigade which could also be deployed. While COMINT alerted the Iraqi leadership that something was

A rare photograph of an Iranian M48A5 from the 16th Armoured Division. A mechanised brigade from this unit was deployed on the southern edge of the marshes for Operation Kheiber. (Tom Cooper collection)

Medical personnel scrambling to evacuate casualties and orderlies from an IRIAF CH-47C (serial 5-4075), deployed in support of ground forces during Operation Kheiber. (Tom Cooper collection)

was never implemented. Border Guards and boat-operating sailors occupied a few marsh-side villages from which boat patrols were despatched, but most of its 1,500 men held a line of fortified police stations along the main route down the eastern bank of the Tigris. To deal with any serious incursions Sultan had in reserve 10th Armoured Division (with 17th Armoured and 24th Mechanised Brigades) while 42nd Armoured Brigade was a permanent reaction force north of the marshes together with the newly formed 66th and 68th Commando Brigades; some 15,700 men with 300 MBTs.[16]

Rashid also kept his regulars out of the marshes whose south-western corner was covered by 19th Infantry Division (108th, 113th, 419th Infantry Brigades) which screened Qurnah. The apparent lack of threat meant the Iraqis made no attempt to fortify this line, but rather relied upon a screen of forward posts which patrolled the marsh edges while the bulk of the division was held back as a reaction force. Within the marshes was a Popular Army sector of

happening around the marshes most probably agreed with the III Corps Chief-of-Staff General Makki, that 'it never crossed my mind that they would cross in that area'. For the Iraqis the Pasdarans' flexible chain of command and logistics arrangements continued to make it difficult for them to determine the enemy plan and later they would begin to conclude, wrongly, there were no chains of command among the militias.[18]

Khyber Begins
The offensive began on 14 February with Task Force Zeid staging a week-long series of diversionary attacks just across the border north-east of Khorramshahr. Sometimes supported by helicopters, these diversions, together with raids and bombardments, were designed to confuse the Iraqi leadership as to the main axes of the offensive and appear to have succeeded.

PART I: BATTLES IN THE MARSHES

The 106mm M40 recoilless gun was another primary means of providing direct fire support to Iranian troops advancing through the Hoveyzeh Marshes. The gunners on the left of this pair have just fired, and a typical trace of smoke drifts away. (Tom Cooper collection)

M151 MUTT jeeps and different variants of Toyota 4WDs mounting TOW ATGMs proved potent direct fire systems, somewhat balancing Iraqi advantages in armour. Although unarmoured, they were capable of facing even the best-protected Iraqi MBTs, primarily because they could target these from stand-off ranges. (Tom Cooper collection)

Following the codewords 'Ya Rasulollah' the first phase of Khyber began on the evening of 22 to 23 February as Task Force Nasr began moving across the marshes for a sub-offensive, reportedly called 'Fatima al-Zahra'. Its two brigades moved along the bunds, sometimes using motorcycles or by boat along the channels, while heliborne commandos struck enemy artillery positions. One bund ran to Beida, at the tip of a sandy peninsula with Sakhra (Sabkha or Sakhrah) some 1.5 kilometres to the south, and then Ajairda (Ajrada or Agirda) where there was a bridge across the Tigris, which was to be seized to provide a bridgehead near the Baghdad–Basra highway.[19]

The spearhead arrived at Beida during the night by boat and seized the undefended village, then began moving westwards to take Sakhra. Inevitably, the attack lost momentum because the boats which had brought in the assault force had to return to pick up reinforcements and supplies, but by dawn the spearhead was close to the river and had taken Ajairda to establish a small bridgehead. Although surprised by the strength of the attack, Sultan reacted quickly and despite the loss of some batteries he was able to bring down heavy artillery fire upon the bridgehead, although many shells exploded into the marshes which absorbed much of the blast and fragments. The Pasdaran used camouflage to blend in with the terrain, but while successful against high performance combat aircraft it was of little use against helicopters, especially the Hinds.

The Border Guards reportedly fought as well as the Army's troops although this was claimed to be '...with bravery born of despair...'[20] Meanwhile helicopters brought in IRIA airborne troops and reinforcements to key areas allowing them to seal the end of the peninsula. Meanwhile, Iraqi air power interdicted the waterways, flying 94 fixed-wing and 135 rotary-wing sorties during the day, to restrict the flow of men and materials, especially anti-armour weapons, to the bridgehead. This had little effect and the absence of Iraqi Forward Air Controllers (FAC) meant there was little Close Air Support (CAS) but the IRIAF – restricted to no more than 100

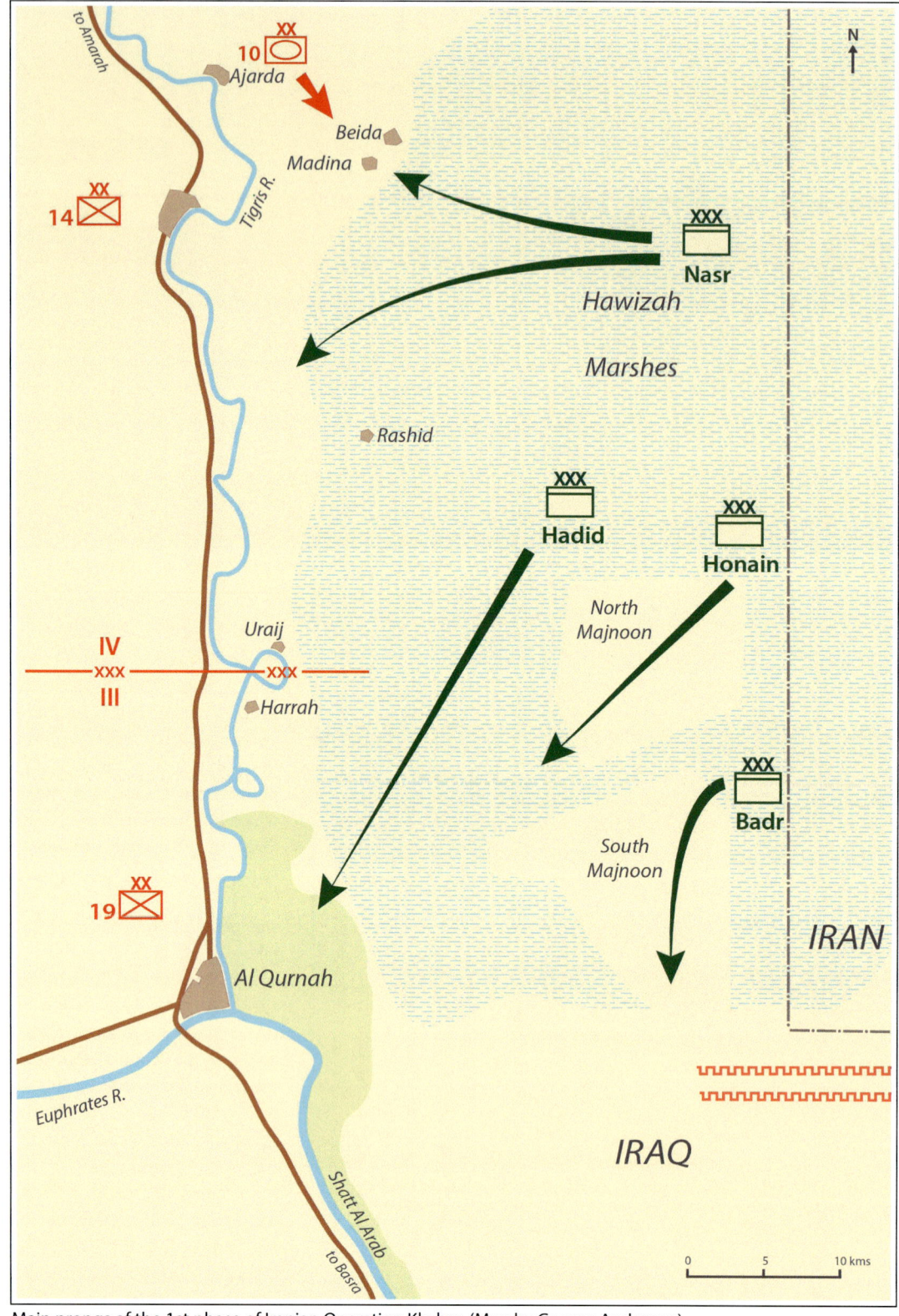

Main prongs of the 1st phase of Iranian Operation Khyber. (Map by George Anderson)

and Uzayr, until the arrival of 10th Armoured Division's 24th Mechanised Brigade, which Sultan swiftly brought south, while its 17th Armoured Brigade swept down the eastern bank of the Tigris – together with 68th Commando Brigade – on a rainy 25 February. The threat along the weak boundary of both corps led Saddam to authorise the creation on 26 February of a new command, East of Tigris Operations Headquarters (ETOH) under Fakhri, who was familiar with the sector and who established his headquarters at Uzayr within seven hours. In addition to 10th Armoured Division he was assigned Sultan's 14th Infantry Division and 18th Infantry Division (95th, 702nd, and 704th Infantry Brigades) while the newly formed 66th Commando Brigade was flown to Uzayr from its training camp, as Fakhri was ordered to end minor operations and prepare for a set-piece counteroffensive.[21]

On 27 February Fakhri launched his counteroffensive, Operation al-Wajib al-Muqaddas (Holy or Sacred Mission) under 10th Armoured Division command, towards Beida. A direct attack was launched by 24th Mechanised and 66th Commando Brigades from Uzayr, while 17th Armoured Brigade with 68th Commando Brigade made a flank attack towards Sakhra. It was heralded in the early hours by a spectacular success for the IrAF whose fighters detected and attacked 50 helicopters carrying a battalion to the Majnoons and claimed eight of them.[22]

sorties by the need to conserve its remaining assets – attempted to interdict IV Corps' convoys driving south. A few sorties temporarily disrupted Sultan's efforts to support his neighbour, but bad weather meant most were ineffective.

But the attackers were in a trap of their own making, scattered along an exposed sandbank and unable to dig deep due to the high water table. Elsewhere along the bank the Pasdaran continued to probe and push, sometimes mortaring the highway. Popular Army units were hastily mobilised to secure the Baghdad–Basra highway

With strong air support – the Iraqis flew 247 fixed-wing and 203 rotary-wing sorties that day – the Iraqi AFVs drove down the narrow bunds, braving RPG fire to crush the infantry in their foxholes, with Sakhra falling on the first day and Beida on 28 February. Yet this was no walkover, and Sultan would later describe the fighting as some of the fiercest he had encountered, with much hand-to-hand fighting. The Pasdaran broke and fled into the marsh, where many were drowned and some electrocuted because Fakhri had placed electrodes in some channels. Helicopters claimed others, as well as

PART I: BATTLES IN THE MARSHES

39 boats, and later 3,000 Iranian dead were buried in a bulldozed mass grave. Fakhri continued sweeping along the east bank of the Tigris from 29 February towards Ajairda with 17th Armoured Brigade with 68th Commando Brigade advanced south while 24th Mechanised Brigade and 66th Commando Brigade moved north from Uzayr to retake Ajairda with strong artillery and helicopter support, then pushed the enemy into the marsh.

A feature of this operation was the first major use of poison gas by the Iraqis – apparently mustard gas – largely against communications, although Fakhri denied their use on 5 March. The Iranians reported 400 chemical casualties by 28 February from agents delivered two days earlier, a figure which soon expanded to 1,100, and there would be other reports of mustard gas being used on 2 and 3, 7, and 9 March, which reportedly caused a total of 6,200 casualties including 1,200 dead. It was especially demoralising to the Pasdaran, who lacked any protection, and as one observed: 'Martyrdom is one thing. Martyrdom with extremities blistered by mustard gas or paralysed by nerve agents is another'.[23]

A more serious threat to the Iraqis emerged in the south where the Majnoon Islands were assaulted, during the early hours of 23 February. At North Majnoon, Jajali led a heliborne assault by elements of 55th Brigade which established a bridgehead. Task Force Honain then expanded this using Pasdaran brought in by boat despite a surprisingly determined defence by the Popular Army defenders. Task Force Badr also faced a strong defence as it staged an amphibious assault upon South Majnoon, but here, as in North Majnoon, the defenders were eventually overwhelmed by the end of 24 February to allow the Pasdaran to begin fighting their way south, and take 20 BTR APCs in the process. Meanwhile Task Force Hadid successfully pushed through the marshes to enter the farmland north-east of Qurnah.[24]

Simultaneously, the Iranians frantically improved communications with the Iranian 'mainland', first using Styrofoam

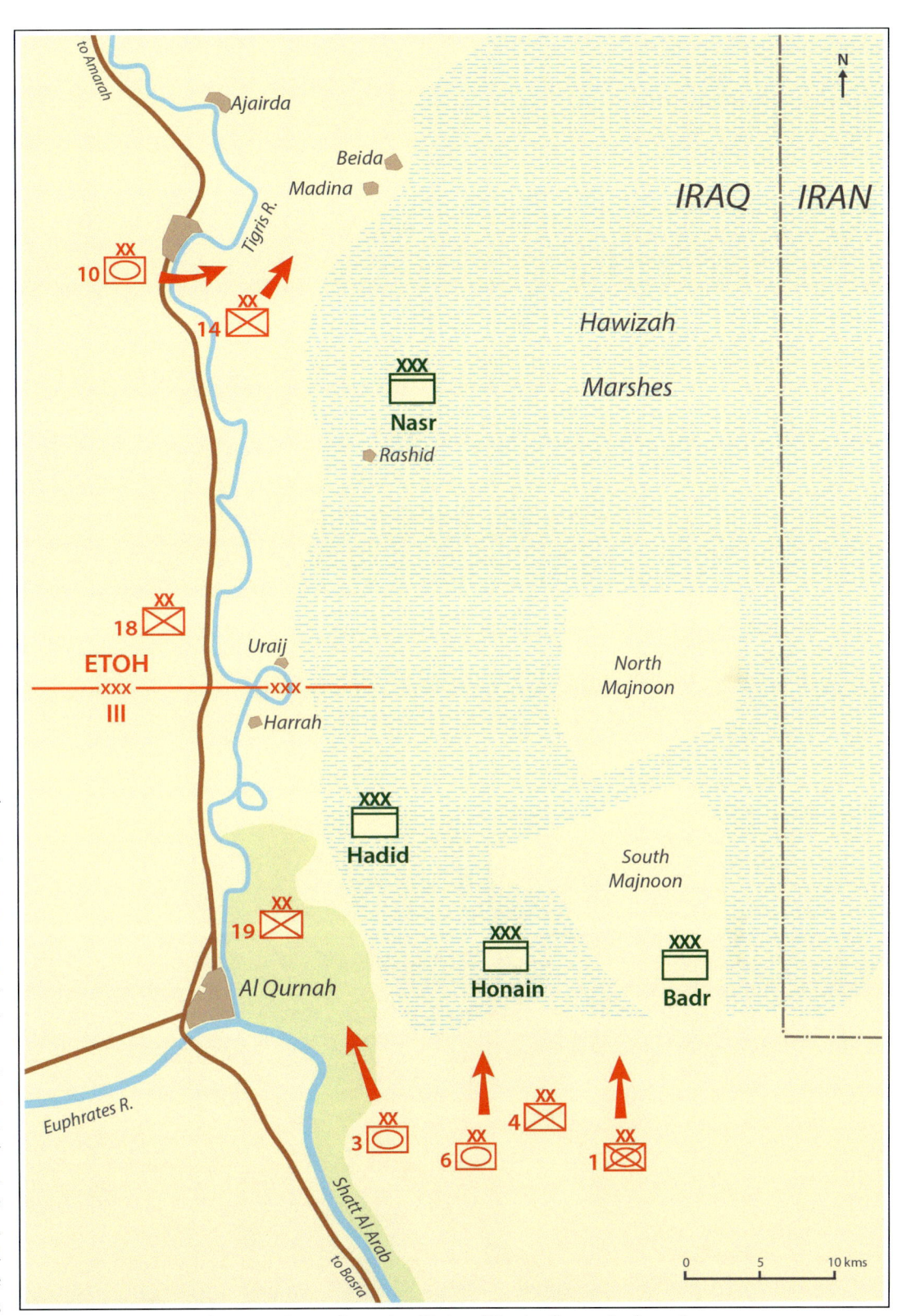

Major Iraqi counterattacks in reaction to Operation Khyber. (Map by George Anderson)

floats to create a 30-kilometre-long supply route to support these two task forces and Task Force Hadid. The IRIA engineers with their bulldozers were joined by Pasdaran engineers, and the men of two Pasdaran divisions, to create a causeway to the main supply base at Talaiyeh. This was extended into North Majnoon by the 15-kilometre 'Khyber (pontoon) Bridge', created from pressurised Styrofoam floatation sections and light metal plates'.[25]

To shield this work, Task Force Fath struck south-west towards the Ghuzail on 23 to 24 February to hit the defensive line from the north, while the IRIA's Task Force Zeid sent its two Pasdaran divisions against the eastern defences which they managed to penetrate. Three days of fierce fighting followed and the Pasdaran tried to bring up their armour, but on 26 February the 6th Armoured Division with 65th Commando Brigade counterattacked and drove them back. The Pasdaran renewed their attack on the night from 27 to 28 February and again fought their way through the defences in several places only to be driven back once more by 1 March. The Iraqi success made work on the land-route to North Majnoon hazardous, although it continued under enemy fire, and owed much to a combination of armour and overwhelming artillery fire while both sides' aircraft were extremely active over this sector, the Iraqis claiming 34 AFVs on 24 February alone.

The Iraqi success made work on bridging the route to North Majnoon extremely hazardous and until the route was complete it was impossible to advance upon the Nashwah Bridge. To maintain the initiative the IRIAA deployed more than 100 helicopters, mostly Bell 214/Agusta Bell 205s augmented by six CH-47Cs and even a few Sikorsky S-61s and the hovercraft of the Islamic Republic of Iran Navy (IRIN), to bring some 2,000 troops onto the Majnoons on 25 February. The IrAAC hit back by using Hinds to interdict the dozens of small craft in the channels while transport helicopters inserted special forces detachments to harass the attackers. The Pasdaran reacted by deploying teams with SA-7 MANPADS, while Oerlikon twin 35mms and Soviet twin 23 mm guns were installed on firm ground on the banks of the marshes and during the day they claimed eight helicopters. Iranian Cobra gunships meanwhile ranged deep into enemy territory hunting dug-in AFVs with some success.[26]

The reinforcements brought the total of troops around the Majnoons to some 55,000 drawn from eight brigades, as the Iranians tried to exploit their success. To the west Hadid was quickly contained

Most Iraqi positions in the Hoveyzeh Marshes looked like this: sand-bagged, or even concrete, machine gun nests. One such reinforced position was usually constructed at each corner of the Iraqi triangular strongpoints, surrounded by 3-metre-high berms. (Albert Grandolini collection)

Heavily camouflaged Iraqi troops in position on the western banks of the Hoveyzeh Marshes. The soldier in the foreground is armed with an RPG-7. (Albert Grandolini collection)

by 19th Division, so that 3rd Armoured Division brought up only 6th Armoured and 418th Infantry Brigades to drive the Pasdaran back into the swamp by 25 February. Attempts by Honain and Badr to push south of the marshes were contained within the Ghuzail the following day by 8th Infantry Division and 4th Mountain Division exploiting the sanctuary of the northern defensive belt. On the night from 27 to 28 February the 4th Division was attacked again by three Pasdaran divisions with armour and heavy artillery support. They pushed a salient into the division's front line but on 1 March the

PART I: BATTLES IN THE MARSHES

An Iraqi ZPU-4 14.5mm KVP heavy machine gun, positioned to protect the road along the Tigris River. Each ZPU-4 had a 40-round ammunition container and could fire 600 rounds a minute to a range of 3,000 metres. (Albert Grandolini collection)

6th Armoured Division again pushed them back. At the same time there was a new attack upon 8th Infantry Division and its southern neighbour, 5th Mechanised Division, but this too was stopped with heavy artillery support.

Work on the 'Khyber Bridge' was completed on 29 February and the Iranians built platforms with anti-aircraft guns in the marshes, while to the east a battery of HAWK (MIM-23B) medium-range surface-to-air missiles was deployed to support IRIAF Grumman F-14 Tomcat interceptors. Political pressure was growing on the frontline commanders and Rafsanjani told the Pasdaran 'we should finish the job right here because sustaining this situation is becoming unbearable'.[27]

As Iranian supplies rolled westward they enabled a division each from Honain and Badr to reinforce Hadid and together, on 1 March, they struck southwards after overrunning a battalion of 19th Division. Their progress towards the outskirts of Qurnah was aided by the fact that Iraqi leaders were reluctant to communicate bad news, indeed the 6th Armoured Division's commander claimed the situation was 'stable' even as his front was split; he had to abandon a number of MBTs which could not be withdrawn. This allowed the Iranians to advance far enough by the end of the day that their shells and even mortar bombs were falling on the outskirts of Qurnah, leading Baghdad to fear it might fall. To prevent this, General Makki, unable to contact Rashid, on his own initiative ordered 6th Armoured Division to send part of its reconnaissance battalion and a battalion of 25th Mechanised Brigade to secure the city. Simultaneously the remaining task forces facing III Corps renewed pressure upon the Iraqi line. As he became aware of the threat, Rashid committed 3rd Armoured Division's 6th Armoured Brigade and hastily despatched reinforcements from 6th Armoured Division and 1st Mechanised Division, together with 701st Infantry Brigade, while the IrAAC's 3rd Wing was ordered to concentrate upon this threat; with the latter flying 252 sorties that day, and the IrAF another 193, the IRIAF – which flew only 20 combat air patrols behind the lines to intercept enemy strike aircraft – was hopelessly overwhelmed. Meanwhile, the Pasdaran advance took them literally into the cannon's mouth for there were numerous battery positions and armoured vehicle laagers organised for all-round defence. But the attackers made little attempt to coordinate operations, indeed most of the orders were extremely vague.[28]

Too many Pasdaran batteries were supporting the infantry with direct fire operations, and few tried to isolate the battlefield, due to shortages of weapons, ammunition and 'intelligence gathering systems.' The Pasdaran lacked armour and soft-skinned vehicles, which meant progress on foot across the open desert was painfully slow and exposed to enemy air attack, the Iraqis flying 212 fixed-wing and 170 rotary-wing sorties this day. The IrAF deployed Dassault Mirage F.1EQs with Saudi-provided 500kg (1,000lbs) bombs fitted with South African Jupiter fuses. According to both sides' accounts this combination proved highly effective against Iranian infantry in the open. Anticipating the problem, Najaf sent bulldozers behind the advancing infantry with orders to consolidate the day's gains by building berms. But by the end of the day they were in a salient exposed to fire from three sides as Iraqi aircraft picked off their supporting tanks and ZSU-23-4 self-propelled anti-aircraft guns.[29]

Hadid's commanders had hoped the enemy would be under pressure from the east, for as Badr moved out the northern defensive belt was struck by Task Forces Fath and Zeid, spearheaded by the Mohammad Rasoolallah and Imam Hussain Divisions respectively, while the 92nd Armoured Division tried to push through the defensive belt. The sheer scale of the assault – some 35,000 troops – surprised the defenders of the 19th Infantry and 8th Infantry Divisions, but their fortifications held this assault. The only Iranian success was a drive by their armour into the flank of the 5th Mechanised Division, which – reportedly – 'inflicted heavy losses', before running out of ammunition and withdrawing for resupply. In turn, the Imam Hussain Division took such heavy losses that it was stopped dead, leaving Task Force Fath to carry the burden, just as Iraqi air power struck its base at Talaiyeh inflicting damage and casualties.

At dawn on 2 March the Iraqis launched a set-piece armour-led counter-offensive, using mustard gas (and possibly Sarin nerve gas), and supported by 140 helicopter sorties, to relieve the pressure on Qurnah, which drove Pasdaran back into the marshes during the morning. However, Rashid's mechanised superiority was neutralised by the terrain which allowed the Iranians to retained control of the bunds and patches of dry ground, including the Majnoons, although he did establish a bridgehead on south-western corner of South Majnoon. In the recriminations following this disaster, the Pasdaran blamed the Army for inadequate support of the attack in the Ghuzail area as replacements, 1,500 from Tehran alone, flooded south.

Saddam Closes the Battle

The Iraqis now sought to regain the Majnoons but had to pause to reorganise their forces. They also flooded part of the marshes, together with some salt-flats, but the Iranians anticipated this and assembled light pontoon bridges to augment their floating bridges and bring in reinforcements. They would use the bridges, boats in the channels and even motorcycles on the bunds to conduct a mobile, aggressive, infantry-based defence, although they had to disperse their forces to avoid Iraqi artillery fire.

Rashid's offensive, spearheaded by 6th Armoured Division, began on 6 March supported by armour and helicopters, the latter flying 390 sorties on the first two days, and interdicting the channels and claiming 20 boats. The defenders consisted of a brigade of 28th IRIA Infantry Division with a Pasdaran brigade, and the marshes restricted the Iraqi advance to narrow causeways where it was vulnerable to enemy anti-armour weapons, yet the Iranians were unable to exploit this advantage.

By 12 March, the Iraqis had succeeded in establishing a bridgehead in the south-eastern corner of Southern Majnoon to secure the easiest westwards approach Baghdad-Basra highway. At this point, Saddam decided to close down the battle, less out of concern for casualties and more from the recognition he lacked sufficiently trained, and self-confident, infantry for the task. He and Rashid also recognised that the bridgehead was extremely exposed and had to be heavily fortified, but the routes into it were exposed to raids by parties of infiltrating Pasdaran. In an effort to secure their communications, a variety of sensors were deployed together with night sights and even searchlights, while electrical cables were run into the water to deter raiders. There was the usual post-offensive squabbling in which the commander of Task Force Faths' Mohammad Rasoolallah Division, Haj Mohammad Ebrahim Hemnat and his deputy Akbar Zojaji, were mortally wounded on 15 March 1984.

During the rest of the month the Iranians maintained pressure upon the sector and even brought in the 92nd Armoured Division at Ghuzail, but this had no more success than the IRGC. The Iranians consolidated their position on the Majnoon Islands and prepared to launch another offensive to take Qurnah. By April 300,000 men had been assembled but, heavy air strikes and artillery bombardments 'destroyed the combat effectiveness and crushed the morale' of these, especially in South Majnoon.[30]

Pasdaran units left the island without permission while IRIA units had to be replaced three times. The final straw came from late March when the Iraqis diverted the flood waters from the Tigris into the western and southern edges of the marshes. Iranian engineers used sandbags, metal plates, gabions (baskets of stones and earth) and riprap (a loose assemblage of broken stones erected in water or soft ground as a foundation) and dug drainage canals leading into the Karun River. But from 5 April up to half of South Majnoon was flooded, partly due to the failure of a levee on its southwest edge of the island, forcing the Iranians to remove their armour and artillery and giving the Iraqis control of some 20 percent of the dry land.[31]

So ended the confusing Operation Khyber – also called 'The Second Battle East of Basra' by the Iraqis – which crippled the Iranians and prevented them from staging any significant offensives for the rest of the year. Khyber played to the strengths of the Pasdaran, their ability to traverse terrain regarded as 'impassable' to most armies and then to infiltrate and to storm defences. However, and although Iranian planning showed continued improvement, little thought was given to exploiting the initial successes and, more importantly, countering the enemy's tank-tipped response. They had tried to overcome firepower by guile and numerical superiority but failed despite sound planning by the IRIA.

The Iraqis commented: 'While the Iranians often scored impressive initial gains, they tended to bunch indecisively once they reached their first objective and they advanced into the killing zones established by Iraq's fixed defence positions and supporting artillery. Thousands of Iranians died pointlessly in this fashion between the first Iranian offensive in mid-February and the end of March.'[32] Predictably the Pasdaran and their political allies in Tehran blamed the IRIA for the failure which they stated was due to the failure to storm the Fish Lake defences.

The Iraqis had recovered rapidly from their surprise, made a rapid appreciation of the situation, reacted quickly and concentrated their forces and firepower on the key areas. After the operation the Iraqis extended their defences, created artificial lakes, flooded the area on both sides of the southern section of the border and dug water tunnels under the Baghdad-Basra highway and the eastern road embankment to exploit the waters of the Tigris for emergency flooding. Yet the nerves of the Iraqi High Command were very raw and that they grew panicky, leading to the use of mustard gas and possibly the nerve agent Tabun on a wider scale; twice against the major supply bases and twice to overcome persistent defence in the Majnoons. The fact that the Iranians were moving slowly on foot made the use of mustard gas especially effective for it is a persistent poison.

This battered Iraqi Type-69 was deployed in support of the III Corps' counterattack from the south – before it was captured by Pasdaran and turned against its former owners. (Tom Cooper collection)

PART I: BATTLES IN THE MARSHES

Loaded with ammunition boxes and food on the rear deck, this BTR-50 was probably used to resupply forward-deployed Iraqi troops. Note the observation tower in the background: because the Hoveyzeh Marshes are flat and devoid of any major features, any observation position represented an important piece of real estate. (Tom Cooper collection)

Operation Kheiber cost the Iranians up to 60,000 casualties. Here, a line of Pasdaran captured by troops of the Iraqi III Corps are paraded for the cameras, their hands tied. (Albert Grandolini collection)

The experience gained by the Iraqi Army was to be distributed rapidly and General Makki was appointed head of the Combat Development Directorate (Muderiat at-Tatweer al-Kitali) which had been established 10 years earlier and was responsible for all military publications, and now had the opportunity to provide formations and the training organisation with the latest lessons. He was succeeded at III Corps by the Shia Major General Fawzi Hamid al-Ali who would defect after the war when sent on a defence course to India. To the north the ETOH was strengthened by creating 35th Infantry Division from some task forces which became brigades.

The Americans estimated that 7,000 Iraqis and 20,000 Iranians died during Khyber. 'Lessons' estimated total Iraqi casualties at 16,000-18,000, including 6,000 dead and 1,140 prisoners, and Iranian casualties at 46,000-56,000 (including 20,000 Pasdaran killed and 20-30,000 wounded). Other sources suggested 40,000 Iranian casualties (15,000 in the first phase) to 9,000 Iraqi, while Ward suggested the IRIA suffered 6,000 dead and the Pasdaran formations 'at least twice that or even 20,000'. Once again it demonstrated a lesson which Tehran was reluctant to learn, that the Iraqis always held the upper hand against the poorly delivered Iranian attacks and eventually the Iranians lost thousands, in exchange for relatively worthless land. It also demonstrated the strategic dilemma facing both sides and the way the war was shaping. Iran had the manpower, but not the material, to support it, while Iraq had the material but lacked manpower which could be used more efficiently through the use of fortifications.

Khyber brought total Iranian casualties after four years to 510,000, including 170,000 dead, while Iraq had suffered 230,000, including 80,000 dead.[33] It provoked new discussions within the SDC and the government on the way forward, and whether or not the Pasdaran should continue major offensives relying on numerical superiority, or should it be used more efficiently in a war of attrition.[34] Rezai still believed the fervour of his men would carry them through and as late as 3 June 1986, he broadcasted: 'We do not need advanced aircraft and tanks for victory. Employment of infantry forces with light weapons, four times more than the number of Iraqi troops, will be enough for Iran to overcome the enemy.'

Nevertheless, the IRGC clearly needed reforms and immediately after Khyber held a seminar, Bonyan-e Marsus ('The Packed Wall'), which reviewed the logistical and manpower arrangements during Khyber. In an acrimonious debate it was decided to rationalise the administrative organisation, reducing the 11 existing regions to five regionally based directorates. This reform was introduced starting in September 1984. Command and control problems were also addressed, and in particular the structure of the brigades with Khyber demonstrating – as European armies discovered during the Great War – that smaller brigades were better. Correspondingly, during the year all IRGC's brigades were reduced from six to three or four battalions. This new organisation was to be subjected to its first test in the next offensive in the marshes.[35]

10
THE SLOUGH OF DESPOND

For nine months the Hawizah Marshes remained a relatively dormant front with the occasional clash between patrols, raids, exchanges of artillery or mortar fire, and helicopter sweeps. However, the Iraqi situation on the Majnoon bridgehead remained precarious and after nine months Saddam attempted to improve it.

The Iraqi Army had now opted for an active defence policy which included limited offensives to improve its positions, aided by a massive arms-spending spree, much of which was funded by oil-rich Gulf States and Saudi Arabia. Fears of an enemy offensive north of the marshes around al-Amarah in the first two months of 1985 saw six such operations, including one in Rashid's III Corps area to regain South Majnoon defended by 3rd Brigade/28th Division, IRIA and Pasdaran companies.

The assault force, drawn from the 49th Infantry Brigade of the new 31st Infantry Division and 28th Brigade/8th Infantry Division – supported by the 65th Commando Brigade – was quietly assembled and a powerful artillery barrage was laid down during the early hours of 28 January 1985. With armoured support the Iraqis struck along the dry corridor between two flooded areas to pin down the defenders, while commandos in assault craft attacked from the flanks and together they recaptured several kilometres of South Majnoon and then held the administrative area in the west against counterattacks. However, the Iranians retained a bridgehead in South Majnoon, and artillery in North Majnoon constantly harassed the new re-conquered territory.

The Iranian response was surprisingly muted, but if Baghdad believed this was due to exhaustion it would soon discover the enemy were conserving their resources. In Tehran a bitter battle of words continued over strategy between the professionals, spearheaded by the IRIA, and the clerical amateurs, including the Pasdaran, who damned the IRIA for Khyber's' failure. Both recognised that Iran's continued numerical superiority in manpower meant it retained the initiative, but the IRIA was acutely aware of Iran's weakness in the arbiters of conventional warfare; armour, artillery and air power, and favoured limited offensives. The clericals, recognising the political kudos of success, dismissed these reservations in favour of a large-scale offensive, and eventually carried the day to forge a new strategy in which Iran would launch strikes which would stretch enemy resources to breaking point then seek a decisive operation.

Offensives were launched up and down the front, but the main blow was again being prepared in the Hawizah Marshes for, despite the appalling losses during Khyber, Rezai and his supporters in Tehran regarded that operation as a cup half full rather than one which was half empty. With the 'Khyber Bridge' still intact and their communications within the marshes steadily improved this boded well for a renewed offensive in the region which would be launched later. The plan was now to strike towards the end of the rainy season in March, when an average of 32mm of rain falls, but before April, when the average tends to fall away.

Both Sides Prepare
During the first months of the year, and shielded by the rains from enemy air power and artillery, a stream of boats built up men and supplies in the myriad of muddy islets where reed banks shielded them from terrestrial observation both visual and by battlefield surveillance radar, as well as from aircraft (although listening posts could detect their engines). The task was eased by the reluctance of

On the first day of Operation Badr, 11 March 1985, the Iranians infiltrated the defences and established bridgeheads on the firm ground west of the Hoveyzeh Marshes. Here an exhausted platoon of Pasdaran takes a welcome rest behind a berm. The radio operator with his distinctive aerial was an obvious target for the Iraqis. (Albert Grandolini collection)

PART I: THE SLOUGH OF DESPOND

News of the Iranian success on the first day travelled like wildfire among their troops. Here a returning boat crew passes on the glad tidings to boatloads of reinforcements sailing rapidly past the reed beds. (Albert Grandolini collection)

the Iraqi Popular Army, supported by Border Guards and the Navy, to patrol aggressively, indeed they were usually content to remain in their bases during the rain or make nominal patrols. By contrast, up to six months beforehand the Iranians aggressively patrolled by boat to push the Iraqis out of the marshes onto dry land. From September the Iranians began extensive engineering work in anticipation of an offensive, building roads and bases east of the marshes and within them flood control measures, as well as further strengthening their logistics by reinforcing the 'Khyber Bridge' route with a second 'stout causeway' to North Majnoon. The network was later expanded through the marshes both by IRIA engineers and the Pasdaran 46th 'Al-Hadi' Engineer Brigade, with pontoon bridges, causeways and narrow footbridges for resupply, and to support the planned offensive. This supported a strong Iranian military presence within the marshes even after Badr.[1]

Outline planning for the offensive began late in 1984 to produce a more ambitious version of Khyber, whose goals were to cut the Baghdad–Basra highway between Amarah and Qurnah, exploiting six bridges over the Tigris including three 60-tonne military bridges, and a fourth over the Euphrates on the outskirts of Qurnah. This would leave the Iranians ready to envelop Basra from the north and from the east, then storm the city. It was also aimed to secure the Majnoons for fear the enemy would use them as a springboard for a renewed attack across the border. These fears were fed by the Iraqi attack on 28 January which established a bridgehead within them. This operation appears to have acted as a catalyst to accelerate Iranian detailed planning, which was apparently completed by 20 February to become Operation Badr.[2]

The execution of the operation was assigned by the Khatam al-Anbiya Headquarters, which divided its total of 115,000 troops into two joint task forces; the IRGC's Najaf, commanded by Colonel Manouchehr Dejkam, and IRIA's Karbala, under Colonel Hossein Hassani-Sa'di. In the first phase the two task forces were to advance through the marshes to secure jump-off positions on the firm ground to the west, around Uzayr, and south. Najaf would then cross the Tigris to establish a bridgehead which would split the enemy

Boatloads of IRGC troops preparing to embark in the fleet of 'little boats', whose sole armament was this 14.5mm KVP machine gun, manned by an elderly, white-bearded Pasdaran. (Tom Cooper collection)

135

MIDDLE EAST@WAR SERIES SPECIAL #1: THE IRAN-IRAQ WAR

The Iranian 'small boat' flotilla did not just deliver men and supplies, but always returned with wounded or carrying Iraqi prisoners – like this group of unfortunates. Some 1,500 Iraqi soldiers were captured during Badr. (Albert Grandolini collection)

Worn out by intensive operations in the first two years of the war, and lacking replacement aircraft, the IRIAF was incapable of providing more than about 40 air strikes in close support for such offensives as Badr. A two-seat F-5F is shown leading a single-seat F-5E into an attack, at an altitude that was typical for Iranian pilots in the war. (Tom Cooper collection)

by cutting the Baghdad–Basra highway, while Karbala would secure the Tigris cultivated area northwest of Qurnah, then a Pasdaran division would cross the Tigris and establish a bridgehead five kilometres deep. In both taskforces the spearhead would consist of Pasdaran, but the need to sew spring crops meant the Basiji element was severely reduced.[3]

The Pasdaran had learned many of Khyber's lessons and for once their divisions and brigades would be only partly committed. Dejkam's Task Force Najaf had some eight brigades of 5th Nasr, 7th Vali Asr, 14th Imam Hussein, 21st Imam Reza, 25th Karbala Divisions (total of 27 infantry battalions), 15th Imam Hassan and 18th al-Ghadir Infantry Brigades (5 infantry battalions), together with the whole of 77th Infantry Division, IRIA (nine battalions). According to the Iranians, artillery support consisted of two gun-battalions and one MLRS battalion of the 22nd IRIA Artillery Group, one of the Pasdaran 40th Ressalat Artillery Brigade and two of Karbala Division. Nominally, this would have meant a total of 90 guns, but such accounts appear to ignore 77th Division's four battalions with another 70 tubes. Overall, Task Force Najaf included about 25,500 Pasdaran and 14,000 IRIA troops.

Hassani-Sa'di's Task Force Karbala had one of the largest concentrations of IRIA troops in the war including all of the 21st and 28th Infantry Divisions (18 infantry battalions), two brigades of 92nd Armoured Division, a brigade of 81st Armoured Division, the 55th Airborne Brigade (five battalions) and the 33rd Artillery Group with five gun-battalions and one MLRS battalion. These were reinforced by 10 brigades of 8th Najaf Ashraf, 17th Ali Ibn Abu Talib, 27th Mohammad Rasoolallah and 31st Ashura Divisions IRGC, the 44th Qamar Bani Hashem Infantry Brigade (four infantry battalions) and 72nd Moharram Armoured Brigade. Total strength was 51,000 IRIA and 26,000 Pasdaran supported by some 320 guns and about 100 MBTs. In addition, the operation received support from the IRIA's 1st Brigade/23rd Special Forces Division, 49 IRIAA helicopters (two AB 206 observation, 12 Cobra gunships, 27 Bell 214/AB 205 transport, eight CH-47 medium transport), and supplies through the 1st Area Support Command. Rezai's confidence was raised by the Pasdarans' preparations for the new offensive which would see them better equipped not only in infantry weapons but also in heavy weapons. To meet the obvious threat from enemy armour the attackers had not only numerous RPGs with a plentiful supply of rockets which, in the absence of anti-armour guided missiles, were augmented with many recoilless rifles; the US-made M40 and Chinese Type-75. Tehran had also addressed the chemical warfare problem and provided the Pasdaran with respirators/gas masks, chemical warfare suits as well as atropine injectors with nerve agent antidotes, and the more immediate threat of drowning was countered by providing each man with a life jacket. However, such was the rivalry with the IRIA that the Pasdaran refused to transfer surplus life jackets to the IRIA – which also complained about a shortage of trucks, although this was another perennial problem for the Iranians.[4]

While a communications infrastructure had been woven through the eastern end of the marshes and ensured some armour and artillery could be moved forward as well as helping the establishment of a fire base on North Majnoon, the planners recognised that projecting this westwards would be difficult. The IRIN could provide hovercraft, helicopters and 150 Gemini rigid inflatable boats, but Hassani-Sa'di recognised that moving his forces, and especially armour, across the marshes and then the Tigris required more, and he estimated that he needed 34 bridges including two more 10-kilometre prefabricated structures. The Iraqi bridges across the Tigris were well defended, so crossing the river would require boats, bridges and hovercraft and his inventory included 490 boats, including twenty 24-metre vessels, 22 BTR-50s and 150 bulldozers. Another major problem was the paucity of artillery ammunition, with sufficient for only 15 days and no more than 20 rounds per 105mm howitzer, 10–12 rounds for other 130mm, 155mm and 203mm weapons and 80 rockets per MLRS.[5]

PART I: THE SLOUGH OF DESPOND

As usual, the IRIAA provided much helicopter support for ground forces during Operation Badr. The IRIAF further reinforced this effort with the help of its own Bell 214As. (Tom Cooper collection)

As so often before and after Operation Badr, CH-47C Chinooks of the IRIAA provided heavy-lift support for forward deployed units, and also participated in CASEVAC and MEDEVAC operations. (via Tom Cooper)

The Iraqis had learned lessons from Khyber and had substantially strengthened their defences along the Tigris. They built high observation towers to look over the banks of reeds, which were cut back and burned nearer the firm ground west of the marshes. Here a line of bunkers was constructed, each surrounded by large barbed-wire entanglements and minefields which, on the marsh edge, extended into the water. Yet the terrain dictated that these defences were extremely shallow, with command posts and artillery all vulnerable to infiltration. A fortnight before the Iranian attack warnings, the defenders were alerted that it might be imminent and there was frantic work building a similar second line along the river's western bank, focusing upon potential crossing points on the river covered by artillery batteries. Anti-landing obstacles were installed at vulnerable sites such as Beida, which had been demolished the previous year, and the Iraqis could also flood large areas in and around the marshes. The blow would land upon the ETOH, now under Brigadier Mohammad Abdul Qadir, after Fakhri returned to Baghdad as Deputy Chief-of-Staff for Operations. Qadir was regarded as a brave and very efficient staff officer but had no close relationship with Saddam and whose relationship with the foul-mouthed III Corps commander, Rashid, was strained.[6] Its Tactical Area of Responsibility stretched from south of al-Amarah, along the marsh's western banks to the borders of Maysan and Basra Provinces on the 31st Parallel, with

The Iranians were also well aware that once the offensive began it would act like a starting gun with both sides racing to build up their forces. Najaf was estimated to be facing three brigades with 10 infantry, one tank and two artillery battalions, while Karbala faced 28 infantry/mechanised battalions (six on Majnoon), three tank battalions and seven artillery battalions (five on Majnoon). However, it was anticipated the enemy could rapidly relocate 21 brigades to face Karbala; 14 (with 55 infantry/mechanised and 14 tank battalions) within 10 hours, four (12 infantry battalions) to Qurnah and a total of 10 artillery battalions, while Najaf could face 14 manoeuvre (infantry and armour) and two artillery battalions. Afterward IRIA historians claimed they had never been optimistic about the prospects of winning this race.

137

While advancing southwards to the front line along one of the Styrofoam floating pathways during Badr, these Pasdaran took time for prayers. (Tom Cooper collection)

32nd and 35th Infantry Divisions, which were formed after Khyber had been contained, and Basra Defence Command under Brigadier Ihsan Kamel Shibib, which covered Qurnah, while 66th Commando Brigade was nearby but not under his command. Each consisted of a single infantry brigade and the equivalent of another in Popular Army units, Brigadier Major General Karim ad-Dabbagh's 35th Infantry Division (formed from Border Guards) which faced Task Force Najaf had only 429th Infantry Brigade augmented by naval coast defence forces equivalent to a brigade, five battalion-size Popular Army sectors and the battalion-strong Marshes Command Forces (Quiadet Quwat Al-Ahwar), a total of some 9,000 men and some 40 guns, and a tank battalion with some 40 MBTs. Shibib, who covered the marshes in Basra Province, had north to south, the 94th, 93rd and 703rd Infantry Brigades with only 18 artillery batteries and one MLRS battery, a total of some 12,000 men and 114 guns and MLRS, while his reaction force was the 66th Commando Brigade. His command did not include an artillery commander and when the Iranian attack began, Qadir assigned him an artillery liaison officer to help coordinate fire plans. Qadir's plan, worked out with the aid of Army Chief-of-Staff General Abd al-Jawad Thanun, was to give ground in the centre but hold the flanks, to contain the enemy on the fringes of the marshes and erode his strength with artillery and air power which would then support a counterattack. The plan was approved by Defence Minister Khairallah and, more importantly, by Saddam himself. Notably, no counterattack forces were assigned to Qadir, but in the north Major General Sabih Umran al-Tarfih's 10th Armoured Division (17th Armoured, 24th and 27th Mechanised Brigades), and the 68th Commando Brigade with some 15,000 troops and 170 MBTs were available. Furthermore, Rashid's III Corps had the usual complement, including the 3rd and 6th Armoured and 5th Mechanised Divisions in reserve – the last having finally been withdrawn from static defensive duties and replaced by the newly established 30th Infantry Division. Brigadier Abd al-Karim Mahmud al-Ithaw's 4th Mountain Infantry Division was on Rashid's left where its 5th Mountain Brigade and 18th Infantry Brigade would be committed to the battle.[7]

Although there had been signs and portents of an Iranian offensive, GMID failed to provide the defending leaders with adequate warning, demonstrating the old adage that it is easy to acquire data but more difficult to analyse it. IrAF reconnaissance monitored Iranian engineering work and by 9 February photographic interpreters reported this included three helicopter bases with 25 landing spots. By 21 February the GMID alerted Saddam to the fact that an offensive in the marshes was imminent and work began on strengthening the defences along the Tigris. But the Iranians succeeded in confusing GMID about the primary axes and the appearance of 77th Infantry Division headquarters and 55th Airborne Brigade together with three Pasdaran divisions (3rd 'Saheb al-Zaman', 14th 'Imam Hossein' and 19th 'Fajr') east of Basra led it to conclude on 23 February that the enemy aimed to strike the Fish Lake Line. The airborne brigade's location,

Making their first appearance on the battlefields of Operation Badr were the few T-72s operated by the IRGC. The tanks in question were all former mounts of the Iraqi 10th Armoured Brigade. They proved urgently needed, because counterattacks by Iraqi armour crushed the desperately secured Iranian bridgehead across the Tigris. (Tom Cooper collection)

PART I: THE SLOUGH OF DESPOND

A T-55 operated by the IRGC moving forward, ready for one of the usually deadly Iraqi counterattacks during Badr. (Tom Cooper collection)

soon followed by detection nearby of the IRIA special forces brigade, seemed to confirm this idea, yet GMID remained uncertain and to cover itself it issued a preliminary warning on 5 March to III and IV Corps together with EOTH. Four days later a new Pasdaran division was identified east of the marshes but the arrival of two brigades for 77th Division led the GMID, on 10 March, to confirm its conclusion that the Fish Lake was the primary objective. Later in the day the Nasr, Vali Asr and Karbala Divisions were observed near the marshes and several brigades were observed to join them.[8]

These were the spearheads of Task Force Najaf but, in a face-saving report on 25 March, the GMID would bewail the fact that Iraqi COMINT failed to provide its usual cornucopia of information in terms of instructions including code words. The report unwittingly underlines the failures of Iraqi intelligence which failed to detect the presence of the enemy task force headquarters, the assembly of boats and new bridging materials, or even a build-up of artillery on North Majnoon aided by the gradual withdrawal of 2nd Brigade from the 28th Division.[9]

The malign influence of these GMID assessments meant that Baghdad's operational direction initially responded to the threat from the marshes as a diversion, indeed the IrAF priority initially remained attacks upon Iranian cities.

Operation Badr Begins

On 11 March, amid a flurry of air raids and scattered artillery bombardments, Pasdaran headquarters issued the go-code which was 'Ya Fatimah al-Zahn' and the attack began that night at 2230 hrs. Security was paramount and when the battalions of Task Force Najaf moved into the marshes from the afternoon of 11 March, according to the Iraqi GMID, the rank and file were informed they were to strengthen the area's defences. Their pre-attack briefing occurred only as they received combat rations and the Pasdaran – according to the IRIA – did not inform their 'regular' colleagues that the offensive had begun until 12 March! There were three thrusts along a 10-kilometre-front between Uzayr and Qurnah using hundreds of small assault boats, fire support being provided by recoilless guns and mortars mounted on flat-bottomed boats or rafts. Heliborne forces from 55th Airborne Brigade and 23rd Special Forces Brigade were inserted on both banks of the river to harass the enemy and were reported to have captured some Soviet-made Scud missiles during this phase. This seems unlikely as these launchers were held far from the battlefield, but if the story is true it may refer to FROG missiles.[10]

The initial Pasdaran success, as an Iraqi after-action report of 21–22 April noted, was due to the narrowness of the defensive belt which exposed the defenders and deprived them of a significant and well-placed reserve. This allowed the Iranians to infiltrate the numerous gaps to isolate then assault the positions, the Popular Army companies being especially vulnerable, although it appears that Shibib's 94th Brigade was virtually destroyed in this operation. During these attacks many commanders were killed and US COMINT reported there was 'a general state of panic and chaos' which helped to clear the Pasdarans' path. Surprisingly, despite (or possibly because of) the GMID alert on 5 March, the report observed that a number of commanders, possibly only Popular Army commanders, went on leave. When he read this report Saddam might have recalled his comment in February: 'Our strength is in the awareness of our soldiers and their strength is the lack of awareness by their soldiers.'[11]

Task Force Najaf broke through to Ajairda and Rashid to control the exits from the marshes as supplies and reinforcements flowed in on a fleet of boats, while the Styrofoam pontoon bridges were used extensively for reinforcements and augmented by footbridges created by lashing rubber boats together and placing planking upon them. The Imam Hussein Division and 77th Division were deployed south of Uzayr but most of Dekjam's troops were to the north, and it was against them that Qadir promptly reacted with 429th Brigade, aided by part of 68th Commando Brigade, and counterattacked to retake Ajairda. During 12 March the fighting in the north intensified into the evening with the arrival of Iranian reinforcements but the initiative had been lost and progress was slow. Ajairda was retaken but the Iraqi troops were conducting a fighting retreat which bought time for 10th Armoured Division to drive down the eastern bank and appear about dawn on 13 March. It counterattacked with heavy artillery support and helped 35th Infantry Division and 66th Brigade to regain Ajairda and Uraij (Ujayrid or Uralje) south of Uzayr, while the following day it recaptured the ruins of Beida.

Task Force Karbala had the greatest success reaching the Tigris on the first day, led by IRIA's 21st Infantry Division and the IRGC's Mohammad Rasoolallah Division, but on the first evening the Pasdaran commander asked his IRIA comrade to relieve two of its seven battalions that were suffering from diarrhoea and malnutrition. On their left the hopes of the Ashura Division and 'Qamar Bani Hashem' Brigade of taking the bridges across the Tigris were thwarted by Iraqi demolitions. Behind them three lightweight

139

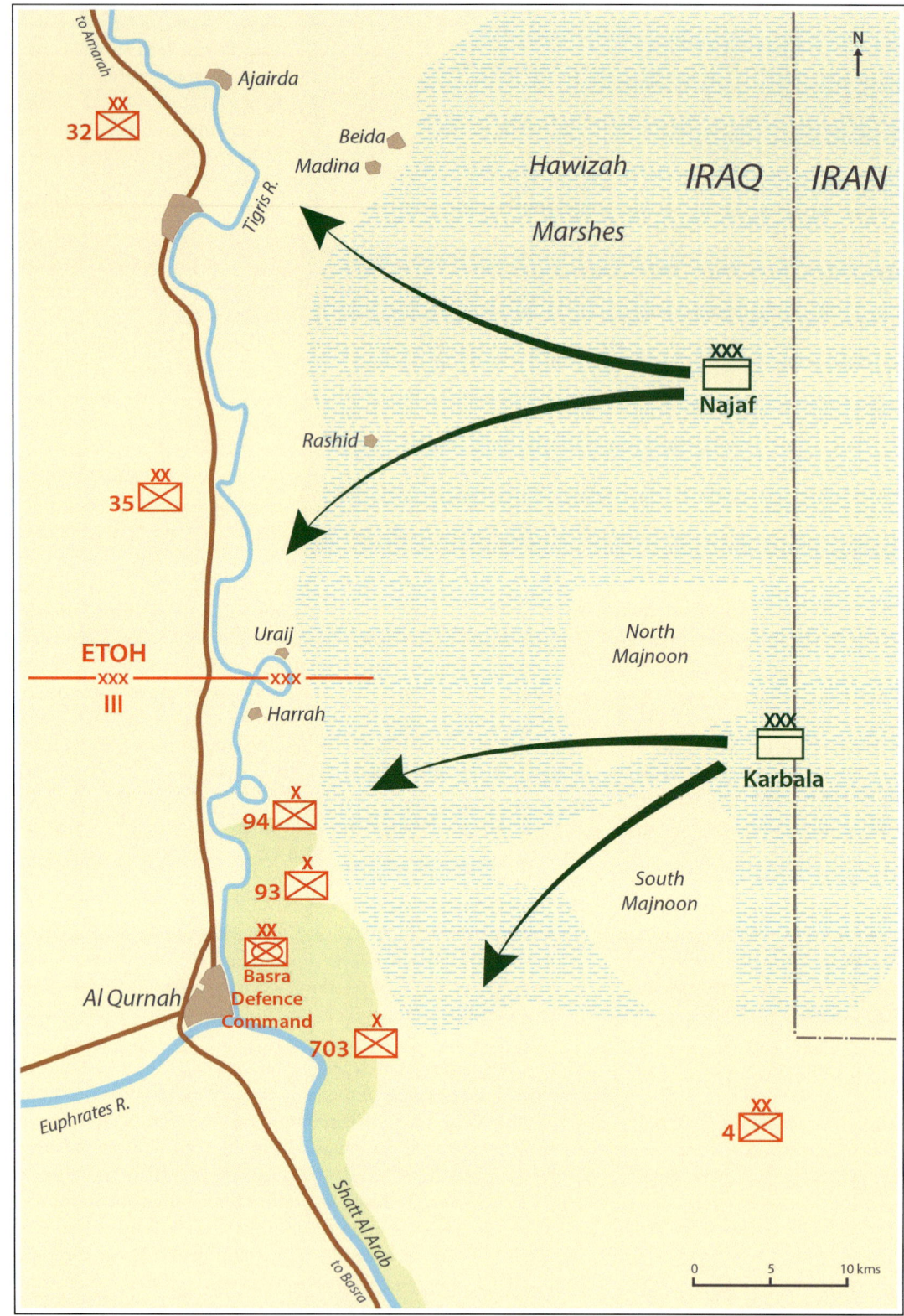

MIDDLE EAST@WAR SERIES SPECIAL #1: THE IRAN-IRAQ WAR

growing support and logistic problems with each kilometre it advanced, and its forces became steadily better targets as they emerged out of the wetlands and onto dry land'.[12]

The bridges began to arrive on the night of 13–14 March and, as they did so, elements of the 55th Airborne Brigade and Mehdi Bakeri's Ashura Division were helicoptered across the Tigris to cut the Baghdad–Basra highway with a bridgehead up to four kilometres deep and 15 kilometres wide into which three battalions of the former and a brigade of the latter were inserted. This success delighted the clerics and politicians in Tehran, although the total haul of prisoners was reported by 17 March at only 1,100. It forced the Iraqis to evacuate neighbouring villages and towns as well as closing the area to civilian traffic while the Ba'ath Party in Maysan and Basra Provinces organised local defence forces based upon the Popular Army to hold towns and cities. Part of the Najaf Ashraf Division later moved into the bridgehead, which was under increasing air and artillery attack, but hopes of moving in the remainder of 55th Airborne and the Special Forces Brigades by helicopter were dashed because of enemy air superiority. The bridges and IRNL ferry service, which included a pair of hovercraft, were under heavy fire making the prospects of a Tigris crossing hazardous.[13]

Iraqi Reinforcements Arrive

Shibib's Basra Defence Force was ordered to prevent the enemy expanding the bridgehead while Rashid was sucked into the battle with Ithawi's 4th Mountain Division transferred northward, Brigadier Iyad al-Futayyih al-Rawi's 6th Armoured Division began to push into the cultivated area northeast of Qurnah, while Brigadier Ali Jasim al-Hayyan's 5th Mechanised Division crossed the Nashwah Bridge and prepared to advance up the west bank of the Tigris to contain the immediate threat.

On 13 March, Defence Minister Khairrallah ordered the General Staff to establish a forward headquarters at Basra under Chief-of-

1st Phase of the Iranian Operation Badr. (Map by George Anderson)

pontoon bridges, one capable of carrying AFVs, were being brought through the marshes to support an assault across the Tigris. Until they arrived Hassani-Sa'di had to content himself the following day by consolidating his gains, aided by the arrival of the Ali Ibn Abu Talib Division to give him control down to the cultivated area north-east of Qurnah. But here, as elsewhere, despite significant improvements in Pasdaran logistics the Iranians still found it difficult to sustain their offensive because of the problems of bringing up heavy weapons. As the advance continued it 'also experienced

PART I: THE SLOUGH OF DESPOND

A ZSU-23-4 Shilka of the IRIA in position and ready for an incoming Iraqi air strike. The weapon proved a formidable foe for low-flying fixed-wing and rotary-wing aircraft during the Iran-Iraq War and highly effective when deployed against exposed infantry formations. (Tom Cooper collection)

The crew of this IRGC-operated BMP-1 optimistically cheered to the cameraman, while their vehicle was moving forward in a cloud of dust to meet another Iraqi counter-attack. (Tom Cooper collection)

Staff Thanun to coordinate the Iraqi response. Thanun brought with him Fakhri and the Deputy Chief-of-Staff for Training, Major General Sa'adi (the former III Corps commander), together with the Head of Intelligence, Brigadier Shukur Shahin (the former 6th Armoured Division commander). The headquarters was established the following day and was promptly visited by Saddam who authorised the use of the recently established Guards Division under Major General Talia Khalil ad-Duri (4th Guards Armoured and 3rd Guards Special Forces Brigades) while 4th Mountain Division was brought up from III Corps, together with 6th Armoured Division and support troops – with the 3rd Armoured Division's headquarters remaining behind the Fish Lake Line. As other reinforcements were arriving Thanun drafted a plan to respond to the threat. Given Fakhri's intimate knowledge of the area and his experience at thwarting Khyber, he returned to Uzayr to assume command of the northern task force which was to crush Task Force Najaf and included the Guards Division (2nd Guards, 10th and 42nd Armoured Brigades, 4th Guards and 702nd Infantry Brigades, and Guards Emergency Force); 10th Armoured Division with its own 17th Armoured, 24th and 27th Mechanised Brigades reinforced by 5th Mountain and 29th Infantry Brigades of the 4th Mountain Division, the divisional headquarters; the 3rd Guards, 66th and 68th Commando Brigades; and the 35th Division's battered 429th Brigade. Altogether some 50,000 men with 450 MBTs.

Sa'adi established his task force headquarters in Qurnah to command the thrust from the west with 5th Mechanised (30th Armoured, 20th Mechanised, 19th Mountain Brigades, the last from the 7th Mountain Division) and the south with 6th Armoured Division (16th Armoured, 25th Mechanised and 18th Infantry Brigades), Shibib's Basra Defence Force (93th Infantry, 65th Commando and 1st Shock Troop Brigades), the headquarters and support forces of 6th Armoured Division – or some 39,000 troops with 270 MBTs. The divisional artillery was boosted by 30 medium and heavy batteries to give some 720 guns, augmented by MLRS and a Scud B brigade (which was then not used). Unsurprisingly, the 35,000 tired Iranians, their 200 guns and a handful of MLRS were clearly outnumbered.

In addition to overwhelming material strength, Thanun was aided by his superior COMINT capability. From 12 March the IrAF joined the 3rd Wing IrAAC in both CAS and battlefield interdiction sorties flying a total of 767 fixed-wing and 530 rotary-wing sorties by the 14th of the month. The vast majority of these hit targets around the marshes. Heavy rain on 14 March reduced operations, but then even the IrAAC-operated Swiss-made Pilatus PC-7 trainers were deployed on airstrips constructed near the battlefield to fly close air support. These light strikers could carry up to 450 kilograms of ordnance – usually consisting of two gun-pods and two rocket launchers, and lacked sophisticated self defence systems: unsurprisingly, the Iranians soon claimed four of them as shot down.

On 15 March the counteroffensive began with Hayyan's 5th Mechanised Division striking the bridgehead on the west bank of the Tigris with powerful support from both the IrAF and IrAAC

MIDDLE EAST@WAR SERIES SPECIAL #1: THE IRAN-IRAQ WAR

The crew of an Iraqi 105mm Oto-Melara Model 56 pack howitzer rest in their position while the gun captain is on the telephone, conferring with superiors. The Model 56 was used by light batteries to augment the normal divisional artillery, which primarily consisted of 122mm howitzers and 130mm guns. (Albert Grandolini collection)

Some IRGC-operated Kashayars (BTR-50s re-engined with US-made diesels) had ZPU machine guns on the rear deck for enhanced air defence. (Tom Cooper collection)

gassed Pasdaran began to give way, and during the night the survivors recrossed the Tigris.

They were to receive no respite, for at dawn of 16 March the main Iraqi counteroffensive began along the eastern bank of the Tigris as their engineers pumped water from the Tigris into the marshes and bank to flood the Iranian defences. During 16 and 17 March the IrAF launched an all-out effort, flying 800 sorties with every available Sukhoi Su-20, Su-22, MiG-23BN and even with Mirage F.1EQs (deployed only as interceptors before February 1984). The IrAAC's helicopter gunships flew another 825 sorties. Unsurprisingly, Fakhri's advance made rapid progress: the Guards Division pushed south from the Uzayr area, inflicting heavy casualties and reaching Rashid by the evening, but there the Pasdaran made a stand, leading to a bitter all-night battle before they were driven out in the early morning, allowing the 35th Infantry Division to mop up. Two Task Force Najaf survivors later said: 'The Iraqis had so much artillery that they would pin us in place – then they would unleash wave upon wave of tanks followed by Republican Guard troops who were very well trained, highly motivated and willing to fight us face to face. We lacked the equipment to stop the Guards' tanks who forced us back.'[14]

Sa'adi made slower progress, led by the 6th Armoured Division supported by the Basra Defence Command, which started north-east of Qurnah, and then advanced through the cultivated belt via Khudr

(which flew 415 and 320 sorties respectively), destroying the pontoon bridges even though Pasdaran teams used SA-7 MANPADs to bring down several of the helicopters involved. The Iranian hope that Dejkam's Task Force Najaf would pin down the enemy rapidly proved forlorn, while the shortage of artillery ammunition and the extreme range from the North Majnoon batteries meant there was little fire support. The defenders were dreadfully exposed in an area with little cover and with little time to prepare anything but the most rudimentary defences. During the evening the isolated and badly

towards Uzayr despite desperate resistance from Task Force Karbala. These attacks caused great concern among the defenders; two of the Ali Ibn Abu Talib Division's five remaining battalions took heavy losses and needed to be relieved by battalions of the 28th Division from the Majnoons. Even then, the IRGC's forward positions were on the verge of destruction already by early afternoon. Although having to fight its way across numerous streams, on 18 March the 6th Armoured Division met Fakhri's spearhead at Hamayoun (10 kilometres north-east of Qurnah) as the surviving Pasdaran

142

PART I: THE SLOUGH OF DESPOND

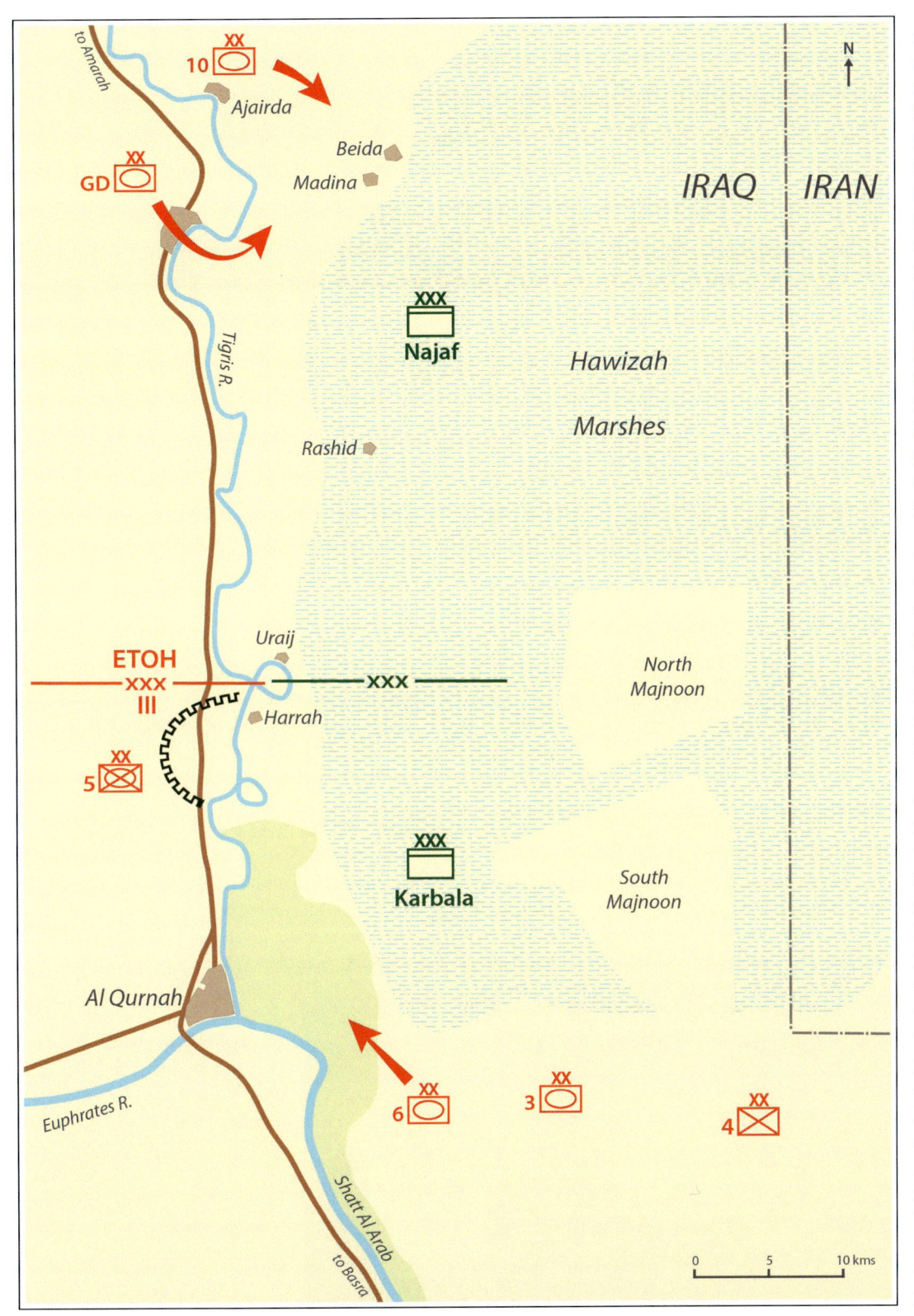

rushed to launch a nocturnal attack in a vain attempt to recover the lost ground. Unsurprisingly, considering all the Iraqi units concentrated in the area, it failed to regain all of the islet, leaving the Iraqis with a toehold on South Majnoon. On the night from 20 to 21 March, as three days of rain began, a new attack was made upon two brigades of the 31st Infantry Division, but again the Iraqi defences held. Indeed, the Iranian counterattack was blasted away to a degree that for all intents and purposes, Operation Badr was over by 23 March.[16]

The Lessons Learned

Two commentators observed: 'Operation Badr was ambitious, but conceived and executed by amateurs incapable of handling its complexities, especially after the normal frictions of war intervened.'[17]

US satellite intelligence estimated a total of 12,000 men from both sides had died, but the Iraqis probably lost 9,000 men including 1,500 prisoners, mostly a battalion of 429th Brigade, while the Iranians probably suffered 17,000 casualties including 3,000 to chemical weapons. Although the IRIA was prepared to participate in the later stages of the operation, and 77th Division received a bridging company from 16th Armoured Division on 12 March, few of its men actively participated in the battle. In turn, 55th Airborne Brigade's strength was reported to have declined following losses during Badr. Material losses were surprisingly low: in the Iranian case because their artillery was never physically threatened, while they deployed little armour; the Iraqis reportedly lost only 45 AFVs and 17 aircraft (including 11 helicopters). However, US intelligence estimated that 260 Iraqi MBTs (a third of their strength) were knocked out by RPGs and recoilless artillery. The IRIAA was extremely active and flew 987 sorties, compared with more than 1,500 from the IrAAC: it launched 23 TOW missiles and evacuated 1,659 wounded, in turn losing 14 helicopters shot down or badly damaged, together with three crewmembers.[18]

Main Iraqi counterattacks in reaction to the Iranian Operation Badr. (Map by George Anderson)

withdrew into the marshes. The seriousness of the defeat is shown by the loss on the same day of the commander of the Mohammad Rasoolallah Division, Haj Abbas Karimi (his predecessor was killed during Khyber). Here, as in the north, the Iraqis captured numerous boats which they used to help mop up the enemy.[15]

In a desperate and belated attempt to relieve pressure on their colleagues, Rafsanjani and the clerics demanded an attack on South Majnoon from North Majnoon. On 18 March, the 3rd Saheb al-Zaman Division was brought down from the Dezful front, and

Well-dug-in troops of the Iraqi III Corps, in position north of Basra. The soldier in the foreground is manning a RPK-74 light machine gun. (Albert Grandolini collection)

Ready to meet a tank-led counterattack is this Iranian anti-armour team, armed with a 106mm M40 recoilless gun mounted on a jeep. Although officially a 106mm weapon, this gun actually used 105mm ammunition: the term 106mm was used to avoid confusion in the logistical chain. (Tom Cooper collection)

The Iraqis, who called this campaign 'The Crown of Battle' (Taj el-Ma'arik), were proud of their achievements in smashing the offensive and in which they had shown determination and resolution, but as usual foreign observers expressed often bitter critique. The British Military Attaché, Colonel R.C. Eccles, probably reflected the views of the other members of the Diplomatic Corps: 'Most observers agree that at face value the resourcefulness and determination shown by the Iranians must have contrasted strongly with an almost incredible degree of Iraqi military incompetence that allowed this to occur.'

Eccles concluded that the Iraqi high command underestimated enemy determination and was surprised by enemy persistence:

'However, the Iraqis quickly assembled an overwhelming counterattack force, at least two armoured divisions strong, which effectively overran Iranians' positions East and West of the Tigris on about 16 March.' He noted that when the international press corps, who were taken on a tour of the battlefield on 17 March saw evidence of heavy Iraqi casualties in men and machines which: 'suggest that the counterattacks may have been conducted hastily and with less than perfect all-arms coordination, but they were nevertheless successful because of the unequalness of the fight.' US intelligence noted that Badr saw poor levels of combined-arms training, with many counterattacking Iraqi tanks lost to RPGs fired from the side and rear due to the absence of close infantry support.[19]

Yet both sides were surprisingly content with their performances. The Iranians were now certain they could exploit terrain to balance enemy firepower superiority while surprise remained a key element in their planning. Iranian Chief-of-Staff Colonel Ismail Sohrabi stated:

Our blitzes are planned so as to make it hard for the enemy to redeploy its forces to the areas attacked. In our various operations, while we aim to avoid sustaining heavy casualties, we seek to surprise the enemy and to wear him out psychologically...We wish to render it almost impossible for enemy commanders to

An Iranian 106mm recoilless gun firing at enemy armour. The biggest drawback of this weapon was the massive back-blast that immediately revealed the weapon's position. Survival of the crew depended on their skill in quickly moving away after firing. (Tom Cooper collection)

plan properly; our operations enable our men to fight an enemy with superior hardware.

Consequently, the politicians and clerics in Tehran remained confident 'Islamic warfare' was the key to success and while the Pasdaran had been unable to cut the Baghdad–Basra highway they had at least reached it.[20] But Rezai explained: 'This tactic has not replaced our previous ones. It keeps the enemy constantly entangled. This strengthens our main tactic, which is launching big and determined operations.'[21]

The Iraqis too were content although the last shots of Badr had barely been fired before Saddam called a meeting in Baghdad on 25 March so the Defence Minister, the Chief-of-Staff, corps and arms commanders could review the lessons learned. The active defence policy was confirmed and the corps were ordered to plan more limited attacks and raids to gain or regain terrain which would improve overall defence and boost morale. The investment in the road network had clearly paid off and allowed the Republican Guard to be deployed in force, aided by a large force of tank transporters, and the Guard was now becoming a strategic reserve. In addition, Saddam was prepared to loosen the reins slightly on his frontline commanders. One decision from the conference was to upgrade the status of the ETOH: this became the VI Corps in the summer of 1985, by when it included the Marshes Command Forces – without the 25th and 35th Infantry Divisions, which were transferred to IV Corps. As compensation the new corps received the 12th Armoured Division, 4th and 25th Infantry Divisions, and – in 1986 – the newly established 40th Infantry Division.[22]

Despite the end of Badr the active defence policy ensured that the marshes continued to echo to the sounds of battle. On 19 March, the 31st Infantry Division and 601st Infantry Brigade staged a raid near South Majnoon and two days later 19th Infantry Division staged Operation Blessed Days of Victory near the same area. An attack by 28th Infantry Brigade (31st Infantry Division) on 27 June gained more of South Majnoon. The new VI Corps was also in action with 2nd Mountain Brigade striking into the marshes on 17 May to wreck enemy bridges, while between 31 May and 2 July the 4th and 25th Infantry Divisions made spoiling attacks to destroy supplies and boats. This provoked Iranian reaction with Operation Mozzafar on 6 June and Tapper 2 at South Majnoon on 7 June, followed by another raid (Tapper 4) on 21 June, while during the second half of June, the 25th Infantry Division IRGC ran Operation Qods-3, and – on 6 August – Qods-5. Raids and minor offensives continued, principally in the Northern and Central Fronts during the rest of the year, often by battalion or company-size units.[23]

To prevent the enemy repeating his attack with greater success the Defence Ministry in Baghdad forwarded a directive from the President's Office on 25 March 1985 demanding the destruction of villages within the marshes and the destruction of both reed beds and palm groves around the edges to strengthen the eastern bank's defences. A committee was established at Uzayr in April to clear the marshes southwards to Qurnah: by the beginning of 1986 at least 21 villages had been razed and some 25,000 people forcibly removed as the Basra-wing of the Ba'ath Party mobilised civilians (including school children) to clear the marshes and the palm groves northeast of Qurnah. A *cordon sanitaire* manned by security police and the Popular Army was then established to prevent infiltrators and deserters, although in January 1987 the Pasdaran moved MLRS teams into the marshes and Baghdad began to plan draining the area. The Iraqi defences were further strengthened by creating earth/sand

An extremely exposed Iranian ZU-23 gun engaging an aerial target. This was a towed weapon that was probably rapidly deployed in response to a threat – or the crew felt very confident. (Tom Cooper collection)

walls 4.5–6 metres high between the Tigris and the Baghdad–Basra highway, and by demolishing almost all the villages and individual houses which straddled the highway – especially in the east – to improve fields of fire. In addition they built a new logistic road alongside the Amara–Qurna road, but 15 kilometres further west. Large armoured forces, at least a division, were deployed between the wall and the desert west of the road for a distance of about 20 kilometres north of Qurna.[24]

11
THE THRIVING ARMOURERS

From the opening shots of Operation Ramadan the southern campaigns were dominated by one inescapable fact, Iran was hamstrung by shortages of modern heavy weapons and ammunition which doomed any conventional trial of strength. However hard the Iranians tried to overcome their weakness through attacking in terrain favourable to themselves, ultimately they still faced such a trial and inevitably would lose, indeed throughout this period Iran had only 1,000 MBTs, 1,400 AFVs and 600–800 guns while Iraq had some 3,000 MBTs, 2,500 AFVs and 1,800 guns.

In part this was because Iran was suffering major economic problems with the cost of the war – estimated at US$163.7 billion by March 1984, of which $53.7 billion was lost by the oil industry. Daily oil exports dropped from 1.3 million barrels to 800,000 in the autumn of 1986, while the world glut meant that prices fell from US$36.71 per barrel in 1980 to US$30.20 in 1982. Even though Tehran exceeded its OPEC production quota of 1.2 million barrels a day with an output of 2.3 million barrels a day, revenues from strong currencies were barely sufficient to cover armament procurements. Consequently, the country's internal transport was decimated, domestic flights cancelled and private car owners allowed only 40 litres of fuel per month. Tehran's only external source of funds was President Muammar Gaddafi who also supplied limited quantities of military equipment. In mid-1983 an American intelligence analyst noted: 'Tehran remains critically short of tanks, aircraft, artillery ammunition and a steady supply of spare parts necessary to keep its equipment fully operational.'[1]

The Shah's attempts at self-sufficiency were continued through the Defence Industries Organisation (DIO) created in 1983, while the Pasdaran established their own weapons manufacturers from early 1984. However, the Iranian factories largely produced assault rifles, RPGs, mortars and mortar bombs, while there was limited production of four-wheel-drive vehicles, communications and chemical protection equipment. Consequently, there was no solution for Tehran but to look abroad: by 1986 it was importing military equipment worth US$2.2 billion a year and signed further contracts worth US$14 billion (see Table 12 for major orders for ground forces equipment).

During the 1970s, the Shah of Iran had established a domestic armaments industry which the revolutionary regime took over under the umbrella organisation of the Defence Industries Organisation (DIO), but this took years to recover from the revolutionary chaos of 1979–1980. The DIO produced many of the small arms, RPGs and mortars but the heaviest weapons which emerged were MLRS, such as the Fajr-3 installed on Japanese-made Isuzu, and then Mercedes, 6x6 trucks. The largest imported weapons included the North Korean-made 240mm M1985 long-range guns. Small arms, mortar bombs, 105mm and 155mm artillery shells were produced too, possibly meeting up to half the requirements in some categories, as were CJ-3B light trucks of Indian design, and gas masks. All of this helped to reduce arms imports. In addition, Iran benefited from the facilities of Iran Electronics Industries (Sana-ey Electronik-e Iran) or IEI established in 1972 which produced the US AN/PRC-77 VHF FM and AN/PRC-105 HF manpack transceiver, and vehicle-based

One of the most important additions to the Iraqi arsenal of the mid-1980s was a batch of Mirage F1EQ-4 fighter-bombers, the first of which reached Iraq in 1983. Equipped with an advanced navigation/attack system and armament of Western origin, they saw intensive service in counterattacks against Iranian offensives. (Hugues Deguillebon collection)

PART I: THE THRIVING ARMOURERS

One of the major reinforcements for the IrAF, acquired in 1984, were the first of an eventual 55 MiG-23ML interceptors. Still not matching the Grumman F-14A Tomcats of the IRIAF, they offered a relatively cheap but effective performance, combined with armament that was unknown to thed Iranians. In one of their first combat operations, a pair of Iraqi MiG-23MLs shot down the Tomcat flown by the leading IRIAF tactician of the war, Hashem All-e-Agha, on 11 August 1984. (Tom Cooper collection)

VRC/GRC-105 systems and later developed tactical encryption systems for them.

Nevertheless, Iran – just like Iraq – remained overdependent upon foreign equipment. Living in the rarefied world of religious mania the clerics and their supporters had succeeded in isolating Iran from its potential Western sources of military equipment and, reflecting the growing economic importance of the Pacific Rim, were forced to turn to the Far East and especially China and North Korea. In 1982, Tehran received the first deliveries under a US$1.5 billion defence contract from China; this included armour, artillery (tube and rocket), infantry weapons, missiles, ammunition and tank engines. Another contract with China followed in 1985: worth some US$3.1 billion, it resulted in deliveries of a similar range of equipment: Beijing is known to have supplied some Type-69 MBTs – derivatives of the Soviet T-54 with a 100mm rifled gun – but Iran appears to have purchased no tank transporters or heavy equipment transporters (HETs) for these.[2] The towed artillery supplied was also often a derivative or development of the Soviet systems and included the Type-83 122mm howitzer, the Type-59 130mm gun (M-46) and Type-81 truck-mounted 122mm MLRS (BM-21). The Type-63 towed 107mm MLRS, however, was a Chinese weapon and was the backbone of Pasdaran divisional fire-support battalions. Later on, the Chinese contracts included 'big ticket' items – such as combat aircraft and associated weapons, long-range surface-to-air and coastal-defence missile systems. The ground forces did receive significant quantities of missile systems, including – starting from 1982 – 6,500 Hongjian (Red Arrow) 73 – or HJ-73 – anti-armour missiles from the first contract and 500 HN-5 MANPADS (Chinese copy of the SA-7) ordered in 1985. Between 1982 and 1985, North Korea is estimated to have supplied artillery, infantry weapons, missiles and ammunition worth US$510. The Soviet Union launched another attempt at rapprochement with Iran in 1986, and this effort resulted in sale of some surplus or second-hand troop carriers, about 100 SA-7 launchers and 400 missiles, but also some ammunition and spares. Up to 2,000 Soviet-made 9K11 Malyutka ATGMs (ASCC/NATO codename AT-3 'Sagger') were delivered by Syria from 1982 and an order to North Korea saw another 4,000 delivered from 1986 until after the war. Syria and Libya provided some heavy weapons but mostly supplied infantry weapons, both individual and crew-served, as well as ammunition; their aircraft joining those of the IRIAF to fly equipment into Tabriz airbase. Eventually, between 1980 and 1987, Moscow is estimated to have provided military equipment and ammunition worth US$11.8 billion to Tehran, including a licence to

Table 12: Major Arms Orders by Iran 1982–1986					
Order Placed	Country	Equipment			Delivered
		Type	Model	Number	
1982	China	MLRS	122mm	100	1982–1987
	China	MLRS	107mm	200	1982–1986
	Syria	MBT	T-55	120	1982
1983	Austria	Towed Arty	155mm	300	1983–1984
	North Korea	Towed Arty	130mm	480	
1984	Argentina	Towed Arty	155mm	10	1984
1985	China	MBT	Type-59	440	1985–1986
	China	Towed Arty	122mm	100	1985–1986
	China	Towed Arty	130mm	100	1985–1986
	China	MLRS	107mm	250	1985–1986
	China	MLRS	122mm	100	1985–1986
	North Korea	MLRS	240mm	100	1985–1990
1986	China	Towed Arty	130mm	120	1987
	USSR	IFV	BMP-1	400	1986–1989
	USSR	APC	BTR-60	400	1986
	Vietnam	MBT	M-48	80	1986–1987
	Vietnam	APC	M-113	200	1986–1987

After a temporary halt during 1980–1982, Iraq continued purchasing additional Sukhoi Su-22M-2, Su-22M-3 and Su-22M-4K fighter-bombers, which became something of a battlewagon for the IrAF during the war with Iran. This Su-22M was operated by No. 5 Squadron. (Tom Cooper collection)

In 1984, Iraq received the second batch of 12 Mi-25 helicopter gunships from the Soviet Union. (Farzin Nadimi collection)

manufacture AK-47 assault rifles. Even so, Iraq remained preferred Soviet client in the region.[3]

China and North Korea also assisted Iran to purchase material covertly in the commercial market apparently under the 'Dermavand' Project, named after Iran's highest mountain. Necessary funding was channelled in 1985 and 1986 through the Belgian Banque Lambert. These arrangements met some of Iran's requirements but there were routinely 100 percent mark-ups, and a single much-prized TOW anti-armour missile worth US$5,500 was sold at US$60,000 to Tehran, while deliveries were irregular and neither quantity nor quality could be guaranteed. Still, such business remained extremely lucrative and thus went on; in 1985 Tehran spent US$100 million with Arab and Swiss dealers to regain captured equipment including M48 MBTs, the dealers earning at least a US$10 million commission. Around the same time, a Syrian attempt to acquire Belgian-made self-propelled 155mm howitzers failed when the vendor demanded US$1 million per gun!

Heavy weapons were the most difficult to acquire. In 1983, a US$440 million contract was placed with the Austrian state-owned company Noricum for 300 GHN-45 155mm howitzers. About 100 of these weapons appear to have been delivered via Libya, but a year after the war ended the Austrian government decided to divest itself of the company. Iran also acquired some Swiss-made Oerlikon twin 35mm AA guns, but these were primarily used to bolster the air defences of the strategically important oil-exporting terminal at Khark Island. US authorities sought to curtail this trade and in November 1985 completed a 'sting' operation which prevented the clandestine shipment to Iran of a huge shipment including 18 F-4s, 46 A-4s, 13 F-5s, and bombs, anti-armour missiles and radars which might have tipped the scales in the Faw Peninsula.[4] Officially at least, most United Nations members respected the arms embargoes imposed upon Iran and Iraq already in September 1980. Unofficially, it was anything but the case: the embargo was simply ignored, often with at least some degree of government support. Iranian oil was widely used to lubricate deals, with such US-allies as Singapore, South Korea and Taiwan willing to provide spares for US-built vehicles and aircraft. Some nations, notably Brazil and France, were willing to supply both sides. During 1984 an Iranian delegation visited Brazil and sought equipment from the aerospace industry and MLRS. Brasilia first granted permission for deliveries of Embraer EMB.312 Tucano training aircraft but then banned exports to Tehran. The Iranians then initiated attempts to acquire Brazilian equipment through Libya which attempted to acquire EE-9 Cascavel armoured cars and EE-11 Urutu APCs – together with spares for them and ammunition for the 90mm guns – but the Brazilian Foreign Ministry blocked these efforts for fear of compromising even more lucrative sales to Iraq.

This contrasted with the US$120 million worth of equipment, including electronic components, supplied by France to Iran from 1983–1987 – at least according to US intelligence reports. The majority of this included 450,000 155mm and 203mm artillery shells, delivered by GIAT – partially via Cherbourg and Zaventem in Belgium, partially via French company Minerve via Saudi Arabia – with false end-user certificates (the latter declared them as ordered by Brazil, Portugal, Thailand and Yugoslavia), in an enterprise that lasted until several months after the end of war. In addition, the French company SNPE supplied Iran with explosives in an enterprise stopped by Paris in March 1986. During the same year, Italian subsidiaries of the French company Luchaire – Consar and S.E.A. – reportedly supplied Iran with ammunition, too.

PART I: THE THRIVING ARMOURERS

During the mid-1980s, Iraq acquired the final batch of SA.342K Gazelle attack helicopters, armed with HOT ATGMs. (Ali Tobchi collection)

Further diversifying its sources of arms, in order to prevent any possible arms embargoes, Iraq acquired three batches, including a total of 75 Messerschmitt-Bölkow-Blohm Bo105 attack helicopters, and then a batch of 16 Japanese-built BK.117B-1 helicopters (developed in co-operation with Germany). The first BK.117B-1s arrived in September 1987. They were primarily used for VIP transport and search and rescue purposes. (Ali Tobchi collection)

Another, perhaps unexpected addition to the IrAAC came from the USA, in the form of 60 McDonnell Douglas MD 500 Defender helicopters. Ostensibly sold for civilian purposes, all saw extensive combat service during the war with Iran, often in combination with Mi-25s. (Farzin Nadimi collection)

Italian sales of military equipment to Iran totalled at about US$350 million in 1983 and US$200 million in 1986. Reportedly, they included 36 OTO Melara 105mm mountain howitzers, Borletti fuzes, 92 Oerlikon Italiana anti-aircraft guns, Marconi Italiana and Selenia radars, Valsella Meccanotecnica SpA land mines and 1,400 Luigi Franchi sights. Late in 1986 Rome's Trade Minister, Mr Rino Formica, confirmed his ministry continued to approve these sales because, he claimed, the government never officially informed him of an arms embargo!

Other European governments were at least as happy to turn a blind eye to the UN-imposed arms embargo. Spain supplied US$280 million worth of ammunition – mostly mortar bombs but also some recoilless artillery – through Syria and Libya until May 1986, and Portugal's Spel did so from 1984 until 1987. Dutch company Muiden Chemie reportedly supplied Iran with US$100 million worth of ammunition from 1984–1987 (all delivered via Austria, Portugal and Yugoslavia), while in 1984 German customs seized 200 tonnes of explosives produced by Sweden's Dynamit Nobel and allegedly destined for Iran via Yugoslavia.

Small arms and ammunition reached Iran from Argentina (which supplied US$31 million worth of equipment), Bulgaria, Cuba, Czechoslovakia, Gabon, Greece, Pakistan, Portugal, South Korea and Nicaragua but many countries also helped the Iranian war machine in other ways. Greece supplied Continental Teledyne engines for M48 and M60 MBTs, Turkey supplied communications equipment, while Singapore illegally sold some 200 Swedish Bofors RBS-70 MANPADS worth US$307 million and also arranged for the delivery of 20mm Oerlikon naval guns. South Korea provided spares while Vietnam provided both spares, AFVs, and even a batch of second-hand Northrop F-5E/B and F-5E fighter-bombers in a US$400 million deal agreed in July 1986.

Tehran also benefited from dual-use equipment, especially vehicles which were ostensibly for civilian use. East and West Germany, South Korea and Japan were major suppliers while India and Sweden each provided 200 trucks, Yugoslavia 500 trucks (including 30 heavy-load vehicles) in 1983 alone. The United Kingdom sold some US$200 million worth of vehicles to Iran, including 3,000 Land Rovers, as Whitehall desperately wriggled to find some way of cashing in on the booming market. During 1985 some US$130 million worth of spares for British-designed AFVs were flown to Tehran and eventually six radars worth US$380 million were sold for 'air traffic control' to replace US-made sensors.

A vast stock of US equipment, worth US$12.2 billion according to Tehran and US$9.9 billion according to Washington – which had been paid for by the Shah before 1979 – remained tantalisingly beyond reach of Tehran. This included M113 APCs, air defence weapons and electronics – and spares for virtually everything. In 1979 Washington offered to buy back this material but Tehran refused and by December 1986 the Americans reported most of the equipment had deteriorated and was useless. A year after the war ended Tehran began moves to recover this cornucopia and in December 1991 the Iran-United States Claims Tribunal in the Hague saw Washington agree to pay Iran US$278 million for defence equipment impounded after Iranian 'students' took US Embassy staff hostage. During the negotiations the tribunal had helped arrange the two sides would pay US$2.3 billion to meet each other's claims, but in 1998 Tehran asked the International Court of Justice to consider its claim that by ending the Foreign Military Sales (FMS) programme to Iran in 1979, Washington should pay US$10 billion in compensation for excessive payments, failure to deliver equipment, unserviceable equipment delivered and storage fees for material in the United States.

That was at least the official side of relations between Iran and the USA. Unofficially, the United States – or 'The Great Satan' – were selling weapons to Tehran all the time between 1980 and 1983, foremost via Israel: reportedly, the latter had supplied US$3.2

Another new weapons system acquired by Iraq in the mid-1980s was the Brazilian-made Astros II (Artillery Saturation Rocket System), about 60 of which were delivered, starting in 1983. Each battery had four AV-LMU launcher vehicles and two AV-RMD transport vehicles, and an AV-VCC fire-control vehicle with Contraves Fieldguard radar. Also known as SS-40, the launch-vehicle had 16 launch tubes, which fired 152kg rockets out to a maximum range of 35km. (Tom Cooper collection)

Although spreading rumours that the IRIAF was non-operational and grounded, the Iraqis knew that the Iranian air force was hitting back at every opportunity. Correspondingly, Baghdad continued purchasing SAMs throughout the war, eventually acquiring over 18,000 of various types during the 1980s. This is a launch vehicle of the Soviet-made 2K12 Kub (SA-6 Gainful) medium-range system. (Joav Efrati collection)

1986, Iran supposedly received 2,008 BGM-71A TOW ATGMs and 238 MIM-23B I-HAWK SAMs in this fashion: unofficial Iranian sources confirmed the delivery of 'about 2,000' TOWs but stressed that all the HAWK SAMs were older MIM-23A which the IRIAF could not use. Similarly, while the CIA requested 4,342 individual items for Iranian I-HAWKs only 3,976, worth US$4.3 million, were actually despatched. Although these supplies were not on the scale which Tehran had hoped for, they undoubtedly helped Iranian forces.[5]

In February 1987 the New York Times published details of alleged US involvement in the 'Damavand' Project and claimed that Washington was aware by early 1984 of efforts by private contractors to supply 39 F-4E Phantoms, 25 AH-1 Cobras, air- and ship-launched missiles together with 150 M48A5 tanks, 50,000 M16A1 rifles and artillery fire control computers. Reportedly funded via Cairo – certainly the closest Iraqi ally of the time – this deal was actually never realised.

By contrast, Iraq had almost uninterrupted access to foreign arms producers although – due to the almost complete destruction of its oil industry by the IRIAF early during the war – Baghdad's economy faced incredible difficulties paying for equipment in the long term. Saddam's bitter enemy, President Assad, cut Iraq's oil pipeline through his country and with his pipelines to Turkey harassed by Kurdish guerrillas, daily oil exports dropped from a pre-war 1.3 billion barrels to 700,000 barrels: this was barely enough to sustain the country, never mind a war. A second pipeline to Turkey was built and when it became operational in 1984 it brought exports to 1 billion barrels a day. However, even after the CIA estimated that the Iraqi oil exports were back to US$2.3 billion, a year later, Baghdad was spending about 245 percent of its oil revenues on imports of military equipment. The reason for this absurdity was simple: since late 1981, bankrupt Iraq was saved by lavishly borrowing money – foremost from Kuwait, but also from Saudi Arabia.

When the war broke out Baghdad had foreign exchange reserves worth US$40 billion. These were quickly depleted and by 1986

billion worth of military equipment – including aircraft spare parts, mortars and ammunition for 105mm tank guns and mortars – to Iran during the same period. The USA became involved with Iran again during the desperate effort to regain influence and free some of the hostages taken by Hezbollah in Lebanon during the infamous Iran-Contra deal (which saw the resulting profit being diverted to support the anti-Communist Nicaraguan Contras). Much of what reached Iran was at least officially declared as 'beyond the shelf life', and again was delivered via Israel. The system worked so that Israel would sell its surplus stocks of older weapons, which in turn would be replaced by deliveries of newly manufactured weapons from the USA. For example, between August 1985 and November

PART I: THE THRIVING ARMOURERS

The longer the war with Iran lasted, the greater emphasis the Iraqis put upon reinforcing their artillery units, until these eventually outclassed the Iranians. The primary divisional guns remained Soviet-designed 122mm howitzers and 130mm guns. The latter were usually available in the form of M-46 guns, one of which is seen here. They could fire up to six 33kg shells per minute over a range of 27km. (Albert Grandolini collection)

down to US$5 billion. Thus, already in 1981 Kuwait City and Riyadh arranged a set of loans totalling US$12 billion, followed by another US$5.5 billion in 1982. By 1986 Iraq had received US$30–50 billion worth of largesse, before the 'Oil Shock' of that year strained the economies of Gulf States to cut back. Furthermore, not only Kuwait and Saudi Arabia, but especially Jordan, all provided safe harbours into which military supplies for Iraq were transported – sometimes by ships organised into outright convoys, usually with official convoys too. Multiple European trucking companies earned handsome profits from organising the transhipment of the contraband from ports like that in Aqaba (Jordan) to Baghdad, during the 1980s.

Indeed, despite the de facto bankruptcy of Iraq, Saddam's prolificacy of spending continued unchecked and from 1981–1986 the country placed orders for arms worth US$32. Annual imports of military-related equipment grew from US$4.3 billion in 1982 to US$7.7 billion in 1986, turning Iraq into the world's biggest arms importer (major acquisitions of ground-forces-related equipment are listed in Table 13). According to US intelligence, the largest supplier was the USSR, which received contracts worth US$12.4 billion – most of that for combat aircraft and missiles – and was followed by France with contracts related just to Mirage F.1EQ fighter-bombers reaching a staggering US$6 billion (those for other equipment added about US$3.8 billion), China with contracts worth US$3.9 billion, and Brazil (US$1.2 billion).

Some of this largesse was not as generous as it appeared; most of the Soviet T-62 MBTs were surplus vehicles which arrived after extensive use with the Soviet Army. The Soviet-designed MBTs were very much lower in quality compared with those of Western manufacturers and the Iraqis sought to incorporate Western technology to improve them, or at least acquire MBTs of Czechoslovak or Polish origin, which were considered as of better quality. While T-62s had infrared searchlights for night operations they lacked laser rangefinders which first appeared in T-72s delivered from early 1983. French laser rangefinders were acquired and fitted

into T-55 MBTs: without the addition of a fire control computer this was of limited effect. Appliqué spaced armour was added to T-55s, and also to BMP-1s, to reduce the effect of shaped charges, initially in commanders' vehicles and then generally applied.

There are many contemporary reports of British Chieftains being used by the Iraqis and even of Kuwait supplying Baghdad from its own inventory. Whitehall was certainly willing to provide Chieftain and its FV4030 derivatives to Baghdad ostensibly through a Jordanian contract, but the Iraqis were all too well aware of the vehicle's limitations and preferred the superior T-72, although there were negotiations with a view to an Iraqi purchase of what would be Challenger 1 with Chobham armour. However, a combination of the British reluctance to supply arms to a country at war, and Iraqi bankruptcy, as well as concern that the arms might be compromised through the Iraqis letting their Soviet allies take a closer look, resulted in related negotiations of 1982–1983 remaining fruitless.

While China supplied MBTs including a derivative of the T-55, the Type-69-I with 100mm smoothbore gun, together with 122mm Type-60 guns as well as Type-83 howitzers, Type-59 130mm guns and the USSR towed D-30 122mm howitzers, neither appears to have provided heavier towed tubes until 1986 when Moscow provided 2A36 Giatsint (Hyacinth) 152mm towed guns together with second batches of 2S3 Akatsiya 152mm and 2S1 Gvozdika 122mm self-propelled howitzers. For heavier towed tubes the Iraqis turned to Western manufacturers and in June 1985 they witnessed a demonstration by France's GIAT of the 155TR towed 155mm howitzer. Unfortunately, while the weapon was demonstrating a high rate of fire with full charges a howitzer exploded and a French non-commissioned officer was killed. Consequently, Baghdad became interested in the Canadian-designed 45-calibre GC-45: already in 1981, an order had been placed for 200 Austria-manufactured GHN-45 howitzers based on this design, and in 1984 an order for a similar number of the South African version manufactured by Denel was placed. Compared with the Soviet D-1 152mm in the Iraqi Army and the US M114 155mm weapon in the IRIA, whose muzzle velocities were 508m/s and 563 m/s, these weapons featured a muzzle velocity of 897 m/s which gave them a range of 29.9 kilometres with Extended Range Full Bore (ERFB) ammunition or 39.6 kilometres with the base-bleed version which were especially hard on barrels. These weapons actually outranged the Coalition field artillery during Operation Desert Storm in 1991. The downside of the situation was that their high performance meant shorter barrel lives. Just as aircraft life is measured in flying hours so gun-barrel life is measured in terms of the number of times it may be fired with the largest number (full charge) of propellant bags or Effective Full

Table 13: Major Arms Orders by Iraq 1982–1986					
Order Placed	Country	Equipment			Delivered
		Type	Model	Number	
1982	China	MBT	Type-69	1,500	1983–1987
	China	Towed Arty	122mm	200	1983–1986
	China	Towed Arty	152mm	200	1983–1986
	France	APC	M-3-VTT	115	1983–1984
	Poland	MBT	T-72	250	1982–1990
	USSR	MLRS	122mm	200	1983–1984
	USSR	Towed Arty	122mm	576	1982–1988
	Poland	APC	MT-LB	750	1983–1990
1983	China	MLRS	107mm	100	1984–1988
	Poland	APC	MT-LB	750	1983–1984
	USSR	Recon	PT-76	200	1984
	USSR	SP Mortar	240mm 2S4	10	1983
	USSR	MLRS	BM-21	200	1983–1984
1984	Egypt	Towed Arty	122mm	120	1985–1988
	Romania	MBT	TR-77	150	1985–1987
	South Africa	Towed Arty	155mm	200	1985–1986
	USSR	Recon	PT-76	200	1984
1985	Egypt	Towed Arty	122mm	210	1985–1989
	USSR	MLRS	122mm	360	1986–1988
1986	USSR	SP Arty	Akatsiya	100	1986–1988
	USSR	SP Arty	Gvozdika	100	1987–1989
	USSR	Towed Arty	152	180	1986–1988
	Yugoslavia	MLRS	262mm	2	1987

Charge (EFC): as of the 1980s, a typical 155mm 52-calibre barrel had a life of 750 EFC while 39-calibre weapons had a life of 2,650 EFC. Guns rarely used full charges but even with limited charges as a projectile moved along the barrel it caused friction on the rifling which was gradually smoothed and made the projectiles less accurate. Tank gun barrels have similar restraints with wear depending upon the type of ammunition used: the 105mm M68 used in IRIA M48s and M60A1s having a life of some 300 EFC with the highest performing anti-armour rounds.[6] The Iraqi Army used huge amounts of artillery ammunition, with the daily rate equivalent to the US Army's weekly rate from the Second World War. This went so far that while it had depots capable of storing up to 300,000 tonnes of ammunition, it suffered periodic shortages.[7] The prime suppliers were Austria, Belgium, Brazil, China, Czechoslovakia, Egypt, France, Greece, Poland, Jordan, Kuwait, South Africa and the USSR. Eventually, even France's Luchaire and Belgium's PRB began supplying 130mm base-bleed shells for Soviet-made guns. Such was the insatiable demand for ammunition that Baghdad asked Italy's Difesa e Spazio if they could supply ammunition for which they did not have a licence! However, with guns from so many sources and with widely differing ballistic performance it was not only difficult to ensure sustained supplies of rounds and charges, but also difficult to organise fire plans, although fire direction computers reportedly reached some batteries by 1985. There were also problems training gun crews and the Iraqis often had to write in Arabic above Russian, Chinese or English language data plates, and these problems were probably shared with Iranian gunners. Unsurprisingly, as the war went on without an end, the Iraqi Army eventually arrived at the decision to start replacing its worn-out artillery pieces instead of just replacing worn-out gun barrels.[8]

The shortage of heavy artillery meant a greater reliance upon MLRS – mostly of Soviet or Chinese origin. Furthermore, a US$600 million contract was placed with Avibras Aeroespacial for 60 SS-40 Astros II MLRS and the first instalment helped to complete development of these weapons. Deliveries began in March 1984 and were completed in 1987 with batteries consisting of four launcher vehicles, a fire control vehicle with Contraves Fieldguard radar and two vehicles to transport spare rockets, with the initial consignment being for 10,000 rockets. In 1986 there was reportedly a US$2 billion contract with Avibras and Engesa for 300 EE-T1 Osario MBTs, 300 EE-9 Cascavael with 90mm and 25mm guns and more Astros II systems including 50–60 of the longer range SS-300 rockets. While the MBTs and some of the other equipment would not be delivered, the contract meant that Iraq would be Brazil's biggest export market, and ammunition sales also proved lucrative for both Chile, Portugal and Spain.

Missile orders were also placed with the trend to acquire basic weapons from the Far East and sophisticated ones from the USSR. In 1985 North Korea received an order for 4,000 of the Susong-Po anti-armour missile, a version of AT-3 Sagger, while the following year China received an order for 1,000 Hong Ying (Red Tassel) 5 or HN-5A MANPADS, a reverse-engineered version of the SA-7. Also in 1986, the USSR received a contract for 3,000 9K111 (ASCC/NATO codename 'AT-4 Spigot') ATGMs comparable with the European Milan system.

In addition to 'big ticket' items, Iraq also received valuable other material. In 1983 an order was placed for 42 LMT Rasit battlefield surveillance radars in France. Another 18 were ordered in 1986 while the following year 10 Thorni-EMI Cymbeline counterbattery radars were ordered and delivered into 1990. Iraq would buy up to 40 percent of France's military exports including legitimate dual-use equipment such as Renault TRM-1000 trucks, while Baghdad also received German Daimler Benz and British Land Rovers together with Saboteur Trooper Mk IV all-terrain transports. Some Laird Centaur half-tracks, based upon the Land Rover chassis, were also supplied but the Iraqis wanted associated mine-laying systems which the British refused to supply.

PART I: THE THRIVING ARMOURERS

An Iranian mechanised battle group, including Scorpion reconnaissance tanks, M60 MBTs and even one 155mm self-propelled howitzer. Such massive formations became a rarity during the mid-1980s because the Iraqi Air Force established air supremacy over the battlefield. (Tom Cooper collection)

Because of dwindling stocks of BGM-71 TOW missiles, the IRIAA decided to mate US-made AGM-65A Maverick guided air-to-surface missiles – actually used by IRIAF F-4Es – to some of its AH-1Js. This is a close-up photograph of such a modification. (Farzin Nadimi collection)

Land mines were supplied to both sides in incredible numbers, Iran having 2.5 million including its pre-war stocks of American ordnance, while Iraq received some 6 million, of which 75 percent were anti-personnel types costing as little as US$10.00. These, used extensively in the southern battlefield, were mainly from Italy's Valsella, BPD Difesa e Spazio and Tecnovar, who were the lead producers of plastic-bodied ordnance of the 1980s. Chile, China, Egypt and the Soviet Union also supplied mines, although the Chinese ordnance were copies of Soviet designs, while Iraq produced the Valmara 69 anti-personnel mine under licence.

Iraq produced limited quantities of small arms, light and medium mortars, together with RPGs. There were also shell-filling plants as well as factories organised by Thomson-CSF to produce the company's communications equipment, and repair depots at national level for hard- and soft-skinned vehicles as well as MBTs. From 1982 chemical weapon production began and by the end of the war Iraq was said to have produced 3,000 tonnes of chemical agents which filled 100,000 bombs, shells and rocket warheads, as well as some missile warheads. Initially the agents consisted of a crude mustard gas (Bis (2-chloroethyl) sulphide) based upon crude sulphur agents, rather than more lethal sesqui and nitrogen agents. Later the Iraqis began to develop nerve agents, such as Sarin and Tabun, which are organophosphates originally developed as pesticides. As a result of a report by a United Nations investigative mission, in April 1984 the United States and the United Kingdom banned the export of chloroethanol, dimethyl-methyl-phosphate, dimethylamine, methyl-phosphonyl-dichloride, methyl-phosphonyl-difluoride, phosphorus-oxychloride, potassium fluoride and thiodiglycol. However, like trucks, many chemical components, had both medical and military usage and could be legitimately exported to Iraq.

12
THE BRILLIANT BLOW

The New Year opened, like 1985, with another Iraqi 'active defence' operation in South Majnoon. Saddam was anxious to regain the island and during the rainy season his engineers used dozens of bulldozers, much earthmoving equipment and hundreds of trucks to drain the island's approaches and to build roads leading into the Fish Lake Line around the Ghuzail.

The Iranians could not help but to be aware of this activity, but Rashid decided to strike before the end of the rainy season when the enemy might expect an attack to exploit the dried ground. The task was assigned to 31st Infantry Division (al-Hussein Force) under Brigadier Yalcheen Omar Abdil and delegated to Lieutenant Colonel Ibrahim Idwan Abib's 28th Infantry Brigade and Colonel Sami Abbas Mujwil al-Rawi's 49th Infantry Brigade, and the attack date was set by Saddam as Army Day, 6 January 1986.

The attack went in on schedule at 0420 hrs and achieved complete surprise with massive firepower and strong air support, including not only gunships but also some of the new Su-25K 'Frogfoot' attack aircraft. The Iraqis stormed forward exploiting water channels as well as bunds to recapture up to half the island in less than two hours, and claimed to have inflicted 4,000 casualties while they suffered minimal losses.[1]

Planning for a New Dawn

Iraqi General Headquarters may have had a secondary motive, to draw the enemy into a bloody battle of attrition for South Majnoon but history repeated itself and the Iranians did not respond. Yet they were not idle and were quietly assembling substantial forces in Khuzestan during the latter half of 1985 as Tehran contemplated its most ambitious offensive at a time when it also faced a major dilemma.

The SDC remained convinced time was on its side and that, like the Union in the American Civil War, it would eventually stretch the enemy to breaking point and had already come tantalisingly close to success in operations Khyber and Badr. But while Iran had a much larger population than its neighbour it could deploy far fewer men, about a million, which was inadequate to achieve overwhelming numerical superiority over the 800,000-man Iraqi Army. The heavy casualties suffered by Iranian forces and the Iraqis' qualitative superiority exacerbated the problem. By the beginning

Led by blue-jacketed men – probably Naval Pasdaran of the 104th Emir al-Mu'minin or the 105th al-Kawthar Brigade – a column of Iranian troops move past a column of vehicles to embark for crossing the Shatt (called the Arvand Road by the Iranians) to open Operation Val Fajr-8. Note the casualties lying on the rear deck of the BTR-50. (Tom Cooper collection)

Iranian SBS commandos not only conducted careful reconnaissance operations on the Faw Peninsula prior to the start of Operation Val Fajr-8, but also led the opening attack of this offensive. Here, they are seen in front of one of the 20 Agusta-Sikorsky AS-61A-4 Sea Kings which were sometimes also used for their insertion behind enemy lines. (Farzin Nadimi collection)

Rafsanjani later explained the SDC's motives:

> Faw was important to us for a number of reasons: First, because with the capture of Faw, Iraq would lose its ability to use the sea, unless they could sneak a boat through Khowr Abdullah (Khawr Abd Allah also Khur Abdollah) under the cover of night. But they would no longer have a military presence in the sea. In addition to that, Iraq no longer could make use of its two oil terminals south of Faw: the al-Amayah and the al-Bakr [sic] oil terminals.

He would later claim that, bearing in mind Khomeini's strict demands for minimum Iraqi civilian casualties, this was an ideal theatre because there were so few civilians.[5]

This was a disingenuous explanation because both oil terminals had been badly damaged by Iranian artillery fire and largely abandoned, while Iranian surface-to-surface missiles were directed at Iraqi cities just as Iraqi missiles struck Iranian cities.[6] Moreover, Iran's control of the Straits of Hormuz stopped Iraqi shipping reaching Umm Qasr (also 'Um Qasir' or 'Om ol-Qasr') which had almost ceased to function as a port. It remained the Iraqi Navy's base, although it posed only a minor threat, and of two dozen missile and torpedo-equipped fast attack craft, about half had been sunk or were decommissioned. By establishing a military presence on the peninsula Iran was clearly demonstrating it could invade Kuwait, which is separated only by the narrow (2 kilometre) Khowr Abdullah from Umm Qasr, and 'persuade' it to abandon the 'oil conspiracy' with the bonus that success would open a new front to Basra. Long after the offensive began, on 23 and 25 February, the Iranians would claim their offensive was designed both to end the interdiction of shipping into Bandar-e Imam Khomeini and Bandar-e Mashur and also to prevent the enemy shelling Khorramshahr and Abadan.

Both Rezai and his clerical supporters in the Pasdaran continued to grow in confidence and they would again spearhead the operation, with training beginning about September 1985. They were slowly learning the lessons from each campaign, like the Allied generals in the First World War and at similar terrible cost. The lessons were dissimilated among the Pasdaran formations, which also received more rigorous combat training, while coordination with the IRIA was improved at the Forward Operational Headquarters. Like the

of 1986 Baghdad and Tehran had 4,500 and 1,000 MBTs respectively while in artillery the figures were 5,000 to 800.[2]

Iraq achieved this largely from gifts and loans provided by Saudi Arabia and the Gulf oil producers, notably Kuwait, as well as limited sales of oil through Turkey. Tehran could still export its oil by sea but its indignation against the Gulf States was increased by what it regarded as their participation in an 'oil conspiracy' to drive down the price of oil by increasing production. With Iran's economy undermined, demands for action grew louder in Tehran, but rather than add to their foes the SDC decided to apply indirect pressure. The Kuwaitis and Saudis were not just bankrolling the Iraqis but also facilitating the movement of arms and equipment. The British Foreign Office, for example, was informed that 110 Chinese tanks and 20–30 APCs were seen moving northwards through Kuwait from Saudi Arabia on 5 March 1983, while on 12 April a convoy of transporters with 400 new Chinese tanks were seen heading towards Basra.[3]

In the mid or late summer of 1985 Tehran decided to cut the Gordian Knot by seizing the al-Faw (also al-Fao or al-Fawr) Peninsula, which lay along Kuwait's northern border and was only 300 to 1,000 metres across the Shatt al-Arab from Iran.[4]

PART I: THE BRILLIANT BLOW

An Iranian Pasdaran commando posing in front of a rush-covered shore with a Kalashnikov assault rifle in his hand. Swimming in the swiftly moving Shatt proved extremely exhausting for combat divers, while a shortage of wetsuits restricted their reconnaissance missions. (Tom Cooper collection)

Boat crews of the Naval Brigade of the IRGC preparing their craft to carry men and supplies across the Shatt. This photograph was taken in one of the ports east of the battlefield, where flotillas of such boats were gathering. In the background is a Japanese-built Iranian Arya class tank landing ship, which was too big to be assigned for this mission. (Tom Cooper collection)

imports could not meet Tehran's requirements for heavy equipment, while a shortage of spares restricted the use of captured equipment, including MBTs for which there were no replacement engines. Despite improved supplies it was impossible to substantially expand either the IRIA or the Pasdaran, and by early 1986 perhaps half the former and two-thirds of the latter were truly combat ready.

The clerics decided they needed a professional soldier in charge and they assigned the task to a Khomeini loyalist, 45-year-old Colonel Hassani-Sa'di, whose joint IRIA-Pasdaran Task Force Karbala had played a major role in Badr and would now play a role in the new offensive. For this and its support operations huge numbers of men were mobilised: one report claims half the IRIA and two-thirds of the Pasdaran – although this may be an exaggeration – while 1,000-strong commando battalions were also established. The demands of the rural economy again meant the new operation would have fewer Basiji, most probably drawn from marsh or coastal villages, and with the well of manpower almost exhausted, from October 1985 women began to be used for rear-area military tasks, and there were plans to send civil servants up to the front. The operation was codenamed Val Fajr-8 (Dawn 8) and preparations began in the late summer of 1985 with major amphibious exercises in the Caspian Sea.

troops of English general Oliver Cromwell, the Pasdaran put their trust in God but kept their powder dry. Yet there still remained a chasm of ignorance between the frontline troops, including the Pasdaran and their political and religious masters. Early in 1986 some 8,000 commanders from division to company level were summoned to Tehran to discuss the war because the leaders at the operational level were unable to make the government and clerics comprehend the frontline situation. They had difficulty drafting and executing plans because the objectives and assigned formations would be changed almost at a whim and there appeared no overall strategic blueprint.

There also remained a severe shortage of heavy equipment, much of which had been lost during the battles around the marshes – together with experienced IRIA personnel. The Pasdaran could improve infantry training, but even Chinese and North Korean

The code name 'Val Fajr' had previously been used exclusively on the Northern and Central Fronts and was part of the deception programme including attempts to attract enemy attention north of Basra. Like Arras in 1917, the wrecked cities of Khorramshahr and Abadan provided excellent cover for assembling much of the assault force, while the numerous coastal date palm groves along the banks of the Shatt, especially near the mouth, allowed boarding points for men and vehicles, and concealed carefully camouflaged pontoon bridging materials. Because the main attack would be launched from the marshes and wetlands of the northern bank of the Shatt al-Arab, the road network south of Abadan between the River Bahmanshir and the Shatt, mostly on bunds, required considerable extension by IRIA engineers, the Pasdaran 44th

157

Abandoned Iraqi defences on the Faw Peninsula. In the background is the rusting hulk of one of dozens of merchantmen trapped inside the waterway at the start of the war, and meanwhile abandoned by its crew. (Tom Cooper collection)

The Iranians captured a number of armoured fighting vehicles – reportedly including up to 30 MBTs – during their initial advance on the Faw Peninsula. Most belonged to the ill-fated 26th Division. T-54/55s like this were quickly turned against their former owners. (Tom Cooper collection)

they were being used for commercial traffic, although in 1987 Iraqi Premier, Taha Yassin Ramadan, would claim that the US had 'doctored' their satellite intelligence which meant that the Iraqis were taken by surprise. Farrokh states that, because the Iranians were conscious that US satellites were observing them, they ran streams of trucks, heavy equipment and troops up and down the roads from the Hawizah Marshes to the Basra front to create a heat signature which not only covered the real movements but helped to confuse first the Americans and then Baghdad. In the build-up for the Faw Peninsula attack the most essential transport movements were made at night but there were numerous accidents and a steady stream of injuries, some of them serious.[8]

There was an extensive reconnaissance effort involving naval frogmen, IRIA special forces, and the IRIAF which used high performance RF-4E Phantoms and F-5E Tigers, while the Pasdaran not only despatched scout units but also used Mohajer Unmanned Aerial Vehicles (UAVs). One encouraging factor was the IRIAF's improvement in combat efficiency after years of decline. Spare parts, acquired either from the black market or from Asian countries, allowed the Iranians to return many aircraft to operational service. By the beginning of Val Fajr-8 Iranian sources indicate 140 combat jets were operational, half of them F-5 Tiger IIs. This allowed the IRIAF to assign 12 Tigers and 12 F-14A Tomcats to support the offensive in Operation Shafagh. Interestingly, the IRIAF directives were issued on 5 January by a committee led by Rafsanjari and included a requirement to provide the Pasdaran with close air support for a minimum of 15 days, extendable to a month. HAWK batteries would also be assigned to provide air defence, and during the offensive they would launch 86 missiles which reportedly hit 52 targets.[9]

'Qamar Bani Hashem' Engineer Brigade augmented by Basiji and the civilian Ministry of Construction often working double shifts. The engineers also prepared a site for the northern end of a pontoon bridge and assembled prefabricated bunkers called suleh, to house command teams and troops, while embankments were built to conceal the preparations; yet it does not appear the Iraqis recognised the significance of this activity.[7]

The chronic shortage of military vehicles which forced both the IRIA and Pasdaran to make extensive use of civilian vehicles, including British-built double-decker buses, helped to conceal the movement of troops and supplies. One source suggests that US photographic analysts who examined images of trucks concluded

A unique feature of Val Fajr-8 was the use of Pasdaran SEAL-type special forces from the two naval brigades who augmented the IRIA teams of 23rd Special Forces Division. Four SEAL battalions were deployed with some 2,400 men, although there was a shortage

PART I: THE BRILLIANT BLOW

By the time that Val Fajr-8 was launched, the IRIAF was only capable of providing about 20 close air support sorties. Most of these were flown by F-5E/Fs from TFB.4 and targeted major Iraqi HQs and supply depots on the Faw Peninsula. (Farzin Nadimi collection)

Boats returning to the Iranian side of the Shatt were usually full of casualties. This photograph shows the evacuation of a gruesomely wounded Pasdaran by his comrades, sometime around 11 February 1986. (Tom Cooper collection)

Iranian Preparations and the Terrain

Crossing the Shatt (called the Arvand by the Iranians) would be a formidable problem and one newly arrived divisional commander was reported to have exclaimed 'May God help us; how can we cross the Arvand?' The IRIA bridging inventory was extended during late 1985, including six pontoon bridges from Germany, while some 3,000 small boats were purchased, mostly from Japan, and distributed among the naval brigades' three boat battalions, but with so many non-swimmers thousands of life jackets were also acquired. The Pasdaran learned from their experiences in the Hawizah Marshes in 1984 and 1985 and were able to practice tactics in conditions of tight security on the Caspian.

of both wet suits and Scuba gear, but despite this the frogmen began a systematic examination of the southern landing sites from September 1985. Small boats would quietly cross the Shatt and insert the SEALs into the smelly and salty water so they could swim to the Iraqi-held coast. Strong currents made this hard work, indeed they could spend only 2–3 hours in the water, and by the time they were recovered the men were exhausted. Some 700–800 missions were made, usually a simple night reconnaissance, but occasionally the men would conceal themselves in reed beds during the day and sometimes they would go ashore, change into civilian clothing so as to resemble local peasants and tour the enemy rear. More than half the missions were reported to be successful, and they provided detailed information on the defences, even to the size of bunker doors!

Hassani-Sa'di decided to give his men the best possible chance of success by launching his assaults when rain would ground enemy airpower and low cloud would reduce its effectiveness. He would first launch diversionary operations around the Hawizah Marshes and towards the upper part of the peninsula while airborne troops raided towards Umm Qasr as well as the Mina al-Bakr and Khowr (or Khawr) al-Amayah Al-Amayah offshore oil terminals which lie some 25 nautical miles (45 kilometres) southeast of Faw City.

The Iranians had some two dozen divisions in Khuzestan Province, some 200,000–300,000 men swelled by 50,000 Basiji. Half the divisions were ostentatiously deployed in large tent encampments either on the eastern shores of the Hawizah Marshes or opposite the Fish Lake Line opposite VI and III Corps to divert enemy attention northwards. In addition, large numbers of worn-out and leaking boats were also assembled on the marsh edges.

MIDDLE EAST@WAR SERIES SPECIAL #1: THE IRAN-IRAQ WAR

The Iranian offensive on the Faw and Iraqi counterattacks set the local fuel depot on fire. The huge, black column of smoke continued rising into the sky for months afterwards and was a clear orientation mark for both sides. (Tom Cooper collection)

Naval commandos of the Emir al-Mu'minin Naval Brigade of the IRGC moving along a trench while supporting the Nooh Task Force's advance between Khor Abdullah and the Mamlaha salt beds. (Tom Cooper collection)

An Iranian anti-tank team mounted on a jeep with a 106mm M40 recoilless rifle approaching a burning Iraqi fuel dump in al-Faw. (Tom Cooper collection)

Another half-a-dozen divisions were assembled opposite al-Amarah to threaten IV Corps.

The main assault would be launched by the equivalent of nine full strength divisions who, with support forces, totalled 97,000 men who were secretly assembled south of Khorramshahr, the majority amid the date palms south of Khosrowabad, under the Khatam al-Anbiya Command. They were organised into Task Force Karbala with 7th Vali Asr, 8th Najaf Ashraf, 19th 'Fajr', 27th Mohammad Rasoolallah, 41st 'Sarallah' Divisions, 57th 'Abolfazl al-Abbas' Brigade; 105th 'Al-Kawthar' Naval Brigade (five infantry, one SEAL, one naval battalion) together with the 1st and 2nd Brigades/21st IRIA Infantry Division, some 48,000 men. Supporting this was Task Force Nooh with some 27,000 men of 14th 'Imam Hossein', 17th Ali Ibn Abu Talib, 25th Karbala Divisions, 104th 'Emir al-Mu'minin' Naval Brigade (Five infantry, three SEAL, two naval battalions). They were supported by the Pasdaran's artillery brigade (believed to be 90th 'Khatam al-Anbiya') and 'Qamar Bani Hashem' Engineer Brigades, and possibly the IRIA 33rd Artillery Group. Although not confirmed by either side, experience in the previous two offensives would have led the Iranians to anticipate chemical attacks. They had quietly acquired chemical protection equipment and it is probable that they had assembled one of the two chemical decontamination brigades to support the operation. There would also be a subsidiary operation by the 1st Brigade/77th IRIA Division with two brigades of 5th "Nassr" Pasdaran Divisions with some 19,000 men.

This subsidiary operation would strike from the mouth of the River Karun to seize the island of Umm al-Rasas (also Omm al-Rasas) as a steppingstone to establishing a beachhead on the peninsula. A pontoon bridge would then be thrown across the Shatt allowing reinforcements to expand the bridgehead while disrupting the movement of enemy reserves down the Basra–al-Faw (Faw City) highway. Iranian sources remain silent upon the ultimate objective of this operation, which may have aimed to provide a springboard for an advance on Basra once the whole of the peninsula was in Iranian hands.

The main blow would be launched across the Shatt from south of Khorramshahr at the southern end of the Faw Peninsula using the two task forces which assembled between Khosrowabad and Arvand Kenar, in the cultivated area around the mouth of the Shatt. Spearheaded by the naval brigades they would cross the Shatt with Karbala on the right and Task Force Nooh on the left to seize and secure the southern end of the peninsula. Pontoon bridges would then be thrown across the Shatt allowing the bridgehead to expand north towards Basra and west towards Umm Qasr to establish a significant, brooding, presence along Kuwait's northern border.

The Faw Peninsula lies south of Az Zubayr and Abu al-Khasib (also Abdul Khassib, Abul Khasib, Abu al-Kasib

PART I: THE BRILLIANT BLOW

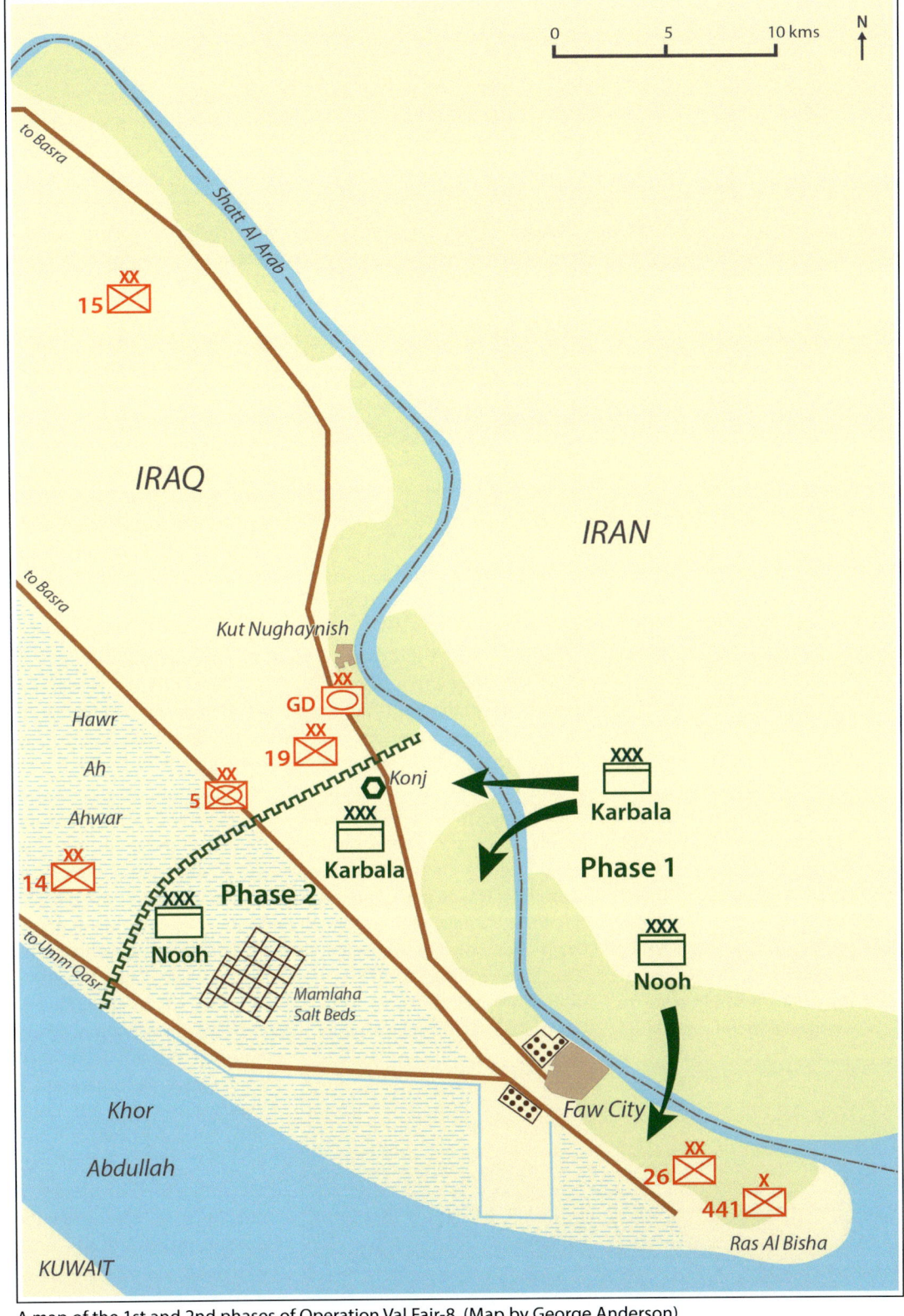

the peninsula is an agricultural area 2–4 kilometres wide down the Shatt coast, where fields and dense date palm groves, surrounded by low mud walls, are watered by numerous irrigation channels. A score of little villages are to be found in this area together with the region's largest town, Faw City, which had some 70,000 inhabitants at the outbreak of the war (although almost all had subsequently fled north). On the northern and eastern outskirts of the town, separated by the Basra–Faw City highway, were oil tanks which had fed the two terminals but were now scorched and twisted metal.

There were numerous paths and small gravel-topped or beaten earth roads on embankments across the peninsula, including one running beside the Shatt, but there were only two major roads which ran northwest to southeast from Abu al-Khasib, one being a 'hard top' (asphalt) coastal highway from Basra to Faw City which is just inland from the cultivated belt. The other ran down the middle of the peninsula to join the Basra road just north of Faw City and until 1985 had been gravel-topped then given an asphalt covering. Some 10 kilometres from Faw City this road ran down the north-eastern side of the Mamlaha (sometimes written Memlaha) salt beds with an evaporator complex consisting of nine salt-extraction ponds in an 8 kilometre by eight-kilometre area divided by a 1.2-metre-high earth bund. The south-western edge of these salt beds was a canal to drain the Hawr ah-Ahwar marshes and this then ran 12 kilometres eastwards to the oil tanks south of the Basra–Faw City highway before taking a 6-kilometre detour to the south then returning almost to the highway.

Another asphalt-topped road ran westwards from Faw City along the peninsula's southern coast, where low tide created wide mud flats, to pass the other side of the ponds before reaching Umm Qasr which lies on the other side of the Khowr Abdullah. The town, which had some 50,000 inhabitants, is separated from Kuwait by a small

A map of the 1st and 2nd phases of Operation Val Fajr-8. (Map by George Anderson)

and Abolkhasib), which are some 10–15 kilometres southeast and southwest of Basra respectively and is bounded in the east by the Shatt al-Arab and in the west by the Khowr Abdullah. It is some 90 kilometres long, ending at the Ras al-Bisha (al-Bisha Cape), and a maximum of 50 kilometres wide and, apart from a six-kilometre-wide strip of firm ground along the east, it consists largely of brackish salt marshes (Hawr ah-Ahwar) which dry out in the summer, except in the west where a strip up to 15 kilometres wide remains permanently flooded. The most densely populated part of

MIDDLE EAST@WAR SERIES SPECIAL #1: THE IRAN-IRAQ WAR

A Bell AH-1J Cobra passing low over the Shatt al-Arab while underway in the direction of al-Faw. The Iraqis amassed an immense volume of anti-aircraft defences on their side of the front line, attempting to close the skies to Iranian fliers. Therefore, their appearance was always a morale-bolster for Iranian ground troops. (Tom Cooper collection)

inlet and was created in 1958 as a naval base which was expanded three years later into the country's only deep-water port. It was completed in July 1967 and linked to Basra by both a highway and a railway running along the western banks of the Khowr Abdullah through Zubayr.

Intelligence Games

The Iraqis were aware of the build-up north of Khorramshahr and Abadan, assisted, probably indirectly, by US satellite intelligence which detected the Iranian build-up north of Basra, but the rainy season clouds had obscured the ground south of the city. Consequently, Baghdad was most concerned by the assembly of some six divisions (50,000 men) in the Susangerd area and concluded the main blow would land around al-Amarah, north of the Hawizah Marshes, in IV Corps or, between there and Qurnah, as with Khyber and Badr, against VI Corps. The Iranians had indeed planned to strike towards Qurnah but only as a diversion, possibly because Rashid's Army Day offensive made a stronger blow impossible by depriving the southernmost prong of a springboard.

But the main blow was always scheduled to fall some 40 kilometres to the south and the Iraqi failure to detect enemy preparations for this blow, despite their superiority in COMINT, was due to a number of factors. Primarily, COMINT proved of little help because the Pasdarans' lack of radios forced them to rely upon landlines or motorcycle couriers, although their reliance upon IRIA logistical support which was better equipped with radios, did pose a security threat. GMID was also being fed false information by double or turned agents including a spy caught in Ahwaz. Pasdaran leader Rahim Safavi noted that the latter 'was under our control and communicated the information that we wanted.'[10]

Iraqi COMINT did detect at least one message which suggested plans for an offensive against the Faw Peninsula but it was not passed on, yet the Iraqi Navy clearly received concrete information about enemy intentions for it withdrew its 'Silkworm' coast defence missiles from a base just south of Faw City. Several senior Iraqi generals visited the Faw Peninsula and reported they could see boats being assembled, extensive road building and gaps in the palm groves for supply dumps, but the head of the GMID since August 1983, Major General Mahmood Shukur Shahin discounted them claiming it was an obvious deception.[11] However, he was not the only one to be mistaken about Iranian intentions. Washington analysed the Iranian concentrations and alerted Saddam through his friend King Hussein of Jordan that the attack upon Faw would be only 'a limited assault'. The main blow, the king said, 'would come later in the central sector.' Knowing the origin of this information, which confirmed reports from their own intelligence organisation, it was little wonder the Iraqis were totally surprised.

Defending the Peninsula

Until April or May 1984 the peninsula was part of III Corps' Tactical Area of Responsibility, but the Operation Ramadan and Khyber offensives demonstrated the Basra-based corps needed to focus on threats from the north and the east. The Faw Peninsula was regarded as being a minor front facing commando raids, starting on 10 May 1982 during Operation Beit-ol-Moqaddas when Iranian naval commandos struck the

Further Iranian advances north of Faw resulted in the capture of this Thomson-CSF Rasit battlefield surveillance radar and a Chinese-made Type-69 MBT. (Farzin Nadimi collection)

162

peninsula's Ras al-Bisha radar station which was used to monitor shipping movements. At the time of the Khyber offensive it was garrisoned by three Border Guard brigades, 238th Infantry Brigade and the Navy, with a brigade of 6th Armoured Division and 33rd Special Forces Brigade available as a reaction force. Khyber demonstrated the Pasdaran could pose a serious threat to such a ragbag of units and in May 1985 the peninsula was placed under the new Shatt al-Arab Operations Headquarters (SAOH) or Quiadet Amaliyat Shatt al-Arab (Shatt al-Arab Operations Command) in Arabic. This covered the western bank of the Shatt al-Arab and the southern coast of the Faw Peninsula to Umm Qasr, but in March or August 1985 this was upgraded to VII Corps.[12]

The corps' first commander was Major General Shawkat Ahmed Atta, the former Director of Military Operations who had drafted the documents which created the EOTH in 1984.[13] By early 1986 this had some 27,000 men under Major General Shawkat Ahmed Atta who had eight brigades with a nominal 15,000 men evenly split between the 15th ('Farooq Force') Infantry Division and 26th Infantry Division. The latter exercised the operational control of the 441st Naval Brigade in the south, but not the 440th Naval Brigade at Umm Qasr.[14]

Both formations were stretched to the limit along the 170-kilometre Shatt front, and even if they had been at full strength, they would have had about 100 men per kilometre in a situation ominously similar to the one the Iraqis faced along the Karun at the start of the Iranian Operation Beit-ol-Moqaddas in 1982. The 26th Division was especially vulnerable with its northernmost brigade holding a 21-kilometre front while the others each had lines of 40–50 kilometres. Baghdad was confident there was no major threat to the peninsula, especially in the south,

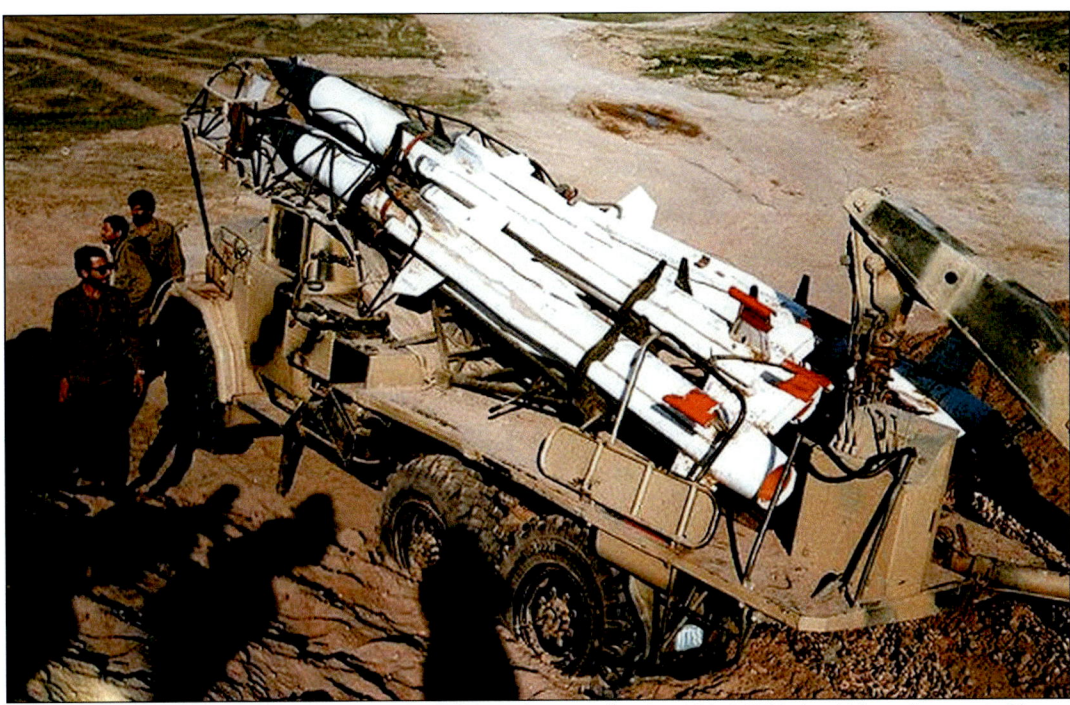

Also captured by the Iranians at Faw was the full complement of an Iraqi SA-6 SAM site. Although operated by the Iraqi Army, these weapons systems were usually reserved for defence of major communication and supply centres in the rear of the Iraqi front. (Farzin Nadimi collection)

This Iraqi ZSU-23-4 became bogged down in the mud and was abandoned by its owners. The Iranians captured the vehicle and one of their troops can be seen conducting repairs on it, but in the light of the ferocity of Iraqi counterattacks, it is unlikely that this Shilka survived for much longer. (Farzin Nadimi collection)

and drained Ata's command of men and equipment to IV Corps especially, where Shawkat was attached until the eve of the Iranian attack as an assistant and potential replacement. While the divisions had commando battalions, and the brigades had commando

A stretcher party of four IRGC Naval commandos crossing a pontoon bridge over the Shatt al-Arab while carrying a wounded comrade to a field hospital. (Tom Cooper collection)

Iranian troops inside the captured Iraqi air defence centre outside al-Faw. This HQ was responsible for the air defence of much of southern Iraq, and its loss was badly felt by the IrAF. (Farzin Nadimi collection)

The Iraqi Air Force hit back at Iranian troops with all available aircraft, from fighter-bombers like this pair of MiG-23BNs – seen deploying FAB 100 bombs to medium bombers such as Tupolev Tu-16s and Tu-22s. (Tom Cooper collection)

companies as reaction forces, Ata lacked a formal 'fire brigade' in the shape of a commando force apart from an ad hoc reserve group of about 1,000 men, possibly drawn from 66th Commando Brigade south of Basra, while his total fire support consisted of only four field artillery battalions (72 guns) and three heavy mortar batteries. During the lull in the fighting in the late summer of 1985 Shawkat persuaded Baghdad to provide him with engineers and heavy equipment. He used them to improve the road network, especially around the cultivated area, and to build a berm, together with bunkers and vehicle shelters, along the eastern side of the Basra–Faw City highway, which would prove a valuable asset during the crisis. He had also improved the road down the centre of the peninsula and built a few switch positions to restrict commando penetrations, but the combination of Defence Ministry indifference and terrain prevented the construction of a defensive system in depth.[15]

Early warning was the first line of defence based upon a string of Rasit battlefield surveillance radars whose antennas were either on masts or the tops of bunkers, but they were designed for use over land rather than water which degraded their performance. These were augmented by searchlights and watch towers for visual observation using night vision goggles. Between the water and the shore were two lines, six metres deep, of wire-covered steel-beam obstacles similar to the 'Czech hedgehogs' deployed on the Normandy beaches by the Germans in 1944. Close to the shore was a line of prefabricated bunkers, usually consisting of a buried steel frame covered with corrugated steel sheets, then concrete or earth and then 50 centimetres of gravel, up to a metre thick. These were sited for all-round defence with wire obstacles and 800–1,000 metres behind them would be command bunkers and artillery battery positions.[16]

The tip of the peninsula was the responsibility of 700 sailors and 500 airmen, mostly technical troops with little or no combat training. The former formed part of 2nd Naval Brigade, with three launchers on earth mounds for Chinese-made CSS-2 'Silkworm' anti-ship missiles, supported by a Garpun ('Plank Shave') surface search radar, or the Chinese Type-352 ('Square Tie'), and a command post. The airmen were from the Southern Air Defence Command, which had a site just north of al-Faw City, possibly linked into the Kuwaiti and other Gulf State air defence systems. It was equipped with French Tigre (Tiger), and possibly the Soviet 'Long Track', air search radars and there were also four surface-to-air missile sites with Crotale and SA-6 'Gainful' missiles, the former supported by Mirador II and 'Straight Flush' search and target acquisition radars.[17]

Holding the southern coast of the peninsula and shielding Umm Qasr was the 1,000-man, relatively lightly armed 441st Naval Brigade raised from Rear Admiral Abd Muhammad Abdullah's under-employed Navy of some 3,000 men, and more of a coast defence militia and guard force than a full brigade, indeed it also supplied men for defending the Hawizah Marshes. The Navy itself had some 30 vessels, none of which had a gun greater than 37mm calibre – which meant they were largely unsuitable for taking part in ground combat.

While officially exported to Iraq as VIP-transports, and supposedly equipped for such purposes only, German-made Bo105 helicopters were actually attack helicopters, usually armed with 20mm cannons and launchers for unguided rockets. They were deployed in large numbers during the fighting at Faw. (Ali Tobchi collection)

Crossing the Shatt

For the Iranians everything now depended upon the weather and the need for low cloud, rain and fog to shield their forces, with the window of opportunity likely to open from late January and, in this case, the rain began to fall during the last three days of the month. Under low, dark, clouds the final preparations began, with the decision to launch the offensive probably made on 8 February, which gave Rafsanjari and Rezai time to travel to the command post, the latter carrying a green banner from the shrine of Imam Reza which he presented to the Karbala commander. The troops moved out during the night from 9 to 10 February after first praying, then having their supper. Their prayers were answered, for from 1800 hrs it began to drizzle, and as the men assembled an hour later the rain grew heavier.[18]

SEALs spearheaded the offensive, but the continued shortage of wet suits weakened their operations. Yet undeterred, they set off in small boats through choppy waters, which capsized one or two boats causing the frogmen to lose their weapons including assault rifles and RPGs. As they sailed, the weather briefly improved and the men entered the water at about 2000 hrs under moonlight obscured by patches of cloud, though within a couple of hours it would turn stormy again with high winds and heavy rain.

Off the Iraqi coast the SEALs lowered themselves into the water, taking up to an hour to swim to the shore, but all had pledged not to return without completing their missions. Many rested in the reeds under radio silence while preparing to penetrate the obstacle belt and enter the bunkers, while others placed demolition charges on obstacles to clear a path for the first infantry wave. The SEALs began isolating the bunkers where many of the defenders were sheltering from the heavy rain or were sleeping. Simultaneously, demolition teams detonated charges on the obstacles, which was the signal for the boats carrying the infantry wave, waiting offshore in overloaded boats, to begin their assault. Yet it was only at 2210 hrs that the Iranian headquarters broadcast the go-code 'Oh Fatemeh

An M192 triple launcher for the MIM-23B I-HAWK SAM. The Iranians developed an elaborate air defence system for Operation Val Fajr-8, in which HAWK SAMs played a major role. (Farzin Nadimi collection)

al-Zahra' to the divisions which then passed it on down the chain of command.[19]

Iranian artillery battalions, with Pasdaran fire-support units, now bombarded the bunkers, which faced a rain of shells from guns and recoilless artillery, rockets and mortar bombs, although some of the Pasdaran fire was a waste of ammunition. The

MIDDLE EAST@WAR SERIES SPECIAL #1: THE IRAN-IRAQ WAR

Table 14: IRGC, Khatam al-Anbiya Command, February 1986		
Corps	Division & HQ	Brigades & Notes
	Direct Combat Support Group (IRIAA)	2 attack battalions (AH-1Js), 2 assault battalions (Bell 214As), 1 reconnaissance battalion (Bell 206), 1 transport battalion (CH-47C)
	33rd Artillery Group	3 battalions of M109; 1 battery of M107; 3 battalions of towed artillery pieces; 1 MLRS battalion (total of about 90 artillery pieces and 12 BM-21s)
Task Force Karbala	21st Infantry Division (IRIA)	1st Brigade only
	7th Vali Asr Infantry Division (IRGC)	
	8th Najaf Ashraf Infantry Division (IRGC)	
	19th Fajr Infantry Division (IRGC)	
	27th Mohammad Rasoolallah Infantry Division (IRGC)	
	41st Sarallah Infantry Division (IRGC)	
		57th Abolfazl al-Abbas Infantry Brigade (IRGC)
		105th al-Kawthar Naval Infantry Brigade (IRGC; including 5 naval infantry, and 2 commando battalions)
Task Force Nooh	14th Imam Hossein Infantry Division (IRGC)	
	17th Ali Ibn Abu Talib Infantry Division (IRGC)	
	25th Karbala Infantry Division (IRGC)	
		90th Khatam al-Anbiya Artillery Brigade
		Qamar Bani Hashem Engineer brigade (IRGC)
Task Force Nasr	5th Nasr Infantry Division (IRGC)	
	77th Infantry Division (IRIA)	1st Brigade only; reinforced by 2 brigades from the 5th Nassr Infantry Division (IRGC)
		104th Emir al-Mu'mim Naval Infantry Brigade (IRGC; including 5 infantry, 3 commando and 2 artillery battalions)
Reserve and Diversionary Forces	81st Armoured Division (IRIA)	1 brigade only
	92nd Armoured Division (IRIA)	2nd Armoured Brigade only
		55th Airborne Brigade (IRIA)

IRIAF personnel reloading MIM-23B I-HAWK missiles onto their launcher. This missile could reach speeds of up to Mach 2.5. Additional rounds for the system were acquired during the so-called 'Irangate Affair' in 1986. (Farzin Nadimi collection)

bombardment and the sounds of approaching boats were the defenders' first warning that they were under threat, and some fled as the leading wave of Pasdaran infantry arrived having endured a waterborne ordeal which would have had many saying their prayers with greater fervour. They happily leaped waist-deep into the water to begin assaulting the bunkers opposite the six chosen beachheads. Some bunkers were engaged from boats offshore and within 30 minutes the first was captured. The infantry then began to push inland, joined by SEALs who stripped off their wet suits into regular uniforms,

PART I: THE BRILLIANT BLOW

Table 15: III and VII Corps Iraqi Army, February 1986		
Corps	Division	Brigades & Notes
III Corps	Corps Troops	8th Border Brigade; 33rd SF Brigade; 65th Commando Brigade; III Corps Artillery Brigade (10 artillery and 5 MLRS batteries)
	11th Infantry Division	45th and 47th Infantry Brigades
	19th Infantry Division	
	30th Infantry Division	
	31st Infantry Division	49th and 109th Infantry Brigades
VII Corps	Corps Troops	66th Commando Brigade (elements), 440th Naval Infantry Brigade; VII Corps Artillery Brigade (4 field artillery battalions, 72 tubes)
	15th Infantry Division	44th, 104th, 501st and 802nd Infantry Brigades
	26th Infantry Division	110th, 111th and 440th Infantry Brigades
Navy		2nd Naval Brigade (CSS-2 AShM)
		441st Naval Infantry Brigade (subordinated to 26th Infantry Division)
Reserve Forces & Reinforcements	Republican Guards Armoured Division	3rd Republican Guards SF Brigade; 4th Republican Guards Infantry Brigade
	5th Mechanised Division	15th and 20th Mechanised Brigades
	6th Armoured Division	16th, 30th and 56th Armoured Brigades; 25th Mechanised Brigade
	14th Infantry Division	
		224th Missile Brigade (2 SCUD battalions, 10 TELs)

while artillery observers, sometimes using captured watch towers, directed fire inland.

North of the Shatt, the 'Oh Fatemeh al-Zahra' go-code triggered a series of diversionary operations which exploded along the front like firecrackers, from the Hawizah Marshes towards Qurnah, and others against the Fish Lake Line, while Basra was also shelled. The attacks on the defences north of the Fish Lake were spearheaded by 2nd Brigade of the 92nd Armoured Division – supported by the Pasdaran of the 12th Qa'em-e Mohamad Mechanised Division: this was certainly a significant commitment of Iran's much-depleted armoured forces. They struck the 19th (Major General Talal Muhammad Salih) and 30th (Brigadier Naijim ad-Din Abdullah) Infantry Divisions of Major General Rashid's III Corps over drier, firmer ground to the south.

Salih's division had been forewarned and, remembering the lessons of its Khyber debut in February 1984, had turned no-man's-land into an artillery-covered killing ground of wire entanglements and minefields, and so the enemy did not come within 150 metres of their positions. Abdullah's division, presumably also alerted, beat off three attacks on the first night almost without breaking sweat, and was not significantly troubled afterwards.

Four days later, from dawn on 14 February, there was an attempt to push the 31st Infantry Division (Brigadier Yalshin Umar Abdil) off South Majnoon with Pasdaran, later supported by 2nd Brigade/92nd IRIA Armoured Division. The Iranians copied the enemy's Army day tactics, using boats to land all over the island and with heavy artillery support from North Majnoon, and they again pushed 49th and 109th Infantry Brigades into a small bridgehead despite vigorous counterattacks.

The main thrust was along the Basra–Khorramshahr highway against 11th Infantry Division (Brigadier Abd al-Zahra Shkara al-Maliki) against (north to south) 47th and 45th Infantry Brigades by brigades of 81st Armoured, 21st and 77th IRIA Infantry Divisions. The Iranians managed to fight their way through heavy artillery fire to take a nearby island, and along the riverbank then gained a foothold in 47th Infantry Brigade's position, inflicting heavy losses. During the afternoon of 11 February, a 5th Mechanised Division counterattack recovered the lost positions and drove back the enemy who then tried to outflank 45th Brigade with an amphibious attack but were beaten off. The attacks upon III Corps were largely repulsed from strong defences using well-rehearsed tactics based upon massive artillery, as well as air, support with the IrAF and IrAAC flying some 984 sorties from 10–12 February, yet it helped to confuse the Iraqi Army command. They probably cost III Corps some 4,000 casualties and the attackers about 8,000.

The Iranians added to the confusion by flying elements of 55th Airborne Brigade from a small air base on Jazireh-ye Dara (Dara Island), some 35 kilometres south of Bandar-e Khomeini in raids against oil terminals and even Umm Qasr itself. The attempt to establish a landing site near the latter was thwarted by vigilant sentries, while fire from the equally alert oil platform garrisons also prevented landings. Yet as reports of heliborne attacks flooded into the peninsula the defenders began to fire wildly and fruitlessly into the skies.

On the Faw Peninsula the bid to establish the northern bridgehead was made by 77th Division and Nassr, which landed on the Iraqi divisional boundary, striking 15th Infantry Division's southern flank unit, the 104th Infantry Brigade. The first landing was on Umm al-Rasas, 'a waterlogged sandbar between Basra and Faw...' which consisted of '... some date palm plantations and the remains of some tiny villages which had once been connected to the mainland by a metal-type pontoon bridge'.[20] With the island secure the Iranians tried to seize this bridge to access the peninsula while beginning the construction of four of their own pontoon bridges across the Shatt. The 104th Brigade fell back into a switch line: the Iranians took 14 hours to overcome it again, by when the 15th Division had assembled reinforcements that finally contained their – meanwhile about two kilometres deep – bridgehead.

The IrAF paid a hefty price while attempting to counterattack Iranian ground forces on the Faw Peninsula. This dramatic photograph shows a burning Iraqi Su-22M-3 going down in flames over the Shatt al-Arab, opposite Abadan in Iran. (Farzin Nadimi collection)

Wreckage of an Iraqi Su-22M-3 (serial 4078) shot down by the Iranians during the Val Fajr-8 offensive. While the Iranians claimed over 70 Iraqi aircraft and helicopters as shot down, the Iraqis admitted only about 16 losses. (Farzin Nadimi collection)

During Val Fajr-8, the IRGC pressed into use even such old weapons as this US-built 40mm M1 L/60 anti-aircraft gun. This weapon could fire 120 rounds per minute and target aircraft out to a range of 7,000 metres. It proved deadly not only against low-flying helicopters, but also against infantry exposed in the open. (Tom Cooper collection)

call upon a stock of 2,000 bombs and 10,000 shells, respectively, delivering 100 of the former and up to 250 of the latter per day.[21] Air attacks were a threat until HAWK batteries came on-stream and claimed 20 aircraft on 11 February forcing the IrAF to operate in strike packages each supported Mirage F.1EQ fighter-bombers equipped with French-made Caiman stand-off jamming pods. Hovercraft and helicopters augmented the boats to move Pasdaran troops, anti-armour teams and artillery across the water as guns on the eastern bank pounded Iraqi defences.

The failure to complete and deploy the pontoon bridges meant the Iranians could not bring over armour or artillery and while many Pasdaran had been taught to drive Iraqi armour, and the Iranians claimed to have captured 120 AFVs by 12 February, the attackers captured few drivable vehicles and those which did fall into their hands were deployed late and often piecemeal in close and marshy terrain where many were destroyed. By now Rashid's III Corps had transferred 6th Armoured Division to support Ata who committed it on the 15 Division front on 12 February together with 3rd Guards Special Forces and 4th Guards Infantry Brigades which had been flown south from Baghdad and rushed by trucks driving at top speed through torrential rain to the new front.

They were hastily assembled to spearhead a coordinated counterattack on the morning of 12 February, but as the companies formed up they were subjected to a fierce rocket bombardment from batteries of Iranian BM-21 Grad MLRS on the other side of the Shatt which delayed their attack and caused up to 30 percent losses.[22] Air strikes with chemical weapons were called in but with the combatants so close some hit friendly troops. They recovered quickly and pushed forward with strong air support, but tanks were

Chaos

Throughout the peninsula some defenders showed resolution which slowed the advance but, as Iranian COMINT confirmed, in many places the Iraqi defences dissolved into confusion and panic. Corps commander Shawkat was slow to respond, partly because many brigade and battalion commanders not only failed to report counterattacks accurately or promptly, but also tried to down-play the scale of the threat – out of a mixture of ignorance and habit. Consequently, Shawkat – who had previously boasted that he would drive any invader into the sea – was slow to recognise the scale of the emerging disaster. However, with daylight the defenders did slowly gain in strength as they determined the enemy's crossing sites and gunners began to range on them with both high explosive and shells filled with chemical agents. These greatly hampered the forward movement of Iranian men and supplies. The decision to use chemical weapons was made on 11 February with their delivery made by 56 aircraft and three battalions of 155m guns which could

PART I: THE BRILLIANT BLOW

One of the Iraqi aircraft lost to the reinforced Iranian air defences was this Mi-25 helicopter gunship (serial number either 2110 or 2121). The helicopter was disabled by ground fire, but the crew managed to land safely. The Mi-25 was subsequently brought to Tehran, where it is still on display. (Farzin Nadimi collection)

Iranian COMINT reportedly intercepted an exchange, apparently between 26th Division and 111th Brigade, which reported the destruction of 110th Brigade and one of its own battalions, and the isolation of half another. The exchange concluded with the two officers exchanging insults as Iraqi troops were captured when their vehicles stopped to ask the advancing Iranians what was happening. But the Iranians found it difficult to exploit the situation due to the shortages of vehicles and limited radio communications – divisions had only 2–5 radio operators while in trying to direct operations from the north bank many commanders became hoarse.[24]

frequently bogged down and the haste with which the counterattack was arranged was reflected in poor coordination. Although Pasdaran positions were penetrated some forward units were exposed, which led to close quarter fighting before the Guards, having suffered severe casualties and the loss of much equipment, were eventually rescued by army units, but their sacrifice ended all hopes of a further Pasdaran advance.[23]

Ata had also received 66th Commando Brigade (Brigadier Bariq Abdallah) which was landed by assault boats on Umm al-Rasas on the evening of 11 February. Supported by 15th Division's artillery and the new Brazilian Astros MLRS, it retook the island after 18 hours of bitter, close quarter fighting. With the loss of their prime bridging point and already suffering from gas attacks, the Iranians recrossed the Shatt.

Potentially the most serious threat came on the southern end of the peninsula as the two task forces exploited the SEAL success, landing half-an-hour after the northern bridgehead and reaching the Basra–Faw City highway by 0300 hrs which was exploited to expand the bridgehead as the defence collapsed in confusion.

Task Force Karbala, led by 1st Brigade/21st Division, and 19th Fajr in the north started well by pushing 26th Division's 111th Brigade northward in a fighting retreat up the peninsula although its commander was captured on 12 February. 7th Vali Asr made a separate landing and linked up with 19th Fajr in the palm groves.

Although the sky over the Faw Peninsula was heavily infested by all sorts of air defences, Iraqi pilots continued flying fierce counterattacks with all available aircraft and helicopters. Here, a Gazelle takes off from one of the forward heliports close to the front, armed with launchers for unguided rockets. (Ali Tobchi collection)

The crews of an Iraqi T-62 tank platoon receiving a briefing on their next mission. Tanks spearheaded every Iraqi counterattack on the Faw Peninsula, but the terrain restricted their operations to the immediate vicinity of roads. (Tom Cooper collection)

In the words of several interviewed Iraqi officers, the Faw Campaign was 'eating' men and machines at an amazing pace. This Iraqi Type-69 is rolling in the direction of the battlefield in March 1986. (Tom Cooper collection)

Despite its command post being overrun and severe losses, the brigade delayed the Iranians long enough for 6th Armoured Division to send down 16th Armoured Brigade with some commandos to stabilise the situation. A major obstacle to the advance was a large bunker on the highway, which they called Konj (Corner), at a point where it met a minor road some 15 kilometres northwest of Faw City and five kilometres south of Kut Nughaymish. It required two brigades to take it and the effort apparently exhausted the attackers who established a berm-based defensive line, some four kilometres long, where they went onto the defensive as growing Iraqi forces came down the coastal highway.

The Meatgrinder

On 11 February the Iraqis began to push southwards along the coastal highway towards the Konj, but mud and mines hastily laid on the roadside verges confined this attack to the road which was blocked with a berm manned by Pasdarans with Basiji in front. The attackers were stopped and driven back in confusion under attack from Cobra gunships which bought time for Iranian engineers to dig an anti-armour ditch. Meanwhile, the Najaf Ashraf Division then began to advance westwards from the highway towards the Mamlaha salt pans, skilfully using TOW and Sagger missiles, as well as towed MLRS, to overcome resistance from road embankments or berms.

Iraqi attacks grew in strength and from 12 February the Republican Guards tried to push south towards the Konj, although progress was disrupted by an accidental IrAF chemical strike. The Guards' T-72 tanks were largely impervious to Iranian anti-armour missiles but were still confined to the road and the immediate surroundings, while due to the Najaf Ashraf advance westwards the Iranians were in an exposed salient, and to shore up the defences the Mohammad Rasoolallah Division and 'Abolfazl al-Abbas' Brigade were brought up; the latter to support Najaf Ashrafs continued advance westwards during the night. In many cases the Pasdaran crawled for up to a kilometre, their progress lit by flares from Iraqi PC-7s, they then surprised the few defenders to fight their way into the salt pans.

But by pushing so far forward, Task Force Karbala exposed the Iranian northern front and on the afternoon of 13 February an Iraqi attack inflicted heavy losses upon the Mohammad Rasoolallah Division and opened the right of the 'Abolfazl al-Abbas' Brigade until the arrival of the 'Imam Hossein' Brigade aided by 23mm anti-aircraft guns which hosed down the attacking infantry. The growing pressure slowly forced the Iranians back towards the Konj, the Pasdaran desperately buying time while engineers of the Construction Ministry hastily threw up a defensive berm which was completed that night, shielded by fierce counterattacks against a newly arrived Iraqi commando brigade. The new defences helped to stabilise the Iranian line whose defenders beat off attacks over the next three days to 15 February, and this would mark the high point of the Iranian advance.

To the south, Task Force Nooh reached the coastal highway at about 0300 hours and, spearheaded by the Karbala Division, moved rapidly towards Faw City rolling up the southern brigades of Brigadier General Mirza Hamza as-Sultani's 26th Division. Karbala was briefly delayed by a half-hearted counterattack which it beat off, and after this token resistance many of the defending officers and men (including Mirza Sultani) reportedly fled in panic abandoning, according to the Iranians, 30 MBTs and Cascaval APCs. Karbala isolated Faw City before dawn, but then the divisional commander defied orders to lead a brigade into the salt pans only to be stopped by 441st Brigade fighting from berms 3–4 kilometres west of the city, although they were unable to prevent the Iranians overrunning the 110th Brigade's command post and a surface-to-air missile base. Meanwhile, the Mohammad Rasoolallah Division on Task Force Karbala's left further isolated Faw City by cutting the secondary road to Zubayr. Joined by the Ali Ibn Abu Talib Division, the Karbala Division assaulted the town during the morning, in heavy rain, to occupy both it and 26th Division headquarters, capturing 950 prisoners and some 40 anti-aircraft guns.

Karbala continued to the al-Bisha Cape which fell just after midnight of 11 February, despite desperate resistance by the Iraqi sailors and marines, but with the 'Silkworm' missiles having been withdrawn to Umm Qasr all the Iranians captured were two launchers and 100 prisoners. Many of the latter had tried to wade the mud flats and been trapped to their waists until pulled out by the Pasdaran after they found their abandoned boots on the shoreline. There are reports that some Iraqi senior officers escaped in hovercraft with key components from the missile and radar systems as well as electronic warfare equipment. Yet the loss of a key Iraqi air defence facility, which the Iranians blew up a few days later, caused temporary panic in the Gulf Arab capitals. Now lacking coastal surveillance radars, the IrAF found it more difficult to interdict enemy maritime traffic in the northern part of the Gulf.[25]

Having consolidated its positions, Task Force Nooh began to push westwards along the Umm Qasr road during the evening of 11 February with its right covered by the Mohammad Rasoolallah Division. Within half-an-hour it ran into determined Iraqi resistance from 441st Naval Brigade, joined by 440th Naval Brigade, which used the Mamlaha salt works as a strongpoint to prevent the enemy advancing up the Umm Qasr road, the reinforced-concrete buildings reducing casualties from air bursts.[26] There was fierce hand-to-hand combat, punctuated by MLRS bombardment, and while the Pasdaran succeeded in taking the salt pans Iraqi reinforcements slowed their advance across the open ground to the north and soon the Iranians were building defensive berms. The Iranian advance was further slowed by the muddy conditions in which both sides fought in slime up to their knees and this accumulated on boots and clothing to such a degree it sometimes made it heavier than the equipment they were carrying in their webbing and haversacks. However, the marshy terrain absorbed the worst effects of Iraqi shells and chemical weapons while Iraqi armour was restricted to the roads and was vulnerable to Cobra helicopter gunships with TOW missiles, as well as anti-armour teams.

A feature of the Iranian operations was the air support it received from both the IRIAF and the IRIAA. They interdicted armour on the roads south from Basra, while transport helicopters deployed Pasdaran 'Zolfagha' anti-armour teams with RPG-7s. This forced the Iraqis to organise Helicopter Combat Patrols, some using the propeller-driven PC-7s often with Border Guard or instructor pilots. Problems bringing forward their artillery forced the Iranians to use air power as compensation, but from 9–18 February Iranian records show an average of 40 CAS sorties a day out of a daily total of 100 combat air sorties. This number dropped to 18 a day until the end of February and then a dozen.[27]

The IrAF interdiction of communications started on 11 February when pairs of aircraft began appearing at five-minute intervals, although they tended to attack from too high and were rarely accurate. Between 9 and 13 February, when rain grounded both sides' airmen for a day, the Iraqis flew 1,198 fixed-wing and 596 rotary-wing sorties, and between 15 and 23 February, despite frequent rain showers and fog, 3,046 fixed-wing and 2,235 rotary-wing sorties. The interdiction campaign was also hampered by air defences and the IrAF had a very limited night attack capability. The Iraqis also struck communications along the Iranian side of the Shatt al-Arab but most of the damage was quickly repaired and the Iraqis were unable to cut the numerous bridges across the canals and channels. The pontoon bridges were also damaged and had to be floated under cover during the daylight hours until the radar of an I-HAWK battery on Abadan Island was repaired on the afternoon of 11 February. It then launched a dozen missiles to claim 10 victories.

Exhaustion sets in

While the fighting raged on, by 12 February Wal Fajr 8 was running out of steam due to shortages of supplies and heavy weapons. On the first night there was chaos on the northern bank because the Iranians underestimated the number of men they needed to move supplies to the boats, forcing commanders to draft command post personnel, including clerics and even follow-up infantry, to carry supplies down the slippery river bank, and then waist-deep through icy water. After three or four hours these men were exhausted.

One of the pontoon bridges had been completed on the night of 7 to 8 February and was assembled underwater with attached containers of compressed air which would raise it to the surface. A combination of rough water, the current, and the need to prepare both banks of the Shatt meant it was not deployed until the night of 10 to 11 February after intense engineering work, and was soon augmented by three others. Some 20,000 troops, many of them engineers with earthmoving equipment, crossed on the first night and IRIA engineers brought stocks of anti-armour and anti-personnel mines which the Pasdaran began to plant on the verges of the main roads while their comrades began to build metre-high embankments and strongpoints to consolidate their hold.[28]

Even with the pontoon bridges Iranian logistics faced a major threat from the IrAF which ensured that from 0700 hrs daylight movement across the Shatt largely ceased until nightfall. IrAF attacks forced the Iranians to partly dismantle the bridges at dawn and bring them under cover of land-based air defences. Boats and hovercraft could operate at all times but had to stop each day when the tide ebbed leaving mudflats which could not bear the weight of vehicles, artillery or even individual soldiers. Unloading was disrupted by poison gas, mostly mustard but with some Tabun nerve agents, hanging around the beachheads to cause some casualties, although the need to wear respirators while undergoing heavy manual labour was probably the greatest problem.[29]

This combination of factors meant that the supply of much engineering equipment, heavy weapons and armour, including MBTs was, according to the Iranians, too little and too late. The Pasdaran also faced the problem of distributing their supplies because the boggy conditions stopped their pick-up trucks. Instead, forward units had to rely upon small quantities brought up by motorcycle, or upon captured weapons and ammunition, although the situation eased when the first pontoon bridge to the al-Bisha Cape was completed on the morning of 13 February, and in the early afternoon BMPs brought ammunition up to the front line, now 20 kilometres long, shielding a 50-square-kilometre bridgehead. Later the second bridge was established between Abu Direh, in Iran, and Maamir, five kilometres north of Faw City, on the peninsula.

Shortly after the initial crisis had passed, Saddam recalled Shawkat to Baghdad about 17 February to face the General Command's investigation committee, but he was not held responsible. In part this was a recognition that his superiors had stripped him of resources, but the fact he had also been a high-school friend of Saddam probably did not affect his defence. He was initially appointed General Secretary of the Armed Forces General Command, but by 1987 the British Defence Attaché reported he was commanding II Corps. He was replaced by former III Corps commander Major General Sa'di Tu'mah al-Jaburi while General Mirza Sultani, the 26th Division's mediocre commander, was relieved (after the war would rise to the rank of lieutenant general and would die shortly after the 2003 invasion of Iraq). He was replaced by the equally mediocre Brigadier General Amjed Mohammed Hassan who would himself be relieved once the situation on the Faw Peninsula had calmed down.[30]

International Concern

The Iranian presence on the north bank of the Khowr Abdullah, only a few kilometres away deeply worried the Kuwaitis. Iranian President Khamenei now warned them not to allow the Iraqis to use nearby Bubiyan Island (Jazirat Bubiyan) – which controlled the waterway – and threatened to confiscate the oil in the Neutral Zone between Kuwait and Saudi Arabia, which was being used to supply Iraqi's customers. On 15 February the Emir of Kuwait, Jaber al-Ahmad al-Jaber as-Sabah, visited the island and publicly declared it to be neutral territory. The Iranian threat increased Saudi fears however, and King Fahd reportedly telephoned Saddam Hussein on 12 February, which led to four high-level meetings in Riyadh and Baghdad during the following fortnight.

In late February the Saudi and the Kuwaiti foreign ministers flew to Damascus to meet President Hafez al-Assad and his Iranian friends to warn them against invading Kuwait. They added that if he failed to restrain Iran he would lose subsidies from the Gulf States. As a result of this battle, Kuwait and – to a lesser degree – Saudi Arabia were under direct threat from Iran as Tehran was quick to remind them, yet paradoxically, Tehran's relations with the West and the Soviet Union improved and on 10 March a planned demonstration outside the Kuwaiti and Saudi embassies was hastily cancelled by the authorities, and when the protestors went ahead the demonstration was broken up by police.[31]

The outbreak of the Iran-Iraq War had made Kuwait and the other small Gulf oil producers acutely aware of their vulnerability, and in May 1981 Bahrain, Kuwait, Oman, Qatar, Saudi Arabia, and the UAE created the Gulf Cooperation Council (GCC). They pledged to cooperate in a number of fields including defence, but the organisation stopped short of being a full alliance.[32] In September and October 1980 the Kuwaiti forces were placed on full alert with a military screen established along the border. Brigadier Muhammed Al-Bader became Head of Operations and a joint command centre was created together with three plans. One was to defend the northern islands with 12 small strongpoints from Sabriya to the main offshore island, Bubiyan, manned by an infantry battalion of 6th Mechanised Brigade. The other two were based on a worse-case scenario in which the Iranians broke through to Basra and sought to invade Kuwait.

When the Iraqis requested a bridgehead in Kuwaiti territory, to thwart an Iranian attack, the battalion on Bubiyan Island was reinforced by a Chieftain MBT company.[33] To further thwart foreign interference, minefields were laid along the coast and a commando unit brought up as a tactical reserve. The air defences were supported by a Decca AR-1 air surveillance/air traffic control radar, a HAWK system and SA-7 Grail launchers. The country's air defences, however, depended upon a manually operated sector operations centre pending the arrival of a Thomson-CSF computerised system. The Kuwaiti Air Force (Al-Quwwat al-Jawwiya al-Kuaitiya) was a small, still poorly-equipped force undergoing expansion: its dozen English Electric Lightning F.Mk 53s were meanwhile replaced by 27 Mirage F.1CK interceptors and six Mirage F.1BK trainers, while 36 Douglas A-4KU Skyhawk light attack aircraft were augmented by a dozen BAC Strikemaster T.Mk 83s. They proved inadequate in a few little-known clashes the IRIAF between 1981 and 1983 and incapable of disputing the IrAF use of Kuwaiti air space when its strike aircraft hunted shipping off the Iranian coast during the Tanker War. The rotary-wing element consisted of eight Agusta Bell 205s, two Bell 206s and 24 SA.342K Gazelles, while there were also two Lockheed C-130 Hercules transports.[34]

Attacks by pro-Iranian terrorists from mid-1983 saw the Kuwaiti armed forces also charged with internal defence plans. The first, 'al-Jeran' (The Neighbours) was to protect Kuwait City and the northern borders, while 'an-Nusar' (The Supporters) covered threats from the south with 80th (Internal Security) Brigade – formed under the Interior Ministry – to defend key sites. Relations with Iraq, which claimed Kuwait was a province, remained tense as the Kuwaitis wished to retain good relations with their powerful northern neighbour without surrendering their independence. They politely declined any Iraqi attempt in 1983 to lease Bubiyan Island – which became a military zone from which civilians were banned. They supported Baghdad's operations clandestinely, provided financial support and allowed convoys of up to 200 trucks at a time to drive northwards twice a week with Military Police escort.

With the nightmare scenario of an Iranian presence close to their borders and shells landing on Bubiyan Island, the Kuwaitis moved the 6th Brigade north in an arc to protect the approaches from Basra and the Faw Peninsula. Four offshore platforms with Rasit radars and electro-optical sensors were established by the Interior Ministry to prevent infiltration. The Kuwaitis were strongly supported by the Saudis who, in late March, declared that an attack upon Kuwait would be 'considered an attack on Saudi Arabia' and would result in full military assistance using the GCC Peninsular Shield force which was on standby at Hafra El Baten in Saudi Arabia. In August 1986, Iranian threats to launch surface-to-surface missiles at Kuwait if it continued its open support for Iraq led to Saudi troops being put on standby for possible deployment into Kuwait. In June, pro-Iranian Islamic fundamentalists were believed to have been responsible for bombs at oil export facilities which caused major fires in pipeline complexes and led Saddam to warn he would not tolerate Iranian-backed destabilisation of Kuwait and would be prepared to send in troops, which the Saudis opposed for fear it would be a tacit occupation.

Baghdad's Dilemma

The Iraqis only gradually recognised that the enemy had opened a new front on the peninsula and awaited a major blow north of the Shatt until a captured IRIAF pilot revealed this was the prime operation.[35] Iraqi losses had been heavy, and while some estimates put them to 16 February at 5,000 and Iranian losses at 8,000–10,000, a more probable figure is 7,000 for the Iraqis and 8,000 for the Iranians (who admitted 800 dead), while the Iraqis had lost 20–25 aircraft.[36] The Iraqis lost three field batteries of 122mm and 130mm guns and up to 60 anti-aircraft guns of various calibres, as well as 1,500 prisoners. The blow to Saddam's prestige, and the corresponding increase in Iranian prestige, as well as diplomatic pressure from Saudi Arabia and his friends in the Gulf dictated his decision to regain the lost ground. But the profligate expenditure of artillery ammunition forced Baghdad to make emergency deals with individuals and manufacturers all over the world, no doubt at exorbitant financial cost.

The GMID assessed enemy strength in the south of the peninsula as 21st IRIA Division with four or five Pasdaran divisions; although the IRIA division was shortly transferred back across the Shatt and there were actually eight divisions and the equivalent of a ninth in the southern tip. To meet the immediate threat Rashid's III Corps lost a significant portion of its strength; 6th Armoured Division had already been committed, but would soon be returned to corps reserve, and was now joined by 5th Mechanised Division. IV Corps was ordered to despatch the Guards Division headquarters, together with 14th Infantry Division and 66th Commando Brigade, the armour coming south by rail.[37] Saddam appears to have visited the front on 12 February and recognised the need for a new front, as with the marsh battles of 1984–1985, so Defence Minister Khairallah set up a forward General Headquarters at ad-Drehmiya camp 25 kilometres southwest of Basra, with the Chief-of-Staff and senior officers to coordinate a counteroffensive after personal battlefield tours.

This would be executed by three tactical headquarters or columns established on 13 February; the Northern Column (ar-Ratl ash-Shamaly) along the coastal highway was under Operations chief Lieutenant General Fakhri and based upon the Guards Armoured Division; the Central Column (ar-Ratl al-Wasaty) was under Major General Maher Abdul Rashid and would drive down the middle road spearheaded by 5th Mechanised Division (15th and 20th Mechanised Brigades) reinforcing the survivors of 26th Division; while the Southern Column (ar-Ratl al-Janoobi) under Major General Talia ad-Duri was around the axis of the Umm Qasr–Faw City road initially with the 440th and 441st Naval Brigades which were soon placed under the newly arrived 14th Infantry Division. Supporting them were three special forces and four commando brigades, and 15 artillery regiments which, along with divisional artillery, gave the Iraqis some 600 tubes together with MLRS and a 'Scud' regiment.

The counteroffensive began on 14 February, preceded by a major IrAF effort to knock out radars and air bases before the IrAF and IrAAC bombarded the bridgehead, which was also struck by 9K57 Luna (ASCC/NATO code name 'FROG-7') artillery rockets.[38] The effort was countered by the fact that the Iranians had brought up two I-HAWK launchers to cover the bridgeheads: these inflicted losses to Iraqi fighter-bombers and forced the IrAF to operate in much more elaborate strike packages. Still, Iranian death rates from air attacks using conventional and chemical weapons in the bridgeheads were estimated at one man per enemy sortie. Chemical weapons were used extensively and frequently proved effective because, although the Koran makes no mention of beards, the tradition was that The Prophet Mohammed had advocated Muslims to grow beards. This led to the practice (sunnah) of beards or at least trimmed moustaches which made it difficult to put on gas masks or to seal them.[39] The effects of chemical weapons were neutralised by the humid conditions and rain, although during February the Iranians reported 45,000 chemical casualties both here and on the northern battlefields and at least 100 were sent for treatment in Europe.

While the Iraqis had eight or nine brigades for the initial attack, the terrain severely limited their deployment to, essentially, a single brigade front of around five kilometres, usually using an armoured or mechanised unit. It rained on most days between 14–18 February and with the ground already largely marsh the battlefield soon turned to churned up mud reminiscent of Third Ypres in 1917, indeed both sides probably suffered badly from Trench Foot. The coastal strip with its fields and palm groves allowed Fakhri to strike on a two-brigade front with a degree of cover, and artillery augmented by Astros MLRS which were especially effective against area targets. The defenders, however, could exploit former Iraqi strongpoints, fields, irrigation ditches and multiple berms.

Fakhri's attack proved a bloody disaster, with his troops coming under intense artillery fire, much of it across the Shatt, and attacks from Cobra gunships. They were quickly stopped and the follow-up forces piled up behind them to provide targets for Iranian gunners and airmen which meant they were only able to inch forward. By early afternoon they had stopped to lick their wounds and to build a new route to facilitate logistics. An Iraqi engineer officer remembered climbing onto an armoured engineer vehicle during the battle and said that while talking to the driver he was shaking with fear. His commander ordered a retreat. 'I had to take it on the only paved road which was very dangerous because it was continuously being shelled and it was heavy, weighing more than 35 tonnes.' There was a mortar battery and he watched as one tube after another was hit. An attack by the Southern Column also suffered heavy losses, partly due to IRIAF attacks, although Iraqi warships tried to interdict the coastal road.[40]

In a coordinated attack on 16 February, Guards Armoured Division had greater success, with artillery fire allowing the mechanised forces to approach within 400 metres of berms, which the IFVs and APCs would try to drive over although this exposed them to RPG fire. In a series of grim and bloody assaults the Iraqis managed to advance 2 kilometres before exhaustion brought them to a halt. Rashid's Central Column encountered well-dispersed Pasdarans with anti-armour missile launchers every 300 metres augmented by mobile 'Zolfaghar' anti-armour teams. From 18 February, these would receive some 500 American BGM-71 TOW missiles which had arrived at Bandar Abbas, followed by another 500 nine days later, most of which were expended against the Central Column. Unsurprisingly, the same managed to advance for exactly 600 metres.

The Iraqi Counteroffensive

On the night of 16 to 17 February the Iranians began a major reinforcement effort while evacuating the wounded and improving defences by inundating land using water from the Shatt and the Khur Abdullah. The refreshed Iranians counterattacked Rashid on the night of 17 to 18 February but were held, although this attack helped to slow the Iraqis whose progress over the next few days was the result of a host of carefully planned small unit actions. On 18 February Iraq reported that Fakhri had been given command of the Faw sector and been replaced by General Saad Tumma al-Jubari.

By 19 February the Iraqi attack had to be abandoned in the face of heavy rain, hail and strong winds after an advance of 5.5 kilometres (3 kilometres by the Southern Column). Both sides recognised they were in an impasse; the Iraqis recognised they would not regain the Faw Peninsula and they began to fortify the southern approaches to Basra with berms stretching for kilometres, while at Friday prayers two days later Speaker Rafsanjani had to admit the Iranians had been forced to reduce their objectives merely to holding the peninsula.

The failure to retake the territory was a profound disappointment to Saddam, leading foreign observers to wonder whether or not it was due to a shortage of trained infantry. Some felt that 100,000 men would be needed to retake the Peninsula, rather than the 50,000 actually deployed. In the aftermath of the campaign they reported he had ordered reforms in training programmes, with dedicated combat training brigades emphasising the training of men to operate in all weather conditions.[41] Such reports may be exaggerated, but the Iraqis reduced the impact of the bitter fighting by exploiting the terrain limitations which limited the deployment of their divisions to brigades in echelon. Like Pétain at Verdun in 1916, the Iraqis rapidly rotated units, with 126 rotations during the campaign, which meant each brigade was in the line for only four or five days.

Yet they still suffered heavy casualties and special trains were organised to evacuate the wounded. There were enforced blood donations, attempts were made to recruit the staffs of leading tourist hotels wholesale, while taxis travelling north from Basra had to carry corpses inside the vehicle and on roof-racks. The consumption of Iraqi war material was prodigious, up to 600 rounds per gun, and because tanks were used for infantry support it is reported that 200 worn-out tank gun barrels had to be replaced.[42] The Iraqis were placing great emphasis upon their artillery but shells tended to bury themselves before detonating, reducing their lethality and it probably led to greater emphasis upon air bursts. Much ammunition was wasted in random or area fire and Iraq desperately searched for replacement shells. The Iranians had their own problems and were finding it difficult to supply the two bridgeheads which may have had up to 70,000 troops between them.

On 20 February, Saddam again returned to the front to assess progress, as the IRIAF completed a series of strikes on forward Iraqi HQs and supply depots, enticing the Iraqis into several air battles east of the Faw Peninsula. Baghdad subsequently boasted about a loss of 45–47 fighters and 10 helicopters, crediting most of these to the Iranian air defences. However, to the present day there is only evidence for about a dozen losses in fighter-bombers, and a similar number of helicopters. Even so, this cost the IrAF several highly experienced pilots and demoralised the reminder: Saddam's standing order for the air force to avoid losses was still in power and most of the air strikes were flown from medium altitude, which greatly diminished their precision. Saddam also ordered the IrAF into another round of air strikes on Iranian urban centres behind the frontline, and into additional attacks on the shipping around Khark Island, thus dissipating instead of concentrating the effort – while opening the skies for the Iranian transport helicopters, which – along with boats – continued bringing supplies and evacuating the wounded. Much more effective was the interdiction campaign ordered by the commander of the IrAF, Major General Hamid Sha'aban. Ultimately, the IrAF flew 18,648 sorties over the Faw Peninsula between 9 February and 31 March (3,000 of these during the first week of the battle), averaging 365 a day.[43]

When Saddam finally granted them permission to run operations at their own discretion, Sha'ban ordered the IrAF to start flying at low altitudes again in order to improve precision of its air strikes: henceforth most fighter-bomber types did so – with the exception of those flying electronic-support missions, and Tu-16 and Tu-22 bombers. Flying low exposed the Iraqis to the full spectrum of Iranian air defences and caused several painful losses – even more so as next to no Iraqi aircrews that bailed out over the bridgeheads survived: furious ground troops tended to spray them with small arms fire as they descended. The Iranians were aided by covert American supplies of I-HAWK missiles that greatly bolstered the half SAM-site that covered the peninsula, but also with spares for aircraft and missiles, augmented by spares from Israel, and it has been reported that the Iranians flew more than 1,000 sorties during the first fortnight. Up to 54 Iraqi aircraft and 20 helicopters were claimed as shot down in the Faw campaign, 20 of which were in the first week. Whatever their actual loss might have been, the Iraqis were meanwhile desperate enough to attempt cutting enemy pontoon bridges with the help of French-made AM.39 Exocet anti-ship missiles deployed from Aerospatiale SA.321 Super Frelon helicopters (one of which was shot down by Iranian fighters), while the Iraqi Navy was also called in to use its Osa-class fast attack craft and their P-15 (ASCC/NATO codename 'SS-N-2 Styx') missiles and claimed 'two supply vessels' as destroyed on 20 February.[44]

Saddam wanted to reduce Iraqi casualties retaking the Faw Peninsula by ordering the avoidance of close quarter combat, and he also ordered III Corps commander Rashid to halt his advance. Rashid was a Takriti whose daughter was married to Saddam's youngest son. There was now an open confrontation between the two, although Rashid was a bit of a glory hound who boasted of stopping the Iranian 1984 offensive. He publicly confirmed the Iraqis had suffered heavy losses and reportedly blamed Saddam for ordering him to halt. Saddam recalled him to Baghdad and re-assigned him a northern corps.[45]

Saddam Calls a Halt

Fakhri appears to have recognised that his troops could do no more, but Saddam was in no mood to listen and demanded a renewed effort to retake the lost ground using leaders who had proven records of defeating the enemy attacks. Following another visit from Saddam on 23 February, General Sa'adi became VII Corps commander, while III Corps commander Rashid – who later told journalists Saddam had rejected his idea for a counteroffensive across the river into Iranian territory – was given overall command of the counteroffensive. Finally, Fakhri took over the Central and Southern Columns which would now form the prime axis for regaining the peninsula. There was some reorganisation of the counterattack forces and while the Northern Column was still autonomous under the Guards Division it began to integrate 19th Infantry Division, whose brigades edged their way towards the north-eastern edge of the Mamlaha salt beds, with a view to replacing it. Meanwhile, poor weather, which lasted until 22 February, gave the Iranians a week to build up supplies and bring in reinforcements.[46]

The Iraqis renewed their counterattack on the night of 23 to 24 February, with Saddam in the command centre, but by now the Iranians had finally managed to bring in a number of batteries, for the first time on the peninsula there were major artillery duels. Rashid's force alone had 100 guns and fire direction observers operating from Pilatus PC-7 spotter aircraft transferred from Helicopter Combat Patrols, but here, as elsewhere along the front, the Iraqis preferred to saturate pre-selected artillery killing zones, indeed, for the first time they relied more on MLRS attacks rather than artillery fire to saturate areas with considerable success. These bombardments could be extremely destructive, although the Iranians had learned to disperse their forces while their counterbattery fire frequently forced the enemy batteries to move their guns.

Even with artillery and helicopter support the advance down the coastal highway was quickly brought to a halt, as the Pasdaran made repeated counterattacks, usually at night in a vain attempt to avoid enemy artillery.[47] The Republican Guards received only limited armoured support and had to fight as conventional infantry, but in this sort of battle they lost their edge and had little hope of success. Eventually, the Guard retreated behind a barrage of high explosive and chemical shells – despite Baghdad's claims about driving a salient 1.35 kilometres long and one kilometre deep into the enemy positions.

PART I: THE BRILLIANT BLOW

The Republican Guard Attacks
The battle continued raging to the south around the Mamlaha salt beds, already saturated with rain and which the defenders had flooded, turning them into marshes to confine Iraqi armour to the bunds and rendering them unable to manoeuvre the Iranians out of their positions. With their attacks channelled into narrow fronts where there was fierce fighting, the Iraqis were vulnerable to anti-armour missiles, especially TOW with its range of 3.75 kilometres. The offensive petered out after a few days. The Central Column made the greatest progress advancing 1.6 kilometres deep and two kilometres wide on 23 February, despite a setback caused by the Iranian COMINT: as a staff meeting was held at the forward command post of the 5th Mechanised Division, this was precisely shelled and numerous officers hit. The dead included divisional commander General Hayyan and several staff officers. This failure temporarily halted its progress once it had taken the 'third embankment' in the salt beds.[48] Despite this, the column advanced a further 2.5 kilometres the next day, while on the night of 26 to 27 February the Northern Column's 19th Infantry Division's attack gained sufficient ground to expose Iranian positions and compel them to move. The campaign now ground to a halt, although the Iraqi Navy claimed success on 26 February in destroying a bridge which the enemy were building between Abadan and al-Bisha Cape. The following day Saddam returned to Baghdad but he had left orders that the campaign was to continue even though it had reportedly cost the Iraqis some 10,000 casualties.

The Central Column with 19th Division inched forward, while the Southern Column took the western section of the salt beds provoking the Pasdaran to make three nights of mass attacks to regain the lost ground. They suffered from the same tactical conditions as the Iraqis however, and their waves of troops dissolved under heavy artillery fire. Further counterattacks were launched along the whole front on the night of 2 to 3 March resulting in heavy fighting which lasted seven hours, with Iraqi artillery turning night into day. Another attack was beaten off on the night of 11 to 12 March as Rashid slowly advanced, but coordination between the columns sometimes failed and on one occasion the Central and Southern Columns exchanged fire. The battle was rapidly approaching an impasse and an attempt by naval and heliborne commandos on the night of 9 to 10 March was eventually repulsed because the Pasdaran had dispersed and camouflaged their forces.

The Front Is Closed Down
On 12 March the Defence Minister and Chief-of-Staff visited the front to assess the situation after 6th Armoured Division failed to draw away reserves following a dummy attempt to cross the Shatt on 7 March. The Iraqi leaders still hoped it might be possible to recapture the whole peninsula but despite knowing that their fire was causing the enemy heavy losses, as confirmed by COMINT which intercepted pleas for help to evacuate the wounded, Iranian resistance continued and progress had slowed. Although the Northern Column conducted raids on the enemy during the night from 23 to 24 March, by 21 March all Iraqi progress had ceased and they could only interdict enemy supply lines, including launching 250 FROG-7 missiles as well as chemical weapons. As the weather improved in late March, the IrAF joined in, but the Iraqis were now concentrating upon building defences.

Between 31 March and 1 April Saddam presided two conferences at the GHQ, the first lasting nine and the second 11 hours. Both were 'post-mortem' and merely resulted in a re-consideration of the future policy. The Iraqi Army clearly had major problems and thus it was decided to rubber stamp a decision made 10 days earlier to alter the way of fighting. With the Iranians driven close to the salt pans, the offensives which were simply causing casualties were now to be stopped and the defences strengthened. The road system was also to be improved while the chance was taken to pull out some of VII Corps' units from the line for reorganisation and training. The corps was reinforced by the 37th and 42nd Infantry Divisions, both led by officers who had distinguished themselves in the fighting. Under such circumstances, the fighting along the frontlines deteriorated into low-level clashes and bombardment: indeed, after the last minor Iraqi attack on 20 September, both sides settled down.

By then the Iraqis were running a massive engineering work, building defensive systems for a later attack including positions for armoured vehicles, artillery and mortars, as well as helicopter landing pads. Civilian ministries were called in to assist with this work and helped to build 1,100 kilometres of road, 1,060 kilometres of defensive works, 16 kilometres of canals and 16 bridges. The General Staff Planning and Operations Departments beginning examining for, and preparing, plans to recapture the peninsula; with 14 working meetings from 14 May 1986 when the order was given

An unusual weapon deployed by the Iranians for the first time during Operation Valfajr-8 was the Mohajeer UAV. Originally based on the design of Israeli UAVs shot down over Lebanon, Mohajeers were primarily designed and deployed for reconnaissance. However, Iran armed several examples with RPG-7s, thus deploying the first ever 'unmanned combat aerial vehicle' (UCAV) in combat. (Farzin Nadimi collection)

The crew of an Iranian ZPU-1 machine gun (single-barrel version of the 14.5mm KPV machine gun) preparing their weapon for action at Faw. (Albert Grandolini collection)

to begin the work. On 16 June a joint service planning group under the Army Minister General Abdul Jabbar Henschel was established which was later joined by VII Corps chief-of-staff.[49]

The victory boosted Iranian self-confidence and Khomeini issued a fatwa demanding the war be ended by the next Iranian New Year (March 1987), but Tehran also continued to reject diplomatic efforts to end the conflict. Val Fajr-8 left the Iranians holding more enemy territory following a brilliant start, but it was strategically almost useless and they were certainly no nearer Basra. As one of their soldiers later said: 'We were full of confidence and were waiting for orders to march to Basrah. Instead, to our great disappointment, we were told to stay put.'[50]

In exchange for 20,000–30,000 casualties (including 400 prisoners) Tehran had taken a bridgehead some 16 kilometres north of al-Faw, they claimed to have destroyed 500 armoured vehicles and 35 artillery pieces. During the summer most of the assault divisions were withdrawn from the peninsula and sent to the assembly camps between Ahwaz and Khorramshahr and were mostly replaced by Pasdaran naval brigades, while some Pasdaran 'Silkworms' were moved into the abandoned al-Bisha Cape missile launching facilities to threaten Kuwaiti oil loading.

Conclusions

Val Fajr-8 demonstrated that Iran could achieve strategic surprise even in the face of US satellite technology and major Iraqi advances in the field of COMINT/SIGINT, and that the Iranian commanders were now capable of running coordinated multi-corps offensives on several fronts. Their troops had demonstrated their ability to fight a successful defence in depth, too. One commentator pointed out:

> Val Fajr-8 constituted the high point of Iran's war effort and has generally been hailed as its most successful operation. It

rekindled the hopes of Iran's leadership — falsely, as it would turn out — that Saddam Hussein's regime was on the verge of collapse.... Although they had failed to completely cut the Iraqis off from the sea (the latter retained a very narrow foothold on the Gulf through Umm Qasr), the Iranians' capture and retention of Faw was a major blow to Saddam's prestige.[51]

Yet ultimately, Val Fajr was an attempt to demonstrate the much quoted claim that 'war is an extension of diplomacy through other means' attributed to military philosopher Carl von Clausewitz. Although often described as an attempt to envelop Basra from the south, the offensive was really Tehran's attempt to break the 'oil conspiracy'. Had it been a serious attempt to threaten Basra then the main force would have been deployed in the northern bridgehead not the southern one. Here it was impossible to exploit the tactical success with rapid and substantial reinforcements of vehicles, without which the Iranians faced a week-long march on foot to reach Basra. This was clearly impossible in the face of superior Iraqi firepower and transport capacities, and the only conclusion left was that the main blow was in the south purely to threaten Kuwait through a significant Iranian presence on the al-Faw Peninsula. But far from cowing the Kuwaitis and Saudis it frightened them into giving Saddam greater financial and diplomatic support as their shield against the Iranians. The Arab League committee (Iraq, Saudi Arabia, Kuwait, Yemen, Jordan, Tunisia and Morocco) met hurriedly in Baghdad on 12 February and denounced Iran's 'intransigent attitude', warning that the new offensive could seriously damage Arab-Iranian relations.[52]

Tactically, it was clear that the Iranians still had much to learn with regards to logistics, for their failure to exploit the initial success was due to their inability to maintain a steady flow of supplies necessary for sustaining an advance. There were some grounds for optimism, for during the course of operations Iranian commanders demonstrated a degree of flexibility, diverting troops and resources from one sector to another when they achieved a breakthrough, in order to reinforce success. Yet ultimately, it reflected Tehran's chronic shortage of armour and artillery as well as the men who could best exploit them. With nothing more to achieve, Tehran reduced the garrison on the peninsula withdrawing the regular units and leaving the equivalent of two Pasdaran divisions, but IRIA engineers, with their Pasdaran and civilian comrades provided them with numerous berms, improved communications and flooded areas to impede enemy movement. Moreover, another five divisions (85,000 men) remained in the Khorramshahr/Abadan area to threaten the Iraqis.[53]

Iraqi casualties were up to 12,000 (including 2,100 prisoners) many of whom were veteran troops and airmen. The Republican Guards lost a third of the men deployed in a bitter battle of attrition. The Iraqis were caught wrong-footed and while they were able to slam the door to contain the threat, the terrain and weather prevented them eliminating it as their leaders undoubtedly hoped. Yet the extent of Saddam Hussein's resolve to retake the Faw Peninsula can be gauged by the number of Iraqi air sorties flown: 18,548 between 9 February and 25 March, compared to 20,011 for all of 1985.[54]

The loss of territory finally convinced Saddam Hussein from July to allow the generals greater initiative possibly to distance himself and the Ba'ath from any disasters which might occur. Although Iraq's total manpower losses were probably half those of Iran, this ratio was unacceptable to Baghdad, partly because its losses included many skilled pilots and technicians who could not be easily replaced, and partly because of the demographic imbalance between the two countries.

The staff received permission to convert the Republican Guard into a military shock force with the Republican Guards Command initially allocated six brigades, only to be tripled in size during the next year, while early in 1987 three divisions were created under the Republican Guard Ground Forces Command. Its troops, and those of the best army units, i.e. the 3rd, 6th and 10th Armoured Divisions with 1st and 5th Mechanised Divisions, were given extensive training in combined-arms operations and offensive tactics. They practised constantly and conducted manoeuvres in corps strength as well as receiving the latest equipment such as T-72 tanks, BMP-1 infantry combat vehicles, GCT self-propelled artillery and GHN-45 and G-5 towed artillery. Stripping the remainder of the army weakened much of it, but the 11 divisions ultimately available, including special forces and Guards, provided an offensive capability described as 'modest' by one commentator who certainly underestimated it.[55] Strategically the idea was sown that Iraq could not achieve victory while remaining upon the defensive and that at some time it would have to resume its own major offensives.

The Iraqi General Staff were not optimistic about the capabilities of the new force. Recognising that its leaders did not possess the personal initiative to conduct operations, the Deputy Chief-of-Staff (Operations), General Hussein Rashid Muhammad at-Tikriti directed the creation of detailed and innovative scripts for every conceivable offensive and counteroffensive operation. The commanders then received the scripts which they would learn by heart and practise for months, often over full-size mock-ups of the terrain in which these operations were to be executed. The units would continually rehearse their missions with units repeating specific tasks until they were word perfect, then these would be repeatedly practised by the units individually, then collectively, so the operation could be performed from memory.[56] The professionalism of the Iraqi armed forces also extended into the air force, which was now under the new, aggressive, commander Major General Hamid Shabban, was allowed to increase the number of sorties per mission and accept the heavier loss rates in return for improved performance.

With the conclusion of the Faw campaign, fighting for almost all of 1986 was confined to the Central and Northern Fronts. There were continued raids and during one, Iran's Operation Karbala 3 on 1 and 2 September, they took the oil terminal and its radar set at al-Ummaya. Yet the Iranians were simply biding their time before renewing their assault upon Basra. It took nine months to prepare for this, but on 24 December they launched Operation Karbala 4, which proved an unmitigated disaster, but was soon followed by Karbala 5 which would prove a decisive blow, but not in the way Tehran had anticipated.

COLOUR SECTION 2

The Chieftain Mk.5/3P remained the major MBT in Iranian service during the mid-1980s. However, with the IRGC taking over the brunt of fighting on the front lines, IRIA formations equipped with the type were held back in reserve, and thus their Chieftains saw even less action. While still wearing the standard camouflage colour of light olive green, applied back in the 1970s, this was badly worn out on most vehicles. Indeed, by 1986, most surviving Chieftains barely showed even their national insignia, applied in the form of a roundel in Iranian national colours, on turret sides and the rear storage box. (Artwork by Radek Panchartek)

Some Iranian M60A1s damaged early during the war were repaired and then repainted. They appear to have been painted in yellow sand overall, although the exact shade of the colour in question is hard to gauge. National marking was still regularly applied on turret sides, but most seem not to have worn any other insignia. (Artwork by Radek Panchartek)

This ex-Iraqi T-62 was captured during one of the 1982 offensives, overhauled, repainted in two shades of green and brought into service by one of the IRGC's armoured brigades. Note the identification marking on the gun tube and inscription. (Artwork by Radek Panchartek)

COLOUR SECTION 2

If they survived long enough, captured Iraqi T-54/55s were overhauled or repaired and repainted before being pressed into service by the IRGC. Their usual new colour consisted of yellow sand only. Most wore not only a large IRGC logo in red but also various inscriptions, in this case a verse from the Quran. (Artwork by Radek Panchartek)

This former Iraqi BMP-1 was captured while still wearing a relatively fresh coat of olive-green overall, probably the colour in which it was delivered from the USSR. It received the IRGC logo, with the inscription 'Islamic Revolutionary Guards Corps' hastily sprayed in white along the side of the hull. (Artwork by Radek Panchartek)

Another of the many captured Iraqi vehicles pressed into service was this ZSU-57-2. The vehicle received a fresh coat of the IRIA's light olive-green overall, and Iranian national insignia on all four sides of the turret. The ZSU-57-2 had two 57mm S-60 anti-aircraft guns installed in an open-top turret, mounted on the T-54 chassis. The guns could elevate up to 85 degrees and were fed from four-round clips. Lack of radar control made them fair-weather weapons, but they proved deadly opponents for helicopters. (Artwork by Radek Panchartek)

MIDDLE EAST@WAR SERIES SPECIAL #1: THE IRAN-IRAQ WAR

Iran acquired 100 ZSU-23-4s directly from the Soviet Union in 1969. They served with air defence regiments attached to each of the Army's divisions. All were painted in light olive-green overall, and had national insignia applied on the hull sides. Like other vehicles of the regular Iranian Army, they should have received four-digit serial numbers – applied in black on the hull front and rear – but, sadly, no details of these are known. (Artwork by Radek Panchartek)

Some of about 300 M113A1s and M113A2s, originally acquired by Iran from the USA in the 1970s, were converted through the addition of a mast for BGM-71 TOW ATGMs, for anti-armour purposes, during the war with Iraq and officially redesignated as M150. As the inscription on its hull side indicates, this vehicle was subsequently assigned to the 201st A'emeh Anti-Armour Unit. This was a dedicated anti-armour outfit of the IRGC, comprising Army equipment handed over to the Pasdaran. Established in 1983, it was expanded to a full brigade by 1987. (Artwork by Radek Panchartek)

Following the successful performance of 10th Armoured Brigade's T-72s early in the war, Iraq placed orders for 250 T-72M1s in Poland, followed by up to 1,000 additional T-72Ms and T-72M1s imported from Czechoslovakia and the USSR. Many went into battle in the mid-1980s still wearing olive green overall, as on delivery. Yellow sand (often bleached into light grey by sun and sand) was crudely applied on some examples, as illustrated here, before the entire fleet was later repainted in that colour. (Artwork by Radek Panchartek)

COLOUR SECTION 2

A reconstruction of a Polish-made Iraqi T-55. The vehicle was equipped with the typical Polish-made storage box on the turret side and a dozer blade and infrared searchlight. The camouflage pattern consisted of the usual yellow sand and blue-green. Iraq purchased several hundred such tanks during the war with Iran, initially because of Soviet refusals to resupply Baghdad, and later because the Soviets were unable to deliver the number of tanks demanded by Iraq. Reportedly, the Iraqis found Polish-built tanks slightly better than those made in the USSR, but not as good as those made in Czechoslovakia. (Artwork by Radek Panchartek)

A reconstruction of one of about 400 Chinese-made Type-69 MBTs (an improved T-54, including a 100mm dual-axis stabilised, smoothbore gun, a laser rangefinder and a new 580hp engine). The tanks were acquired in 1983–1985 to replace losses from the first two years of the war with Iran. As in the case of all the T-54s and T-55s operated by the Iraqi Army in the 1980s, they were camouflaged in standard colours of yellow sand and blue-green, and most had side-skirts made of rubber. No turret numbers or any other kind of insignia are known to have been applied, although many Type-69s were seen and photographed by international journalists in the Faw area in 1986, most with their turrets loaded with the crew's personal belongings and ammunition boxes. (Artwork by Radek Panchartek)

Clear photographs of Iraqi ZSU-57-2s remain relatively rare, and thus very little is known about their camouflage patterns and insignia. This artwork is based on several stills from a TV documentary broadcast in Iraq in the early 1980s, showing an example apparently painted in yellow sand, with stripes of blue-green applied in a zig-zag pattern down all four sides of the turret. (Artwork by Radek Panchartek)

MIDDLE EAST@WAR SERIES SPECIAL #1: THE IRAN-IRAQ WAR

Only three out of the first 140 AH-1Js built for Iran were modified to the full configuration compatible with BGM-71 TOW ATGMs before the fall of the Shah in 1979, and thus the majority of the fleet serves until today armed only with the 20mm M197 gun and 3.75in unguided rockets. All are painted in dark yellow sand and dark earth over, and pale grey under. The original crest of the IIAA (applied below the cockpit) was usually replaced by the so-called 'Onion' – the official crest of the Islamic Republic of Iran in the form of a stylised word 'Allah', applied in red or white in the same place. Service titles were often applied, not only in two different positions but also in two different colours, as shown here. (Artwork by Tom Cooper)

When the Iranian Army depleted its stocks of BGM-71 TOW anti-tank missiles, the idea was born to install AGM-65A Maverick, electro-optically guided air-to-surface missiles on some of the IRIAA's AH-1Js instead. This modification proved successful and was deployed in combat. The AGM-65As taken over by the Army for this purpose were usually crudely over-sprayed with green in order to make them less conspicuous. The AH-1J depicted here is otherwise wearing the standard camouflage pattern of dark yellow sand and dark earth, and the usual national and service insignia, though with its 'Onion' applied in white. Note the replacement frame for the front cockpit hood, left in forest green. (Artwork by Tom Cooper)

A reconstruction of a Bell 214A Esfahan of an unknown IRIAA unit, as seen in the Abadan area in 1986. By the time of the Iran-Iraq War, this helicopter received the full service title applied in the usual place on cabin doors, and the 'Onion' in black. Early during the war, many IRIAA Bell 214As went into combat still wearing the last three of their serials applied in large orange digits on the top of the nose and cabin doors. Note that the top sides of main rotor blades on all helicopters of this type were also painted dark yellow sand. (Artwork by Tom Cooper)

COLOUR SECTION 2

Between 1977 and 1984, the IrAF, and then the IrAAC, received a total of 35 SA.342L, 56 SA.342K and 20 SA.342H Gazelle helicopters. Most received the camouflage pattern depicted here, consisting of sand, chocolate brown and olive drab on upper surfaces and sides, and light blue under. More than 80 saw combat service during the war with Iran, but their attrition was heavy because their 'glasshouse' type of cockpit proved vulnerable even to small-arms fire from the ground. Usual armament consisted of four HOT ATGMs, but 20mm cannons (installed on the right side only) and various pod for unguided rockets (usually 68mm) saw widespread service too. (Artwork by Tom Cooper)

The Mi-25 was probably the best-known helicopter gunship in IrAAC service during the war with Iran. At least two batches of 12 helicopters each were delivered to Iraq, one in 1980 (known serials in the range 2110–2119) and another in 1984 or 1985 (serials in the range 4493 and upwards). All were camouflaged in the standard pattern for Mi-25s exported to a number of foreign customers, including Afghanistan, Libya, Nicaragua and Mozambique, and consisting of yellow sand and green on upper surfaces and sides, and light admiralty grey (BS381C/697) on bottom surfaces. Their 9M17P Falanga (AT-2 Swatter) anti-tank missiles were usually painted in dark olive-green. Other frequently deployed armament consisted of UB-32-57 pods for 57mm unguided rockets. (Artwork by Tom Cooper)

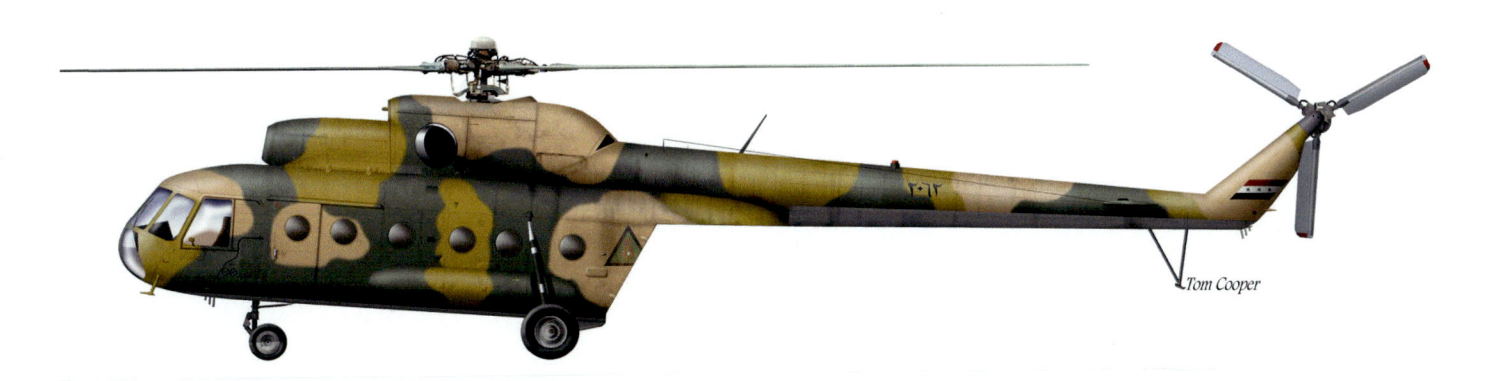

A reconstruction of an Iraqi Mi-8T as seen on a photograph from the early 1980s, but too poor for reproduction. This helicopter – said to have been frequently used for the deployment of Iraqi special forces behind Iranian frontlines – was apparently delivered wearing the usual olive-green colour on upper surfaces and sides, and light admiralty grey (BS381C/697) on bottom sides, and then camouflaged through the application of irregular splotches of sand and apple green. Unusually, no large Iraqi national flag was applied on the rear of the cabin: instead, it received only a single set of national markings, and a small serial (2062) in black on the boom. As often in the case of Iraqi Mi-8s, rear cargo doors were completely removed in order to enable rapid embarkation and disembarkation of troops and cargo. (Artwork by Tom Cooper)

13
IRAN'S LAST CHANCE

Iraq's fortunes were at a nadir after Iran captured the southern Faw Peninsula in Operation Val Fajr-8 and this was reflected in pessimistic briefings from the US Central Intelligence Agency (CIA). Looking at the implications the Agency noted on 12 March 1986: 'The situation is more ominous for Baghdad than at any time in the struggle.'[1] The same document further said that the already low Iraqi morale might decline further under the burden of heavy casualties and added: 'In any event the initiative now belongs to Iran, but Tehran must act soon, otherwise chances for success will diminish as Baghdad recovers and builds new defenses.'

The CIA's assessment continued with the observation that further Iranian attacks could lead to a series of setbacks for the overstretched Iraqi Army (IrA), which in turn could collapse and cause the fall of the regime, and concluded that Tehran might be able to hold its gains indefinitely: 'Even if Iran is pushed out of Al Faw eventually, it could make this so costly in manpower and equipment for Baghdad that the Iraqi Army would be seriously weakened.'[2]

A fortnight later, another of the CIA's assessments asked 'Is Iraq Losing the War?' and suggested the answer was positive – if Baghdad continued to pursue the objective of ending rather than winning the war.[3] The perspicacity of CIA analysts would be variously demonstrated or undermined over the next two years, but the tone was undoubtedly reflected in chancelleries and intelligence agencies all over the world.

Meanwhile, from the late summer of 1986 the Iranians spoke openly of preparing for a new offensive, with Speaker Hojatolislam Ali Akbar Rafsanjani claiming on 10 September that the current mobilisation would be completed within four days. On 16 September Iran's Supreme Leader, Ayatollah Ruhollah al-Musavi al-Khomeini received senior Army officers and leaders of the Islamic Revolutionary Guards Corps (IRGC, or 'Pasdaran'), all leave was cancelled while medical facilities throughout the country were placed on the alert. Five days later President Ali Hosseini Khamenei publicly spoke of exploiting the Majnoon oil fields if Iraq failed to provide restitution for war damage, and with 600,000 men at the front it was widely believed that the offensive would be launched on 22 September, the sixth anniversary of the Iraqi invasion.

But that day saw only a huge parade in Tehran, although the Iranians began a series of probes in the marshes the following day.

These soon petered out and the opening of the rainy season at the beginning of November washed away the immediate threat.[4] In fact the rains exacerbated the Iranians' tactical problems because the Iraqis had flooded a 20-kilometre-long strip covering the southern approaches to the Fish Lake Line to the international border, and a further 10 kilometres into Iranian territory. Iran's bombastic claims

A rare photograph of one of the few PT-76s operated by the Iraqi Army in the 1980–1981 period. The troops wearing orange berets indicates its assignment to one of the commando or special forces units. (via Ali Tobchi)

One of at least 110 GHN-45 155mm guns that Iraq obtained from Austria via Belgium, in 1984–1987. (Photo by Ted Hooton)

184

PART I: IRAN'S LAST CHANCE

A reconnaissance photograph taken by an RF-4E Phantom II reconnaissance fighter of the IRIAF, showing the Karbala-4 area of operations. The point of crossing of the Karoun River (left) and Shatt al-Arab waterways. (Farzin Nadimi collection)

Another reconnaissance photograph taken on the same occasion. The arrows show the launching points of Iranian forces. The residential area visible in the centre of the photograph is Abadan, with parts of Khorramshahr also visible at the bottom left. (Farzin Nadimi collection)

An Iraqi-operated S-60 57mm anti-aircraft gun, in position east of Basra in 1986 or 1987. Notable is the elaborate network of trenches and bunkers around its sangar. (Tom Cooper collection)

were no cunning plan to confuse the Iraqis, but rather reflected the turmoil within Tehran over the operational planning.[5]

The Great Barrier: The Fish Lake Line

The greatest Iranian problem was to overcome the strongest fortifications in the Middle East, the 20–25-kilometres-deep Fish Lake Line. Two writers noted that from the air:

> … could be seen the gun parks and the bunkers, the 'scrapes' bulldozed out to protect vehicles, the raised dykes topped with tarmac roads ….(and the)… secondary defensive lines out of interlocking circular positions, laagers of earth with tanks and artillery inside …[6]

The backbone remained the so-called Fish Lake, but the Iraqis had learned the folly of trying to defend the frontiers during 'Ramadan al-Mubarak' in 1982. In the following 50 months the defences around this anti-armour feature were expanded as 400 million cubic metres of heavy clay were excavated at a cost equivalent to $1 billion. The defences were based upon berms; earth embankments 2–3 metres high and 200–800 metres apart, with the removed earth creating a ditch which hindered infantry and AFV attacks. The height of the berm provided good fields of fire and effective defence even if the surrounding area was flooded in the rainy season.[7]

The backstop positions north of the lake were expanded to create a belt of berm-based battalion positions in a right-angle shape, many of these strongpoints having ramps onto which main battle tanks (MBTs) or infantry fighting vehicles (IFVs) could be driven to augment the defenders' firepower. The strongpoints were at the centre of improvised command, control and communication (C3) systems using battlefield surveillance radars, ground movement detectors and image intensifiers to provide early warning of attack. This belt consisted of 27 triangular battalion strongpoints, organised chequer-board style, between a pair of roads to provide rapid movement of reserves. The northern part of the belt facing the marshes had 15 strongpoints, while the eastern element consisted of 12 strongpoints which 'overhung' the northern approaches to the Fish Lake. In each case two company positions were on the frontline berm covered by a third company position in the rear. Many of the strongpoints augmented infantry weapons with light anti-aircraft guns such as the ZSU-23-4, a 23mm self-propelled quad-barrelled gun, which could prove devastating against infantry. These positions also helped to shield the water pumping stations at the head of the Fish Lake.

In front of them, covered by outpost positions, were at least half a kilometre of minefields and wire obstacles, barbed wire fences or single coils of barbed wire. The original minefields were some 350 metres deep, but they were steadily extended to 600 metres with a mine every metre; a quarter of the mines being anti-armour while the remainder were anti-personnel, notably Italian 'bouncing' mines.[8]

About a dozen strongpoints were constructed along the lake's western bank, especially covering the 8-metre-wide causeways designed for Iraqi mechanised counterattacks, with another three strongpoints and two anti-armour ditches providing in-depth defence of the Iraqi entrances. South of the waterway, and bisecting the Basra–Khorramshahr highway, were lines of semicircular company strongpoints, often with 5-metre walls, stretching into the cultivated area which ran along the Shatt. This defensive belt was some 10 kilometres long and six kilometres deep with each berm line fronted by a waterway; either an enlarged irrigation channel or a small tributary of the Shatt such as the rivers al-Duaiji (also 'Da'iji/Diaiji/Du'ayji/Du'ayi/Doeeji') and Jasim ('Jasem'). Behind the fortifications were a myriad of berm-based positions; laagers for mechanised reserves, fire bases for tube and rocket artillery, headquarters and supply dumps, all linked by a growing web of hard- and gravel-topped roads, usually on embankments, for reserves supported by 9P148 Konkurs anti-armour vehicles with two AT-4 'Spigot' and three AT-5 'Spandrel' anti-armour missiles. The artillery had a dedicated communications network, and it is reported that the Iraqi Army had some Soviet 'Pork Trough' (SNAR-2) counterbattery radars as well as British Cymbeline counter-mortar radars.

The southern flanks of these defences were covered by garrisons in company strongpoints on the narrow islands of the northern Shatt. West of Umm Rassas was Umm Twaila (or Tawila or

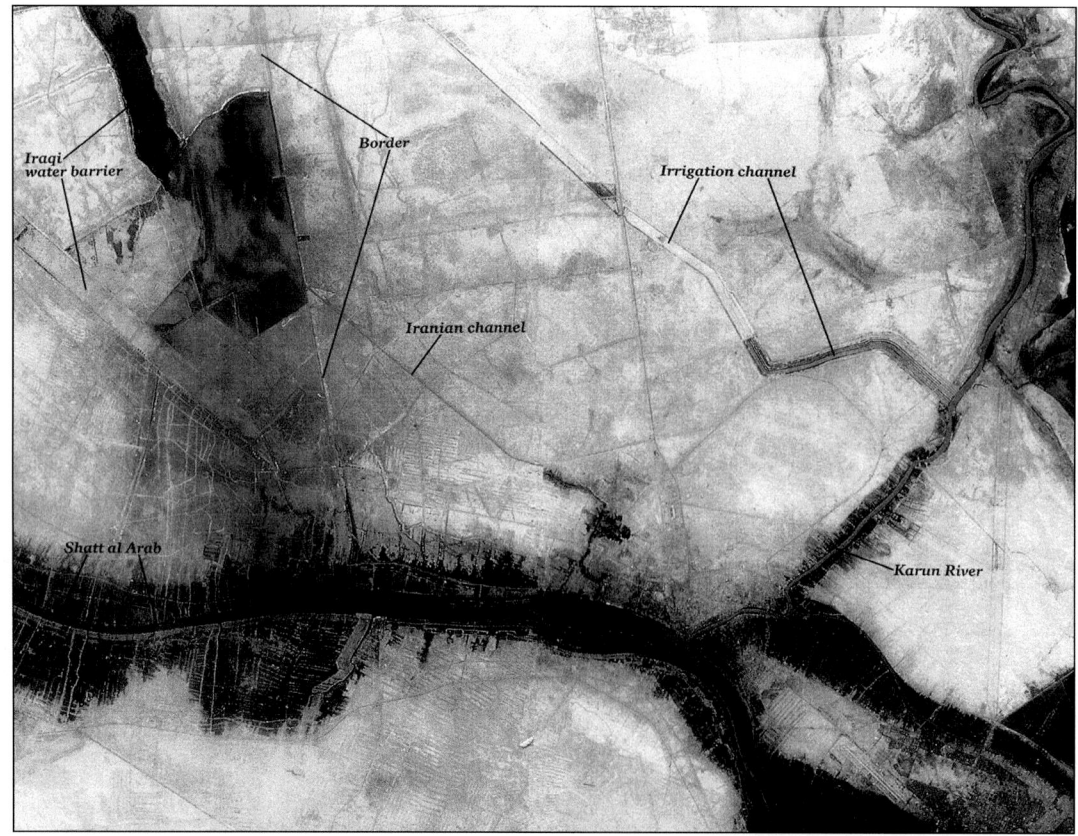

A SPOT satellite photograph (as used by the Iranians for their operational planning) from September 1987, showing the area between Fish Lake (left upper corner), Shatt al-Arab and the Karoun River – the centrepiece of Iranian offensives in 1987. (Tom Cooper collection)

While often dehumanised and belittled as 'cockroaches' conducting 'human wave attacks', and certainly poorly trained, the Pasdaran infantry proved one of the most effective branches of the Iranian military and were much feared even by Iraqi generals. Here an IRGC officer is briefing his troops before the next operation. (Tom Cooper collection)

A view inside the Khatam al-Anbia headquarters of the Iranian forces. Notable is a large wallmap, made up of reconnaissance photographs taken by IRIAF and SPOT satellites. (Tom Cooper collection)

Tuwayiah or Omotiavil) which extended past the defences covering the highway, and Umm Salhia (or Ujayrawihah or Salehieh) which reached almost the outskirts of Basra. They were described by Aldridge, the British Military Attaché, as 'sandbanks' and separated by a narrow and shallow creek. Approaching these fortifications, the attacker had first to navigate through inundations with a kilometre-wide zone extending from the Hawizah Marshes (Hawr al Hawizah) around the Zayed (also Zayd and Zaid) Salient. To the south were other inundations which extended some 20 kilometres northwards from the Shatt to cover most of the area between the southern Fish Lake, which merged with this zone in the south, and into Iranian territory north of the Basra–Khorramshahr highway, to create an area of some 200 square kilometres.

The northern bank of the Shatt was the weak point of Basra's shield. The frontier ran north to south almost to the Shatt, but along the bank was an Iraqi salient. This was literally an island with inundations to the north and east, and the Shatt to the south, while from the Fish Lake canals designed to control flooding ran down to the Shatt. The groves on both sides of the Shatt had made Iraq the world's prime producer of dates, but farmers had long abandoned this fertile strip and years of war had left the groves with blackened and broken palm trees.[9] The flooding was deep enough to slow infantry but shallow enough in places to cause assault boats to run aground. The edges of the inundated area were lined with multiple lines of wire entanglements, liberally laced with mines, and with electrodes linked to Basra's electric power stations; all covered by shallow trench positions.

Overcoming defences on this scale was not impossible and, since 1917, has been achieved with or without significant armoured support. Beginning with short, overwhelming artillery bombardments upon a narrow front; these were rapidly followed by assaults involving combined-arms groups operating flexibly to infiltrate, isolate and then overwhelm surviving positions. The Coalition Forces demonstrated this in 1991, with the added support of precision-guided munitions. However, five years earlier the Iranians lacked both skills and weaponry, and it was unclear how they would – already suffering serious shortages of heavy weapons and ammunition – achieve this goal.[10]

Target: Basra

In the aftermath of Val Fajr-8 Iran's Supreme Defence Council (SDC) agreed that the strategic level objective should be to take Basra, a predominantly Shi'a city. Correspondingly, from May to August 1986 military leaders conducted a series of operational level studies to determine ways of cracking the city's defences. The 'maximalists', led by Pasdaran commander Mohsen Rezai, wanted a frontal assault from the east to bulldoze through the Fish Lake defences. The 'minimalists', led by the commander of the Islamic Republic of Iran Army (IRIA), Colonel Ali Sayad Shirazi, were more cautious: they pointed out the strong defences and overwhelming enemy superiority in armour, artillery and air power compared with Iranian inferiority in all three. Shirazi, who appears to have had some support within the Pasdaran, wanted a well-planned, well-coordinated, two-prong offensive; one by the IRIA from the Hawizah Marshes southwards against, and around, the Fish Lake Line; and the second by the Pasdaran along the Faw Peninsula following an amphibious assault across the Shatt. However, the problems experienced by the Iranians while striking from the Hawizah Marshes, demonstrated by 'Kheiber' and 'Badr', forced the IRIA to accept an assault upon the Fish Lake Line from the east as one element, and in conjunction with an attack from the Faw Peninsula.

While the Pasdaran were willing to accept the IRIA's indirect concept, they believed in the supremacy of their men's revolutionary and religious fervour and demanded a greater share in the enterprise. There was no doubt that some of their leaders recognised that they were materially handicapped and they accepted the truth of the IRIA's demands for greater Pasdaran professionalism to augment revolutionary zeal. Nevertheless, dispute developed: this tore apart old alliances and brought Shirazi into an increasingly vitriolic conflict with Rezai. According to different reports, at one point in time they came to blows.[11] Shirazi insisted on improving overall direction by introducing Army standards of planning and preparation, but the clerics naturally favoured Rezai over any professional military officer, no matter how devout and devoted. Ultimately, Shirazi was dismissed on 4 August 1986 in favour of Southern Forward Operational Headquarters (SFOH) commander, Colonel Hossein Hassani-Sa'di, who had directed Val Fajr-8.

It was thus the Pasdaran influence that resulted in the plan – placed before the SDC on 8 September – which called for simultaneous attacks along and across the Shatt. This was formally accepted in October but became subject to clerical and political tinkering with demands for the offensive to coincide with the Islamic Summit Congress scheduled in December in Kuwait. Brigadier Qasem Ali Zahirnejad (Khomeinei's representative in the SDC), and Armed Forces Chief-of-Staff Colonel Ismail Sohrabi, together with President Khamenei, wished to strike earlier. Furthermore, the Pasdaran, backed by Rafsanjani, persuaded Khomeini that the offensive would strengthen Iran's status in the Islamic world, and thus the overall command was given to the IRGC's Haj Ahmad Kosari.

Rafsanjani was a strident advocate for the offensive – foremost because this was likely to offset his support for the secret 'Irangate' arms-for-hostages-deal with the United States. The details had been revealed as the radicals jockeyed for position in the run-up to the parliamentary elections scheduled for the spring of 1988 when no one could afford to be seen as 'soft'. Khomeini was obviously ill and politicians were staking out their post-mortem positions. While Rafsanjani was the leading candidate to replace the Ayatollah as head of state, there was another contender for the position of Khomeini's successor as religious leader: Ayatollah Husseini Ali Montazeri. Montazeri's relative and Pasdaran Chief-of-Staff, Mehdi Hashemi, revealed details of 'Irangate' in public with the aim of giving Montazeri's opponents the excuse to arrest 200 of his supporters in October 1986. In turn, Hashemi was tried and convicted of treason on 10 December. One commentator observed that this would explain why the offensive 'proved to be the worst managed Iranian attack since Iran's offensives in 1984'.[12] In December various Iranian politicians demanded the offensive be brought forward to put greater pressure upon the Arabs during the summit in Kuwait: certainly enough, they had also been seeking a public diversion from the purge of Montazeri's supporters.

With the end of the harvest, Tehran planned to create 500 new Basij 'battalions' with 100,000 men to fill out the Pasdaran formations. However, only 300 of these (including about 60,000 combatants) were actually established.[13] Even Rafsanjani had no desire to throw untrained men at enemy fortifications and demanded that the Basiji be given up to a year's training – although they usually received only three months before mobilisation and up to three months at the front.

Operation Karbala-4 (al-Yawm al-Adheem)

By December 1986 some 200,000 men (13 divisions) were concentrated north of the Shatt, of whom 60 percent were Pasdaran and Basiji. The new offensive was designated Operation Karbala-4 and envisaged the Shatt al-Arab itself being the main axis of attack towards Basra. It would include a direct attack from south of Shalamcheh across the Shatt, where the Iran-Iraq border follows the waterway. Another prong was to follow up the Basra–Khorramshahr highway. The amphibious assault would repeat Val Fajr-8, with bridgeheads re-established opposite Umm al-Rassas ('Om al-Rasas' or 'Omorrasas' in Farsi) – the long island running from opposite Khorramshahr to opposite the frontier. The Iranians may have had a second stage contingency plan to exploit success in the northern Faw Peninsula with a second cross-Shatt assault from Minoo ('Minu') Island. This was intended to help the besieged troops in the Faw Peninsula bridgehead to fight their way northwards and increase the southern threat to Basra. To divert enemy attention there would

While often belittled by foreign observers, Iraqi Tu-22 operations were very intensive during several periods of the war with Iran. They included the bombardment of the major assembly points of the Iranian ground forces with some of heaviest bombs of Soviet and Iraqi manufacture. (Tom Cooper collection)

PART I: IRAN'S LAST CHANCE

Officers of one of the IRGC's naval brigades, leaning on one of countless earthen berms constructed by both sides, trying to make out the positions and intentions of the Iraqis opposing them. (Farzin Nadimi collection)

Pasdaran of the Imam Hossein Division at their gathering point near Jufayr, east of Basra. (Photo by M. H.)

BGM-71A TOW-armed AH-1J Cobra attack helicopters remained the most potent anti-armour asset in the Iranian arsenal throughout the war with Iraq. This example was photographed at a forward base near Ahwaz in November 1986. (Farzin Nadimi collection)

be a heliborne landing in the Umm Qasr area, at which two Scud missiles would also be fired during the operation. The initial Iranian objective on the south bank of the Shatt was the ruined refinery complex of Abu al-Khasib, west of the River Abu Fulus (or Abu Floos), whose capture would allow them to enfilade the defences south of the Fish Lake.

Task Forces Najaf and Quds would strike north of the Shatt, the former was north of the flooded area, while the latter would strike along the highway. The Shatt would be crossed by Task Force Karbala from the Khorramshahr area (this included 18 brigades of the IRIA and the IRGC, with 52,000 troops), leap-frogging the Shatt islands, and Nooh from Minoo Island south of Abadan (the latter included 14 brigades with 49,000 troops, supported by two artillery brigades and two engineer brigades of the Pasdaran; see Table 16 for order of battle). The Islamic Republic of Iran Army Aviation (IRIAA) provided 112 helicopters – including 24 Bell AH-1 Cobra gunships – to support this operation. The prospects for the landing were good as the channel is less than half-a-kilometre-wide, narrower where it is constrained by the islands, and the water moves slowly so that once the bridgehead was secured a pontoon bridge could be thrown across.

The concept was essentially what Val Fajr-8 might have been – if the clerics had seriously intended to strike towards Basra – but it suffered the same serious deficiencies as the earlier operation. If the Pasdaran established bridgeheads they would require rapid reinforcement and heavy weapons to reach Basra in the face of Iraqi artillery deployed at the Fish Lake Line. The same would also be able to engage the northern thrust which would have to cross the inundations before reaching the line's outposts.

Because the Iranians expected a massive reaction from the Iraqi Air Force (IrAF) and knew they could expect little support from the exhausted Islamic Republic of Iran Air Force (IRIAF), they established a significant concentration of ground-based air defence assets, including five MIM-23B I-HAWK battalions of surface-to-air missiles (SAMs). These were augmented by two British-made Rapier systems, anti-aircraft artillery units including 30 Oerlikon 35mm guns supported by 10 Sky Guard radars, and the IRGC's 95th Moharram Air Defence Brigade.

As with Val Fajr-8 there was an extensive reconnaissance effort involving McDonnell Douglas RF-4E Phantom II reconnaissance jets of the IRIAF, special forces of the IRIA, Pasdaran scouts and even UAVs. But the IrAF, possibly cued by US intelligence reports based upon satellite imagery, was also conducting its own reconnaissance effort and on 23 December brought back photographs of major enemy troop concentrations facing III and VII Corps.[14] Anticipating an assault, starting in mid-October 1986, the IrAF began interdicting communications and concentrations in the Khorramshahr-Abadan area: such attacks proved highly effective and eroded Iranian military engineering and road construction capabilities by 75–85 percent.[15]

On 22 December 1986 the General Military Intelligence Directorate of Iraq (GMID) reported the enemy had forward-deployed 25 helicopters and that they had completed preparations for an offensive in the south.[16] Baghdad therefore placed its forces on alert and the IrAF – flying up to 194 fixed-wing sorties – heavily

189

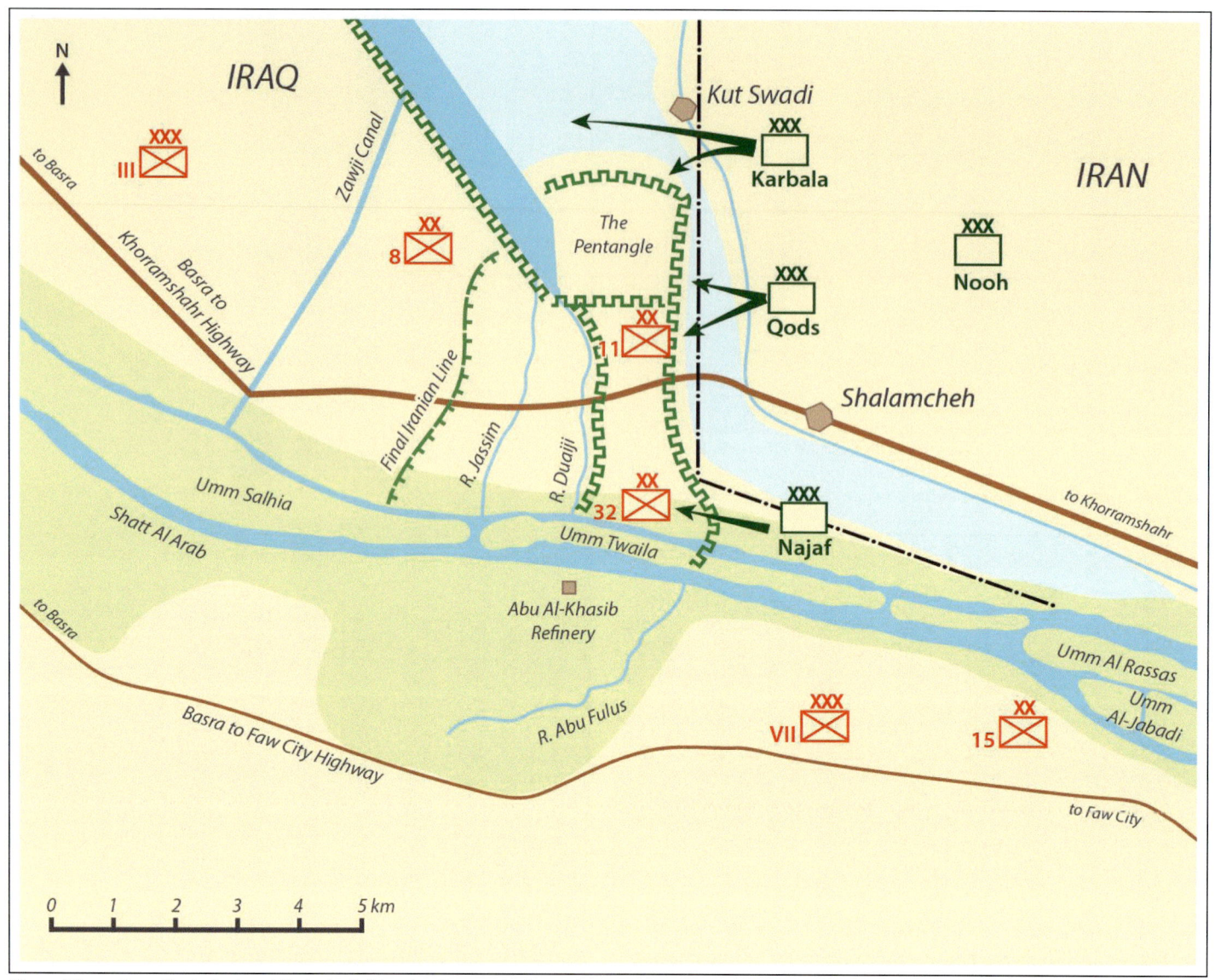

Map of Operations Karbala-4 and Karbala-5. (Map by George Anderson)

bombed the whole assembly area and continued to do so until 26 December 1986. Many of the attacks in question were flown by Tupolev Tu-22 bombers of No. 18 and No. 36 Squadrons, IrAF, which made extensive use of the heaviest bombs in Iraqi arsenal, like the 3000kg FAB-3000 and 9000kg FAB-9000.[17]

Battle of the Red Night

With the Iraqis on full alert the Iranians were left without a choice but to move out. At 22:30 on 23 December 1986, they launched their assault over formidable obstacles. To reach the Fish Lake Line their infantry first had to cross a flooded area two-to-three kilometres wide to reach the frontier, then four kilometres of dry land, before forcing its way across four small rivers each backed by a fortified berm. Across the Shatt, the VII Corps of the Iraqi Army, commanded by Lieutenant General Maher Abd al-Rashid ('Maher'), had already created a killing zone along the northern coast of the Faw Peninsula opposite Umm Rassas and Umm al Jababi (Omolbabi) with bunkers, watchtowers, barbed wire entanglements and mines amid the date palm groves.[18] His northern sector was still held by Brigadier Qays Muhammad Ali's 15th Infantry Division, which had seven brigades opposite the Iranian bank, with the 104th Infantry Brigade holding the islands, and reserves of a mechanised brigade, reconnaissance and divisional commando battalions. These were supported by 15 corps batteries giving the 28,000 men some 160 guns and a FROG battery.

The operation was opened by an assault of frogmen and SEALs of Sajjad Brigade IRGC, across the waters to Umm Rassas and Umm al Jababi, in fibreglass assault craft and rubber dinghies. On the western side of the waterway, the Iranians were caught totally exposed and machine gunned in a hail of bullets. About 175 were killed: some of them only after being caught and then buried alive without injuries, but with their hands tied.[19]

The second wave followed with grim determination, landing a blow on the 104th Infantry Brigade and taking the defenders by surprise. Contrary to their usual tactics, the Pasdaran made little attempt to infiltrate the defences. Instead, they resorted to piecemeal frontal attacks, exposing themselves to murderous crossfire that caused terrible loss of life among the massed men and follow-on forces. They gained a foothold on the River Abu Fulus, but then became struck in between Iraqi defences, hamstrung as much by the haphazard preparation as by minimum support from their own artillery and that of the regular Army. The reed beds provided little cover, while many boats were sunk or smashed and reduced the flow of reinforcements to a trickle. Early the next morning, a combination of Iraqi air strikes, helicopter attacks and artillery barrages smothered the Iranian guns on the far side of the Shatt al-

PART I: IRAN'S LAST CHANCE

Table 16: Order of Battle for Operation Karbala-4, December 1986		
Corps	Division	Brigades
Iran		
Task Force Najaf	92nd Armoured Division IRIA	2 brigades
	3rd Sahel ol-Zaman Division IRGC	3 brigades
	7th Vali Asr Division IRGC	3 brigades
	31st Ashura Division IRGC	3 brigades
Task Force Qods	5th Nasr Division IRGC	3 brigades
	10th Seyyed ash-Shohada Division IRGC	3 brigades
	17th Ali Ibn Abu Talib Division IRGC	3 brigades
	33rd al-Mahdi Division IRGC	2 brigades
	41st Sarallah Division IRGC	3 brigades
	57th Abolfazl al-Abbas Division IRGC	3 brigades
	16th al-Hadi Brigade IRGC	
	48th Fath al-Mustaqil Brigade IRGC	
Task Force Karbala	92nd Armoured Division IRIA	1 brigade
	21st Infantry Division IRIA	2 brigades
	14th Imam Hossein Division IRGC	3 brigades
	25th Karbala Division IRGC	3 brigades
	27th Mohammad Rasoolallah Division IRGC	3 brigades
	32nd Ansar al-Hossein Division IRGC	3 brigades
	33rd al-Mahdi Division IRGC	1 brigade
	64th Suduqu Brigade IRGC	
	106th Sajjad Naval Brigade IRGC	
Task Force Nooh	8th Najaf Ashraf Division IRGC	3 brigades
	19th Fajr Division IRGC	3 brigades
	21st Imam Reza Division IRGC	3 brigades
	30th Beit-ol-Moghaddas Division IRGC	3 brigades
	104th Amir al-Mo'menin Brigade IRGC	
	105th Kowsar Naval Brigade IRGC	
Support Forces	22nd Artillery Group IRIA	
	33rd Artillery Group IRIA	
	90th Khatam al-Anbiya Artillery Brigade IRGC	

Table 16: Order of Battle for Operation Karbala-4, December 1986		
Corps	Division	Brigades
	91st Hadid Artillery Brigade IRGC	
	40th Sahel az-Zaman Engineer Battalion IRGC	
	43rd Imam Ali Engineer Battalion IRGC	
	2nd Combat Support Group IRIAA	
	3rd Combat Support Group IRIAA	
	4th General Support Group IRIAA	
Iraq		
VII Corps	1st & 2nd Commando Brigades, VII Corps Artillery Brigade	corps troops
	15th Infantry Division	22nd, 104th, 111th, 238th, 436th, 702nd, 802nd Infantry Brigades
	6th Armoured Division	25th Mechanised Brigade
III Corps	1st & 2nd Commando Brigades, III Corps Artillery Brigade	
	11th Infantry Division	23rd, 45th, 47th, 81st, 421st, 422nd, 429th, 501st Infantry Brigades
	3rd Wing IrAAC	

Arab. Lacking electronic countermeasures to penetrate dense Iraqi air defences, the IRIAF was only able to provide 23 attack sorties; none of these deeper than eight kilometres behind the front line. On the contrary, the intensity of the Iraqi artillery fire 'turned night into day' – which is why this became known as the 'Battle of the Red Night'.

The Iraqis then launched counterattacks that regained part of Umm al-Arassas, while containing the threat to the offshore islands. Finally, an attack by elements of 6th Armoured Division and the 66th Special Forces Brigade, from the morning of 25 December 1986, drove the enemy into the water.

Table 17: Order of Battle for Operation Karbala-5, January 1987		
Corps	Division	Brigades
Iran		
Task Force Karbala	14th Imam Hossain Division IRGC	3 brigades
	25th Karbala Division IRGC	3 brigades
	33rd al-Mahdi Division IRGC	3 brigades
	41st Sarallah Division IRGC	3 brigades
	83rd Ramadan Armoured Brigade IRGC	
	18th al-Ghadir Infantry Brigade IRGC	
	16th Armoured Division IRIA	1 brigade
	21st Infantry Division IRIA	2 brigade
	92nd Armoured Division IRIA	1 brigade (3rd)
Task Force Qods	10th Seyed o-Shohada Division IRGC	3 brigades
	17th Ali Ibn Abu Talib Division IRGC	3 brigades
	19th Fajr Division IRGC	3 brigades
	27th Mohammad Rasoolallah Division IRGC	3 brigades, 1 mech. battalion
	32nd Ansar al-Hossein Division IRGC	3 brigades
Task Force Najaf	3rd Saheb az-Zaman Division IRGC	3 brigades
	5th Nasr Division IRGC	3 brigades, 1 mech. battalion
	7th Vali Asr Division IRGC	3 brigades
	21st Imam Reza Division IRGC	3 brigades
	31st Ashura Division IRGC	3 brigades
	155th Shohada Division IRGC	3 brigades
	85th Moharram Mechanised Brigade IRGC	
Task Force Nooh	8th Najaf Ashraf Division IRGC	3 brigades, 1 mech. battalion
	9th Badr Division IRGC	3 brigades
	57th Abolfazl al-Abbas Division IRGC	3 brigades
	12th Qa'em-e Mohammad Mechanised Division IRGC	2 brigades
	29th Nabi al-Akram Brigade IRGC	
	90th Khatam al-Anbya Artillery Brigade IRGC	
Support Forces	22nd Artillery Group IRIA	
	33rd Artillery Group IRIA	
	90th Khatam al-Anbiya Artillery Brigade IRGC	
	91st Hadid Artillery Brigade IRGC	
	40th Saheb az-Zaman Engineer Brigade IRGC	
	43rd Imam Ali Engineer Brigade IRGC	
	1st Combat Support Group IRIAA	
	2nd Combat Support Group IRIAA	
	3rd Combat Support Group IRIAA	
	4th General Support Group IRIAA	

PART I: IRAN'S LAST CHANCE

Iraq		
III Corps	1st & 2nd Commando Brigades, III Corps Artillery Brigade	
	2nd Infantry Division	39th, 116th, 423rd, 435th Infantry Brigades
	8th Infantry Division	3rd, 9th, 22nd, 28th Infantry Brigades
	11th Infantry Division	23rd, 45th, 47th, 81st, 421st, 422nd, 501st Infantry Brigades
	19th Infantry Division	82nd, 108th, 427th Infantry Brigades
	32nd Infantry Division	44th, 48th, 101st, 102nd Infantry Brigades
	1st Mechanised Division	34th Armoured Brigade
	3rd Armoured Division	6th & 12th Armoured Brigades; 8th Mechanised Brigade
	5th Mechanised Division	26th Armoured, 15th & 20th Mechanised Brigades
	12th Armoured Division	37th Armoured & 46th Mechanised Brigade
	6th Armoured Division	25th Mechanised Brigade
	18th, 83rd, 94th, 101st, 478th, 702nd, 703rd, 706th Infantry Brigades	
	65th Special Forces Brigade	
	3rd Wing IrAAC	
AFGC	10th Armoured Division	17th & 42nd Armoured Brigades, 24th Mechanised Brigade
	Medina Manarawah Armoured Division Republican Guards	2nd & 10th Armoured Brigades, 14th Mechanised Brigade, 3rd Commando Brigade Republican Guards
	Baghdad Infantry Division Republican Guards	4th, 5th, 6th, 7th Infantry Brigades Republican Guards
VII Corps	15th Infantry Division	76th Infantry Brigade
	68th Special Forces Brigade	
	19th Infantry Division	82nd, 108th, 427th Infantry Brigades
	32nd Infantry Division	44th, 48th, 101st, 102nd Infantry Brigades
	1st Mechanised Division	34th Armoured Brigade
	3rd Armoured Division	6th & 12th Armoured Brigades; 8th Mechanised Brigade
	5th Mechanised Division	26th Armoured, 15th & 20th Mechanised Brigades
	12th Armoured Division	37th Armoured & 46th Mechanised Brigade
	6th Armoured Division	25th Mechanised Brigade
	18th, 83rd, 94th, 101st, 478th, 702nd, 703rd, 706th Infantry Brigades	
	65th Special Forces Brigade	
	3rd Wing IrAAC	
AFGC	10th Armoured Division	17th & 42nd Armoured Brigades, 24th Mechanised Brigade
	Medina Manarawah Armoured Division Republican Guards	2nd & 10th Armoured Brigades, 14th Mechanised Brigade, 3rd Commando Brigade Republican Guards
	Baghdad Infantry Division Republican Guards	4th, 5th, 6th, 7th Infantry Brigades Republican Guards
VII Corps	15th Infantry Division	76th Infantry Brigade
	68th Special Forces Brigade	

The Glorious Day

Task Force Karbala's failure meant that Task Force Nooh's operations were confined to some brief, half-hearted, probes by two naval brigades on the far bank of the Shatt before being abandoned. On the north bank of the Shatt, the assault upon Major General Tali Khalil Ruhayyim al-Duri's III Corps fell, once more, on 11th Infantry Division (total of eight brigades, augmented by a tank battalion and two commando battalions, supported by 32 batteries of corps artillery, which gave it 25,000 troops with 290 guns). This Iraqi concentration was struck from the north by 11 brigades of Task Force Najaf – which sought to outflank the highway defences from the north – while 89,000 troops of the 19 brigades of Task Force Quds advanced along the highway, or along the waterway's island, supported by two IRIA artillery groups.

Outnumbered 2:1, the Iraqis again relied upon their artillery augmented – at dawn – by air power. The IrAF flew no fewer than 361 fixed-wing sorties on 25 December 1986, while the Iraqi Army Air Corps (IrAAC) provided 110 rotary-wing sorties. Task Force Najaf did penetrate the northern part of the first defensive line, forcing the Iraqis to withdraw to the second line, but just before noon an Iraqi counterattack retook the positions after a 14-hour battle. The Iranians retreated back across the inundations covered by 21st IRIA Division (assigned to the Task Force Karbala).

By dusk on 25 December, after 39 hours fighting, it was all over and the Shatt reportedly ran red with blood from between 9,000 and 12,000 Iranian casualties (including only 200 prisoners). The IRIAA had also lost nine helicopters. The Iraqis suffered some 3,000 casualties but were clearly victorious and thus this attack went down in their history as 'The Glorious Day' (al-Yawm al-Adheem). The Iraqi success did much to raise their morale: the Iraqi corps commanders claimed to have killed 83,000 men, creating a complacent atmosphere in Baghdad, where Saddam Hussein al-Tikriti and his circle believed the enemy would not be capable of any major effort for another six months. In Tehran, the disaster was such that the entire operation was explained as 'attempts to destroy enemy artillery on the south bank of the Shatt'. Rafsanjani – still convinced of the value of mass attacks – launched a hunt for scapegoats and blamed the country's military leaders. Nevertheless another, even deadlier, offensive was to follow in a matter of two weeks.[20]

Operation Karbala-5 (al-Hassad al-Akbar)

The Karbala-4 disaster should have been a wake-up call for the Iranian leadership: instead, Iranian accounts indicate it 'plunged the Supreme Command into crisis'.[21] To the 'hawks', the best way to achieve their dreams and destroy Iraq continued to be a direct offensive upon Basra, as espoused by IRGC leader Mohsen Rezai. Hassani-Sa'di's position was unclear but his experience in Val Fajr-8 was likely to have made him more sympathetic to the IRIA viewpoint.[22]

Basra remained a prime objective both as a large, historic city and port whose loss would undermine Saddam's prestige. He would clearly wish to hold it at all costs and this provided the Iranians with a good opportunity to grind down the Iraqi army. However, top leaders in Tehran were becoming acutely aware of the fact that their country possessed finite resources. As Rafsanjani put it: 'In our opinion, there exists no other solution better than accelerating the war operations based on our calculations made so far. The country's general situation and its economic conditions imply bringing this problem to an ultimate point as soon as possible.'

Pressure to end the war was fed by the Iraqi air and missile offensive in the 'War of the Cities', which was eroding Iranian morale amid growing demands for an end to the threat. Tehran's prime objective remained the destruction of the Iraqi war machine and demoralisation of Saddam's regime, while Shi'a clerics hoped to force out Basra's Sunni inhabitants and replace them with 500,000 Iraqi Shia exiles and refugees when they occupied the city. Furthermore, Iranian leaders were determined not to let the enemy regain the initiative – especially not on the Faw Peninsula – and were hoping to exploit winter's heavy rains to restrict enemy superiority in the air and in armour. Unsurprisingly, for the new offensive – codenamed Karbala-5 – the IRGC was again to provide the spearhead. On the contrary, the IRIA was expected to 'sit out' an offensive in which it had little confidence except through providing artillery, engineer, and helicopter support.[23]

In what Tehran began claiming would be the 'final battle', the objective was to break the stalemate with an assault on the southern Fish Lake Line, aiming to drain the defenders' lifeblood and allow an advance which would also allow a breakout from the Faw Peninsula bridgehead in direction of Basra. Before the attack Rafsanjani said:

> Our aim is to completely destroy the Iraqi war machine. Here, near Basra, Saddam cannot do anything but fight, for the fall of Basrah is tantamount to his own death. We want to settle our accounts with Iraq at Basra's gates, which will open and pave the way for the final victory we have promised.

Encouraged by the perceived success of Task Force Najaf during Karbala-4 and based on extensive aerial reconnaissance – including the use of UAVs – detailed planning began on 27 December 1986. However, detailed plans were drafted by the SFOH – or Khatam ol-Anbiya – Headquarters literally on the eve of the assault. Unknown to them, the Iranians were assisted by an error of the US intelligence services: these failed to monitor adequately sales of the specialised equipment needed to read Land Satellite (Landsat) imagery. This equipment was received in 1986 and allowed the Iranians to use satellite imagery to prepare their offensives.[24]

The successes and failures of operations on this front since 1985 were carefully examined, and during the summer and autumn exercises were held in the marshes along the Caspian Sea with the aim of determining the most effective way of crossing the flooded zone between the Fish Lake and the border. The involved infantry were well-armed, well-equipped and were led by a large core of experienced junior- and non-commissioned officers, and given very clear briefings of their tactical objectives. Nevertheless, because of the strength of the Iraqi defences, and Tehran's diminutive artillery train, tactics were rendered subtly irrelevant: instead, the Pasdaran aimed to bulldoze through the southern defences and outflank the Fish Lake.[25] Unsurprisingly, Iranians sources indicate significant unrest among the IRGC's leadership about the prospects of success. The commander of the Imam Hossein Division told his men to rely upon their faith for, '…nothing but a miracle will help us!'[26] Furthermore, during a conference of top generals attended by Rezai, on 8 January 1987, Ahmad Gholampour – commander of the Task Force Karbala – laid out the stark choices:

- authorise the offensive immediately before the enemy discovered its imminence, or
- disperse the troops back to their camps.

His objections resulted in 'considerable discussion' between Rezai and his advisors before the order to attack was issued late that night – essentially with the aim of raising political prestige during the Kuwait conference.[27]

For Karbala-5, the Iranians concentrated four corps-sized task forces – Karbala, Qods, Najaf, and Nooh – forces under the command of Khatam ol-Anbiya Headquarters, with some 215,000 men (see Table 17 for an order of battle). Task Force Karbala totalled 18 brigades and 70,000 men that were planned to strike across the broadest part of the inundated area – the point where this merged with the southern Fish Lake – to create bridgeheads on its western bank. Meanwhile, Qods – which totalled 15 brigades and 62,000 troops – was to strike across the narrower inundated area into the exposed Iraqi salient, and then push westwards around the southern edge of the Fish Lake. Once there, it was to link up with Karbala and advance westwards to Basra. Nineteen brigades of Najaf – a total of about 78,500 troops – were to strike along the northern bank of the Shatt, leaving Nooh in reserve with 12 infantry brigades and one of the Pasdaran's artillery brigades (a total of 51,500 troops). All combined, the IRIA and IRGC could contribute about 570 artillery pieces and some 40 multiple rocket launchers to the operation. Further support was to be provided by two Pasdaran engineer brigades and about 250 MBTs from the Army and Pasdaran's armoured- and mechanised brigades, and mechanised battalions equipped with BTR-50 APCs, variously known as 'Raksh' and 'Kashayar'.[28] The IRIAA assembled a record number of 131 helicopters, including 28 Cobra gunships (only 10 of these armed with BGM-71 TOW anti-tank guided missiles), to provide much-needed direct support, and 12 Boeing CH-47C Chinook transport helicopters to bring in supplies and reinforcements as well as evacuating wounded.[29]

Overall, there was little doubt that Karbala-5 was a hastily-arranged gamble, lacking crucial fire support and armour – despite an attempt to increase helicopter support. Its success depended upon flexible execution and close cooperation between the IRIAA and the IRGC. The latter was next to impossible, especially considering that even the headquarters of different task forces rarely communicated between each other: instead, they relied upon the SFOH for coordination. Unrecognised by the Iranians was also the fact that the flooded terrain largely restricted their deployment along the Basra–Khorramshahr highway – the key to supporting the main assault – in turn creating a situation similar to that which faced the British XXX Corps in September 1944 during Operation Market Garden. Correspondingly, the Iranian thrust was exposed not only to fire from the west and the north but also from the south across the Shatt, and to the fire from Iraqi positions on the islands, while the assault force was weakened because five divisions had been battered only a fortnight earlier and had barely received replacements.

Nevertheless, preparations went ahead and were largely successful thanks to thick cloud cover and then dense fog, starting from 7 January 1987. These helped conceal resulting troop concentrations from US reconnaissance satellites.

Ya-Zahra!

The signal for the start of the attack, 'Ya-Zahra', was transmitted by the SFOH at 01:00 on 9 January 1987; with the offensive scheduled to start at 02:00 after clouds obscured the moon. Around midnight it began to rain, yet when an officer of the 'Imam Reza' Division expressed his concerns about the change in weather to his divisional commander it was suggested that the rain was a blessing from God.[30]

In front of this unit was the III Corps of the Iraqi Army – still under the incompetent Duri, whose territory of operations extended across the Shatt to cover the area opposite the Shalamcheh and the offshore islands. Duri had no fewer than 130,000 troops of the 2nd, 8th, 11th, 19th and 32nd Infantry Divisions. These held the main frontline, with the 3rd Armoured Division and the 5th Mechanised Division and several commando brigades in reserve. Further behind was the 10th Armoured Division (behind the Fish Lake), officially assigned to the Armed Forces General Command (AFGC).

Holding the southern part of Fish Lake was 8th Infantry Division (Brigadier Nawfal Ismail Khudayyir), while 32nd Infantry Division (Brigadier Dawood Salman) held the offshore islands and the northern shore of the Faw Peninsula.

Unknown to the Iraqis was that the main Iranian blow would again fall upon 11th Infantry Division, now under command of the future Chief-of-Staff of the Iraqi Army, Brigadier Abdul Wahid Shannan ar-Rabat ('Shannan'). This unit still totalled about 24,000 men in eight infantry brigades. The main position of this unit was just east of the bottom of the Fish Lake and called 'the Pentangle' (Panj-zelee) by the Iranians. This area – its eastern side leaning on the lake, its two northern and eastern sides facing inundations, and the southern flanked by a canal – was held by 421st and 429th Infantry Brigades. The higher points in the flooded area to the north were held by 422nd Infantry Brigade – which was little more than a screen. The area to the south was covered by 23rd, 45th and 47th Infantry Brigades, the 501st Infantry Brigade held the Duaiji Line in the rear, while 81st Infantry Brigade was in reserve together with a tank battalion and the corps and divisional commando battalions. The division was supported by 32 artillery batteries, comprising 190

A group of Iraqi soldiers with a suitably decorated BTR-50, seen during the later stages of what they termed 'al-Hassad al-Akbar'. (via Ted Hooton)

An IRIAA AH-1J Cobra, armed with rocket launchers, passing above Iranian position in the Shalamcheh region, during Operation Karbala-5. (Farzin Nadimi collection)

A scene from one of several bridgeheads established by the Pasdaran on the western side of the Fish Lake on 9 and 10 January 1987. (Albert Grandolini collection)

tubes, and some 50 MBTs, while air defence was provided by four light gun batteries and two 'Grail' platoons.[31]

Further south, on the Faw Peninsula, Maher's VII Corps sill had the 15th Infantry Division on the bank opposite Abadan, and could enfilade the attackers with some 160 guns as well as multiple launch rocket systems (MLRS).

The primary Iraqi problem was neither the lack of troops, nor that of firepower – but complacency. After successfully defeating Karbala-4, the defenders convinced themselves that they had substantially weakened the enemy. With generous leave policies still in place many units were understrength. To compensate, brigade commanders reduced the strength of their forward units, while some reserves were not alert. These problems were known not only to the Iranians but also to Saddam's Jordanian friend, King Hussein, who flew to Baghdad to warn Saddam. The Iraqis, who anticipated only raiding parties, appear to have ignored these warnings, although fear of raiders made the defenders nervous on the night of 8–9 January 1987 as it began to rain. Correspondingly, they began firing flares in an attempt to detect enemy activity. It was these flares which detected the 'Imam Reza' Division forming up on Umm Rassas 30 minutes before H-Hour and prompted its commander to order an immediate attack.

Martyrdom Junction

As some 50,000 Pasdaran advanced on a 25-kilometre front, the Iraqi outposts fell back. In the north, the Iranians waded or swam the inundated areas to outflank many of the smaller positions, and it appears there was little serious fighting beyond the Fish Lake. Early in the morning, the IRIAF flew 30 attack sorties: while these hit numerous Iraqi headquarters and significantly bolstered the morale of ground troops, they also alerted the enemy.

On the right flank of Task Force Karbala, the IRGC's Imam Hossein and Sarallah Divisions landed on the western bank of the Fish Lake and secured part of the embankment covering the southern causeway. Troops from Sarallah then forced their way down the causeway to take the southern strong point by 05:00 in the morning. Engineers supporting them then got a single T-55 tank across the causeway – just in time to face the first counterattack launched by the 5th Mechanised Division, the 66th Special Forces Brigade and the 8th Mechanised Brigade of the 3rd Armoured Division. Acting as a mobile pillbox, this single T-55 was to provide the centrepiece of Iranian front lines for the next two days. Manned by successively

PART I: IRAN'S LAST CHANCE

An Iraqi BMP-1 captured by the IRGC during the opening blows of Operation Karbala-5. (Photo by S. E.)

This MT-LB APC was also captured by the troops of one of the IRGC's naval brigades, and instantly deployed against its former owners. (Photo by S. E.)

Fierce resistance forced the commitment of Qods' Ansar al-Hossein Division, while – despite an Iraqi counterattack – the Seyed o-Shohada Division penetrated the Pentangle by 11:15 (and the Iraqis admitted this later the same day). Interestingly, Tehran subsequently claimed taking 287 prisoners of war on the first day, and 610 on the second day, of Karbala-5 – indicating that many other Iraqis escaped the onslaught.

Meanwhile, the 'Imam Reza' Division – supported by one mechanised brigade of the IRGC – led the envelopment by Task Force Najaf along the Shalamcheh Salient, by striking southwards, while the 'Nasr' Division advanced westwards despite fierce resistance from the isolated 47th Infantry Brigade.

Iranian Tactics

During the Iran-Iraq War, and ever since, there was, and still is, much talk about so-called 'human wave' assaults by the Iranian military. While there is little doubt that such attacks were launched – spontaneously and at minor scale – by a few Iranian commanders for different reasons, time and again; in reality the IRGC's Pasdaran and Basiji units relied upon constant infiltration – or 'swarming' – by night to overcome the massive fortifications of the major Iraqi front lines during this phase of the war. Indeed, according to multiple Iraqi officers interviewed over time, it was the Iranian infantry and its tactics that they feared the most.

With these tactics, the Iranians sought to encircle enemy positions and then push 200 to 500 metres deep within them, and thus effect what they called the 'attack from within'. Once in such a position, the Pasdaran would take strongpoints under fire with their heavy weapons – including anti-tank armament – 'drench' them with fire from automatic weapons, and thus isolate them before an assault by the Basiji. The latter generally showed strong disregard for any kind of tactical finesse and often expended their limited ammunition supply – in turn leaving themselves defenceless to Iraqi counterattacks. By contrast, Pasdaran assaults succeeded much more often because their experienced junior officers and NCOs directed attacks upon each formation's well-defined objectives – even if uncertain of their next objective. Throughout the entire war, it was foremost the lack of entrenching tools and fire support, as well as Iraqi artillery barrages

replaced crews – brought over the lake by Kashayar APCs, together with ammunition and fuel – it proved crucial in defeating several Iraqi counterattacks. The IrAF flew about two dozen air strikes attempting to hit it, but to no effect: the muddy terrain absorbed the effects of ordnance that detonated, while dozens of bombs failed to explode at all. Before long, like a lethal garden, the area was dotted by dozens of unexploded bombs. The Iraqi artillery fire grew to such intensity, and caused so many casualties, that the place became known to Iranians as the 'Martyrdom Junction': even the wounded were reluctant to seek evacuation across the causeway. Ultimately, after reportedly firing more than 300 shells, the gun of the lonesome T-55 overheated to the point of blowing up, forcing the crew to evacuate the tank. Ironically, while not a single tanker was killed while using this vehicle, its last crew was martyred while trying to take cover outside the vehicle, by one of the rare bombs dropped by Iraqi fighter-bombers at Martyrdom Junction that did explode, two days into Karbala-5.[32]

Meanwhile, the Pentangle was struck from the north by the Seyed o-Shohada and Ali Ibn Abu Talib Divisions from Task Force Qods, and by the 'Ashura' Division of Task Force Najaf from the east.

Troops of one of the naval brigades of the IRGC inside the completely ruined village of Duiji, early during Operation Karbala-5. (Photo by S. E.)

Burned hulks of military trucks and smashed buildings were all that was left of the Iraqi military base in Duiji. (Photo by S. E.)

and air strikes on Iranian communication lines that hampered their ability to consolidate positions they have reached.

Over time, a pattern developed in which the Iranians would attack after dusk and spend most of the night reducing Iraqi centres of resistance, before the dawn brought an Iraqi response. Starting at first light, the Iraqis would react with a rain of shells; air and mortar bombs, air and ground launched rockets; prior to launching their counterattacks while the Iranians were trying to hold captured positions. Provided enough of them survived, they would continue the process of eroding the defences the next night. Iranian artillery and mortar batteries were active in forcing Iraqi troops to run a gauntlet during daylight, and one Iraqi general later referred to the battle in early 1987 as 'The Somme of the Iran-Iraq War'.[33]

Trading Hot Punches

From dawn of 10 January 1987, the Sarallah Division and the newly deployed Karbala and Mohammad Rasoolallah divisions absorbed Iraqi counterattacks and then, during the evening, pressed forward through the Pentangle defences, collapsing the salient by the end of the day. This success was based on a major violation of Iraqi radio security noted not only by the Iraqi intelligence, but also by the Iranian intelligence.[34] The next day, the Iranians claimed to have taken 1,000 prisoners and that the survivors fell back upon the River Duaiji, although 5th Mechanised Division (Major General Salah Aboud Mahmoud) launched counterattacks to support the beleaguered infantry. Undertaken by the 25th Mechanised Brigade of the 6th Armoured Division and the 34th Armoured Brigade of the 1st Mechanised Division, this counterstroke was channelled by muddy terrain to the bridges over the Duaiji, and thus easily held up by the Pasdaran that were abundantly supplied with light anti-armour weapons.

Left without a choice, the Iraqis – who remained in possession of aerial dominance over the front lines – flew fierce airstrikes on the concentration points behind the Iranian front lines. Between 9 and 12 February, the IrAF flew 662 sorties, including about a dozen by Tu-22 bombers. These began deploying even Nassr-5 and Nassr-9 bombs – Iraqi copies of the Soviet-made FAB-5000 and FAB-9000 bombs. Furthermore, the IrAAC flew 433 helicopter sorties, the vast majority over the Basrah area. The Iranian fire support remained weak and the GMID – which had largely assembled the enemy ORBAT by 12 January 1987 – noted that the Iranian artillery was restricted to an average of about 100 tubes firing no more than 5,000 rounds a day.[35]

Duri tried to stabilise the situation during the next two days using counterattacks by Brigadier Salman Hamid Abbdullah's 3rd Armoured Division, aiming to contain the Task Force Karbala's bridgehead. However – and contrary to what the Iraqi propaganda claimed – he failed to drive the enemy into the Fish Lake and the 12th Armoured Brigade even lost its commander on 10 January. To prop up the southern front, Duri then brought in the 8th, 20th, 46th Mechanised and 65th Special Forces Brigades, the latter supporting 8th Division's counterattacks on the Fish Lake bridgehead. However, IRIAA AH-1s hit back with TOWs and claimed many armoured vehicles, despite the intensive activity of IrAAC anti-armour teams composed of Mi-25s and either Hughes MD.500s or Aerospatiale SA.342 Gazelles.[36]

Duri thus proved unable to prevent the further Iranian build-up along the Duaiji, which brought the troop strength to about 65,000, but also enabled Iranian engineers to construct causeways across the inundated areas; these were used to bring in supplies, move some armour and redeploy artillery. In the light of Iraqi air strikes, this proved a risky business – as witnessed by a group of journalists the Iranians attempted to bring up to Shalamcheh. Nevertheless, the IRIA and the IRGC managed to concentrate their artillery on a relatively narrow, 5-kilometre front and during the night from 11 to 12 January they unleashed a hurricane of fire upon the defenders. When the barrages lifted the Pasdaran and Basiji swept forward in numbers and, acting upon improved tactical training, penetrated multiple Iraqi positions. The few strongpoints not overrun immediately were isolated and exposed to a combination of artillery and machine gun fire. Although the Iraqis did manage to disrupt this attack and then regain some positions with the sheer volume of their fire on the next day, the Iranians continued pumping men and material into

One of the embarkation points for IRGC units on the eastern side of the Fish Lake. (Albert Grandolini collection)

A group of Pasdaran mopping up a recently captured Iraqi position, including an operational T-55, during Karbala-5. (Albert Grandolini collection)

The Pasdaran cheering the crew of an AH-1J Cobra underway low over their positions along the embankment of the Fish Lake, on 5 January 1987. (Tom Cooper collection)

MIDDLE EAST@WAR SERIES SPECIAL #1: THE IRAN-IRAQ WAR

Many of the lighter bombs dropped by Iraqi fighter-bombers failed to detonate when hitting the muddy battlefields of Karbala-4 and Karbala-5. This French-made example was photographed during the latter operation. (Farzin Nadimi collection)

As during Karbala-4, the IrAF deployed its Tu-22 bombers in strikes on the major assembly points of Iranian troops involved in Karabla-5. Their primary armament consisted of such massive bombs as the FAB-5000 and FAB-9000, or their locally manufactured copies, Nassr-5 and Nassr-9. (Tom Cooper collection)

A photo of an Iraqi-made Nassr-9 – a copy of the FAB-9000, which the Iraqis calculated packed about 60 percent of its original's punch – on display in front of the then IrAF HQ in Baghdad. (via Ali Tobchi)

the frontline and kept their momentum. By the morning of 12 January, the Iraqi 426th Brigade was forced back, thus turning the entire frontline of the 11th Division right. In this fashion, the Iranians opened a way forward along the highway from Basra to Khorramshahr.[37]

Meanwhile, the advance of Najaf's 'Imam Reza' Division along Twaila Island was slow and bloody but the Iranians secured this piece of real estate by the same morning.[38] A force of some 3,000 from the Nasr Division then crossed the Shatt near the wrecked Abu al-Khasib refinery on 12 January. This bridgehead was contained by the 76th Infantry and 68th Special Forces Brigades from the 15th Division, and driven out by 14 January – with help of a heliborne landing on the islands.[39]

At the AFGC, the Chief-of-Staff Lieutenant General Abd al-Jawad Dhanoon (also 'Dhannan/Thanoon/Zanun') was being urged by his Operations Chief, Major General Nizar Abdel Karim al-Khazraji, to use III Corps' reserve (including the 3rd Armoured and 5th Mechanised Divisions), and 10th Armoured Division to stage a counteroffensive sweeping down from north of the Fish Lake to roll up the enemy. Dhanoon dithered, partly because it would mean seeking Saddam's permission to commit the armour, and partly because Duri had committed much of his armoured reserve piecemeal and was unable to extract it. At best the corps commander was mediocre and ignored advice, never tried to anticipate the enemy and always reacted to Iranian attacks. His command style was to shout down radios and telephones threatening death and damnation if his bewildered subordinates did not immediately resolve the latest crisis. The constant

PART I: IRAN'S LAST CHANCE

One of the embarkation points for Pasdaran and Basiji units during Operation Karbala-5. Whenever identified by the Iraqi defenders, such areas were heavily bombed by the IrAF. (Photo by E.S.)

factories and offices. Eventually, even Tehran had to admit that only 200,000 followed the call – and that was probably an overestimate. As the appeal was issued Rafsanjani visited the forward battle headquarters and encouraged further efforts, but by 11 February all of the divisions had been battered, with the IRGC alone losing 974 company, battalion, brigade and divisional commanders.

Lethal Skies

The long nights and low cloud cover of mid-January and early February 1987 had provided at least some shelter from Iraqi air power. However, whenever the weather permitted, the IrAF was airborne. Between 13 and 17 January, its pilots and those of the IrAAC flew 1,600 and 1,289 sorties, respectively, most over the Basra front. The Iranians reacted with their integrated air defence system, which included MIM-23B I-HAWK SAM-sites deployed east of the Karoun River, and these claimed both a MiG-23 and a Tupolev Tu-16 bomber on the first day of the offensive (the latter while underway at 40,000ft/12,200 metres, and because a pair of Mirage F.1 fighter-bombers equipped with French-made Caiman pods for electronic countermeasures failed to appear).[44]

The presence of HAWKs – reinforced by clandestine US deliveries of spares – restricted the Iraqi airpower over the battlefield, even more so because these were linked with Skyguard anti-aircraft artillery systems. The Iranians took some time to move their air defence system and eventually, by 13 February 1987, their ground troops were operating at the very edge of it. This in turn exposed them not only to additional air strikes, but also to the full force of Iraqi attack helicopters. On the other side, in response to repeated – even if few in numbers – Iranian air strikes on their headquarters, the Iraqis felt forced to deploy at least one SA-2 SAM site within the sector protected by the VII Corps.

Baghdad later announced that during January and February 1987 its air force lost up to 50 combat aircraft – or 10 percent of its total strength – together with numerous experienced pilots. However, such a loss rate was never confirmed by official documentation and has since been fiercely denied by all available Iraqi sources.[45]

The IRIAF had meanwhile increased its operational strength, but with fewer than 60 fully operational fighter-bombers, it was usually on the defensive. Held back for defence of critically important installations deeper inside Iran, its F-14s were not used for attack purposes and rarely approached the front lines. Even more problematic was the status of the IRIAF's early warning radar network which, by this time in the war, was not only badly damaged by earlier fighting, but also in state of disrepair. Combined with extensive knowledge about this network provided to the Iraqis by Iranian defectors already before the war, and Tehran's failure to at least rebuild if not reinforce the IRIAF's radar-equipped units,

deployment and rotation of brigades aggravated the situation, for with some 100 brigade movements during Karbala-5, junior commanders had no time to familiarise themselves with the situation before they entered the line and many became casualties while personally trying to find out what was going on.[40]

During 12 January, Defence Minister Adnan Khairallah Talfah inspected the battlefield and ordered the Medina Manarwah Armoured Division of the Republican Guards – which was still undergoing training – to be sent south, indicating the fate of the offensive would now be determined by the size of reinforcements each side could bring up.[41] Success was also determined by the logistical organisation, and in this regard the more experienced staff of the Iraqi Army and well-maintained supply links proved more successful. However, the concentrated Iranian artillery fire – estimated with exaggeration by one Iraqi at 5,000 tubes – proved daunting even for experienced troops and left many shell-shocked.[42] Furthermore, Khairallah authorised the use of chemical weapons. However, with the two sides closely entangled they could be deployed only against the enemy communications and supply dumps: these were subjected to repeated airborne mustard gas strikes. One Iranian survivor noted he never encountered fighting as ferocious as that in Karbala-5 and added: 'I really did not want to fight'.[43]

Indeed, the sheer exhaustion of combatants on both sides resulted in a decline in fighting between 13 and 16 January. Nevertheless, the Imam Reza and Shohada Divisions – reinforced by multiple Basiji battalions – made another push. They forced the 45th and 478th Brigades to withdraw and secured the headquarters of the Duaiji sector. Encouraged, the Iranians committed their reserves from the Task Force Nooh and deployed the Abolfazl al-Abbas Infantry Division and Qa'em-e-Mohammad Mechanised Division, together with the Nabi al-Akram Infantry Brigade and Khatam al-Anhiya Artillery Brigade without success. By that time, casualties were so heavy that already on 13 January 1987, the Ministry of the IRGC called upon citizens to register for the 'Division of the Prophet Mohammed' in hope of raising 500,000 men from mosques,

201

this resulted in the Iranians gradually losing the big picture of the situation over the front lines.

On the contrary, bolstered by spares obtained during the Irangate affair, the IRIAA remained airborne over the battlefield and used BGM-71 TOW ATGMs as often as possible, keeping the Iraqi armour at bay. Indeed, the activity of Iranian Cobra attack helicopters was such that the Iraqis rushed to the front lines shells equipped with anti-helicopter proximity fuses, which could match TOW's 3.75km maximum range. At least according to Iraqi sources, such shells proved highly effective.[46]

Republican Guards to the Rescue

On 14 January 1987, the Pasdaran began pushing into the 11th Infantry Division's left flank through half-burned palm groves, slowly forcing it out of the Duaiji Line and into the Jasim Line. This was a brutal frontal attack, leaving behind a ghastly trail of bodies – and body parts – along the berms crossed by Iranian troops. However, this success of the IRGC led to momentous changes the following day, when Saddam chaired a meeting of the AFGC attended by Defence Minister Khaiallah, Chief-of-Staff Dhanoon, his Operations Director Khazraji, III Corps' commander Duri, the Director of Military Planning General Mohammad Abdul Qader, and 11th Infantry Division's commander General Shannan al Rabat. Saddam demanded to know what had happened and received a vague response from Dhanoon. Khazraji was franker, pointing out that he, Dhanoon and Qader had all been in III Corps' forward command post and seen that Duri was nervous, shouting and cursing. He said Duri failed to recognise the true situation and was confusing Shannan. Duri's response was confused, and he accused Dhanoon of failing to assist him. The two were soon exchanging angry words whereupon Saddam and Khaiallah stormed out of the meeting. Saddam soon expressed his wrath with Dhanoon: he was retired on the spot and replaced by Lieutenant General Saad ad-Din Aziz. Duri was ordered to exchange positions with the commander of V Corps, Dhiya ad-Din Jamal; while the Director of Operation Khazraji was given the command of I Corps. Finally, Commander of IV Corps, Thabit Sultan at-Tikriti, was replaced by Mohammad Abdul Qader. However, instead of taking over, Qader did not go straight to his new headquarters, but remained assigned to his old command – 11th Division, where he created additional defences in the rear until the situation stabilised, and acted as advisor to Shannan, who focused upon containing the enemy.[47]

Meanwhile, the arrival of 47th and – probably – 48th Infantry Brigades boosted the 11th Infantry Division, while the 5th Mechanised Division shored up its right with 94th, 702nd, 703rd, and 706th Infantry Brigades, as well as the 37th Armoured Brigade (whose commander was killed on 15 January 1987). Similarly, the Baghdad Republican Guards Infantry Division – supported by the 2nd Republican Guards Armoured Brigade of the Medina Division – struck the Fish Lake bridgeheads together with 18th Infantry Brigade.

Iranian progress was already very slow by the time Saddam finally did visit the front, on 17 January 1987, but the Duaiji Line had almost been lost. Correspondingly, he demanded the rest of 'Medina' together with 'Baghdad' to stage a counterattack the following afternoon. The Guards tried to make their way forward along roads clogged with traffic and reached the front only around dusk, only to discover that nobody had a clear idea what was going on. Nevertheless, the counterattack was launched early the following morning and briefly held up the IRGC, even if failing to prevent them from taking the last strongpoints of the Duaiji Line.

On the contrary, after bringing in additional reinforcements, five divisions of Task Force Qods – supported by three tank battalions – used this area as a springboard for their new attack towards the Jasim. Despite heroic resistance from 18th, 44th and 704th Brigades, the Iranians punched through, took 2,010 prisoners, and established a kilometre-deep bridgehead on 19 January 1987.

The next day, the Seyed o-Shohada and Sarallah Divisions renewed this assault by attempting another breakthrough, but this

This group of Pasdaran wearing gasmasks was photographed while they were in the process of outflanking the Duaiji Line by moving through the palm groves. (Farzin Nadimi collection)

A still from a rare video showing an Iranian military bulldozer in the process of erecting one of a myriad of earthen berms used as primary combat positions by both sides on the southern frontlines of the Iran-Iraq War. (Tom Cooper collection)

PART I: IRAN'S LAST CHANCE

A grim scene from a shallow Iranian trench opposing the Jasim Line in early 1987. (Tom Cooper collection)

The crew of a North Korean-made M1978 Koksan 170mm self-propelled guns deployed on the frontlines near Basra in 1987. The vehicle was left as painted and marked on delivery – including its overall olive-green colour livery and Red Star insignia. (Tom Cooper collection)

Firing the Koksan resulted in a powerful wave of overpressure, as illustrated by this image from 1987. (Tom Cooper collection)

time they were held by 18th, 83rd, 101st, 704th Infantry Brigades (controlled by the 8th Infantry Division), and the 10th Guards Armoured Brigade. While the Iranians retained their bridgeheads on the shores of the Fish Lake and the Shatt, the Iraqis meanwhile frantically threw up a new defensive position behind the Jasim Line along the Zawji (Dual) Canals, which helped to feed the Fish Lake from the Shatt. The Guards were again committed and their counterattacks helped to restrict enemy progress. In comparison, the Iranians made little attempt to fortify their hard-won ground although their engineers did build berms alongside the main roads to conceal their traffic from enemy artillery observers.

Behind the Jasim Line there was hectic engineering activity directed by the Sandhurst-trained GCHQ Logistics Chief, Lieutenant General Salim Hussein. He ordered several flooded areas to be drained and the construction of additional berms and roads. Two berm-based defensive positions were built at 5-kilometre intervals behind the Jasim Line with 'Baghdad' and 5th Mechanised Divisions manning the first, while 12th Armoured and 3rd Armoured Divisions manned the second, using these as the basis for counterattacks. On 22 January 1987 there was a new assault upon the Jasim Line where 2nd Infantry Division (Brigadier Ahmad Rakan) had been brought in to hold the northern section on the right of 5th Mechanised Division, while 32nd Infantry Division had been moved north from the Shatt to hold the southern section leaving 11th Infantry Division in the middle like the meat in a sandwich. Fresh units launched successive night attacks and by the afternoon of 23 January the Iranians claimed 2,235 prisoners.

After stopping the initial wave of Iraqi counterattacks, the Iranians relaunched their offensive. Progress was painfully slow as the Iraqis resisted fiercely with the Pasdaran having to storm each position. Nevertheless, by 26 January 1987 Tehran claimed to have secured a bridgehead across the Zawji Canals and the Iraqi engineers were forced to quickly build another defensive belt behind the waterway. On the night of 27/28 January Task Force Qods tried to break out of this bridgehead using the Sarallah Division while Task Force Karbala launched diversions with the Imam Hossain and al-Mahdi divisions, reinforced by the Najaf Ashraf Division from 'Nooh'. This time, the Iraqis contained the situation by the following morning: indeed, 5th Mechanised Division and Baghdad, with 12th Armoured Brigade finally overran the enemy bridgehead on west bank of Fish Lake later that day. The fighting between 27 January and 1 February involved 1,554 IrAF and 995 IrAAC sorties and then a brief pause descended upon the battlefield allowing 'Medina' Division of the Republican Guards to be withdrawn.

By now the Iraqis had suffered some 10,000 casualties, indeed so heavy that on 21 January Saddam called for volunteers between the ages of 14 and 35, while university students and any of their physically fit lecturers under the age of 35 were told to enrol as officer candidates. Yet the pressure was severe enough for Saddam Hussein to send additional Guards units, while Maher's VII Corps not only provided artillery support but also a division as a backstop to III Corps' right. Eventually, some 50 Iraqi brigades, including eight Guards, became involved in the battle, and there were reports that the dead were being ferried back to Baghdad in disguised vehicles, or kept in cold storage to regulate their release to relatives, while trains carrying casualties were being unloaded short of Baghdad.[48]

The Iranians maintained the pressure but by the end of the month the offensive was clearly running out of steam due to supply problems and the Pasdaran's shortage of both heavy equipment and command skills to exploit their successes. They had secured a 10-kilometre bridgehead inside Iraq and were within 12 kilometres of Basra, indeed they could see the eastern suburbs – but were exhausted. However, Iran brought the city under artillery and missile fire which did force the Iraqis to evacuate much of the civilian population.

Final Attempt

On the night of 31 January to 1 February 1987, the Karbala Task Force made a last effort around the Zawji Canals. The Imam Hossain and al-Mahdi divisions assaulted, and reportedly achieved their greatest success on, the frontline held by the Iraqi 11th Division, where the gun line was reached. Nevertheless, the attackers were eventually driven back from the canals in a hard-fought battle with heavy Pasdaran losses to air power: the Iraqis are known to have flown 492 fixed-wing and 345 rotary-wing sorties on 1 February 1987 alone.

With the Iranians shooting their bolt and forced to pause and lick their wounds, the fighting died down for nearly a fortnight, during which the Iraqi 2nd Infantry Division relieved the battered 11th. As soon as they were ready, they counterattacked again, this time against the northern side of the Iranian salient, while the III Corps assaulted along the western side of the Fish Lake before turning south to the Jasim River. This enterprise began as a combined-arms operation, but its components quickly devolved into private battles as the infantry and armour became separated and struck out at diverging angles with inadequate artillery support. The Iraqis lumbered forward so slowly in frontal assaults that they were rapidly stopped, although the pressure was sufficient to force the Iranians to abandon their Fish Lake bridgehead by 2 February. The counterattack regained some 20 square kilometres of territory to pinch out the enemy salient by 7 February. Furthermore, this operation strained the Iraqi army to breaking point because, '...the Iraqi high command reduced its reserves to such a low level that, had the Iranians achieved a major breakthrough, it would have found itself short of reserve forces to stop the enemy'.[49]

After seven weeks of bitter fighting the Iranians were still outside Basra in terrain consisting '...of marsh, flooded terrain, and date palms, most of which had been reduced to stumps'.[50] There was intense, but inconclusive, fighting until mid-February, during which the Iraqis did not perform well while attempting to advance. On the contrary, their army was ever more reliant upon defensive fire, water barriers, and high-performance fixed-wing aircraft – operations of which were frequently hampered by bad weather. Indeed, some secondary positions were virtually abandoned, together with much equipment and ammunition, and this may be why a number of Iraqi officers were reportedly executed.[51] However, the Iranians remained confined to their bridgehead, which was, meanwhile, barely a kilometre wide in some places.

There was one more, brief, flare-up after the Iranians belatedly brought down armour and artillery from the Sumar front. On the night from 22 to 23 February the Imam Hossain Division spearheaded an assault along the Basra–Khorramshahr highway hitting the 39th, 116th, 423rd and 435th Brigades of the 2nd Division and pushing them back by two kilometres. However, this assault then came under sustained artillery fire from the west and south which, together with counterattacks of the 5th Mechanised Division and aerial activity (including 304 fixed-wing and 234 helicopter sorties between 23–25 February), helped smother the attack. Even the commander of the Imam Hossain Division, Hajj Hoseyn Kharrazi, was killed, apparently by an RPG round.

A trail of destroyed equipment and wrecked vehicles left behind by the Pasdaran in the aftermath of Karbala-5. (Albert Grandolini collection)

Loss of Strategic Initiative

On 26 February 1987, Tehran officially ended Karbala-5. This was a decision which finally recognised Iran's failure to achieve its war objectives – regardless of the cost. Certainly enough, a new Iranian attack struck 2nd Infantry and 5th Mechanised Divisions on the night from 28 February to 1 March 1987 and broke through in several places. However, the Baghdad Infantry Division of the Republican Guards counterattacked and restored the line within 12 hours. Another similar attempt

The wreckage of one of up to 30 IrAF aircraft (a Su-22M-3 in this case), shot down by Iranian air defences during Karbala-4 or Karbala-5. (Tom Cooper collection)

launched during the night of 3 to 4 March against 2nd Infantry Division in heavy rain and high winds, went as deep as three kilometres before it was stopped on 11 March, when Iranian commander Ahmad Rakan was killed.

Tehran was, meanwhile, facing pressure from new Iraqi attacks upon its cities and was diplomatically isolated even by Moscow and Damascus. Starting with 12 January 1987, the IrAF bombed 62 Iranian cities and towns in 42 days, reportedly killing more than 6,000 people. This led to retaliation with artillery barrages against Basra in late January, encouraging a further flight of the civilian population from the city. A journalist visitor in late April noted: 'Parts of Basra are now completely deserted; and there is widespread damage from Iranian shelling, with many buildings (damaged) either by direct hits or shattered by shrapnel. Basra no longer functions as a city and this clearly can be counted as a propaganda coup for the Iranians'.[52] To help relieve the pressure, III Corps' new commander, Lieutenant General Dhiya Ad-din Jamal, launched a counteroffensive around the Jasim River on 1 March. IrAF commander, Air Marshal Hamid Shaaban at-Takriti, meanwhile closely cooperated operations of his branch and this ensured aerial reconnaissance information that was swiftly passed down to field commanders. However, while regaining a third of the ground lost in Karbala-5, this counteroffensive also caused excessive losses.[53]

Meanwhile, Tehran proclaimed a triumph claiming to have taken nearly 2,900 prisoners and captured 220 AFVs and 85 guns as well as 155 square kilometres. An indirect confirmation of the gains were repeated strikes by heavy artillery and, reportedly, MLRS upon Basra's suburbs. However, while theoretically gaining a springboard for a future assault upon the city, Karbala-5 was another Iranian defeat – at both operational and strategic levels. It was only in

CaptiVictorious Iraqis with captured Pasdaran following what Baghdad named 'The Great Harvest', in March 1987. (Albert Grandolini collection)

regards of internal policy that it provided a boost for Rafsanjani who had been smeared by his opponents over the Irangate affair which had been publicised over the past months.

The cost was heavy; it was estimated that the Iranians had suffered 52,000-62,000 casualties (including 17,000 dead) and, while this figure may be exaggerated, the slaughter of the Basij must have been especially severe. Many of those lost, especially on the Iranian side, were veterans and the Iranian authorities now faced great difficulties finding volunteers for the Pasdaran and Basiji with quotas allocated to regions, towns and ministries. The well of courage and dedication, even within these revolutionary shock troops, had been drained low and there was a reluctance in their ranks to make further attacks. This reflected declining national morale among the war-weary population at a time when declining oil revenues, ebbing cash reserves and arms embargoes were sapping the Iranian war machine. One commentator noted: 'Undeniably, Iran sorely needs a vast influx of new weaponry, at the very least a sustained infusion of spares to mobilise its air force, artillery and armour.' Despite huge amounts spent on the black market, and what it was able to squeeze out of President Ronald Reagan in clandestine shipments, Iran still has not been able to amass sufficient new hardware to exploit its tactical superiority.[54]

The Iraqis – who called this battle 'The Great Harvest' (al-Hassad al-Akbar'), lost over 40,000 troops (including about 6,000 dead), up to 30 aircraft, over 700 tanks and other armoured vehicles, 250 artillery pieces and 1,400 other vehicles. This was a high price, but they prevented an Iranian breakthrough and imposed upon their enemy the growing and demoralising realisation that Iran lacked adequate material resources. Perhaps more importantly: while his forces had just about contained the threat, Saddam felt forced to encourage greater professionalism between his commanders, and raise the morale of his nation. When the Iranian New Year ('Norouz/Nowrouz/Nowruz') ended without a clear-cut victory on 20 March 1987, he organised mass demonstrations in Baghdad. Unsurprisingly, this prompted commentary like 'the fact that his government regarded not being defeated as victory was a testimony to the static defence to which it had become wedded over the past five years'.[55] Somewhat unfairly, another foreign observer concluded 'Ultimately, Iraq's generals prevailed... in spite of the forces under their command rather than because of them'.[56] On the contrary, the British Military Attaché in Baghdad, Aldridge, summed up 'The battle was large-scale, bloody, prolonged by local standards and horrendous in its casualties to both sides'.[57]

Operation Karbala-8

Understanding the danger of losing the strategic initiative, in April 1987 Iran launched a series of minor offensives – Karbala-7, Karbala-9 and Karbala-10 – on the northern front, aiming to pin down potential Iraqi reinforcements, but also as a reprisal for air attacks. Furthermore, knowing the last offensive caused the draining of the flooded area between the Fish Lake and the border, while waiting for the ground to dry, the IRGC commenced preparations for one last push towards Basra – Operation Karbala-8. In order to expand the salient south of the Fish Lake and improve their tactical position – perhaps also to prepare a bigger jump-off point for the next offensive – the IRGC assembled about 46,000 fresh troops. Clearly, most of the involved divisions were still licking their wounds, and thus additional divisions were brought in, resulting in a concentration of 10 divisions and their following deployment:

Task Force Karbala, some 45,000 strong, was to strike from the northern bridgehead on the Jasim, north-westwards across the Zawji Canals and then roll up the southern section of the Fish Lake defences to the lower causeway.[58]

Task Force Qods, about 20,000 strong, was to strike down the causeway.

On the Iraqi side, 2nd Infantry Division had been relieved by the 8th, which now held the southern part of the Fish Lake, while 19th Infantry Division faced the northern face of the Iranian salient, with 32nd Infantry Division on its right and two brigades of 5th Mechanised Division in reserve. On 1 April GMID noted unusual vehicle movements in the southern zone from late March, while on 31 March two spies reported troops forming up for an attack. Nevertheless, knowing the enemy had suffered heavy casualties, the Iraqis were convinced the Iranians were left with only 60 artillery pieces and complacently failed to expect a major assault.[59] Thus, the Iraqis did nothing when hundreds of pick-up trucks were used to deploy Pasdaran and Basiji within 1.5 kilometres of their jump-off points, and then made their final approach on foot.

Ya Saheb az-Zaman!

The code-word Ya Saheb az-Zaman ('Oh Lord of the Era' or 'Hidden Imam') was issued during the night of 6 to 7 April 1987, and troops

Table 18: Order of Battle for Operation Karbala-8, April 1987

Corps	Division	Brigades
Iran		
Task Force Karbala	8th Najaf Ashraf Division IRGC	
	10th Seyed o-Shohada Division IRGC	
	17th Ali Ibn Abu Talib Division IRGC	
	19th Fajr Division IRGC	
	25th Karbala Division IRGC	
	27th Mohammad Rasoolallah Division IRGC	
	31st Ashura Division IRGC	
	33rd al-Mahdi Division IRGC	
	83rd Ramadan Armoured Brigade IRGC	
Task Force Qods	21st Imam Reza Division IRGC	
	32nd Ansar al-Hossein Division IRGC	
	18th al-Ghadir Brigade IRGC	
Iraq		
III Corps	5th Mechanised Division	26th Armoured & 27th Mechanised Brigades
	8th Infantry Division	106th, 418th Infantry Brigades
	19th Infantry Division	44th, 417th Infantry Brigades
	32nd Infantry Division	29th, 41st, 73rd, 117th, 441st Infantry Brigades
Reinforcements	Hammurabi Armoured Division Republican Guards	8th & 17th Armoured, 15th Mechanised Brigades Republican Guards
	Medina Manarwah Armoured Division Republican Guards	2nd & 10th Armoured, 14th Mechanised Brigade Republican Guards
	Baghdad Infantry Division Republican Guards	4th, 5th, 6th, 7th Infantry Brigades Republican Guards

of the Task Force Qods launched their assault. Almost instantly, they established bridgeheads around the southern causeway with two battalions each of the Imam Reza Division and al-Ghadir Brigade, but these were unable to continue their advance due to intense artillery fire.[60] Similarly, Task Force Karbala's attack with 10 battalions was pinned down for two hours by prompt artillery fire and before it could hit positions of the 19th and 32nd Divisions, even if not before the Pasdaran forced their way into two of former's strongpoints.

On 10 April, Karbala attempted to exploit its penetration through deployment of 30 battalions, supported by a battalion of MBTs and APCs each from the IRIA's 81st Armoured Division, and about 70 artillery pieces. Simultaneously, Task Force Qods renewed its attempts to force the causeway through 8th Infantry Division. However, in all of these cases, the hard-won gains were swiftly obliterated by armour-led counterattacks launched with strong air support. The IrAF flew over 300 fixed-wing sorties and the IrAAC another 206 by helicopters on 8 and 9 April, deploying chemical weapons in abundance. The IRIAA appeared only occasionally, while the IRIAF held itself back. Correspondingly, the only available means of air defence were a few batteries of ZSU-23-4 Shilka self-propelled guns, and about a dozen MANPAD-teams equipped with SA-7s. Unsurprisingly, the Iranians found themselves exposed to continuous counterattacks and one Pasdaran later commented: 'It was just like we were sitting near an airport and airplanes easily approached and calmly dropped their loads along with leaflets telling us to go back to our homes'.[61]

Like so many times before, the conclusion was unavoidable, that the IRGC-officers were the architects of their own misfortune: they rarely – if ever – coordinated operations with the IRIAF and even when Grumman F-14A Tomcat fighters were flying combat air patrols 20–30 kilometres behind the front lines, would not call upon them to help. Such failures were a result of a combination of factors, including pride, shortage of VHF radios, and the fact the Pasdaran were often not sure of their exact location. Indeed, not a few supply columns were destroyed because they were sent in the wrong direction.[62]

Ultimately, the assaults of Karbala-8 were broken off after a gain of only a kilometre in three days of fighting. Nevertheless, the Iraqis were getting anxious. Just after midnight on 9 April 1987, the Soviet Military Attaché sought a special meeting with Iraqi military leaders to forward information from Moscow that at least four Pasdaran divisions and several brigades had received boats, bridges and other crossing equipment, which might suggest that Karbala-8 involved not just a crossing of the Fish Lake but also attacks either in the Hawizah Marshes or across the Shatt al-Arab.[63] For Baghdad it was vital to nip the offensive in the bud. On 11 April, a crushing response was unleashed in the form of three divisions of the Republican Guards and 10 brigades of the Army: Ibrahim Abdel-Sattar Muhammad's Hammurabi Republican Guards Armoured Division, Ahmad Ibrahim Hammash's Medina Republican Guards Armoured Division and Kamil Sajit Aziz's Baghdad Republican Guards Infantry Division. Provided with overwhelming air- and artillery support they restored the situation to that before the last Iranian attack by noon. They not only took many prisoners but also dashed all of Tehran's hopes of success. Certainly enough, the IRGC did receive some support from IRIAA Cobras this time: these flew over 50 combat sorties. Similarly, the IRIAF fighter-bombers hit several Iraqi headquarters and communication facilities. But that was not enough. The IrAF flew over 350 sorties in support of ground troops, and successfully interdicted Iranian communications between Shalamcheh and Khorramshahr. While suffering some 2,000 casualties, the Iraqis thus held the enemy 15 kilometres short of Basra and boxed them into a salient exposed to artillery fire from three directions. In turn, while suffering some 6,500 casualties – or about 10 percent of the assault force – the Iranians failed not only to develop a viable springboard to Basra, but were left with the realisation that no further advance was possible.[64]

The Iraqi Air Force dominated the skies over the battlefield during Karbala-5. This MiG-23BN was photographed while flying very low above Iranian positions. (Farzin Nadimi collection)

Post Scriptum

Karbala-8 brought total Iranian casualties since late December 1986 to more than 85,000 and forced even the biggest hawks in Tehran to finally accept the reality: Iran lacked the material resources to end the war with a conventional blow. In despair, Rezai wrote a letter of resignation to Khomeini in April 1987, blaming – amongst other reasons – the lack of national support for the war effort. The Ayatollah refused his request: Rezai remained in his position until August 1997 when the government accepted his second resignation letter.

Grudgingly, the religious-political leadership in Tehran admitted that the IRIA's generals had been right all along with their doubts about the country's ability to take Basra. In turn, the regular military overplayed its hand when demanding of religious-political leaders and the IRGC to recognise the fact that the impasse with Iraq could only be resolved through the means of diplomacy. This was something absolutely unacceptable for the clerics and their supporters, both of whom desperately insisted on a military solution. Eventually, a solution was found in emphasising the northern front lines, and thus buying time until the situation in the south would be favourable enough to renew the assault upon Basra. It was a massive gamble based on assumptions that the Iraqis would remain as passive as they had acted for the last five years. While appearing rational, it made no allowance for any changes in Saddam's strategy. Correspondingly, and before long, a steady stream of IRGC divisions began flowing northward.[65]

Rezai re-appeared in late June 1987, to reveal this new strategy with remarks that the Basra-offensives had 'put the war's decisive stage behind it… and (the war) has now entered a stage to determine the future of Iraq… (The coming struggle will be) a series of limited operations and a series of bigger ones. We have plans to organise, train and arm popular forces inside Iraq…This is the new front'.

Essentially, and years too late, Tehran decided to start supporting opposition to Saddam inside Iraq, notably the Kurds, in an attempt to weaken and destabilise the regime, erode and disperse its military strength – before renewing major attacks.[66]

A grim scene from one of the battlefields of the Iranian Karbala offensives, showing dozens of bodies of the Pasdaran, probably killed by Iraqi chemical weapons. Although nearly breaking the back of the Iraqi army, ultimately, these operations destroyed the offensive power of the IRGC. (via Tom Cooper)

In Baghdad, commanders around Saddam had already decided that only offensive operations would bring a favourable conclusion to the war. Even then – and as insurance against a new thrust around the Hawizah Marshes – they added another 32 kilometres of fortifications to extend the existing 88-kilometre line to cover Amarah.[67] On 5 March 1987, Saddam had held a top-level meeting lasting five hours in Baghdad. Those attending included the Defence Minister Khairallah, a senior member of the Ba'ath Party Ali Hassan Al Mejid, and Information Minister Latif Nasif Jassem. The meeting reportedly considered strategy and raised concerns about the future for Iraq in a war of attrition. It decided to meet this situation by expanding the Republican Guard, escalating the Tanker War, and making even more extensive use of weapons of mass destruction.[68]

14
TWO ARMIES

With the failure of Karbala-8, a year-long lull descended upon the southern battlefield – no doubt to the relief of the troops on both sides. But while there was some relief from danger there was none from discomfort. Therefore, the generals tried to ensure their men were never idle – for constant activity prevented them brooding.

During the day there were rear defences and roads to be both built and maintained as trucks brought men and supplies to the dumps at the rear; running the gauntlet of enemy artillery, heavy mortars, MLRS or roving helicopter gunships which targeted bottlenecks such as crossroads and the approaches to bridges. Safety from enemy fire was to be found in trenches and dugouts – with one Iraqi soldier recalling that as he went along the road all he could see was the heads of soldiers sticking out of the ground.[1] At the front both sides kept their heads down, with the daily monotony broken by the crack of a sniper's rifle aiming at the unwary, or the occasional harassing mortar bomb or shell. At night, seen through the green light of image intensifiers, the front resembled an ants' nest. Supply convoys and replacements would file to the front line, whose garrisons would send forward work parties, ration carriers and reliefs to the advanced positions within the barbed wire and minefields. There, with every sense alert to raiders, the men spent the night laying mines, repairing or extending barbed wire entanglements, against a background of harassing fire which might suddenly concentrate upon tracks, bottlenecks or areas where the enemy knew, or suspected, there would be work parties. In the morning came the mournful task of counting and evacuating the casualties to hospital, or to the grave, and accounting for material losses.[2]

Both sides would stand-to before dawn and once the men had been stood down, around 05:00 in summer, they would have morning prayers. Daily prayers were the norm for both sides, but the Iraqi Army avoided formal Friday prayers although there was nothing to stop men using civilian mosques.[3].

Then came breakfast which, for Iranian troops, usually consisted of sweet tea, feta cheese and flat bread, very occasionally accompanied with scrambled eggs; while Iraqi troops would have cheese, milk, tea or soup cooked by squads in the front line, augmented by dates and onions. Lunch would be between noon and 13:00 although, for Iranian troops, it depended upon how well-supplied they were, or where they were fighting. If a hot meal was available it was cooked rice with lentils, or stews. A good treat was rice with chicken or cooked meat. Where they were unable to get a hot meal they used canned food, of which the most sought-after was tuna in oil. Dinner was around 20:00 to 21:00 and often consisted of abgoosht (a meat stew with chickpeas and beans), or thick Persian soups, but during the summer men settled for watermelon or grapes with feta cheese and bread.

The Iraqis tried to organise hot meals for both lunch and dinner. This was cooked at the front whenever and wherever possible, but sometimes combat operations forced the meals to be merged. They consisted of rice, cooked vegetables with tomato sauce, and meat which was either beef or mutton – although twice a week this was replaced by chicken. Lunch was often augmented with dates or onions, while all meals included fruit depending upon the season. The men also received date syrup (dibis) or sesame syrup (rashi) during winter or on cold days to raise calorie levels. All meals were accompanied by universally-loved brown Army Bread baked in military bakeries from high-quality whole-wheat flour. This was famous for its unique taste and texture. Where the front line was some distance away it was cooked in mobile field kitchens, one per company, and then driven to the units on the frontline in insulated

The crew of an IRIA-operated Chieftain seen with their vehicle later during the war. Because of heavy attrition during earlier operations and of increased rivalry with the IRGC, they saw ever less action in 1986 and 1987. (via S.S.)

To shield themselves and their equipment from the summer heat, the crew of this IRIA-operated ZSU-23-4 improvised a sun shield atop the turret of their vehicle. (via E.S.)

Due to lack of replacement equipment and the poor quality of arms hurriedly acquired from China and North Korea, the Iranians were forced to make extensive use of armament captured from the Iraqis. This photograph was taken during the testing of French-made Milan ATGMs. (via E.S.)

containers. Where intense combat was anticipated each unit would receive a week's supply of dry food.

Keeping this food edible, and equipment serviceable, was always a problem – regardless if in winter or in summer. The winter mist and rain forced men to repeatedly oil their weapons, but ammunition was often ruined, and the Pasdaran had problems with their telephone cables. Flooding created soft, clinging mud which could enter mess tins and give food a gritty taste. It slowed movement by foot or vehicle and worked its way into the operating rooms in the forward casualty posts and field hospitals. There were similar problems during the summer when the sun baked the ground so that vehicles or groups of men created plumes of dust which attracted the unwelcome attention of artillery observers. Sandstorms from north-westerly winds created drifts on the roads and could rapidly fill a trench while the men had to clean their weapons twice a day despite wrapping them in cloth.[4]

Heat, humidity and dust all affected the men and hardware to a greater or lesser extent. Indeed, during the summer the heat around noon could distort the gun barrels of MBTs. Therefore, and unless urgently required, all combat activity tended to take place before 10 o'clock in the morning and after 3 o'clock in the afternoon. Dust was the most serious problem, especially for electronic equipment (such as radios); although the Russian practice of using rotas to exchange modules eased the problem for Iraqi troops – while increasing demand in the supply system. Radio communication was affected by static electricity caused by dry air and sandstorms affecting FM communications in the day and AM communications after midnight. A problem for AFV crews of both sides was that Russian and Chinese vehicles were designed for Arctic-like conditions and closed-down crews frequently suffered heatstroke.[5]

After more than six years of bloody fighting the two armies, especially the Iranian, had changed significantly since September 1980.[6] Tehran's policy was summed up by the chant 'Jang, jang ba pirouzi' ('War, war until victory'), with which Pasdaran, Basiji and even Iraqi PoWs greeted Rafsanjani as he mounted the podium at the Tehran University Friday Sermon (formerly football) ground, on 4 July 1988, knowing the war was already lost.[7]

The Iranian Forces

Tehran's command structure remained very much the same as of 1982, with Khomeini the ultimate decision maker and nominal head of the SDC, whose members included the President Khamenei, and Premier Mir-Hossein Moussavi together with the Defence Minister. Military personnel included Colonel Hussein Jalili and Revolutionary Guards Minister Mohsen Rafighdust, as well as the

Ayatollah's professional representative on the council, Brigadier Zahirnejhad. The service chiefs included Armed Forces Chief-of-Staff, Colonel Sohrabi, IRIA commander Shirazi, and the Ground Forces Commander Colonel Hussein Hassani-Sa'di, the Pasdaran leader Mohsen Rezai and his Deputy Ali Shamkhani, together with the Air Force and Naval commanders. In May 1987 Khomeini promoted 10 senior officers for outstanding wartime service, with Zahirnejhad becoming a Major General, while Sohrabi, Shirazi, and Hassani-Sa'di, together with IRIAF commander Colonel Mansour Sattari becoming Brigadiers.[8]

The SDC was supported by a Joint Staff, drawn from the conventional and unconventional forces augmented by the National Police and the Gendarmerie, responsible for military planning and cooperation and operational control of all forces. It was based upon the US system with Personnel and Administration (J1), Intelligence and Security (J2), Operations and Training (J3), Logistics and Support (J4), Liaison (J5). The executive arm of the SDC was the Headquarters Western Operational Area, organised on similar lines to the Joint Staff but with Gendarmerie and National Police representatives. To ensure political reliability there was an SDC representative – usually the senior Pasdaran commander, together with Khomenei's personal representative. Decisions made by the SDC were executed through task force headquarters by the operations headquarters (OHQ) of which three faced the Iraqis; Northwest (NWOHQ) at Urumiyeh (or Urmia), West (WOHQ) at Kermanshah and South (SOHQ) at Ahvaz. These three were also known as Ramadan, Hamzeh Seyyed ash-Shohada and Karbala, respectively.

Furthermore, there was Headquarters East Operational Area at Torbat-e Heydariyeh to secure the eastern frontier. These were usually IRIA/Pasdaran commands but the northern ones also had a strong police/gendarme presence. They were subdivided into 3–8 sectors whose operations might be coordinated by permanent task force headquarters.

It has been estimated that by 1987 out of 9 million men aged 18–45, Iran had 1.28 million in uniform.[9]

Although the IRIA, administered and supported by the Defence Ministry, had lost much prestige since the Iranian Revolution, especially among the politicians, it remained a formidable force which had been steadily expanded. The basic structure remained based upon the 16th, 81st and 92nd Armoured Divisions, and 21st, 28th, 64th and 77th (Mechanised) Infantry Divisions. Between 1981 and 1982 the 88th Armoured Brigade, the 30th, 58th and 84th Infantry Brigades were expanded into divisions followed in 1983 by the 23rd Special Forces Brigade, but the 37th Armoured, 40th Infantry and 55th Airborne Brigades were unchanged and a 45th Special Forces Brigade was created. This gave the IRIA 45 brigades, including 16 armoured/mechanised, 24 infantry and five special forces/airborne brigades. The majority of these were deployed with 11 divisions on the Northern and Central Fronts.

Many of these units were filled out with temporary reservist or 'Qods' battalions, usually two or three at a time, with the 84th Brigade reported to have created a total of 20 such units during the war. The IRIA, whose strength was estimated by US intelligence in July 1987 as 243,000–279,000, also provided a broad range of specialist services including the five pre-war artillery groups (11th, 22nd, 33rd, 44th, and 55th) – each of six or seven battalions – and engineer battalions.[10]

Depending on the task in question, the IRIAA usually forward-deployed one of its five aviation groups – 1st (Kermanshah), 2nd (Masjed Soleiman), 3rd (Kerman), 4th (Esfahan), and 5th (Ghale-Morghi) – to major headquarters. Each was usually organised into one attack battalion, one or two assault battalions and one battalion of support aviation. The downside of the IRIA's expertise was its reliance upon Western equipment – primarily American and British – for which the stream of spares had been dammed when the two governments damned Tehran for its diplomatic waywardness.

Inferior equipment from China and North Korea had to be used even by the IRIA which re-equipped three former Chieftain battalions – including the 293rd/3rd Brigade/92nd Armoured Division – with North Korean Chonma-ho Is, based upon the T-62. The quality of East Asian products was inferior to that of Soviet and Western manufacturers, Saddam being told during a meeting on 27 June 1988 of North Korean bombs detonating after being in the sun for only six hours. While Iraqis could afford the luxury of cancelling contracts for poor-quality of Chinese and North Korean ammunition, Iran could not: after all, China was estimated by US intelligence to be providing 60–75 percent of Iran's arms requirements.[11]

Part of the IRIA and Pasdaran needs were met from the domestic military industry base established by the Shah, but by early 1987 Iran's whole industrial base was suffering steady erosion. Refining and electrical generation capacity were down by a third, although during the winter of 1986/1987 daily power cuts were reduced from up to seven hours a day to two.[12] Incompetence, but foremost endemic corruption with Ministry of the IRGC, meant that millions allocated for vital military production ended in private pockets: indeed most of the money allocated for domestic military production in 1987 was squandered or stolen and only the most minor projects were started. This was so successfully concealed that Rafsanjani learned of it only in the summer of 1988.[13]

Additional money had to be spent on the illicit trade in spares and equipment not only from the 'commercial' market but also from many of Uncle Sam's Asian allies, such as South Korea and Singapore, but also foes – like Vietnam. Even this was insufficient and the inventory of serviceable Western equipment slowly declined, the greatest problems being with artillery and helicopters; the former slowly wearing out to reduce battery strength by up to half, while the latter were most dependent upon scarce spares.

In part this explains why the IRIA was no longer the Iranian spearhead in favour of the Pasdaran and Basiji. The bemused professionals despaired of the slapdash planning and preparation of the Pasdaran but recognised their bravery. A former university student and conscript tank commander who served until October 1982 noted 'They were not worried about dying, and when they were issued steel helmets they would not wear them'. He noted they took heavy casualties, but '…even so, they were very cheery and always making jokes'.[14]

By 1987 the Pasdaran, administered and supported by their own ministry, had become grimmer but also more professional; few would not accept a helmet, but many would wear a green or red bandana and a symbolic wooden or plastic key to heaven around their necks. At battalion level, despite heavy casualties, they were formidable opponents who were skilled in infiltration and the use of light and heavy weapons. However, at divisional and task force level their leaders still had much to learn, especially about all-arms operations. The core of the Pasdaran remained light infantry with divisions having been reorganised to a dozen rifle battalions and one artillery battalion with a dozen 122mm howitzers or 130mm guns, augmented by 122mm MLRS; a heavy support battalion

MIDDLE EAST@WAR SERIES SPECIAL #1: THE IRAN-IRAQ WAR

with 120mm heavy mortars, recoilless artillery, air defence weapons and 107mm MLRS; a small reconnaissance battalion, and a company-size engineer battalion.[15] There were 26 named and numbered infantry divisions each of some 6,500 men together with 43 brigades including special forces, each of about 1,400 men – but, the clerics' ambition was to create a separate modern army to offset the 'conservative' IRIA.[16]

Tactical requirements resulted in the decision that any brigades not expanded into infantry divisions were converted into specialised formations – including six engineer- and two armoured/mechanised divisions in SOHQ, together with one armoured brigade (each with 40 tanks) and two mechanised brigades (with 20 tanks each).[17] There had also been a substantial expansion in specialised support brigades with four artillery-, two anti-armour-, four air defence-, and four engineer brigades, while the threat from chemical weapons saw two brigades converted into chemical decontamination units. The Pasdaran naval forces were also substantially increased during the 1980s, and five brigades of marines and SEALs were created together with coast defence artillery brigades. Pasdaran strength is generally given at around 500,000 although US intelligence estimated only 275,000 were deployed along the western front.[18]

Most of the T-55s operated by the Iranians as of 1987–1988, were originally captured from Iraq during earlier offensives, especially during the fighting for Khorramshahr, in 1982 – like these three examples (including a Chinese Type-69 with its distinctive side skirts). A number of them suffered additional damage over the following years, to a degree where, by 1988 the Iranian industry was badly lagging with necessary repairs. (Farzin Nadimi collection)

A group of Pasdaran meeting reinforcements that arrived on the frontline. (via S.S.)

In February 1987 the IRGC was reorganised again: from five directorates created in September 1984 into 15 commands, mostly provincial based, each of which would support specific Pasdaran formations. Curiously, their autonomy had been steadily curtailed as the war progressed and until well into the mid-2000s.[19] Generally, the quality of the Pasdaran formations rapidly declined from 1987 due to the cumulative effects of heavy losses among junior leaders and non-commissioned officers, but also to emigration.[20]

Further to the IRIA and the IRGC, there were also the Gendarmerie of 40,000 – largely consisting of police and border-protection units with counterinsurgency duties in Iranian Kurdistan. They were divided into provincial based districts; subdivided into regiments and companies, with most of the men assigned to small posts. In border districts, especially those in Kurdistan, each regiment had a 'strike unit' – or an intervention force – varying from a battalion to a company.

All the branches of the Iranian military had one severe problem in common: their logistics. A sophisticated, US-developed, computer-supported inventory system was sabotaged during the revolution and it took a great deal of time getting back on track. One consequence of this success was for the IRIAF to realise it had twice the number of critical spares that it had believed. However, in other services it was the sheer size of the war with Iraq that created immense backlogs at repair centres. In order to speed-up the re-delivery of vehicles to their units, so-called 'cannibalisation' of spares became widespread practice, and especially in regards of sophisticated equipment. Every single hour of 'down time' between major offensive was used to repair damaged or captured equipment, and to resupply and re-equip units. This, in turn, made it difficult to launch and to sustain multiple simultaneous offensives. Attrition

A typical scene of IRGC troops within recently captured Iraqi positions during the lull in fighting in the second half of 1987. Notable is increasing use of steel helmets. (via S.S.)

was massive: by 1987, the US intelligence estimated that the IRIA and the IRGC lost 1,000 MBTs, 500 APCs and IFVs, and 550 artillery pieces in the war.[21] Only about 150 MBTs and 120 APCs, 400 guns and 2 million shells and mortar bombs were either refurbished or acquired during the same period.[22] This forced the Iranians to increasingly rely upon inferior equipment of Russian design but Chinese or North Korean production. The 88th Armoured Division, for example, had to be built-up with Libyan-supplied T-55s and T-62s instead of the originally planned Shir Irans. Overall, the war left Iran in possession of some 1,040 MBTs, about 1,400 APCs and IFVs, 630 towed- and 230 self-propelled guns, and about 100 truck-borne MLRS, but only half of these were serviceable on average.[23] Curiously, just a few months later, and following information-exchange with Iraqi General Security Intelligence Directorate, the US intelligence agencies corrected their assessments to about 1,800 towed- and self-propelled guns (including about 500 assigned to IRGC units), with 70–75 percent serviceability. A further 400 tubes were stored in unserviceable condition.[24]

By contrast, the Iraqis estimated that Iran still possessed 1,700 MBTs, of which 300–400 were operated by the IRGC, and about 50 percent were serviceable. Furthermore, the Iraqis noted that the tanks in question had main guns with seven different calibres, which imposed serious supply problems. Both the Americans and Iraqis agreed that the Iranians had 1,400 APCs and IFVs.[25]

Serviceability problems, and maintaining regular maintenance schedules, were also the primary problem of the IRIAA. This entered the war with 864 aircraft and helicopters but was down to about half

As in many other wars, reading letters from home – or writing them – was one of the favourite occupations of troops on both sides of the Iran-Iraq War. (Photo by Bahman Jalali)

The diet of Iranian troops on the battlefields of the war with Iraq was rather austere. These two Pasdaran are sharing a can of cherries and some flat bread. (via S.S.)

Until the heavy losses they suffered during Operations Karbala-4, 5, and 8 – primarily caused by massive use of Iraqi chemical weapons – the Pasdaran were generally in high spirits and cheerful. This group was photographed during preparations for an attack on the Duaiji Line. (via E.S.)

Wreckage of an IRIAA Bell 214A shot down during the fighting in early 1987. The Iranians carefully recovered all such remnants and following the war they were either used for spare parts or even completely rebuilt. (Farzin Nadimi collection)

this number by 1987 – and many of older types were nearing the end of their useful airframe lives. Actually, the Iranian Army Aviation could still call upon 105 AH-1J Cobras (of which about a third could deploy TOWs), 90 Agusta Bell 206 reconnaissance helicopters, 210 Agusta Bell 205 and Bell 214A transport and assault helicopters, and 35 of the Italian-built CH-47C Chinook heavy lifters.[26]

Except for the air force, all other branches of the Iranian military were short on radio communications and navigational equipment. While providing a degree of security, this made C3 extremely difficult.

This perilous military position of Iran was reasonably well-known to the Commander of the US Central Command, Marine Corps General George B. Crist, who accurately informed the Senate Armed Services Committee in March 1988 that Iran lacked the military resources for another major offensive. He said Iran had overstretched itself in its last assault on Basra and was having problems finding enough new recruits. It had also been seriously weakened economically by the intensified Iraqi air attacks on more than 30 cities.[27]

The Iraqi view of the enemy was revealed to foreign defence attachés in two briefings which showed Baghdad regarded the Pasdaran as the prime threat: 'The Regular Iranian Army was identified as poorly led, badly equipped, secularly motivated and therefore confined to a supporting and diversionary role'.

This must have been a personal disappointment to the British Defence Attaché in Baghdad, Colonel B. Aldridge, who had trained the Iranian Army for 2½ years from 1976, the last three weeks under the Khomeini regime.[28] One reason why the IRIA was relegated to 'a supporting and diversionary role' was the reluctance of both Pasdaran and Basiji to become involved in static defence: their commanders preferred short offensive operations – no matter how bloody.

Financing the War

To pay for military equipment both sides depended upon oil. Iranian oil exports had been halved in 1986 to some 800,000 barrels a day, but by early 1987 had risen to 1.5 million barrels a day. Refining capacity had also risen to 100,000 barrels a day, but the international price of oil dropped to a record low.[29] As the international price steadily declined both sides ignored the oil cartel's attempts at regulating oil prices through production quotas and actually increased production. In the last quarter of 1986 both sides averaged around 1.6 million barrels per day (MMBD) each month. During 1987 Iranian production for the first three quarters averaged 2.27 MMBD per month, declining to 2.26 MMBD in the last quarter and 2.00 in the first two months of 1988 – by which time the battered and mismanaged oil industry provided only 10 percent of Gross National Product (GNP; compared with 38 percent in 1979).[30]

By contrast Iraqi production averaged 1.93 MMBD in the first three quarters of 1987, reached 2.56 MMBD in the last quarter and 2.45 MMBD in the first two months of 1988; it provided 40 percent of GNP by 1987 compared with 50 percent when the war broke out.[31]

Iraqi exports through oil pipelines steadily rose during 1987–1988 while the so-called 'Tanker War', together with raids on oil targets inland, saw Iranian oil exports by sea adversely affected. With both sides' economies in melt-down there were few major arms purchases involving ground forces' equipment in 1987–1988 – apart from one to Iraq from Egypt, agreed at the beginning of 1987, with deliveries from April. This included about 100 T-55s, an unknown number of APCs and towed artillery, four SA-2 air defence batteries, 12 Embraer EMB.312 Tucano trainers and 10 Gazelle helicopters. This was not enough to replace the losses the Iraqis suffered during operations Val Fajr-8 and Karbala-5, which – according to US intelligence estimates – had cost Baghdad 800 armoured fighting vehicles.[32] Iraq's military creditors were growing restive, with the country's debt estimated at $40 billion by the end of the war, while foreign exchange reserves fell from $36 billion in 1980 to $3 billion in 1987 (in comparison, Iran's declined to $5.5 billion).[33] Paris was meanwhile making token delays in delivering equipment, while by March 1988 China was demanding payment for mortar fuses and threatening not to make further supplies if the money was not forthcoming (eventually, Beijing did not carry out the threat).[34]

Nevertheless, Iraq continued receiving substantial quantities of new equipment from earlier orders, and thus managed to increase the total number of its MBTs to 6,600; that of APCs and IFVs to about 4,000; the number of towed artillery pieces to 2,200, and that of self-propelled guns to 300 – in addition to 276 truck-borne MLRS.[35] Furthermore, in the light of lessons learned on the battlefield the Iraqis began modifying their Soviet equipment; to meet the threat from RPGs they provided their vehicles with appliqué armour (30mm steel plates for T-72 MBTs and multi-layer armour for T-55 MBTs; 35–40mm steel for BMP-1 IFVs), improved passive night sights, and steel 'skirts' to protect the sides of vehicles. Chinese Type 69 MBTs received laser rangefinders. However, adding armour to

Starting in 1986, the Iraqi Air Force began exercising constantly increasing pressure upon the Iranian economy. This in turn forced the IRIAF to keep most of its remaining interceptors reserved for the defence of strategic areas such as Khark Island. This F-4E from TFB.6 (Bushehr) was photographed while flying a combat air patrol over a pair of tankers bound for Khark. (Farzin Nadimi collection)

the T-55 reduced its power/weight ratio from 16 horsepower-per-tonne (hp/t) to 14.7 hp/t.[36]

The Iraqi Forces

According to one estimate, by 1987, out of 2.6 million Iraqi men aged 18–45, almost 1.7 million were in uniform. However, the shallow well of manpower meant many Iraqis had to serve several times, on various fronts, where up to three men per family were deployed.[37] Those in higher education were exempt from conscription until the Faw campaign when Saddam drafted 125,000 university lecturers and students.[38]

As of 1987, the strength of the Iraqi Army was estimated at 875,000, including up to 480,000 reservists. There were also some 4,800 Border Guards who were used for counterinsurgency duties, which was also a role of the People's Army (al-Jaysh ash-Shabi, also 'Popular Army'). This Baath Party paramilitary organisation had grown from 75,000 to 100,000 during the war, and while it proved a failure in conventional operations it was perfectly capable of guarding lines of communications and hunting deserters even in the Hawizah Marshes. Between 1985 and 1988 at least 195,000 Iraqis – including a few women (most of whom served as medical staff or in rear echelons) – were recruited, usually co-opted or coerced by commissars, and trained.[39].

The foreign military presence in Iraq remained limited. About 1,200 Soviet, Bulgarian, Czechoslovak, East German, Hungarian and Polish military advisors were present, primarily within local maintenance facilities. France provided some 65 advisors; foremost in relation to various of its arms sales; Yugoslavia had a group of about 100 military advisors (and more than 5,000 civilians) working on further development of hardened air bases; while some 110 Indians, and about 185 Egyptians and Jordanians served as instructor pilots with the IrAF and the IrAAC.[40]

The Iraqi Army was meanwhile organised into more than 40 divisions (Firka), of which five were armoured, two mechanised, and 33 infantry. These controlled a total of 26 armoured, 16 mechanised, 132 infantry, six special forces (al-Quwwat al-Khassah), and 16 commando (al-Maqhawer) brigades. The Navy provided another two brigades of marines.[41] Armoured divisions averaged 13,800–14,800 men (against an establishment of 18,500), while the figures for mechanised and infantry divisions were 14,250–15,200 (19,000) and 15,750–16,800 (21,000) respectively. Manpower shortages meant the brigades were also under their authorised strength: in the case of armoured brigades they had 1,800–1,900 against an establishment of 2,400; a problem exacerbated by generous leave entitlements. Some 60 percent of the Iraqi Army, including the majority of its armoured and mechanised forces, were on the southern front.[42]

Baghdad's three original corps (I, II and III) were overstretched as new fronts opened up and four more (IV, V, VI and VII) were created between 1982 and 1986, often by expanding an ad hoc operational headquarters. Also created in Wasit Province on the central front was the reservist I Special Corps – deployed in between II and IV Corps. Each corps had a number of divisional headquarters and reserve brigades augmented by two commando brigades and strong support forces. These included an artillery brigade headquarters, usually with battalions of towed artillery and truck-borne MLRS, an air defence brigade with battalions of 'Gainful' SAMs and light anti-aircraft guns, a reconnaissance battalion with BDRM-2 and APCs, an anti-armour battalion with vehicle-mounted missiles or occasional anti-tank guns, engineer, bridging, signal and chemical defence battalions.[43] There were also four surface-to-surface missile brigades; two equipped with R-17E/SS-1b Scud C and its al-Hussein derivative (223rd and 224th), one with Luna-M/FROG-7s (225th), and one with Brazilian-made Astros long-range MLRS (226th).

An increasingly important feature in Iraqi operations was the IrAAC. Under the command of Major General al-Hakam Hassan Ali, this comprised four wings:

- 1st Wing, based at Kirkuk, supporting I and V Corps;
- 2nd Wing, based at Taji, supporting II and I Special Corps;
- 3rd Wing, based at Basra, supporting III and VII Corps; and
- 4th Wing, based at Amara, supporting IV and VI Corps.

These wings had six attack squadrons equipped with Mi-25s and Gazelles; four reconnaissance squadrons with Alouette III, Messerschmitt Bölkow-Böhm Bo.105s and MD.500MFs; 10 transport squadrons with Mi-8T/MT and Mi-17s; one heavy transport squadron with Mi-6s, and two squadrons equipped with Pilatus PC-7 light strikers (nominally assigned to the Border Guards). Each squadron usually totalled 8–15 aircraft or helicopters, but some units operated up to 35. Each wing controlled three to six squadrons and several detachments. As of 1987, US intelligence estimated the total strength of the IrAAF at 40 PC-7s, 40 Mi-25s and 55 Gazelles, 35 Alouette IIIs, 30 Bo.105s, 26 MD.500s, and 217 Mi-8/17s.[44]

One of the most important developments for the Iraqis was the significant improvement of relations with the USA. Washington restored diplomatic relations with Baghdad in November 1984 and grew sympathetic with Iraq: Tehran's virulent hatred of the USA – 'The Great Satan' – prompted the Americans to support 'the enemy of my enemy'. However, for many of the crucial decision-makers in Washington (and their friends in London and Tel Aviv) – and despite the fact that the Iraqis did not accept any kind of 'comrades' (Soviet advisors) at any of their headquarters – the country was regarded as a 'Soviet client' and thus the US support for Iraq remained limited to provision of intelligence and some financing.[45]

The Iraqi chain of command of General Command of the [Iraqi] Armed Forces (GCAF) briefly remained as it was following the changes during Karbala-5 – i.e. under the leadership of Saddam and Defence Minister Adnan Khairallah Talfah (Khairallah). Yet Saddam was not satisfied, possibly feeling his new command team was too defensive. Correspondingly, on 14 July 1987 he instigated another reshuffle. Chief-of-Staff Lieutenant General Saad el-din Aziz shared the fate of his predecessor and was retired after barely six months at this post. He was replaced by commander of the I Corps, Khazraji. Saddam also appointed a new Director of Operations, former Guards Corps commander, Major General Hussain Rashid al-Tikriti, while his predecessor Thabit Sultan, a former IV Corps commander, was demoted to Brigadier and assigned a brigade.

Khazraji was a very capable officer, and former Military Attaché in Moscow, who recognised passive defence alone would not win the war, and advocated offensives at operational level in order to regain strategic initiative and defeat the enemy. Hussein Rashid appears to have held similar views – which in turn were reflected by his appointment, on 17 November, of former 5th Mechanised Division commander Salah Aboud Mahmoud (Aboud) to command III Corps.[46]

The changes reflected the fact that Saddam had gradually eased his political control and allowed professionalism rather than political reliability to determine promotion. He continued routinely rotating corps commanders to prevent them establishing a power base, but still enabled their work, and the work of their staff, to grow more professional.[47]

Meanwhile, GCAF established fortified forward bases, with airstrips, on all the major fronts and assign to each corps and division command the equivalent of the Red Army's Representative of the General Staff – to assist the commander and monitor the situation for the General Command Headquarters (GCHQ). For example, Qader was attached to Shannan's 11th Infantry Division already during Karbala-5.

Heavy casualties and the need for technical expertise forced a loosening of Ba'ath Party control, and where once only Ba'athists were admitted to military academies now admission was open to all men provided they had shown no hostility to the Party. Professional and technical schools provided most staff officers although some officers were still selected because of connections to officials or the Party. However, the loosened Party control eased the promotion path for mid-ranking officers.[48].

The improvement in quality was reflected in Colonel Aldridge's annual report of May 1987 when he noted the Iraqis had recently moved 24 brigades in a four-day operation which called for 'road transport and dexterous staff work'.[49] Nevertheless he felt the Iraqi military leadership had made a number of errors: 'For the past four months the greater part of the Iraqi Army and all its strategic

With Baghdad having nearly unlimited access to the international arms market, and dozens of countries being ready to deliver almost everything requested, Iraqis troops were – by far – the better supplied on the frontlines of the Iran-Iraq War. This soldier was photographed while guarding stocks of small-arms ammunition. (Albert Grandolini collection)

In an attempt to improve the mobility of their artillery – and much like the Egyptians about ten years earlier – the Iraqis mounted some of their artillery tubes (in this case a 130mm M1954 gun) atop the chassis of T-55 tanks. (US Department of Defence)

PART I: TWO ARMIES

The crew of an IrAAC Mi-25 with their mount (serial 2121) – which belonged to the second batch of this type delivered to Iraq in around 1984. (via Ali Tobchi)

This PC-7 armed with gun-pods and rocket launchers was photographed by Iranian troops while underway over the Hawizeh Marshes, in late 1987. Appearance of such aircraft over hotly-contested battlefields was a clear indication of Iraqi aerial dominance by this point in the war. (Farzin Nadimi collection)

Sold as 'training aircraft' to Iran and Iraq alike in the mid-1980s, Swiss-made Pilatus PC-7s saw widespread service as combat aircraft in Iraq. Officially assigned to the Border Guards, they were operated by two squadrons of the IrAAC and – as visible in this still from a video – were armed with gun-pods and rocket launchers. (Tom Cooper collection)

ground force reserve have been dragged into a battle of attrition… Other sectors of the front, including the north, had been weakened through losing units rotating into the Basra battlefield'.[50]

He noted that Iran's choice of Basra as the main battle site had proved a major setback for Iraq because it lacked space for tactical mobility and forced the Iraqi Army to conduct static defensive positions with armour used as pillboxes, '…and with no ground-to-air communications for Close Air Support… Close combat has made the extensive use of CW (Chemical Warfare) impossible'.

Furthermore, Aldridge noted that during 1986–1987 the Iraqis had anticipated the main Iranian effort would be east of Baghdad on the central front, and in anticipation of this maintained their strategic reserve in this area. But; '…it was wishful thinking, the Iranians were not to expose their unprotected 'infantry' to 80 miles of open ground'.

In fact, during 1987, Khazraji and Aziz redistributed reserves and by Karbala-5 the strategic reserve, with some 15 brigades of Republican Guards, was in three areas around Basra. Unsurprisingly, these were deployed – with distinction – to recapture Iraqi forward positions during Karbala-8.[51]

Expansion of the Republican Guards

No army can endure a prolonged conventional conflict unscathed. The constant stream of casualties erodes overall quality because the best soldiers – those ready to stand up and fight while risking their lives – are most often the victims too. With no end of fighting in sight the majority are left willing to march in step performing basic duties to survive, but with little enthusiasm and less initiative. Consequently, the successful conduct of war increasingly depends upon the elite minority to act as the spearhead. Unsurprisingly, by 1987, both Iran and Iraq were critically short of such men, and the morale on both sides was generally low.

Iraq's limited manpower meant that after serving their time the conscripts were transferred to the reserves, but then frequently found themselves being drafted back to the front. Thousands went absent without leave or even deserted. Incomplete figures suggest up to 5 percent of Saddam's army came under these categories (see below) by 1987 leaving him in a similar situation faced by Marshal Philippe Pétain with the French Army 70 years earlier – although without any mutinies. Like the poilus, the Iraqi troops were willing to defend their homeland, as the Karbala offensives clearly demonstrated, but at command conferences throughout the war Saddam expressed doubts about their offensive spirit.

Khazraji recognised that self-confidence increases morale – which, like Pétain, he sought to restore through instilling offensive spirit upon his troops. Correspondingly, he began pulling divisions out of the line for retraining. During the second half of 1987 and through early 1988, no fewer than 96 brigades had been honed sharp. This policy would certainly bear fruit during the summer of 1988 when Iraqi infantry divisions, including one unit of elderly reservists, distinguished themselves in offensive operations.

But autocrats often place greater faith in military organisations which appear to reflect the political-social ethos of the regime. Saddam was no exception. Back in May 1986, he ordered a major expansion of the Republican Guard (al-Haris al-Jamhuri). The result was that this grew to four brigades (1st and 2nd Armoured, 3rd Commando, and 4th infantry) – then commanded by his son-in-law, Brigadier General (later Major General) Hussein Kamal al-Majid ('Kamel al-Majid'). A year later, Saddam decided to double the number of brigades, and then create eight to ten divisions. Correspondingly, a headquarters for the Republican Guards was established under Major General Iyad Futayyih ar-Rawi, on 25 July 1987.[52]

Most of the new units and formations were created from scratch, although 10th Armoured Brigade was transferred to the Guards to become 10th Republican Guards Armoured Brigade, while the Army remained the prime source of personnel. However, there was no wholesale transfer of men and units such as the Imperial German Army's creation of *Mobiledivisionen* from existing formations in 1917–1918 – because the Iraqis correctly concluded that this would dilute overall Army capabilities. When the Defence Ministry issued the order to raise a unit it would assign a few officers and administrative staff for the headquarters. Once activated the headquarters were assigned further troops, as well as equipment, with unit expansion often accelerated by temporarily assigning companies from Army battalions or brigades to accelerate the process. The Guards attracted both university students and the Army's best officers, non-commissioned officers and men, with Army officers nominated by Baghdad ordered to report within 72 hours otherwise the brigade or division commander would be punished.[53]

Until the expansion Ba'ath Party membership had been a prerequisite for joining the Guards. Indeed, the Faw battles of 15–25 February 1986 saw two battalions of the Guards losing 175 killed – all of whom were Party members. With the expansion this criterion no longer applied, but Party affiliation was essential for

In 1987, the first Iraqi unit equipped with T-72 Ural MBTs – 10th Armoured Brigade – was transformed into a centrepiece of the Republican Guards Corps. This photograph from earlier during the war shows tankers of the 10th with one of their vehicles. (Albert Grandolini collection)

A T-72M1 of one of the newly established armoured brigades of the Republican Guards Corps, seen in the Basra area in 1987. (via Ali Tobchi)

promotion – and political reliability remained a factor in selecting senior commanders. Indeed, political reliability remained a factor in selecting senior commanders such as Brigadier Ahmad Hammash al-Tikriti who was appointed first commander of the 'Hammurabi' Division in September 1986. As with the remainder of the expanded Iraqi Army, the abilities of the new divisions were restricted by the general shortage of fully trained staff officers.[54]

During 1986, 11 new brigades of the Republican Guards were created and organised into four divisions; Hammurabi, al-Medina al-Munawwarah (or 'Medina') and Tawakkalna all-a-Allah' Armoured Divisions, and Baghdad as infantry division.[55] The following year another eight brigades were created while 1st Republican Guards Armoured Brigade was re-designated the 17th Republican Guards Armoured Brigade, and two special forces formations were created;

'Nebuchadnezzar' Infantry – and the Special Purposes Division headquarters ('SP Division'). The latter was an elite special forces command rather than a traditional division.

In the following months the last three brigades were created to fill out the new divisions and give the Republican Guards the strength of 103,000 men.[56] All these divisions were grouped into the same Republican Guards Corps, initially under future Operations Chief, Major General Hussein Rashid, and later Lieutenant General Ayad Futayyih al-Rawi (Rawi) – a Saddam loyalist even after the Allied invasion of 2003.

Another new weapon introduced in 1986–1987 was the 122mm 2S1 Gvozdika self-propelled howitzer. They were assigned to armoured divisions of the Iraqi Republican Guard. (via Ali Tobchi)

Units of the Republican Guards received extensive training in standard military disciplines. Troops assigned to them were sent to a vast training area at al-Habbaniyah in al-Anbar Province (separate from the former RAF Habbaniyah), constructed in the aftermath of the Arab-Israeli War of October 1973 using Egyptian, Indian, Pakistani, Soviet and Yugoslav experiences. In addition to the usual training ranges, this area offered enough manoeuvring space for entire brigades, and even divisions, to train simultaneously. The units received not only training for combat in daylight, but by night too, and were lavishly equipped. Kamel al-Majid took great care to ensure that the Guards received whatever they requested.[57] It was this intensive training and strict discipline which moulded men from a variety of backgrounds into formidable combat units aided by superior weaponry and a very well-organised logistic system.

Abu Khalil

'Abu Khalil' – the generic term for the Iraqi soldier – was generally a nationalist that opposed the 'hukm al-malali' ('mullah rule'). However, war weariness and frequent exposure to combat eroded his nationalism and led to dereliction of duty or even desertions. Furthermore, sharp divisions within the army remained – those between officers and other ranks, between conscripts and volunteers, Army units and those of the People's Army, commissars and frontline troops, Arabs and Kurds, Sunni and Shi'a, men of urban and rural backgrounds, and between people with different educational standards. The patronage played its part too, and all of this strongly influenced the life at the front.[58] Morale was maintained through divisional recreation areas – which included barbers and cafés – where the men could rest and unwind, but foremost through generous leave entitlements. The latter meant that every Iraqi soldier could enjoy a 7-days leave for every 31 days on the frontline. However, this resulted in a situation where up to a quarter of a unit was nearly always absent. Furthermore, officers – who also used their men to perform personal errands – often manipulated the leave entitlement in return for money and favours. Others sold fake documents – like identity papers for absentees or deserters, or documents permitting leave. Such manipulations became so serious that in 1986 the Ba'ath Party Military Bureau – which was attached directly to the Presidential Office – asked Military Intelligence to monitor the practice and discipline of officers and commissars involved.[59, 60]

On the contrary, in the case of the Republican Guards units, there were dramatic changes in this regard. Foremost, officers and other ranks were entitled to significant rewards – including money and consumer goods – for heroism. The rates were for example 1,500 Iraqi dinars (equivalent to US$465 at contemporary exchange rates) for recovering bodies from no-man's-land, while taking a prisoner earned 5,000 dinars (US$1,550). A successful military operation might earn an officer 6,000 dinars or US$1,860, and the most senior officers a Mercedes automobile, while a corporal might earn 1,000 dinars or US$300. Further benefits included land, apartments, cars, and educational privileges – and these were provided to the families of 'martyrs' (those killed in action). However, the families often needed the assistance of the local Ba'ath Party which also intervened when disputes arose between widows and the 'martyr's' parents or siblings. The system was extremely bureaucratic – especially when it came to collecting the salaries of the missing or captured. In practice such financial rewards were rare, with medals and citations more usual, although some medals had social benefits. All awards were approved by Ba'ath Party commissars, who worked along an extremely bureaucratic system: while this created opportunities for both corruption and patronage, commissars were present at every level – from platoon to corps command and training camps – their omnipresence seems to have kept the situation under control, at least during the war with Iran. Some problems were experienced by families of those who fell: they often required assistance of the local Ba'ath Party's branch, which also intervened when disputes arose between widows and the martyr's parents or siblings.[61] Unsurprisingly, an Iraqi writer later summarised: '…the experience of conscription, training, and battle brought a generation of men from different social and communal backgrounds together on unprecedented scale and forged a sense of Iraqi patriotism and generational solidarity.'[62]

As well as better-paid and – trained – troops, units of the Republican Guards also received a formidable artillery element. By late May 1988, each division had 34 guns – most of these self-propelled pieces – plus two MLRS battalions.[63] The primary equipment of their armoured formations were the recently acquired T-72M1 MBTs, equipped with the 2A46 gun (instead of the older

Adnan Khairallah (centre) – the highly popular and certainly effective Minister of Defence of Iraq – seen during a visit to the HQ of the II Corps Iraqi Army, together a Bo.105 helicopter, in 1987. Khairallah was a qualified pilot and often flew PC-7s on his own. (via Ali Tobchi)

Pictured from the left General Sultan Hashim, the Minister of Defence, on his left is General Abdul Wahid Shanan Al Rebat, Chief of Army Staff, behind them Major General Abdul Raheem Al Janabi, Commandant of the Military Academy. (Ted Hooton collection)

2A26M), and the 1A40 fire control system (instead of older TPD-K1 laser rangefinder). The T-72M1 had a V-46-6 diesel engine, TPN-3-49 gunner's night sight, and TVNE-4B driver night observation device. It also had improved protection with combination armour on the turret and another 16mm of steel armour plate on the front.[64]

Crises in Morale

Because the well of Iraqi manpower was so shallow, life at the front for Abu Khalil became a lethal kismet of death or mutilation from which the only means of escape seemed to be going absent without leave or desertion. The only alternative were self-inflicted wounds which would not arouse official suspicion. Following the Faw Peninsula setback and a central front defeat at Mehran, the Military Bureau of the Ba'ath Party in October 1986 produced a report on the desertion problem, which concluded the revolution had failed to instil a belief in the Iraqi nation or to break the conscript's traditional loyalty to his clan or tribe or ethnicity.[65] By early 1987 desertion had reached epidemic proportions with some men repeatedly deserting even though they knew their families would suffer. On 28 March 1987, during a discussion on operations in the Basra area, Saddam was informed that 24,952 soldiers had left their positions between 1 December 1986 and 20 March 1987.[66]

Desertion was most acute on the northern front were there were numerous Kurdish paramilitaries serving, while in the central front's II Corps one brigade lost 756 – or a quarter of the men![67] On the southern front the Ba'ath Party Southern Bureau noted that the Faw campaign '…resulted in a large number of deserters from the army and they increased the crime in (Basra) by stealing.'

In the latter years of the war the Bureau had to deal with 67,522 deserters; of whom 58,943 surrendered in an amnesty, 432 were shot while trying to escape, and 193 were executed.[68]

The regime reacted by holding families as hostages: already since 1982, wives, children and parents of deserters could be jailed, while other members of the family would be denied government employment or access to higher education. In December 1985 a decree stated that wives of those who had been absent for more than six months had to seek a formal separation. This could be annulled if the soldier returned, but a second desertion would see it turned into divorce. To deter desertion, commissar-led, Party-manned execution squads in combat dress with red armbands, were stationed in the rear. They were always from different regions from the one in which they were stationed. The soldiers deeply resented these men with their clean boots.[69]

Medical attention is a key factor in military morale and the British attaché reported a serious shortage of medical expertise in the battle zone – which frequently led to amputations. His predecessor, Colonel R. C. Eccles, bemoaned the lack of defence sales activity but noted a British company had won a contract for 15,000 pairs of crutches and a follow-on order for 30,000 – although a Swedish company had received a larger order in 1986. In January 1987 General Motors of Canada was asked to quote for 10,000 cars with specifications demanding control by men with one arm (left or right), one leg (left or right), or no legs.[70]

Yet even after six years of war, as Aldridge noted, no wounded were seen in cities and towns. He ascribed this to the Arab tradition of hiding those who were not in perfect physical and mental condition. The seriously wounded, especially the maimed and disfigured, were kept in specialised medical facilities – which locals often described as 'hospital prisons' (although families were allowed to make frequent visits).[71]

Saddam Hussein during a visit to the frontlines of the Iran-Iraq War. (M.H. collection)

Iranian Experiences

Demoralisation was to be found on both sides of the line. Morale was lowest among the IRIA, whose offensive spirit had been steadily eroded by a government which clearly favoured the Pasdaran and regarded the 'Artesh' – as the IRIA is colloquially known until today – with profound suspicion. Ever since 1982, most of the army's units were assigned defensive duties on quiet sectors of the front which allowed Tehran to limit their supplies and make little attempt to improve their living conditions.

The Iranians also suffered from poor medical facilities, especially in the frontline field hospitals where many died of wounds and infection. Medical supplies, such as dressings, were allowed to run out entirely before bureaucrats would attempt to replace them. A mortally wounded battalion commander, abandoned without treatment in a provincial hospital, wrote in a final letter to his parents: 'They are killing us'.[72].

While there remained widespread support for the goals of the Islamic Revolution a combination of factors slowly eroded morale, especially among the Pasdaran. Curiously – and despite its claim for its rule to be based on popular support – the regime's leadership appears to have been blithely unaware of both the problem and its causes. By contrast Iraqi intelligence began to assemble accurate reports of shaky morale.[73]

Boredom and despair, but also war weariness and heavy casualties, as well as poor protection of Iran's border with Afghanistan and Pakistan in the 1980s, resulted in a widespread and serious problem with drug-addiction (mostly with cannabis/hashish, rather than cocaine/heroin). As early as of 1982, the 21st Division IRIA became colloquially known as, 'The Junkies', amongst the troops.[74]

Heavy casualties, hollow claims that the martyrs were all in heaven, growing national resentment against incompetence and corruption, inevitably reflected in what was effectively a citizen army – the IRGC – too. What added to the butcher's bill was the selection of many military leaders on basis of religious and ideological purity, rather than professional and organisational ability. The men were quick to identify those with inadequacies, and – reportedly – 'happy to help them find them a fast path to martyrdom'.[75]

The troops were aware of the corruption and incompetence, and all but the most devout Pasdaran despised it. However, although defections from IRGC units are known, there appear to have been no execution squads keeping Iranian troops at the front. Furthermore, the nation as a whole did not learn about the problem until after the case-fire of 1988. Then it turned out that while many members of the Iranian Parliament ('Majlis') were aware of individual problems, they remained silent for patriotic, or other, reasons; it was only in September 1988 that they felt free to speak. Combined with reports that he had misappropriated defence funds, this resulted in dismissal of the Minister of the IRGC, Mohsen Rafiqdoust.[76] The worst effect of corruption was the failure to expand military production. However, tales emerged of troops being sent infected sheep meat, ammunition being so poorly stored that it became useless, or the lack of replacement tyres for frontline vehicles while IRGC depots had immense stocks.

Actually, alarm bells should have rung in Tehran already in 1986, or at least by January 1988, when it was announced that a 100,000-strong 'Mohammed Corps' would be formed. Instead of noticing a clear lack of popular enthusiasm despite official propaganda, the system obviously failed to understand, and accept, that the recruitment-drive did not achieve even a third of the aimed-for figure. By that time not just the urban middle classes preferred sending their 16-year-old sons abroad; even the provincial peasantry was no longer rushing to join the Basiji. Overall, only about 350,000 Iranians volunteered for service with the IRGC in early 1988 – compared with twice that number a year earlier.[77]

Even so, Saddam could not afford to be complacent anymore: he knew the Iranians had come back from similar reverses in the past. He was also concerned that the lack of action on the southern front after the spring of 1987 could erode the troops' combat capabilities (see below). This was to prove an incentive for Saddam to seek morale-boosting operations.[78]

15
SADDAM'S FIRST BLOW

Tehran's Karbala debacle raised Saddam's hopes that he could regain prestige with his own offensive and thus end a morale-eroding lull on the southern front. Inevitably he looked at the southern Faw Peninsula whose loss he keenly felt. Related thoughts had predominated the front's generals all the time since the summer of 1986.

Although that offensive had always been a political action first and foremost, rather than a military operation, for Tehran the high hopes raised by Val Fajr-8 had been rapidly sucked into the peninsula's marshes: neither Kuwait nor Saudi Arabia ceased providing support for Iraq. The Iranians thus attempted increasing pressure: a battery of the 1st Naval Region's 26th Salman Coast Defence Missile Brigade was transferred from Sirri Island to Faw and reorganised as the 36th Assef Coast Defence Missile Brigade. This unit began firing Chinese-made CHETA YJ-6/C.601 (HY-2 Silkworm) anti-ship missiles at tankers underway off the Kuwaiti coast.[1] Furthermore, a battery of 170mm North-Korean-made Koksan self-propelled guns also crossed the Shatt for this purpose: through its deployment on Faw, it was not only capable of shelling the Iraqi naval base of Umm Qasr, but also reach most of Kuwait.

In the largest urban area, Faw City, the office of the Tehran-backed Supreme Assembly of the Islamic Revolution of Iraq (SAIRI) was established under Hojatoleslam Mohammed Baqr al-Hakim, with members of the exiled Hakim family whose 'military arm' consisted of Hakim's bodyguard under a thug called Abu Ali Mowla. Its offices were used by Pasdaran students who aimed to complete their education at its library. Meanwhile, during the last quarter of 1987, President Khamenei authorised national mobilisation and ordered all the students, mullahs, and civil servants to, 'breathe the smell of the war fronts'. Under cover of the rainy season at the end of the year, wild rumours began making circles about 20 Pasdaran divisions and 200 battalions of Basiji assembling for a new offensive in the south.[2]

From the point of view of the Iraqi military, the elimination of this 'buzzing mosquito' at Faw would have provided significant, strategic level advantages through re-opening the Iraqi approach to the waters of the northern Persian Gulf. At the operational level, it would free troops necessary to reinforce III Corps, and remove a major threat to Kuwait's oil industry – both directly, by eliminating enemy fire bases; and indirectly, by removing the threat of Iranian mines (like the one that damaged the Kuwaiti tanker SS *Bridgeton*, on 24 July 1987, or the US Navy's guided missile frigate USS *Samuel B Roberts*, on 14 April 1988).

Iraqi Preparations to Recapture the Faw Peninsula
For Saddam, as one commentator observed: 'This was his last chance to rectify these losses that had happened along the borders of Iraq.'[3] The work on 'Plan 2' – the recapture of the peninsula – began on 16 June 1986, when a planning cell was established in Baghdad. Presided over by the future Defence Minister Major General Abdul Jabbar Shanshall, this prepared an outline further developed by the staff of Lieutenant General Maher Abd al-Rashid's (Maher) VII Corps. Originally the offensive was scheduled for the autumn of 1986, but this deadline had to be abandoned allowing the plans to be refined in 14 meetings, always chaired by Saddam, and including representatives of the IrAF and the Iraqi Navy, with detailed work by an AFGC planning group with VII Corps.[4]

Saddam was paranoid about secrecy, so the AFGC planning group which he chaired initially consisted only of Guards Corps commander Iyad Futayyih al-Rawi (Rawi), his Chief-of-Staff, and his intelligence officer. During the summer of 1987 the cell was expanded to include the Army's Operations Chief Hussein Rashid. However, Army Chief-of-Staff Khazraji was still largely excluded although he did receive an outline briefing. Coordination of the planning group's and VII Corps' activities was conducted by Lieutenant General Raad Majid al-Hamdani, who frequently flew between Baghdad and Basra. It was only gradually that additional officers were drawn in, including Lieutenant General Najm-ad-Din Abdallah Muhammad who became Logistics Chief (Deputy Chief-of-Staff for Logistics) in July 1987 and learned of the plan during an AFGC meeting on 27 September 1987.

There was an intensive reconnaissance effort to provide a detailed picture of the berm-based defences as well as the locations of headquarters, batteries and bridges. Iraqi planning was greatly aided by COMINT, while both the United States and the Soviet Union provided intelligence derived from satellite imagery – which showed the defences in considerable detail. Yet most of the reconnaissance work was done by the IrAF, which had been reorganised and re-equipped after Val Fajr-8. For this purpose, the air force used aircraft like MiG-25RB, Mirage F.1EQ and Su-22s.

The MiG-25 had an integral AFA-70 or AFA-72 film camera augmented by an AFA A-E/10 and a Romb 4A communications ELINT system and was used more for 'strategic' or general reconnaissance. The Mirages, which assumed the bulk of IrAF reconnaissance tasks from 1986, were equipped with 400-kilogram Dassault COR-2 reconnaissance pods, with four vertically-mounted Omera 35 cameras with focal lengths of 40–600mm, an Omera 70 panoramic camera, or by Sagem Super Cyclope Infra-Red Line Scanner (IRLS) to detect camouflaged targets through their radiant heat. Later these were augmented by Dassault Systems' AA-3-38 Harold and Raphael-TH pods, the former being a 680-kilogram film system with Omera 38 camera (with a focal length of 1,700mm which could provide 2m resolution at ranges of 100 kilometres for long-range optical reconnaissance). The latter, *Radar de photographie Aerienne Electrique a Transmission Hertzienne*, was a state-of-the-art I/J (also known as X)-Band 10 GHz Side Looking Airborne Radar

PART I: SADDAM'S FIRST BLOW

A pre-delivery photograph of a Mirage F.1EQ manufactured for Iraq, equipped with the COR-2 reconnaissance pod. (Tom Cooper collection)

This pair of Iraqi-operated Type-69-IIs was photographed sometime in late 1986 or early 1987. Notable is the unusual light earth colour used to camouflage the example in the foreground (turret number 31). (via Ali Tobchi)

(SLAR) in a 600-kilogram pod which used synthetic aperture and pulse compression techniques to penetrate up to 100 kilometres, and then transmitted the data in real time data to ground stations. The Su-22 used KKR-1TE/2-54K (*Kombinirovanny Konteiner Razvedy*) reconnaissance pods. These were 6.79 metres long, 59cm in width and 58cm in height, with a loaded weight of 800 kg. They featured an AND a-39 f/100 vertical and oblique 80mm film camera with a focal length of 100mm for use at 500–5,000 metres, and a PA-1 with an oblique camera which had a focal length of 90.5mm, for low-level operations up to 1,200 metres.[5] In addition to manned aircraft the Iraqis also used Mirach 1000 UAVs, while the interpretation of film images was aided by the purchase in 1986 of French panoramic stereoscopes.

Frontline units did some probing, notably to determine the location and area of minefields as well as wire entanglements, while special forces companies were rotated through VII Corps for reconnaissance behind the enemy lines. Unit 999 – the Military Intelligence Directorate's elite unit specialising in the most sensitive of clandestine reconnaissance missions – usually had its troops operating in the cultivated area.

Most of the troops who had contained the Iranian assault were withdrawn during the summer of 1986, leaving VII Corps with five infantry divisions (2nd, 7th, 14th, 15th, and 26th), and two naval infantry brigades (440th and 441st Naval Infantry Brigades) – for a total of 95,000 troops. Of these, only the 7th and 26th Infantry Divisions, and the two naval brigades – faced the bridgehead.

Plan 2²

'Plan 2', aimed to regain the peninsula at minimum cost. Its first draft envisaged the main blow by Maher's reinforced corps with Rawi's Guards Corps in reserve. However, Saddam's desire to test his 'Praetorians' meant Rawi's corps joined the assault force and the Iraqi leader then deliberately encouraged competition between the two corps as to who would take Faw City.[6] Furthermore, an agreement was reached for the two naval brigades to support the Guards, and – later on – to use a heliborne commando brigade in attempt to capture Silkworm launchers deployed at the Cape Bisha (Ras al-Bisha).

The recovery of the peninsula was originally scheduled for October-November 1986, but this was abandoned due to the Iranian Karbala offensives, which forced Saddam to prop up the defence with Guards units scheduled for the assault on Faw. When this threat was contained preparations were resumed as 'Plan 22'.[7]

The planning and operation were de facto dictated by the terrain. Much of the western side of the peninsula was covered by tidal salt marshes – including a permanently flooded 15-kilometre strip – and the Mamlaha salt beds (64 square kilometre area of extraction ponds subdivided and surrounded by 1.2-metre-high earth bunds). The only permanently firm ground was a six-kilometre-wide strip in the east of the peninsula, and even this had numerous irrigation channels through dense date palm groves and fields in a two-to-four-kilometre belt alongside the Shatt al-Arab. There were three 'hard-topped' (asphalt covered) roads; the highway along the Shatt al-Arab, from Basra to Faw City; another down the middle of the peninsula which later joined the highway; and a third along the Khor Abdullah in the western part of the peninsula from Umm Qasr to Faw City. East of the Basra–Faw City highway was a gravel-topped coastal road running along the edge of the cultivated areas. In between these were countless paths and small, gravel-topped, or beaten earth, roads on embankments. Along the western side of the southern length of the Basra–Faw City highway lay the strategic oil pipeline which provided a degree of cover from fire coming from the salt beds.

The terrain and defences dictated an infantry assault, with mandatory powerful artillery support, in a set-piece offensive like those launched by the Allies in 1917, rather than a Second World War manoeuvre battle. The gunners would first have to neutralise the defences, then support the infantry assault while simultaneously conducting counterbattery work. There was a debate over whether to assault at midnight or in the morning, but all agreed that the assault troops should assemble at night. Eventually the planners opted for an attack after the usual dawn alert when the defenders had been stood down and were having breakfast. It was officially estimated that the offensive would be completed within three days, but there were pessimists – possibly including the 7th Division's commander, Major General Saad Abdul Hadi (Hadi) who feared it would take five days before the whole peninsula down to the Cape Bisha was again in Iraqi hands.

Rawi's main axes would be the central road and the one which ran along the Khor Abdullah from Umm Qasr which he would exploit to swing eastwards like a closing door. The Guards would be the hammer to Maher's VII Corps anvil, the latter advancing southwards between the Basra–Faw City highway and the road running alongside the Shatt.

The offensive was to develop in three phases. After a hurricane bombardment, the two corps would bulldoze their way forward, with infantry first establishing a line beyond the Mamlaha salt beds. They would then insert armoured and mechanised divisions to exploit this success taking the attackers to the outskirts of Faw City – which Maher would then storm. It would be a stand-alone offensive with no immediate follow-on, but its success would determine whether or not there were further offensives on the southern front.

Constructing the Battlefield

Hopes were soon dashed of an amphibious assault behind enemy lines, aimed to ease the advance along the Umm Qasr–Faw City road, because Navy commander Major General Ghaib-Hasson Ghaib reluctantly had to concede he lacked dedicated amphibious warfare vessels. From 1977 to 1979 Poland supplied Iraq with four Project 773K ('Polnocny-B') class medium landing ships (LSM), giving a nominal 'lift' of a battalion. But at the outbreak of war IrN *Nouh* and *Atika* were being refitted in Basra where they remained for the duration of the war as moored MLRS batteries supporting the Fish Lake Line. The IrN *Janada* and *Ganda* were in Umm Qasr but the former was sunk by AGM-65A Maverick missiles from an IRIAF Phantom in November 1980, while *Ganda* could carry only a company. The shallow waters and wide mud flats made it impossible to use FACs to carry the troops, in contrast to the invasion of Kuwait in 1990.[8]

Starting with 14 May 1986, an equivalent of eight Iraqi engineer battalions – about 6,000 troops – began improving the local infrastructure through expanding and reinforcing roads, adding battery positions and AFV laagers, ostensibly to strengthen the defences. Over time, these units were augmented by personnel and equipment from the Ministries of Housing, and Petroleum as well as Irrigation, and Construction who together provided 350 requisitioned bulldozers and earthmovers. To build roads, each engineer company had up to three earth movers, three bulldozers, six digger vehicles and six road rollers, and could create roads at the rate of up to three kilometres per hour.[9] They drained potential assembly sites with 16 kilometres of channels and added 1,100 kilometres of roads as well as 16 bridges. To shelter the troops, and provide fire platforms for MBTs, the engineers created 1,060 kilometres of earthworks and would assemble 139,000 cubic metres (111,000 tonnes) of earth, sand and gravel near the major axes to create new causeways through the marshes, while firing positions increased from the second half of 1987.

The planners also examined ways to help the advance and support the capture of objectives using special equipment provided by Iraq Military Industries – which was under Major General Hussein Kamel Hassan. Apart from command tanks, all T-72s could be fitted with a bulldozer blade to push through berms and minefields, while engineers deployed 30-tonne bridges and fabric mats to help soft-skinned vehicles cross the marshes. Each divisional engineer battalion had MTU-20 or, in armoured units, Czech MT-55, Armoured Vehicle Launched Bridges (AVLB) and six GSP ferries, each with a carrying capacity 52 tonnes, augmented by PTS tracked amphibious trucks with a capacity of 10 tonnes.[10]

The Iraqis assembled four Guards divisions (Hammurabi and Medina Armoured, Baghdad and Nebuchadnezzar Infantry) with 19 brigades, and four Army divisions (1st Mechanised, 6th Armoured, 7th and 26th Infantry Divisions) with 24 brigades. The Medina and 26th Infantry Division were assigned largely supporting roles in the forthcoming campaign for which the corps received numerous artillery, engineer, logistic and medical units. The Guards would have to operate in the marshes and had to extemporise solutions to their problem of transiting the marshes or cratered roads. They created raised footpaths from the timber of empty ammunition cases or qugh wood (Khashab al-qugh) ladders. The infantry received snowshoe-like footwear to distribute weight more evenly and each man carried a thick sponge cushion which could be linked up and thrown across a minefield to provide safe passage. Tides moved mines in the marshes and to deal with this movement gabions

PART I: SADDAM'S FIRST BLOW

In preparation for their counteroffensive on Faw, the Iraqis constructed an elaborate system of roads, berms, firing ramps, and firing positions for their artillery. The latter (this photo shows a battery of 130mm M1954 guns) was to play the dominant role during the opening minutes of the attack. (Albert Grandolini collection)

(baskets filled with stones) were prepared to create a physical barrier on either side of cleared lines.

Because VII Corps would have to advance through the cultivated zone, with its myriad of irrigation channels, it would clearly make slower progress than the Guards whose sector was wider and 'more open' and who had received more intensive training. Maher would also come under fire from across the Dhatt from artillery and mortars which would further restrict his advance. There was extensive preparation with each corps having its own remotely located training area, resembling their objectives, where troops rehearsed day and night and in all weather conditions. Training emphasised combined-arms operations, rapid response to threats, and mutual support among the corps. There were numerous war games for both officers and NCOs using maps and sand tables both to familiarise them with taking their objectives and rehearsing alternative tactics.

Confusing the Enemy

To confuse the enemy, the Director of Military Intelligence Lieutenant General Sabir Abdul Aziz ad-Duri (also 'Sabir ad-Duri'), rolled out a deception plan which began with suggestions of an offensive by IV Corps on the central front in Amarah area. Correspondingly, Major General Sadallah Khalil's Nebuchadnezzar Republican Guards Infantry Division and General Thamir Sultan Ahmad's ('Thamir Sultan') 1st Mechanised Division were both deployed in this area before secretly being sent to the Faw Peninsula. Once there, the Nebuchadnezzar was to largely act as the Guards Corps reserve. Other units of the Guards and VII Corps were ostensibly transferred to III and IV Corps, neither of which was informed that these units were not under their command anymore. Later they too were quietly sent to the peninsula, with tank transporters and low-loaders sometimes moving several guns at a time.

Baghdad's apparent concern with the Northern and Central Fronts created an Iranian response which played into Iraqi hands. Baghdad's and the international media had long raised the fear of a new Iranian offensive on the southern front and in early 1988 the Iraqis used this as an excuse both for continued preparation work on the Faw Peninsula and for concentrating troops around Basra. Aware of this the Iranians decided to encourage the Iraqis with an ostentatious build-up on the Faw Peninsula as a diversion for a major offensive – Val Fajr-10 – around Halabja on the northern front. Trucks, mostly empty, streamed across the Shatt bridges. However, the bluff was quickly detected by Unit 999 and Iraqi COMINT, allowing Baghdad to exploit this both by weakening the Iranian garrison and providing a reasonable excuse for an Iraqi build-up. It also provided a plausible reason to pull Khudayyir's 6th Armoured Division out of its training area and return it to III Corps.[11]

The Iraqis then skilfully turned the concept on its head following the success on the northern front in March 1988 – when Val Fajr-10 threatened Iraq's most important hydro-electric project. This threat was regarded seriously by Iraq's military leaders for the first half of the year, but Saddam's gaze remained on the Faw Peninsula. Thus, and in response, Baghdad

As of early 1988, the T-55 (and its variants manufactured in Czechoslovakia, Poland and China) still formed the backbone of the armoured and mechanised battalions assigned to all of the Iraqi infantry divisions. This example survived most of the war with Iran while retaining its original camouflage pattern in sand and dark blue-green. (via M.H.)

225

Despite numerous visits to the frontlines and extensive conferences, Saddam kept the timing for the counteroffensive on Faw secret to a degree where even the most important of the generals involved did not know when it would start. (via M.H.)

despatched half the Baghdad Division, reinforced by 24th and 25th Republican Guards Infantry Brigades, to 'meet the threat'. The Iraqi 'concern' was reflected by a well-publicised appearance on the northern front by Defence Minister Khairallah on 16 April 1988, who flew south that evening. But the Guards units barely had time to unpack their kit bags before they were on the way back south, to the bewilderment of the many Iraqi generals unaware of the planned offensive.[12]

Even more bewildered was VI Corps commander, Lieutenant General Yaljin Umar Adil, when he was telephoned on 15 April by Operations Chief Hussein Rashid, and told to take leave even though he knew he was not entitled to any. Part of the Baghdad Division had been under his command and he knew it was undergoing extensive training. Realising something was 'up', when this division moved south he asked, 'why?' However, fearing a possible arrest for his inquisitiveness, Adil eventually decided to stop asking question and instead began his 'leave' with trepidation. In turn, on the next day he received a telephone 'invitation' to become the Guards Corps' alternate commander. He did not arrive until 09:30 on 17 April 1988 but quickly became thoroughly familiar with the plans and would have replaced Rawi if he had been wounded.

Tight Secrecy

The Iraqis realised that with the enemy fully committed in the north there was no better time to strike in the south, and Saddam turned optimistic enough to telescope the first and second phases so the latter would be on Y-Day not Y+1.[13] On 12 April 1988, in conditions of tight security, Saddam chaired a meeting of senior commanders which provisionally scheduled the offensive for 17 April, the first day of the holy month of Ramadan for Islamic year 1408. For this reason the offensive was re-designated Operation Ramadan Mubarak – the same code name selected by the Iranians for their first offensive on Iraqi soil in 1982. Another advantage of this date was that a number of the defenders were expected to have been withdrawn to go on pilgrimage within Iran, while others might be on leave with their families. The decision was confirmed on 16 April when Saddam met his son-in-law, Guards Director General Kamel al-Majid, Chief-of-Staff Khazraji, the Operations Chief Hussein Rashid, and Intelligence Chief Aziz ad-Duri. Saddam arrived with the date to launch the assault, worked out previously by the army staff, and fearing the room might be bugged wrote it down on a piece of paper which he passed around the room. This set Y (Yom) Day for 17 April with S (Sifr or Zero) Hour at 06:30 and after the others agreed, Saddam tore up the paper and sent word south.

He and Khairallah then flew to the General Command South Operations Centre which opened on the outskirts of Basra at 23:00 on 16 April and included the Directors of Artillery and Engineering, representatives of all arms and associated commands and featured extensive radio and landline communications. Each corps received one of Saddam's sons, nominally to show the nation's leaders were at the front, but also to act as personal observers as division and brigade commanders were informed of S-Hour/Y-Day only 20 hours beforehand and battalion commanders even later. But before dawn the assault force, with a nominal 183,000 men, 910 MBTs, 1,100 guns and 100 attack helicopters was ready. Extremely tight security reasons led to the maintenance of the generous leave entitlements and thus many of involved units were at least 10 percent understrength.

Assembling the Strike-Force

The assembly of the assault forces, organised by Logistics Chief Abdallah Muhammad under tight security, had begun on 13 April 1988. Half of the assault force brigades began assembling, together

A reconnaissance photograph taken by an Iraqi MiG-25RB and showing one of the Iranian pontoon bridges spanning the Shatt al-Arab. (Ahmad Sadik collection)

with 40 artillery (two self-propelled) battalions and thousands of tonnes of supplies. Their movement was concealed by four days of poor weather.

The assault corps were organised in echelon with Rawi's Guards Corps first having Baghdad Infantry and Medina Armoured Divisions, together with 26th Infantry Division – the last largely for consolidation – while the Hammurabi Armoured Division was in the second echelon. The Nebuchadnezzar Infantry Division was in the potential third echelon, but although available as a tactical reserve, many of its brigades – together with part of Brigadier Waad Allah Mustafa Hanoush's (Mustafa Hanoush) Republican Guards SF Division – were assigned to the other Guards divisions.[14] This reflected the Guards' shared organisational flexibility: they actually inherited this practice from the experience with the Army turning its divisions into task forces whose strength could be modified to meet unexpected situations or perform new tasks.

The Baghdad Division, under former 11th Infantry Division commander Lieutenant General Abd-al-Wahid Shannan ar-Ribat ('Shannan'), and Medina under Lieutenant General Ahmad Ibrahim Hammash ('Hammash'), had 11 brigades while the follow-up forces of Lieutenant General Ibrahim Abd-Al-Sattar Muhammad's ('Sattar') Hammurabi would follow up with four brigades (see Table 19 for order of battle during Operation Ramadan Mubarak). Major General Sadallah Khalil's Nebuchadnezzar remained in reserve. Rawi thus had 67,500 men with 315 MBTs, while Maher's VII Corps had 101,500 men with 285 MBTs.

The latter was also organised into two echelons. The first was Khudayyir's 6th Armoured Division and Hadi's 7th Infantry Division with a total of 15 brigades. The second echelon consisted of Major General Thamir Sultan's 1st Mechanised Division (transferred from IV Corps) with six brigades. They were supported by 31 artillery (two self-propelled) battalions and, six MLRS battalions with BM-21s and Astros, augmented by five batteries of Chinese 107mm light MLRS. There were also 12 batteries of 120mm heavy mortars, and a battalion of FROG-7 surface-to-surface missiles. This gave some 1,160 x 105mm, 122mm, 130mm and 152mm tubes, 140 MLRS and 72 heavy mortars.[15]

A Lonesome Outpost

Following the heady days of Val Fajr-8, the Iranian garrison on the Faw had been steadily stripped, until it was down to fewer than 20,000 troops and 100 MBTs. The IRIA troops were the first to re-cross the Shatt during the spring of 1986, followed by both Pasdaran task force headquarters and all seven divisions for eventual commitment to the Karbala offensives in summer of the same year. Iraqi intelligence calculated that there were two Pasdaran divisions and a naval brigade on the peninsula, deployed in echelon with four brigades on the front line and three deployed south of the Mamlaha salt beds. Actually present was only the 8th Najaf Ashraf Division IRGC – whose three brigades returned to Faw after Karbala-8, three naval brigades of the Pasdaran, and about 1,000 Basiji. Two of Najaf Ashraf's brigades were in the front, with the third and two naval brigades acting as reserve in the rear. These troops were supported by some 20 batteries

Equipped with a hodgepodge of vehicles and equipment of US (M113 APCs), Soviet (BMP-1 IFV), East German (W50 truck), Chinese, and North Korean origin, the Pasdaran of the Najaf Ashraf Division were not only outnumbered, but also hopelessly outgunned by attacking Iraqi forces. (Tom Cooper collection)

One of the IRGC's artillery batteries deployed at Faw was equipped with North Korean-made Koksan self-propelled guns. (via S.S.)

Table 19: Order of Battle for Operation Ramadan Mubarak, April 1988		
Corps	Division	Brigades
Iraq		
Republican Guards Corps	Corps Troops incl. Republican Guards Corps Artillery Brigade	
	Hammurabi Armoured Division Republican Guards	17th Armoured, 15th Mechanised, 12th Commando, 20th Infantry Brigades Republican Guards
	Medina Manarwah Armoured Division Republican Guards	6th Infantry, 10th Armoured, 11th Commando, 16th Special Forces Brigades Republican Guards; 440th & 441st Naval Infantry Brigades
	Baghdad Infantry Division Republican Guards	4th, 5th, 7th Infantry Brigades, 3rd Special Forces, 21st Commando Brigades Republican Guards
	Nebuchadnezzar Infantry Division Republican Guards	8th & 9th Armoured, 19th Commando, 22nd & 23rd Infantry Brigades Republican Guards; 110th & 11th Infantry Brigades
VII Corps	Corps Troops, 1st & 2nd Commando Brigades of VII Corps; VII Corps Artillery Brigade	
	1st Mechanised Division	1st & 27th Mechanised, 34th Armoured, 102nd, 108th, 701st Infantry Brigades
	6th Armoured Division	16th & 30th Armoured, 25th Mechanised, 14th, 95th, 104th, 107th, 429th, 802nd Infantry Brigades
	7th Infantry Division	19th, 27th, 38th, 39th Infantry, 66th & 68th Special Forces Brigades
	3rd Wing IrAAC	
	4th Wing IrAAC	
Iran		
	8th Najaf Ashraf Division IRGC	3 brigades
	104th Emir al-Mu'minin Naval Brigade IRGC	
	105th al-Kawthar Naval Brigade IRGC	
	106th Sajjad Naval Brigade IRGC	
	94th Sha'ban Air Defence Brigade IRGC	
	2nd Combat Support Group IRIAA	

with 114 guns, including a battery of Koksan self-propelled 170mm tubes and 13 MLRS, all augmented by the 94th Sha'ban Air Defence Brigade IRGC, a battalion of 98th Sahib az-Zaman Engineer Division, and members of the 26th Salman Coast Defence Missile Brigade.[16]

Iraqi deception plans appear to have had some success because from late March 1988 many of the Iranian artillery batteries war withdrawn from the Faw Peninsula, together with some Pasdaran units. The remaining men were mostly lowgrade older troops and volunteers who had little or no preparation for gas attack. They occupied an extensive defensive system built after the capture of the peninsula and based upon flooding and berms, but lack of manpower meant that numerous positions were incomplete.[17] Berms running north to south were designed to channel enemy armour while those running east to west were resistance-lines, often studded with bunkers and dugouts. Dozens of earth ramps were built so MBTs could augment the defender's firepower. To further channel an Iraqi assault using the Basra–Faw City highway as an axis, parts of the western peninsula were flooded.

There was a buffer zone some three kilometres deep between the Iraqi positions and the first line of defence, and in the east the attacker would have to cross a kilometre of inundations 0.6 metres deep. These areas, and the marshes in front of the first line of defence, featured extensive barbed wire entanglements and minefields. A double line of west-east berms up to 50 metres apart and studded with bunkers and dugouts ran right across the peninsula and was the first line of resistance. On the eastern end, some 350 metres behind these defences, lay a six-kilometre-long flooded anti-armour ditch, between 25 and 60 metres wide, covered by bunkers and dugouts, artillery and AFV positions, and which acted as a second line of defence.

About a kilometre behind that was a similar ditch, 'The Counter Attack Canal', some 40 metres wide which was designed to be the jump-off point for counterattacks directed with the aid of a chain of 20-metre-high observation towers. Within the marshes the Mamlaha salt beds had been turned into another second line of resistance. Behind these positions the eastern approaches to Faw City had been restricted through two flooded areas around the Basra–Faw City highway. One was 3.4 kilometres long and 1.8 kilometres wide; the other – just north of the city – was 2.5 kilometres long and up to 1.5 kilometres wide. A smaller inundation and a 40-metre-wide flooded ditch covered the approaches from the west. The defences were controlled from a headquarters in Faw City linked by underwater landline and a microwave relay tower to Iran. Physical communication with the

Iranian homeland was across the Shatt, which the winter rains had raised to its highest level since 1954.[18]

The garrison was supplied by a fleet of some 1,500 small boats and the two bridges; a pontoon bridge north of Faw City, and a bridge south of the city, while at the time of the Iraqi attack work was under way to build another bridge into Faw City. This was similar to the 900-metre-long so-called 'pipe bridge' at Be'ssat, south of Faw City, which was constructed from two layers of oil pipelines and Styrofoam, laid so the tides flowed through them, and whose roadway could accommodate MBTs. A Pasdaran division and 3rd Brigade/92nd Armoured Division IRIA were in reserve ready to cross the Shatt and the IRIAA had some 40–50 helicopters ready to support operations in the south.

The Iranians probably heard the increased noise raised by convoys of newly arrived vehicles, but rain or drizzle from 10–14 April prevented detailed observation. There are claims that from 14 April there was a comprehensive Iraqi programme to jam enemy radars but the accuracy of this claim is uncertain. It is only certain that the Iranians were taken by surprise: their intelligence may have received some indications of Iraqi plans, but any warnings they passed on appear to have been ignored. The first intimation of the offensive came at 05:30 as Iraqi special forces began to attack the pontoon bridges across the Shatt which, from 05:45 were also engaged by Iraqi guns, with a battalion assigned to each bridge. Finally, the southern bridge was cut in two by a pair of IrAF Su-22M-4s, which deployed Kh-29 (AS-14 Kedge) laser-guided missiles for this purpose.[19]

Operation Ramadan Mubarak
A 45-minute bombardment by guns, MLRS and mortars opened a relatively cool day with a maximum temperature of 34° Centigrade with a 29 kilometre/hour wind. The first berms disappeared under a curtain of fire and steel from most tubes while 130mm and 155mm guns, sometimes aided by observation helicopters, engaged batteries, troop concentrations and headquarters. Iraqi artillery benefited from improved training, moving more quickly in response to requests from the front, and efficiently shifting and concentrating fire on centres of resistance. The Iraqis also augmented their Brazilian Astros II SS-30 MLRS with 18 SS-40s, each vehicle firing 16 x 152 kilogramme 180mm calibre rockets up to 35 kilometres, with a cluster munition warhead of 20 anti-armour/anti-personnel bomblets.[20]

In addition to conventional shells the Iraqis made extensive use of chemical warheads: mortars, guns and BM-21 MLRS were estimated to have fired up to 2,000 warheads, while the CIA estimated that about 100 tonnes of chemical agents were used in the bombardment contaminating the Shatt. The Iraqis especially targeted the rear areas because the support troops had little chemical warfare defence training and little in the way of protective equipment.[21]

The US Defence Intelligence Agencies' Lieutenant Colonel Rick Francona, who had confirmed the use of sulphur mustard gas ('Agent HD') and Tabun, or Agent GA, semi-persistent nerve agents from 1983–1984, now reported the use of Sarin, or Agent GB, non-persistent nerve agents. During his visit to the peninsula after the battle he discovered numerous atropine injectors and decontamination fluid on vehicles, as well as the absence of insects and birds. His report to Washington led to a brief suspension of cooperation with the Iraqis. Towards the end of the war the former head of Iraqi military intelligence, General Wafiq as-Sammarai, claimed the campaign was the first use of Agent VX – a persistent nerve agent which surprised and terrified the defenders, and which necessitated the equipment of the Iraqi troops involved with both atropine injectors and special tablets to counter the effects.[22] However, several reports suggest a changing wind blew some nerve gas into the Iraqi lines, possibly those of 7th Infantry Division, reportedly killing almost 200 and forcing the survivors to wear gas masks which, in warm weather, proved extremely fatiguing.[23]

The IrAF and IrAAC also delivered chemical agents, the former using 250 and 500 kilogram bombs with chemical agents, reportedly including VX, but also mustard gas which could be spread 100 metres from the point of impact. Mi-8 helicopters, operating in teams of three, carried either bombs with 220 litres of chemical agent (usually nerve gas), or spray tanks with a capacity of 1,000 litres. Nevertheless, most of the IrAF ordnance consisted of 'iron bombs': about 45 fighter-bombers and helicopter gunships used these to target headquarters, key batteries and the Iranian approaches to the pontoon bridges. The IrAF committed five squadrons in direct support of the offensive; during the day 'Saddam's Falcons' would fly 330 sorties and drop 655 tonnes of bombs, as well as 13 guided air-to-surface missiles, in missions which included interdicting enemy road and rail communications in south-western Iran. The IrAAC would fly 218 gunship sorties on the first day.[24]

The roar of the bombardment concealed the Iraqi troops' initial movements and this was further obscured by extensive smokescreens as well as clouds of gas. Mine clearance was an important role and brigade engineer companies had Soviet- and Iraqi-made hand-held, and Soviet DIM vehicle-mounted, detectors although few were effective against non-metallic mines.[25] They could use the traditional method of lifting mines with hand tools or the Soviet UR-77 rocket propelled line charge trailer which could clear a 90-metre-long lane, 6–8 metres wide, from a distance of 150 metres. Bangalore Torpedoes were used too. Each rifle company had an 8–12-metre wide path marked with distinctive coloured flags. Armoured and mechanised units had Russian-built tank-mounted KMT-4 mine ploughs (one per platoon), and KMT-5 mine rollers (one per company).[26]

The infantry were close behind them ready to suppress enemy fire with their heavy weapons which augmented the artillery with great success. When the guns switched to a rolling bombardment on the enemy's second line, at 06:30, the Iraqi infantry were quickly into the first berms, many were breached with the remainder pock-marked by shell holes and covered with stunned survivors and the dead. Rawi's guardsmen faced more formidable problems advancing through the marshes to overcome the first defensive system and then the heavily defended Mamlaha salt beds. Hammash's Medina Division advanced in two echelons on the Iraqi right wing along the coastal road and shoreline from Umm Qasr to Faw City, with Shannan's Baghdad Division its left. Yet within six hours Rawi had almost all of the first berm line, apart from the coastal section where 16th Republican Guards Commando Brigade – from the Republican Guards SP Division – made slow progress through waist-deep water while advancing bare-footed and partially dressed.

Hammash's centre and left – 6th Republican Guards Infantry and 11th Republican Guards Commando Brigades, supported by 10 T-72s – made faster progress and 6th Republican Guards Brigade swung south to isolate the enemy coastal defences. In their rear, engineers quickly repaired the road to help insert 10th Republican Guards Armoured Brigade, which made such rapid progress towards Cape Bisha that plans for the two Navy brigades to make an amphibious assault on the peninsula's southern coast were abandoned and instead they accompanied the tanks.[27]

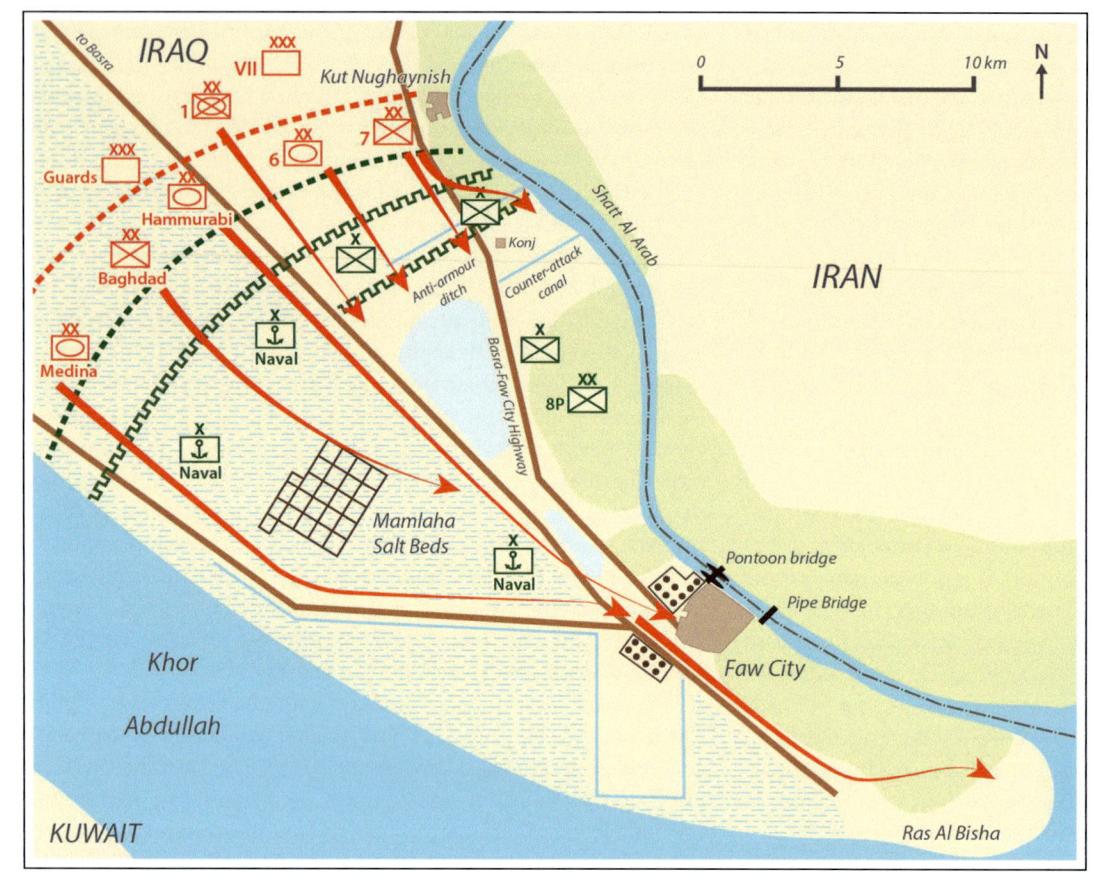

A map of the Iraqi Operation Ramadan Mubarak, in April 1988. (Map by George Anderson)

There was fierce resistance from the Iranians, who used RPGs extensively, forcing some tank crews to use personal weapons to drive them off, but the tanks eventually overran the southernmost Silkworm battery with the assistance of a naval brigade. The rest of the division followed through and within 14 hours had secured the southern coast; with the Iraqi flag being raised over Cape Bisha at 19:00 on 18 April 1988. To their disappointment, the Iraqis found the coast defence and surface-to-air missile sites all empty.

Meanwhile, 6th and 11th Republican Guards Brigades masked the Mamlaha salt beds to support Shannan's Baghdad Division, which brought up its reserves and stormed the salt beds in an intense close-quarter battle, with anti-armour missiles used as 'bunker busters'.

Plan 22 had envisaged the Medina and Baghdad Divisions completing the conquest of the outer defences by the end of Y-Day, opening the way for Sattar's Hammurabi on Y+1. But at noon on Y-Day Saddam rang Sattar and informed him his mission was now to take Faw City. Sattar saw his opportunity, drove back to the Centre and pressed to bring his division forward ahead of schedule. The two Guards division commanders fully supported him and persuaded Saddam to agree, and during the early evening Hammurabi was brought into the line north of the salt beds. It was substantially reinforced with all of the Nebuchadnezzar Division's infantry and commandos, who arrived after a forced march of 27 kilometres through the marshes carrying all their equipment.

Sattar attacked at 20:00 on Y-Day, fighting his way down the Basra–Faw City highway led by 20th Republican Guards Infantry Brigade, while 12th Republican Guards Commando and 19th Republican Guards Infantry Brigades – together with 17th Republican Guards Armoured Brigade – isolated the town from the south by 14:00 on 18 April. While Sattar planned a full-scale assault led by 12th and 20th Brigades, Khairallah – realising the scale of the enemy collapse – urged him to send just 20th Brigade into the city, but immediately. The unit jumped off at 15:00 and – later aided by the other brigades – took it within an hour. The 4th Republican Guards Infantry Brigade then became the garrison.

Khudayyir's Problems …

The first day's success encouraged Baghdad to accelerate the operation and on the night of 17 to 18 April 1988 Maher was shocked to receive a call from Saddam informing him that the honour of taking Faw City would now go to Rawi's guardsmen. In a back-door attempt to flaunt Saddam's order, the VII Corps Chief-of-Staff Major General Qaidar Mohammad Saleh, rang his opposite number, Major General Ibraheem Ismael, and sought permission to take Faw City. But Ismael refused, arguing it was Saddam's order. Salt was rubbed into the wound when the Guards banned a preliminary bombardment by VII Corps artillery.

The decision taken by Saddam and Khairallah was made after telephone consultations with Maher, and was neither an attempt to increase the regime's prestige nor a personal snub: it reflected VII Corps' weak performance compared with Rawi's guardsmen – despite opening with great promise.

Although Maher advanced across firm ground he had first to traverse a mine-strewn no-man's land with steel obstacles, old palm trunks and battle debris ranging from wrecked AFVs to anti-armour missile guidance wires which could tangle wheels tracks. Maher's left also had to fight through the palm groves of the cultivated area and their numerous irrigation ditches, which could provide enfilade fire into his spearheads. A further complication was that he was confined to two axes; the Basra–Faw City highway and the coastal road running through the palm groves, so that delays caused congestion. Maher's artillery preparation, directed by Brigadier Abd al-Hadi Mohammed Saleh, may have been judged inadequate, for the gunner would be dismissed on 18 May 'for not fulfilling his set duties according to the Blessed Ramadan plan…' and also 'for not taking to task the commanders who did not fulfil their duties correctly…'

Nevertheless, Hadi's 7th Infantry Division and Khudayyir's 6th Armoured Division rapidly captured the first berm line – in spite of slow progress through the palm groves under increasing mortar, artillery and MLRS fire from across the Shatt, which caused severe congestion along the coastal road. One of the infantry brigade commanders became increasingly pessimistic and claimed his unit was 'finished', but Khazraji came over to Maher's headquarters to find out what was slowing the advance and soon dismissed the demoralised brigade commander. Khazraji believed he had solved

PART I: SADDAM'S FIRST BLOW

the problem, but 7th Division's progress remained glacial and by the end of the day it had still not reached its Y-Day objectives.[28]

The lack of progress effected the advance of Khudayyir, who would later claim he was ultra-confident of success and had six infantry brigades in addition to his integral armour. His confidence was well-placed. He took the first berm in 12 minutes, aided by a tank company he had moved right up to the berms. Ironically Maher did not at first believe Khudayyir's report, but the latter just continued pushing; he sent 107th and 429th Brigades up to the 'Counter-attack Canal' where they were exposed from the east. Further in the rear, 16th Armoured Brigade was held up at the anti-armour ditch because bulldozers had difficulty pilling up the soft sand to create a causeway.

Eventually Khudayyir's tanks crossed, but he had now fallen behind schedule. In an attempt to make up lost time, and gambling on enemy demoralisation, he brought up his wheeled BTR-60 APCs which had better traction in the sand. Heavy fire from the palm groves on his left – where Iranians were still fiercely resisting Hadi's 7th Infantry Division – created a space up to 300-metres wide and the 107th Brigade had to enter the palm groves to shield his left. Khudayyir's advance eventually picked up pace and was joined by 30th Armoured Brigade, but at 00:35 on 18 April Saddam, fearing that Maher would take Faw City, ordered him to stop on exposed ground forcing the brigades to go into laager for the night. At dawn the 30th Armoured Brigade renewed its advance while 25th Mechanised Brigade was brought up to relieve 16th Armoured Brigade. At noon, they were all ordered to withdraw because of Saddam's order, and this ended Khudayyir's contribution to Ramadan Mubarak.

… and Maher's Final Push

Meanwhile, Maher tried to break the impasse on his left by bringing up his second echelon formation, Thamir Sultan's 1st Mechanised Division (whose tanks had been providing fire support for the other divisions). It had been scheduled in the second and third phase operations but now crossed the main ditch to advance on a three-brigade front and assigned one of its infantry brigades to support 7th

Although involving quantitatively and qualitatively far superior forces, and although proceeding at a high pace, the Iraqi counteroffensive on al-Faw was anything but a one-sided affair, especially on the eastern side of the peninsula, as mines and Iranian anti-tank teams still managed to knock out a number of Iraqi army tanks. (Farzin Nadimi collection)

A Soviet-made Kh-29 (AS-14 Kedge) guided missile, as used by the Iraqis to knock out Iranian bridges spanning the Shatt. (US DoD)

Division. However, Khudayyir's advance exposed his right as it tried to cross the 'Counter-attack Canal' while craters and un-cleared minefields restricted AFV movement. Thamir Sultan decided to use the remnants of the oil pipeline west of the highway to cover his advance but first brought up tree trunks and 20,000 filled sandbags to repair his communications, while engineers built ramps as fire platforms for MBTs and lifted mines around the highway. The 7th Division had three brigades in defensive positions (including 27th and 102nd Infantry), which 1st Mechanised Division took over, together with its three integral brigades, and he learned that 6th Armoured Division had sent an infantry and a commando brigade into the palm groves.

There was fierce resistance from the former Iraqi strongpoint which the Iranians called the Konj, and this stopped a VII Corps' commando brigade which suffered heavy losses. At 09:00 on 18 April, 7th Division finally secured the last of its Y-Day objectives and Maher now ordered Thamir Sultan to assume operational command of its brigades and resume the advance; for which he received the battered VII Corps' commando brigade. Sultan moved 102nd Infantry and 34th Armoured Brigades to cover 6th Armoured Division as congestion built up on the highway behind, due to Iranian mortar fire, and then decided to use 1st Mechanised Brigade as his spearhead, to outflank the Konj and reach the next anti-armour ditch. Moving out at dawn, his units reached the pontoon bridge al-Maamir, which had been destroyed by the IrAF and which was held by Guard special forces. Meanwhile, the 27th Mechanised Brigade was brought up and drove down the coastal road only to be stopped 1.5 kilometres from Faw City when Khazraji rang to remind him of Saddam's decision and ordered Sultan to mop up the palm groves – although this duty was soon passed to the newly arrived 2nd Infantry Division which had been hastily brought in to secure the eastern flank.

It was another comment on Maher's poor performance that Rawi was assigned the task of securing the two bridge sites. Part of 3rd Republican Guards SF Brigade was flown into the northern site but encountered no resistance as they captured a few exhausted and naked Iranians on the shore where they had tried to swim the Shatt. Rawi had also planned to take the southern Pipe Bridge at Bessat, and on the evening of 17 April planned an air assault by his reserve 21st Republican Guards Commando Brigade, but the plan was abandoned by midnight due to bad weather.

The End

From the Iranian point of view, the Iraqi assault caused a catastrophe; the opening bombardment decimated the first defending echelon on the berms and inflicted heavy losses on the second echelon, while chemical weapons disrupted the rear echelons. The use of new gases especially stunned the defenders and prevented them from regrouping.[29] Massively outnumbered and outgunned, the defenders lacked heavy weapons; TOW teams did knock out a number of MBTs but spent their ammunition stocks very soon too. The palm groves provided some cover, but with Iraqi pressure growing the commander of Najaf Ashraf was left without a choice but to order a fighting withdrawal towards the bridges. While some troops continued to fight desperately news of the northern bridge's destruction further demoralised the defenders and the retreat became a rout. Jostling crowds of men fled across the damaged Pipe Bridge and in the panic some fell, or were pushed off, and drowned. Only then did the Pasdaran issue a demand for top cover from the IRIAF, but – taken by surprise – the latter was unable to provide more than 42 CAS sorties. F-4 Phantom IIs from Bushehr flew 20 top cover sorties for the final retreat on 18 April. Reports from involved Iranian pilots indicate they felt 'drowned in the sea of Iraqi aircraft': the IrAF was present above the battlefield in such numbers, that there was no chance of success in air combats.

'Ramadan Mubarak' achieved its objectives within 35 hours. Nevertheless, the Republican Guards still suffered 1,086 casualties. Total Iraqi casualties were probably about 4,000 men and 20 AFVs while the Iranians probably suffered 5,000 casualties and 2,000 men taken prisoner, with the loss of all their heavy weapons. A delighted Saddam gave his top commanders Mercedes automobiles and on 19 April he went on a pilgrimage to Mecca. That day Rawi's corps was withdrawn northwards and Maher was given total responsibility for the peninsula. He remained bitterly and volubly disappointed at being thwarted at Faw City and, despite being father-in-law to Saddam's youngest son he received only minor awards. When he continued protesting he was replaced by Lieutenant General Mohammad Abdul Qader and placed in the reserve Office of the Warriors (Deirat al Muharebeen) where he retained all his privileges.[30]

Iraq's Navy commander, General Ghaib, was also disappointed as his only hope of winning glory was dashed. Nevertheless, he was less vocal. He had committed most of his surviving 41 FACs, patrol boats, landing craft and hovercraft as well as a small squadron of Super Frelon helicopters from Umm Qasr.[31] FACs claimed to have hit one of three Iranian vessels approaching the peninsula and the Medina Division received fire support from one of these vessels and the coast defence batteries. IrAF Super Frelon helicopters under naval operational control were primarily deployed for maritime surveillance, although two were kept in readiness armed with AM.39 Exocets for anti-shipping operations.[32]

The defeat, coming after years of supposed victories, was a severe blow to Iranian morale. It took place at a politically sensitive time: Khomeini was seriously ill, while Tehran had complacently assumed that years of defensive strategy had left Baghdad incapable of a major offensive. The deep divisions between the regular forces and the Pasdaran reopened, with each side blaming the other for the disaster and the search began for scapegoats. A number of IRIA and Pasdaran commanders were dismissed, with the clerics' biggest scalp being that of the Chief-of-Staff of the Armed Forces Brigadier General Ismail Sohrabi. He was replaced by his 42-year-old deputy, Brigadier General Ali Shahbazi and relegated to the position of 'military consultant' to the Supreme Defence Council.[33]

Interestingly, while other clerics were blaming top regular military commanders for the defeat, Khomeini criticised all the leaders of the armed forces for 'becoming too arrogant', driving even Rezai into public admission of making mistakes. Nevertheless, the Pasdaran commander in the south, Ali Saleh Shamkhani remained in place and in September 1988 became the Minister of the IRGC: indeed, when that ministry was merged with Defence Ministry, he – briefly – became the first Pasdaran in charge of the Iranian regular armed forces.

The literal 'dot' on the 'I' was delivered by the Americans; as the Iraqis mopped up on al-Faw, on 18 April 1988, the US Navy launched its Operation Praying Mantis, aiming to find and sink Iranian Navy warships involved in attacks on international merchant shipping in the lower Persian Gulf. In the course of two naval actions, two Iranian warships were sunk and a third crippled, and Tehran received a strong lesson in modern warfare. Overall, operations Ramadan Mubarak and Praying Mantis isolated Iran on the international scene, while greatly boosting not only Iraqi, but also Saudi Arabian and Kuwaiti confidence. On 27 April 1988, Riyadh cut diplomatic links with Tehran, allegedly over the Iranian refusal to limit the number of pilgrims for the Hajj from 155,000 to 45,000.[34]

16
IRANIAN BURNOUT

Both sides recognised that the Faw offensive had created a seismic change in fortunes, and a delighted Saddam authorised preparations for a new offensive from the Fish Lake Line; although he reluctantly accepted it would need a month's preparation.

For Iran's SOHQ the loss of the peninsula was especially alarming because it was soon obvious it would face a major new blow which it had little chance of warding off. Opposite the northern end of the Fish Lake Line there remained a flooded area fed by the waters of the Hawizah Marshes, and controlled by the River Arayedh which ran southeast from its southern point into the Karun watershed. This shielded the northern part of SOHQ's front but Karbala-8 had left the Pasdaran in the southern part holding a salient, like a chicken awaiting the axe, with the tip of this salient projecting beyond the southern edge of the Fish Lake into the enemy lines. This tip was exposed to fire not only from an arc around the western edge of the salient but also, like the rest of the salient, from across the Shatt. The experience of the Faw Peninsula had demonstrated that this fire against the forward defences would be overwhelming.

Shifting the Schwerpunkt

If Iran was to retain its bridgehead within southern Iraq, this tip of the salient had to be either abandoned completely or held as a lightly manned breakwater whose garrison would be adequate to prevent its loss to a surprise attack. The clerics in Tehran, and the Pasdaran political allies, obstinately refused to do either and insisted instead the salient be held in force: the Shia martyrdom ethic ensured it would be a huge tomb. Behind the berm-lined salient were a succession of small rivers on whose eastern bank the defenders had raised more berms to replace the levelled Iraqi ones on the western side. SOHQ's only hope was the defensive system between the rivers Jasim and al-Duaiji – which ran five kilometres from the southern edge of the Fish Lake to the Shatt – to provide the illusion of defence in depth. This could be approached through ground usually flooded and always covered in dense barbed wire entanglements and minefields.[1]

The berms were supplemented by trenches and dugouts and linked by an extensive network of communication trenches, but the whole defensive system was only a kilometre or two deep. It could not be outflanked due to Iraqi-made inundations coming from the southern part of the Fish Lake and stretching to, and across, the international border. However, this flooded area also restricted access to the defences to the ground around Basra–Khorramshahr highway, which could be interdicted by artillery from across the Shatt. To the north lay the impregnable Iraqi defences, the double line of battalion strongpoints which acted like a balcony facing more berm lines, studded with ramps for MBTs, beyond which the attacker could strike westwards across firm ground which was ideal for armoured and mechanised forces.

Manning these defences was more difficult because from mid-1987, 11 of the 19 Pasdaran divisions used in the Karbala offensives, together with 18th al-Ghadir Infantry Brigade – a total of 80,000 men – had been sent north for Val Fajr-10 around Halabja.[2] Nor was the defence helped by a 10day amphibious exercise codenamed Zulfikar-3 (the sword of the Iman Ali), which had begun on 21 May, to demonstrate that Iran remained a significant naval power – but involved an airborne brigade and other troops who might have acted as a reserve, and elements of the dwindling IRIAF.

Controlled by the headquarters of the Task Force Karbala, the defences consisted of two IRIA divisions (see Table 20 for order of battle), with three divisions and three brigades of Pasdaran.[3] Facing III Corps were 2nd Brigade/21st Infantry

One of the few 155mm M109 howitzers still operated by the 33rd Artillery Group IRIA as of 1987–1988. (E.S. collection)

Division IRIA and 12th 'Qa'em-e Mohamad' Mechanised Division IRGC, and the reinforced 3rd Brigade/92nd Division, while facing the Guards was the 14th 'Imam Hossein' Division and a mechanised brigade of 30th 'Beit-ol-Moghaddas' Division, reinforced by elements of two Pasdaran infantry brigades. The Iranians had two infantry battalions in the salient, seven on the River Jassim and another seven on River Duaiji. In the rear, straggling across the border, were two Pasdaran infantry brigades (minus battalions with 'Imam Hossein') and a mechanised brigade of the IRGC. The remainder of Iranian forces in this area consisted of two formations: the 1st Brigade/92nd Division (which was on the border around Shalamcheh with the remainder of 'Beit-ol-Moghaddas'), and the battered 8th Val Fajr Division IRGC, still recovering from the hammering on the Faw Peninsula. Other infantry elements totalled about 10 battalions. These forces were supported by three IRIA and Pasdaran artillery groups – including a battalion of Brazilian Astros MLRS – with a total of 130 guns (30 self-propelled), and some 50 MLRS augmented by six heavy mortar batteries. The air defence brigade had several batteries of 30mm guns; there was a substantial engineer force of 20,000 men; and a Pasdaran chemical decontamination brigade brought the total strength to 90,000. A total of about 280 MBTs was available, about half of which were serviceable, but the poorly-trained Pasdaran crews would be no match for Iraqi armoured brigades.

Operation 'Tawakkalna ala Allah (1)'

The Iraqi staff, therefore, could be confident of success as they began planning what became Operation Tawakkalna ala Allah.[4] As with 'Ramadan Mubarak' initial planning was conducted by the local command, with Lieutenant General Salah Aboud Mahmoud's (Aboud) III Corps given the go-ahead on 30 April to eliminate the threat which had been aimed at Basra for the past six years. Even as the last Iranian stragglers on the Faw Peninsula were being rounded up Aboud took the first steps by ordering the northern part of the Fish Lake to be drained dry.[5]

The planners could be fairly certain of favourable weather, indeed after April 26 there was no significant rain in the region and the temperature steadily rose from the mid-30s Centigrade at the beginning of May to the 40s by the middle of the month.[6] Together with the Iranian-built Muqdad Canal, designed to drain the Fish Lake and the former inundated areas to the southeast, the former Karbala-5 battlefield and Iranian territory to the east was dried up and much became a mine-ridden man-made wilderness of rusting barbed wire entanglements on metal posts. It also made it easier to move the mechanised formations in which Iraq had absolute superiority: the area east of the lake is flat and dusty. The sun posed a logistical problem for both sides as high salinity levels in the ground water meant large amounts of potable water had to be shipped in.

Aboud had had two armoured divisions, two mechanised divisions and seven infantry divisions, but needed a mechanised division and five infantry divisions to garrison the strongpoints to secure the flanks and the jump-off positions. His plan was based upon a frontal assault spearheaded by Rawi's Guards Corps which would strike along the Basra–Khorramshahr highway to take Shalamcheh as well as Twaila Island on the northern Shatt. His corps would strike eastwards towards the Ahvaz–Khorramshahr road shielding Rawi's northern flank from the enemy around the Zayed (also Zaid or Zayd) Salient. Work progressed rapidly, possibly based upon a III Corps contingency plan, and by 10 May Saddam could issue a directive setting Y-Day for 1 June.[7]

Five Guards divisions, with some 70,000 men, left the Faw Peninsula and assembled east of Basra between 10–17 May (for complete order of battle during this operation, see Table 20), while Rawi's staff began detailed planning. He had two armoured, one infantry and one special forces divisions, which had all been 'blooded' on the Faw Peninsula. Correspondingly, he decided to deploy the full force: Rawi's attack would begin on a two-division, 11-brigade, front. Medina (reinforced by 12th Republican Guards Commando Brigade) would strike the salient on his right while Baghdad (reinforced by 16th Republican Guards Special Forces Brigade) on the left would cross the southern Fish Lake. Once they had broken through, Hammurabi would exploit the success with 17th Republican Guards Armoured and 15th Republican Guards Mechanised Brigades. Khalil's Nebuchadnezzar Republican Guards Infantry Division would again act as reserve while Mustafa Hanoush's 26th Republican Guards Naval Commando Brigade would spearhead an amphibious operation to regain Twaila Islands – with commandos and infantry units including Khalil's 22nd Republican Guards Infantry Brigade.

Aboud's plan was based upon a similar two-pronged attack organised into three phases, using two battle-hardened divisions with 11 brigades. In the first phase a commando and an infantry brigade would cross the drained Fish Lake and establish a bridgehead from which Mahmoud Faizy would then launch his two mechanised brigades in echelon to sweep eastward to the frontier, eventually stopping on the middle River Arayedh. On the left, Tahir, reinforced by one of Mahmoud Faizy's mechanised brigades, would also establish a bridgehead on the eastern bank of the Fish Lake using an infantry brigade of 8th Infantry Division; from this an armoured and a mechanised brigade would sweep through the area north of the Muqdad Canal to the frontier in the second phase. The success would be consolidated by eight brigades of the 8th Infantry Division and the 11th Infantry Division under Brigadiers Natiq Shaker and Sami Abbas respectively; Mahmoud Faizy and Tahir would establish a covering bridgehead in Iran as far east as Shalamcheh in the third phase using the River Arayedh to shield his left.

The Iraqis had only 20 days to transfer troops and equipment, expand ammunition and supply dumps, prepare for the amphibious assault and ensure detailed reconnaissance of the enemy positions. Aboud had to organise much of the preparatory work including new approach roads to the western bank of the Fish Lake, firing positions for two tank battalions of 8th and 11th Infantry Divisions (for direct fire support) and strong points so that armoured and mechanised brigades could do the same. The staffs made extensive use of sandtray models to plan their operations and to brief subordinates while each corps created a full-scale replica of the defences upon which the troops could practise their assault both day and night.

Advance by Fire

The assault force consisted of 136,500 men with 680 MBTs, supported by a powerful artillery train.[8] Aboud would be supported by 25 artillery battalions (450 tubes), including two MLRS battalions (36 BM-21s each with 40 tubes) and 12 heavy mortar batteries (72 120mm mortars), and two regiments of FROG surface-to-surface missiles. Aboud augmented this firepower by reorganising the brigade mortar companies into Mortar Nodes, deployed some 200 metres apart. These 750 82mm tubes on a four-kilometre front received 200 bombs per platoon for this task, and were to provide support for the assault troops for 45 minutes just before S-Hour. Afterwards, they were to fire into the enemy rear until the infantry had taken the positions whereupon they would re-join their brigades. Rawi's troops would be supported by 28 artillery battalions (504 tubes), some firing from across the Shatt, including some MLRS batteries and a FROG battalion, although the Astros batteries were not used because they had expended almost all their ammunition.

Furthermore, each corps had two organic engineer battalions and each division had an engineer battalion, while Rawi also received an extra bridging battalion and, like the Iranians in the Hawizah Marshes, sections of foam were available to create lightweight bridges. The amphibious assault would use 134 fibreglass and metal boats, capable of carrying some 1,350 men, 55 rubber dinghies carrying 350 men, and would be supported by 11 GSP ferries and 12 PTS amphibious transporters. There would again be extensive use of chemical weapons and each corps had a chemical defence company with Soviet DDA-53 or DDA-66 decontamination trucks for clothing, ARS-12 or ARS-14 area decontamination vehicles and BRDM-2RKh chemical reconnaissance vehicles.[9]

The offensive was preceded in early May by intense aerial preparation: after deploying two wings with 60 fighter-bombers at al-Kut and Ali Ibn Abu Talib ABs, the IrAF flew 308 attack sorties on 24 May 1988 alone – which the IRIAF could counter with only about a dozen.

Maskirovka

These attacks and obvious enemy preparations meant the Iranians could view the coming days with foreboding. However, they were uncertain whether or not the enemy meant to strike east towards the border or north into the Hawizah Marshes. To increase their confusion the Iraqi Army staff staged diversions on other fronts, while Saddam brought Y-Day forward to 26 May 1988, and pushed S-Hour back three hours from the usual 06:30 to 09:30, by which time the enemy would have stood down with many men assigned to work parties. The spur-of-the-moment decision was apparently because he had convinced himself the enemy had divined his plans after SIGINT reported plans to reinforce the southern positions.[10]

Saddam managed to confuse not only the enemy but his own generals too. In

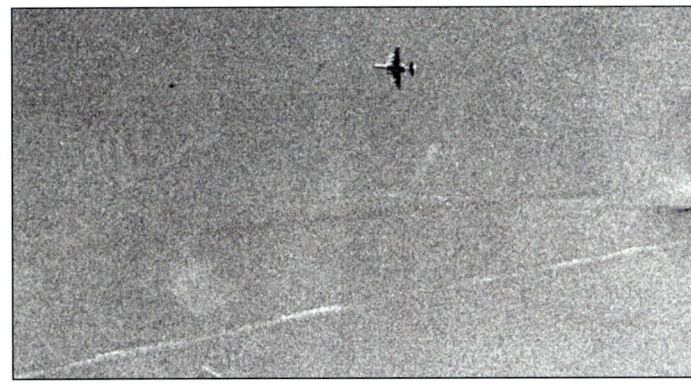

Operation Tawakkalna ala Allah (1) saw the first combat deployment of the Sukhoi Su-25 in the environment for which this type was originally designed: provision of close air support for conventional mechanised formations on the advance. This Iraqi Su-25 was narrowly missed by an Iranian MANPAD. (Farzin Nadimi collection)

As usual during the later stages of the Iran-Iraq War, the Iraqi artillery played a dominant role in Operation Tawakkalna ala Allah. The crew of this gun was photographed just seconds before opening fire. (Albert Grandolini collection)

Iranian troops scrambling for cover, as medics run to assist the injured, while their positions are blanketed by Iraqi artillery fire. (Farzin Nadimi collection)

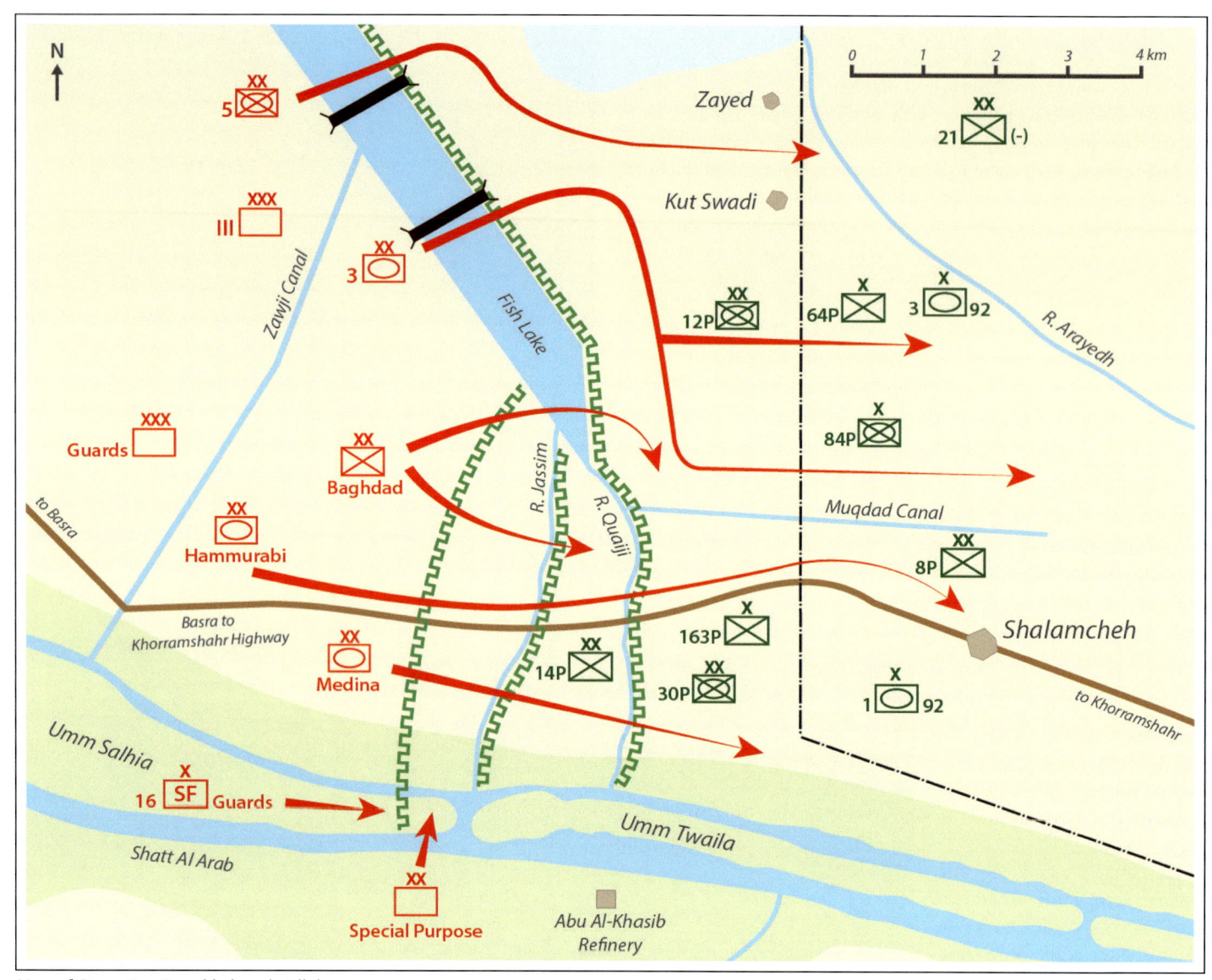

MIDDLE EAST@WAR SERIES SPECIAL #1: THE IRAN-IRAQ WAR

Map of Operation Tawakkalna ala Allah.

the early afternoon of 24 May Rawi was summoned to a meeting of the Advanced General Command Headquarters to discuss final arrangements. Then, at 20:00 Operations Chief Hussein Rashid and Planning Chief Qader flew in by helicopter from Baghdad to inform him that Saddam had decided to change the timings. Aboud was not informed until 01:00 on 25 May, although he may have had a hint earlier because during the afternoon he ordered the 3rd IrAAC Wing to intensify reconnaissance.

The combination of the dry season and Iraqi shelling covered most of the battlefield with immense clouds of dust and smoke, helping to conceal, in this photograph, an advancing Iraqi infantry assault. (Farzin Nadimi collection)

A fire mission being conducted by an Iranian 175mm M107 self-propelled howitzer. By 1988, far too few of such artillery pieces were left in operational condition to match the Iraqi artillery. (via E.S.)

A still from a video showing a T-72 of the Republican Guard advancing during Operation Tawakkalna ala Allah (1). (Tom Cooper collection)

T-72s represented the backbone of the armoured units of the Republican Guards and led most of its offensives in 1988. This example was captured on a video during an advance on Shalamcheh. (Tom Cooper collection)

Despite the last-minute chaos, the bombardment began on schedule at 09:30 on 25 May and achieved total surprise. The IrAF and the IrAAC began striking behind the lines, the former deploying large numbers of brand-new Sukhoi Su-25K ground-attack aircraft for the first time. The bombardment was controlled by the corps artillery brigades with a dedicated communications network extending down to forward observers at company level. At corps and division level were gun battalions, some with ballistic computers to help make rapid adjustments in targeting or weight of fire, as well as MLRS battalions, all ready to provide general fire support.

In its initial bombardment the artillery sought to saturate Iranian headquarters, command posts (from battalion to division level), artillery and air defence positions, and engineer units, while MLRS also targeted supply dumps, communication choke points and operational level reserves. Multiple FROG missiles were fired at key enemy headquarters. This barrage of high intensity was maintained until the assault units crossed their jump-off lines and began sweeping into the enemy rear to disrupt the movement of reserves.[11]

While the operational level onslaught was already going on, artillery battalions assigned to specific brigades opened fire at Iranian anti-armour positions and observation posts, tank and mortar positions, minefields, and reserves. Once all targets had been engaged the brigade commander authorised support of neighbouring units. The Iraqi gunners had grown in skill in delivering massive fire, in counterbattery capabilities and in shifting fire. By contrast only the IRIA possessed the skills for these tasks but lacked the materials, while Iranian target acquisition and attack had been eroded and often relied upon 'blind fire' techniques or striking potential targets selected from a map.[12]

Infantry Leading

Exposed to the hail of fire, the Iranians sought cover in their trenches, foxholes and dugouts. Before long, an ominous melon smell warned them of chemical weapons, including nerve agents, which the Iraqis used extensively. Forward positions were hit by cyanide and nerve agents that worked quickly – but dispersed quickly too. Rear areas were hit by slower-dispersing mustard gas to prevent the enemy forming up for a counterattack. Most of the chemicals were delivered by BM-21s (their warheads contained a small amount of explosive and three plastic bottles containing 8–12 kilograms of chemical agents that could be mixed and matched). Sarin ('Agent GB') was delivered by 120mm mortars, but also by artillery pieces of 130mm, 152mm, and 155mm calibre; 130mm and 155mm artillery shells were used to deploy mustard gas; while Agent GF was delivered by 152mm and 155mm shells. Under threat, the Iranians scrambled to use their atropine injectors and donned gas masks, but with temperatures reaching up to 41°C, these proved too hot to wear for any length of time.

Meanwhile, Iraqi mine-clearing teams – deployed already the previous evening – were clearing lanes for the infantry, enabling rifle units to move forward, followed by engineers that widened the lanes for tanks. Medina Division advanced in battalion-sized, all-armoured battlegroups which included mine-clearing tanks and AVLBs. The threat to the armoured fists from anti-armour missiles remained a concern and they had top priority for direct support fire. However, the missile threat was mitigated by the difficulties of destroying MBTs which proved very robust: already the October 1973 Arab-Israeli War demonstrated that success depended less upon accuracy and more upon high rates of fire. Iranian ground-based TOW teams often had to spend four missiles to destroy a tank; Iraqi teams regularly required 6–8 Milan or HOTs, while teams equipped with Soviet-made AT-3 Saggers required up to 30 missiles for one kill.[13] To decrease this threat, the Iraqis let their infantry and commandos lead the attack with MBTs and IFVs providing fire support from the flank and the rear.

Intensive bombardment raised immense clouds of smoke and dust. These were further enhanced by smoke screens to conceal the infantry while this was advancing through the wire and over the berms, and began destroying forward Iranian positions.[14]

In the north, infantry of the III Corps required 30 minutes to cross the Fish Lake and establish bridgeheads around the exits of two causeways. Both were then reinforced by GSP ferries, before the engineers threw bridges across the lake and started clearing obstacles to allow the armoured forces to cross with little incident, regroup on the eastern side of the lake and push towards the frontier. Mahmoud Faizy drove south-eastwards while Tahir helped to clear the eastern bank and then pushed into the Pentangle both to threaten the Diaiji defences and to support Sattar's Hammurabi Division.

Hammash's Medina Division found most of the defenders of the salient dead or stunned, and thus quickly swept south of the Fish Lake to take the Jassim defences by 10:42; while Sattar's Hammurabi Division was brought up and by 11:07 its 17th Republican Guards Armoured Brigade had punched a 500-metre breach through the enemy lines. At 12:50 the Baghdad and Medina Divisions began to push into the Duaiji defences while Sattar pressed on and broke through the last defensive system at 13:25. He then drove to the border and joined Tahir to envelop the enemy in between. The dry ground, and a considerable dose of professionalism in combined-arms operations, enabled the Iraqis to advance fast, although – reportedly – at least one Iraqi armoured unit ran into major problems while advancing without adequate infantry support.[15]

Pasdaran on the Run

The Iranians initially fought well, inflicted 'significant' casualties, and even launched several counterattacks and took some prisoners. However, the Iraqis reacted with additional artillery barrages and emergency CAS provided by helicopters, quickly suppressing most resistance. Therefore, only one of the Iranian counterattacks north of the formerly inundated area briefly halted the Iraqis before the IRGC started to crack: artillery barrages and chemical weapons had killed or incapacitated many of the defenders, and demoralised the rest. Attempts at a fighting retreat thus quickly dissolved into a rout, during which Pasdaran commanders showed a great predilection to commandeer vehicles and speed their way to safety.

With the defence dissolving Tahir and Sattar pushed eastwards to the frontier, which they crossed at 14:45, then went on to take the Iranian border town of Shalamcheh. However, when Hammurabi pushed reconnaissance forces beyond the frontier towards Khorramshahr fierce resistance forced them to return.

Meanwhile, the Medina's 16th Special Forces Brigade of the Republican Guards worked its way along the Shatt's northern islands to take Twaila Island, while SEALS from the 26th Naval Commando Brigade Republican Guards secured bridgeheads. Reinforcements were initially ferried across the Shatt by boats and barges, some carrying MBTs and APCs, until engineers threw a pontoon bridge across by 15:00. Supported by the 16th and 22nd Brigades of the Republican Guards, the naval commandos quickly overwhelmed the defenders and by 18:00 all the islands had been recaptured to conclude 'Tawakalna ala Allah' – within just eight and a half hours instead of the anticipated 28. Iraqi casualties remain uncertain but probably included no more than 3,000, although they certainly suffered significant material losses; one US military attaché that witnessed this operation from the rear counted about 70 knocked out Iraqi AFVs, including T-72 MBTs, being towed to the rear after the offensive.[16]

The offensive was a disaster for Iran, the military of which lost up to 10 percent of its heavy equipment – including about 100 MBTs and 150 guns. However, Iraqi claims of inflicting 400,000 casualties were wildly exaggerated: the actual figure was closer to about 6,000, including a few prisoners.

Khomeini remained defiant. On 28 May 1988, he addressed the new Majlis (elected on 8 April) and appealed to his troops stating their losses did not matter for when they '...began treading this holy path, they have lost nothing to be worried about, nor have they suffered any loss of which they should repent…. The outcome of the Iraqimposed war will be determined on the battlefields, not through negotiations.'[17]

Nevertheless, damage was already caused. Recruiting reportedly dropped by 70 percent, and there were protest rallies which the IRGC had to suppress. Eventually, even Khomenei was forced to recognise that the war was lost and a political solution inevitable. In this regard, he feared the reaction of the Pasdaran and hard-line clerics, and thus needed a lightening-rod: as Khomeini's representative in the SDC, Rafsanjani had been 'de facto commander-in-chief', but on 2 June 1988, Khomeini ratified this formally, appointing him officially as the commander-in-chief of all Iranian armed forces. However, the terminally ill Ayatollah was so much out of touch with reality, that he demanded Rafsanjani end the war by military means within six months.

Even if unaware of there being no chance of an Iranian victory before this appointment, Rafsanjani was no fool. As soon as he learned the truth, he concluded that his primary task would be to persuade Khomeini to accept a diplomatic solution. In the meantime, he publicly recognised that it would take three or four months to reorganise and regroup Iranian forces and created a unified command under his supervision. While considering – but rejecting – a plan to merge the IRIA with the IRGC, he was able to side-line Rezai – with help from Shabazi, who was not only a fully trained staff officer, but also a staunch Khomeini loyalist with close links to the IRGC.[18]

Recovering the Majnoons

With everybody in Tehran knowing that Khomeini was about to die, most of the top Iranian clergy and politicians began jockeying for position, and nobody was eager to become associated with another bloody and ultimately futile offensive. The only area where Iran was still able to exercise pressure upon Iraq was in the north.

The massive Iraqi deployment of chemical weapons resulted in heavy casualties for Pasdaran and Basiji units in 1986–1988. This in turn caused the recruitment of Iranian volunteers to drop by 70 percent, denying the IRGC even the ability to provide effective defences on the southern front. This photograph shows a captured Iraqi T-55 being used by Iranian clergy during one of the recruiting drives. (Photo by Mamhoud-Reza Kalari)

PART I: IRANIAN BURNOUT

Jeep-mounted 106mm M40 recoilless guns were often the only means of fire-support for lightly armed Pasdaran and Basiji. (Photo by E.S.)

An AH-1J passing low over Iranian positions in the Shalamcheh area in May 1988. (Albert Grandolini collection)

Khairallah fully supported a follow-on attack upon North Majnoon, but he did not anticipate it would be practical for another three months. Inpatient, Saddam then ordered IV, VI, and III Corps, and the Republican Guards to retake the islands, while the I Special Corps was to launch a diversion on the central front.

Hussein Rashid was enthusiastic, especially as work on draining the Hawizah Marshes meant armour could be moved further forward. Moreover, the enemy had withdrawn their artillery from the Majnoon Islands and all thought that Shabazi's inexperience would help exploit recent successes.[23]

On 1 June 1988, the AFGC met again, and the corps commanders were informed that the next offensive would be to recover the Majnoon Islands on or about 25 June. The Guards would strike the islands, supported by VI Corps, while III Corps would encircle the enemy east of the marshes. Anticipating the war to last for another 18 months, on 5 June 1988 Saddam wrote to Khazraji, advising him that the decision had been made to go-ahead with the Majnoon offensive so that Iraq could exploit its recent successes before the enemy could interfere. He demanded intensified reconnaissance and a comprehensive electronic warfare plan but would include artillery fire to erode enemy strength.[24] Detailed planning for what became Operation Tawakkalna ala Allah 2 began on 12 June 1988. However, its execution was then disrupted by what became the final Iranian offensive of this war.

Correspondingly, the JCS assembled four IRIA divisions and 15 IRGC divisions, together with 17 brigades of Pasdaran and Basiji – a total of some 220,000 men – between Mahabad and Kermanshah.[19]

The Iraqis recognised this threat and a concern over the northern front was clearly expressed when Saddam chaired a meeting of the AFGC on 26 May 1988. Chief-of-Staff Khazraji and his Operations Chief, Hussain Rashid, were especially worried that only half of Iraq's infantry – 64 brigades (including commandos) – were with I and V Corps in the north. Both corps commanders were seeking reinforcements, including up to three Guards divisions, but Saddam was reluctant to strip the southern front.[20] On the other hand, he was surprised at the enemy staff's failure to transfer troops from the north to the south along Iran's poor railroad network, while optimistic about the prospect of defensive operations in the north, and concluded that the despatch of four or eight divisions would be no guarantee for a major success. Commenting that this would force the southern front upon the defensive, and anxious to exploit the success of operations Ramadan Mubarak and Tawakkalna alla Allah, Saddam concluded that striking in the Majnoon Islands was a preferable option.[21] Hussein Rashid agreed with this idea, commenting that the VI Corps – then under Major General Yaljin Omar Adil – had already drafted a plan for securing South Majnoon but had been told to wait until the northern front had settled down.[22]

Iran's Lame Response: Operation Beit-olMogaddas-7

Rafsanjani's first weeks as Commander-in-Chief of the Islamic Republic's armed forces were a nightmare, for his troops faced a trial as terrible as that of September 1980. Indeed, the fear that those events would be repeated was omnipresent in the minds of many civilian and military leaders in Tehran.

The southern front was in the biggest crisis since the heady days of 1982, with powerful, combat-hardened Iraqi forces now poised to drive deep into Khuzestan Province. The defenders were battered and demoralised, and lacking troops and equipment. Realising the strategic peril, Rafsanjani authorised the stripping of the northern front and about a dozen divisions had begun the long, slow, trip; first eastwards to Tehran then southwards over the poor transport network. Even by the end of the Iran-Iraq War, most units were still in central Iran.

MIDDLE EAST@WAR SERIES SPECIAL #1: THE IRAN-IRAQ WAR

Unable to permit the enemy to threaten the oilfields of Khuzestan again, Rafsanjani was enough of a realist to recognise he lacked the material strength to push the Iraqis back to the Fish Lake. Yet, as he observed to a press conference on 14 June 1988, that the enemy had now advanced beyond the Fish Lake Line and was exposed. Reconnaissance by Pasdaran and – probably – IRIA special forces showed the armed and mechanised spearhead of Tawakkalna ala Allah had been withdrawn and infantry divisions were throwing up defences along the frontier and around Shalamcheh. Whether or not Rafsanjani knew the Guard Corps was being transferred to the southern banks of the Hawr al Hawizah is unknown, but he did recognise a small window of opportunity had opened to catch the enemy off guard. He hoped to buy time as the Iranian Foreign Ministry sought a diplomatic solution.

'The Homeland is in Danger' was a slogan which many a demoralised military and clerical leader had hoped would spur the demoralised troops to further heroic sacrifice. However, despite the energetic efforts by the imams, the troops were all too well aware that the war was lost. In addition to Iraqi chemical weapons, morale was also affected by the weather; during May the temperature steadily rose into the mid-40s centigrade, reaching 49° on 13 June. This was especially trying for infantrymen whose canteens held only enough water for a couple of hours and, with fighting likely to take place under a scorching sun, medical advice was being given to prevent the men falling prey to heatstroke, including 'use your headscarves to prevent direct sunlight on your heads and faces'.[25]

For a fortnight SOHQ frantically reorganised its units and rushed down supplies – together with whatever reinforcements it could lay its hand on – usually in trucks driving through the night without headlights. Some 70 artillery pieces, and a few battalions in replacements and reinforcements reached the front, but the IRIAF meanwhile was down to a point where it could only provide eight fighter-bombers and its SAM-sites to provide support.[26]

Ya Aba Abdellah!

The Iranian troops moved out at dusk of 12 June 1988, following receipt of the code-phrase 'Ya Aba Abdellah'. Dubbed Operation Beit l-Moqaddas-7 – in memory of the great victory of April-May 1982 – their assault began at 23:30, with an attempt by four understrength IRGC divisions and one armoured brigade (some 20,000 troops and 160 MBTs in total) along a 15-kilometre frontline around Kut Swadi.

An RPG-team of the IRGC in action against advancing Iraqis. (Farzin Nadimi collection)

A column of BMP-1s carrying Pasdaran towards the forward operational area at dusk on 12 June 1988. (Albert Grandolini collection)

Their assault was supported by 120mm mortars, some 175 artillery tubes, and 22 or 23 attack sorties by the IRIAF.[27]

The area that came under attack was referred to by the CIA as 'The Step': it was occupied by the 8th, 11th, and 19th Infantry Divisions of the Iraqi Army – some 50,000 veterans of defensive successes. These held newly constructed defences that lacked the depth and the combination of minefields and barbed wire that shielded the Fish Lake defences. There are strong indications that their garrisons had been a 'little lax' following recent victories perhaps even 'demob happy'. Furthermore, it is certain that the Iraqi intelligence failed to obtain enough information to warn the defenders – perhaps because most of the attacking formations relied on landlines and couriers, rather than radio communications.

The first inkling of trouble was a succession of reports from Brigadier Majid Mahmud Hussein's 19th Infantry Division at 21:30 that enemy truck convoys were driving into positions in Iran beyond artillery range. Just 105 minutes later, at 23:15, the short Iranian bombardment began and soon many forward positions of Hussein and his northern neighbour, Brigadier Natiq Shaker's 8th Infantry Division, were overrun. The Pasdaran briefly regained their old offensive spirit to drive 9–10 kilometres into the Iraqi line around Kut Swadi, inflicting heavy casualties – including destruction of 30 MBTs and the capture of about 700 prisoners. However, the Iraqis were not cowed.

III Corps commander Aboud ordered the remaining strongpoints to hold out even if encircled, and quickly alerted his gunners. Although many batteries had been withdrawn for training and had to be ordered to re-join their units, a mass of artillery units moved to the threatened section of the frontline. One saving grace for the Iraqis was that the northern part of the Fish Lake Line – the double line of strongpoints – was still manned as a jump-off line for Tawakkalna ala Allah 2. This ensured defence in depth while other units were training around the Fish Lake. Furthermore, assembly of Rawi's corps near the strongpoint line in anticipation of Tawakkalna ala Allah-2 meant that first his batteries and then his brigades were available to respond to Baghdad's demand for a counteroffensive.

Iraqi Counterattack

Within hours, Aboud assembled a force of 10 brigades, totalling 45,500 troops and 315 MBTs, including Tahir's 3rd Armoured Division (6th, 12th Armoured, 8th Mechanised Brigade); Mahmoud Faizy's 5th Mechanised Division (26th Armoured, 15th, 20th Mechanised Brigades); and Brigadier Sami Abbas' 11th Infantry Division (23rd, 45th, 47th, 501st Infantry Brigades). These troops were originally to spearhead a counteroffensive he planned to launch at noon. However, his subordinates began launching counterattacks and contained the threat already by 08:00. Abbas was ordered to use one brigade to reinforce 8th Division's beleaguered strongpoints then struck around Bubyan at 05:00 to begin retaking the lost northern positions, secure the eastern bank of the Fish Lake and allow batteries to deploy there. There was little impediment to Iraqi movement for the IRIAF provided only token support: a lone dawn strike package of eight aircraft with iron bombs was nearly drowned in a combination of about a dozen Iraqi interceptors and dozens of SAMs. Two aircraft were shot down and two others badly damaged. By contrast, most of the 170 IrAF and 240 IrAAC sorties flown on 13 June encountered next to no resistance from Iranian air defences.

As the counterattacks were launched, Aboud completed his planning. Tahir would strike across the Fish Lake – as in Tawakkalna ala Allah 1 – while Mahmud Faizi would strike eastwards on the southern flank towards Kut Swadi and the Muqdad Canal. Natiq Shaker's 8th Infantry Division (reinforced by Abbas' infantry brigade, 65th SF Brigade and 34th Armoured Brigade from 1st Mechanised Division) was to regain the rest of its lost positions around Bubyan. Khudayyir's 6th Armoured Division and Thamir Sultan's 1st Mechanised Division would remain in reserve. Throughout the morning Iraqi artillery fire pounded the enemy, inflicting heavy casualties on troops who were often in exposed positions in the desert, and Iraqi SIGINT began picking up a growing stream of pleas for supplies and reinforcements.

Aboud arrived at Majid Mahmud Hussein's 19th Division's headquarters to use it as a forward command post. Meanwhile, Saddam arrived at III Corps headquarters at 10:00 – with most of the Iraqi Army's senior command team to look over his shoulder – concerned that the gains of Tawakkalna ala Allah might be lost, and that Tawakkalna ala Allah-2, might have to be cancelled. Aboud quickly reassured him and said that the lost ground would be retaken by his counteroffensive which would start in less than two hours. Saddam was not totally convinced and took out insurance by alerting Rawi to be ready to launch a counteroffensive by dusk if Aboud's attack failed.

The Pasdaran were well aware of Aboud's preparations, which were completed by 11:30. One of them, Ahmad Dehqan, wrote in his diary: 'I have a bad feeling. I think something bad is going to happen tonight. Everybody shares the same feeling. Qasem has put his head on his knees at a dugout. I want to say something, but change my mind...'[28]

Meanwhile, the IrAF and the IrAAC were roaming the skies: most of the 213 sorties flown by the air force, and 391 by helicopters, between 14 and 15 June 1988 were undertaken over this battlefield. They de facto blocked any kind of Iranian movement during daylight hours, destroyed vital supplies of ammunition and water, and debilitated the attackers' ability to fight. At 11:30, about 360 Iraqi artillery pieces and 760 mortars opened the preparatory bombardment as the armoured brigades moved out followed by the infantry both in armoured vehicles and on foot. The Iraqis quickly closed with the enemy and there was fierce fighting as the cracked-lipped Pasdaran defenders rapidly ran out first of anti-armour missiles and then of RPG rounds. This allowed the tanks and troop carriers to get ever closer and attack from the flanks, gradually – but with increasing speed – pushing the Pasdaran back towards the Iraqi frontier.

By 16:30, it was all over, and the surviving Iranians were back on their start lines.

Guards in the Flank

Meanwhile, the Republican Guards Corps had swung around to face the threat and at 16:30 Rawi's Chief-of-Staff, Ismael, telephoned Aboud to say that the corps was ready to join the advance to the international frontier and would attack at 17:00. Aboud informed him that his troops were already on the frontier, but that he was willing to withdraw them and allow the Guards to retake the frontier positions provided there was a 30-minute delay so he could withdraw his men and avoid friendly fire.

When Saddam learned of this he was delighted both at the selflessness of the III Corps commander and the close degree of cooperation between the Army and the Guards. He ordered Rawi to place his forces under III Corps – the only occasion ever that the Guards came under Army command. The Guards commander drove to 19th Division headquarters but still sought a role. Aboud

Iraqi troops inspecting the bodies of fallen Pasdaran found on one of the Majnoon Islands after they were recaptured. (via S.S.)

tactfully convinced him there was no need and he could return to the reserve. At 18:00 Aboud signed off the counteroffensive and soon received a congratulatory telephone call from Saddam.

Once Beit al-Moqaddas-7 was over, the Iranians talked-up the result claiming to have inflicted 18,000 casualties (the figure was probably 2,500) and taken up to 2,100 prisoners (it was probably fewer than 1,000) and described it as 'the first sweet fruit' of Rafsanjani's appointment. The new Iranian commander-in-chief exploited the opportunity to claim he planned more extensive operations and appropriate responses to the recent Iraqi successes.[29] In reality, the Iranians lost about 4,000 troops – or a quarter of their strength – and had achieved nothing except to further weaken their forces. A CIA report from June 18 noted:

> The concentration of (Iraqi) armour in the marsh area is the largest since the battle of Kursk in 1943 between German and Soviet armies. Iraq can launch an offensive at any time; Iranian forces are in a poor position to defend against an attack out of the 'step' area particularly if Iraq, as in recent battles, uses extensive artillery and chemical bombardment.[30]

17
END GAME

With the Iranian counteroffensive crushed, detailed planning and preparations for Tawakkalna ala Allah-2 were renewed on 12 June 1988. They involved only nine meetings, each chaired by Saddam, with the agreed outline developed into detailed plans involving the various commands, the IrAAC, and the air commands, and completed by 15 June.

The objective was to regain the last large bloc of territory still in enemy hands, the economically important Majnoon Islands in the Hawizah Marshes, which one Iraqi journalist described thus 'Vast areas of water stretch as far as the eye can see... recurring dust storms make visibility difficult'.

Waters of the southern marshes were usually one-and-a-half metres deep, while in the north they usually evaporated under the summer sun. The Iranians had created a lake on the eastern edge of the marshes to help flood Iraqi territory and impede an assault upon the Majnoons; while the Iraqis had begun extensive drainage work to reduce the cover provided by the reed banks to enemy operations, and to deprive deserters and their supporters of their marshy sanctuary. They also began digging a drainage ditch, the 30-metre-wide Qutaiba Canal, along the frontier which also augmented III Corps' forward defences and helped to drain the flooded area. However, high levels in the rivers feeding the marshes in 1988 had meant water seeped along the edges of the marshes, leaving a strip of boggy ground some 3.5 kilometres from the edge, to hinder the assembly and movement of armoured/mechanised forces.

Preparing to Retake the Majnoons

The Iraqi plan envisaged Rawi's Guards Corps sweeping through the Majnoons from south to north, using powerful artillery preparation and protective fire. It was a difficult task for, despite extensive work to drain the marshes and the summer sun evaporating the waters, the attackers still had to advance across deep, reed-lined and mine-infested waters which required an amphibious element to the assault. This drive would be supported by a heliborne landing of a special forces battalion behind the enemy lines to isolate forward-deployed Iranians and maintain contact with VI Corps (Major General Yaljin Umar Adil). The latter was to strike east from al-Uzayr (also Uzair) for some 15 kilometres to isolate North Majnoon from the north as well as to divert enemy forces. Aboud's III Corps would shield Rawi's right by sweeping northwards from 'The Step' through Talaiyeh (also Shabhabi) and Kushk towards Hoveyzeh and the River Karun to prevent intervention by enemy forces around Ahvaz and Khorramshahr.[1]

Rawi's Republican Guards totalled about 61,000 men (see Table 20 for order of battle) in 13 brigades controlled by the Hammurabi Republican Guards Armoured Division, Medina Republican Guards Armoured Division, Baghdad Republican Guards Infantry Division, and Mustafa Hanoush's Guards Special Forces Division (with elements of the Nebucadnezar Republican Guards Infantry Division). While part of the assault would come from the Ghuzail – the exposed salt flats north of the Fish Lake strongpoint line, along the strip linking South Majnoon – most of it would be through, or over, the marshes. Once the island was secure a similar assault would be made upon North Majnoon. They would be supported in the west by VI Corps, with 18,000 men in six brigades under the control of the 25th Infantry Division.[2]

Rawi would be covered by Aboud's III Corps with 61,500 men, leaving 8th and 19th Infantry Divisions to cover the frontier, and strike northwest from 'The Step' with Thamir Sultan's 1st and Mahmud Faizi's 5th Mechanised Divisions, Tahir's 3rd Armoured Division and 6th Armoured Division (now under Brigadier Hussein Hassan Adday) and 41st Infantry Division. The original plan called for two brigades (infantry and commando) supported by an armoured brigade to establish a bridgehead where 'The Step' turned northward. This would be exploited by an understrength armoured

Iraqi troops resting after bringing one of their Czechoslovak-made OT-62 APCs up to the starting position for the next offensive towards the end of the war with Iran. (Albert Grandolini collection)

Table 20: Order of Battle for Operation Tawakkalna ala Allah 2, June 1988		
Corps	Division	Brigades
Iraq		
Republican Guards Corps	Corps Troops incl. Republican Guards Corps Artillery Brigade	
	Hammurabi Armoured Division Republican Guards	8th & 17th Armoured, 15th Mechanised Brigades Republican Guards Corps
	Medina Manarwah Armoured Division Republican Guards	2nd & 10th Armoured, 14th Mechanised Brigades Republican Guards Corps
	Baghdad Infantry Division Republican Guards	4th, 5th, 6th, 7th Infantry Brigades Republican Guards Corps
	Special Purposes Division Republican Guards	3rd & 16th Special Forces, 26th Naval Commando Brigade Republican Guards Corps
III Corps	Corps Troops, 1st & 2nd Commando Brigades of III Corps; 65th & 66th Special Forces Brigades; III Corps Artillery Brigade	
	1st Mechanised Division	34th Armoured, 1st & 27th Mechanised Brigades
	3rd Armoured Division	6th & 12th Armoured, 8th Mechanised Brigades
	5th Mechanised Division	26th Armoured, 15th & 20th Mechanised Brigades
	6th Armoured Division	16th & 30th Armoured, 25th Mechanised Brigades
	41st Infantry Division	82nd, 105th, 112th Infantry Brigades
	8th Infantry Division (defensive only)	
	19th Infantry Division (defensive only)	
	3rd Wing IrAAC	
	4th Wing IrAAC	
VI Corps	Corps troops; 1st & 2nd Commando Brigades of VI Corps; VI Corps Artillery Brigade	
	25th Infantry Division	87th, 103rd, 428th Infantry, 68th Special Forces Brigades
Iran		
	92nd Armoured Division IRIA	3 brigades
	21st Infantry Division IRIA	3 brigades
	8th Val Fajr Division IRGC	3 brigades
	12th Qa'em-e Mohammad Mechanised Division IRGC	3 brigades
	14th Imam Hossein Division IRGC	3 brigades
	19th Fajr Infantry Division IRGC	3 brigades; redeployed during offensive
	30th Beit-ol Moghaddas Armoured Division IRGC	1 mechanised brigade
	64th Suduqu Brigade IRGC	
	84th Zafar Mechanised Brigade IRGC	
	85th Hejrat Mechanised Brigade IRGC	
	163rd Fateme-ye Zahra Brigade IRGC	
	33rd Artillery Group IRIA	
	90th Khatam al-Anbiya Artillery Brigade IRGC	
	91st Hadid Artillery Brigade IRGC	
	2nd Combat Support Group IRIAA	

division and a mechanised division to drive 30 kilometres through Kushk to cut the Kushk–Jeghir ('Jofeyr') road and to seal the eastern bank of the marshes. The two divisions would then push beyond Jeghir and occupy ground to the east, to seize enemy supply dumps, while the mechanised division would send its armoured brigade to seize the eastern end of the Kheiber Bridge which led to North Majnoon.

The assault force thus consisted of a nominal 140,000 men with 850 MBTs, but due to the continuance of generous leave entitlements it was probably 126,000 men and 750 MBTs. Its artillery train was remarkable: it consisted of 39 field and medium battalions (702 guns), an MLRS battalion (18 pieces), 16 heavy mortar batteries and two FROG battalions with the 225th Missile Brigade headquarters. The IrAAC deployed 3rd and 4th Wings and could provide 100 troop-carrying helicopters for Rawi, in addition to gunships. The IrAF provided three strike wings, a bomber squadron, and a squadron of Mirages equipped for photo reconnaissance and electronic warfare. Meanwhile, as usual by this point in the war, the Iraqis were de facto free to roam the battlefield almost unchallenged, as Iranian air power reached its nadir.

As petty bickering between Iraqi generals continued, Rawi pressed to strengthen operations on his right and may have hoped to exploit Aboud's 'unselfishness.' On 15 June 1988, the latter withdrew the assault units from the front for training, and three days later – after Beit-ol-Mogaddas-7 – he attended a AFGC meeting, chaired by Khairallah, still clearly shaken by the Iranian attack. It was suggested, probably by Khazraji, that as insurance against a repeat of Beit alMoqaddas-7, Aboud should keep one of his mobile divisions on his right flank and that one of Rawi's formations would replace it for the drive across the border. Rawi rightly opposed a scheme which would see his forces advancing on two axes when he wished to advance solely upon South Majnoon. Once again Aoud came to the rescue suggesting he use three rather than four mobile divisions – by leaving 5th Mechanised Division on watch in the south. He also proposed having another corps headquarters ready to take over 8th and 19th Infantry Divisions, together with 5th Mechanised Division, if the Iranian threat returned. Correspondingly, General Mohammad Abdul Qader's IV Corps was warned it might be deployed for this task.

Thus, Aoud redrafted his plans so the thrust from the bridgehead would now be by the understrength (minus one brigade) armoured division reinforced by an infantry brigade, and push up to 44 North, while the mechanised division (also minus a brigade) would be sent north. This was agreed on 19 June 1988 when Y-Day was set for 25 June with S-Hour at 04:15.

Remnants of the Remnants

Just as the Iraqis had relied upon berm-based defences so did the Iranians who established their FEBA some two kilometres inside

A medic evacuates an injured soldier from the position of one of the few IRIA units deployed on the southern frontlines, while under Iraqi artillery fire. (via Tom Cooper)

In too many cases during the final battles on the southern frontlines of the Iran-Iraq War, Iranian defenders were left with little choice but to wait for Iraqi infantry and armour to enter their frontlines before firing back. Here a group of Pasdaran tensely monitor the situation in front of their position. (via Tom Cooper)

their own country. Behind the usual wire entanglements and minefields were four hastily constructed berms, one-behind-the-other to a depth of some five kilometres, with high observation towers built into the forward berm to provide early warning of enemy intentions. These poorly built and shallow defences were manned by two or three tank battalions of 3rd Brigade/92nd IRIA Armoured Division (50 MBTs), 2nd Brigade/21st IRIA Infantry and 15 Pasdaran battalions; the battered remnants of divisions which had taken part in the abortive counteroffensive and were still licking their wounds.

The islands, which had similar defences, had been expanded since the failure of Val Fajr-8 as part of an extensive Iranian effort to strengthen the southern front. Despite the departure of so many Pasdaran troops, the Iranians had been filling the marshes since the summer of 1987 to double the size of the islands, which now extended to within 5.5 kilometres of the Iraqi positions on the marsh's western bank. They had also extended logistical facilities between Ahvaz and Khorramshahr with numerous camps, supply depots and repair shops and a much-improved road system; activities the CIA interpreted as preparations for a new southern front offensive.[3]

The Kheiber Bridge still crossed the frontier from the Shaheed Bassim road junction to link North Majnoon with Iran. The island was held by the 85th 'Hejrat' Mechanised Brigade, reinforced by 13 Pasdaran battalions, of which one or two were deployed along the western edge of the marshes. South Majnoon was held by the IRIA's 3rd Brigade/23rd Special Forces Division, reinforced by two Pasdaran battalions and a tank battalion from 92nd Armoured Division, a total of some 8,500 men with 25 MBTs and some guns – of which most of the latter had been withdrawn to the Iranian 'mainland'. The Iranians faced the new threat with no more than 30,000 men with 75 MBTs, supported by 18 artillery battalions now down to 200 guns with limited ammunition. SFOHQ was no doubt anxiously awaiting the arrival of reinforcements from the north, apparently heralded by the deployment around Ahvaz of 19th Fajr Division IRGC with some 6,000 men. It was a forlorn hope, for the Americans observed the Iraqi build-up and, on 18 June, the CIA reported a significant increase in artillery south of the marshes and the deployment of 2,200 AFVs.[4]

Start Basins

During mid-June 1988 there was intense preparatory work behind the Iraqi lines with units again rehearsing assaults on courses specially created to resemble their initial objectives, while amphibious assaults were practised in the Hawr al Hammar, north-west of Basra.[5] Much effort was expended to overcome the problems of operating in the marshes and the surrounding boggy ground. Rawi required extra bridging material, together with boats, and had to be helped out by the resources of General Headquarters and the Iraqi Navy, the latter providing 136 seagoing barges and landing craft as well as some hovercraft. Some 48 hours before Y-Day Rawi had assembled 1,680 aluminium and rubber assault boats, some 220 with support weapons.

The problem of launching the Iraqi 'armada' was that the moment boats began assembling along the marsh edge embankments they faced the threat of artillery fire which could inflict heavy losses. A civilian engineer came up with the solution of creating dry docks (the Iraqis called them 'start basins' (Ahwadh al-Intilaq)) behind the embankments, in which the boats and the men assembled shortly before S-Hour when holes would be blown in the embankment, filling the dry docks, and allowing the boats to float into the marshes. Rawi's mechanised battalions were stripped to provide a flotilla of 138 BMP-1 amphibious IFVs, augmented by a fleet of 48 GSP amphibious ferries from the Military Engineers' Directorate, while the divisional engineer battalions provided 12 Czech MT-55 AVLBs. The Directorate also provided a 500-metre pontoon bridge which was augmented by Styrofoam floats: 2,700 small ones to form footbridges and 830 large ones to support light vehicles.

Aboud concealed his preparations behind a berm built just behind the corps' frontline berm-based defences, where walled laagers were created in the angle of 'The Step' to assemble the armoured units. Engineers also had to prepare routes through III Corps' defences, extend the road network and prepare to bulldoze gaps through the berms. Aboud also had problems with the boggy terrain around the marshes which he would have to traverse to reach Kushk, and this task was assigned to two engineer battalions. They assembled heaps of rock and dry earth which were brought up at night, during which they secretly created along the northern part of 'The Step' 18 12-metre-wide, firm passages through the soft ground

An Iraqi mortar crew in action in the dust and heat of the summer 1988. (Albert Grandolini collection)

A BMP-1 operated by the IRGC, seen in mid-1988, somewhere on the southern front of the Iran-Iraq War. (Albert Grandolini collection)

at 200-metre intervals up to the enemy FEBA, five kilometres inside Iran. In addition, narrower paths were constructed for the infantry and there was more material to create passages beyond the enemy FEBA. To ensure the enemy could not raise the level of water in the marshes, Aboud also arranged with the civil authorities to breach one of the embankments and allow water to drain into the Shatt al-Arab.

While the IrAF and Special Forces probed the marshes to learn all they could of the defences, the planners paid particular attention to deception. This effort was largely carried out by VI and III Corps who planned diversions, dummy frontal assaults and amphibious assaults upon the islands, and even encirclement. The first active operations began as soon as the Iranian counteroffensive had been contained and, on 16 June 1988, Rawi's guns began probing the enemy by fire to determine his reactions. Up to 20 batteries, augmented by FROG missiles were delivering 20-minute barrages at a time. The response was encouragingly weak and when the Guards' batteries repeated their probe the following day there was no reaction as the Iranians decided to conserve their limited ammunition.

What man proposes, God disposes and while there had been some cooling since mid-June with the temperature dropping into the low-40s centigrade, on the afternoon of 24 June, the winds picked up. A very strong north-westerly wind started to blow causing an easterly surge in the marsh waters which overflowed the southern and eastern banks. Flood waters covered III Corps' three western passages and threatened the fourth. Aboud's prayers were answered by dusk for the winds had died down and the flooding stopped before it reached the fourth passage and thus caused only a minor setback. That evening he and Rawi were summoned to 41st Infantry Division headquarters where they met Saddam who passed on his final instructions while final preparations for the offensive were arranged. The temperature the following day was 40° Centigrade, although the wind had increased to 30km/h rising to 40km/h when the temperature dropped to 38° Centigrade. On 26 and 27 June 1988, the temperature rose to 44° Centigrade as the wind declined to about 24 km/h.[6]

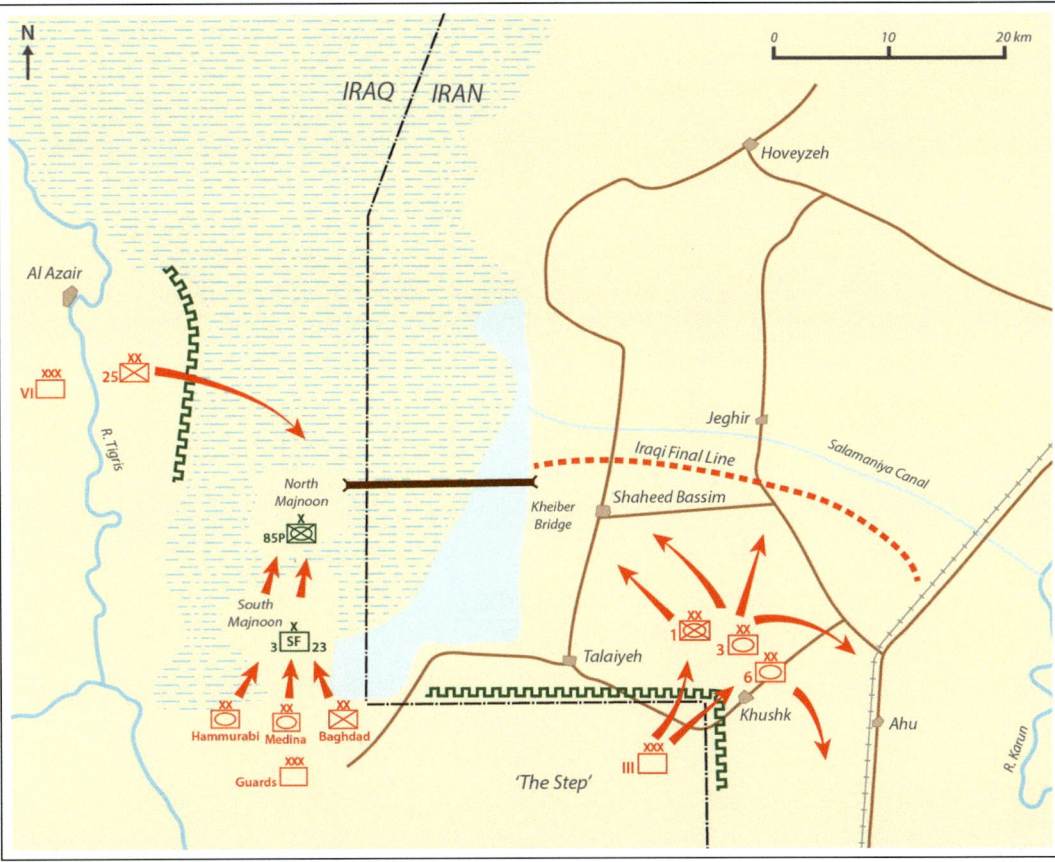

Map of Operation Tawakkalna ala Allah-2. (Map by George Anderson)

Operation Tawakkalna ala Allah 2

At 03:45 hours of 25 June 1988, the Iraqis opened their half-hour preparatory bombardment, paying considerable attention to the disruption of Iranian reserves. Even so, the barrage left the waters covered with dead and stunned fish. Unlike the previous offensives, which were launched into largely barren and sparsely populated terrain, Tawakkalna ala Allah 2 had significant impact upon Iraq's post-war economic recovery plans – for the Majnoon oil fields would be a major contributor. For this reason the bombardment relied less upon lethal chemical agents and more upon those which ensured temporary incapacity, such as riot control and CS gas, to prevent the oilfield being contaminated. Riot control agents and CS gas came from 82mm and 120mm mortar bombs, while 152mm howitzers fired shells with CS – although more lethal agents were used against the enemy rear network as far north as Hoveyzeh.[7]

Proceeded by airstrikes including two squadrons of Tu-22 bombers and two of Su-25 fighter-bombers, the assault went in at 04:15 with the Guards Corps advancing northwards up the land bridge to South Majnoon in three parallel columns, with (west to east) Sattar's Hammurabi, Hammash's Medina, and Shannan's Baghdad Divisions – each led by an infantry brigade supported by three IrAAC squadrons of Bo.105s, Gazelles and Mi-25s. T-72 tanks were brought across the marshes on GSP ferries and began providing fire support, while Hanoush's SP Division on the right provided two commando brigades which boarded boats around midnight, floated out of their dry docks without incident when the embankment was blown, and then sailed some three kilometres to land on the island's western bank and attack enemy batteries.

As they landed in the west, the Iraqi second echelon – two infantry brigades in BMPs – began landing on the eastern side. They were delayed by failing engines, and poor navigation aggravated by poor communications. Despite the problems they had pulled the fangs of the defence by the time the third echelon arrived at S+2, with one armoured brigade brought in by GSP ferries and the other by pontoon bridge. Together, the Guards brigades mopped up to take 1,000 prisoners and a number of MBTs which they turned against their former owners, and by 07:30 the Iraqi flag flew over the island.

The Iraqis then rushed to organise defences and prepare for the next phase of the offensive, as their engineers assembled pontoon bridges to bring in heavy support and also built earth embankments to facilitate the movement of support forces. After two hours, Rawi began assaulting North Majnoon from 09:30 with two of Shannan's infantry brigades, supported by Sattar's and Hammash's mechanised brigades fighting their way across the embankment linking the two islands, landing at 09:40.

Once they established a bridgehead, the second echelon followed with the two commando brigades and an armoured brigade on GSPs, while at 14:40 no fewer than 57 Mi-17 helicopters landed a commando battalion six kilometres inside Iran – east of the marshes near the Shaheed Bassim junction, to block the Kheiber Bridge's mainland exit. The landing zone came under heavy fire but the Guards suffered light losses and began eliminating those batteries which did not withdraw. The isolated Iranian garrison stubbornly fought on for 10 hours as Iraqi engineers built two causeways from South Majnoon to consolidate their grip. Eventually, the island was secured by 19:30. During this final phase, the Guards were assisted by VI Corps which, despite fog, pushed forward with two infantry brigades of the 25th Infantry Division to clear the marshes west of the Majnoons by taking the Iranian-held sandy promontories within the marshes before reaching North Majnoon.

Some of the Majnoon defenders undoubtedly escaped along the myriad of minor paths along embankments but there was no

MIDDLE EAST@WAR SERIES SPECIAL #1: THE IRAN-IRAQ WAR

A HOT ATGM-armed Gazelle of the IrAAC (serial 4237) underway low over forward Iraqi positions. Together with Mi-25s and MD.500s, the type played an important role in providing support for Iraqi offensives in 1988. (Albert Grandolini collection)

A rare photo of a nearly intact Iraqi Bo.105 attack helicopter captured by US troops in 2003. The type saw intensive service on the southern frontlines during the last three years of the Iran-Iraq War. (via Pit Weinert)

A still from a video showing an Iraqi Type 69-II advancing in the direction of Iranian positions south of the Majnoons, in June 1988. (Tom Cooper collection)

their laagers. The redrafting of plans on 19 June reduced the impact of the loss of passages due to flooding, and by 04:50 the spearheads were on the edge of the enemy defences and requesting a lifting of fire. An infantry brigade and a commando brigade, supported by an armoured brigade, took most of the first three berm lines in just over an hour. The last, some three kilometres away, had fallen after another hour's fighting to establish the bridgehead Aboud was seeking. Now 3rd Armoured Division, reinforced by an infantry brigade, broke out at 08:00 and pushed north along the Kushk–Jeghir road 'to the east up near the edges of marsh', to envelop the enemy. While Pasdaran formations around it were falling apart, the 92nd Armoured Division desperately resisted in a fighting retreat, aimed at shielding Ahvaz, but lost its commander, Major General Muhammad Ali Shafiee. The Iraqi 1st Mechanised Division (minus its armoured brigade) followed and while 6th Armoured Division masked the Iranian forces around Khorramshahr, it joined 3rd Armoured Division's advance to the ancient Salamaniya Canal, which the Iranians had reopened and linked to the Karun, then stopped in a landscape of wreckage lit by numerous fires. One of the 1st Division's mechanised brigades took the Shaheed Bassim junction, which was the entrance to the Kheiber Bridge, relieving the Guards commando battalion. In total, the Iraqis had thus taken 800 square kilometres of Iranian territory, together with about 1,000 prisoners and much equipment, before they continued to mop up and push probes northwards to Ahwaz, keeping the enemy off balance.[8]

The advances of Rawi and Aboud were greatly aided by air support. On 25 June 1988, the IrAAC flew 266 gunship sorties while the IrAF flew 247 attack sorties. Their activity continued in similar fashion on the next day, with the IrAAC flying 161 gunship sorties over the battlefield. During mop up operations of 27 and 28 June, the IrAF still flew 221 combat sorties and the IrAAC another 238. By contrast, the IRIAF managed meagre 35 combat sorties on 25 and 26 June.

sanctuary for them. Aboud's artillery also began its preparation at 03:45, and 30 minutes later three divisions – from west towards east: 1st Mechanised, 3rd Armoured, and 6th Armoured – advanced from

248

Telescoping the Conclusion

The collapse of Iranian resistance meant Aboud was able to telescope the second and third phases: within two hours his men were between Jeghir and Kushk rounding up as many prisoners as they could, 1st Mechanised Division receiving an infantry battalion to help them in this task. This division reached Shaheed Bassim at midday, while 3rd Armoured Division went onto Jeghir some 20 kilometres across the border. Then, in response to a query from Saddam, who was visiting III Corps forward command post, Aboud sent a brigade of 3rd Armoured Division to Ahu rail station to cut the Ahvaz–Khorramshahr highway and rail line and destroy as much stored material as possible. The division also pushed ahead to the Salamaniya Canal to seize and demolish two bridges which crossed it. A trench-digging machine was brought forward in the early afternoon and used to break embankments leading from Iran to North Majnoon, while observation towers in the captured enemy defences were demolished. Meanwhile, 3rd Armoured Division spent the afternoon emptying or destroying enemy supply dumps. Finally, at 18:00, Aboud gave the order for a general withdrawal across the border.

This final action, made to demonstrate the Iraqi acceptance of the modified UN Resolution 598 – which was to be the basis of a ceasefire – still provided sufficient opportunity for transfer of the booty to Iraq. Namely, the Iraqis actually remained on Iranian territory for the entire 26 June and withdrew only when the last piece of captured equipment and the last prisoner of war had been sent across the border. In their wake, they left carefully laid minefields and then plugged the gaps in their defensive berms. Indeed, during the General Army Command meeting on 27 June, Aboud was criticised for not bringing back more prisoners due to slipshod searching for scattered Iranian troops.[9]

The Iraqis claimed, probably accurately, that their offensive had mauled between six and eight Iranian divisions, resulted in the capture of 5,000 prisoners (nearly 1,650 by Aboud), 57 MBTs, 24 AFVs and large quantities of weapons, while inflicting up to 9,000 casualties. In return, by 27 June 1988, the Iraqis had suffered 368 killed (including 69 dead of the Guards Corps) and about 900 wounded. However, there were reports in which the 25th Division might have also suffered heavy casualties.[10]

Immense Booty

There was no Iranian reaction to the Iraqi offensive into the Hawizeh Marshes. Instead, Tehran bitterly complained about the extensive use of chemical weapons by Iraq – which eventually proved to be one of the major reasons for increasing numbers of young Iranians becoming reluctant to volunteer for military service. Having denied the use of such weapons for years, on 1 July 1988 the Iraqi Foreign Minister Tariq Aziz publicly admitted it but added a claim that the Iranians used chemical weapons on many occasions, too. Responding to Western criticism, Aziz added 'There are different views on this matter from different angles. You are living on a civilised continent. You are living on a peaceful continent.'[11]

Overall, since March 1988, the Iraqis had claimed the capture of 1,298 MBTs, 155 IFVs, 512 guns, 6,196 mortars, 5,550 light guns and pieces of recoilless artillery, 60,694 rifles, 454 trucks and 1,600 light vehicles and trailers – in essence nearly all of the heavy weapons of the Iranian ground forces. In comparison, about 570 MBTs, 130 BMP-1s and Scorpions, 300 APCs, 320 towed guns and 45 self-propelled guns, and 300 anti-aircraft guns were put on display in Baghdad in July the same year – and, certainly enough – many of these had been captured early during the war. Nevertheless, related publications resulted in reports about the complete exhaustion of the regular Iranian military, and de facto the demise of the IRIAF. Similarly, Iranian oppositionals in Iraq estimated that Iran would require US$15–20 billion spent over five years to rebuild its forces.[12]

The Nail in the Coffin: Tawakkalna ala Allah-4

With the conclusion of Tawakkalna ala Allah 2 the southern front now became a backwater, although one in which the Iranians were constantly on the alert for new thrusts towards Ahvaz or Abadan. The central front, reinforced by Rawi's corps, now became the focus of Iraqi efforts; beginning at Mehran with Operation Tawakkalna ala Allah-3 from 12 July, followed from 22 July 1988 by Operation Tawakkalna ala Allah-4. The latter became one of the biggest ever Iraqi offensives on this part of the frontline.

Together these operations not only inflicted heavy blows upon the Iranians but forced them to disperse their forces and delayed the passage of large troop contingents from north towards the south. A crumb of comfort for Tehran was the destruction of a major incursion by the Iraqi-backed Iranian émigrés of the Mujahideen eKhalq (MeK, also MKO) or National Liberation Army (NLA).

Tawakkalna ala Allah-4 provided Aboud's III Corps with one last 'hurrah'. Although minor in comparison to the three earlier

An Iraqi Type-69-II in hull-down position near the Iranian border, summer 1988. (via Pit Weinert)

Amongst the Iranian artillery pieces captured by the Iraqis towards the end of the war are this 35mm Oerlikon GDF-001 anti-aircraft gun (centre) and 155mm M1/M59 'Long Tom' field howitzer (right side). (Albert Grandolini collection)

operations with this title, it allowed him to complete the disruption of the enemy infrastructure in the south. On 23 July 1988, the 3rd and 6th Armoured, 1st Mechanised, 8th, 11th, 19th and 30th Infantry Divisions crossed the border to carve out a 25-kilometre-wide and 65-kilometre-deep bridgehead, only 25 kilometres southwest of the provincial capital Ahvaz. The operation was led by Brigadier General Tahir's 3rd Armoured Division, which overran the major Iranian camp around Hamid during the night. Tahir was killed in a helicopter crash, but this remained the only setback for the Iraqis, and thus they were left free to plunder and then destroy the enemy logistics depots before withdrawing unhindered across the border.[13]

The Last Hurrah

The elections of April 1988 in Iran had reflected Khomeini's growing public antipathy to conservative traditionalists and resulted in a Majlis dominated by more liberal representatives. Amid growing tensions between the hawks and new parliamentaries – clashes between them were prevented only by Khoemini's intervention, on 24 May – the Iraqi attacks into Iran prompted large numbers of Iranians to follow renewed calls to arms. Even the Majlis closed to allow its members to go fighting, while thousands of civil servants, clerics, and students left for the front: they all arrived much too late.

Furthermore, there were more pressing economic reasons for ending the war. Already in March 1988, the Budget and Planning Ministry warned that in the light of dwindling revenues the current rate of military expenditure could be maintained only with a 25 percent cut in social expenditure. Rafsanjani's promotion in the aftermath of Tawakkalna ala Allah-1 saw the Iranian Foreign Ministry intensify its efforts to seek a diplomatic solution. The United Nations had proposed a ceasefire agreement as Resolution 598 – which Iran accepted in February 1988 – but Tehran mistrusted the international organisation. It was Khomeini, who sought to neutralise the IRGC's influence and opposition to its acceptance through appointing Rafsanjani as Commander-in-Chief – who saw this as the basis for ending the war.[14]

On 30 June 1988, the same day Mir Hussein Musavi was appointed the Prime Minister, that Tehran officially conceded that it had suffered major military reverses – which it blamed on the Superpowers' 'unholy alliance'. On 3 July the American cruiser USS *Vincennes* shot down, in error, an Iranian airliner with the loss of 290 lives. Tehran requested an emergency meeting of the UN Security Council.

The UN body was that month chaired by West Germany, one of the few European countries which had provided soft-skinned vehicles – but no arms – to the combatants, and its relative neutrality made it acceptable to Tehran. Resolution 598 was redrafted to include the establishment of a commission of inquiry into the war's origins and was generally accepted on 20 July 1988. A few days later German Foreign Minister Hans Dietrich Genscher publicly rebuked Iraq both for starting the war and for using chemical weapons and – by establishing his credentials as an independent – he cemented Germany's position with Iran. Baghdad was less welcoming, but Saddam – who now had military superiority – was willing to accept a diplomatic solution knowing he had leverage through the equivalent of a $2 billion debt to Bonn.

On 14 July 1988 Iran's leaders met and agreed to accept Resolution 598, the cabinet ratifying this decision the next day in a meeting attended by Rafsanjani, while on 16 July Khomeini wrote to express his agreement. This decision was passed to the UN within 24 hours and Khomeini formally announced it to the nation on 20 July, adding that accepting it: '...was more deadly for me than taking poison. I submit myself to God's will and drank this drink for His satisfaction.'

The decision astonished the world. Indeed, on 17 August the CIA had to write a report explaining its failure to predict it. It admitted its analysts had failed to anticipate it but, in an example of bureaucratic face-saving, claimed a minority of them had recognised Iran's growing interest in diplomacy and the amount of support for Rafsanjani.[15]

Saddam was more reluctant to accept the ceasefire, for he believed the enemy were only playing for time. Furthermore, he was determined to achieve his pre-war aims of gaining territory and controlling the Shatt al-Arab. Yet by late July it was obvious there was a strategic impasse and the two sides quickly began to hammer out a UN sponsored ceasefire. A corresponding agreement was

Jubilant Iraqi Army troops cheering the cease-fire that ended eight years of war with Iran in August 1988. (via Ali Tobchi)

reached on 8 August to take effect at 03:00 on 20 August 1988 with a UN military observer group as the controlling body.

While many of post-war estimates put the war dead at 300,000 or more (sometimes to over 1 million), and while no official figures were ever made available for Iraqi casualties, on 18 September 1988, Islamic Guidance Minister Mohammed Khatami said the country had lost 123,220 combatants and 11,000 civilians killed. The Army lost 35,170 dead and the Pasdaran 79,664.[16]

After eight years of bloody conflict the war ended virtually where it had begun. There would be no diplomatic agreement between Baghdad and Tehran until 1990, when Saddam sought to recoup his diplomatic and economic loses with the disastrous invasion of Kuwait. This delayed a full repatriation of prisoners until 1993. Meanwhile, in 1991, the Iraqi military was taught a sharp lesson in modern military sciences by a collection of US and European armies which had been preparing for a high intensity conflict for 40 years.

MIDDLE EAST@WAR SERIES SPECIAL #1: THE IRAN-IRAQ WAR

COLOUR SECTION 3

Photographs of Iraqi T-72s from 1987–1988 are extremely rare. Those of surviving examples from the original batch of 125 tanks delivered in 1980 – even more so. This example was last seen in summer 1988, mostly re-painted in yellow sand, with only minimal touches of blue-green. (Artwork by Tom Cooper)

This almost brand-new T-72M was captured by the Iranians sometime in 1987. Most of the vehicle was painted in green overall, but front parts of the turret and most of the gun were camouflaged with mud, or grey sand colour. The vehicle only received only a turret number (113) before it was sent to the frontlines. (Artwork by Tom Cooper)

By 1988, most of the vehicles assigned to units of the Republican Guards Corps were painted in yellow sand overall. Polish-supplied T-72Ms were originally painted in a 'cardboard' colour, but this rapidly faded in the sun and sand. They received various identification insignia, including front and rear ends of fenders trimmed in white, and about 60-centimetre long 'ID-stripes' in white, green or black on their skirts. Some T-72Ms received the inscription 'Assad Babil' (Lion of Babylon) instead. Insets show (left upper corner) complex tactical insignia used by the Medinah Manarwah Armoured Division, Tawakkalna ala Allah Armoured Division, and Nebuchadnezar Infantry Division respectively. If applied, these were placed on the rear of the turret-stowage box, together with individual identification – or the 'turret number' of the tank in question, and the letter 'J' (short of 'Jaysh', Army). (Artwork by Tom Cooper)

COLOUR SECTION 3

The majority of other heavy vehicles of the Iraqi Army were repainted in yellow sand overall by 1988. This T-55 had its fume extractor painted in yellow, with a white strip: this was one of the most widespread methods of identification for Iraqi tanks in this war. Furthermore, it had its tactical unit insignia applied on the turret. Sadly, the background to the latter remains unknown. (Artwork by Tom Cooper)

Probably belonging to the same mechanised battalion of an unknown Iraqi brigade – and captured by the IRGC on the same occasion as the T-55 shown in the previous profile – is this BMP-1. Painted yellow sand overall, it also wore its unit's tactical insignia: the red and white square was applied near the centre of the vehicle instead of further towards the front as was more usual. Insets show tactical unit insignia of various other Iraqi brigades. Sadly, no background to these are currently known. (Artwork by Tom Cooper)

This BMP-1 was captured by the IRGC during Operation Karbala-5 and instantly pressed into service against its former owners. Uncharacteristically for 1987, it was still camouflaged in yellow sand and blue-green, indicating it might have been in service with the Iraqi Army since the early 1980s. It is possible that this BMP-1 also received the large turret number '21' applied in white or yellow. (Artwork by Tom Cooper)

MIDDLE EAST@WAR SERIES SPECIAL #1: THE IRAN-IRAQ WAR

By 1988, the Iraqi Army had received its first batches of BMP-2s, and these saw some service during final stages of the war with Iran. As far as is known, all of these were painted in the same fashion as the Polish-made T-72Ms. This example would have been assigned to one of the brigades of the 3rd Armoured Division, the tactical insignia of which was applied on the side of the front hull. The meaning of the yellow 'bar' directly above it remains unknown. (Artwork by Tom Cooper)

Another new appearance in the Iraqi Army of the late 1980s were Chinese-made YW-531 APCs. Apparently operated by mechanised brigades of infantry divisions only, all seem to have been painted in dark sand colour overall, and most received their parent-unit's tactical insignia applied on the forward hull. (Artwork by Tom Cooper)

This BMP-1 seems to have survived in service with the IRGC for long enough to receive at least three different sets of inscriptions over time. As well as the 'Onion' (stylised word 'Allah'), applied in white atop the gunner's hatch on the turret and in light blue on the front of the hull, these included various citations from the Qoran, applied in black and red along the hull. (Artwork by Tom Cooper)

COLOUR SECTION 3

Indicative of significant problems with identification friend or foe on the battlefields of the Iran-Iraq War, where both sides used vehicles of the same or similar design, this T-55 operated by the IRGC received large ID-markings. As well as Iranian national colours applied around the smoke extractor, it had a large national flag of the Islamic Republic of Iran applied over most of its rear turret. Inscribed on the turret's side was another citation from the Qoran. Otherwise, this T-55 seems to have retained its original coat of olive-green (probably applied well before it was captured from the Iraqis), over which wide stripes in mint-green were applied to enhance its camouflage. (Artwork by Tom Cooper)

North Korean-made, and Iranian-operated, self-propelled M1979 Koksan 170mm guns became notorious during Iranian offensives on Basra in 1987 when they randomly shelled the city. Firing rocket-assisted projectiles, they could shell targets out to 60 kilometres away – which made them the world's longest-range field artillery pieces in service. Operated only by the IRGC, they retained their original colour of olive green with a strong bluish touch – and even Red Stars made of iron – while wearing no other insignia at all. (Artwork by Peter Penev)

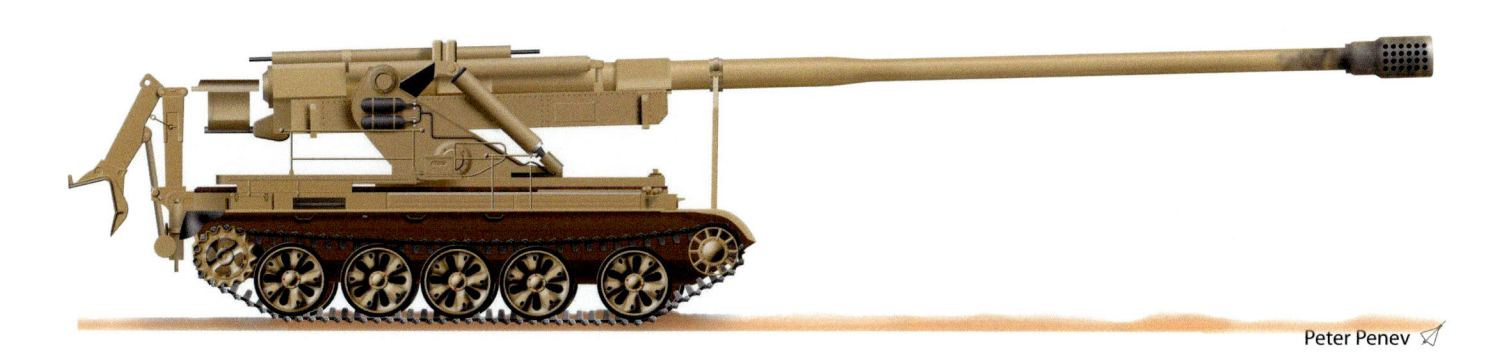

Manufactured by the Second Machine Industry, and installed on a Chinese Type-59 tank chassis, the Koksan guns were only exported to Iran. However, a few IRGC-operated M1979s were captured by Iraq during the campaigns of 1988 and re-painted as shown here. It remains unclear if any of these saw combat service by the end of the Iran-Iraq War. (Artwork by Peter Penev)

MIDDLE EAST@WAR SERIES SPECIAL #1: THE IRAN-IRAQ WAR

A reconstruction of an Iraqi Mi-25 ('Hind') helicopter gunship. Its serial number – 2148 – confirms the delivery of a third – previously unknown – batch of this type to Iraq during the 1980s. Their camouflage colours included yellow sand and green on upper surfaces and sides and were applied in the same pattern as examples exported to a number of other customers (amongst others: Afghanistan, Libya, and Nicaragua). Notable is that the large national flag applied on the front of the cabin of this second batch of Iraqi Mi-25s was slightly narrower than that applied on the first batch. (Artwork by Tom Cooper)

While exported by the USA to Iraq for agricultural purposes, 30 Hughes (later McDonnell Douglas Helicopter Systems) MD 500D helicopters were all taken up by the Iraqi Army Aviation Corps and saw intensive combat service during the last three years of the war with Iran. As far as is known, most were painted in yellow sand overall, although some did receive a more complex, three-colour camouflage pattern reminiscent of that applied on many Iraqi Mi-17s. Armament confirmed as deployed by IrAAC MD 500Ds included FN ENTA TMP-5 pods for twin 7.62mm machine guns (shown here), 12-tube FZ launchers for unguided 2.75in rockets and Brandt 22x68 launchers for 22 68mm unguided rockets. (Artwork by Tom Cooper)

Iraq acquired a total of no fewer than 75 Bo.105Ds, and at least four Bo.105Cs, manufactured by Messerschmitt-Bölkow-Böhm in West Germany, and at least 24 CASA-made Bo.105Ps. A few of these served for SAR purposes, while a handful was equipped as VIP-transports, but most of the Bo.105Ds served with the IrAAC as scout and attack helicopters. A few received Swiss-made 20mm Oerlikon KAA cannon installed under the cabin, but their primary armament consisted of HOT ATGMs, and various pods for unguided rockets, such as Brandt 22x68s. (Artwork by Tom Cooper)

PART II
THE FORGOTTEN FRONTS

18
THE OPENING OPERATIONS

Background

While the Southern Front was the decisive theatre of the Iran-Iraq War, its Northern and Central Fronts attracted relatively little attention.

The warfare in this part of the world has always been dictated by the local terrain. In contrast to the flat battlefields of the south, the terrain stretching north from the Hawizah Marshes is characterised by ridges that gradually merge into the Zagros Mountains (Kuhha-ye Zagros), some of which climb to more than 2,000 metres above sea level. The Northern Front ran from the tri-border area between Iran, Iraq and Turkey, with fighting touching the Iraqi provinces of Arbil, as-Sulaymaniyah, Diyala, and northern Dahuk and the Iranian provinces of Azerbayejan-e-Gharabi, Kordestan, Kermanshah and northern Ilam. There are two major lakes in this area: Lake Dukan (Buhayrat Dukan), 100 kilometres north-west of the town of Sulaymaniyah, and Lake Darband-i-Khan (Buhayrat Darband-i-Khan), about 20 kilometres south-west of it.

The Central Front touched the Iraqi provinces of Diyala, Wasit and Maysan and the Iranian provinces of southern Ilam and northern Khuzestan. Here the elevations are lower, averaging 500–2,000 metres above sea level. Indeed, on the Iraqi side of the foothills they drop into terrain that features sand dunes and descends to the northern tip of the Hawizah Marshes in al-Amarah area. Eastern Diyala Province is characterised by extensive marshes fed by numerous tributaries of the Tigris descending from the Zagros Mountains – including Hawr Suwayqiyah in the south – that stretch for some 150 by 110 kilometres. To the east of the marshes is a narrow strip of ground, some 10–13 kilometres wide and averaging about 250–400 metres above sea level. This runs parallel to the border with Iran to a point just south of the Mehran Salient. Eastern Wasit and Maysan consist of undulating terrain broken by low hills and crisscrossed by waterways. This is an area suitable for manoeuvre and mechanised warfare, although high ground on the Iranian side tends to restrict movement eastwards.

The Fronts' Infrastructure

The terrain restricts cross-border commercial transport to a handful of roads, while movement into Iran is restricted to a limited number of passes through the mountains. Furthermore, mountainous terrain means that communications are often disrupted by weather; rains cause flooding and landslides, while snow can block roads for weeks. Due to the lack of interest in cross-border connections, most of the road networks constructed during the 1950s and 1960s run parallel to the frontier, following different valleys. Nevertheless, roads remain essential due to the scarcity of railways, most of which are either single-track, or have narrow gauge lines, limiting their capacity.

During the reign of the Shah Mohammed Reza Pahlavi, Iran built a number of major military installations to control border crossings – such as Orumiyeh, Sanandaj (also known as Sinnah), and Khermanshah (renamed Bakhtaran in December 1981 but later reverting to its original name). Further north is a main road linking Arbil (or Erbil), Shaqlawah, Rawandiz (or Rawanduz), to Piranshahr, Urumia (or Orumiyeh), while Sulaymaniyeh is connected to

The towering Zagros mountains in western Iran. (Mark Lepko collection)

Lake Dukan in north-eastern Iraq. (Mark Lepko collection)

The imposing Zagros Mountains run like a curtain along the western side of the Mesopotamian plains. (Mark Lepko collection)

to Eslam Abd-e Gharb, then Ilam, Mehran and Dehloran. This splits near Musyan, with one branch going east to Dezful and the other following the frontier through Fakkeh (or Fakke or Fuka) to Bostan, then Susangerd and Ahwaz.

Population

While terrain was one factor affecting military operations, another one – especially along the northernmost part of the border between Iran and Iraq – was the population. Most numerous in this part of the world are Kurds: an ethnic group that is culturally, historically and linguistically classified as belonging to the Iranian peoples, but the majority of whom are Sunni Moslems.

Often described as, 'the largest ethnic group without a state', the Kurds are split into numerous tribes and clans and speak dozens of different dialects, some of which are akin to foreign languages. With Kurds being successfully integrated (though not assimilated) into the Ottoman Empire, their nationalism emerged only during the First World War, when Young Turks launched a large-scale deportation of Kurds. The Treaty of Sévres promised at least autonomy, if not outright independence for the Kurds, and a Kingdom of Kurdistan was declared in Iraq from 1922 until 1924. However, traditional disunity between major Kurdish tribes, intensive efforts of Kemal Atatürk, and complaints by numerous other minorities living in the same area – including Arabs, Christians and Yezidis – all conspired to prevent the establishment of a viable state. Multiple Kurdish uprisings which erupted over the following decades were bloodily supressed, first by the British, then by the Iraqis. In the 1970s, Kurdish nationalism led to several insurgencies with their leaders openly challenging traditional feudal authorities. Divisions between them ensured that Baghdad and Tehran always had a strong foundation of support within 'Kurdish' territories.

In 1974 the Kurdish Democratic Party (Partiya Demokrat a Kurdistane; KDP) under Mullah Mustafa Barzani and his sons Idris and Masoud, launched an uprising.[1] The KDP was actually a conservative organisation, based upon the tribal system and emphasising personal leadership. Tehran provided clandestine, even if large-scale military support for this rebellion, openly threatening both Iraqi national unity and the economy. Although initially highly successful, this insurgency was crushed by the Iraqi military in the

Kirkuk via a highway that continues in the form of a secondary road eastwards towards Penjwin, and then to Marivan (or Dezh Shapur). Closer to the border with Iran, only one secondary road connects the eastern shore of Lake Darband-i-Khan with Halabja, from where a few tracks cross the frontier to Nowsud. On the southern side, Sulaymaniyeh is connected with the Baghdad-Kirkuk and Babgdad-Baquba highways via a network of secondary roads. The highway connecting Baghdad with Basra runs along the Tigris through al-Kut, al-Amarah and al-Qurnah.

In the area along the central sector of the border between Iran and Iraq, Diyala is connected to Baghdad by a main road that branches eastwards at Khanaqin. One link leads to Qasr-e Shirin and Sar-e-Pol-e-Zohab before becoming a secondary road to Eslamabad-e Gharb. In between major roads there are a significant number of gravelled, or simply beaten earth, roads, some of these extending beyond the borders. Towns like Badrah (northern Wasit), and at Tib (also 'Teeb'; in central Maysan) are crossroads for the road networks on the Iraqi side, while inside Iran Mehran and Musiyan are their offshoots.

Deeper behind the border, on the Iranian side, the road network is much poorer. There is only one main road running from Suma

PART II: THE OPENING OPERATIONS

Mustafa Barzani, seen during the uprising of 1974–1975. (Mark Lepko collection)

Jalal Talabani (right) at the HQ of the PUK. (Mark Lepko collection)

managed to steadily extend its influence into Arbil, becoming the primary resistance force against Iraqi authorities.

Events of 1979

The Iranian-supported KDP revolt of 1974–1975 polarised not only the Kurds, but the whole of Iraqi society too. Many Iraqi Shi'a were sympathetic, to a degree and decades later, after the fall of the regime of Saddam Hussein at-Tikriti (Saddam), – the Shi'a-dominated government in Baghdad granted full autonomy to the northern regions.

In the meantime, Saddam – despite helping negotiate the Algiers Treaty and granting autonomy to the Kurds – tended to describe them as 'saboteurs' and considered them a threat to Iraq's unity.[3] He received considerable support for his actions against the Kurds from different parties within Iraq, a British journalist later noted: 'Even anti-government exiles wax indignant at the Kurds' treacherous behaviour during the Gulf war.'[4]

Therefore, while the Algiers Treaty had helped Iraq crush the revolt, it remained a thorn in Saddam's side, a sign of national weakness in comparison to Iran, and one in which he had been intimately involved. Consequently, he was determined to reverse it as soon as possible. A suitable opportunity offered itself in 1979, when the revolution in Iran toppled the Shah Reza Pahlavi, to be replaced by a cleric-led administration under Ayatollah Ruhollah al-Musavi al-Khomeini (Khomeini). The post-revolutionary chaos, power struggles, a counter-coup attempt and massive purges of the military left Iran in such chaos that it appeared unable to defend itself. Indeed, only two months after the Shah was forced to leave Iran, Kurdish nationalists – who wholeheartedly supported the revolution to that point – were denied the seats in the newly established Assembly of Experts in Tehran. As a result, the Democratic Party of Iranian Kurdistan (KDPI), and the leftist Revolutionary Organisation of Kurdish Toilers (Komala) launched an uprising against the Iranian revolutionary government and by late April, sectarian fighting broke out between Kurdish and Azeri factions, resulting in hundreds of casualties.

As the violence spread, many Kurdish conscripts from the regional military garrisons brought the strength of the KDPI's insurgency to about 30,000 fighters, colloquially known as Peshmerga (Death Defiers). The insurgency brought most of Kurdistan and Gharei under control, leaving Tehran controlling only the major population

aftermath of the Iranian withdrawal following the Algiers Treaty of 1975. Afterwards, Iraqi authorities dispersed up to 200,000 Kurds into resettlement camps scattered throughout the country. The Barzani family went into exile to reorganise, Mustafa dying in 1979 in the United States, while many of their followers fled to Iran. In July 1979 the Barzani brothers, seeing an opportunity to renew their armed struggle, moved to Iran which began supporting the PDK the following year.[2]

Meanwhile, a new Kurdish leader appeared in the form of Jalal Talabani, a moderniser who sought to establish a modern democracy based upon socialist ideas. Forced into exile in Iran by Barzani's forces in 1964, Talabani played little part in the 1974–1975 revolt, but in May of the latter year established a new group in Damascus, named the Patriotic Union of Kurdistan (Yekêtiy Niştîmaniy Kurdistan; PUK), as an umbrella organisation for like-minded Kurds to offer a modern alternative to the Barzani's vision. The resulting division between the KDP and the PUK was as much as political as it was ethnic: KDP-supporters spoke the Kurmanji dialect, while those of the PUK spoke the Sorani dialect. When Talabani's men pushed into the KDP's heartland of Arbil and Dahuk, in 1976–1977, fierce clashes erupted, causing a deep rift within the entire Kurdish nation. The PUK failed to dislodge the KDP, but over the following years

centres, and even these had to be supplied from the air. That the uprising had popular support became obvious in March 1979, when the traditional Kurdish capital of Mahabad, in Gharei, was taken by combined forces of Abdu Rahman Ghassemlou, the KDPI's leader and the local Kurdish Sunni religious leader, Sheikh Ezzadin Husseini.[5]

The two locally based units of the Islamic Republic of Iran Army (IRIA) – the Urumia-based 64th Infantry Division and Sanandaj-based 28th Infantry Division – tried to contain the threat, but their ranks had been drained by post-revolutionary purges. Furthermore, the clerics placed greater faith in the emerging Islamic Revolutionary Guards Corps (IRGC, also Sepah-e Pasdaran-e Enghelab-e Eslami, or Pasdaran). The Pasdaran were initially too fragmented to provide effective resistance, and even by the end of 1979 still operated only in platoons and companies of up to about 80 men. They reacted by deploying a large force, but this was ambushed while marching upon the Kurdish-held town of Paveh and suffered grievous casualties.

Undaunted, the new government of the Islamic Republic of Iran (IRI) declared a 'Jihad' (holy war) and issued a fatwa (religious edict), declaring the Iranian Kurds and their key leaders 'enemies of the state'. Fearing Iraqi support for the Kurds, and finding out that Ghassemlou had been joined by Talebani's PUK operating from the Iraqi province of Suleymaniyah, Tehran even recalled military officers who had received extensive training in counterinsurgency (COIN) operations from US advisors in the 1960s and 1970s. In August 1979, the Iranian military – supported by McDonnell Douglas F-4E Phantom II fighter-bombers from the Tactical Fighter Base 3 (TFB.3) of the Islamic Republic of Iran Air Force (IRIAF), near Hamedan, Bell AH-1J Cobra, and Bell 214A Esfahan helicopters of the Islamic Republic of Iran Army Air Corps (IRIAA) – was unleashed upon the Kurdish-held town of Mahabad. In the course of a three-day long siege the Kurds were soundly defeated.

Despite the failure to secure Mahabad, by the end of the year the KDPI still controlled territory up to 75 kilometres east of their Gharbi Mountains heartland while Husseini's enclave extended 50 kilometres from the Iraqi border.[6]

Meanwhile, Saddam began claiming that Iran had failed to honour the Algiers Treaty and – starting in May 1980 – began deploying troops to 'liberate' territory claimed by Iraq, causing a series of low-intensity clashes along much of the border. The Iranian response was weak and confused, but in early June 1980, the Iraqi Military Intelligence (GMID) reported large concentrations of the KDP in the Sardash area. Correspondingly, No. 1 Squadron of the Iraqi Air Force (IrAF), based at al-Hurrya Air Base near Kirkuk was ordered to deploy eight Sukhoi Su-20 fighter-bombers for a strike against one of the Kurdish bases inside Iran. This attack was flown on 4 June 1980, and caused not only considerable losses to the Kurds, but also an uproar from Tehran. It was also a signal for both sides to resort to use of air power to support their respective interests and ground forces in what became a series of small-scale operations along the border.

On 7 September 1980, the 16th Armoured Brigade of the 6th Armoured Division, Iraqi Army, seized the plateau of Zayn al

The more crises and internal and external threats Iran faced in 1979 and 1980, the more opportunity the local Shi'a clergy found to recruit the population. Ultimately, this enabled the 'Mullahs' to secure their rule over the entire country – and to become influential in regards of military-related affairs. (Albert Grandolini collection)

A group of volunteers of the future Islamic Revolutionary Guards Corps, listening to the lecture of their preacher. (Albert Grandolini collection)

PART II: THE OPENING OPERATIONS

II, with the aim of seizing additional territory and helping overthrow Khomeni, or at least to enforce a re-negotiation of the Algiers Treaty from a favourable position.

Iraq Invades

While Saddam's primary objectives were within the province of Khuzestan, in south-western Iran, he was determined to secure key areas in the northern mountains and the foothills of the Zagros Mountains too. For this purpose, the Iraqi Army deployed its I Corps (commanded by Lieutenant General Mohammed Fathi Amin) and II Corps (Lieutenant General Abadallah Abd al-Latif al-Hudaythi) (for a detailed order of battle of these and other involved forces, see Table 21). Saddam did consider assisting the rebellion of dissident Iranian Kurds but feared this might encourage Iraqi Kurds to launch their own uprising, and thus ordered Amin to focus upon counterinsurgency (COIN) operations. Indeed, the I Corps even had to transfer some of its troops under the command of the II Corps. This left it with its 11th Infantry Division on the defensive in the north, while the 7th Mountain Division advanced along the Penjwin-Marivan and Halabja-Nosud roads, with the aim of 'retaking' areas occupied by the Iranians in 1975. Latif's units bore the brunt of the cross-border operations. The emphasis of these was an attack on Qasr-e Shirin by the 8th Infantry and 6th Armoured Divisions, while the 4th Mountain and 12th Armoured Divisions were to take Naft Shahr and Summar, respectively and threaten Kermanshah. The 2nd Infantry Division (reinforced by 37th Armoured Brigade from the 10th Armoured Division) was to secure the Mehran Salient, and threaten Ilam, while the remainder of the 10th Armoured Division was sent to reinforce the III Corps in Khuzestan.[7]

Central section of the frontlines of the Iran-Iraq War was stretching from the Lake Urumia in the north, to Dezful and Bostan in the south. (Map by George Anderson)

Qaws. Three days later, Brigadier General Hisham Sabah al-Fakhri's 10th Armoured Division took the Saif Sa'ad enclave. Meanwhile, Iran continued sliding ever deeper into chaos, and thus Saddam decided to launch an invasion of the country, codenamed Qadisiyya

MIDDLE EAST@WAR SERIES SPECIAL #1: THE IRAN-IRAQ WAR

The IRGC crushed the Kurdish uprising in north-western Iran in blood, often summarily executing any captured enemy fighters, as well as any activists or suspects it could lay its hands upon. (Mark Lepko collection)

A map of the Qasr-e Shirin sector. (Map by George Anderson)

Nominally, the IRIA had three divisions and two brigades facing what became the Northern and Central Fronts. However, the Urumia-based 64th Infantry Division, and Sanandaj-based 28th Infantry Division were in no condition to deploy and initially remained unengaged. Latif thus faced the Kermanshah-based 81st Armoured Division, reinforced by the 40th (Srab) and 84th (Khorramabad) Independent Infantry Brigades. Eventually, the 2nd Brigade of the Ahwaz-based 92nd Armoured Division was redeployed to the Central Front lines at a later stage.

All the units were severely under strength due to neglect and purges, even though augmented by the Border Guards, Gendarmerie, Police, civilian volunteers and Pasdaran. Their initial resistance was weak apart from the odd Border Guard post, some of whose garrisons fought to the death. Generally, there were too few Iranian troops near the frontier, while the IRIA's battalions were very slow to deploy westwards.[8]

As in Khuzestan it thus fell upon Iranian air power to prove as the greatest obstacle to the Iraqi progress. The IRIAA operated an entire Combat Support Group – totalling about 24 each of AH-1Js, Bell 214s and a company of Boeing CH-47 Chinook transport helicopters – deployed at Kermanshah. Indeed, the first IRIA reinforcements to the border were deployed with the help of helicopters on 14 September 1980. Immediately afterwards, Iran's president, Abol Hassan Bani-Sadr, ordered a ceasefire in the Kurdish region, to allow his troops to concentrate on the Iraqi aggression. Ironically, the Revolutionary Guards ignored his order and continued fighting the Kurds, so that only a weak screen of the IRIA's ground troops protected the border. Bani-Sadr also offered the KDPI a ceasefire, so he could concentrate on the west.[9]

Khomeini eventually found a solution in offering the KDP a deal: its 800 Peshmerga still active in Iraq, and about 5,000 men under arms in Iran, should fight the KDPI and the PUK, in exchange for money and arms. The full repercussions of this decision were to become obvious only years later.

The IRIAF was present foremost in the form of Northrop F-5E Tiger II fighters from the TFB.2 (Tabriz) and F-4E Phantom IIs from TFB.3. Operating with the support of Forward Air Controllers and Direct Air Support Centres assigned to Army units and major headquarters, respectively, this proved highly effective in knocking out dozens of Iraqi vehicles. Indeed, their activity during the weeks before the war, and then the first weeks after the Iraqi invasion grew to a degree where the Iraqis were forced to redeploy batteries of SA-6 Gainful surface-to-air missiles (SAM) from Baghdad to the vicinity of the border in order to bolster their air defences. However, while the air power proved effective in destroying much of the Iraqi oil industry, and thus blocking fuel supplies for the front, left on its own it was insufficient to prevent the invaders from establishing good blocking positions from which they could beat off spasmodic and uncoordinated Iranian attacks.[10]

Hindered by complete chaos in their state and the military, and the Kurdish uprising in the north, the Iranians were slow to react. Furthermore, they also misinterpreted Iraqi attacks upon their border posts as an Iraqi attempt to support the Kurds in a similar fashion to what the Shah did in Iraq in 1974–1975.

PART II: THE OPENING OPERATIONS

Table 21: Order of Battle for Iraqi Invasion of Iran, Northern and Central Fronts, September 1980

Corps	Division	Brigades
Iraq		
I Corps	2nd Mountain Division	3 brigades
	4th Mountain Division	3 brigades
	7th Mountain Division	3 brigades
	8th Infantry Division	4 brigades
	11th Infantry Division	4 brigades
	12th Armoured Division	4 brigades
	31st Special Forces Brigade	
	32nd Special Forces Brigade	
II Corps	3rd Armoured Division	4 brigades
	6th Armoured Division	4 brigades
	10th Armoured Division	4 brigades
	31st Special Forces Brigade	
Iran		
	29th Infantry Division (Sanandaj)	4 brigades (-)
	64th Infantry Division (Urumia)	4 brigades (-)
	81st Armoured Division (Kermanshah)	4 brigades (-)
	40th Independent Infantry Brigade (Sarab)	
	84th Independent Infantry Brigade (Khorramabad)	
	2nd Brigade	from 92nd Armoured Division

During the opening Iraqi strike of the war, a formation of MiG-21bis from No. 47 Squadron bombed the Iranian Army base in Orumiyeh. The aircraft flown by Lt Ra'ad Hamid was blown up by the premature detonation of its bombs, and the pilot killed. (Tom Cooper collection)

A group of Iranian Army soldiers with the ejection seat of Ra'ad Hamid's MiG-21bis. (Tom Cooper collection)

A still from a video, showing Iraqi T-55s lining-up prior to start of another advance into Iran, in late September 1980. (Tom Cooper collection)

Another early loss of the Iraqi Air Force over the central front was this Su-22, claimed shot down on 24 September 1980, in the Marivan area. (Tom Cooper collection)

Qasr-e Shirin Sector

Dominating a prominent salient into Iraq, Qasr-e Shirin was a town about 20 kilometres from the border in between fertile, undulating plains in the west, and the Zagros Mountains in the east: overall good tank country, broken by relatively few low hills and ravines. Most of the population fled in the days before the Iraqi invasion, while the most important position was the Baytaq Pass, a narrow defile through which ran the road to Kermanshah.

Commandos of the 32nd Special Forces Brigade cleared the way for the 6th Armoured Division and 8th Infantry Division during the night from 22 to 23 September 1980, by securing a bridge near Emam Hassan and key peaks around Sar-e Pol-e Zahab. The 25th Mechanised Brigade (6th Armoured Division) then isolated Qasr-e Shirin from the north-east, while the 30th Armoured Brigade pushed eastwards on Sar-e Pol-e Zahab. As the Iraqis progressed deeper into

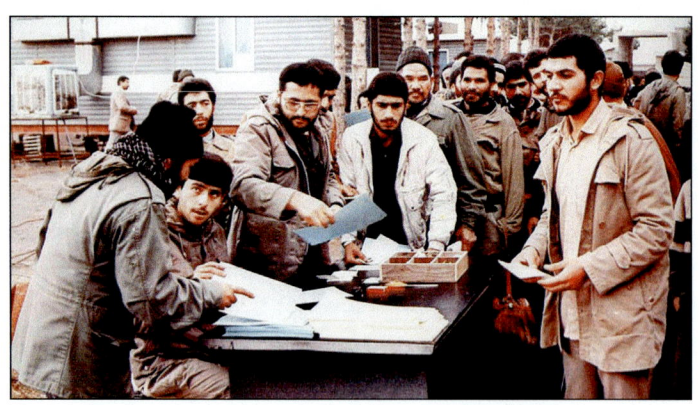

MIDDLE EAST@WAR SERIES SPECIAL #1: THE IRAN-IRAQ WAR

The Iranian Army had only around 11,000 troops deployed along the central and northern sectors of the front lines at the start of the war. However, the Iraqi invasion prompted dozens of thousands of Iranians to volunteer for military service. (Albert Grandolini collection)

Iran they used tactics based on strong artillery support used to ease the progress of the infantry. This became ever more important as the IRIA began deploying its highly effective artillery groups. Worse still the Kurds, whom Baghdad believed would regard the Iraqis as liberators now began harassing their advance.

Nevertheless, the two Iraqi brigades pushed down the road before running into elements of an IRIAF mechanised infantry platoon and two companies with about 25 main battle tanks (MBTs). These delayed them for two days, and Qasr-e Shirin thus fell only on 27 September 1980.[11]

Assault on Gilan-e Gharb

The only major IRIA formation in this part of Iran – 81st Armoured Division – took two days to bring at least its 1st Brigade into operational order. This was deployed westwards from Kermanshah. Its 3rd Brigade moved out of its barracks on the next day and then quickly stopped the advance of 25th Mechanised Brigade on Sar-e Pol-e Zahab. Similarly, a weak battalion group was enough to stop the first Iraqi attack on Gilan-e Gharb.

The Iraqi caution in these operations was remarkable, considering their superiority in heavy weaponry. According to US intelligence assessments, the Iraqi Army had 282 MBTs against 42 Iranian as of mid-October 1980, and its 183 artillery pieces were facing some 65 Iranian. However, the Iraqis were critically short on infantry: after their 30th Armoured Brigade suffered heavy losses – mostly to nocturnal Iranian counterattacks – it had to be reinforced by two battalions of 3rd Infantry Brigade.[12] Meanwhile, the 8th Infantry Division pushed on Gilan-e Gharb, with the 22nd Infantry Brigade advancing from the south towards the Kojar Pass, and the 3rd Infantry Brigade on the Sisar Heights in the north. However, these forces proved inadequate: the need to protect their lines of communication meant the two Iraqi brigades were unable to take the town.

Further south, Brigadier General Muhammad Ismail al-Weis led his 12th Armoured Division towards Sumar. His unit was a recently converted infantry formation, and Weis had to relinquish his 37th Armoured Brigade to the 2nd Infantry Division. However, in turn he received 10th Armoured Brigade (Colonel Mahmud Shukr Shahin) from the General Headquarters (GHQ). Even then, his advance was led by 46th Mechanised Brigade – which, after colliding with elements of 2nd Brigade of the 81st Armoured Division at Nafte-Shah – required two days of bitter fighting to punch through towards Gilan-e Gharb. Meanwhile, Shahin's brigade supported 4th Mountain Division's advance on Sumar, which was reached by the morning of 24 September, while 5th Mountain Brigade (Lieutenant Colonel Sultan Hashim Ahmad) cleared the way for Shukr Shain by advancing over the Haran Plateau, then supporting the capture of Sumar, before pushing on Gilan-e Gharb.

This combination of five brigades – further reinforced by the 18th and 29th Infantry Brigades – eventually managed to break through and briefly took Gilan-e Gharb on 28 September. However, they were forced out in a matter of few hours.[13]

The primary reason for this failure was the habit of Iraqi drivers of bunching their vehicles like a flock of sheep whenever under fire, rather than dispersing them. Despite losing their top pilot – Major General Mansour Vatanpour, who was shot down and killed – attack helicopters of the IRIAA thus found a 'target rich environment' and exploited the opportunity to score dozens of kills.[14]

This bought the time for 81st Armoured Division IRIA to start implementing its defensive plan 'Abuzar' (one of Prophet Mohammed's companions, Hazrat Abu Zar Ghaffari), and deploy its forces in delaying operations along a 600-kilometre-wide frontline. Reinforced by Border Guards, Gendarmerie, Pasdaran and Kurdish tribesmen, the Iranian Army then launched increasingly stronger counterattacks while divisional artillery harassed the invader joined by fierce fixed-wing and rotary-wing air support. Eventually, the Iraqis were not only stopped, but also by mid-December 1980 found themselves exposed to the first Iranian counteroffensive – the primary benefit of which was to keep the enemy in their positions until snow ended operations in that year.[15]

M60A1 MBTs and an AH-1J Cobra attack helicopter of the Iranian Army seen in a forward base in the central sector of the Iran-Iraq War, in late 1980. (Tom Cooper collection)

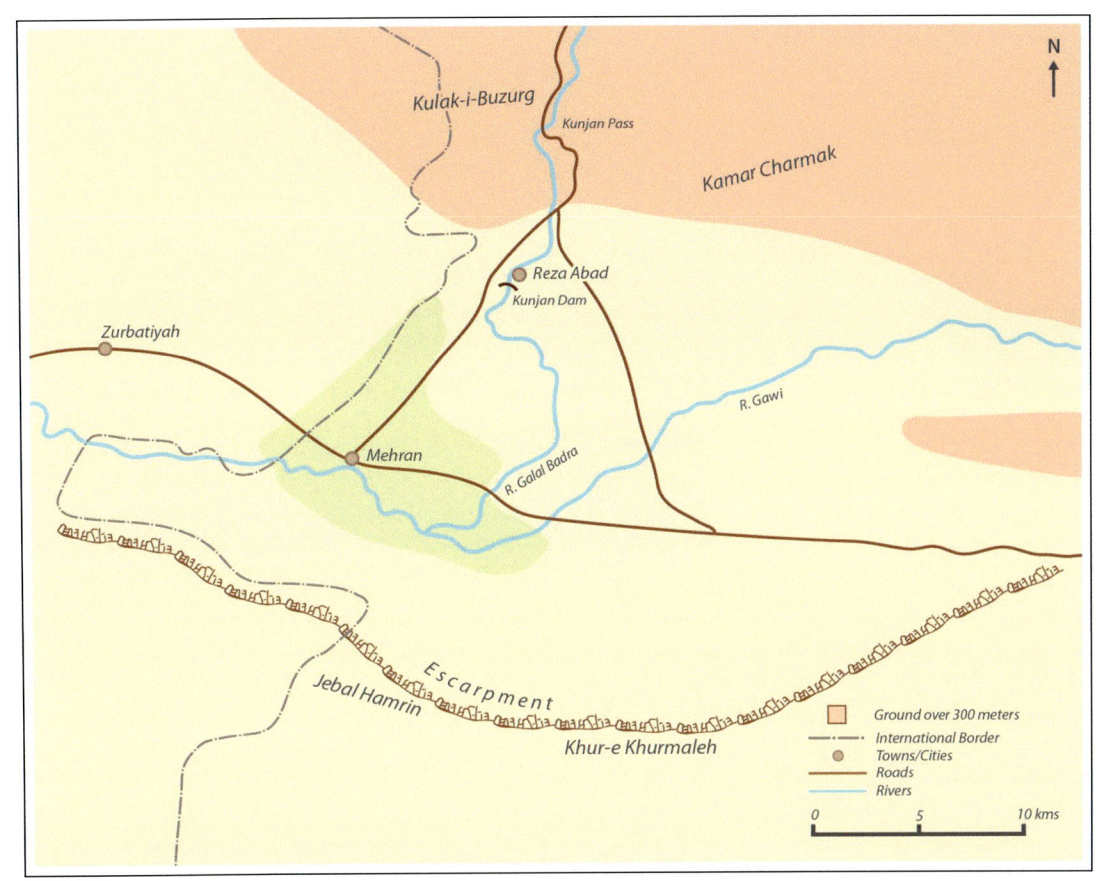

PART II: THE OPENING OPERATIONS

Mehran Sector. (Map by George Anderson)

Mehran Sector

An important Iraqi objective was the town of Mehran, with a population of about 75,000. This occupies a pincer-like salient into Iraqi territory, pointing in the direction of Baghdad, some 150 kilometres to the west. Furthermore, its occupation was to protect the fertile fields of Diyala Province and al-Kut (Kut al-Imara), with their citrus groves and orchards, some 75 kilometres away and result in the capture of the Kunjan Dam on the River Galal Badra.

Mehran was defended by a weak battalion battlegroup of 1st Brigade, 81st Armoured Division, which faced overwhelming odds – in the form of Brigadier General Hazim Sulayman al-Barhawi's 2nd Infantry Division. Barhavi deployed his 4th Infantry Brigade and elements of 33rd Special Forces Brigade north of Mehran towards Konjam Cham Pass and captured the dam on 24 September 1980. His main attack – involving 36th Infantry and 37th Armoured Brigades – came along the main road and was held for two hours at a berm-covered anti-armour ditch. Nevertheless, he entered the town on the morning of 24 September.

As the defenders withdrew eastwards, the Iraqis followed into a river-crossed plain with numerous ridges and defiles, which were easy to defend. This slowed the invader's advance to a crawl, with little artillery or air support. The Iraqi problems were increased by their own commando attack on the Galal Badra irrigation dam, which flooded much of the area.[16] Unsurprisingly, 2nd Infantry Brigade was still three kilometres from Ilam by the end of September and had no prospect of proceeding – especially once the Iranians solidified their positions.[17]

In early October, 8th Infantry Division (including 3rd, 22nd, and 23rd Infantry Brigades) took over responsibility for the Qasr-e Shirin sector, while the 2nd Infantry and 4th Mountain Divisions did the same in the south. Latif then ordered the demolition of buildings in Qasr-e Shirin, Gilan-e Ghab and Sumar, to use their timber and girders to build fortifications and thus tighten the grip. All of his positions were to receive overhead protection and were dispersed to reduce the impact of artillery and air strikes. Furthermore, his units withdrew as many of their non-combat elements as possible to reduce the strain on supplies. Even then, the Iraqis in the Mehran area were clearly overstretched, and by the end of 1980 had to be reinforced by a battalion-sized battlegroup from 12th Armoured Division.[18]

Battle for Dezful

On Latif's right Major General Adnan Kadum's III Corps operations into the southern part of Iran's Ilam Province and the northern part of Khuzestan – centred around Major General Abdul Hamid

Saddam and King Hussein of Jordan inspecting tanks (including an M60A1 MBT) captured early during the Iraqi invasion of Iran. (Tom Cooper collection)

The first Iraqi soldier taken prisoner of war by the Iranians in the Ilam area, in late September 1980. (via Ali Tobchi)

265

A still from a video showing an Iraqi T-62s involved in the advance on Dezful, in late September and early October 1980. (Tom Cooper collection)

An SA.342 Gazelle attack helicopter of the Iraqi Army Air Corps underway low over the frontlines west of Dezful, in October 1980. (via Ali Tobchi)

F-5Es from the Tactical Fighter Base 4 (TFB.4) played a crucial role in the defence of Dezful and their home base. During 15 days of the Battle for Dezful, between 27 September and 11 October 1980, they flew 324 attack sorties, and claimed the destruction of 170 Iraqi tanks and other armoured vehicles, forcing the invaders into a retreat. (Tom Cooper collection)

Despite success, the Battle of Dezful proved costly for the IRIAF's TFB.4: at least four of its F-5Es – including the example shown here (presented to foreign journalists as 'an Iraqi') – were shot down by Iraqi ground defences. (Albert Grandolini collection)

at-Tikriti's 1st Mechanised Division (including 1st and 27th Mechanised, and 34th Armoured Brigades) – aimed to complete control of the Iranian frontier road system. This push did pose a threat to Dezful too, although the Iraqis insist they never planned to capture the city.

On 20 September 1980, Saddam replaced Kadum with Lieutenant General Ismael Tayeh an-Niami, and then reinforced III Corps with Major General Sabah al-Fakhri's 10th Armoured Division (including 17th and 42nd Armoured, and 24th Mechanised Brigades).[19] Sabah used 24th Mechanised Brigade to isolate the battlefield from the north by striking from Tib, while 17th Armoured Brigade – followed by 42nd and supported by 24 artillery batteries – took Musiyan and then attacked Eyn Kush. The local IRIA garrison consisted of 2nd Brigade from the 92nd Armoured Division, but this had only five serviceable MBTs and three M113 APCs with TOW launchers. Although anti-armour missiles took a heavy toll of Iraqi tanks, Dasht Abbas fell on 26 September, enabling invaders to push on to Dezful. Upon reaching the Khark River they found two out of three bridges demolished, while the surviving construction was only suitable for pedestrian traffic. Relentless air strikes by F-5Es from the nearby TFB.4 – including extensive use of CBUs – then caused such losses that the Iraqi commanders soon found themselves lacking troops and equipment to cross the river. The Iranians are known to have flown 324 sorties against this area within a fortnight, and to have lost seven aircraft to air defences. This campaign proved at least sufficient to discourage any kind of Iraqi ambitions with regards to Dezful. Instead, the III Corps limited its activities in this area to shelling. Even a battery of LUNA-M (FROG-7) rockets was deployed for this purpose. At least six of its weapons were fired, causing around 470 casualties.

After regrouping, the Iraqis attacked Dehloran on 13 October; although managing to enter the town they were quickly driven out. Indeed, between 14 and 16 October, a brigade-sized element of 92nd Armoured Division launched a series of counterattacks that struck the 10th Armoured Division's left flank. The 42nd Armoured and 24th Mechanised Brigades counterattacked and recovered the lost ground, claiming the capture of 136 armoured vehicles – including 84 MBTs – in the process. During this fighting Iran's Major General Muhammad Reza Ziaie was killed.

The Dezful sector then became quiet. The IRIA deployed its 21st Division (created from two former Imperial Guard divisions) to reinforce defences, together with a battalion of M60 MBTs from the 77th Infantry Division, and a battalion of marines. However, the Iranian operations remained purely defensive by nature – which puzzled the Iraqis. Before long, there was talk about replacing the two mechanised divisions of the II Corps with 11th Infantry Division.

The Crawl on Shush

Further south, 1st Mechanised Division – supported by 12 artillery batteries including one of BM-21 multiple launch rocket systems (MLRS), took the border town of Fakkeh and – supported by 34th Armoured Brigade – then pushed across hilly terrain towards Shush. The Iraqis thus concentrated a force of more than 200 MBTs and 200 artillery pieces to attack an area protected by a mere 62 tanks and a dozen towed and self-propelled guns of the IRIA.[20] However, their advance was extremely slow; they first concentrated upon neutralising a handful of border posts before beginning to crawl

The Shi'a clergy did much to bolster the morale of the Iranian combatants right from the first days of the war. Here the future 'Supreme Leader of the Islamic Revolution', Ayatollah Sayyid Ali Hosseini Khamenei, is seen with an officer of the Iranian Army during one of his visits of the frontlines. (Mark Lepko collection)

eastwards and eliminating the IRIAF's forward ground installations – including several radar stations.

This slow advance created a threat to the northern flank of III Corps as it advanced through Susangerd, and prompted the 3rd Armoured Division to send its 12th Armoured Brigade northeast from Amarah for a 40-kilometre flanking movement – to threaten the defenders from the south. While capturing the IRIAF's crucial radar site, on 2 October, the push was blocked near Chenaneh not only by the 37th Combat Group, but also two infantry battalions of 21st Division and the reconnaissance regiment of 92nd Armoured Division. The last significant Iraqi operation in this area in 1980 saw the 3rd Armoured Division inflict heavy losses upon the 2nd Brigade of the 92nd Armoured Division, leaving the Iranians demoralised. In turn, this enabled the Iraqis to establish good defensive positions along the upper Khark River, opposite Shush. However, they failed to secure the sand dune belt to the south which runs northeast of Bostan – because the III Corps on their right was bogged down in fighting around Susangerd.

Iraqi I Corps in the Winter of 1980–1981

Despite their initial success, the Northern and Central Fronts remained relatively tense during the winter of 19801981, because Iraqi positions were constantly harassed by Iranian artillery and infantry raids. By 14 January 1981, reports emerged about the 18th Infantry Brigade of the 4th Mountain Division and the 50th Armoured Brigade of the 12th Armoured Division showing signs of 'stress'; the few infantry units available were insufficient to properly secure the foothills around Ilam and the local road network became too dangerous even for movement of armoured fighting vehicles. The Iranians repeatedly infiltrated teams of jeep-mounted TOWs behind Iraqi positions and knocked out at least 35 MBTs over time. Local Iraqi units also suffered from a lack of 130mm ammunition: their M-46 guns had to be replaced by 122mm pieces transferred from mountain divisions until sufficient stocks could be built-up.

Lacking other solutions, Iraqi Army Chief-of-Staff, Lieutenant General Abd el-Jabbar Shahshal, suggested attaching Kurdish guerrillas to armoured units. The Director of the General Military Intelligence Directorate (GMID), Brigadier General Abdul Jawad Dhannoun, supported this idea through a proposal to establish the so-called 'al-Jaf Group' – made up of about 1,500 Kurdish fighters

The first phase of the Iran-Iraq War was one of great crisis for the Iranians. They had too few troops to occupy more than the most sensitive points along the frontlines and had suffered heavy casualties. These Iranian infantrymen were photographed while evacuating an injured comrade. (Albert Grandolini collection)

from the Halabja area. However, Saddam not only preferred a much larger operation, but also recognised the threat of the Iranians destroying invading forces piecemeal.[21]

Overall, reflecting the priority on COIN – by direct or indirect means – the I Corps launched only two minor offensives during the winter of 1980–1981. In mid-December 1980, it struck southwest from Penjwin, attempting to capture the communications hub of Marivan and pre-empt any conventional threat to Sulaymaniyah. Advancing through rain, low cloud and mist on 18 December, it pushed some 50 kilometres into the foothills of the Zagros Mountains, encountering only weak resistance from 3rd Brigade of 28th Infantry Division, taking some 775 square kilometres with little loss. The Iranians reacted with air strikes and claim to have established air superiority over the region, which they should have held until the end of the war. However, the IRIAA lost at least one AH-1J, together with its pilot, Major General Sharif Ashraf.[22]

Later the same month, 4th Mountain Division advanced two kilometres across the border from Halabja to the road junction of Nowsud (Nowdesheh), in support of the KDPI. The Iranian garrison – consisting of IRIA troops with some Pasdaran – was quickly driven out and the KDPI-leader Abdu Rahman Ghassemlou established his headquarters there. The Iranians counterattacked in Operation Mohammad Rasoolallah, on 2 January 1981, advancing some 5–6 kilometres despite bitter cold, strong winds and heavy snow – only to be pushed out by an Iraqi counterattack.[23]

Despite the difficult weather, I Corps of the Iraqi Army staged another offensive around Nowsud and Penjwin, aiming to pin down enemy forces and erode their strength. On 21 January 1981, 38th Infantry Brigade of 7th Infantry Division launched one raid, followed by another – involving 39th Infantry Brigade – on 15 February. Following the thaw, Iranian attacks pushed back the Iraqis and on 29–31 May 1981 they struck 4th Mountain Division in the Penjwin sector but were held by 29th Infantry Brigade. A similar effort in the Nowsud sector had the same effect. The Iranians attempted again on 2 July 1981 but lost most of their gains to Iraqi counterattacks. The campaigning season in that year ended on 10 November, when 4th Mountain Division staged a successful pre-emptive attack on Iranian concentrations in the Nowsud region, despite heavy snow and low temperatures.[24]

II Corps' Problems

Starting from the night of 4/5 January 1981, the Iranians launched a small, diversionary offensive near Mehran and regained a few hundred metres of high ground in the upper valley of the Galal Badra. Five days later, they opened a month-long offensive by the Pasdaran – apparently their first large-scale offensive – targeting positions of 2nd Infantry Brigade, 2nd Infantry Division of the Iraqi Army. This resulted in the Iranians gaining control of the 12-kilometre-long Meimak Heights near Saif Saad. The success emboldened the Pasdaran to use large-scale infantry assaults as their battle-winning tactics in the future. Combined with the Iranian Operation Hoveyzeh, the IRGC's attack caused serious concerns for Saddam, who was worried that the Iranians might penetrate all the way to Baghdad. Certainly enough, Iranian harassing and diversionary operations not only confused the Iraqi leadership but eroded the morale of their troops. Correspondingly, Defence Minister Adnan Kharaillah paid a three-day visit to the front, between 5 and 7 February 1981, as a result of which the brigade commander Lieutenant Colonel Muhammad Juwad Kadhum and one of his company commanders were executed; the division commander Brigadier General Hazem al-Barhawi was replaced by Brigadier General Jawad Asad Shitna, while the commander of II Corps, Lieutenant General Taha ash-Shakarji was replaced by Lieutenant General Abd al-Jabar Abd ar-Rahim al-Asadi.[25] Furthermore, Saddam visited this frontline on 6 March, accompanied by King Hussein of Jordan, who witnessed the entry of the Jordanian 'al-Yarmouk Force' into the line.[26]

The rest of 1981 saw the II Corps concentrating primarily on the Qasr-e Shirin sector, where the Iranians launched several attempts to regain the town. The first was a week-long attack in the Dana Khushk heights, launched on the night of 22 to 23 April by the 7th Ghadir Brigade IRGC, supported by a tank battalion of 81st Division IRIA. The sector, which included peaks dominating the approaches to Qasr-e Shirin, was held by Major General Salem Hussein al-Ali's 8th Infantry Division, and Brigadier General Nizar Abd al-Karim al-Khazraji's 7th Infantry Division, which replaced the 4th Mountain Division. The 8th Division's 3rd Infantry Brigade had just replaced 22nd Infantry Brigade and was still unfamiliar with the territory, while other defenders were overstretched, tired and lacking reserves. Unsurprisingly, they were pushed back and it took the II Corps' major effort to retake Dana Khushk. This counterattack began on the night of 27–28 April 1981. The two infantry divisions were reinforced by the Republican Guards Brigade, 32nd Special Forces Brigade and the 6th Armoured Division, and saw the 7th Division fighting its way into the Dana Khushk from the south, while three other divisions swept along the road from Qasr-e Shirin to Sar-e Pol-e Zahab to regain most of the lost terrain. Even then, the Iranians retained their grip on Gilan-e Gharb and took 500 prisoners.[27]

Another Iranian attack – launched on the night of 3–4 September 1981 – drove 8th Infantry Division from much of the Sisar Heights, while 7th Infantry Division lost much of the Dana Khushk and the Kojar Pass. Further north, 6th Armoured Division had to bring forward two brigades to stabilise the situation but it was the deployment of 32nd Special Forces Brigade that re-established the Iraqis in the Sisar range. The 7th Infantry Division – reinforced by the Special Forces Battalion of the Republican Guards – sought to regain the lost ground in the Dana Khushk, but with only limited success. Eventually, Baghdad had to accept that its Qasr-e Shirin garrison was exposed, and from mid-October 1981 it began withdrawing troops from this area to reinforce the Dezful sector. Furthermore, 6th Armoured Division positioned its 25th Mechanised Brigade forward, while the remainder of its units were redeployed up to 16 kilometres further west. This was a rather humiliating development considering that they faced only one depleted IRIA armoured brigade and various minor Pasdaran units.[28]

Operation Matla al-Fajr

On the Central Front, the year 1981 ended with a major Iranian offensive, Operation Matla al-Fajir (Rising of Dawn), launched on 11 December. Advancing through heavy rain, 81st Armoured Division, 58th Commando Brigade, and a reinforced 7th Ghadir Pasdaran Brigade (totalling 14 battalions), attacked 2nd Infantry Brigade of 12th Armoured Division in the Summar sector. The following morning, the Iranians also assaulted the front and the right flank of 7th Infantry Division at Gilan-e Gharb and Qasr-e Shiring sector. As the battle descended into hand-to-hand fighting, the Iranians not only drove back the Iraqis, but also thwarted all counterattacks. Only the second Iraqi effort – a counterattack by 12th Armoured Division (now commanded by Brigadier General Talal Khalil ad-Duri) – on the evening of 17 December 1981, regained most of the

Illustrating the kind of problems both sides faced during the fighting in the northern sector of the Iran-Iraq War, this photograph shows a column of IRGC troops navigating one of the endless mountain chains in January 1982. (Tom Cooper collection)

lost ground. Nevertheless, fighting continued and it was only on 5 January 1982 that the Iraqis retook the last of their lost positions. Even then, the Iranians caught their breath and struck again, this time to the south, starting on 5 January, retaking Gilan-e Gharb. However, their thrust against Naft Shah was repulsed.[29]

In an attempt to bolster the morale, Saddam then gave a speech claiming his army could take any place. In order to demonstrate this, 10th Armoured Division was ordered to take Dehloran. This created a task force centred around 17th Armoured Brigade, and attacked during the night of 28–29 May. The Iraiqs took the town, but lacked infantry to hold it and were forced to withdraw only 12 hours later.[30]

Further south, the III Corps spent most of the winter of 1980–1981 strengthening defensive positions, improving the roads and constructing supply dumps. Sorkheh was developed into a major stronghold, but then the Iraqis recognised that two mechanised divisions were unsuitable for holding the area and forward-deployed reserve brigades in their place.

The Iranian side of the frontline was held by 1st Brigade of 21st Infantry Divison (Dezful sector) and 2nd Brigade of 92nd Armoured Division (Shush sector). These totalled only some 100 MBTs and some 70 artillery pieces, and thus did very little. Between 3 and 21 April 1981, 21st Infantry Division attacked the two Iraqi reserve brigades and took their positions, but then the front went largely quiet for the rest of the year.[31]

19
PRIVATE WARS

Although part of a greater struggle, many operations by both sides on the Northern and Central Fronts had the characteristics of private wars. These were fought in a wide range of terrain and, unlike the big battles on the Southern Front, were characterised by the absence of a continuous line.

In areas where they were constructed, frontlines wound high into the mountains, until reaching elevations and areas where they rather resembled scattered battalion and company strongpoints. Most positions in the mountains were based on stone breastworks (sangars); except in the summer, these were bitterly cold and vulnerable to heavy snow falls or torrential rains that occasionally triggered avalanches or land slips. The latter two also kept both sides constantly busy with repairing their roads.

Fighting in such terrain required top physical fitness – not only because of the rugged terrain but also due to the rare air and frequent supply problems. Four-wheel-drive vehicles could move supplies over many of the minor roads and even hillside tracks but, with few helicopters for resupply, mule trains remained the prime means of moving food and ammunition. The mountainous terrain also presented radio communication problems: the use of FM radios was restricted by limited horizontal and vertical line-of-sight, while UHF radio signals could be 'bent' to leap over mountain tops – all provided the transceivers were positioned high enough. Multiple peaks would usually thwart their transmissions.

Iranian Army Organisation

On the Iranian side the defence was originally based upon scattered, understrength, IRIA formations augmented by gendarmerie and police. New command arrangements were created under the Supreme Defence Council (SDC), with representatives of the government and the armed forces, and between 1984 and 1986 when several brigades were expanded into divisions. The IRIA Ground Forces command then created two Forward Operational Headquarters (FOHQ); the Northern (NFOHQ) with headquarters in Torbat-e Heydariyeh, northwest of Urmia, with a forward HQ near Sumar; and the Central (CFOHQ) at Kermanshah. The right wing of the Southern Front (SFOHQ) was semi-autonomous.[1]

Iranian troops with a Chieftain MBT, somewhere in the Dezful sector, in 1981. (via N.S.)

An Iranian soldier guarding four Scorpion light tanks, somewhere on the central front, during the first winter of the Iran-Iraq War. A squadron of Scorpions was assigned to the reconnaissance regiment of each Iranian Army division. (via N.S.)

The NFOHQ controlled the 28th, 30th and 64th Infantry Division IRIA, the 11th Artillery Group and – later on – the 23rd Special Forces Division, with a total of some 80,000 troops by 1988. The CFOHQ eventually received the 58th and 84th Infantry; the 81st and 88th Armoured divisions; 37th Armoured, 40th Infantry, and 55th Airborne brigades; and 191st Combat Group and 44th Artillery Group – with a total of about 91,000 troops. The Dezful sector controlled the 16th Armoured, 21st and 77th Infantry divisions, and 22nd Artillery Group with a total of no fewer than 61,000 troops, but would often detach brigades to the Southern Front.[2] The IRIAA usually operated detachments from the 1st, 2nd, and 3rd Combat Support Groups (CSGs) and the 4th and 5th General Support Groups (GSGs) close to the frontline. All major Army formations were usually reinforced with ad hoc Qods battalions before they began benefitting from the expansion of the IRGC.

The Dezful sector was often 'milked' to aid its neighbours: at least one brigade of 16th Armoured Division and one or two brigades of 21st and 77th divisions were usually attached to the SFOHQ, while in 1984 they were temporarily joined by most of the NFOHQ's 28th Division and a brigade of the 81st Division. The security situation in the north necessitated the return of the 28th Division in November 1984, but the poor transport network meant such movements took an inordinate amount of time. For example, moving 81st Division to new positions in CFOHQ took almost two months. Therefore, most of the IRIA divisions acted as static sector commands.

Gendarmerie and Pasdaran

Supporting the IRIA was the Iranian Islamic Gendarmerie under the Interior Ministry and responsible for law enforcement in rural areas and border patrols. It strength had dropped from 75,000 before the revolution to 40,000 (mostly due to conscripts leaving) and it was organised into some 250 companies assigned to 16 districts – each with two to five 'regiments.' The Gendarmerie was primarily armed with small arms, mortars and light anti-armour weapons, but had a few BTR-60 wheeled APCs, and excellent communication systems. Therefore, it was often deployed to support combat operations in the north.

The Gendarmerie also shielded the road network near the border from guerrillas and special forces but proved not particularly successful due to the terrain. The IRIA berated the Gendarmerie paramilitary force for its failures, and a number of minor operations to take heights to the west were motivated by necessity to keep related problems in check, as much as with the crushing of the Kurdish revolt (which ended only in 1983).

As in the south, the Revolutionary Guards began deploying ever larger light infantry formations within the NFOHQ and CFOHQ, starting in 1982, but they never deployed as many of their troops in these areas as they did in the south. Through mid-1980s, the Pasdaran created specialised support formations – such as artillery and engineers – from infantry units. It was during this period that the 45th Javad ol-Aemeh and 46th al-Haadi Engineer Divisions, and the 89th Moharram Artillery Brigade came into being. There followed specialised infantry formations like the 6th Imam Sadeq Commando Division, the 77th Nabbovat Commando and 622nd Beit-ol-Moghadddas Mountain Brigades. Even then, the number of such formations remained very limited; as of 1988 US intelligence assessed the total IRGC manpower with the NFOHQ at only 20,000, and that with the CFOHQ at 30,000. By contrast, the

Pasdaran formations in Dezful sector alone totalled about 68,000. It was only following the disastrous attempts to take Basra – operations Val Fajr-4/5/8 – that Tehran decided to switch attention to the Northern Front and transferred about a dozen divisions and brigades (total of about 100,000 troops) from the SFOHQ to the NFOHQ.[3]

Raids and Reconnaissance Operations

The rugged terrain in the north provided opportunities for deep reconnaissance, raiding and sabotage operations. At first the Iranians used special forces teams from 23rd Commando Brigade, sometimes reinforced by teams from 55th Airborne Brigade. However, the IRIA's participation in special operations was gradually restricted. Instead, it was its SIGINT base at Sanandaj – which had staff fluent in English, different Kurdish dialects, Arabic and Russian – which became ever more important.[4]

It was the Pasdaran which assumed the lead in special operations. In the mid-1980s, they established their 66th Vali-ye-Amr and 75th Zhafar Special Forces Brigades (both were part of Pasdaran military intelligence). Furthermore, as Tehran's relations with the Iraqi Kurds improved, in 1986 the Ramadan Guerrilla Warfare Headquarters (RGWHQ) was established. Supported by the IRIAA, this command of the IRGC included its two special forces brigades and the 67th Brigade, trained specifically to attack oil pipelines. However, this unit launched only a few operations before Turkish diplomatic pressure forced Tehran to stop targeting such installations; indeed, it might have resulted in disbandment of the latter unit.

Nevertheless, the RGWHQ organised cross-border supplies for the Iraqi Kurds and began co-ordinating their operations to a degree where nearly all major Kurdish operations of the late 1980s appear to have been devised in, and directed from, Iran. Furthermore, this headquarters supported such non-Kurdish groups as insurgents of the Dawa Party and had one of their units attached to the 9th Badr Division IRGC.

Many commando operations on the northern sector of the frontlines involved heliborne insertion of the involved troops. Here an IRGC-unit is waiting its turn to embark upon a CH-47C Chinook helicopter of the IRIAA. (IRIAA)

This photograph shows a Bell 214A helicopter of the IRIAA deploying troops on another 'strategically important' peak. (IRIAA)

Iraqi Reorganisations

On the Iraqi side I and II Corps were initially responsible for command and control on the two fronts. However, as the Iranians recovered and began exercising pressure upon the whole frontline, the Iraqis found themselves forced to reorganise. After realising that the II Corps held a frontline of no less than 460 kilometres, Saddam ordered the establishment of IV Corps under Major General Hisham Sabah al-Fakhri, with its HQ in al-Amarah. This took over the 1st Mechanised and 10th Armoured Division from the III Corps and became responsible for operations in Wasit and Maysan Provinces. The II Corps' front was reduced to southern Diyala, while the I Corps' frontline was limited to operations in Arbil, Sulaymaniyah and northern Diyala.[5]

The lack of a separate command for the relatively quiet Wasit Province remained a problem. In 1984 the responsibility for this

PART II: PRIVATE WARS

The year 1982 was one of major Iranian victories on several battlefields of the Iran-Iraq War. This Iraqi OT-62 (Czechoslovak-made variant of the BTR-50 APC) slipped off a bridge during one of the often paniced retreats. (via N.S.)

A group of captured Iraqi troops seen at one of the collection points behind Iranian lines in 1982. (via N.S.)

area was transferred to the East of Tigris Operations Headquarters (ETOH), but the growing threat in the Hawaizeh Marshes saw it returned to the south. Finally, in September 1986 a unique solution was found in establishing the I Special Corps, headquartered in al-Kut under Lieutenant General Ismael Tayeh an-Nuaimi. Nauaimi controlled three volunteer divisions and a special commando brigade consisting of retired officers and reservists, most of them older than 39.[6]

While such reorganisations helped improve the control of conventional operations, the Northern Front in particular continued facing a growing unconventional threat, especially in the form of Iranian-supported Kurdish insurgency. The need both to run a counterinsurgency campaign and interdict Kurdish supply lines across northern Iraq led to the creation of Northern Operations Headquarters (Quaidet Amaliyat ash-Shamaliyah, NOHQ) under Major General Dhiya ad-Din Jala, in the summer of 1985. This was responsible for operations along the Turkish border in Arbil, Dahuk and Ninaws provinces, and was later upgraded to the status of V Corps (HQ in Arbil). Unlike the Southern Front, local commanders were frequently rotated. This was Saddam's decision, aimed at preventing officers from creating power bases. However, others were removed for failures – including brave, staunch and proven members of the Ba'ath Party – like Major Generals Taha Nuri Yasi ash-Shakarji and Sultan Hashim Ahmed al-Jaburi at-Tai. Furthermore, Major General Abd al-Aziz Ibrahim al-Hadithi was killed on 22 January 1988, when his helicopter crashed in bad weather.

The greatest changes took place in 1987–1988, when former commander of I Corps, Nizar Abd al-Karim al-Khazraji became Chief-of-Staff and began to reorganise the Iraqi Army in preparation for driving the Iranians back across the border. Although a Ba'athist, Khazraji was an extremely able commander, and a key feature of his new strategy was to create a massive GHQ reserve by stripping most of the corps' reserves – a concept which Saddam accepted but which had to be 'sold' to the corps commanders. Most accepted this but II Corps' Lieutenant General Shawkat Ahmed Ata and I Special Corps neighbour Lieutenant General Ismail Taya al-Nuaimi remained strongly opposed. Saddam's reaction was to replace Ata (a competent but overcautious officer who lost the Faw Peninsula in 1987) with Kamel Sajet Aziz al-Janabi and Nuaimi (one of Iraq's longest-serving officers), and then another retiree – Lieutenant General Kamal Jamil Aboud. Another, more delicate, command problem occurred before the 'Tawakkalna ala Allah 3' in the summer of 1988. The IV Corps commander Lieutenant General Muhammad Abd al-Qadir Abd al-Rahman had been responsible for much of the earlier planning for this operation, but Director of Operations, General Hussein Rashid

273

Al-Tikriti and the Director of Military Intelligence General Sabir al-Duri – who may have feared that another success by Qadir would make him the next candidate for the post of the Army's Chief-of-Staff (which they also coveted) – wanted him transferred to VII Corps, and replaced by the equally competent Lieutenant General Ayad Khlil Zaki. Defence Minister General Adnan Khairallah Telfah (Kairallah) wanted Qadir to remain in place at least until the new offensive finished. Eventually a compromise was reached; Qadir remained at IV Corps acting as standby for Ayad Khlil Zaki.[7]

T-55 MBTs of the Iraqi Army in a typical position surrounded by earthern berms, somewhere along the central frontline in 1984 or 1985. (Tom Cooper collection)

Expansion of the Iraqi Army

Iraq's original dozen divisions were inadequate for a prolonged war, and new ones were created – most of these infantry formations. Furthermore, the crisis on the Southern Front in summer of 1982 saw three divisions from I and II Corps (4th Mountain, 6th Armoured, and 11th Infantry) sent south. As compensation the 17th Armoured Division was formed in II Corps.

Between 1982 and 1986, 26 division-sized formations were created in the Northern and Central Fronts. Many were raised by expanding ad hoc formations like Ash-Shib Force (18th Division), Arbil Defence Force (23rd Division), Kirkuk Defence Force (24th Division), Jilat Force (25th Division), Darband-i-Khan Force (36th Division) and Shahibi Force (37th Division). Others – including the 43rd, 44th and 45th – were divisional task forces (Kiadat Kuwat) sometimes controlling brigades on an ad hoc basis, but with smaller support elements. Nominally, each new division had three brigades and often a commando battalion; in reality, the divisions acted as task force headquarters which could control up to 10 or more brigades with up to 26,000 troops. During a review of Northern Front operations on 26 May 1988, Khazraji noted that of 132 infantry brigades (including 16 special forces/commando formations) about half were within the NFOHQ, of which I Corps had 42, while V Corps had 15.[8]

Each corps had its own troops, including an artillery brigade, an air defence brigade, reconnaissance, engineer and bridging battalions. Corps commands also created up to two commando brigades as their intervention forces, and often augmented these with

Youthful troops of one of the many of ad hoc units of the Iraqi Army converted into regular divisions in the mid-1980s. Many of the resulting divisions were armed with older weapons and lacked their full complement of artillery and other support elements. (Albert Grandolini collection)

some of GHQ's special forces formations – created from the three original units. Commando brigades of I and V Corps were used for COIN operations too. Ground troops were supported by the Iraqi Army Aviation Corps (IrAAC), which provided units equipped with gunships and transport helicopters, but also squadrons equipped with Pilatus PC-7 light attack aircraft. Nominally, 1st Wing was headquartered in Kirkuk (it supported I and V Corps); 2nd Wing in Baghdad (it supported II and I Special Corps); and 4th Wing at Amara (it supported IV and VI Corps).[9]

Khazraji's demand for strengthening GHQ reserves was reinforced when the Iranians launched their Val Fajr-10 offensive around Lake Darband-i-Khan in March 1988. The destruction of 43rd Division created the need to reinforce I Corps and 28th Infantry Division, 70th and 80th Armoured Brigade (17th Armoured Division), and 46th Mechanised Brigade (12th Armoured Division) were all rushed up from II Corps, together with corps troops from IV Corps.[10] Their arrival helped to stabilise the front while the Iraqi Army was running a number of major offensives on the Southern Front in summer 1988.

For covert operations Baghdad relied upon its special forces, but also had two units of the GMID, created with Egyptian assistance in 1984, Units 888 and 999, each of some 800 officers and other ranks. The former unit was responsible for gathering intelligence and running sabotage operations with the help of sympathetic Iranians and Iranian Kurds; the latter unit was a deep reconnaissance formation similar to the British Special Air Service.[11] Finally, the GMID developed an extensive SIGINT infrastructure – although this proved less effective in tracking IRGC units – primarily because of Iranian chronical shortage of radios.

Iraqi Paramilitary Organisations

The Iraqi Army was supported by two paramilitary organisations. The 48,000-strong Border Guard (operated by the Ministry of Defence since February 1980, before reverting to the Ministry of Interior in March 1985), was organised into 24 brigades with three battalions of light infantry each. The Border Guard often supported the military in conventional and COIN operations, and – in low-level urban security duties – was augmented by the police and the Popular Army of the Ba'ath Party (al-Jaysh ash-Shabi).[12]

Rural areas of northern Iraq were the responsibility of the Kurdish militia – or Command of the National Defence Battalions (NDBs), nicknamed the Fursan Salahuldin (Saladin's Knights) – but also known as 'Young Donkeys' amongst Kurdish insurgents. Originally raised in the 1960s, the NDBs were primarily for internal security duties but they were also to attract men who might otherwise join the insurgents.[13] The NDBs were usually raised voluntarily – sometimes under pressure – by tribal leaders anxious to demonstrate their loyalty to Baghdad, or to strengthen their local standing. By 1987, there were 147 NDBs with – nominally – some 205,000 troops, or some 10 percent of the Kurdish population. Their number continued increasing and by August 1988 no fewer than 321 battalions may have been operational, totalling 412,636 troops. Correspondingly, starting in 1986, some NDBs were grouped into divisional-sized commands known as National Defence Headquarters, of which six were created within the areas of responsibility of I and V Corps by the end of the war.[14]

Each NDB was under the command of an advisor/consultant (Mustashar), selected by the clan or tribal leader, who – like all the troops – received a salary and was also paid for each man on his roster (which encouraged inflated strength returns). Indeed, one battalion was disbanded by the General Security Department (GSD) when it was discovered to have only 90 men and not the 500 claimed.

Many Kurds joined the NDBs to avoid being drafted into the Iraqi Army, but they had no enthusiasm for Baghdad and suffered a high desertion and absenteeism rate; 82,957 in the NFOHQ between August 1985 and March 1987. Unsurprisingly, five of battalions were disbanded for such reasons in 1987 alone. The GSD closely monitored the NDBs for signs of rebellion or defection, with suspected Mustashars sometimes being executed – one after he planned to assassinate the V Corps commander! To reduce the risk of defection or desertion, NBDs were frequently rotated between different areas, but this did not help; defections continued, and thus drastic consequences were introduced for families of deserters – including deportation and/or imprisonment. On the other hand, those that did join the NDB were considered pariahs among the Kurds. Correspondingly, their reliability was always of concern to the Ba'ath Party, which in October 1986 bitterly complained about their commitment, willingness to surrender, provide intelligence to the enemy, and to destroy or sell military equipment.[15]

The Ba'ath Party exercised the control over two 'elite' Kurdish COIN units – each of about 1,000 troops. One was the Emergency

A group of combatants of the MEK/MKO seen during their training. This organisation was widely publicised by the Iraqis in an attempt to discredit the government in Tehran through presenting example Iranians fighting on the side of Iraq. (Albert Grandolini collection)

The MEK/MKO included many females and was keen to present these in public. The group was foremost a political force and was rarely deployed in combat before 1988. (Albert Grandolini collection)

Force and responsible for urban COIN, while the other was the Special Unit, operated by the General Security Directorate (Amn), and responsible for rural counterintelligence. To counterbalance these two, the Ba'ath created the Light Battalions in 1984, but these, 'soon became a haven for deserters and volunteers looking to make a living and obtain arms'.[16]

Iranian Exiles

The two Iraqi fronts facing Iranians in the north and centre received the mixed blessings of the presence of the National Liberation Army (Artesh-e Azadibakhsh Melli Iran) – the military arm of the Mujahideen e-Khalq Iranian resistance movement. The NLA was founded on 20 June 1987, led by Massoud Rajavi but actually commanded by Mahmoud Ataii, this was considered a terrorist organisation in Iran, but rapidly grew in size. By 1988, it included 10 full divisions with 35 combat and support brigades (two entirely staffed by female personnel). Nominally totalling about 180,000 troops supported by armour, artillery and engineering units, the NLA was actually about 20,000 strong, and little more than a politically led militia raised from defectors, émigrés and a few prisoners of war, lacking professional leadership and training. Over time, and due to participation in some conventional operations, some of its units matched those of the IRGC's Basiji and Pasdaran. However, most of the NLA spent the war inside camps around Baghdad, passing time by posing in highly publicised parades – described as 'inefficient' and 'scruffy' by most of foreign observers.[17]

20
THE CENTRAL FRONT 1982–1987

By the New Year of 1982 the newly established IV Corps held a salient west of Dezful and Shush some 75 kilometres long and 40 kilometres deep, which then merged near Bostan into a narrow (20 kilometre) wide strip of Iranian territory leading into the Hawizah Marshes. Sandy desert seemed to secure the northern and southern flanks although the Iranian Operation Tarigh al-Qods had demonstrated this was not impassable, especially not for the Pasdaran. Meanwhile, II Corps still under Aziz at Ba'qubah was left with (north to south) 8th Infantry, 7th and 2nd Mountain Divisions with 12th Armoured Division. It was in this area that the Iranians launched their first major offensives on the Central Front, resulting in several disasters for the Iraqis.

Early in 1982, Tehran decided to cut off out what it perceived as the 'Iraqi cancers in its holy territory' with two major consecutive offensives: Operation Fatah al-Mobin (Clear or Undeniable Victory) – usually called Operation Fatah – and Operation Beit-ol-Mogaddas. The former was to hit IV Corps' salient opposite Dezful and Shush, while the latter was to hit III Corps.

The battlefield stretched between the River Doveyrich (Duveryrij/Dwayrij/Doiraj), some 8–16 kilometres to the east, and the River Kharakeh (Karkha or Kharkha), some 50 kilometres deeper inside Iran. On its norther side were the foothills of the Kabirkuh, some 200–500 metres high and occupied by the Iranians, while in the south was a belt of sand dunes around the Mishdagh Hills. The terrain in between was largely open, undulating ground, but behind the northern face of the Iraqi salient was the Movazi Ridge.

Operation Fatah al-Mobin

Iranian planning was in the capable hands of the IRIA's Chief-of-Staff, General Sayed Shirazi, a shrewd tactician who was nominated Commander of the Ground Forces, and was aided by the fact that the Iranian positions overlooked the enemy defences. Due to the Southern Front being a tougher nut to crack, Tehran decided to launch Fatah, a double envelopment of IV Corps, first. Once this had sucked in enemy reserves the Iranians would strike into the underbelly from the south to isolate, then annihilate, the enemy. Preparations began in December 1981 and to secure Pasdaran support, Shirazi successfully enlisted the help of President Ali Hosseini Khamenei, which meant the main theme of a Pasdaran commander seminar held in Tehran during January 1982 was cooperation with the IRIA together with organising and controlling mass attacks.

Four task forces were created (see Table 22 for details) with Qods and Nasr in the north, and Fajr and Fath in the east. The northern assault consisted of six IRIA brigades and four Pasdaran divisions and was supported by an independent tank company and the 44th Artillery Group (total of 17 batteries with 100 artillery pieces).[1] The eastern assault was to involve six IRIA brigades and seven Pasdaran

Sayed Ali Shirazi, Chief of Staff of the Iranian Army. (Tom Cooper collection)

divisions and was supported by 33rd Artillery Group (12 batteries with 70 guns). All the troops involved in the assault used full-scale mock-ups of Iraqi strongpoints to practice attacks. The assault force totalled some 47,000 Army, 65,000 Pasdaran and 10,000 Basiji troops, supported by 270 MBTs, 170 artillery pieces, 64 attack and assault helicopters, and 12 Boeing CH-47C Chinook medium transport helicopters.[2]

Iraqi Preparations

Iraqi intelligence quickly detected signs of Iranian preparations and the assembly of a dozen IRIA brigades. However, the shadowy presence of the Pasdaran was at least as much a reason for uncertainty as for anything else. COMINT played a major role in Iraqi intelligence, and this proved capable of decrypting some of the IRIA's codes. However, the Pasdaran lacked radios and relied upon landline communications or couriers, which the Iraqis were unable to monitor. The GMID should have been able to gauge precise Iranian intentions through the assembly of bridging equipment,

MIDDLE EAST@WAR SERIES SPECIAL #1: THE IRAN-IRAQ WAR

Large-scale operations by the Iranian ground forces on the central and northern fronts of the war with Iraq were usually supported by one or more of the IRIAA's Combat Support Groups, each of which included a company of Boeing CH-47C Chinook heavy helicopters. (IRIAA)

but it remained uncertain as to whether this was a diversion or a major thrust. To make sure, in early March 1982, Baghdad provided Fakhri with substantial reinforcements – including 3rd Armoured Division (Brigadier General Juwad Assad Shetna) and 10th Armoured Brigade, together with several artillery batteries from GHQ and III Corps' reserves, while II Corps also sent its 9th Armoured Division south.

Fakhri already had 1st Mechanised, 10th Armoured (Brigadier General Thabit Sultan), 11th and 14th Infantry Divisions holding the northern shoulder of the salient, and 1st Mechanised Division (Brigadier General Thamir Hamad Mahmoud) the southern shoulder. Part of the 11th Infantry Division held the sector covering Bostan, while the 14th Infantry held the line into the Hawizeh Marshes. However, neither they nor Fakhri's reaction force – 32nd Special Forces Brigade – would be involved in the disaster. Overall, the salient's defences ran along the River Kharkhekh, from Dasht-e Abbs in the north to Mishdagh Hills in the south, and were manned by 86,000 troops supported by 1,500 MBTs, and 400 artillery pieces.

The III Corps' experiences had demonstrated the inadequacy of mechanised formations in static defence, so the mechanised divisions were given eight infantry brigades – many of them staffed by reservists recently recalled to the colours. Sultan deployed not only five infantry brigades but also his two armoured brigades in static positions on his left, leaving only the 24th Mechanised Brigade

Once mobilised and deployed on the frontlines, the Iranian Army became capable of putting sizeable formations of its armour on the battlefield – including weak brigades equipped with British-made Chieftain MBTs, two of which are seen in this pre-war photograph. (Albert Grandolini)

in reserve. Hamad had three infantry brigades and one mechanised brigade in line behind one of largest minefields ever constructed by the Iraqis, while his reserve – 1st Mechanised and 34th Armoured Brigades – was east of Fakkeh. All of their defensive positions consisted of the usual triangular battalion-strongpoints, which in the east and south were buttressed with berms. Because the Iraqi Army was overstretched, many of the key communication hubs behind the lines were held by Popular Army troops, a somewhat slender reed, a large number of which were reportedly incorporated in 1st Mechanised Division's defences.[3]

The Onslaught
Anticipating an attack on the Iranian New Year (Norouz), 21 March 1982, the two Iraqi divisions launched a pre-emptive attack, Operation al-Fowz al-Azim (Glorious Victory). In the course of

PART II: THE CENTRAL FRONT 1982–1987

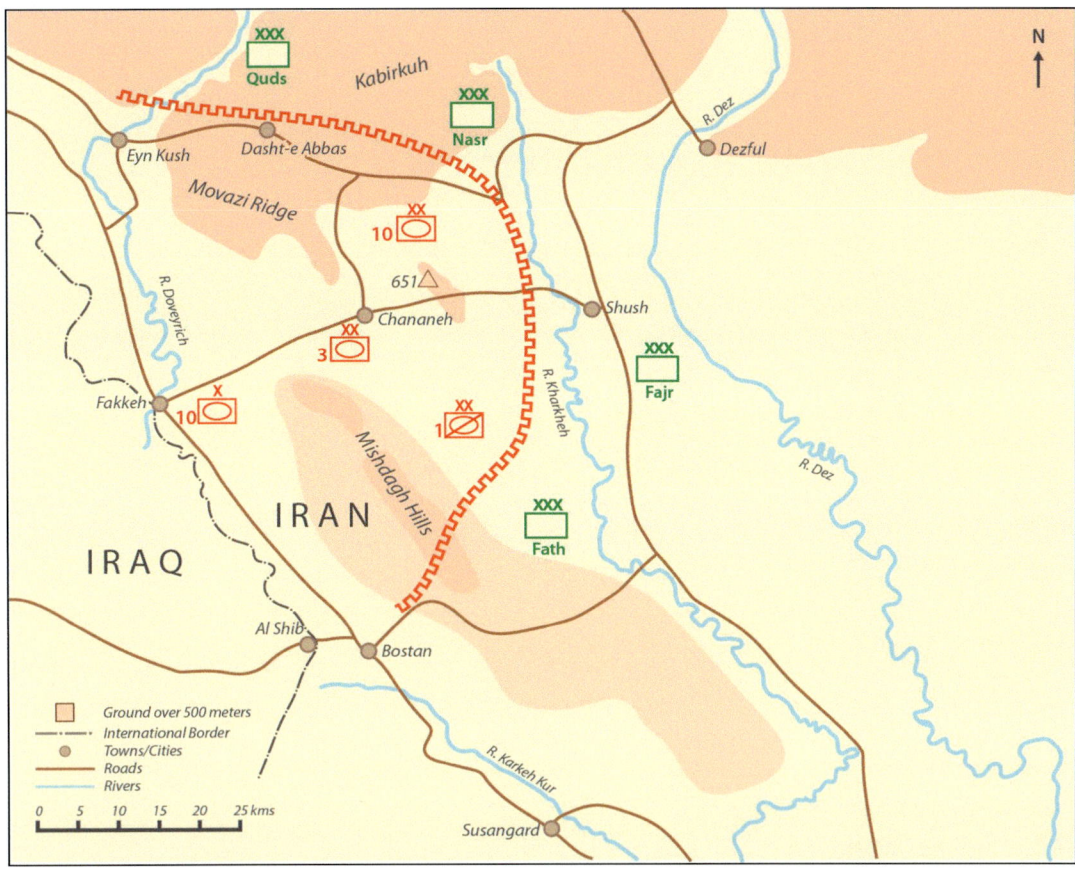

A map of the area in which Operation Fatah al-Mobin was undertaken. (Map by George Anderson)

While relatively small in total numbers of available tubes, and often suffering from lack of ammunition early during the war, the Iranian artillery played a crucial role in supporting offensive operations. This photograph shows a pair of M109A1s early in the morning before a major fire operation. (Albert Grandolini collection)

Iraqi complacency was dashed at 0330hrs on 22 March 1982 – exactly 18 months after their invasion and the day after Norouz – when the Iranians launched Fatah with a stunning blow from the north. Operating as battlegroups some 15 kilometres apart, Iranian task forces – spearheaded by Pasdaran light infantry – exploited the hilly terrain to infiltrate Iraqi positions, then used the hills to shield them from armoured counterattacks, while enjoying fire support of the IRIA. Careful reconnaissance enabled the Iranians to target positions manned by reservist units, and religious fervour carried the advancing infantry – which advanced in 1,000-strong, brigade-waves at half-mile intervals, urged on by mullahs who showed no regard for their own safety – ever further forward. An Iraqi officer later said; 'They came at us like a crowd coming out of a mosque on a Friday. Soon we were firing into dead men, some draped over the barbed wire fences, and others in piles on the ground, having stepped on mines'.[5]

Actually, the Iranian attack was much more sophisticated, and included a heliborne landing of Iranian Special Forces behind positions of 10th Armoured Division. These overran Iraqi batteries on Hill 651 which had been shelling TFB.4 and Dezful, and destroyed or captured up to 30 130mm M-46 guns. Simultaneously, IRIA's 21st Infantry Division and 84th Infantry Brigade punched holes in the Iraqi line and isolated both of Sultan's armoured brigades before capturing the road junction of Chananeh,

this enterprise, run from 19 to 21 March, each division deployed one brigade-sized task force. The 1st Mechanised Division's 34th Armoured Brigade drove 15 kilometres deep before withdrawing, and both sides lost heavily but the Iraqis calculated that their efforts had been successful. They did not anticipate a new assault, but the Iranian timetable was not significantly affected.[4]

just 200 metres from 3rd Armoured Division's command post. The Iranian armour, fighter-bombers and helicopter gunships hit hard with everything available. The IRIAF flew at least 95 combat sorties, to which the IRIAA added over 100; their crews, and the Army's tanks claimed between 320 and 400 Iraqi tanks knocked out during the morning. The luckless defenders were thus assaulted from all directions and pinned down; subsequent estimates concluded that

Table 22: Order of Battle for Operation Fath al-Mobin, March 1982		
Corps	Division	Brigades
Iran		
Task Force Qods	84th Infantry Division IRIA	3 brigades
	92nd Armoured Division IRIA	2nd Brigade
	14th Imam Hossein Infantry Division IRGC	3 brigades
	41st Sarallah Infantry Division IRGC	
Task Force Nasr	21st Infantry Division IRIA	1st, 2nd, 3rd Brigades (10 battalions)
	58th Infantry Brigade IRIA	
	7th Vali-e-Asr Infantry Division IRGC	3 brigades
	27th Mohammad Rasoolallah Infantry Brigade IRGC	
Task Force Fajr	77th Infantry Division IRIA	1st, 2nd and 3rd Brigades
	17th Ali Ibn Abu Talib Infantry Division IRGC	
	33rd Ali Mahdi Infantry Division IRGC	
	35th Imam Hassan Infantry Division IRGC	
	46th al-Haadi Infantry Brigade IRGC	
Task Force Fatah	92nd Armoured Division IRIA	1st Brigade
	37th Armoured Brigade IRIA	
	55th Airborne Brigade IRIA	
	3rd Saheb az-Zaman Infantry Division IRGC	
	8th Najaf Ashraf Infantry Division IRGC	
	25th Karbala Infantry Division IRGC	
Other units	33rd & 44th Artillery Group IRIA	
	2nd & 3rd CSGs, IRIAA	
Iraq		
IV Corps	Corps troops, including IV Corps Artillery Brigade	
	1st Mechanised Division	34th & 51st Armoured Brigades; 1st & 27th Mechanised Brigades; 93rd, 96th, 109th & 426th Infantry Brigades
	10th Armoured Division	17th & 42nd Armoured Brigades; 24th Mechanised Brigade; 55th, 99th, 423rd & 505th Infantry Brigades
Reserves	3rd Armoured Division	6th & 12th Armoured Brigades; 8th Mechanised Brigade
	9th Armoured Division	35th & 43rd Armoured Brigades, 14th Mechanised Brigades
	10th Armoured Brigade	
	5th Border Guards Brigade	
	2nd Wing IrAAC	

90 percent of the Iranian attacks overran their objectives.[6] Facing Iranian summons to surrender, the commander of 42nd Armoured Brigade, Colonel Iyad Futaykh Khalifa ar-Rawi, reacted by issuing each of his officers two hand grenades – one for the enemy and one for themselves. His unit took three days of bitter fighting to break out, followed by 17th Armoured Brigade.

The collapse of the Iraqi northern line exposed both of Thamir Hamad's mechanised brigades which were both mauled in 'clumsy and confused' attempts at mobile defence. Despite Saddam's demands that units stand or fall in their positions, the northern defenders began to abandon the hills, and retreated some 10 kilometres compounding Fakhri's woes. Their withdrawal allowed the Iranians to bring their guns onto the heights and strike the Iraqi rear. The IrAF and IrAAC attempted to intervene, and their pilots claimed as many as 196 Iranian MBTs but most of their sorties were ineffective due to general confusion on the ground.

Iraqi Collapse

Despite the air support, Fakhri recognised he was in a desperate situation and ordered both divisions to make an orderly withdrawal, starting with 10th Armoured Division. However, Thamir Hamad then wrecked the plan. He had always been a weak commander and exacerbated the crisis by moving his headquarters to the rear. Just as the northern forces began to withdraw, he ordered his two

PART II: THE CENTRAL FRONT 1982–1987

An Iranian Army Chieftain MBT passing by a column of captured Iraqi troops during Operation Fatah al-Mobbin. (Tom Cooper collection)

The Iranian counter-offensives in 1982 were better supported than ever before. Amongst others, the IRIAF deployed its British-made Rapier SAMs to improve the protection of ground forces. This firing unit was photographed somewhere in the Urumiyeh area in March 1982. (IRIAF)

reserves, usually dissolved into frontal assaults on strongest Iranian positions and were stopped with ease.[7]

Heavy losses forced Fakhri to rob Peter to pay Paul; he stripped 1st Mechanised Division of troops used to prop up the frontlines, in turn weakening positions of this unit. Renewed Iranian attacks on 23 March 1982 then forced him to deploy elements of 3rd Armoured Division to shore up the 1st Mechanised and re-route the 10th and 12th Armoured Brigades to face a new threat coming from the Mishdagh Hills. The two units counterattacked on 24 March, with heavy artillery support and several FROG-7 rockets, but the Iranians counterattacked and isolated the 12th, forcing it to fight out of the encirclement. The only positive action of the Iraqis on this day was the IrAF's effort to stop the advance of 25th Karbala Division IRGC on Chenaneh; this was hit by up to 150 strikes and forced to entrench.

Crisis for Saddam

On 24 March 1982, Saddam Hussein arrived on the front leading a high-ranking delegation (including the Defence Minister and Chief-of-Staff). He dismissed Thamir Hamid and then personally supervised the restoration of the situation for three days. Amongst others, he ordered a redeployment of a brigade from 12th Armoured Division in Khorramshar, and another from 7th Infantry Division at Qasr-e Shirin. Such measures proved ineffective and Saddam was nearly captured when his convoy was ambushed while inspecting the frontline.[8]

The situation further deteriorated during the night of 24–25 March, when the Iranians hit Fakhri's right flank with a powerful concentration of 88th and 92nd Armoured Division, 55th Airborne Brigade and several of the IRGC's brigades.[9] A night later, the Iranians hit the 1st Mechanised Division too, inflicting heavy casualties. However, their supply system collapsed again and thus they lost the momentum and were unable to exploit the chaos they caused. Nevertheless, by the morning of 27 March, the Iranians liberated Hill 651 and thus completed the elimination of the Iraqi threat to TFB.4. In a matter of a few hours, the IRIAF then brought in a battery of MIM-23B I-HAWK and British-made Rapier SAMs; this soon inflicted losses to the IrAF.[10]

remaining brigades to do the same. As soon as he learned the news Fakhri ordered the brigades to remain in place, but the confused troops panicked. Hamad then lost all semblance of control of his men and they abandoned positions held since October 1980, fleeing to Fakkeh which became a scene of utter chaos. The situation was brought under control only once the Iraqi officers finally realised that the Iranians had halted – probably because their own supply system had collapsed.

With 3rd Armoured Division headquarters under attack, Fakhri had to cover the withdrawal by personally directing counterattacks. Initially, he used 10th Armoured Brigade's T-72s and 24th Mechanised Brigade to support the 17th and 60th Armoured Brigades, artillery barrages and MLRS to stop the Iranian advance on Eyn Kush on 22 March 1982. However, the increasingly desperate situation in the south led to most of his units being redeployed there and being replaced only by the Mechanised Brigade of the Republican Guards. Counterattacks by this formation, and other

281

Eventually, Saddam was left without a choice but to authorise construction of new defences closer to the international border, along a 20-kilometre-long strip anchored on its southern side on the dune belt, before arcing north of Bostan and Fakkeh, and then following the River Doveyrich. The Iranians followed the Iraqi withdrawal for a few kilometres before starting to consolidate their gains on 29 March. Immediately afterwards, they began moving most of their forces further south – to the Ahwaz-Abadan theatre of operations.

The Iraqis exploited the resulting end of the battle by scrutinising their officers. Reportedly, several of Thamir Hamid's subordinated were jailed or executed. By contrast, any criticism of Fakhri was muted; he retained his command until 1983 when he was appointed the Head of the Intelligence Agency (Mukhabarat) and replaced by Lieutenant General Thabit Sultan Ahmed.

A dramatic photograph taken during one of many ad hoc infantry charges by IRGC volunteers, sometime in 1982. While often initiated by little more than frustration, and giving birth to the legends about 'human wave tactics' early on, over time the Pasdaran learned how to direct and control such attacks – and the Iraqis learned to fear them. (Tom Cooper collection)

Aftermath

Operation Fatah al-Mobin was a tremendous victory – bigger than the Iranians had ever expected. It effectively swept IV Iraqi Corps out of Iran, mauled two armoured divisions and one mechanised division – a total of 12 brigades – and captured up to 15,450 prisoners, 320–350 MBTs, about 100 other AFVs, 165–200 guns and an entire battery of SA-6 SAMs. The booty allowed the Pasdaran to create their first 10 artillery batteries and their first armoured brigade on 1 April 1982. An emboldened deputy commander of 21st Division IRIA exclaimed, 'Now we are going to write our own manuals, with absolutely new tactics that the Americans and British and French can study at their staff colleges'. Although Joint Chief-of-Staff, General Zahir-Nejad, officially disavowed any offensive intentions by his government, this success caused many in Tehran to focus their attention upon the Shi'a holy city of Karbala, only 80 kilometres south of Baghdad – or even advancing all the way to Jerusalem.[11]

Fatah al-Mobin enabled the IRGC to launch a diversionary attack against the new defences of IV Corps' southern flank, during 30 March – 1 April, in support of the great Iranian offensive in Khuzestan – Operation Beit-ol-Mogaddas. This attack resulted in the Pasdaran pushing through positions of 34th Armoured and 606th Infantry Brigades in direction of Fakkeh, before being stopped by the corps commando battalion. The IRGC then launched a new attack from the south, during the night of 5 – 6 May, broke through, inflicted heavy casualties upon 34th and 51st Armoured, 27th Mechanised and 426th Infantry Brigades, before reaching the international border. However, the Iraqis held onto Fakkeh.[12]

Ultimately, the Iranian victories at Khorammshar and east of Fakkeh caused Saddam to surrender most of his ill-gotten gains from 1980. The II Corps was forced to abandon Qasr-e Shirin, Sumar and

An Iranian soldier with a 9M14 Malyutka (AT-3 Sagger) ATGM. Large numbers of such missiles were deployed by the Iranian military starting in 1982. Some were captured from Iraqi stocks, while others were imported via Syria and Libya. (via N.S.)

Operation Fatah al-Mobin was one of most successful Iranian offensives of the Iran-Iraq War. It resulted in the capture of dozens of thousands of Iraqi troops and hundreds of armoured vehicles. This Iranian guard is watching over several hundreds of Iraqi prisoners of war in March 1982 (Albert Grandolini collection)

PART II: THE CENTRAL FRONT 1982–1987

Mehran to withdraw to better defensive positions inside Iraq. Shortly afterwards, partially because of the failure of the first Iranian attempt to take Basra (Operation Ramadan Mubarak), the corps then found itself exposed to probes against its 14th Infantry Division on 6 August, and its 12th Armoured Division on 8 August 1982.[13]

Operation Moslem Ibn Akil

Following the bloody disaster of Ramadan Mubarrak, the Iranian SDC met in mid-August 1982 to discuss its next move. This time, the clerics were more amenable to the JCS's suggestions about striking a more exposed section of the front and selected positions opposite Sumar. These were based upon the 320–400-metre-high Haran Hills, straddling the border and pierced by the River Gangir (Kangir). This area was dominated by Mandali – a major communication hub, linked by a hard-topped road to Baqubah, some 45 kilometres further west, and then to Baghdad, only 120 kilometres away. Mandali also controlled a network of minor roads along the frontier and across the northern marshes, 50 kilometres east of Baqubah, and to the HQ of II Corps in Mansouriyah.

The area was garrisoned by 12th Armoured Division (Brigadier General Shawkat Ahmed Atta), who knew the Iranians had begun assembling forces around Sumar but was uncertain about their intentions. Saddam is known to have visited Baqubah on 12 September, but without any useful results.

Commanded by Colonel A. Rostami, the Iranian forces involved in the operation named Moslem Ibn Akil (after the martyred cousin of Imams Hassan and Hussain) included the 4th Brigade of 81st Armoured Division IRIA, part of 55th Airborne Brigade, 27th Mohammad Rasoolallah and 31st Ashura Divisions IRGC, and 18th al-Ghadir and 21st Imam Reza Brigades IRGC – for a total of 33,000 troops, supported by 50 MBTs and 100 guns. The IRIAF prepared all the F-4Es of TFB.3 for this operation, while the IRIAA forward-deployed one of its Combat Support Groups.[14]

Fire in the Hills

Although the defenders were alert, the attackers exploited the terrain to infiltrate enemy positions at 18 points along a 35-kilometre-wide front on the Haran Hills during the night of 30 September – 1 October 1982, and then push on for up to two kilometres. Reinforced by brigades from 7th Infantry Division, Shawkat Ahmed Atta counterattacked and regained the terrain, but the Iranians attacked again during the following night and punched through, reaching the heights on both sides of the river. Counterattacks by 37th Armoured Division and 46th Mechanised Brigades prevented further advances and left the Iranians with a meagre booty of about 110 prisoners and a dozen tanks.

Nevertheless, Rostami regrouped his forces and attacked again during the night of 5 – 6 October, this time reaching suburbs of Mandali. Somewhat shaken, the Iraqis counterattacked on 10 November, using the new 17th Armoured Division's 59th and 70th Armoured Brigades, and Atta's 50th Armoured Brigade, plus four squadrons of IrAAC to push the enemy 10 kilometres away from Mandali.

Iranians collecting Iraqi troops captured during Operation Moslem Ibn Akil. (Tom Cooper Colection)

A BRDM-2 armoured reconnaissance car equipped with six launchers for 9P133 Malyutka (AT-3 Sagger) ATGMs, was one of hundreds of Iraqi vehicles captured by the Iranians during the first half of 1982. As indicated by its insignia, it was subsequently pressed into service with the IRGC. (Albert Grandolini collection)

A week later, 81st Infantry Division IRIA spearheaded a renewed attack, but this was stopped by well-prepared Iraqi artillery and multiple counterattacks. Ultimately, the Iranian forces claimed the capture of 12 AFVs and 20 artillery pieces, while IRIAA gunships were credited with destruction of 25 AFVs. While successful in defence the Iraqis had little to show, but issued obscure claims to the foreign press, for example, that one of their 'Mi-24' helicopters had shot down an IRIAF F-4 Phantom II using a Soviet-made AT-6 anti-tank guided missile (ATGM).[15]

Operation Moharram al-Haram

Muslim Ibn Akil fanned the embers of tensions between the IRIA and the IRGC, leading to bitter arguments over tactics. The professional Iranian officers accused the militias of poor training and slapdash style of fighting, while the Pasdaran complained about the lack of revolutionary zeal among the military leadership. Eventually, Speaker of the Iranian Parliament (and future President of the IRI), Akbar Hashemi-Rafsanjani, announced that the new Iranian policy would be to 'hit the enemy with restricted blows'.[16]

A corresponding offensive was then planned for the area south of Dehloran, with the intention of eliminating the Iraqi-controlled enclave around Musiyan (Musian) and obtaining a bridgehead for advance on Amarah during the holy month of Muharram. Hence, the operation in question was named Muharram al-Harram (Holy Muharram). The SDC may have had a political motive for the operation because the captured terrain might later win concessions at the negotiating table. To execute the attack it transferred two brigades of 21st Infantry Division IRIA, together with 25th Karbala and 30th Beit-ol-Moghaddas Divisions IRGC, from the south. These helped establish the Task Force Zafar, which consisted of one armoured and four infantry divisions, two brigades of Pasdaran and two IRIA infantry brigades, for a total of 51,000 troops (including about 9,000 regulars). The IRIA provided support in the form of 51 artillery batteries and 2 MLRS batteries (300 artillery pieces), and five tank battalions (with M60s and Chieftains), while the IRIAA added 46 helicopters (including 16 AH-1Js, of which eight were armed with BGM-71 TOW ATGMs). For further details on involved units, see Table 23.

The northern prong of this offensive aimed to cross the frontier and take the road hub at Tib, and the nearby high terrain. The southern prong was to cross the border and capture the ridge north of Abu Ghirab (Abu-Qarrab or Abu Ghorab).

Facing them on a 50-kilometre front was IV Corps of the Iraqi Army, including 10th Armoured Division (Major General Thabit Sultan Ahmed) on the left, facing Musiyan; 20th Infantry Division (Brigadier General Farouk Twafiq Abdur Razak) on the right, while Fakkeh was shielded by 1st Mechanised Division. Primary defence positions consisted of two lines of mutually-supporting strongpoints running along a riverbank, which – combined with minefields, ravines and water courses – were expected to channel the attackers into killing zones. Infantry was deployed forward and expected to fall back under pressure along pre-planned lines; drawing the enemy into open areas where armour could counterattack. This force totalled about 48,000 troops, 340 MBTs and 180 artillery pieces on the Musiyan front, and some 34,000 troops, 380 MBTs and 150 artillery pieces on the Fakkeh front.[17]

Fighting in the Rain

The Pasdaran opened their assault in heavy rain during the night of 31 October – 1 November 1982. The Najaf Ashraf and Karbala Divisions advanced on the right of the 30-kilometre-wide frontline, while Ali Ibn Abu Talib and Imam Hossein Divisions pushed on the left. The defences collapsed under the onslaught, and the Iranians drove forward for 5–8 kilometres, taking Tib and the Bayat oilfield in the process. Thabit Sultan launched his well-rehearsed counterattack during the afternoon of 2 November, but this became bogged down in mud, and resulted only in

Table 23: Order of Battle for Operation Muharram al-Harram, 1982

Corps	Division	Brigades
Iran		
Task Force Zafar	21st Infantry Division IRIA	1st Brigade
	77th Infantry Division IRIA	3 brigades
	84th Infantry Brigade IRIA	
	8th Najaf Ashraf Infantry Division IRGC	3 brigades
	14th Imam Hossein Infantry Division IRGC	3 brigades
	17th Ali Ibn Abu Talib Infantry Division IRGC	3 brigades
	25th Karbala Infantry Division IRGC	3 brigades
	30th Beit-ol-Moghaddas Armoured Division IRGC	3 brigades
	35th Imam Hassan Infantry Brigade IRGC	
	44th Qamar Bani Hashem Engineer Brigade IRGC	
	33rd Artillery Group IRIA	
	44th Artillery Group IRIA	
	1st & 4th CSG IRIAA	
Iraq		
IV Corps	Corps troops, including IV Corps Artillery Brigade	
	1st Mechanised Division	34th & 51st Armoured Brigades; 1st & 27th Mechanised Brigade; 93rd, 96th, 109th & 426th Infantry Brigades
	10th Armoured Division	17th & 42nd Armoured Brigades; 24th Mechanised Brigade; 423rd, 501st, 606th & 701st Infantry Brigades
	20th Infantry Division	44th, 420th & 435th Infantry Brigades

PART II: THE CENTRAL FRONT 1982–1987

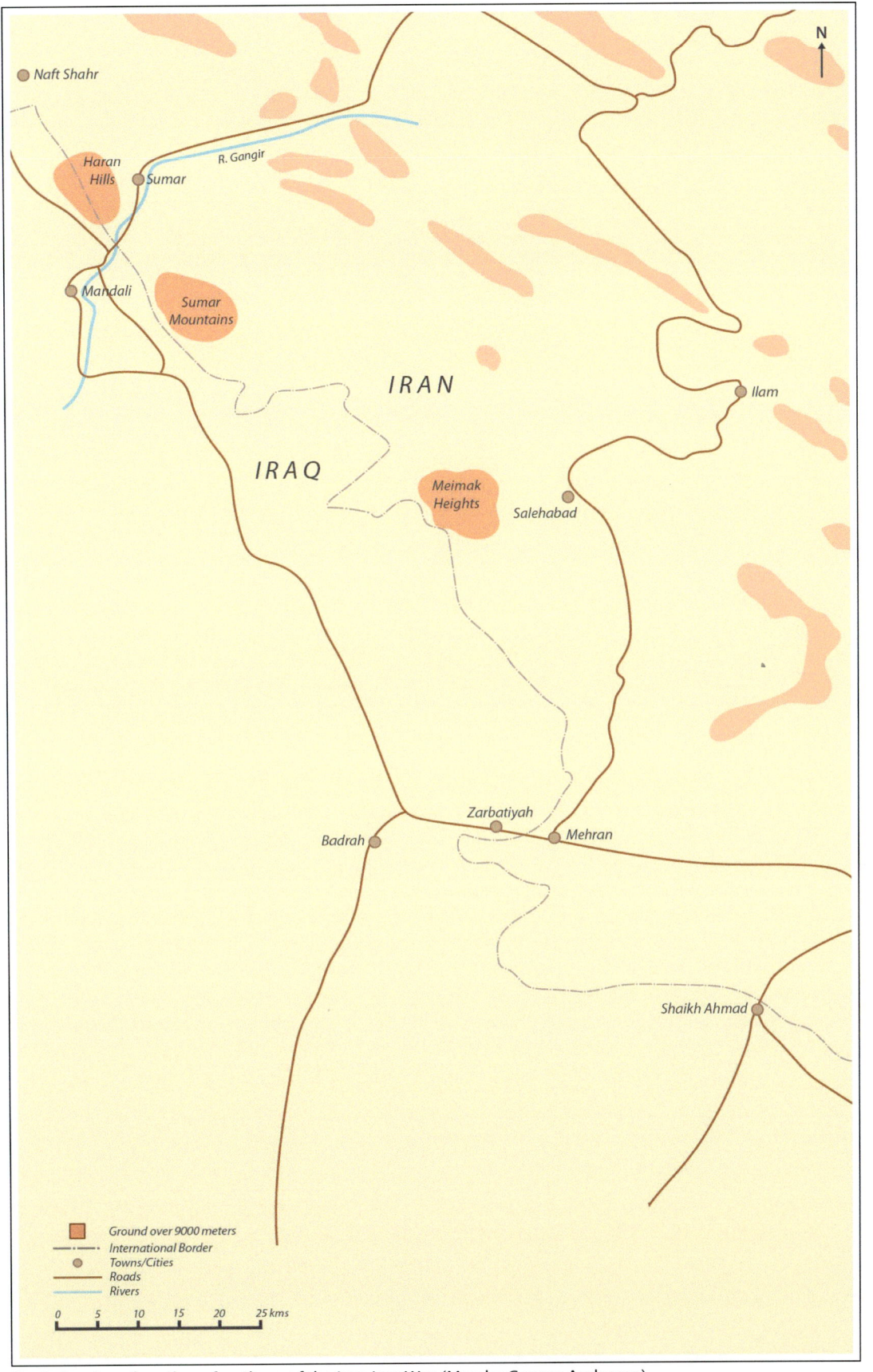

IRIAA is known to have carried 2,194 troops and 85 tonnes of supplies to the frontlines, while evacuating 1,521 wounded. Its TOW-equipped Cobras reportedly destroyed 107 enemy vehicles. However, Fakhri's new 60th Armoured Brigade and commandos helped contain their further breakthroughs. Finally, the Iraqis launched an all-out counterattack on the night of 9–10 November and regained some of the lost ground within the following 15 hours, before their counterattack was virtually washed away by rain. Eventually the Iranians managed an advance of up to 10 kilometres deep into Iraq and regained about 440 square kilometres of their own territory. Tehran subsequently claimed the capture of 3,000–3,500 enemy troops and 14 MBTs (including 9 T-55s), but the operation clearly failed to reach its objectives. Still, for the clerics, Fatah al-Mobbin and Muharram 'demonstrated the best way forward' and strongly influenced the operations of the year 1983.[18]

Val Fajr Moghaddamati

Despite the disappointment of 'Muharram' on the Fakkeh front, in early 1983 the SDC demanded a new assault to outflank the Doveyrich line, take Fakkeh and then, in a surfeit of ambition, to advance along a minor road across the marshes to Amarah. Dubbed Val Fajr Moghaddamati (Dawn Prelude) this eventually became the first of a series of operations codenamed Val Fajr (Dawn).[19]

Commanded by Colonel Mohammed Baqeri, the Iranian forces were concentrated for an attack from north and south towards Fakkeh and included two task forces: Karbala and Najaf. These included four divisions of the IRGC, two brigades of 16th Armoured Division IRIA, and 84th Infantry Brigade, as well as detachments from 21st Infantry Division, 23rd Special Forces and 55th Airborne Brigades. The concentration totalled some 60,000 troops (including 25,000 from IRIA), and was supported by 200

Central sector of northern frontlines of the Iran-Iraq War. (Map by George Anderson)

the recovery of Tib. In the south, Muharram opened badly as the attackers ran into an extensive minefield that inflicted crippling casualties and ended the attack almost as soon as it began.

The Iranians continued attacking on 4, 6, and 8 November, expanding their bridgehead by taking more of the high ground. The

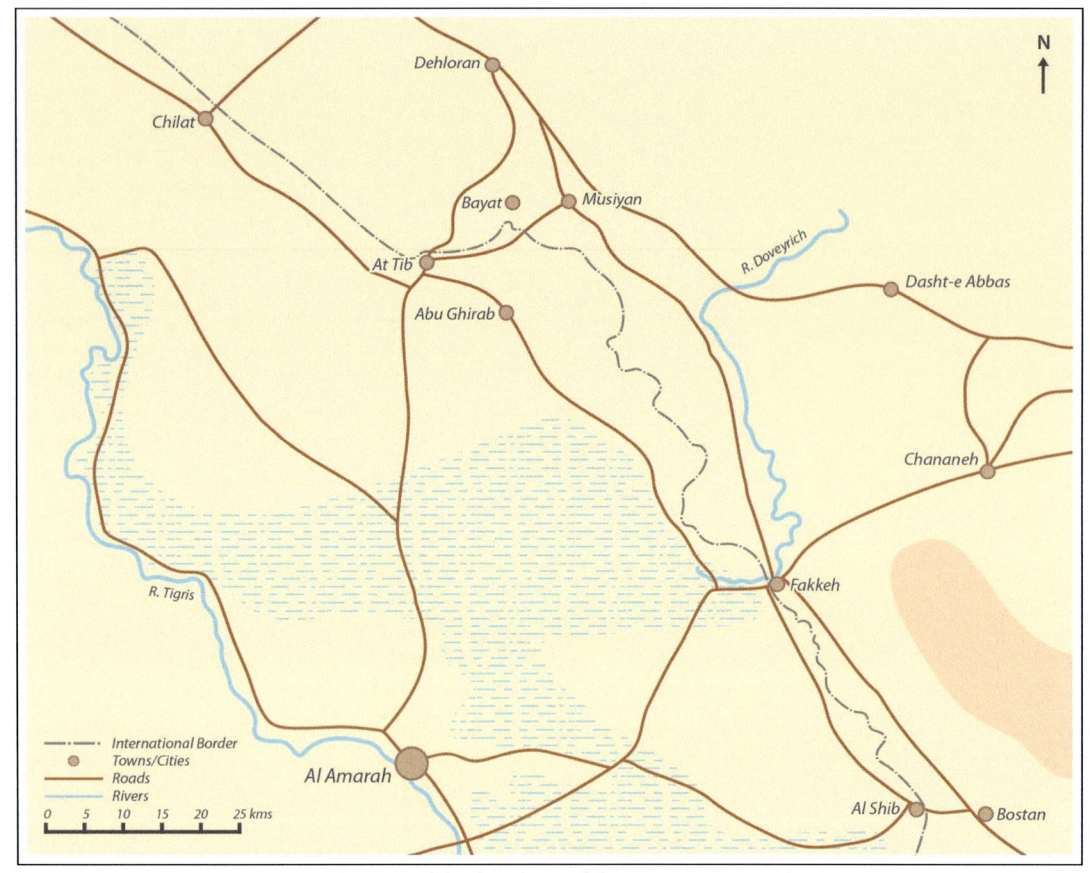

The Amarah area: southern-central sector of the frontlines of the Iran-Iraq War in the period 1982–1987. (Map by George Anderson)

MBTs, 58 helicopters (including 18 AH-1s), and 33rd and 55th Artillery Groups IRIA (21 batteries, of which 12 were self-propelled) with 150 guns.

Fought in an area of sandy desert dunes northwest of Bostan, this battle would be the baptism of fire for the 18th Infantry Division (commanded by Brigadier General Hashim Ahmed), which held a 15-kilometre line around Al-Shib (Sheeb). This was a large formation, including three brigades (95th, 702nd, and 704th Infantry), with 15,000 troops, 72 guns and 18 BM-21 MLRS. Furthermore, the Iraqi COMINT had alerted the defenders, which resulted in the redeployment of Brigadier General Hussein Rashid Muhammad's 3rd Armoured Division, together with 36th Infantry, 65th and 68th Special Forces Brigades. Finally, the GHQ added 49th and 108th Infantry Brigades. All of the Iraqi artillery in this area was put under the command of the corps artillery brigade, together with most of 1st Mechanised Division's artillery.[20]

The Iranians opened their attack in heavy rain just before midnight on 6–7 February 1983, with Karbala's Saheb az-Zaman and Vali Asr Division probing across the dunes south of Fakkeh, into a sector held by 702nd and 704th Infantry Brigades. Well-constructed and extensive defences easily held off the attacks, but the Iranians relaunched their assault in the morning and their spearheads reached the road connecting Fakkeh with Shib before they were driven back by 12th Armoured Brigade of 3rd Armoured Division.

Fakhri's centralisation of his artillery paid dividends and his gunners inflicted heavy losses, especially among the Basiji, while the IRIA's failure to assemble an adequate stock of shells limited their preparation and counterbattery fire. When Iranian pressure became too great, Fakhri's troops were deliberately withdrawn to entice the enemy forward and expose them to mechanised counterattacks, involving up to three brigades which drove back the enemy.

Iranian offensives on the central front of late 1982 often saw intensive deployment of IRIAA helicopters. Here a typical formation of Bell 214As is seen passing one of the local mountain peaks. (Farzin Nadimi collection)

Despite significant success during earlier fighting, by 1983 the Iranian air force began showing clear signs of exhaustion. Because of this, and because of the growing strength of the Iraqi Air Force, ground-based means of air defence – like this IRGC-operated ZSU-23-4 Shilka self-propelled AAA – became ever moreimportant for the defence of the battlefield. (via N. S.)

Pasdaran punched through the position of 60th Armoured Brigade and 501st Infantry Brigade, and then drove 20 kilometres deep into Iraq. Early in the morning of 11 April, the Iraqis launched a divisional counterattack, spearheaded by 42nd Armoured Brigade. However, they regained only the southern part of the lost terrain. Nevertheless, the Task Force Najaf was thus out of steam and its offensive over.

Further south, Task Force Karbala penetrated the positions of 51st Armoured and 108th Infantry Brigades, aided by hand-to-hand fighting. To prevent the collapse of their frontline, the Iraqis deployed the 65th Special Forces Brigade as 1st Mechanised Division and 34th Armoured Brigade launched a counterattack supported by 87 attack sorties of the IrAF. However, this effort failed to regain the lost positions. Fakhri now decided to concentrate his forces and coordinate all of their operations with that of the newly arrived 3rd Armoured Division (commanded by Hussein Rashid Muhammad), which now controlled 10 brigades.

Supported by another 150 attack sorties of the IrAF, and heavy artillery support, this counterattack was launched on 15 April and saw the Iranians withdrawing after only a few hours – their AH-1s claimed destruction of up to 56 AFVs, while losing a third of their number to Iraqi air defences. Certainly enough, the Iraqis took another two days of mopping up to regain all of their positions (and collect about 1,000 prisoners), but Val Fajr-1 was over by 17 April 1983. US intelligence estimated the Iraqis suffered 6,000–8,000 casualties and the Iranians 15,000. Shortly afterwards, Rafsanjani indicated that his country's losses were too high and that in future greater care should be taken to prevent unnecessary losses.

Obviously failing to learn the lesson of reinforcing success rather than failure, the Iranians rushed in reinforcements of one armoured brigade and six infantry brigades, and attacked again during the night of 7–8 February. This time they did manage to cut the Fakkeh–Shib road, despite heavy air strikes in the course of which the IrAF deployed its new Dassault Mirage F.1EQ fighter-bombers for the first time, while IrAAC helicopters flew up to 150 sorties a day. By contrast the IRIAF played next to no part in this operation.

When his third attack failed, and struggling to regain the initiative, Baqeri then committed two brigades of 16th Armoured Division IRIA on a 1.5-kilometre-wide front, starting on the afternoon of 9 February 1983. These ground their way through Iraqi positions and beat back a counterattack of 12th Armoured Brigade. However, when the dawn broke, they found themselves exposed and unsupported in an open plain. Whether due to incompetence of the IRIA staff, or Pasdaran failure, this provided the Iraqis with a splendid opportunity for a corps-sized counterattack. Spearheaded by 3rd Armoured Division and 1st Mechanised Brigade of the Republican Guards, this saw 250 Iraqi MBTs sweeping along the frontier from the northwest before smashing into Iranian ranks, leaving up to 100 MBTs and 80 APCs knocked out or abandoned intact in its trail.

Val Fajr Moghaddamati thus ended with a defeat and then the usual – bloody – bickering before the Iranians realised they could not gain anything, and went onto defensive on 17 February 1983. By then, the Iranians had suffered 8,000 casualties – including about 1,000 prisoners of war – while the Iraqis lost about 6,000.[21]

Val Fajr-1
Despite the failure of Val Fajr Moghaddamati, Rafsanjani persuaded the SDC to launch a new attack; Valr Fajr-1. This used the same task forces but reinforced to more than 100,000 troops (including 40,000 from the IRIA), nearly 200 MBTs and more than 300 artillery pieces, as outlined in Table 24. The IRIA added 31 helicopters (including nine AH-1s). Crucial Iraqi units remained 10th Armoured Division and 20th Infantry Division, commanded by Thabit Sultan Ahmed and Farouk Tawfiq Abdur Razzak, respectively, while 1st Mechanised Division continued to shield Fakkeh.[22]

The Iranian assault began during the night of 10–11 April 1983, with Task Force Najaf attacking on a 32-kilometre-wide front against 20th Infantry Division. Despite heavy casualties, the

Val Fajr-3
Undaunted by this failure, the SDC prepared their next offensive – Val Fajr-3 (for Val Fajr-2, see next chapter). This was to be undertaken further north, with the aim of eliminating an Iraqi-held enclave that remained after the abandonment of Mehran in May 1982. Mehran lies in the broad east to west valley of the River Gawi; this is only some 30 metres wide with its southern boundary sharply defined by a steep escarpment of the Jebal Hamrin/Khur-e Khurmaleh. The northern part consists of the Kamar Charmak mountains, which are up to 1,290 metres high and are cut by the Kunjan Pass through which flows the River Galal Badra, a subsidiary of the Gawi. A cultivated area extends for some 10 kilometres north of the town to the border, with a narrower band on the southern banks of the Gawi extending another 10 kilometres.

The north-eastern approaches to the town are via a web of streams and irrigation canals across which the main highway to Kermanshah runs. Further east this road then runs up the Gavi Valley, before crossing an escarpment. Some 10 kilometres north of Mehran there is a crossroads with one road running westwards across the border to Badrah through Zurbatiyah (Zorbaitiyah). A second road bypasses Mehran to link up with the highway some 15

MIDDLE EAST@WAR SERIES SPECIAL #1: THE IRAN-IRAQ WAR

Table 24: Order of Battle for Val Fajr-1, April 1983		
Corps	Division	Brigades
Iran		
Task Force Najaf	77th Infantry Division IRIA	2nd Brigade only
	37th Armoured Brigade IRIA	1 battalion only
	55th Airborne Brigade IRIA	
	58th infantry Brigade IRIA	
	84th Infantry Brigade IRIA	
	5th Nasr Infantry Division IRGC	1 brigade
	11th Amir al-Momenim Infantry Division IRGC	
	19th Fajr Infantry Division IRGC	1 brigade
	27th Mohammad Rasoolallah Infantry Division IRGC	1 brigade
	31st Ashura Infantry Division IRGC	1 brigade
Task Force Karbala	21st Infantry Division IRIA	2nd and 3rd Brigades
	7th Vali Asr Infantry Division IRGC	1 brigade
	8th Najaf Ashraf Infantry Division IRGC	1 brigade
	41st Sarallah Infantry Division IRGC	
	55th Artillery Group IRIA	
Iraq		
II Corps	65th and 66th Commando brigades, II Corps Artillery Brigade	
	1st Mechanised Division	34th & 51st Armoured Brigades, 1st & 27th Mechanised Brigades, 108th Infantry Brigade
	3rd Armoured Division	6th & 12th Armoured Brigades; 8th Mechanised Brigade
	10th Armoured Division	17th & 42nd Armoured Brigades; 24th Mechanised Brigade; 38th, 48th Infantry Brigades
	20th Infantry Division	60th Armoured Brigade; 44th, 420th, 435th & 501st Infantry Brigades

kilometres east of Mehran. The town itself is only some 80 kilometres north of the Baghdad–Basra highway at al-Kut. Indeed, the IRGC's garrison of Mehran was in peril because of its proximity to major roads inside Iraq.

For their attack, the Pasdaran assembled the reduced 5th Nasr Infantry Division and reinforced part of 41st Sarallah Infantry Division, together with brigades from 11th Amir all-Momenin, 17th Ali Ibn Abu Talib, 21st Imam Reza and 40th Sarab Divisions, plus a battalion from 27th Mohammad Rasoolallah Division IRGC. Supported by 4th Armoured Brigade of 21st Division IRIA, and a battalion from 84th Infantry Brigade, the forces involved totalled about 35,000 troops.

Mehran was the bailiwick of II Corps under Lieutenant General Mohammed Fathi Amin (transferred from I Corps); the 2nd and 22nd Infantry Divisions had established strong defences along the western edge of the irrigated area, and then in an arc west of Mehran. The GMID was aware of the enemy build-up but concluded the Iranian attack would be launched north of Zurbatiyah. To make sure, Baghdad boosted Amin's reserved with 1st and 2nd Brigades of the Guards Corps, and also launched a pre-emptive attack by two mechanised brigades on 29 July 1983 in vain.[23]

However, their hopes were soon dashed, for the Iranians struck out of the Mehran area during the night of 29–30 July and in a new fashion; with armour in the lead. The Pasdaran infantry meanwhile encircled and isolated a battalion of 417th Infantry Brigade: positioned high in the hills, this unit was usually supplied by helicopters only. It was authorised to break out during the night of 8–9 August 1983. The Iranians were also successful against 2nd Infantry Brigade, and an attempt by the Iraqi 38th Infantry Brigade to help was so badly handled that its commander was subsequently executed for incompetence – although his ATGM teams managed to hold enemy tanks. The next day, supported by multiple strikes of F-4Es from TFB.3, the Iranians pushed the enemy across the border and occupied most of Kulak-i-Buzurg, while taking about 400 prisoners. The Iraqis also employed their air power; with up to 150 attack sorties on 31 July alone.

Fathi Amin organised a corps counterattack on 2 August, deploying both Guards' brigades, together with corps commandos, and elements from his own 7th Infantry, 12th Armoured and 17th Armoured Divisions. While recovering much of the lost territory, this effort was eventually abandoned on 4 August 1983.

With Saddam demanding the recovery of Mehran, Amin reorganised his troops and attacked again during the night of 5–6 August 1983. This time, 8th Mechanised and 12th Armoured Brigade of 3rd Armoured Division, and 48th Infantry Brigade set out to isolate the town from the north, while the reinforced 70th Armoured Brigade (17th Armoured Division) pushed from the south. After encountering fierce resistance, both attempts were abandoned on 9 August. Meanwhile the Iranians began pushing into Iraq in the south towards Zurbatiyah but were stopped outside the town by Iraqi reinforcements hurriedly withdrawn from their counterattack, the Iranians, however, still managed to secure Kulak-i-Buzurg.

By the time both sides stopped combat operations Iraqi casualties were estimated at 10,000–17,000; Tehran claimed victory although suffering between 15,000 and 25,000 killed or injured. Some Iranian casualties were caused by chemical weapons deployed by the IrAF during this offensive, however, such operations had little effect due

PART II: THE CENTRAL FRONT 1982–1987

to failure to allow for wind conditions. The Iraqis also deployed the mustard gas, which was heavier than air and tended to roll down the heights away from Iranian positions.

Val Fajr-5 and Val Fajr-6

With neither side undertaking any major operations on this sector of the border for the rest of 1983, it was only in February of the following year that the Central Front became active again. However, operations Val Fajr-5 and Val Fajr-6 were diversionary attacks against the positions of II and IV Corps, intended to draw Iraqi attention away from the actual big offensive – Operation Khaiber.[24] Val Fajr-5 was launched on the night of 15–16 February 1984, with two IRGC divisions attacking the well-entrenched 2nd Infantry Division on the right flank of II Corps. While highly successful in using dry riverbeds to infiltrate enemy defences, the Pasdaran were subsequently cut to pieces by artillery and air power, followed by a counterattack by the 12th Armoured Division, launched during the night of 19–20 February.

Val Fajr-6 exploited dense fog when three IRGC divisions (18th al-Ghadir, 25th Karbala and 105th Qods) struck the newly established 25th Infantry Division, on the northern side of IV Corps, during the night of 21–22 February 1984. Although storming numerous positions and isolating others, the Iranians were then struck heavily by a counterattack from 24th Mechanised and 42nd Armoured Brigades of 10th Armoured Division, and the following night lost all the ground they had gained. The IRGC's southern attempt aimed at Al-Shib was an even briefer affair, and only offered the units of the Iraqi Popular Army an opportunity to distinguish themselves.[25]

'Quiet' Years

With both sides busy fighting big battles in the Hawizeh Marshes, the spring and summer were quiet; in September 1984, however, the Iranian CFOHQ was sharply criticised by everyone from the IRIA to the local gendarmerie over the security of the border between Ilam and Dehloran where there had been numerous ambushes by Iraqi special forces. Therefore, on 30 September 1984, decision was taken to launch Operation Ashura – or Val Fajr-7 – against a 20-kilometre front of Iraqi bridgehead on the Meimak Heights, west of Salehabad.

Assembled under Task Force Najaf, the assault group consisted of 1st and 3rd Brigades of the 81st Division IRIA, 84th Infantry Division, and a brigade each of 5th Nasr, 21st Imam Reza, and 32nd Ansar al-Hossein Divisions, and the 29th Nabi-y Akram Brigade IRGC. During the night of 17–18 October 1984, the Iranians infiltrated positions of II Iraqi Corps around Saif Saad all the way to their artillery emplacements. However, stubborn defence by 22nd Infantry Division and a counterattack by elements of 12th Armoured Division quickly secured the situation. Another Iranian

Long columns of IRGC combatants on the march during the Operaiton Val Fajr-5, in February 1984, in the Mehran area. (IRGC)

attack, launched on 20 October, overran a battalion of 4th Infantry Brigade, resulting in the loss of some heights west of the border road.

By coincidence, only a day earlier, Saddam and new Army Chief-of-Staff, Lieutenant General Abd al-Jawad Dhanun, paid a two-day visit to the corps and authorised the deployment of the newly established Hammurabi Guards Armoured Division to the II Corps' area. On 22 October this unit launched a counterattack, but despite strong air and artillery support failed to regain all of the lost ground and called off their attack. As Cordsman noted, this kind of Iranian attack posed serious problems for the Iraqis for it meant that Iraq had '...the alternative of either ceding the loss or counterattacking and sustaining casualties for relatively unimportant objectives.'[26]

The Central Front remained quiet in 1985, with both sides conducting only minor raids to improve their positions or disturb the enemy. Most related Iraqi operations were a part of Saddam's 'dynamic defence policy'. They began with 606th Infantry Brigade (16th Infantry Division) taking key heights north of the Mandali–Sumar road, on the night of 30–31 January 1985, to prevent the Iranians from shelling nearby Iraqi towns and villages. A more ambitious operation resulted in the capture of heights in the Mehran sector, during the night of 11–12 February, by 2nd Infantry Division and commandos; and 434th Infantry Brigade (12th Armoured Division) in the Saif Saad sector. Similar raids were launched by II Corps during July and August. The IV Corps launched such raids in February, July and September 1985.[27]

The Iranians launched several raids of their own, primarily against II Corps around Qasr-e Shirin (operations Zafar-1 and Zafar-3, Qods-1 and Qods-2, all undertaken in June 1985, and followed by Qods-5 in August). However, their largest attack was Operation Ashura-2, which struck 114th Infantry Brigade of 37th Armoured Division on 15 August, and Ashura-3, which hit 108th Infantry Brigade of 1st Mechanised Division, in Fakkeh sector only a day later. Qods-3 followed in July, Qods-4 in early August and

An Iranian strongpoints on a dominating peak – in this case Hill 402 – of the northern frontlines. (IRIA)

Ashura-4 in October 1985. While inflicting casualties and gaining some ground, none of these enterprises was of any great significance.

Following a winter lull, raiding was resumed on the night of 6–7 April 1986, when IV Corps struck the Tib sector. Two days later, part of 1st Mechanised Division launched a similar mission in the Doveyrich River Valley, while on 13 April, 29th Infantry Division raided enemy bases in the Hawizah Marshes. Larger operations followed on 30 April, when 1st Mechanised and 10th Armoured Divisions took an area 12 kilometres deep and 21 kilometres wide in the Fakkeh-Chenaneh sector and repelled a counterattack by 16th IRIA Armoured Division, launched during the night of 2–3 May. There was a similar attack during the night of 8–9 May, when 1st Mechanised and 20th Infantry Divisions captured a 100 square kilometre sector in Doveyrich Valley, despite a counterattack by the IRGC supported by IRIAA Cobras.[28] Some of the raids may have been intended as diversions, prompted by Iraq's loss of the Faw Peninsula during Operation Val Fajr-8 in February 1986. The loss of this critical piece of terrain – and the failure to regain it – undermined Saddam's political ambitions and hurt his prestige both at home and abroad. Saddam's gaze thus fell on Mehran – lost during Val Fajr-3, which, he believed, might prove a useful bargaining chip in exchange for Faw. Furthermore, in the light of repeated Iranian announcements of another 'final' offensive for 19 May 1986 (the anniversary of the death of Ali, Prophet Mohammed's nephew), he feared that the Iranians might use Mehran for a large-scale attack across the Tigris River.

Heroes' Revenge

The task of regaining Mehran – Operation Heroes' Revenge – fell upon Lieutenant General Zia Tawfik Ibrahim's II Corps. Tawfik actually feared he would be exposed to a repeat of Val Fajr-3 over the same terrain and would have preferred to strike further south towards Dehloran, where he might take high ground which was easier to hold. However, he was overruled and delegated the planning to his Chief-of-Staff, Brigadier General Ayad Khlil Zaki, who dusted off the plans to regain Mehran developed after Val Fajr-3. Zaki intended to envelop the town from the north with 4th Commando, 49th Armoured, and 94th Infantry Brigades under his personal command, and from the south by a force consisting of 5th Commando, 70th Armoured and 417th Infantry Brigades commanded by Brigadier General Nawfal Ismail Hammadi. The GHQ's 606th Infantry Brigade acted as reserve. These units totalled some 25,000 troops, supported by 250 MBTs. They faced about 10,000 defenders from a brigade each of 21st and 84th Divisions IRIA.[29]

Tawfik's troops moved out on the evening of 16 May 1986. Zaki's northern force quickly pushed 4th Brigade of 21st Infantry Division back and secured the high ground by 18 May. Ismail's tube and rocket artillery inflicted heavy casualties upon 84th IRIA Division, which was manning nine 4-metre-high berms across the valley and broke through to reach the town by dusk on 17 May. There followed two days of bitter street fighting, by the end of which the Iraqis had established a 15-kilometre-deep bridgehead of 160 square kilometres inside Iran. This was protected in the north by the peaks around Reza Abad, overlooking the town and covering the northern crossroads. However, the Iraqi advance up the Gawi Valley was held some 3–4 kilometres short of the eastern road junction, leaving the Iranians in control of communications from the east. This was to prove a serious mistake.[30]

Karbala-1

Saddam's offer to exchange Mehran for Faw was brusquely rejected by Tehran, which almost instantly ordered its military into a counterattack. Probing operations had already begun on the morning of 19 May, notably in the north, where a brigade of 5th Nasr Infantry Division IRGC struck 59th Armoured Brigade in the Kunjan Dam area. The Iraqi positions held, but Tawfik's armour-heavy force was unable to push into the nearby heights to prevent the Iranians from assembling larger forces there. During the following six weeks, the Iranians rushed to prepare Operation Karbala-1. For this purpose, Task Force Najaf was redeployed to this area, and filled with about 20,000 Pasdaran and Basiji from numerous local units. Several IRIA units – including 44th Artillery Group – followed, totalling about 12,000 troops, 100 MBTs and 37 helicopters (including 10 AH-1s; for further details on involved units, see Table 25).

Meanwhile, Nawfal Ismail's 17th Armoured Division was given responsibility for the salient, but he fell ill and his replacement restricted all patrols to within 20 kilometres of Mehran, thus hindering chances of detecting Iranian preparations.[31] The northern front of the salient was held by 417th and 443rd Infantry Brigades, while 425th and 705th Infantry Brigades entrenched themselves in the east. 59th and 70th Armoured Brigades were held in reserve. Overall, the garrison totalled some 22,000 troops, supported by around 180 MBTs.

The 17th Armoured Division found itself under fierce pressure from 10 June 1986. Tawfiq requested air support, but because Saddam forbade direct requests to the IrAF, these were delayed and the few fighter-bombers which did appear proved ineffective.

PART II: THE CENTRAL FRONT 1982–1987

Table 25: Order of Battle for Karbala-1, May 1986		
Corps	Division	Brigades
Iran		
Task Force Najaf	5th Nasr Infantry Division IRGC	1 brigade
	10th Seyed o-Shohada Infantry Division IRGC	1 brigade
	17th Ali Ibn Abu Talib Infantry Division IRGC	1 brigade
	25th Karbala Infantry Division IRGC	1 brigade
	27th Mohammad Infantry Division IRGC	2 brigades
	41st Sarallah Infantry Division IRGC	1 brigade
	15th Imam Hassan Infantry Brigade IRGC	
	21st Imam Reza Infantry Brigade IRGC	
	662nd Beit-ol-Moghaddas Infantry Brigade IRGC	
	84th Infantry Division IRIA	1 brigade
	44th Artillery Group IRIA	
	1st & 2nd CSG IRIAA, 4th GSG IRIA	
Iraq		
II Corps	65th Commando Brigade, II Corps Artillery Brigade	
	17th Armoured Division	59th & 70th Armoured Brigades; 417th, 425th, 443rd & 705th Infantry Brigades
Reserves	606th Infantry Brigade	
	2nd Wing IrAAC	

Shirazi conferring with several commanders at an IRIAA forward base. Note the three AH-1J Cobras and a single Bell 206 in the background. (Tom Cooper collection)

struck the positions of 443rd and 705th Infantry Brigades around Hill 233, east of Reza Abad. The defenders resisted tenaciously, but lost heavily and conducted a fighting withdrawal, covered by armour. The famous commander of 70th Armoured Brigade, Colonel Jawhar Kalil – nicknamed 'The Wolf' – was killed while leading a counterattack. Similarly, 100 air strikes by IrAF, and 33 by IrAAC, as well as deployment of the 65th Special Forces and 606th Infantry Brigades from the reserve, were in vain: by 2 July, the Iraqis were forced back, almost to the border. It was only during the second phase of Karbala-1 – launched on 4 July with the aim of pushing westwards into Iraq – that the Iranian assault was finally stopped. The Iraqis suffered about 3,000 casualties (including more than 1,000 prisoners) leading Saddam to relieve Tawfik and replace him with Lieutenant General Abd as-Sattar Ahmed al-Muaini.[33]

Crisis of Morale

The failure to regain the Faw Peninsula, followed by the loss of Mehran, caused a major crisis in the morale of the Iraqi armed forces. However, it also acted as a catalyst for radical reforms which had been needed for years. The generals' muted grumbling about Saddam's meddling in military issues increased when the Iranians exploited their earlier success to capture additional heights west of Mehran, during the night of 16–17 September 1986. This time it took the deployment of 94th and 118th Infantry Brigades of the new I Special Corps to stabilise the situation.[34] Eventually, Saddam was forced to call an Extraordinary Congress of the Ba'ath Party. Little has emerged about the deliberations, but the Iraqis did decide to introduce major changes in recruitment and strategy. Now the army would conscript more officers from university students to improve the overall quality, while their generals would adopt a more active strategy. Progress was certainly made, but it was given real momentum by Khazraji's appointment as Chief-of-Staff, in 1987.[35]

Moreover, Saddam seems to have had second thoughts about holding Mehran, and reportedly decided to abandon the town on 30 June. Consequently, the assembly of the Iranian assault forces not only proceeded unhindered but also largely undetected.[32]

Whether or not Saddam's decision to abandon Mehran was communicated to local commanders became purely academic, as during the night of 30 June–1 July 1986, the Seyed o-Shohada, Ali Ibn Abu Talib, Karbala and Mohammad IRGC Infantry Divisions

Iranian troops inside one of the Iraqi positions captured during Operation Karbala-6 in January 1987. (Albert Grandolini collection)

Meanwhile, raiding continued, but on 14 October 1986, the Iranians struck II Corps at Qasr-e Shirin again, pushing 21st Infantry Division off several key heights. This time, it took an intervention by 68th Special Forces Brigade and a corps commando battalion to recover the ground.[36]

Karbala-6

During the latter half of 1986 the SDC was pre-occupied with preparing its 'war-winning offensives' on Basra; Karbala-4 and -5. However, diversions were planned to support these operations; and the SDC came to the decision to launch a diversion, Operation Karbala-6, in early 1987, to regain Naft Shahr, northwest of Sumar and thus remove one of the burrs in Iran's skin.

Naft Shahr lies near the border, on the northern bank of the Kanga Kush, across the Khanaqin-Sumar road – at the mouth of a gently sloping river valley to the east and a narrow gorge to the north. The Iraqis held the eastern side of the gorge, and a line due south to the point where the salient protruded into Iraq. This road went around the western base of a height, and control of that height and the road would provide a valuable springboard for an assault upon Al Miqdadiyah, but it was poor tank country. With most of the IRGC's units busy fighting for Basra, Karbala-6 was one of the rare IRIA-led operations from this period of the war. The army deployed 2nd and 3rd Brigades of 21st Infantry Division, 3rd Brigade of 77th Infantry Division, an unknown brigade of 84th Infantry division, elements of 58th Infantry Division and 55th Airborne Brigade. The IRGC element was confined to two brigades of 31st Ashura Infantry Division, reinforced by several battalions of Basiji. Overall, the Iranians concentrated about 30,000 troops, supported by one tank battalion and 17 artillery battalions (about 185 guns and MLRS). They faced 16th and 22nd Infantry Divisions commanded by Brigadiers Abd Mutlak al-Juburi and Tariq Radi Hassan, respectively, who had six brigades with about 19,000 troops.

Bad weather forced several postponements and helped alert the defenders. Once the assault began, during the night of 13–14 January 1987, Iraqi defences channelled the attackers, spearheaded

Lacking replacements for earlier tank losses, the IRIA was forced to keep its obsolete M47 Patton MBTs in service with the 77th Infantry Division throughout the war. (via N.S.)

PART II: THE CENTRAL FRONT 1982–1987

Iranian army troops carrying an injured comrade on a makeshift stretcher made from two G3 assault rifles. (Albert Grandolini collection)

capture a useful height; Nasr-2, which – supported by 30 IRIAA helicopters and some air strikes of the IRIAF – hit 22nd Infantry Division to gain some ground in the Meimak Heights; Nasr-3, which struck 29th Infantry Division in June; and Nasr-6, which hit 22nd Division between Sumar and the Meimak Heights, in August 1987. Furthermore, during the night of 19–20 December 1987, two Pasdaran brigades – reinforced by some commandos – assaulted positions of the 29th Division along the Doveyrich River, apparently with some minor success.[39]

by the 77th Division's brigade and Ashura's Pasdaran (supported by few captured Iraqi tanks), into killing zones.

What happened next is uncertain. Some reports assume that Iranian regulars recognised the nature of this operation as a diversion, and did not press home their attack, prompting reports about 'half-hearted' efforts.[37] Yet it was the IRIA which cracked open the Iraqi defences in several places. The IRGC, which lacked armour, failed to reinforce spearheads on time. Isolated, these had to fight their way back to their start line. Another attack hit the Iraqi 16th Infantry Division during the night of 17–18 January, but any gains were quickly lost to counterattacks. A day later, the Iranians called off their operation; while claiming to have taken up to 260 square kilometres of Iraqi territory, they failed to take Naft Shahr or to divert any enemy troops from the south.

This time, it was the Pasdaran who were made scapegoats. An observer from 77th Infantry Division IRIA commented that while the final approach was supposed to be made silently, the Basiji opened fire, forcing Army commanders to launch their assault before schedule.

Karbala-8

On 9 April 1987, the Iranians launched their next offensive on the Central Front, Operation Karbala-8. This time, it was the IRGC that intended to improve Iranian Kurdish positions and to divert Iraqi resources northwards. Once again this was a short operation, involving only two divisions. Unsurprisingly, it was broken off within two days, despite taking three heights near Suleimaniya. Rather tragically, it prompted the Iraqis into launching chemical weapon attacks on 20 Kurdish villages, on 15 April 1987.[38]

For the rest of the year, central frontlines remained largely quiet, other than minor clashes. These included operations like Karbala-9, launched against II Corps in the Qasr-e Shirin area to

21
THE NORTHERN FRONT 1982–1987

Baghdad's decision to abandon most of its conquests inside Iran left I Corps on the defensive during the period 1982–1987, with a conventional role shielding Sulaymaniyah and a counterinsurgency role containing the Kurds. The year following the Iraqi withdrawal of 1982 was relatively quiet on the Northern Front until signs of an imminent Iranian offensive led to a pre-emptive operation by the newly established 24th Infantry Division. This began during the night of 26–27 July 1983, east of Qala Diza, and resulted in seizure of two 2,300-metre-high peaks in the Jabal Balgha range. While this success came at a heavy cost – because 28th Infantry Division IRIA was alerted on time – the Iranians failed to regain the peaks.

However, between July 1983 and early 1988, the primary battlefields of the Northern Front were the Haj Umran Pass and the Sulaymaniyah-Penjwin-Marivan roads (where Chwarta became the virtual 'eye of the storm'). These were tantalizingly close to the PUK's eastern sanctuaries of Basilan and Jafati Valley. The events in the two sectors between 1983 and 1987 will be described geographically rather than chronologically to ease understanding.

Still led by Dr Abdul Rahman Ghassemlou, the KDPI remained a major thorn in Tehran's side, although driven back towards the border with Iraq. Having forced the KDPI out and into camps in the Rawandiz Valley, just inside Iraq, in 1983 the Iranians prepared a 'final settling of accounts' with Ghassemlou.

The pre-war garrison of Piran Shahr had been part of the 64th Infantry Division IRIA, most of which was committed to COIN operations, leaving only its 132nd Infantry Battalion behind. Consequently, substantial reinforcements were needed for the offensive – codenamed Val Fajr-2. These included 2nd Brigade of 77th Infantry Division, 105th Mechanised Battalion of 92nd Armoured Division IRIA, and a brigade of 33rd al-Mahdi Division IRGC on the northern side. To the south of Piran Shahr were a brigade of 8th Najaf Ashraf Infantry Division, 14th Imam Hossein Infantry Division and a part of 105th Qods Infantry Brigade – all IRGC. This gave the Iranians about 45,000 troops, including the Barzani-led KDP of about 800, and some 200 Iraqi Shi'a 'Mujahideen'. The Kurds not only acted as infantry, but also as scouts and porters of supplies, while the artillery of 64th and 77th Division was bolstered by that of 33rd Artillery Group (a battalion each of 130mm howitzers and

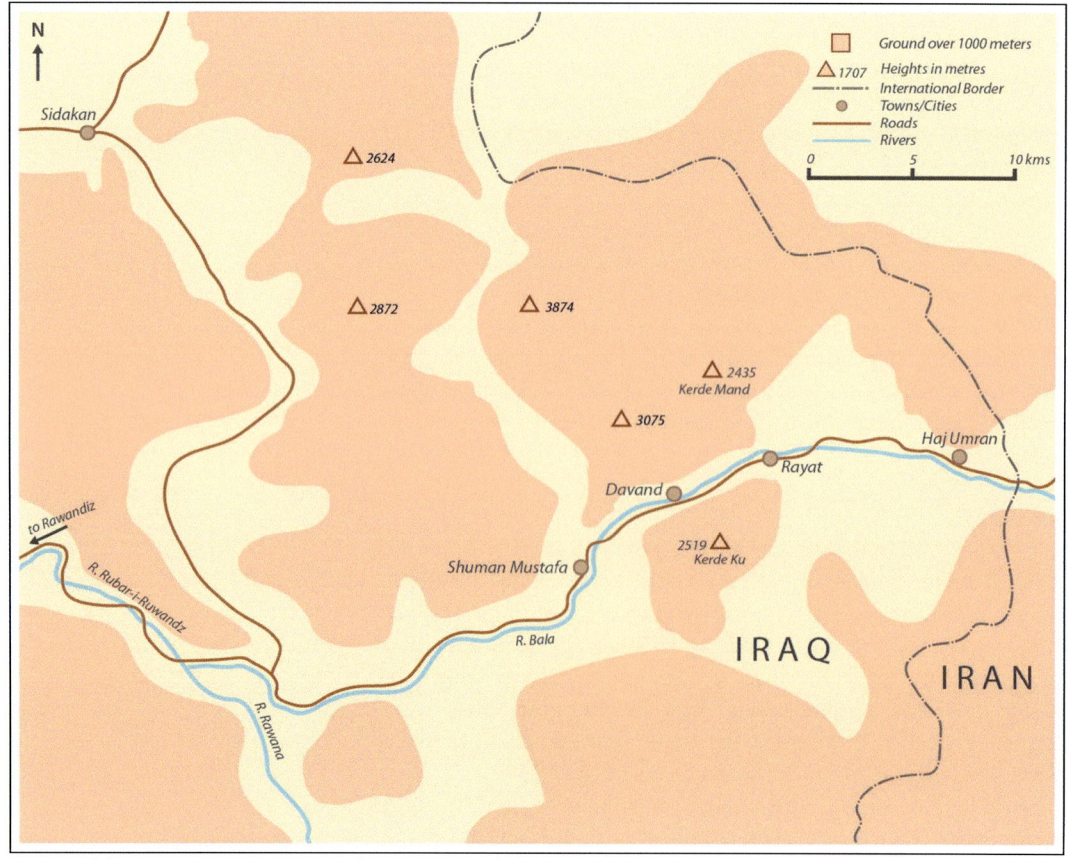

Haj Umran Sector, 1983–1987

The Haj Umran Pass carries the main road from northwest Iran through Piran Shah, then along mountain ranges at an elevation above 2,000 metres, to Arbil and then Kirkuk. From Kirkuk the road continues southwards in the general direction of Baghdad, but it also meets the highway eastwards to Sulaymaniyah. The pass itself runs between two border massifs with Haj Umran (also Haj Omran) at its mouth. To the north is the 3,874-metre-high Shuman Mustafa (Chumanmostafa) and the River Bala (Balak), which wends down the eastern side of the spur, then westwards to join the River Rawana (Rawand or Rubar). To the south is a massif up to 3,587 metres high, with outcrops dominating the road which then goes up the Rubar-i-Ruwandiz valley, to the town of Rawandiz.[1]

A map of the Haj Umran sector. (Map by George Anderson)

PART II: THE NORTHERN FRONT 1982–1987

To accelerate the advance of the IRGC forces in the Haj Umran sector in July 1983, the IRIAA made extensive use of its helicopters to deploy light infantry on dominating peaks. (via N.S.)

Many of the combatants deployed during the Iranian offensives on the northern sector of the frontlines in 1984 were either Basiji, mobilised form the local population, or KDP Kurds. Here a group of them is preparing for action after being brought to their starting position by one of the omnipresent Toyota 4WD pickups. (IRGC)

MLRS). Furthermore, the IRIAA deployed about 30 helicopters from the 4th CSG in support (these evacuated 260 injured soldiers and 39 civilians during this operation, while delivering 40 tonnes of supplies).

The KDP Kurds discovered that the pass was defended only by 23rd Infantry Division's 91st Infantry Brigade, supported by 4th Border Guards Brigade, and the PUK. However, Iraqi spies in Iran alerted the commander of I Corps, Major General Niima Faris al-Mihyawi. The only uncertainty was when, and where, the main blow would fall.

The attack came during the night of 21–22 July, with the Iranians crossing the border in combined formations of IRIA, IRGC and KDP on multiple points along a 30-kilometre-wide frontline – primarily through infiltration – to envelop the valley. The main blow came from the south with the rapid seizure of many peaks which the defenders had been unable to garrison.

The push down the road, into the mouth of the valley, faced fierce resistance. This came not only from the KDPI, but from Iraqi helicopter gunships, and – reportedly – mustard gas shells fired by artillery. Whether or not the latter were really deployed, it had little effect because of terrain and weather. Iranian helicopters proved far more effective than those of the Iraqis, who even used two Ilyushin Il-76 transports to bomb Iranian positions, dropping their bombs from the rear loading ramp, though with little effect.[2] Iraqi counterattacks also proved unsuccessful, and by 26 July the Iranians had advanced 10 kilometres, taking not only Haj Umran, but also 43 villages and Height 2435 (or Kerde Ku). In the south, the Pasdaran even overcame stiff Kurdish resistance to take Mount Kerde Mand (Kerdemand), and its western heights, which overlooked the town of Rayat, west of Haj Umran.

Two days later, on 28 July 1983, the Iraqis launched their first heliborne assault on Mount Kerde Mand. Supported by air strikes (including some by PC-7s) and artillery, and a mechanised force which isolated the peak, Mi-8s lifted two battalions from 66th Special Forces Brigade, and the special forces battalion of the Guards Corps. The initial landing was unopposed, but once on the ground the troops faced fierce resistance and it took them until the next morning to secure the mountain. As soon as the area was secure, special forces troops were relieved by a brigade of 23rd Infantry Division – which lost the peak shortly afterwards, in early August 1983, to an Iranian counterattack. Eventually the fighting fizzled out, leaving the Iranians and their KDP allies holding the key heights dominating the eastern Haj Umran road, while the Iraqis held the heights in the lower valley. Some idea of the scale of the fighting may be gained by the fact that 77th Infantry Division IRIA expended 22 tonnes of 105mm field artillery ammunition and 1,435 mortar bombs in a single day.

Iranian Success

For the Iranians, Val Fajr-2 was a rare successful offensive. The IRIA, the IRGC and the KDP not only recovered 195 square kilometres of Iranian territory but also captured 220 square kilometres of Iraq. They had also cut the main KDPI supply line and forced their survivors to flee westwards, often leaving behind their families, most of whom – up to 20,000 – were held in detention camps in southern Iran. The Iranians gave Barzani's KDP control over the Haj Umran camp area, and they brought in their families from Khaneh, while that town itself was given to the Iraqi Shi'a dissident Dawa Party and Hojatolislam Mohammed Bakr Hakim of the Supreme Council of the Islamic Revolution for Iraq, which was created in 1982.

The Iranian successes in Kurdish territory prompted ever more Kurds to defect from the Iraqi Army and, in August 1983, Baghdad admitted that up to 48,000 Kurdish fighters were absent without leave and might have joined the anti-government insurgency. Nevertheless, the effects of Val Fajr-2 were limited and the Iraqis understood this operation was designed to stretch the Iraqi Army

A PC-7 light striker seen while overflying forward Iranian positions during Operation Val Fajr-2. (Farzin Nadimi collection)

while a larger one, Val Fajr-4, was launched in the south. Yet the Iraqis were always worried that the northern dams might be captured or destroyed, leading to severe flooding in central and even southern Iraq.

Operation Qader

While 1984 remained quiet on the Northern Front, in 1985 the Iranians belatedly decided to exploit the success of Val Fajr-2 with Operation Qader (Almighty God). This was to be launched northwards from Haj Umran towards heights 2624, 3874 and 3075 using 77th Infantry Division's 1st Brigade in combination with elements from 23rd, 28th and 64th Divisions and 55th Airborne Brigade IRIA. The IRGC provided a brigade from 8th Najaf Ashraf Division together with the 105th Qods and 155th Seyed ol-Shohada Brigades, which were to advance from Kerde Mand towards the high ground opposite Shuman Mustafa to tighten control of the Haj Umran Pass.

The Iranians struck at dawn on 15 July 1985 and initially they had little success against 431st, 433rd and 438th Infantry Brigades of 23rd Division. Saddam was concerned enough to send a delegation from the GHQ, including Khairallah and the Operations Chief, Lieutenant General Hisham Sabah al-Fakhri. Soothing messages were sent south, but on 16 July the Iranians renewed their attack, driving back the defenders until they reached the lower slopes of heights 2624, 2873 and 3874. Now even the Sidakan Valley was under threat, and GHQ had to despatch reinforcements in the form of commando brigades and artillery units from III, IV and VI Corps for a counterattack launched by Brigadier General Iyad Khalil Zaki al-Bayati's 33rd Infantry Division. Attacks by 428th Infantry Brigade, on 25 July, and by IV Corps' 2nd Commando Brigade, three days later, retook high ground south of the road. Yet during the night of 28–29 July, the Iranians struck at 703rd Infantry Brigade, who held the attack when reinforced by VI Corps commandos.

After a three-day break the Iraqis launched counterattacks. During the night of 1–2 September 1985, the III Corps' commando brigade attacked in the 33rd Division sector and on the night of 6–7 September, 66th Special Forces Brigade secured Height 2030.

Despite this setback, on 9 September the Iranians renewed Qader, striking positions of 23rd and 33rd Divisions on a 50-kilometre front. Armoured forces, with elements of 55th Airborne IRIA Brigade, pushed from Rayat, while infantry advanced towards Sidakan to outflank the enemy. Already on alert – partially with help of intelligence provided by Kurds – the Iraqis held this attack. After the front quietened down, the 66th Special Forces Brigade regained a number of peaks – including Height 2435 – in a combined operation with the PUK during the night of 17–18 September, the front then quietened down again.

Karbala-2

While the rest of 1985 remained quiet in the north, during the second half of April 1986, V Corps began raiding Iranian and Kurdish positions near the border. The success of these attacks encouraged a larger operation by 33rd Infantry Division during the night of 10–11 May 1985. This took ground above 2,000 metres, encouraging plans for a major assault upon Kerde Mand. This began during the night of 13–14 May in constant rain and regained not only Kerde Mand, but also Kerde Ku and then drove off all Iranian counterattacks.

During the summer of 1986, the IrAF staged a strategic air campaign against towns behind the frontline. With the IRIAF unable to respond, the SDC decided to retaliate on the ground by taking the entire Haj Umran Valley. Saddam, concerned about another Val Fajr-8 publicly appealed to Iran – in August – not to implement its threat to launch a final offensive, and on 3 August produced a Four Point Peace Plan, but the Iranian response was to launch Operation Karbala 2.

On 1 September, two division-sized task forces; the northern with three brigades from 9th Badr, 10th Seyed o-Shohada, and 155th Divisions IRGC, and the southern with three brigades from 12th Qa'em-e Mohammad, 21st Imam Reza and 105th Qods Divisions, came down the heights and into the valley on either side of the road to Piran Shahr. Due to poor Iranian coordination, and good Iraqi aerial support, the defenders – including 98th, 604th and 807th Infantry Brigades of 33rd Infantry Division in the north, and 91st Infantry Brigade in the south – experienced no problem stopping each attack and within two days Karbala-2 was abandoned with Kerde Man still in Iraqi hands.

Youthful gunners of an Iraqi artillery unit, in 1985. (via Ali Tobchi)

PART II: THE NORTHERN FRONT 1982–1987

Karbala-7

After a lull due to winter, the Iranians decided to support Karbala 6 on the Central Front with a diversion which would push further down the Haj Umran Pass. Karbala 7 was launched during the night of 3 to 4 March 1987 by 64th IRIA Infantry Division supported by KDP Kurds. The Iraqi 91st Infantry Brigade fought well and initially contained the assault, but then the Iranians broke through and secured not only Kerde Mand, but advanced for 1–2 kilometres in the direction of Shuman Mustafa. This time, the counterattacks by units of V Corps failed to recover the lost ground, highlighting problems caused by the spread of the Kurdish insurgency, and laid the foundation of the Anfal campaigns (see next chapter). Lacking troops to bolster their success, the Iranians were forced to limit their activity to a few raids for the remainder of 1987. The biggest of these was Operation Nasr-7, launched on 5 August by four IRGC brigades which struck 24th Infantry Division's positions around Qala Diza, inside Iran and drove the Iraqis back across the border. A similar attack upon 23rd Infantry Division – Operation Nasr-9, launched on 23 November 1987 – was less successful.

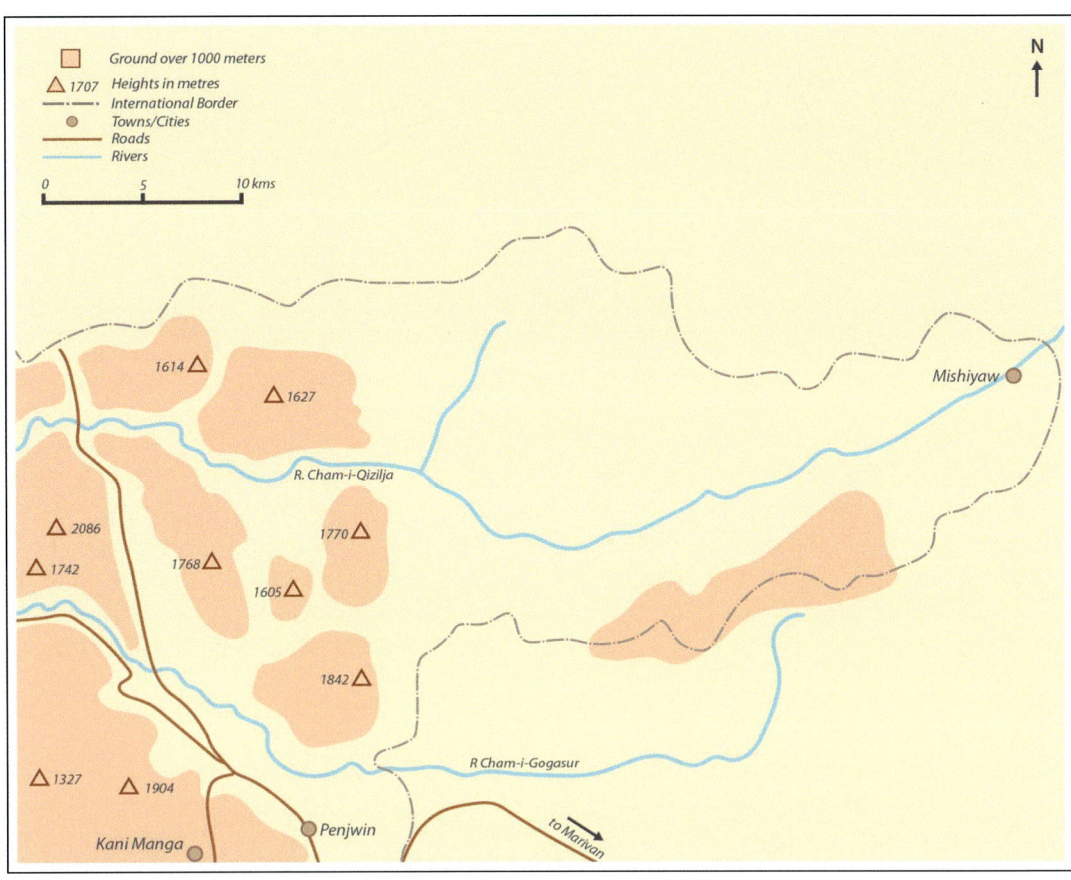

A map of the area in which Operation Val Fajr-4 was conducted. (Map by George Anderson)

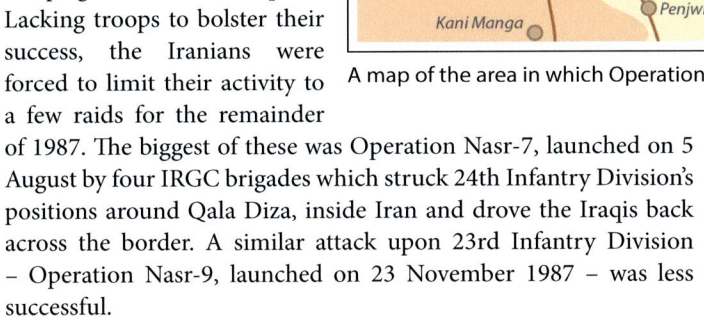

Chwarta Sector, 1983–1987

The Chwarta Sector is entered through the Mishiyaw Salient, a valley beneath peaks of up to 2,000 metres. Running on an east-west axis through the salient is the Chami-Qizilja (Aw-e Rashia) River, which flows into the Nahr Siwayl. The latter runs past several heights, ranging from 1,605 to 2,086 metres, to join the Lower Zab River (al-Zab Saqir) inside a valley north-east of the town known as Chwarta (Churwartah or Chuartah). The latter is about 25 kilometres from Sulaymaniyah and a tantalising 50 kilometres from the Iranian border. The terrain is rugged and there are only a few good roads, indeed even today most 'roads' in this region are mere dirt tracks. The one connecting Chwarta with Sulaymaniyah continues eastwards, passing through the village of Mawat, before crossing the border to join the Iranian frontier road linking Sar Dasht and Baneh. Another road runs northwest from Marivan, across the border to Penjwin, through the valley of the Gogasur before turning south into the intensively cultivated valley north of Lake Dharband-I Khan. Thirty-five kilometres southwest of Penjwein is Halabja.3

Val Fajr-4

The Chwarta Sector had been relatively quiet for nearly two years, before the Pasdaran – supported by the KDP – decided to launch an impromptu attack on the northern face of the salient on 16 September 1983. During the following three days they took a number of key heights that proved as useful jumping-off points. To complete the neutralisation of the KDPI, the Iranians planned their first major offensive in this sector, Operation Val Fajr-4. This involved the envelopment of the Mishiyaw Salient using Task Force Hamzeh with 30,000 men divided into four battlegroups:

- Hamzeh-1 (two brigades of 14th Imam Hossein IRGC Division and 2nd Brigade from 21st IRIA Infantry Division)

- Hamzeh-2 (3rd Brigade from 28th IRIA Infantry Division, a tank battalion from 88th IRIA Armoured Division, and part of 44th Qamar Bani Hashem IRGC Engineer Brigade) were to deliver the major blow from the north

- Hamzeh-3 (two brigades from 8th Najaf Ashraf IRGC Infantry Division, 2nd Brigade from 28th IRIA Infantry Division)

- Hamzeh-4 (1st Brigade from 28th IRIA Infantry Division) with KDP.

Hamzeh-1 and Hamzeh-2 were to deliver the major blow from the north while the other two battlegroups would strike from the south. Fire support was provided by 11th Artillery Group IRIA (27 batteries with 105mm and 203mm guns, and three MLRS batteries), the 3rd and 4th Combat Support Groups IRIAA (total of 42 helicopters).

The Iranian objective was to slice off the salient and take the heights overlooking Marivan in the west, thus preventing the Iraqis from shelling Baneh and Marivan. The secondary objective was

Youthful Basiji taking a short break prior to continuing their advance towards the next peak during Val Fajr-4. (Albert Grandolini collection)

Cheerful IRGC troops atop an Iraqi T-55 MBT captured during Operation Val Fajr-4. (Albert Grandolini collection)

to clear the valleys of the KDPI and further disrupt its last major supply line into Iraq.

Meanwhile the I Corps, commanded by Major General Maher Abd al-Rashid, was badly overstretched. The sector was held by 4th Infantry Division, which was then reinforced by 7th Infantry Division – commanded by Brigadier General Sultan Hashim Ahmed – from II Corps. The salient was now defended six brigades and some Border Guards.

The Iranians opened their attack during the night of 19–20 October by infiltrating and then overrunning forward Iraqi positions. Much of 5th Infantry Brigade collapsed, opening the way for the Pasdaran to take Mishiyaw Salient, five KDPI camps, and heights including 1614, 1768 and 2086. A night later, the Iranians put even more pressure upon the defenders, and during the night of 23–24 August, they widened the frontline by assaulting most of 4th Infantry Division. Although degenerating into hand-to-hand fighting, their attempt to completely isolate 5th Infantry Brigade failed in the face of a counterattack which retook Height 1904 and Kani Manga, northeast of Penjwin. During the battle Iraqi helicopters deployed part of 65th Special Forces Brigade behind enemy lines to interdict communications, while Iraqi airmen flew 122 air, and 39 helicopter sorties, some at night. Although causing heavy casualties, this effort was in vain and the Iraqis evacuated Penjwin on 29 October 1983, although their artillery prevented the enemy from occupying the town.

During the night of 2–3 November 1983, Hamzeh-2 struck 7th Infantry Division, forcing it away from Height 1900, but the main Iraqi defence line held firm. This allowed Saddam to send the Guards' Special Forces Brigade to retake Height 1900 during the night of 4–5 November.

In the south, the Iranians vainly attempted to occupy Penjwin, on 6 November 1983, but the town remained in no-man's-land. Three nights later, two divisions of the IRIA and seven of the IRGC struck both 4th and 7th Infantry Divisions but failed again. Emboldened, corps commander Maher Abd al-Rashid and his divisional commanders then publicly informed Saddam that, '... they had succeeded in a model defence campaign to cause the Iranians a major defeat, and decimated their forces.'[4]

Yet the Iranians had not only captured the Qizilja and Gogasur Valleys, but also some 650 square kilometres of Iraqi territory, pushing the defenders to within 10 kilometres east of Chwarta. Furthermore, Val Fajr-4 had certainly attracted substantial Iraqi strength, and when it concluded each of two Iraqi divisions controlled up to 10 brigades (including four special forces units), making their command at least challenging, if not difficult. Furthermore, in the wake of Val Fajr-2 in the north it helped encourage the growth of the Kurdish rebellion in northern Iraq.

Val Fajr-9

Val Fajr-4 left the Iranians only 40 kilometres from Sulaymaniya and poised to reach at least the Lower Zab Valley. For the SDC this was an excellent opportunity to 'spook' the Iraqis and divert them as Iran launched its offensive on the Faw Peninsula, Val Fajr-8. Nevertheless, the Iraqis realised this was a diversion thanks to their Kurdish scouts and COMINT.

PART II: THE NORTHERN FRONT 1982–1987

The Chwarta Sector. (Map by George Anderson)

the night of 24–25 February. The thin Iraqi line was soon overwhelmed, but the 34th Infantry Division managed to hold most of its major positions, while commandos and Kurdish NDBs launched counterattacks to recover peaks overlooking the Zab Valley.

Further south, 27th Infantry Division found itself exposed to another attack, but successfully held its lines, encouraging its commanders to launch a counterattack and regain terrain ranging from 1,800 to 2,100 metres – especially all the peaks lost during the October-November 1983 campaign.

The 34th Division counterattacked during the night of 5–6 March 1986, through cloud and continuous rain (which turned to snow on the higher ground), with helicopter and artillery support. While it was not completely successful, it did regain many of the heights and cleared the area up to the border by 14 March. Reinforced by the Guards' Special Forces Brigade and NDBs, 27th Infantry Division counterattacked during the night of 20–21 March and retook additional heights. Finally, both divisions launched another attack during the night of 27–28 March and recovered most of the lost ground. Nevertheless, the Iranians were barely five kilometres from Chwarta, and had extended their hold down the western slopes of the last heights before Sulaymaniyah, which lay only 15 kilometres away.

Spearheaded by the 57th Albolfazl al-Abbas Infantry Brigade – supported by 105th Qods, 110th Boroujerdi, and 155th Brigade IRGC and a brigade of 28th Infantry Division – the Iranians attacked into the Katu range around heights 1543 and 1451 during

Karbala-10

Determined to maintain pressure, the Iranians prepared their next offensive – Karbala-10 – aiming to take Mawat, some 30 kilometres to the northwest to provide better communications for the pro-Barzani Kurds. The attack would be launched by Task Force Ramadan (110th Boroujerdi Infantry Brigade and 9th Badr Infantry Division, totalling about 12,000 troops), and KDP forces, which faced V Corps' 34th and 39th Infantry Divisions. Karbala-10 also

Iranian Army troops and the Pasdaran made extensive use of RPG-7s for attacks on Iraqi fortifications during operations Val Fajr-9 and Karbala-10. (Tom Cooper collection)

Some of the Iraqi POWs captured during Karbala-10. (Albert Grandolini collection)

envisaged two sub-operations: Nasr-1, run by Task Force Ramadan, and a combined PUK/Iranian commando – Operation Fath-5.

The Iraqis had been aware of the impeding blow since 20 April but lacked details. Consequently, when the Pasdaran assaulted three nights later, they quickly captured some 20 villages and heights east of the Lower Zab, 1972 and 1897, which dominating the confluence of the rivers. Despite the IRGC concentrating a total of 77 infantry battalions, Karbala-10 was contained in early June 1987 with the help of reinforcements rushed from Baghdad.

Nasr-4, -5, -7, -8 and -9
Dissatisfied with results of Karbala-10, the SDC transferred the sector to the headquarters of Task Force Najaf, while Brigadier General Ali Siyed Shirazi personally planned the next offensive – Operation Nasr-4. Launched during the night of 20–21 June 1987, this attack took the remaining heights around Mawat and the village of Zhazaya, pushing 39th Infantry Division back across the Lower Zab. Three nights later, Task Force Najaf launched Operation Nasr-5, this time driving back the southern flank of 34th Infantry Division.

Saddam reacted by rushing reinforcements – including the Guards Baghdad Infantry Division, and 3rd and 16th Special Forces Brigades. These helped 34th and 39th Divisions to counterattack during the night to 26 June and regain some heights but left the Iranians overlooking Mawat and the nearby Lower Zab Valley.

Rafsanjani claimed these successes were 'as important as those at Faw Peninsula, because… Suleymaniyah is an entrance gate to other parts of Iraq', but while the Iranians were now closer to Sulamaniyeh, and only 100 kilometres from Kirkuk and its oil fields, they could not exploit their successes. Task Force Najaf also launched its third operation, Nasr-7, from the night of 4–5 August 1987 using parts of 7th Vali Asr and 27th Mohammad Rasoolallah IRGC Infantry Divisions, which managed to push 24th and 39th Infantry Divisions from additional heights.

There were two additional Iranian 'land grabs'; operations Nasr-8 and -9 at the end of 1987. During the night of 20–21 November, brigades from 11th Amir al-Momenin, 12th Qa'em-e Mohammad, 21st Imam Reza, 57th Abolfazl al-Abbas, and 155th Seyed ol-Shohada IRGC Infantry Divisions attacked the new 44th in Mawat sector and pushed it back, taking Height 1107 (called Mount Girdarash by the Iranians) in the process. By contrast, Nasr-9 was a vain enterprise launched during the night of 21–22 September by 2nd Brigade 64th IRIA Infantry Division.

22
IRAN'S LAST CHANCE

Following the bloody failures around Basra, and with the passing of Khomeini's deadline for 'final victory' by 31 March 1987, the SDC reconsidered its strategic options. Finally concluding that taking Basra was extremely unlikely, it decided to switch the strategic focus northwards, and press deeper into northern Iraq with Kurdish support. A key factor for this decision was the existence of extensive areas – 'sanctuaries' – held by the PUK around Suleymaniyah. Calculating that by opening routes to these, Iran could secure a massive enclave inside Iraq to threaten not only Suleymaniyah but also the northern oil fields, the SDC decided to switch its prime strategic objectives from the Southern to the Northern Front. Consequently, nearly a dozen IRGC divisions began making their way from southern to northern Iran. Due to the nature of the ramshackle communications system, it took them months to complete this journey and they did not assemble until late 1987. When they arrived many divisions were broken up, often with one brigade being deployed in a separate sector possibly to 'stiffen' their IRIA garrisons. Their arrival was an omen of a radical change in the Iranian strategy in this war, because the Northern Front had largely been a backwater for conventional operations during the past seven years.

Beit-ol-Mogaddas-2, -3 and -6

The first attempt to reach the 'sanctuaries' was Operation Beit-ol-Moghaddas 2, launched from the Chwarta area on 15 January 1988, with the aim of reaching the PUK-controlled Jafati Valley. Five brigades struck southwest from Height 1107, driving 39th and 44th Infantry Divisions back towards the Lower Zab Valley by 21 January. Further tightening their grip on Mawat, the Iranians then established a bridgehead across the Zab (between heights 1707 and 1827) adding another 130 square kilometres of Iraqi territory.

Two months later, on 15 March 1988, brigades form 5th Nasr and 31st Ashura IRGC Infantry Divisions on the right, and 12th Qaem-e-Mohammad IRGC Infantry Division (reinforced with 35th Imam Hassan and 48th Fath al-Mustaqil Brigades) on the left, stormed the southern heights and occupied the area southwest of Mawat, around Height 1827.[1]

With the road to the sanctuary still blocked, Beit-ol-Moghaddas-6 was launched from 16 to 18 May, using brigades from three divisions, which took Height 1827 from 44th Division. However, once there, the Iranians could not advance any further. Even so, their total gains included another 25 square kilometres of sparsely populated territory and 750 prisoners.[2]

Chief-of-Staff Khazraji was not pleased about the performance of the 38th Infantry Division in the Lake Dukan area and made his views clear when he evaluated the defence at a conference with Saddam. He described the performance of 448th Infantry Brigade as 'terrible' and noted 76th and 442nd Infantry Brigades were isolated and had to be resupplied by helicopters, and while although increasing the number of brigades deployed in the Qalat Dizah sector from three to seven, Khazraji demanded additional reinforcements.[3]

The Iranian success prompted an adverse reaction from Turkey. Ankara was then controlled by secular Sunnis, who were always suspicious of Iran's theocratic Shi'a regime – and even more so to the Iranian success in northern Iraq. Turkey therefore threatened to close the border and – following an air attack on 27 March 1988 – reinforced its garrisons in the adjacent area.

Lake Darband-i-Khan

While the Iranian government might be concerned about the closure of the border, the I SDC was more interested in the sector to the

Troops of one of the IRGC's naval brigades marching into the hills in the Chwrata area in January 1988. (via N.S.)

MIDDLE EAST@WAR SERIES SPECIAL #1: THE IRAN-IRAQ WAR

The task of resupplying infantry brigades cut off by the Iranian offensives of early 1988 proved a very dangerous one: a number of IrAAC Mi-8/17 helicopters were shot down by the Iranians while hauling 'beans, bullets and gas' for Iraqi ground troops. (IRIA)

Bad weather concealed much of the Iranian troop movements on the northern frontlines in January–May 1988. (via N.S.)

the river are heights 1108 (Shakh-e-surmer) and 1306 (Shakh-e-shemiran). In March the temperature in the region averages 17°C but can drop to 5.5°C; during the summer, it rises rapidly to 39.5°C. Given the predominance of Kurds in the region, this front had naturally attracted insurgent presence; indeed, these were covertly present in the town for nearly 30 years. In May 1987, this prompted the Iraqi authorities to bulldoze two of the town's quarters, although the population had meanwhile swelled by 60,000 refugees.

Since Operation Tahrir al-Qods in February 1984, the Iranians had launched several attempts to support the Kurds in Halabja. Most of these resulted in minor gains, while Operation Val Fajr-9 (see Chwarta section) ended with an Iraqi defensive success.[5] Realising the Halabja sector was relatively lightly protected, the Iranian commanders believed they could link up with the PUK-controlled sanctuary in the Qara Dagh Heights. The resulting plan – codenamed Operation Val Fajr-10 – envisaged deployment of no fewer than nine infantry divisions of the IRGC, one of the IRIA and 11 brigades, for a total of 130,000 troops (see Table 26). In the north, Task Force Qods was to sweep down through the fertile area and cut the road between Sayyid Sadiq and Khurmal. In the south, Task Force Samene-al-Aeme would strike westwards to take heights 2322 and 2945 then sweep down their slopes to take Halabja. Meanwhile, Task Force Fath would complete Halabja's isolation from the south. Following intensive preparations, the IRIAF was to provide eight F-4E Phantoms from TFB.3 and additional F-5Es from TFB.4 for support of this operation. The IRIAF readied no fewer than 49 helicopters – including 16 AH-1s. The Iraqis were forewarned about the coming attack – in part by increasing activity of the Iranian artillery – but did little to reinforce its three divisions deployed in this area.

south, around the town of Halabja (also Halabcheh), a town of some 70,000 people, mostly Kurds. This sector was separated from Iran by the 1,500 to 3,000-metre-high Shamran range, which stretches for 60 kilometres from Penjwin to the River Sirvan. Halabja is in the centre of a fertile belt arcing around the Daraband-i-Khan Lake, only some 20 kilometres from the border – as the crow flies. The lake held three billion cubic metres of water but was subject to frequent slope failure requiring constant repair. On its southern end a 128-metre-high, 445-metre-long, US-designed dam was constructed in 1961. This generated nearly 40 percent of Iraqi's electricity. German and Japanese companies launched the work on replacing its two original 800kW generators with two 83MW units in 1983, but this work was completely only in 1990.[4]

Shielding the approaches to the southern part of the lake from Iran are a series of 1,600 to 2,900 metre heights, of which the most important are 2945 (Sindravi) and 1802 (Shakh-e Balambo). Across

Val Fajr-10

The Iranian assault began during the night of 13–14 March 1988, with raids by Iranian commandos (Operation Zafar-7) from the Qara Dagh sanctuary towards Khurmal, with the aim of opening a route towards the Iranian border. Task Forces Qods and Samene-

Table 26: Order of Battle for Operation Val Fajr-10, April 1988		
Corps	Division	Brigades
Iran		
Task Force Qods	41st Sarallah Infantry Division IRGC	
	105th Qods Infantry Division IRGC	
	39th Nabi al-Akram Infantry Brigade IRGC	
	44th Qamar Bani Hashem Engineer Brigade IRGC	
	48th Malek-e Ashtar Infantry Brigade IRGC	
Task Force Samene-ol-Aeme	25th Karbala Infantry Division IRGC	
	27th Mohammad Rasoolallah Infantry Division IRGC	
	31st Ashura Infantry Division IRGC	
	15th Imam Hassan Infantry Brigade IRGC	
	100th Ansal ar-Rasool Infantry Brigade IRGC	
	125th Abu Zayr Infantry Brigade IRGC	
	129th Mayssam Infantry Brigade IRGC	
	142nd Infantry Brigade IRGC	
	77th Nabbovat Commando Brigade IRGC	
	87th Ressalat Artillery Brigade IRGC	
	40th Saheb az-Zaman Engineer Division IRGC	
	84th Infantry Division IRIA	
	55th Airborne Division IRIA	1 brigade
Task Force Fath	9th Badr Infantry Division IRGC	
	10th Seyed o-Shohada Infantry Division IRGC	
	32nd al-Husayn Infantry Division IRGC	
	33rd al-Mahdi Infantry Division IRGC	
	18th al-Ghadir Infantry Brigade IRGC	
	57th Abolfazl al-Abbas Infantry Brigade IRGC	
	49th Muslim Ibn Aqil Infantry Brigade IRGC	
	127th Meghdad Infantry Brigade IRGC	
	11th & 44th Artillery Groups IRIA	
	1st and 2nd CSG, 4th GSG IRIAA	
Iraq		
I Corps	Corps troops, 65th, 66th, 68th Special Forces Brigades, I Corps Artillery Brigade	
	27th Infantry Division	72nd, 119th, 806th Infantry Brigades
	36th Infantry Division	106th, 238th, 426th, 602nd Infantry Brigades
	43rd Division Task Force	87th, 423rd Infantry Brigades
Reinforcements	10th Armoured Division	17th, 42nd, 70th & 80th Armoured Brigades; 24th & 46th Mechanised Brigades
	28th Infantry Division	78th, 412th, 417th Infantry Brigades
	34th Infantry Division	72nd, 76th, 424th, 504th Infantry Brigades
	40th Infantry Division	82nd & 98th Infantry Brigades
	1st Wing IrAAC	

A post-Iran-Iraq-War photograph of Lake Daraband-i-Khan. (Mark Lepko collection)

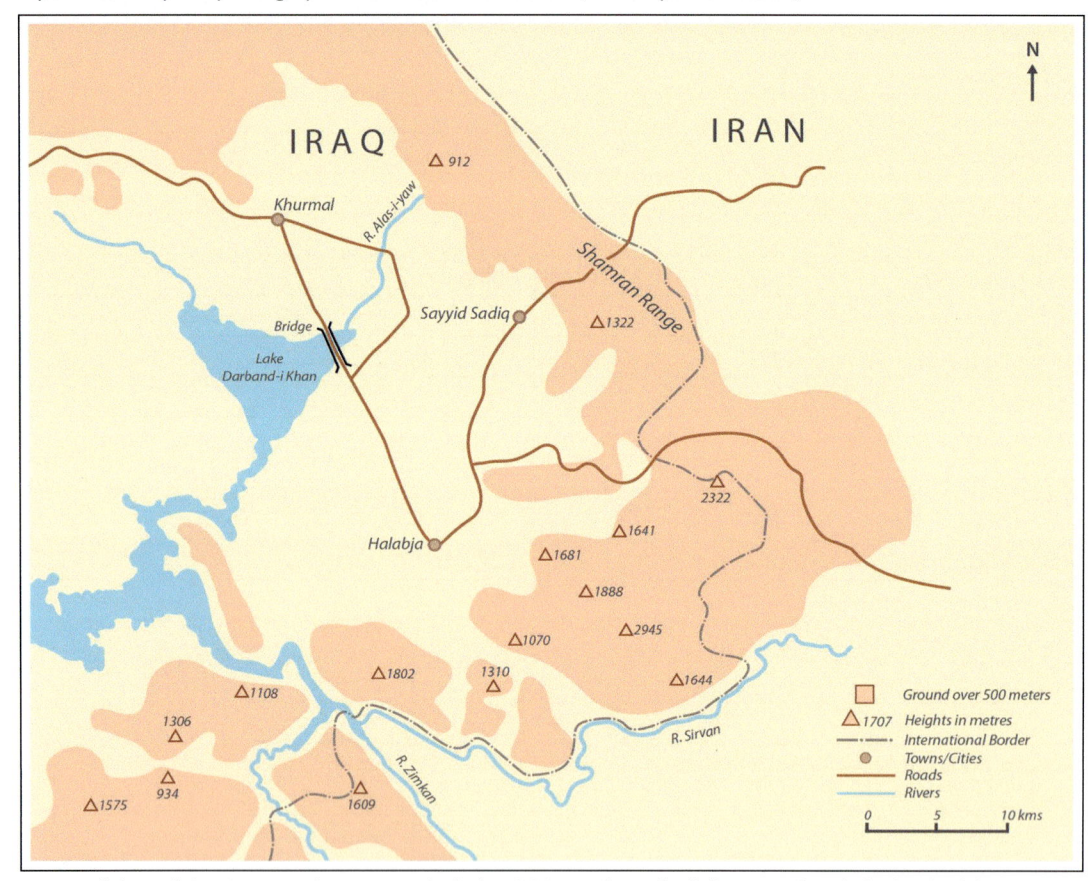

A map of the Halabja Sector – the area in which the IRGC sought its final chance to break the back of the Iraqi armed forces, in early 1988. (Map by George Anderson)

588 sorties while helicopters moved forward 5,778 troops and 177 tonnes of supplies and evacuated 4,808 wounded and civilians during the offensive.

Under this onslaught, the Iraqi 43rd Infantry Division fell apart. It not only suffered over 4,000 casualties, but also had its headquarters overrun and its commander captured – together with up to 1,700 of his troops and about 200 armoured fighting vehicles. Consequently, by 16 March the Pasdaran and PUK were entering Halabja. Meanwhile, Task Force Fath took Zimkan and then stormed Height 1802.[7]

Facing less pressure, 27th Infantry Division managed to hold most of its frontline but had to swing back its right flank to keep the Iranians outside Sayyid Saddiq, pending the arrival of reinforcements from II Corps – including 28th Infantry Division, 70th and 80th Armoured Brigades (17th Armoured Division), and 46th Mechanised Brigade (12th Armoured Division). The IrAF and the IrAAC fought back as intensively as they could; fighter-bombers flew 104 sorties on 19 March 1988 alone, while helicopters are known to have flown 613 sorties between 16 and 19 March.

When all of this showed little effect, Saddam ordered the IrAF to deploy chemical weapons against major Iranian concentrations in and around Halabja. These were launched starting on the morning of 16 March 1988, and included more than 50 MiG-21s, Mirage F.1EQs, PC-7s and Su-22s. The brunt of the bombs filled with nerve agents fell upon Halabja. Tragically, very few Iranian troops were in the town, but nearly 4,000 civilians – men, women and children – perished. The carnage increased when the Iraqi artillery then bombarded the town with a mix of high explosive and gas-filled shells.[8] Khazraji would later claim that neither he, nor any military leader, was involved in the decision which was taken by Saddam, Majid and military production chief Hussein Kamel; while Saddam denied all knowledge of the decision and blamed Khazraji.

The horror of Halabja overshadowed the rest of the campaign, with the advance slowing by 19 March as the Iranians outran their

al-Aeme then assaulted positions of 27th and 43rd Divisions, while Fath attacked 36th Infantry Division, positioned on the boundary between I and II Corps.[6] The Iranians overran or outflanked the mountain strongpoints, with many defenders fleeing westwards, as 'Qods' brushed aside the 43rd Division's mountain defences and swept down to take Khurmal. Its success exposed the defences on Height 1322, and so the Iraqis' line of mountain bastions fell like a row of dominoes. The Iranian advance was aided by air support with the IRIAF flying the first of 99 sorties from the morning of 15 March, with its F-4Es using domestically produced Shahin-2 air-to-ground rockets for the first time. The Cobra gunships of the IRIAAC flew

PART II: IRAN'S LAST CHANCE

Column of the Pasdaran on in the Halabja area in March 1988. (Farzin Nadimi collection)

Troops of one of the IRGC's naval brigades seen in positions recently captured from the Iraqis, during Operaiton Val Fajr-10. (Farzin Nadimi collection)

Pasdaran bringing their wounded back to their starting positions. (Farzin Nadimi collection)

The Iranian Army deployed two of its Artillery Groups (the 11th and the 44th) in support of Operation Val Fajr-10. This photograph shows an M109 155mm self-propelled howitzer on the march towards the front. (via N.S.)

supplies. Task Force Qods reached towards Sayyid Sadiq but were held along the Alas-i-yaw, while the Qara Dagh sanctuary was still 35 kilometres away. Meanwhile, Iraqi reinforcements from IV and V Corps poured to fill the gaps in the breached frontline. The exhausted Iranians began to dig in after advancing up to 30 kilometres to the lake's eastern shore down to the Zimkan having taken 3,000 prisoners.

The second phase thus began on 27 March 1988, when Task Force Fath launched Operation Beit-ol-Moghaddas-4 against 36th Infantry Division, using T-72 MBTs captured only days previously, but were beaten off. During the night of 9–10 April, the Iranians opened Operation Beit-ol-Moghaddas-5 in the Penjwin sector, seized many heights and inflicted heavy losses upon 27th Infantry Division. Further south, Task Force Qods (meanwhile including IRGC's divisions Seyed ol-Shohada and Mohammad Rasoolallah and brigades al-Ghadir and Abolfazl al-Abbas) infiltrated across the Zimak during the evening of 10–11 April, to hit 36th Infantry Division. They reached heights 1108 and 1306 to extend their grip along the lake's eastern shore for a further five kilometres to the mouth of the Zimkn Valley. However, this attack petered out by 19 April 1988, primarily because of events on the Southern Front.[9]

In early April Baghdad was apparently sending all the units it could find as reinforcements, including half the Guards Baghdad Division and 24th and 25th Guards Commando Brigades.[10] On 16 April 1988, Defence Minister Adnan Khairallah made a highly publicised appearance in Suleymaniyah, but his visit and the 'reinforcements' were designed to divert Iranian attention from the Faw Peninsula where Iraq struck on 17 April.

The shock of this offensive immediately ended Iranian operations around Lake Darband-i Khan, but Iraqi firepower had already thwarted Iranian ambitions. The IrAF was now flying some 224 combat sorties a day, aided by 31 artillery battalions (560 guns), allowing the defenders to rebuild their defences by

305

MIDDLE EAST@WAR SERIES SPECIAL #1: THE IRAN-IRAQ WAR

A CH-47C Chinook helicopter of the IRIAA seen while unloading casualties collected at a forward position during Val Fajr-10 in March 1988. (Tom Cooper collection)

Iranian troops inside a trench in the Halabja area. (via S.N.)

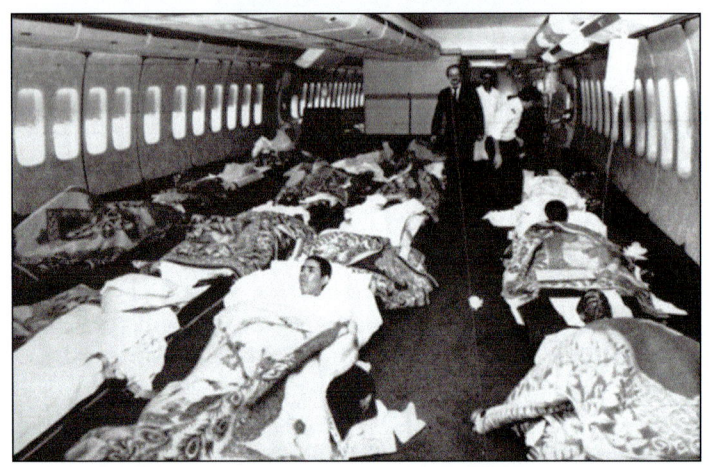

The number of casualties caused by the massive deployment of chemical weapons by the Iraqi military in 1987 and 1988 forced the Iranians to send some of the injured for treatment at specialised facilities abroad. This photograph shows a group of wounded flown to Vienna International on board a Boeing 747 of IranAir. (Albert Grandolini collection)

A lot of overhaul and maintenance of Iranian military vehicles, and captured Iraqi ones, in Iran was undertaken in small, privately owned workshops, often under the most rudimentary conditions. (via N.S.)

early April and gradually they began to push back the Iranians, making much use of chemical weapons, to stabilise the Halabja sector. The Iraqis noted that the Pasdaran were increasingly splitting their divisions into assault and follow-up units, a concept first used by the Imperial German Army in 1918.[11]

Saddam's Discussions

Val Fajr-10 prompted a number of conferences in Baghdad, in the course of which Saddam noted the Iranians now had large forces deployed in the north. He credited this to I and V Corps pinning down the enemy, and therefore ordered a number of spoiling operations, aimed to have maximum effect for minimum casualties. Uncertain whether or not to reinforce I Corps, he said: 'We have to ask if the enemy's concentration in that area provides us with an opportunity to strike it in a serious way, to confront and crush them?' There were two ways to achieve this aim; either by a decisive battle, or a war of attrition. Eventually, Chief-of-Staff Khazraji, convinced him to continue the planned offensives on the Southern Front, and once they were completed, use the victorious forces to strike on the Central and then Northern Fronts; advice which Saddam heeded.

The situation on the Northern Front was again discussed on 26 June 1988 during talks about strategy. Saddam appeared pessimistic while Khazraji was optimistic, as was the Operations Chief Lieutenant General Hussein Rashid. The former explained: 'We have sufficient forces, with a simple manoeuvre, we can be a real threat to the enemy in his current position.'

A sceptical Saddam, who was worried 28th Infantry Division would be isolated, asked: '"Why Halabja?" and added, 'I don't feel comfortable. What does Halabja mean to us?' Khazraji countered by pointing out the propaganda value, while Khairallah said the front could be secured by adding another two brigades to the eight already deployed. However, the meeting ended without a decision.[12]

PART II: IRAN'S LAST CHANCE

A group of Iranian civilian experts and military officers inspecting an unexploded Iraqi bomb. Gauging by its shape, the weapon in question was probably made by the Spanish company Expal, and based on the Mk.82 design of US origin. (Albert Grandolini collection)

Wearing a gas mask, this Iranian soldier demonstrates the effects of the Iraqi chemical weapons – in the form of dead birds collected around the battlefield. (Albert Grandolini collection)

Only a day later, Saddam presided another meeting of his senior commanders. This time, Khazraji pointed out that the Halabja front had been reinforced to 13 brigades, while Khairallah suggested the use of six of these for recapturing the town. This idea was eventually accepted, with the operation in question being limited to 21 days for immediate objectives, and seven for the further ones.[13]

The Iraqi Riposte
In fact the Iraqi worries were pointless, for the stunning Iraqi victory on the Faw Peninsula of mid-April 1988 ended all major Iranian offensive activity on the Northern Front. Indeed, the deteriorating situation in the south forced the Iranians to begin withdrawing troops to meet the new threats.

This threat would increase with the Central Front's Operation Tawakkalna ala Allah-3, and to exploit the increasing enemy weakness a new offensive was planned in the north. Operation Mohammad Rasul Allah (Mohammed, the Messenger of God) aimed to regain all the lost territories around Lake Daraband-i-Khan, around Chwarta and the Haj Umran Pas.

The Mawat sector was the first to feel Iraqi revenge when Major General Sultan Hashim Ahmed's I Corps attacked at dawn on 14 June using 4th, 7th and 44th Infantry Divisions, reinforced by commandos. These advanced in divisional columns to strike five mountain ranges. After 16 hours hard fighting, most of the peaks were in Iraqi hands exposing the Iranians in the valleys. The attack continued on 17 June with the divisions storming a dozen peaks (the 44th Infantry Division distinguished itself by taking Height 1897 which dominated the Mawat valley). Iranian counterattacks were beaten off with support of armour, artillery and from the air, and the Pasdaran were left with little other choice but to retreat while blowing up bridges and culverts, as well as laying extensive minefields.[14]

The Iraqis now expanded the scope of the operation, using their reinforcements including 10th Armoured Division and 28th Infantry Division. The 39th Infantry Division, reinforced by commandos, special forces and armour, attacked the Mawat valley on the evening of 29 June and began fighting its way to the border where it was joined on 9 July by 46th Infantry Division. On the night of 9–10 July the 27th Infantry Division struck in the Penjwin sector and began working its way through the mountains to the border, severely damaging the former Pasdaran armoured division, 30th 'Beit-ol-Moghaddas'. To stiffen the front, brigades of 28th Infantry Division IRIA with a brigade of 25th Karbala Division, and part of 23rd Special Forces Division IRIA, counterattacked on the night of 12–13 July but were driven back. The V Corps' contribution was on the night of 4–5 July when 24th Infantry Division, supported by commandos, armour and artillery attacked between the Haj Umran–Rawandiz road and Lake Dukan, through terrain of up to 2,300 metres height. The well-coordinated attacks ensured that by the end of the day the Iraqis had totally regained the pass, despite a rear-guard action by a brigade of 64th Infantry Division, a special forces battalion IRIA, two Pasdaran battalions and Gendarmerie in the heights shielding the road to Piran Shahr.

From mid-June 1988, around Lake Darband-i-Khan, the 36th Infantry Division had begun attacks aimed at regaining the heights southeast of the lake; while 34th Infantry Division struck towards Sayyid Sadiq. Strong defences meant that the Iraqis made little progress. Defence Minister Khairallah now returned to the front and sought a renewed attack, for which corps commander Sultan Hashim Ahmed transferred 10th Armoured Division from the north and reinforced it with four infantry brigades. It was brought in beside 34th Division and launched a surprise attack in the Sayid Sadiq sector on 12 July, overcoming defences. However, its further advance was eventually stopped by Iranian demolition work on the roads, which were also cut by deep trenches and covered from the heights.

Meanwhile, there was intense diplomatic activity as the United Nations sponsored a ceasefire; to accelerate this as his forces disintegrated, on 15 July Rafsanjani announced the withdrawal of Iranian forces from Iraqi territory, which began the next day. This opened the way for the 34th Division to retake Halabja and eased the Iraqi advance towards the border. Siriwn was liberated by 15 July, and by 20 July 1988 the Iraqis had reached the border. Simultaneously, 36th Infantry Division retook the border heights to end the conventional war in the north.

23
THE KURDISH FRONT 1980–1988

The low-intensity operations of the Kurdish Front sprawled across the tri-state border with fighting in eastern Turkey even before the Iran-Iraq War. The Kurds represented around 15 percent of Turkey's population and their determination to seek autonomy had seen major revolts throughout the life of Kemal Atatürk, founder of modern Turkey, with hundreds of thousands of Kurds displaced and Istanbul banning Kurdish culture. From 1980, Turkey described the minority as Easterners (Doğulu). In the 1970s the Kurds were split between those who sought autonomy through political action, which had some success, and the Kurdistan Workers Party (Partiya Karkerên Kurdistan) or PKK, which launched 'armed struggle'. The PKK's war against Turkey grew ever more intense through the late 1970s and early 1980s. With the Iranian Revolution in 1979 the Kurdish struggle rolled across the border into north-western Iran, as described above.

The Iraqi invasion of 1980 prompted Ghassemlou and his KDPI to reposition their headquarters to the Iraqi village of Sunn, near Halabja. Strengthened by Baghdad's arms and supplies and exploiting Iran's problems with the Iraqi invasion and insurgencies in north-western Iran, in April 1981 he struck towards Lake Urumia, Mahabad, Naqadeh, Bukan and Saqqez with 7,000–12,000 Peshmerga. In Sanandaj, they encircled 64th Infantry Division's 1st Brigade. After a month-long siege, the brigade ran out of ammunition and had to surrender, having lost nearly half the garrison, but killing nearly 2,000 of the attackers.[1] The 64th Infantry Division's 3rd Brigade in Marivan held out and, with his men exhausted and short of supplies, Ghassemlou was forced to withdraw.

Gambling that the KDPI's offensive had run out of steam, Bani-Sadr concentrated his limited military resources against the uprising in the nearby Azerbaijan province instead. However, this handed more ammunition to his critics, and in June 1981 he was dismissed by Khomeini. Immediately afterwards, Tehran concentrated 100,000 troops (including about 30,000 Pasdaran, several thousand Gendarmes, and Barzani's supporters) for an offensive against about 15,000 KDPI Peshmerga. Spearheaded by the IRIA 16th Armoured Division, this force struck westwards and took the Ghassmelou by surprise recovering Sanandaj and then lifting the siege of Marivan, before securing the main road network by taking Saqqez, Bukan,

Kurdish people of northern Iraq. After more than 20 years of almost-constant insurgency against the central government in Baghdad, much of the local society was militarised and most of the young men under arms. (Mark Lepko collection)

PART II: THE KURDISH FRONT 1980–1988

Shirazi with KDPI leaders. (IRGC)

Mahabad, Piranshar, Naqadeh and Urumia. A wave of brutal repression over the local population followed, but despite this setback Ghassemlou planned to launch a new offensive in 1982 with intention of establishing a 'Liberated Kurdish Zone.'

The Iranian Army's Chief-of-Staff, General Shirazi, beat him to the punch. In April 1982, he preempted the KDPI offensive by reinforcing Mahabad, and securing Bukan, Saqqez and Sanandaj. Unsurprisingly, the Peshmerga's attempt to take Mahabad on 26 June was defeated. Although Kurdish insurgents subsequently controlled large parts of the countryside, the Iranians controlled at least most of the valleys.

In mid-September 1982 the Iranians renewed their offensive to clear the main road south of Lake Urmia along the border through the Gharbi Mountains, between Piran Shahr and Sar Dasht, as well as Baneh to Saqqez in the KDPI heartland, and through the 25-kilometre-deep enclave from the frontier. Shirazi used 40,000 men of the IRIA's 16th Armoured, 28th and 64th Infantry Divisions, and a similar number of Pasdaran and Gendarmerie, in a series of small but powerfully supported offensives. Casualties were heavy on both sides – but especially amongst the Iranians. As one of the veterans of the 28th Division recalled: 'The word was the Peshmerga were born with a rifle in their hands. Their aim was fantastic. They were ambushing us all the time. Lots of our soldiers were killed by head-shots'.[2]

While some roads were secured, the KDPI held the Sar Desht-Baneh section. Nevertheless, even this meagre success encouraged the SDC to end the Kurdish threat once and for all, and Shirazi was assigned four IRIA and six IRGC divisions, supported by 300 guns, about 100 MBTs and 50 helicopters for a new offensive.[3] During the second week of March 1983, Iranian Special Forces deployed by helicopters to block routes from Iraq, while the main body swamped dissident territory south of Lake Urumia. Ghassemlou's attempts to simultaneously fight a mobile guerrilla war and static defence proved disastrous, and within days the Peshmerga were short on ammunition and forced to withdraw into the mountains. The KDPI now controlled only Baneh and the smaller towns of Oshnavieh and Gavileh, which Ghassemlou decided to retain with defensive operations based upon his Iraqi bases and headquarters in the Haj Umran Pass.

But Shirazi gave him no time to regroup and on 22 July followed up with Operation Val Fajr 2 (see above), in the course of which the Peshmerga were driven out of Iran. During the following years, the surviving members of the KDPI were limited to acting as auxiliaries to the Iraqi Army, before an internecine struggle resulted in a disillusioned Ghassemlou seeking safety in exile in Austria, but he was assassinated in Vienna in 1989. As for Husseini, he decided that discretion was the better part of valour and ceased any kind of military activities against Tehran. He went into exile in Sweden, in 1991 and died there 20 years later.

Iraq's Kurdish Kaleidoscope
Recognising the impotence of the KDPI, Baghdad subsequently rerouted its support to the PUK. However, if Tehran began 1983 believing it had neutralised the Kurdish threat, Saddam Hussein faced a growing threat.

The Kurdish Front in Iraq covered the border provinces of Dahuk, Arbil, Sulaymaniyah and Diyala, and also touched the inland provinces of Niniwa (round Mosul) and at-Tamim (around Kirkuk), although the latter two were predominantly populated by Arabs and Turkomen as of that time. This area is characterised by terrain over 500 metres above sea level, with mountains in the east, and numerous streams and minor rivers. Many of the slopes were wooded, with meadows and stony fields at their base, the exception being the fertile uplands of the Germain (Gamiyan) – or 'Warm Country' – the fertile high plain around Qadir Karam, southeast of Kirkuk.

In 1980, Iraqi COIN efforts were centred around three divisions (4th Mountain, 8th and 11th Infantry) deployed in Arbil and Dahuk provinces, and two (2nd and 7th Infantry) deployed in Suleimaniyah province, augmented by Border Guards and Police.[4] Saddam did not rely purely upon military force, but adopted a policy of 'divide and rule' which skilfully exploited the fragmentation of Kurdish society. This meant he was able to withdraw many army units urgently needed for the war with Iran.[5] Left to the paramilitary forces, the security in the Kurdish areas slowly declined.

The decline began in 1980 when the KDP joined the National Democratic and Patriotic Front – an alliance of anti-Saddam organisations including the Communists and the Kurdistan Socialist Party, which also encouraged any action against the PUK. In April 1981, the Front launched an offensive in Arbil Province against its competition, but the PUK hit back very hard and destroyed most of the Communists. Nevertheless, the kaleidoscopic nature of Kurdish relations meant that only 16 months later the KDP and PUK staged a joint operation in Suleymaniyah.[6]

The departure of the Iraqi Army and the reluctance of the paramilitary forces to run serious COIN operations in the mountains deprived the government of the symbols of power; teachers, medical staff, administrators of protection. Self-preservation compelled local people to withdraw to safety in the larger, and better protected, urban conurbations. Into this power vacuum came the Peshmerga who brought their own administrators, teachers, and doctors to extend their influence from the remotest mountain villages down the slopes to ever larger communities to create liberated areas. The weakness of the counterinsurgency forces eased supply problems for the Kurds; they were unable to provide effective control of the 5 to 30-kilometre-deep belt along the border which had been cleared of some 500 villages – the majority in Sulaymaniyah Province – and 200,000 people forcibly resettled in the south with thousands of other Kurdish civilians after the 1974–1975 revolt. Some of these now began to return and were joined by exiles from Turkey and Iran, while Baghdad actually transferred some refugees north to camps around the city of Arbil. The PKK were also attracted into northern Arbil and Dahuk.[7]

The elimination of the KDPI suited the Barzanis, whose Peshmerga began to extend their control of the border in Arbil Province. This process was further boosted by Iraqi setbacks of 1982, when Baghdad's cancellation of cultural concessions sparked protest demonstrations in Iraq's Kurdish cities and increased skirmishing between Kurds and Iraqi security forces. Nevertheless, the primary threat for Iraqi authority as of early 1983 remained Jalal Talabani, who had thousands of men under arms in Suleymaniyah and Arbil.[8]

With the KDPI's fortunes clearly on the wane, Talabani needed a strong ally to shield himself from Iranian vengeance and reluctantly made common cause with Saddam. An agreement was hammered out on 10 December 1983 in which Talabani pledged not to attack Saddam's forces, and vowed to drive the 'Persians' across the border and fight them in their country – provided Baghdad left him alone. Talabani went further and agreed his Peshmerga would act as Kurdish Border Guards, although some 3,000 reportedly defected to the KDP in protest. A formal ceasefire was signed on 3 January 1984, but Saddam sought to convert this into a long-term political solution and dangled the carrot of a renewed commitment to Kurdish autonomy, with Talabani as acknowledged Kurdish leader. For the time being, Saddam was willing to accept Talabani's pledges at face value, but he was aware the PUK was sponsored by Saddam's sworn enemy – Syrian President Hafez al-Assad. Correspondingly, the strongman in Baghdad aimed to buy time until he could settle accounts with the Kurds. Unsurprisingly,

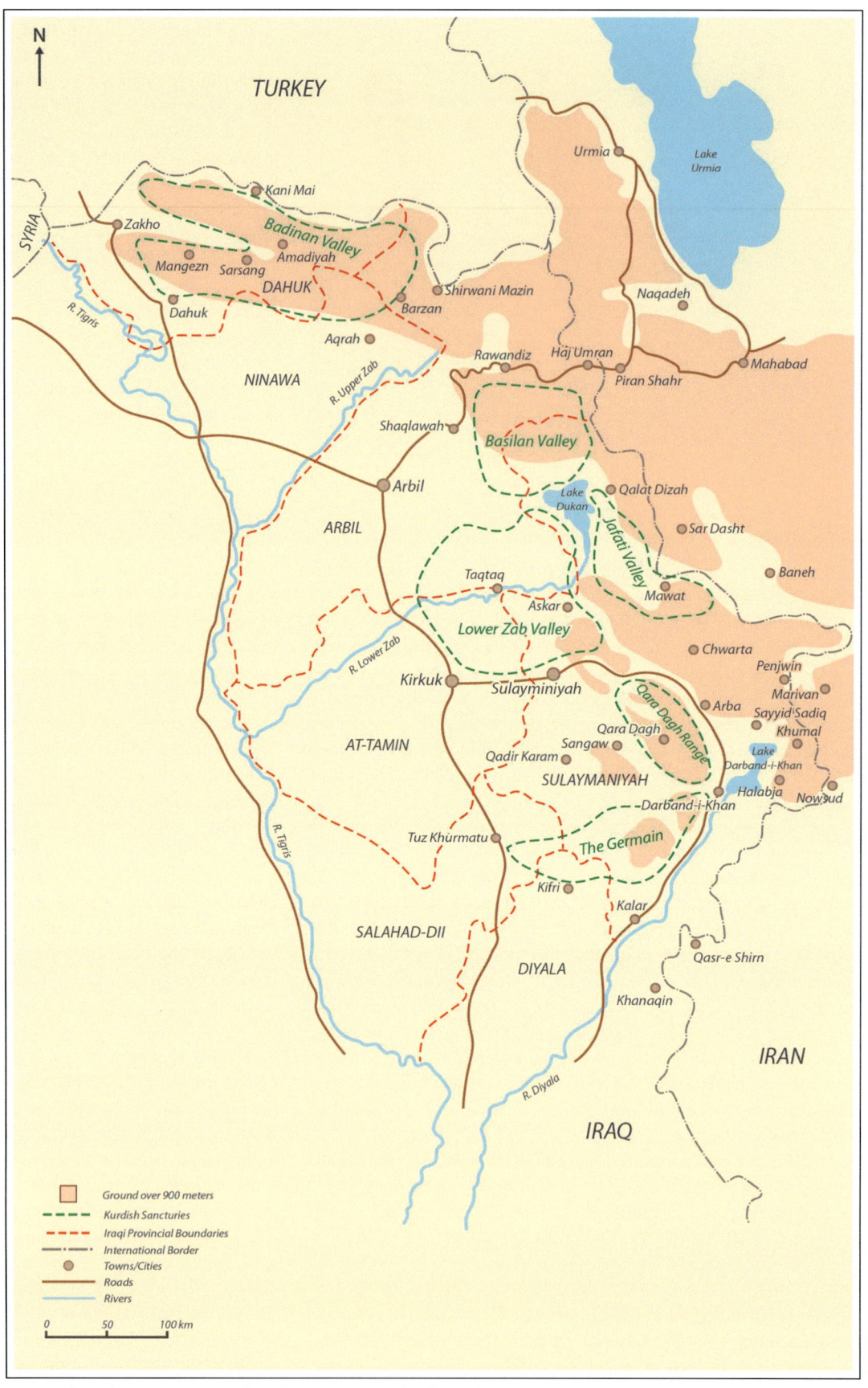

A map of north-eastern Iraq and north-western Iran, both predominantly populated by the Kurds: this was the scene of one of one of most important 'sideshows' of the Iran-Iraq War. (Map by George Anderson)

his Foreign Minister, Tariq Aziz, warned the Kurds: 'If you help us, we will never forget it. But, if you oppose us, we will never forget it. And, after the war is over, we will destroy you and all your villages completely.'

PART II: THE KURDISH FRONT 1980–1988

Despite such threats, Talabani remained reluctant to join Saddam's 'National Progressive Front'. Combined with his demands for oilfields around Kirkuk to be considered a part of Kurdistan (although that area was largely inhabited by Arabs and Turkomen), this became an insurmountable hurdle, and ultimately led to the collapse of the agreement, in 1985.

Meanwhile, a new player entered Iraq's Kurdish front when Barzani decided to capitalise upon Val Fajr-2 and seek support from his rival Talabani's sponsor – President Assad – who in turn was in dispute with Turkey over construction of a hydro-electric power scheme on the upper Euphrates. Assad, who was already supporting the PKK, decided Barzani could help put pressure upon Ankara by providing 'sanctuaries' for the PKK in northern Iraq. Barzani agreed and soon the PKK was striking into Turkey from its new bases. The furious Turks quickly concluded a joint security agreement with Iraq, on 20 April 1983, which granted them permission to enter Iraqi territory in so-called 'hot pursuit operations.' A suitable excuse for such incursions was available in the form of a major pipeline Iraq used to export its crude via Turkey – to pay for its war effort against Iran.[9]

The pipeline and the Oil Road, which ran parallel to it, were protected with barbed wire and a 15,000-strong force of Fursan. The installation was of obvious interest for Turkey, which was happy to accept cash from related construction contracts and transit fees – especially in exchange for Saddam's promises of joint action against the Kurds. Indeed, Turkey went a step further and depopulated the frontier region along a 25-kilometre strip, and created barriers to movement including wire entanglements, minefields and free-fire zones to shield the Iraqi pipeline. Further protection was available in the form of 60,000 troops of VII Corps of the Turkish Army, part of the Malatya-based 2nd Army. The HQ of this corps delegated operations against the PKK to the Hakkari-based 3rd Infantry Division, which controlled no fewer than eight brigades: 2nd Commando, 5th Mountain Commando (often temporarily augmented by 1st Commando), 6th, 16th and 70th Mechanised, 6th Infantry, 23rd Security and 34th Border. There were also two Jandarma (Gendarmerie) mobile brigades and a special operations battalion.

Two Kurdish militants in northern Iraq in the mid-1980s. Both are wearing a mix of civilian clothes and military fatigues. Their armament consists of a PKM machine gun (left) and a Dragunov sniper rifle. (Albert Grandolini collection)

The PUK consisted of a mix of older veterans of earlier Kurdish uprisings and many youngsters, mostly armed with different variants of the omnipresent AK-47/AKM-family of assault rifles. (Albert Grandolini collection)

The first Turkish cross-border raid was undertaken from 25 to 29 May 1983, when two commando brigades launched a cordon-and-search operation near Dahuk. For the Peshmerga, which enjoyed several years of relative immunity, this came as a terrible shock, then in addition to the Iraqi pressure from the south, they were now facing Turkish forces in the north.

A second Turkish incursion followed on 25 August, and resulted in the capture, execution or imprisonment of many Iraqi Peshmerga. This instilled such Kurdish dread of Ankara, that when one of their splinter groups captured and held hostage two Turkish airmen who had crashed in northern Iraq, the hostages were returned to Turkey. The threat also meant the Kurds tended to leave the oil pipeline untouched.

Meanwhile, Saddam's attention was focused upon the east. He was incensed at KDP participation in Val Fajr-2 and Val Fajr-4, which boosted Kurdish morale and secured safe supply lines to Barzani's forces. To hinder any expansion of the KDP, on 22–28 June 1983 Baghdad summoned all Kurds in the north born between 1963 and 1964 to report for military service. Furthermore, on 30 July 1983 Saddam's troops went through resettlement camps and villages around Arbil, arresting every man they could find, including members of the Fursan. Some 5,000–8,000 were then paraded through Baghdad and most were executed, with Saddam later observing: 'They betrayed the country and they betrayed the covenant, and we meted out a stern punishment to them and they went to hell.' The camps were then sealed off for a year with the families depending upon food being smuggled in.[10]

Meanwhile, Tehran urged the Barzanis to reinforce their forces in northern Iraq with their Peshmerga who had settled in Iran after 1975. The Barzani brothers were reluctant, fearing they were being pushed into a hostile environment before they were ready. Unsurprisingly, this led to a cooling of their relations with Tehran, where the clerics distrusted the secular and nationalist nature of the KDP. Nevertheless, Barazni's forces did support an attack by two Pasdaran brigades which advanced from Nowsud towards the Darban-i-Khan Dam in Feburary 1984.

Despite the ceasefire the PUK, or renegade elements within it, appear to have renewed operations against the Iraqis during the summer of 1984 – although other PUK units continued to fight alongside the Iraqi Army. Baghdad retaliated by deploying five divisions for an advance into PUK areas, razing several villages to the ground. This act strained relations between Talabani and Saddam but helped to shape events which broke the ceasefire – because, at the same time Tariq Aziz visited Ankara to sign another cross-border security agreement which now allowed Turkish forces to remain in Iraq for up to three days.[11]

The Turks promptly launched another cross-border offensive into Dahuk Province, leading Talabani to denounce the agreement as anti-Kurdish. His relations with Baghdad deteriorated rapidly and resulted in a formal end to the ceasefire in January 1985. Fighting resumed with raids around the cities of Arbil and Kirkuk. Saddam's desperate last-minute attempt to contain the Kurdish threat by offering an amnesty on 13 February 1985 was ignored by both the KDP and PUK.

The Kurdish Zenith, 1985–1987
Strengthened through control of the border area, the Kurds began deploying their forces closer to population centres. By May 1985, it was estimated that the Peshmerga controlled about a third of the Kurdish territory in Arbil, Dahuk and Sulaymaniyah, while the Iraqis effectively controlled only the urban centres and oilfields.[12] By the autumn of 1986, the Iraqis lost further areas. The KDP, supplied through the Haj Umran Pass, controlled all of northern Dahuk and Arbil, and the 150-kilometre-long section of the Turkish border. Similarly, the PUK – also supported by the Iranians – controlled most of the high ground of Sulaymaniyah Province, including the border territories south of Qalat Diza and as far west as Kirkuk.

The winter of 1985–1986 brought some respite for Iraq, although Iranian commandos exploited growing Kurdish territorial control to mortar Sulaymaniyeh on 3 March 1986. The 45th Infantry Division staged a small counteroffensive from 25 to 30 April against the KDP around Shirwani Mazin, but its claims of success were overoptimistic. Barzani's Peshmerga soon began raiding along the Iraqi-Turkish pipeline, and on 15 May 1986 about 1,000 of them even took Mangezn (Mangesh or Mangezh) – a small garrison south-east of Zakhu – capturing some 800 defenders. An Iraqi counterattack, spearheaded by a mountain brigade reinforced by Republican Guards, armour, special forces, Fursan and helicopter gunships, was ambushed and defeated on 19 May with another 800 prisoners taken.

The situation forced the Iraqi Army to rebuild its forces in Kurdish territory, establishing two divisional task forces; the 38th at Zakho (Zakhu) and 45th north of Arbil. These managed to recover Mangezn. However, Baghdad remained reliant upon 30,000 Turkish troops to protect the northern part of its pipeline, while the terrain along its south-eastern border prevented Ankara from successfully sealing it.

The Peshmerga's successes meant Iraqi maps showed signs of growing Kurdish sanctuaries. These were usually marked red even on official Iraqi maps and described as 'areas Prohibited for Security Reasons' (or, more usually: 'Prohibited Areas'). All the inhabitants of these areas were considered hostile – even more so because communications in between such areas were subjected to frequent ambushes. The situation reached the point where Ali Hassan al-Majid later commented that it was impossible to travel from Kirkuk to Arbil, except in an armoured vehicle.[13]

The armament of the Peshmerga improved significantly during this period too. While initially armed with small arms and a few RPGs, they now obtained mortars and even some radios. The Peshmerga were professional fighters who received a small salary and usually served 15 to 20 days at a time, with equal spells at home to work their lands. They were augmented by many military-aged men (and some women) of the Civil Defence Force – a lightly armed militia.

There were differences between the two leading Kurdish resistance organisations. The KDP, which eventually had 15,000 Peshmerga and 30,000 militia, focused upon controlling the population; while the PUK, which grew to about 4,000 Peshmerga and 6,000 militia, seemed more interested in controlling territory and creating a conventional army. The KDP had dual military-political 'Branches': the 1st and 2nd in Arbil and Dahuk, and 3rd and 4th responsible for the Kirkuk area and Sulaymaniyah Province. The PUK had five sanctuaries in and around Sulaymaniyah, with its headquarters within the Jafati valley village of Yakhsamar, and four Regional Commands which were also responsible for military and political activity. The 1st and 2nd were responsible for operations in Sulaymaniyah Province, while the 3rd and 4th were active in neighbouring Balisan and Smaquli Valleys and responsible for operations in Arbil Province.[14]

Smuggling was a way of life for the Kurds, who exploited the numerous pathways and goat trails to bring supplies and recruits from Iran. Supplies would be delivered to isolated buildings or caves for later distribution, sometimes using the ubiquitous Nissan Coaster pick-up truck, but Kurdish peasants were also encouraged to store 10 percent of their produce for the fighters. A captured Peshmerga told the Iraqis he and his friends had used a civilian vehicle to drive across the border all the way to Isfahan in central Iran – and back. They then infiltrated through the mountains

PART II: THE KURDISH FRONT 1980-1988

Kurdish militants with the wreckage of a downed Iraqi helicopter (including remnants of a UV-32-57 rocket pod). (Tom Cooper collection)

The PUK invested heavily in creating the semblance of a conventional military. Here a group of its combatants are seem during training on a 120mm mortar. (Albert Grandolini collection)

and supplies to reach us, no help for our wounded, no roads out of the territory that we had liberated. Iran was our window to the world.'[16]

Talabani sought a rapprochement with Tehran and in October 1986 they signed an agreement on economic, political and military cooperation leading Baghdad to call PUK-members 'Agents of Iran'. Meanwhile, Talabani and the Barzanis sought common ground for a future Kurdish state – a task eased by the death in January 1987 of Idris Barzani, leaving Masoud as undisputed KDP leader. The Kurdish factions then hammered out agreements for both political and national unity to provide a compromise acceptable to Iran between provincial autonomy and full independence. In February 1987 they created the Kurdistan National Front, and three months later a joint command. In early September they agreed to fight for a Kurdish state which would be in a confederation with a future democratic Iraq. This was acceptable to Tehran which steadily increased aid, and also forwarded Syrian supplies for the PUK, which together supported further Kurdish offensives. They continued to be allies with the Kurdish Socialist Party, which had 1,500 Peshmerga, and the Shia resistance Al Daawa. The latter would ultimately contribute to the Anfal catastrophe.

Fath Operations

Most operations involved interdicting traffic to erode enemy strength, gain equipment and dominate or control roads, as well as expanding 'sanctuaries' by controlling villages near the roads. But in 1986–1987 there were a series of offensives codenamed Fath. Fath-2 struck Lake Dukan's hydro-electric facilities, while Fath-4 saw Iranian commandos and the KDP claiming to have destroyed an important air defence radar near Arbil. Fath-5 and Fath-7 aided Iranian Army operations around Chwarta by attacking 27th Divisions' supply lines, and in a separate operation during May the PUK took Taqtaq, on the Kirkuk–Dukan Dam road, and held it for 10 hours. Fath-8

without interruption and when asked how he had avoided the Iraqi line he asked: 'What line?'[15]

For the Iranians the rapprochement between the Barzanis and Talabani was a mixed blessing. Both were secular and nationalist, which aroused Iranian fears that success might encourage them to support their Iranian brothers. Therefore, Tehran sought a degree of control through a formal agreement with the two parties and encouraged closer cooperation between them. Geography strengthened Tehran's hand, for as Deputy PUK commander Naywshirwan Mustafa Amin noted: 'There was no way for food

Table 27: The 'Fath' Offensives (October 1986–September 1987)				
Operation	Began	Provinces	Kurds	Other
Fath 1	10.10.86 (to 13.10.86)	Arbil, Sulamaniyah	PUK	66 Bde IRGC
Fath 2	29.10.86	Sulamaniyah	PUK	75 Bde IRGC
Fath 3	14.11.86 (to 19.11.87)	Dahuk	KDP	75 Bde IRGC
Fath 4	11.3.87 (to 22.2.87)	Arbil, Sulamaniyah	KDP	75 Bde IRGC
Fath 5	14.4.87 (to 20.4.87)	Sulamaniyah	PUK	75 Bde IRGC
Fath 6	17.6.87 (to 28.6.87)	Arbil	KDP	75 Bde IRGC
Fath 7	17.6.87 (to 28.6.87)	Sulamaniyah	PUK	75 Bde IRGC
Fath 8	19.7.87	Dahuk	KDP	75 Bde IRGC
Fath 9	9.8.87	Sulaymaniyah	PUK	75 Bde IRGC
Fath 10	3.9.87 (to 5.9.87)	Arbil	KDP	75 Bde, Daawa

Turkey's secular Moslem regime was also acutely sensitive to the activities of the Iranian theocrats. Following Karbala-7 it notified Tehran that it would not permit the capture of the Kirkuk and Mosul oilfields, emphasising the point by bombing Kurdish villages in Iraq, which led to Rafsanjani's hasty visit to Ankara, and adopting a conciliatory approach as described above.

Yet the Ramadan Headquarters continued to direct Kurdish operations, with the Fath offensives followed by the Zafar (Triumph or Victory – in Arabic and Farsi) series, starting on 15 August 1987 and continuing until mid-March 1988. These claimed a number of significant successes; Zafar-2 saw the Kifri defences penetrated, while Zafar-3 was a pre-emptive attack upon 36th Infantry Division as it prepared to strike the Qara Dagh ridge. Zafar-4 damaged the electricity network in the town of Dahuk.[19]

There would be three operations during 1988, beginning with the wide-ranging Zafar-5. This overran the bases of 38th Infantry Division and three NDB battalions around Kani Masi on the Turkish border and took the road bridge near al-Amadiyah. It also led to the downing of an Su-22 and the capture of its pilot (1st Lieutenant Ali Hameed al-Jabouri of No 109 Squadron was shot down on 15 January but his subsequent fate is unknown).[20] Zafar-6 disrupted traffic at the crossroads town of Sangaw; while Zafar-7 was undertaken in support of the Iranian Operation Val Fajr-10 and claimed to have destroyed 423rd Infantry Brigade, from 43rd Infantry Division, during attacks on Khurmal.

was staged around Atrush and the last operation, Fath-10 struck V Corps rear, and supply links for 33rd and 45th Divisions.

An increase in Kurdish activity in the Mawat sector, following Fath-1 and Fath-2, prompted the 39th Infantry Division to launch a month-long offensive starting on 7 November 1987. It claimed to have cleared 200 square kilometres allowing Iraqi engineers to build hard-topped roads.

Meanwhile, in September 1987, KDP forces took the Iraqi town of Kani Masi on the Turkish border, while combined PUK and Iranian forces operating behind the Iraqi lines around Mawat took some 260 square kilometres of territory south of the Little Zab. In October the Iranian 67th Brigade, supported by some 2,000 PUK, made a mortar and MLRS attack upon the Kirkuk oil field, which they claimed reduced the flow of oil by 70 percent. It appears to have had little effect, and by now 1.5 million BPD were flowing northwards.[17] Few of the Kurds were enthusiastic about fighting Iran's proxy war and especially against the pipeline which would provoke Turkish retaliation, so ceased their attacks upon the pipeline and focused upon fighting Saddam.

The Fath offensives would be the highpoint of the new Kurdish insurgency, aided by Operation Karbala-7 (see above), which further strengthened communications from Haj Umran. Tehran could be very satisfied with its Kurdish allies whose activities had even helped Operation Karbala-6 on the Central Front. These attacks resulted in US intelligence estimates from June 1987, in which the Kurds controlled 2,072 square kilometres of territory. In addition to inflicting up to 2,000 casualties, they also brought in much booty, including about 100 mountain guns and recoilless rifles, 82mm and 120mm mortars, 107mm MLRS of Chinese origin, ZPU-4 quad anti-aircraft machine guns, SA-7 Strella MANPADS and even – in the case of the PUK – 11 T-55 MBTs.[18]

Kurdish fears of Turkish retaliation after the Iranian attacks upon the oil pipeline were well founded. In its campaign against the PKK and its Iraqi infrastructure, Ankara's 2nd Army maintained a fluctuating force of 12,000–20,000 men around the border, and in March 1987 they launched a major offensive against the PKK and, on 4 March, bombed Kurdish villages in Iraq.

Turkish concern about the PKK was increased by the deaths of 180 civilians and 260 Kurds between 1984 and 1986, leading to increased pressure on the Kurds both in Turkey and Iraq. Ankara revealed in November 1986 that its troops had twice crossed the border in hot pursuit of Kurdish guerrillas, and there had also been 20 cross-border air attacks.

Baghdad Strikes Back

With Iraq's red-white-black banner flying only over the larger population centres, by 1987 it was clear radical changes were required in counterinsurgency policy. Counterinsurgency was a joint responsibility between the corps commanders and the Ba'ath Party's Northern Bureau in Kirkuk – initially under Sa'adi Mahdi Saleh and then Muhammad Hamza al-Zubeidi (responsible for a population of 3,760,244, of whom 2,064,712 were Kurds).[21] The Army deployed about half-a-dozen infantry brigades, and a similar number of commando/special forces brigades, with some 30,000 men, augmented by some nine Border Guard brigades (18,000 troops), who reverted to their own command in March 1985 but remained under Army operational control.[22]

The backbone of counterinsurgency remained the Kurdish NDBs which scouted, escorted convoys, manned roadblocks, patrolled in the countryside or were transported to remote bases by helicopter. As Kurds they were familiar with the usual hiding places, and usually conducted searches of homes and farms, and captured suspects who were turned over to the authorities.

Much of the Iraqi COIN effort remained passive and reactive. A blockade with fortified checkpoints was established around each Kurdish sanctuary area, where people, animals and vehicles were searched to prevent them from importing food and medicine. Usually only women were permitted to move between the zones.[23]

PART II: THE KURDISH FRONT 1980–1988

Along the roads, and around the cities and towns, were fortified bases from which convoy escorts, and reaction forces to assist smaller beleaguered bases or convoys under attack, would depart. Many of these were brick or concrete structures surrounded by sandbags and barbed wire, but at Nizarkeh in the eastern suburb of Dohuk, was a huge concrete structure – built to Soviet design in the 1970s – protected by a battery of four anti-aircraft guns mounted on the roof. Some sites were firebases which divided prohibited areas into target zones which might be shelled at any time. However, even the biggest guns in the Iraqi arsenal had a limited reach.[24]

Although Iraqi documents indicate the GMID exploited the fractious nature of Kurdish political and tribal relations to enrol many agents, and they produced abundant intelligence, it was little used. There were no major attempts to penetrate the 'sanctuaries'; retaliatory actions struck easy targets near the roads, with buildings demolished and the surviving inhabitants transferred to resettlement camps close to military bases. Helicopters were used by commandos, special forces and Kurdish Special Units for raids into enemy territory, against headquarters and supply dumps, to lay mines along Kurdish infiltration routes, or for infantry and Fursan search operations looking for supply dumps; but the men rarely stayed overnight.

The deterioration in Iraqi security occurred under Zubeidi, who appears to have replaced Saleh sometime in 1984. As the Kurds grew bolder there was a full-scale review in about March 1986, and Zubeidi was told to turn the situation around within six months. Yet despite the lack of improvement he was given another six months, by which time the security situation had reached a nadir. His failure influenced Saddam's decision to make radical changes; a decision also influenced by the presence of the Shia resistance movement, Al Daawa, in Kurdistan where it claimed 1,000 of its members were active. Another factor was KDP and PUK support for Karbala-7, with Talabani talking of seceding from Iraq, but the fuse was lit with success on the Basra front where the Iranian offensive Karbala 5 was defeated in March.[25]

Chemical Ali
Saddam had long supported the policy of 'active defence' in conventional operations (partly to offset the Iranian war of attrition), and now he wished this policy to apply against the Kurds. On 15 March 1987, after Karbala-7, he presided over a five-hour meeting of the Armed Forces General Command, which was attended by his cousin Ali Hassan al-Majid – a member of the Regional Command of the Ba'ath Party and President of the General Security Office – dubbed 'Chemical Ali'. Former head of the General Security Directorate (Amn), he was described as being of use when Saddam needed somebody without a heart and is known to have had some success against the Kurds in Sulaymaniyah in October 1985.[26]

Saddam (like Hitler) always admired ruthlessness, which he equated with effectiveness, and on 18 March 1987 the Revolutionary Command Council and the Ba'ath Party's Regional Command jointly appointed Majid as new head of the Ba'ath Northern Bureau. Within a fortnight he was granted extraordinary powers, 'for the purpose of protecting security and order, safeguarding stability, and applying autonomous rule in the region'. His decisions were mandatory for all

A column of the PUK combatants moving amongst the mountains of north-eastern Iraq in 1987. (Albert Grandolini collection)

A group of Pasdaran embarking a Toyota 4WD for a drive to the frontlines. The Iranians attempted to support several of the operations run by Kurdish insurgents in north-eastern Iraq in 1987. (via N.S.)

315

Table 28: The Zafar offensives, August 1987 – March 1988				
Operation	Began	Provinces	Kurds	Other
Zafar 1	15.8.87 (to 18.9.87)	Dahuk	KDP	75 Bde, Daawa
Zafar 2	5.10.87 (to 7.10.87)	At-Tamin, Diyala	PUK	75 Bde, Daawa
Zafar 3	5.10.87 (to 17.11.87)	Sulaymaniyah	PUK	75 Bde
Zafar 4	20.11.87	Dahuk	KDP	75 Bde
Zafar 5	13.1.88 (to 17.1.88)	At-Tamin, Dahuk, Diyala	KDP	75 Bde
Zafar 6	24.2.88	At-Tamin, Sulaymaniyah	PUK	75 Bde, Daawa
Zafar 7	13.3.88	Sulaymaniyah	PUK	75 Bde, Daawa

state agencies, military, civilian and security – including the GMID and the Popular Army.

Majid was well briefed about the situation and later told aides he gave himself two years to succeed. He began publishing decrees, directives and orders; clearly showing he intended not only to destroy the Kurdish resistance but to crush those Kurds who refused to accept Iraqi rule. He would later tell a court: 'I am the one who gave orders to the army to demolish villages and relocate villagers. The army was responsible for carrying out those orders, I am not defending myself. I am not apologising.'

Majid at first lacked the resources to implement his plans, but one of his earliest decisions was to double the number of NDBs which were placed under operational control of the GMID-controlled 1st National Defence Headquarters and warned '...we will push you to your target until you all get killed.'[27]

Majid waited only for the spring thaw to begin his new policy with a three-phase operation in 1987 against PUK which he described as 'village collectivisation'. An ominous feature of this plan was the use of chemical weapons – which would earn Majid the nickname of 'Chemical Ali' (Ali Kimyawi) – and for which he was hanged in January 2010 having been convicted of eight capital crimes. He readily admitted the use of chemical weapons commenting: 'I will kill them all with chemical weapons. Who is going to say anything? The international community? Fuck them!'

However he was not alone: Saddam had discussed the idea that the IrAF use its 'special arsenal' (chemical weapons) against Kurdish headquarters and bases, and Defence Minister General Adnan Khairallah Talfah (Khairallah) suggested 'Whatever we cannot defeat, we should use special ammunition to secure areas'. Unsurprisingly, there are reports that the Iraqis used chemical weapons against the Kurds around Haj Umran starting already on 18 August 1983.[28]

The use of air power against the Kurds was as old as modern Iraq – which the British controlled during the 1920s and early 1930s, through 'air policing'. A Turkish incursion around Rawandiz, and post-war defence cuts, led to the decision that the Royal Air Force (RAF) would be used in an aerial policing role, predominantly against the Kurds. The Colonial Secretary, Winston Churchill, and the RAF Chief-of-Staff, Sir Hugh Trenchard, discussed the use of chemical weapons against the Kurds, but did not put this policy into practice. Churchill noted on 17 August 1921, 'The only weapons which can be used by the Air Force are bombs and machine guns'. In addition to 98.5 tonnes of high explosive bombs, the British also deployed those filled with phosphorus.[29]

Possibly influenced by Turkish cross-border operations, all of Majid's offensives would follow a pattern in which he would 'lasso' a Prohibited Area using commando/special forces – to cordon the remoter areas – and conventional forces exploiting the road networks. He would then draw the 'noose' tight to capture the majority of the inhabitants and transfer them to resettlement camps, raze their villages and farms to the ground and often take away most of the adult males (including young teens and old men) for interrogation, often followed by execution. But occasionally NDB commanders, and more rarely Iraqi officers, would take pity on the wretched Kurds and save their lives. The NDBs were more interested in loot, including livestock, cash, gold, watches, as well as rugs, mattresses and blankets, picture albums and even toothpaste!

Majid's 'Collectivisation'

Plans for the 'collectivisation' were published on 13 April 1987 by V Corps' Lieutenant General Khalil Ibrahim Talia al-Durri (Talia al-Durri). Phase I (21 April – 20 May 1987) and Phase II (21 May-20 June 1987) would assault the PUK 'sanctuaries' with the General Security Directorate (Amn) to prepare deeper penetrations in a later Phase III. Truckloads of explosives were assembled to ensure that no Kurdish villages would remain standing, while 200 civilian bulldozers were commandeered, and any officer who left even a wall standing would have to return to finish the job. Wells were to be filled in, electricity cables were to be ripped out and the area left so that no farming could be carried out.[30]

The first phases were clearly preparatory and focused upon villages near the major roads east of Mosul, even those already under government control with Fursan garrisons, as well as the smaller road networks within the 'sanctuaries'. Stringent restrictions were imposed on all grain sales in the region and upon the transport of food between the provinces. The offensive was heralded by chemical weapon attacks on the PUK heartland of the Jafati valley and the 2nd and 3rd Malabands on 15 April; possibly in retaliation for a renewed PUK offensive, but it helped put the Peshmerga on the back foot. They had anticipated chemical weapon attacks and suffered few casualties but failed to warn the civilians, of whom some 400 died. In the next few months chemical weapons were delivered into the valley and its neighbours by gun, MLRS, high-speed combat aircraft and the Pilatus light attack aircraft.

On 21 April 1987 Majid's plan went into effect all over Kurdistan, with 661 villages affected; 219 around Arbil, 122 in the Germain and 320 throughout Sulaymaniyah Province, token compensation sometimes being offered to families of the 200,000 displaced. The campaign ended on 20 June, and aircraft then periodically flew over the affected areas to extinguish activity once detected. While Saddam and Majid felt they had made a good start – having cleared the main roads from Mosul-Arbil-Kirkuk-Tuz Khurmatu, and from the Darband-i-Khan dam to Kalar and the road network around Kifri – they were not completely satisfied. Some army officers were shocked at the brutality of the orders, indeed Talia al-Durri reportedly refused to destroy some of the villages fearing these actions would only stiffen resistance. The relocation effort was poorly managed, inadequately funded and was extremely discriminatory while some resettlement camps did not exist.

With conventional operations now absorbing much of the Army's energies and resources, Majid had to focus upon administrative action to maintain pressure upon the Kurds. On 3 June he informed I, II and V Corps and intelligence and counterintelligence organisations, that all human activity was banned in 1,000 Kurdish villages, and those aged 15 to 70 who failed to show allegiance to the regime would be shot together with their animals. On 20 June he sanctioned Fursan pillaging of villages, and from 29 September tightened the screw by reducing food rations for Kurdish civilians outside the 'sanctuaries' to the bare minimum. The blockade of those areas was tightened, with greater vigilance at check points, shutting Kurdish grocery stores and carefully monitored stocks at restaurants, bakeries and cafés. A planned national census for 17 October was also 'weaponised'; for those whose names were not included were deemed hostile to the regime, although many in the remoter areas were totally unaware it was being conducted.[31]

The Kurdish reaction to Majid's 'collectivisation' was a new series of raids, and the PUK's 2nd Malaband struck out of the Jafati Valley in mid-April, overrunning dozens of outposts.[32] This and the increasing use of Daawa troops strengthened Majid's case for more resources, but he pressed on with those he had, and his success meant that in the wake of Iraqi victories on the Basra front in operations Ramadan Mubarak and Tawakkalna ala Allah 1 the improved strategic situation allowed Saddam to provide the resources for the murderous Anfal campaigns. He observed at a meeting sometime in June or July 1988 'That will teach (the Kurds) a painful lesson; so next time before they think to raise the issue against us they will think twice as they remember the pain that they have suffered in this lesson.'[33]

Anfal Campaigns

The offensives took their name – an-Anfal – from the 8th Sura of the Koran, which refers to the 'spoils of war' which are due to the righteous from the infidel once they are driven them from their land. The prime target would be Talabani's PUK, which would suffer seven of the eight offensives, for a variety of reasons including its 1985 'betrayal', its proximity both to the front and key communications routes, as well as its high physical profile occupying key valleys and uplands.[34]

The decision to begin the campaign was apparently taken by Saddam at a meeting in February 1988 attended by Defence Minister Khairallah, Chief-of-Staff Lieutenant General Nizar Abdel Karim General Nizar Abdel Karim and Alwiya al-Khazraji, GMID head Saber Abd al-Aziz and, of course, Majid. The Army assigned the initial operation to I Corps under Major General Sultan Hashim Ahmed al-Tai, who had just been transferred from VI Corps (on 3 March 1991 Hashim would negotiate the terms of the ceasefire after Desert Storm). Majid's strategy focused upon the PUK 'sanctuaries' which could support Iranian Army operations and were also targeted because they were more visible and easier to access from surrounding road systems. He intended to burn out the heart of PUK resistance, working his way clockwise through their central Sulaymaniyah 'sanctuaries' and then finish off the northernmost.

Intelligence of a PUK plan to take the Lake Dukan dam made the PUK headquarters in the Jafati valley the first target, and Hashim was given operational control of the V Corps' 4th Mountain and 33rd Infantry Divisions, which would attack from the north, while his own 24th Infantry Division and 1st Commando Brigade struck from the south.

Anfal-1

The Peshmerga within the Jafati valley did not fear chemical weapons as they were equipped gas masks and atropine injectors, and MANPADS for defence against enemy aircraft. However, this made them complacent while the departure of Talabani in a vain attempt to gain support from Washington meant his deputy, Naywshirwan Mustafa Amin, was in charge. Before dawn on 23 February the PUK positions came under artillery and MLRS bombardment, and at dawn I Corps pushed northward and east, as V Corps drove south. PUK forces were able to delay them for three weeks until 18 March, when they retreated eastward through a corridor left open by the Iraqis as an escape route.

Anfal-2

A sense of urgency was brought to the Anfal operations by the Iranian offensive around Halabja (Val Fajr-10), and the Iraqis feared the enemy were trying to reach the Qara Dagh 'sanctuary' to create a massive enclave which would threaten Sulaymaniyah.[35] They launched Anfal-2 on 22 March south of the Chamchamal–Sulaymaniyeh highway around Qara Dagh, and cut the lines of communications to PUK forces threatening the Kirkuk area. The defenders were the PUK's 1st Malaband, some Iraqi Communists and up to 400 Pasdaran who had dispersed for fear of chemical attack. The attack was directed by Major General Iyad Khalil Zaki, who was assigned the 43rd Division Task Force and 28th Infantry Division – both of which had to leave substantial forces on the eastward-facing front – as well as three Special Force brigades (65th, 66th and 68th) and the 1st National Defence Headquarters. The offensive opened with MLRS launching chemically-tipped rockets; these panicked the civilian population who fled, soon followed by the Peshmerga, and by 1 April the operation was over.

Anfal-3

Following another brief pause the Iraqis continued their campaign into the Germain. It appears a scratch force of elements from I Corps was put together under special forces officer Brigadier General Bareq Abdullah al-Haj Hunta, with the new 50th Division Task Force controlling three infantry brigades (417th, 443rd, 444th), and three Special Forces brigades (65th, 66th, 68th) as well as the 1st National Defence Headquarters and Emergency Forces (the general would be executed in 1991 for the hasty and chaotic withdrawal from Kuwait). The open countryside was not good guerrilla country, but the remnants of 1st Malaband had little choice but to defend the area as it was main recruiting ground for the PUK Peshmergas.

The offensive began on 7 April and appears to have omitted the usual chemical screen, possibly because the open ground was suitable for mechanised forces to cross quickly. Qadir Karam fell on 10 April. The exhausted Peshmerga were short of supplies and faced overwhelming force, causing morale to collapse and many surrendered, and although one or two groups held out for five days the campaign concluded on 20 April.

Anfal-4

Having purged the area south of the Kirkuk–Sulaymaniyah highway, Hashim and Majid now looked north. The valley of the Lesser Zab around Taqtaq had been briefly held by PUK a year earlier. At a meeting on 13 April the PUK leaders decided the Peshmerga would retreat, taking the surviving civilians north of the Kirkuk–Sulaymaniyah highway. One column, led by 1st Malband headed for Askar in the Lesser Zab valley to set up a new base.

Shortly after their arrival, a chemical attack by the IrAF at dusk on 3 May caused general panic and confusion. A force of Iraqi troops, including 10th Armoured (reinforced with two infantry brigades) and 46th Infantry Divisions, with I Corps' 1st Commando Brigade and three Special Forces brigades (65th, 66th and 68th), plus Fursan, attacked at dawn on 4 May. There was little prolonged resistance, but at one point Hashim had to bring in some 700 Emergency Force troops by helicopter. Many Peshmerga escaped northward in carts drawn by commandeered tractors, and by 8 May the fighting was over and 138 Kurdish villages were abandoned. Up to a third of the population, many of them women and children, had disappeared.

Anfal 5–7

The destruction of the PUK was almost complete, and its remnants filed into Iraq's northeast Arbil Province to hold the Balisan Valley, running the gauntlet of 24th and 39th Infantry Divisions west of Lake Dukan. The rugged valley was defended by PUK 3rd Malband, the Socialist Party of Kurdistan, Iraqi Communists and some KDP. They began to stockpile food and ammunition in anticipation of a prolonged struggle.

The I Corps was again responsible for mopping up the last PUK resistance and committed 23rd, 24th and 39th Infantry Divisions, four commando/special forces brigades and the ubiquitous Fursan. There were few civilians in the region as many had fled from the sustained gas attacks that had begun in May 1987 and were renewed at dusk on 15 May. Following a week-long lull the IrAF launched a sustained chemical assault from 23 May.

The initial assault on 16 May took 20 villages but encountered fierce resistance and petered out inconclusively by 7 June. The V Corps' Brigadier General Yunis Muhammad al-Zareb was now authorised to complete clearance of the valley in two simultaneous operations, Anfal 6 and 7. Plans for the operations were drawn up by V Corps as early as 30 May but was subject to postponement pending the outcome of Tawakkalna ala Allah-2, which would be launched on 25 June 1988. Only on 23 June did Saddam authorise the next stage, but a further postponement was ordered on 29 June to build up resources. On 20 July Khazraji stated the operation had been postponed until after the Feast of 'Id al-Adha (i.e after 25 July), possibly because on 17 July Iranian President Ali Khamenei notified the United Nations that he was willing to accept UN Security Council Resolution 598. Two days earlier Rafsanjani had announced Iran's intention to withdraw its forces in Iraq and began to do so the following day. These announcements were a shock for the PUK because they regarded it as breaching the October 1986 Teheran agreement; this had stipulated that neither party would make a unilateral deal with Baghdad. Iran accepted Iraqi terms for a ceasefire on 8 August.

On 26 July the Peshmerga decided to conduct a partial withdrawal behind a rear-guard. As this began the IrAF began a new campaign, using chemical weapons, to drive the Peshmerga up the mountains and cluster bombs to drive them down. On 26 or 27 August the remaining Peshmerga contingents in the Balisan Valley fled. The ceasefire with Iran was announced on August 7. I Corps, however, continued mopping up operations until 26 August.

Anfal-8

The remoteness of the KDP's sanctuary in the Badinan valley, and the difficult surrounding terrain, meant that this was the last Anfal target. The offensive was authorised on 28 July, and planning was completed on 16 August. Assembling the resources took time; in a letter to Saddam on 7 August, an impatient Majid urged him to finish the KDP, but the following day the ceasefire with Iran was announced.

The KDP claimed it had 8,000 Peshmerga and 36,000 militia. Iraqi intelligence put KDP Peshmerga strength at 2,600, augmented by up to 300 PUK Peshmerga, 220 Iraqi Communists, and some 70 Kurdistan Popular Democratic Party (a KDP breakaway group). To ensure success the 38th and 45th Infantry Divisions were joined by 29th and 41st Infantry Divisions, transferred from VI Corps following Tawakkalna ala Allah-2, to give 16 brigades including four of commando/special forces. Each division organised two task forces with strong Fursan support; the 29th Infantry Division alone controlling 16 NDBs.[36] Some 100,000 men supported by up to 500 guns and overwhelming air power helped to ensure success, but the commanders had to be careful not to provoke the Turks. Formidable engineering resources had to be assembled both to support the advance and to destroy up to 400 villages.

The IrAF was responsible for deploying chemical weapons, reportedly mustard gas and Sarin nerve gas, during this offensive but it also made extensively use of 'iron' and cluster bombs. The chemical weapons were used not only against individual KDP bases but also against some 49 villages – with aircraft reportedly covering strips 60 miles wide and 20 miles deep – causing panic among both civilians and Peshmerga whose morale broke as they tried to save their relatives.

The Iraqi advance involved (west to east) 38th, 29th, 41st and 45th Divisions with a large number of tank, artillery and MLRS battalions in support. This advance met scattered resistance, which largely ended by dusk on 26 August when Barzani apparently ordered his fighters to cease resistance, although some ignored the order. The last shots were fired on the border on 6 September, and that afternoon, to Majid's fury, Iraqi radio announced 'a general and comprehensive amnesty for all Iraqi Kurds...both inside and outside of Iraq' with the exception of Talabani.[37] The security forces lost 31 dead, including 18 Fursan, and captured 13,395 Kurds, including 1,574 Peshmerga. This figure included 3,063 men – many of whom were executed – who were deemed part of the Kurdish resistance ('saboteurs'). Even villages that had once been regarded as loyal suffered, many because they did not participate in the 1987 census: their failure was regarded as evidence of the deepest treason.

The Anfal campaigns reportedly involved 14 infantry divisions and two Guards divisions which, with other forces, totalled 250,000 men, or 33 percent of the Iraqi ground forces. It is worth noting that they also allowed the Turkish Army to put pressure upon the PKK. It is claimed that the campaigns destroyed more than 4,000 villages, displaced a million people and caused 182,000 to disappear.[38] Yet within three years, Kurdish resistance was reignited following the Coalition's Operation Desert Storm and quickly carved out a fully autonomous region, under Barzani, recognised by Baghdad in 2005. That same year, in an act of tremendous irony, Talabani, who had been denied amnesty '...because of his wilful and repeated violations of law and order, even after he was granted opportunities to reform his ways' – became Iraq's president and remained so until a stroke forced him to resign in 2014. He refused to sign death warrants for Majid, who had been sentenced to death together with Hashim, and while the former would pay the ultimate penalty, the general had his sentence commuted to 15 years of imprisonment.

24
THE LAST BATTLES 1988

The general lull on the Central Front lasted some 18 months, with the focus of operations during the spring of 1988 switching to the Northern Front and Iran's Operation Beit-ol-Mogaddas-5. As late as 26 May Saddam, who was worried by enemy progress on the Northern Front, was determined the Central Front would remain on the defensive, rejecting even a IV Corps proposal for an advance in the Tib sector to improve the line. The Guards, he said, could contain any local Iranian threat and line adjustment would consume, rather than release, troops.[1]

In June he changed his mind as he recognised that the recapture of the Majnoon bridgehead in the Tawakkalna ala Allah-2 offensive meant Tehran had lost all the ground it had won since 1982 and was in a desperate situation. The Iranian ground forces, especially the Pasdaran, were utterly demoralised, with the mere threat of gas attack capable of causing panic, and they lacked the means to resist having lost vast amounts of equipment. When Saddam met his commanders on 27 June, Khazraji, backed by Khairallah, proposed targeting the IRIA to prevent a post-war threat, the Defence Minister noting the lightly-equipped Pasdaran would achieve nothing without IRIA support.[2]

Saddam agreed as part of a strategy of clearing 'the Persians' from Iraqi territory in three stages; a IV Corps thrust to push back the enemy on the Tib-Fakkeh front and secure Amarah, then I and V Corps would remove the enemy enclave around Mawat, and finally II Corps would strike in the Sanuba and Saif Saad Plateaus between Sumar and Mehran. The objective of the next stage, Operation Tawakkalna ala Allah-3, was to smash the enemy south of Dehloran.

Operation Tawakkalna ala Allah-3

The plan envisaged one heavy blow around the hotly contested town of Fakkeh and a second around Tib. The northern part of the battlefield would be in the area of the Abu al-Gharb Plateau, which overlooked the River Doveyrich. This one-to-five-metre-deep river provided a 10–15-metre-wide shield running southwards in an undulating plain crisscrossed with river valleys.

Detailed planning began on 27 June and was based upon two offensives; by IV Corps in the north and the Guards Corps in the south. IV Corps, now under Major General Iyad Khlil Zaki, had seven divisions to attack north-eastwards around Tib and Abu Ghirab, with 29th and 20th Infantry Divisions breaking through in the first phase to seize the high ground and aid the recapture of Iraqi territory to the Doveyrich. This would also allow 1st and 5th Mechanised Divisions to push into enemy territory supported by two armoured and two commando brigades, as well as 2nd Infantry Division. The 18th and 32nd Infantry Divisions would be in reserve and the corps would be supported by seven engineer battalions as well as 34 artillery battalions (612 guns and MLRS) and a FROG battalion.

The Guards under Lieutenant General Iyad Futaykh Khalifa al-Rawi would have the Medina Manarwah Armoured, Baghdad Infantry, Nebuchadnezzar Mixed and Special Operations Divisions deployed between Abu Ghirab Plateau and Fakkeh to drive eastwards. Medina was to swing north up the road towards Musiyan

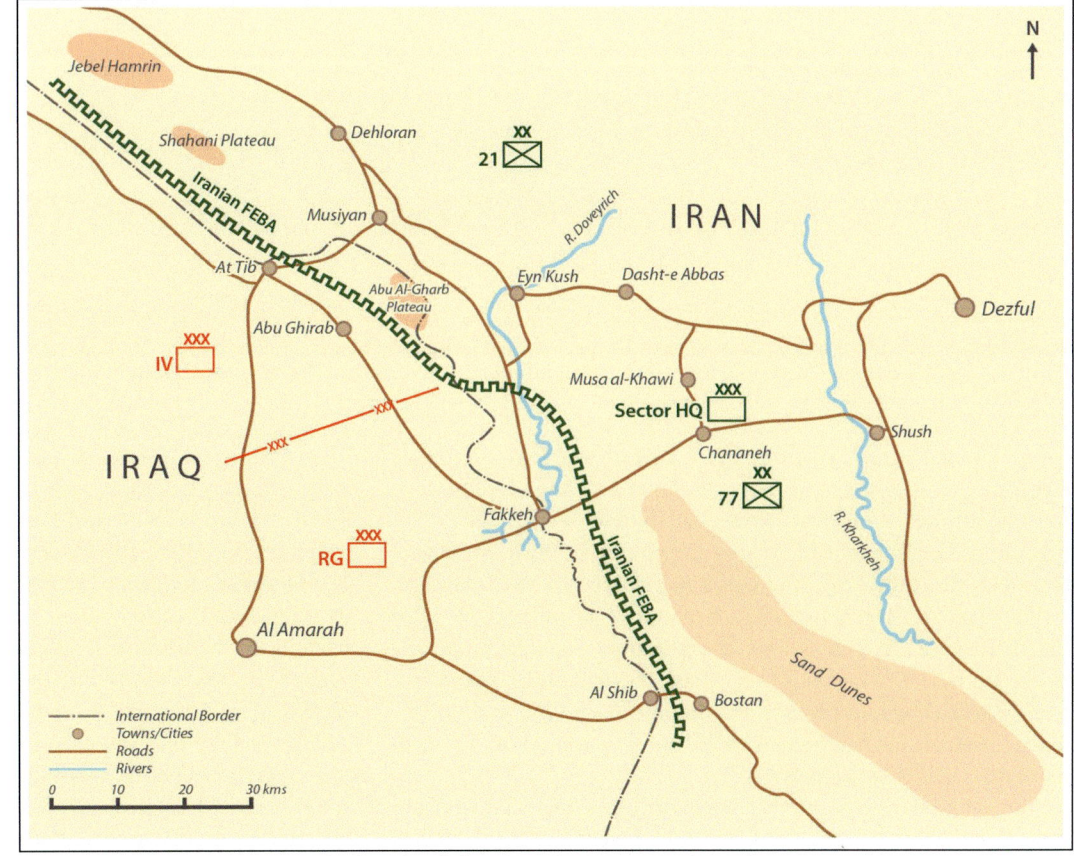

Map of the Iraqi Operation Tawakkalna ala Allah-3. (Map by George Anderson)

IRGC troops in the mountains around the Abu Ghirab Plateau in early 1988. (via N.S.)

By 1988, the IRGC operated a small artillery unit equipped with 2S1 Gvozdika self-propelled 122mm howitzers. Here is one of them in action on the front near Dehloran. (via N.S.)

before taking the road east through Eyn Kush and Dasht-e Abbas, targeting enemy reserves, artillery concentrations and headquarters. It would also relieve a special forces battalion of 16th Special Forces Brigade of the Republican Guards Corps in the Eyn-e Kush area to isolate the battlefield. The corps had some 200 MBTs and an artillery train of 20 gun and MLRS battalions (360 tubes and MLRS) together with a FROG battalion. The two corps would be supported by the 4th IrAAC Wing with 140 helicopters, including 40 gunships, while the IrAF would provide 150 aircraft in six CAS and one air defence squadrons augmented by electronic jamming and photo-reconnaissance detachments.[3]

The defences were largely under the IRIA's SFOHQ and as 16th Armoured Division had moved north to cover the Mehran sector this left the Guards and IV Corps facing the 21st and 77th IRIA Infantry Divisions respectively, each of two brigades. They were augmented by a brigade each of 84th Infantry and 23rd Special Forces Divisions IRIA, and Pasdaran, together with Gendarmerie supported by 55th Artillery Group with 21 artillery battalions (the 21st Division's 2nd Brigade and probably 77th Division's 3rd Brigade were not with their parent units). The defences exploited the natural strength of the western foothills of the Jebel Hamrin, while in the south there were berms and deep minefields, the defenders having six brigades in the front line and two in reserve.

The artillery preparation on 12 July began at 06:45 and as usual was short; lasting only 30 minutes. The assault began in challenging conditions with intense heat (45ºC) and high winds which created sandstorms in the south. But this did not prevent the Guards completing Phase One by 11:00 using four infantry and a commando

PART II: THE LAST BATTLES 1988

Table 29: Order of Battle for Operation Tawakkalna ala Allah-4, July 1988		
Corps	Division	Brigades
Iraq		
Republican Guards Corps	Corps troops; Artillery Brigade Republican Guards Corps	
	Baghdad Guards Infantry Division	9th Armoured Brigade; 14th Mechanised Brigade; 4th & 7th Infantry Brigades, 21st Commando Guards Brigades
	Guards Special Operations Division	15th & 18th Mechanised Brigades; 3rd & 16th Special Forces Guards Brigades
	Hammurabi Guards Armoured Division	8th Armoured, 29th Mechanised, 5th Infantry Guards Brigades
	Medina Manarwah Guards Armoured Division	2nd & 10th Armoured, 6th Infantry Guards Brigades
	Nebuchadnezzar Guards Mixed Division	17th Armoured; 11th & 12th Commando; 22nd & 23rd Infantry Guards Brigades
	1st Wing IrAAC	
II Corps	Corps troops; II Corps Commando Brigade; II Corps Special Forces Brigade	
	5th Mechanised Division	26th Armoured; 15th & 20th Mechanised; 505th Infantry Brigades
	10th Armoured Division	17th & 42nd Armoured; 24th Mechanised Brigades
	16th Infantry Division	99th & 604th Infantry Brigades
	17th Armoured Division	59th & 70th Armoured; 99th Mechanised Brigades
	21st Infantry Division	59th Armoured; 90th, 423rd, 430th, 706th Infantry Brigades
	22nd Infantry Division	70th Armoured; 93rd, 425th, 706th Infantry Brigades
	28th Infantry Division	78th, 412th, 417th Infantry Brigades
	2nd Wing IrAAC	
I Special Corps	10th Commando Brigade; IV Corps Commando Brigade; I Special Corps Artillery Brigade	
	1st Special Infantry Division	1st, 2nd, 3rd Infantry Brigades
	2nd Special Infantry Division	4th, 5th, 6th Infantry Brigades
	3rd Special Infantry Division	7th, 8th, 9th Infantry Brigades
	12th Armoured Division	50th Armoured Brigade
	unk. Infantry Brigade	
Iran		
Northern Forward Operational Headquarters		
	16th Armoured Division IRIA	1st, 2nd, 3rd Armoured Brigades
	58th Infantry Division IRIA	1st, 2nd, 3rd Infantry Brigades
	81st Armoured Division IRIA	1st, 2nd, 3rd Armoured; 4th Mechanised Brigades
	84th Infantry Division IRIA	1st, 2nd, 3rd Infantry Brigades
	88th Armoured Division IRIA	1st, 2nd, 3rd Armoured Brigades
	37th Armoured Brigade IRIA	
	55th Airborne Brigade IRIA	
	127th Meghdad Infantry Brigade IRGC	
	33rd Artillery Group IRIA	
	44th Artillery Group IRIA	
	1st & 3rd CSG, 4th GSG IRIAA	

brigade as the defence collapsed, allowing the exploitation to begin. The mechanised forces quickly reached the River Doveyrich by 13:00 and, aided by the Guards Special Forces, seized the bridges. Other special forces were flown 12 kilometres inside Iran to Musa al-Khawi, using 40 helicopters, and they held until relieved by 2nd Armoured Brigade of Medina Guards Division at 16:00 hours. IV Corps was similarly successful attacking on a 60-kilometre front and completing Phase One in 75 minutes. Phase Two was completed two hours later at 10:30 and by 16:00 it controlled Musiyan, in operations greatly aided by the IrAAC.

The success excited Saddam who kept moving from one corps headquarters to the other, and he now ordered the Guards to send 2nd Armoured Brigade of the Medina Division south to Chananeh to overrun the sector headquarters. Meanwhile Nebuchadnezzar was to send a mechanised brigade, and Baghdad an armoured brigade, to secure arms dumps. The units moved out at dawn on 13 July and by midday had secured their objectives against slight resistance. Around the same time, IV Corps was ordered to send 5th Mechanised Division to take Dehloran, which the enemy had abandoned, and it did so during the morning of 13 July.

Advances of up to 45 kilometres left Iraq briefly in control of some 400 square kilometres of Iranian territory, including Dehloran, but Saddam was no longer interested in seizing ground; only in destroying Tehran's means of continuing the war. On 13 July 1988 he threatened to invade southern Iran if the Iranians did not abandon their Kurdistan enclaves including Halabjah. With Iran now down to an estimated 200 tanks and short of military equipment, the next day Rajsanjani announced that all Iranian forces would withdraw from occupied Iraqi territory north of Haj Umran, the last major piece of Iraqi territory which they held.[4] In the south the Iraqis mopped up, and on the afternoon of 15 July withdrew, taking 5,000–7,000 prisoners and military booty including 90 MBTs, 60 APC/ICVs and 130 guns.

Tawakkalna ala Allah-4

On 18 July 1988, the 20th anniversary of Ba'ath rule, Saddam Hussein again called for peace negotiations and claimed Iraq had no territorial claims. He warned that he would not give the Iranians time to rebuild their forces and would continue to attack economic targets. Iran faced enemy victories and heavy losses, a growing fear of chemical weapons and attacks on her cities, threats from Western naval power and diplomatic isolation.

The previous day Iran's President Khameini wrote to the UN Secretary General, Javier Perez de Cueller, requesting a ceasefire and accepting UN Resolution 598. According to one press report the decision was reached in an eight-hour meeting between Khomeini and some 40 of his leading officials and commanders. The deciding factor was the statement by the Pasdaran commander Mohsen Rezai that the war could be won only after another five years of conflict. In fact, the country was nearly bankrupt, having used up most of its foreign reserves, and its industry was on the verge of collapse. The currency was almost worthless and oil markets were turning to other producers. Moreover, the regime itself was becoming unpopular and this threatened the Revolution.

But Iraq refused to accept the initial Iranian ceasefire proposal, claiming the Iranian acceptance was ambiguous for Khomeini had not publicly indicated he would agree to a ceasefire. Also, Saddam Hussein refused to accept continued Iranian mobilisation. He underlined his point by a series of air attacks upon Iranian industrial targets. This forced Iran to appeal to the UN Security Council, but on 20 July Khomeini himself issued a public statement accepting the ceasefire. He said 'Taking this decision was more deadly than taking poison. I submitted myself to God's will and drank this drink for his satisfaction.'

Saddam remained anxious to exploit the successes of the first three Tawakkalna ala Allah offensives, and in anticipation of a fourth such offensive from 14 July he transferred Rawi's Guards Corps north from Maysan Province to Diyala Province, where it was inserted between I and II Corps. The corps had steadily gained experience since retaking the Faw Peninsula, and the combination of expertise and equipment made it the most formidable command on the Iran-Iraq frontline. Saddam was planning one last 'harvest' of Iranian military power to bring Iran to heal, and to buy time he refused to implement the ceasefire and demanded face-to-face talks on all aspects of a peace agreement.

The new offensive, Operation Tawakkalna ala Allah-4, was the most ambitious and also the largest offensive launched by the Iraqi Army. It included four corps headquarters (I Special, II, III and Republican Guards) with 20 divisions, twice the strength of the one which crossed the border in September 1980, deployed on a front 170 kilometres long and 70 kilometres deep.[5] Units involved were to advance for up to 70 kilometres into Iran through mountainous terrain, in between peaks more than 2,000 metres high. The objective was to wreck the enemy ground forces and to take as many prisoners as possible to exchange for the thousands of Iraqi prisoners, while simultaneously regaining all lost Iraqi territory. Each corps was ordered to complete operations within 72 hours; with photographic reconnaissance and COMINT providing a detailed picture of the enemy forces and defences.

The Guards Corps was to take Sar-e Pol-e Zahab and Gilan-e Gharb but II Corps was to launch the main blow on a 120-kilometre front from north of Mandali to Mehran, taking the Sanuba Plateau, which dominates the Sumar Valley, and the Saif Saad Plateau within 72 hours. I Special Corps had a secondary role to secure the Mehran area but be ready to support its neighbours. The Southern Front's III Corps would also participate in the erosion of enemy strength.[6] Preparations began on 14 July with extensive aerial photography and scouting, and in addition to the arrival of the Guards, II Corps was reinforced by 10th Armoured Division, 7th and 8th Infantry Divisions from I Corps, and 5th Mechanised Division from IV Corps. Tawakkalna ala Allah-4 was scheduled to begin on 25 July 1988, but Y-Day was then brought forward to 22 July to pre-empt any diplomatic effort to end the war before Baghdad was ready.

Rawi, on the Iraqi left, had the Hammurabi and Medina Armoured Divisions, the Baghdad Infantry Division and Nebuchadnezzar Mixed Division. Furthermore, he had two brigades of Tawalkalna ala Allah Armoured Division, 24 artillery battalions (432 guns and MLRS), a FROG battalion, 18 heavy mortar batteries (108 x 120mm tubes), and a combat engineering battalion. Baghdad, north of Qasr-e Shirin, was to take Sar-e Pol-e Zahab and raid the nearby headquarters of 81st Infantry Division IRIA, and also to strike its most forward supply bases to destroy heavy weapons and vehicles. Hammurabi and Medina would advance along the valleys on Baghdad's right. Meanwhile the Special Operations Division would capture Gilan-e Gharb in a heliborne assault and hold it until relieved by a mechanised brigade of 5th Mechanised Division, advancing from Mandali through Sumar, which would be handed to the MeK. Nebuchadnezzar would be in reserve.

II Corps, under former Special Forces commander Major General Kamel Saji Aziz, was organised as detailed in Table 29. His units included 10th Armoured Division, 5th Mechanised Division, 16th, 21st, 22nd, and 28th Infantry Divisions, an armoured brigade from 17th Armoured Division, two independent armoured brigades, a commando brigade, 20 artillery battalions (with 360 guns and MLRS), 12 heavy mortar batteries (72 tubes), a FROG brigade and five engineering battalions. It was to advance on six divisional fronts:

- 21st Infantry Division to take the Zayn al Qaws Plateau then advance upon Ghila e Gharb and headquarters of 58th Infantry Division IRIA

- 5th Mechanised Division, flanked by 16th Infantry Division, was to take the Sanuba Plateau then push on to Ghilan e Gharb

- 10th Armoured Division was to strike into the Sumar Valley to take both 88th Armoured Division IRIA's headquarters and WOHQ forward headquarters

- 28th Infantry Division was to cover the right flank of 10th Armoured Division

- 22nd Infantry Division was to take the Saif Saad Plateau and then 84th IRIA Division's headquarters during the night from 23 to 24 July

- The remainder of 22nd Infantry Division, supported by a brigade from 17th Armoured Division, a commando and a special forces brigade, would take the Meimak Heights.

I Special Corps would secure Mehran and from 30 June, it took over this sector from IV Corps; it was substantially reinforced from 14–18 July, and in addition to 1st, 2nd and 3rd Special Infantry Divisions it had one armoured brigade, one infantry and two commando brigades, 12 artillery battalions (216 guns), 3 heavy mortar batteries (18 tubes), and three engineering battalions. Its 2nd Special Infantry Division had already taken the Shahabi Plateau on 30 June and now it would occupy the mountains north of Mehran down to the Kunjan Dam and the mountains to the south down to Dehloran. There was the usual powerful air support with the 2nd and 4th IrAAC Air Wings providing 180 helicopters, while the IrAF deployed 125 aircraft in five CAS squadrons, a multi-role squadron with Mirage, and an air defence squadron, as well as electronic warfare and photo-reconnaissance detachments.

This front was also largely an IRIA bailiwick under NFOHQ with five IRIA divisions (three armoured, two infantry) with 16 artillery battalions (200 guns/MLRS) and some smaller Pasdaran formations. In the Qasr-e Shirin/Sar-e Pol-e Zahab area was 81st Armoured Division, some Pasdaran brigades and six artillery battalions. In the Gilan-e Gharb area was 58th Infantry Division reinforced by 37th Independent Armoured and 55th Airborne Brigades, Sumar had 88th Armoured Division, at Sar Ney was 84th Infantry Division, and in Salehabad was 16th Armoured Division. The presence of two armoured divisions in mountainous terrain unsuitable for armour was an interesting commentary on Iran's strategic perspective and its growing shortage of resources.

The Last Attack

The attack began before dawn on 22 July 1988 as Iraqi engineers began clearing passages through minefields. The work was largely complete when the artillery preparation began at 06:25, paving the way for the infantry assault after 50 minutes. The combination of powerful artillery support, more than 1,000 tubes and MLRS, together with well-rehearsed tactics meant that most of the frontline positions were in Iraqi hands by 10:00 and their mechanised forces pushed into Iran as the temperature rose to 50°C with large amounts of water needed to prevent heat exhaustion.

In the Guards Corps the reinforced 'Baghdad' Division struck the Sisar Heights northeast of Sar-e Pol-e Zahab, and it was its armoured brigade which broke through the defences which were cleared by its infantry brigades. Its mechanised brigade took the pass leaving the commandos and armoured forces to follow the road to Sar-e Pol-e Zahab. Pausing only to refuel and refill ammunition lockers 'Baghdad' renewed its advance eastward the following day with its 9th Armoured Brigade taking an IRIA base and destroying all the equipment. Hammurabi advanced along the Qasr-e Shirin to Sar-e Pol-e Zahab road, seizing both towns and was then leapfrogged by Medina which continued south on the route to Eman Hassan. Once Emam Hassan had been captured, Medina turned southeast towards Ghilan e Gharb where, on the evening of 23 July, part of 16th Special Forces Brigade of the Republican Guards Corps was landed by 100 helicopters behind the 81st Infantry Division's headquarters, which it soon captured with artillery and gunship support (the troops were flown up to 70 kilometres in the deepest Iraqi heliborne operation of the war). That evening they were relieved by the Guards Special Operations Division from the north, and the II Corps' 5th Mechanised Division from the south.

Iraqi armour, including T-62M MBTs, covered by a US-made Hughes MD 500 helicopter, advancing in July 1988. (Albert Grandolini collection)

A Mi-25 helicopter gunship of the IrAAF returning from a combat sortie in support of Operation Tawakkalna ala Allah-4 in July 1988. (via Ali Tobchi)

The II Corps fought a series of private divisional wars which are described from north to south, watched carefully not only by the corps commander but also Saddam. The reinforced 21st Infantry Division struck from Qasr-e Shirin to clear the Zayn al Qaws Plateau in three hours, then advanced upon Gilan-e Gharb which it also took after a short, sharp, fight. 5th Mechanised Division struck out north of Sumar to take Sanuba Plateau then pushed eastwards. The infantry overran the defences, then 20th Mechanised Brigade pushed deep into enemy territory to outflank the Sanuba Plateau from the south, isolating it by the afternoon to cause panic and confusion among the enemy. Behind it 26th Armoured Brigade advanced and quickly took Zarneh, while 16th Infantry Division mopped up the Sanuba Plateau. Meanwhile, 5th Mechanised Division pushed on to Gilan-e Gharb from the south through the night of 23–24 July and relieved the Guards in the town, whose isolated garrison now surrendered.

The 10th Armoured and 28th Infantry Divisions broke into the Sumar Valley outflanking enemy strongpoints to penetrate the defences, with many strongpoints isolated. In the early hours of 23 July, the 10th also took 88th Division's headquarters near Sumar, and on the night 24/25 July took the NFOHQ forward command post. On its right 28th Infantry Division, which had returned from I Corps, crossed the Talkhab River and collected much booty including some Scud missiles.

The 22nd Infantry Division took the Saif Saad Plateau during the morning of 23 July, then advanced upon the village of Sar Ney where it overran 84th Division's headquarters on the night of 23–24 July. One of its brigades then advanced south to the village of Salehabad where it linked up with I Special Corps forces on 25 July. The 17th Armoured Division headquarters, with 22nd Division, commando and special forces brigades, had actually attacked first on the evening of 21–22 July to take the Warzin Plateau, easing its task the following day of isolating Sar Ney by taking the Meimak Heights.

To the south, following the 2nd Special Division's success in taking the Shehabi Plateau on 30 June, the I Special Corps attacked on the night of 19–20 July. The seasoned troops overran the enemy defences in the mountains east of Mehran aided by powerful artillery support, and on 24 July its commandos struck the enemy defences in the Kunjan Dam sector opening the way for its armoured brigade. The brigade, with 2nd Special Division's commando battalion, pushed north from Mehran to attack Salehabad on 25 July with 50th Armoured Brigade (12th Armoured Division), and captured the 16th Armoured Division's headquarters after several hours of hard fighting. The corps then linked up with II Corps' 22nd Infantry Division. The corps' secondary operation was southeast of Mehran along the Iranian frontier road towards Dehloran, overcoming rugged terrain and numerous rivers with blown bridges, to complete their mission on 27 July. 2nd Special Forces Division's commander, Major General Salman Shuja Sultan, was killed in a plane crash.

Curiously, the largest Iraqi offensive in the war is largely ignored by most historians. Iranian casualties are unknown, although it is known that Major Generals Mostafa Pazhubandeh and Reza Nikkah were killed on 22 July. The Iraqi booty was reported to be 12,000 prisoners, 270 MBTs, 240 APC/ICVs, 250 guns (50 self-propelled) and 20 surface-to-surface missiles. This marked the end of Iraqi operations on the Central Front, but the last battle in this region would be de facto an episode of the Iranian civil war.

The Odyssey of the NLA

The fuse was already lit by the Iranian success on the Faw Peninsula, Val Fajr-8, in early 1986. This raised French doubts about Saddam's ability to win the war and pay his massive debts for French equipment and led to a diplomatic rapprochement with Tehran. France, which had once offered Khomeinei sanctuary, was the natural home for Iran's exiled politicians, including former President Abol Hassan Bani-Sadr and his son-in-law, the leader of the Iranian Mujahideen e-Khalq, Massoud Rajavi. The latter were drawn from the Liberal/Left secularists who, with the elimination of enemies within the armed forces, posed the greatest internal threat to the Islamic Revolution.

Driven underground, the MeK hoped Bani-Sadr would rally the secularists, but these hopes were dashed when Khomeinei dismissed Bani-Sadr in in June 1981. The MeK then began a ferocious bombing campaign against the leaders, killing President Muhammad Ali Rajai and Prime Minister Muhammad Javed Bahonar, but like all terror campaigns this rebounded, for it appalled traditional supporters such as the young middle class and skilled working class, who reluctantly supported the Islamic Revolution – for patriotic reasons – after the Iraqi invasion. In February 1982 the MeK's central committee were killed, and within months the organisation's military allies were destroyed when the Ghotbzadeh (or Qutbzadeh) Plot was uncovered. The survivors fled abroad to Paris and Baghdad, and by the end of 1982 the Iranian clerics felt confident that the threat had been contained and eased political repression but remained wary of the threat resurfacing.[7]

Paris may have hoped a potential secular, pro-Western, opposition would return to Tehran and overthrow the government. The émigrés, however, spent more energy bickering among themselves, and by 1986 the French government had probably concluded that,

PART II: THE LAST BATTLES 1988

as was noted 'The....Mujahedin was always better at publicity than at fighting'.[8]

Rajavi promoted the wife of a crony to the position of co-leader and then married her. Subsequently he fell out with both his wife and Bani-Sadr, established a personality cult, and – 'for ideological reasons' – then purged the movement of all his critics, which lead to additional desertions.[9] Another reason for dwindling émigré support was the closer relations between the MeK and Iraq, Rajarvi meeting Iraqi Foreign Minister Tariq Aziz in January 1983. Eventually, Paris decided it had backed the wrong horse and with numerous Iranian-sponsored kidnappings of its citizens abroad, as well as bombings within Metropolitan France, the new government of Jacques Chirac sought a rapprochement with Tehran amounting to appeasement. As part of this policy they expelled Iranian Mujahideen leader Masoud Rajarvi from his headquarters in Paris in June 1986, and following earlier contacts with Saddam, who would exploit the MeK, he now moved to Baghdad.

A year later he created a conventional army, the NLA (Artesh-e Azadibakhsh Melli Iran), whose baptism of fire was in the Northern Front on 3 July 1987, when a detachment struck in the Sar Dasht area east of Qalat Dizah to close a Kurdish supply route. The NLA took some peaks in a 15-hour battle, and the day saw several cross-border raids into western Azerbaijan, Ilam and Khuzistan Provinces. Similar operations continued throughout the year, 99 operations being claimed by the end of the year. They led Baghdad to conclude that the NLA would be best deployed on the Central Front. Its first operation was launched on 27 March 1988. Codenamed Rising Sun, it saw a surprise attack by 12 'brigades' against 3rd Brigade of 77th Infantry Division IRIA, west of Shush, close to the Fakkeh-Dezful road. Rajavi claimed to have taken 1,000 square kilometres and captured 500 prisoners and four MBTs.[10]

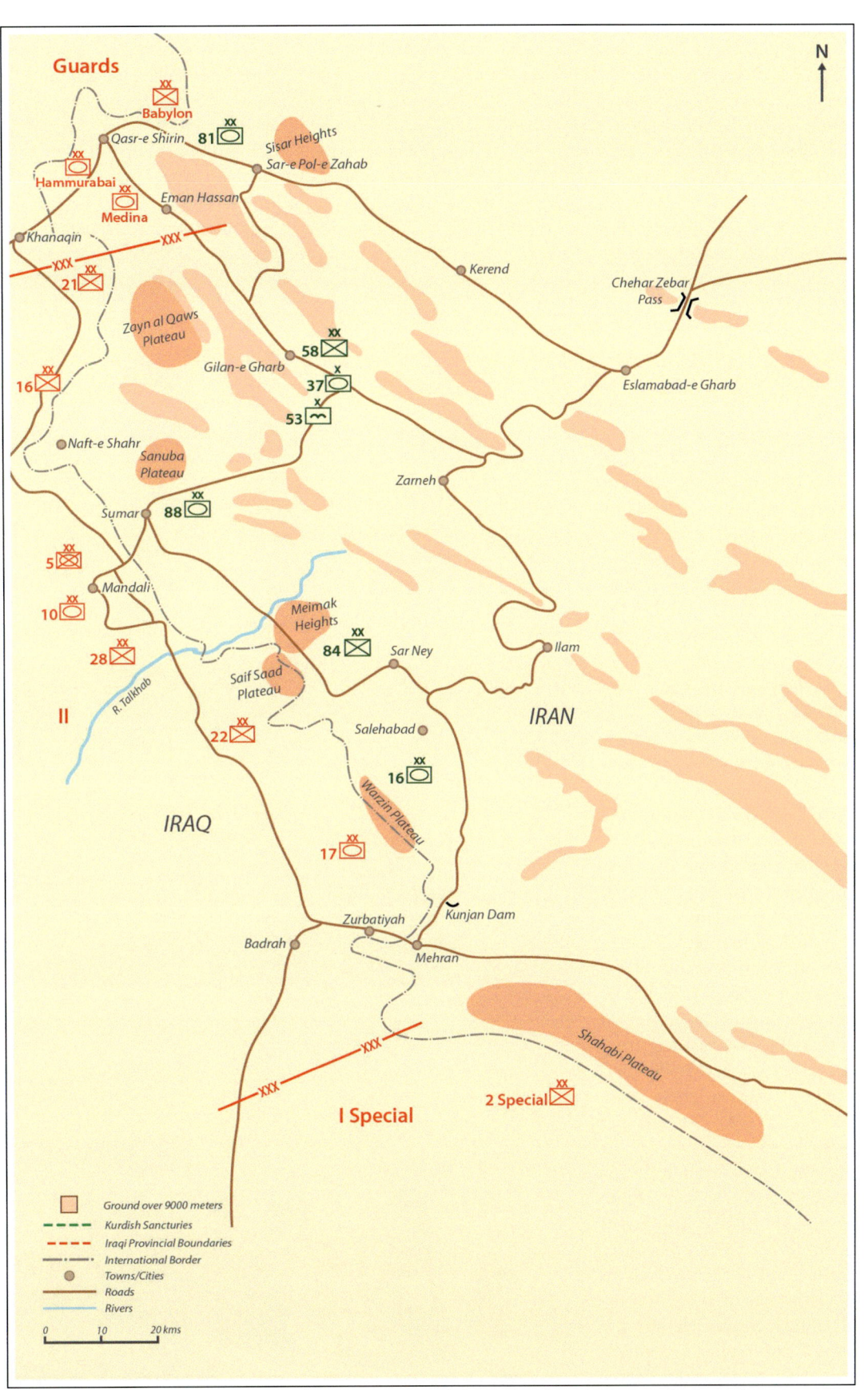

A map of the area that was the scene of Operation Forougheh Javidan. (Map by George Anderson)

The success fed Rajavi's ambitions and, to strengthen his political hand, he opted to seize an Iranian town which would be a beacon for domestic discontent. Mehran was the most obvious objective and the NLA began preparations for Operation Chelcheragh (Chandelier) (Most accounts say this was Operation Forty Stars but it was actually Chandelier.) Ataii was aided by the staff of Iraq's II Corps, for Baghdad undoubtedly welcomed a diversion as it was about to launch Tawakkalna ala Allah-2 in the Hawaizah Marshes. While the MeK would later claim it struck independently, there is no doubt the NLA was supported by 17th Armoured Division and II Corps' artillery. This provided a heavy bombardment against the defences of 11th Amir al-Momenin Infantry Division IRGC, supported by 2nd and 3rd Brigades of the IRIA's 16th Armoured Divison (some 20,000 troops).

The attack on 18 June was launched by 22 NLA 'brigades' (probably 11,000 men) but it was almost certainly the Iraqi troops who actually assaulted the defences and pushed back the defenders. The attackers beat off a major counterattack on 21 June, to secure Mehran the following day, aided by 530 fixed and rotary-wing sorties. The NLA claimed it suffered only 310 casualties, an indication that it actually took a secondary role, before extending its control to key bridges which it blew up, but after three days it withdrew across the border. A considerable amount of booty was acquired, the NLA claimed it was worth $2 billion, including 38 Chieftain MBTs, 30 guns (half of these self-propelled), and large numbers of Toyota trucks as well as 1,500 prisoners.[11]

Acutely aware that the war was now drawing to a close, the MeK pondered its options, and Rajavi decided to gamble on exploiting Iranian demoralisation by sending the NLA deep into Iran, to test popular support, in Operation Forougheh Javidan (Eternal Fire). Once again II Corps provided assistance, moving the NLA northwards to its Sar-e Pol-e Zahab bridgehead, but with the possible exception of special forces, the Iraqi Army intended to sit on the side-lines, partly to ensure there were no obstacles to the planned ceasefire.

Saddam's attitude was ambiguous, for he was willing to support anyone who might undermine Iran's theocratic regime, but if it failed he had no intention of tying Iraq to a political corpse. He and the Iraqi Army leaders recognised that the NLA could never reach Tehran under its own power (or at least they said so to Rajawi, who would never listen), but were still willing to provide artillery and air support, although the latter would suddenly cease when

the NLA's fortunes turned, according to General Makki. The MeK leadership talked of marching upon Tehran, a distance of 600 kilometres, but their initial objective was to establish a bridgehead around Qasr-e Shirin, Sar-e-Pol-e-Zahab, Kerend, Islamabad and Kermanshah, establish a provisional government and encourage their supporters to rally.

The advance by 16 'brigades', with some 7,000 men and women supported by 35 EE-9 Cascaval wheeled reconnaissance vehicles, began at 15:30 on 25 July under NLA deputy commander Maryam Rajavi and Chief-of-Staff Mahmoud Atai'I, in five task forces under themselves, Deputy Chief-of-Staff Mehdi Bara'i, Ebrahim Zakeri, Mehdi Eftekhari and Mahmoud Mahdavi who found themselves facing Pasdaran and Basiji. The NLA drove eastward down the road from Qasr-e Shirin led by a fast-moving 'brigade' which took Kerend by 19:00, driving out the 127th Meghdad Brigade IRGC. The attackers now paused as reports flooded in of enemy troops assembling, and the NLA strengthened its positions by securing

An EE-9 Cascavel armoured car advances into Iran in July 1988. (Albert Grandolini collection)

A column of MT-LB APCs of the NLA, on the start of their advance into Iran. (Albert Grandolini collection)

PART II: THE LAST BATTLES 1988

A scene from the MEK/MKO's 'highway of death': following a series of fierce strikes by the IRIAF and the IRIAA, the road to Eslamabad was left clogged full of burned-out tanks, vehicles and the bodies of the NLA. (Albert Grandolini collection)

heights around the town on 27 July. However, its southern flank remained exposed and its supply line to Qasr-e Shirin was very narrow. The following day saw increasing Pasdaran attacks with air support, and COMINT indicated the enemy was trying to isolate the task force which withdrew across the border on the night of 28–29 July.[12]

Operation Mersad

The Iranians feared an NLA operation, and on 22 July 1988 President Khamenei warned 'that a group of hypocrites, two-faced and evil persons may appear in the country supported by foreign propaganda, who may try to break our national pride'.[13]

Pasdaran of the 27th Rasoolallah Infantry Division IRGC during a break in fighting, in the Soleimaniyah area, in June 1988. (via N.S.)

Tehran might have believed that divine fortune ensured the regime's survival at this point. The Iraqi offensives had wrecked the IRIA and while the NFOHQ forward command post was reformed on 29 July it had only the remnants of the IRIA's 58th, 81st, 84th Divisions and 55th Airborne Brigade, which could offer only token resistance. But earlier in the month Tehran had decided to move its reserve of relatively fresh Pasdaran divisions from the Northern Front to prop up the battered Southern Front. Poor communications slowed the response. Nevertheless, by late July some 115,000 battle-hardened Pasdaran troops were flooding south and southeast, placing them across the NLA's planned line-of-advance. Other Pasdaran formations came up from the Central Front, as Tehran planned their annihilation in Operation Mersad (Ambush) directed by Lieutenant General Sayyad Shirazi. This operation would use much of the IRIA's remaining armour while the IRIAA deployed 45 helicopters, including a dozen gunships, while three IRIAF CAS squadrons with F-5 Freedom Fighters were also deployed. The helicopters, three of

327

which would be damaged, moved 3,360 troops and evacuated 388 wounded. Iranian air power claimed 29 APCs.

These troops were placed under Task Force Najaf-2, which first tried to stop another NLA column of five 'brigades' advancing from Kerend upon Eslamabad-e Gharb on 25 July, but the Najaf-2 garrison were driven out of Eslamabad by 22:00. Yet the three 'brigade' garrison quickly came under growing pressure, during the next three days, from the 5th Nasr, 17th Ali ibn Abu Talib Infantry Divisions, and 43rd Imam Ali Engineer Division IRGC in the north. From the south the 8th Najaf Ashraf, 25th Karbala, 27th Mohammad Rasooallah and 57th Abolfazl al-Abbas Divisions were reportedly attacking. By 27 July these had been joined by 71st Ruhollah Division and 155th Shohada Divisions, with 89th Moharram Artillery Brigade tightening the noose around the NLA, which was driven back across the border on the evening of 28 July.

Meanwhile, Eslamabad had barely fallen when the NLA pushed a 'brigade' forward towards Kermanshah. They were briefly held at the Chehar Zebar Pass by 33rd al-Mahdi Infantry Division, some 25 kilometres from Kermanshah, then pushed on only to be held by the newly arrived 31st Ashura and 32nd Ansar al-Hossein Divisions. The exposed NLA had no option but to withdraw during the morning of 28 July, pursued by the victorious defenders of the pass together with 9th Badr Division and 45th Javadol-A'emmeh Engineer Division.

Despite its claims, the NLA received little popular support in the areas which it 'liberated' because it was too closely associated with the Iraqis – making it abhorrent to patriotic Iranians. Rajavi's gamble had been a total failure; admitting the loss of 1,263 dead and missing, and 994 injured. The NLA also lost 72 AFVs, 21 122mm guns and 612 other vehicles. Over 1,000 of its combatants were taken prisoner too, so that Rajavi had lost nearly half his army. Surprisingly, Tehran talked-up the NLA advance, claiming it threatened towns and cities far beyond its control. Whether or not this was panic, or a cynical ploy to encourage MeK supporters to expose themselves remains uncertain, but it did cause a wave of arrests inside Iran, and during the autumn between 1,000 and 5,000 were executed including many NLA prisoners.

Whatever happened inside Iran afterwards was a different story. Operation Mersad was the final act of the eight-year-long, bitter and bloody, Iran-Iraq War.

COLOUR SECTION 4

Iran acquired 150 M48A5 Patton II MBTs, all equipped with the British-deigned 105mm guns, during the 1970s. Most of these went into the battle still painted in olive drab overall. However, many received disruptive camouflage patterns applied in medium green. This reconstruction is based on several photographs of different vehicles from the mid-1980s. (Artwork by Peter Penev)

Each Iranian division included a reconnaissance regiment equipped with a company of British-made, Alvis FV101 Scorpion light tanks – a total of 250 of which were acquired in the late 1970s. All of these were originally painted in light olive green overall. Scorpions proved reasonably effective during the first two years of the war, when some of the more-skilled Iranian commanders used them to flank Iraqi armoured formations. One of the Iranian units equipped with Scorpions distinguished itself during the early fighting in the Ilam area, where it managed to temporarily stop the advance of the Iraqi 2nd Infantry Division. (Artwork by Peter Penev)

Based on the chassis of the PT-76 light tank, the MT-LB was originally developed as the armoured variant of the MT-L artillery tractor. In Iraqi service it was often armed with a ZU-23-2 anti-aircraft gun installed on the rear part of the hull. The Iranians captured about a dozen MT-LBs during the offensives of 1986–1987 and pressed them into service as APCs. Most were painted in dark sand overall, though some had a disruptive camouflage pattern in green, applied in very different forms. (Artwork by Peter Penev)

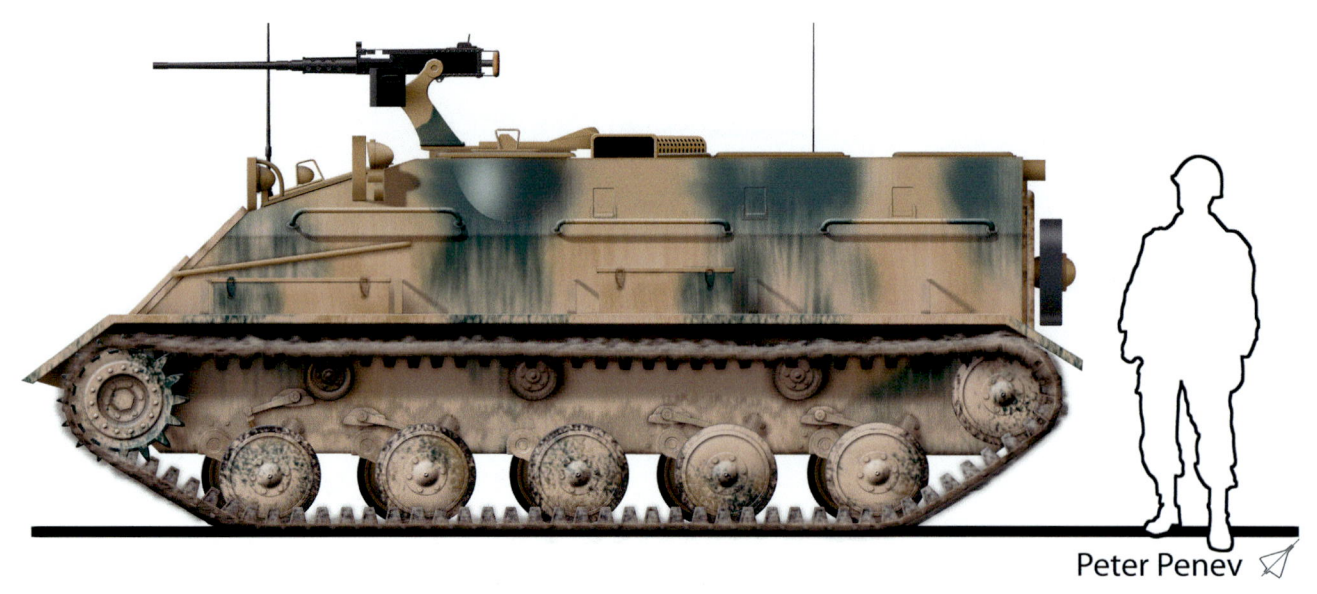

MIDDLE EAST@WAR SERIES SPECIAL #1: THE IRAN-IRAQ WAR

The OT M-60 (*oklopni transporter*, or armoured carrier) was the first APC to enter serial production in Yugoslavia. Iraq purchased 190 slightly improved M-60Ps in the mid-1980s, but very little is known about their service. Gauging from the few available photographs, all were painted in the standardised Iraqi Army camouflage pattern consisting of yellow sand and blue-green, and retained their US-made 12.7mm Browning M2 machine gun as primary armament. (Artwork by Peter Penev)

The BRDM-2 amphibious scout car was the primary reconnaissance vehicle of Iraqi mechanised formations. The vehicle proved highly popular for its easy maintenance and reliability. This example shows how most Iraqi BRDM-2s appeared early during the war, painted in the standardised Iraqi Army camouflage pattern of yellow sand and blue-green. (Artwork by Peter Penev)

Later during the war with Iran, most Iraqi BRDM-2s were painted in yellow sand only – a colour that rapidly bleached into different shades of grey-sand. Many received the tactical unit insignia of their parent formations – one example of which is illustrated in the inset. (Artwork by Peter Penev)

330

COLOUR SECTION 4

The 2S1 Gvozdika self-propelled howitzer made a relatively late appearance in the Iran-Iraq War. While based on the extended chassis of the MT-LB
The 2S1 Gvozdika self-propelled howitzer made a relatively late appearance in the Iran-Iraq War. While based on the extended chassis of the MT-LB
carrier, they were equipped with a modified variant of the 122mm 2A18 towed howitzer. Gvozdikas became the primary equipment of two batteries
in each artillery battalion of every armoured division as of 1987. All the examples known to have been operated by the Iraqis as of that time were
painted in yellow-sand overall, and seem to have worn no special insignia. (Artwork by Peter Penev)

The Iranians captured about a dozen 2S1s in 1986 and 1987, and the IRGC pressed them in service – usually after enhancing their camouflage
through the addition of a disruptive pattern in green. This is a reconstruction of a Gvozdika operated by the IRGC in 1988. (Artwork by Peter Penev)

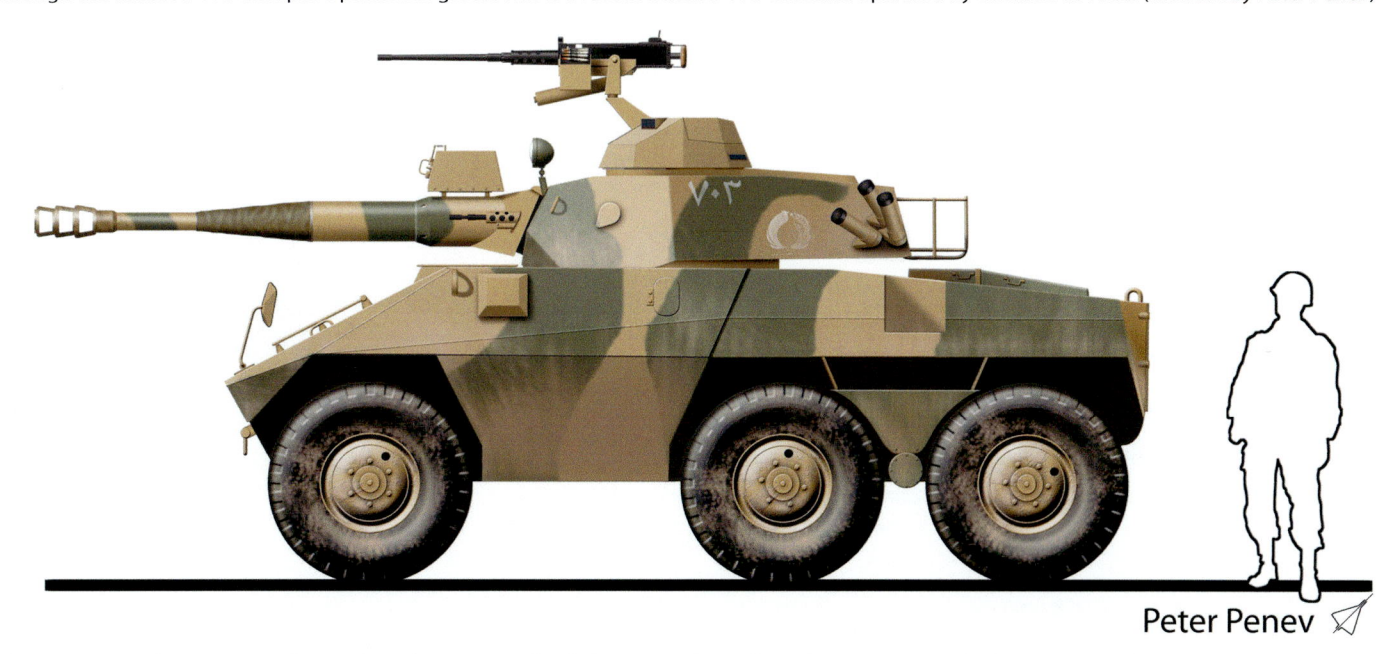

The EE-9 Cascavel (Portuguese for 'Rattlesnake') is a six-wheeled armoured car of Brazilian origin, 364 of which were acquired by Iraq in the 1980s.
At least a company worth of EE-9s was donated to the NLA and deployed during its advance into Iran in July 1988. Atop the sand as primary colour,
some received disruptive camouflage patterns in light green, and others in dark green. Most NLA vehicles had the crest of the MEK/MKO applied –
either on the sides of the forward hull, or on the turret side. (Artwork by Peter Penev)

MIDDLE EAST@WAR SERIES SPECIAL #1: THE IRAN-IRAQ WAR

Peter Penev

The M107 self-propelled howitzer was based on the chassis of the M578 light recovery vehicle. The lightly protected body (the armour was only 13mm thick), carried the 175mm cannon, installed on the rear of the vehicle without any armoured protection – in turn offering more space for movement of the crew. The Iranians acquired only 38 M107s (and 38 similar M110s, armed with a 203mm howitzer) in the 1970s, but these were in much demand because they outranged most artillery pieces in Iraqi service. As far as is known, most went into battle still painted in olive drab overall, over which disruptive patterns in sand (as shown here), or other shades of green, were applied. (Artwork by Peter Penev)

Peter Penev

With Iran acquiring no fewer than 430 self-propelled artillery pieces of this type, the M109A1s were the most important element of the artillery groups of its army. Its primary armament consisted of the 155mm M185 howitzer. All vehicles were originally painted in light olive green overall. Never refreshed during the war with Iraq, their colour frequently dilapidated into various shades of grey-green and sand. (Artwork by Peter Penev)

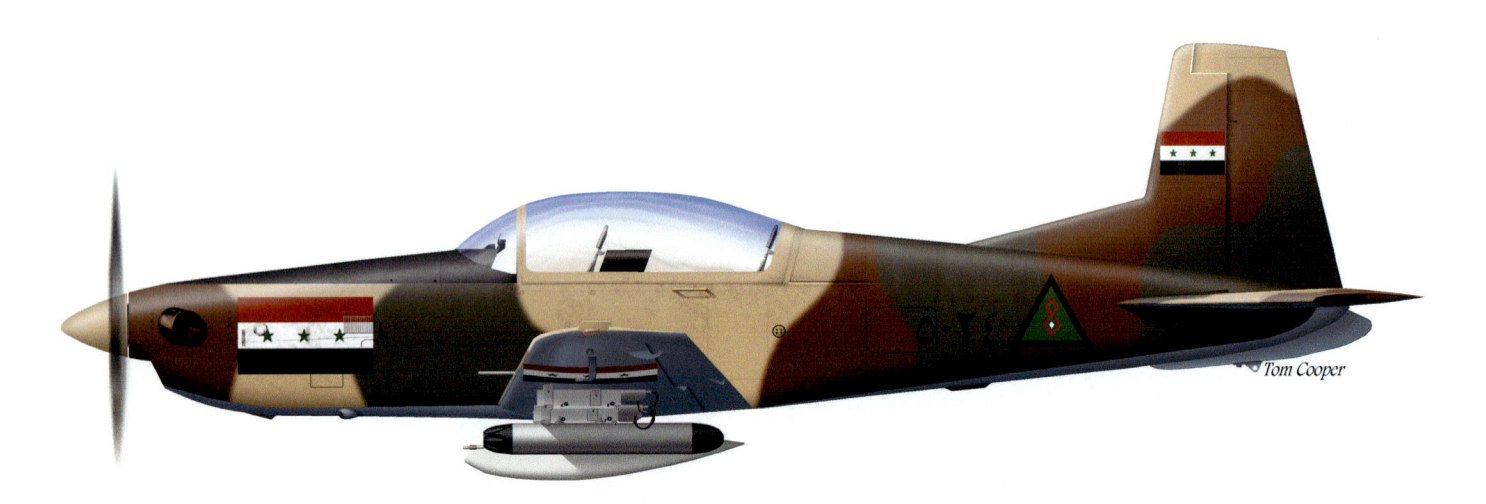

Tom Cooper

The Pilatus PC-7 was a two-seat basic trainer aircraft, sold by Switzerland to both Iran and Iraq – starting in 1983. The Iraqi Army Aviation Corps was quick in adapting some of its 52 PC-7s for COIN purposes. The first unit equipped with the type became operational in 1984 and was deployed to fight Kurdish insurgents in the north of the country. It had all of its aircraft camouflaged as shown on this example (serial number 5024, c/n 170/9043). Colours used seem to have been of French origin and included Brun Café (similar to BS381C/388 Beige), Brun Noisette (similar to BS381C/350 Dark Earth) and Gris Vert Fonce (similar BS381C/641 Dark Green) on top surfaces and sides. Undersurfaces were probably painted in a colour similar to Celomer 1625 Gris Bleu Moyen Clar (light blue-grey). The second IrAAC unit of PC-7s was operational by 1986, by when PC-7s became frequent sights over the northern and central battlefields of the Iran-Iraq War. Their usual armament consisted of FN ETNA TMP-5 twin 7.62mm machine-gun pods and Matra F2 pods for six 68mm SNEB unguided rockets. (Artwork by Tom Cooper)

COLOUR SECTION 4

While playing a prominent role on the southern battlefield early during the war, most IrAAC SA.342 Gazelles were re-deployed towards the north later during the conflict. With anti-armour warfare being of lesser importance in these areas, they were frequently armed with 20mm GIAT M621 cannon (installed on the right side of the helicopter only), and Brandt 68x12 or 68x22 launchers for 68mm SNEB unguided rockets. Some examples had improved exhaust pipes, illustrated in the inset, to decrease their exposure to infrared homing MANPADs. (Artwork by Tom Cooper)

With southern battlefields proving too dangerous for them, most of about 50 SE.316C Alouette IIIs Iraq acquired in the 1970s served on the northern and central battlefields, where their significant 'hot and high' capabilities were of advantage. The type was equipped with the APX-Bézu 260 gyro-stabilised sight, which enabled the deployment of AS.12 ATGMs. Many Iraqi Alouette IIIs received improved sand filters installed on their engine intakes during the second half of the 1980s. (Artwork by Tom Cooper)

In addition to the well-known Bell 214A Esfahan, no fewer than 335 of which were purchased by Iran in the 1970s in several major variants, the IRIAA also deployed about 70 Agusta-Bell AB.205A utility helicopters (essentially an export variant of the UH-1H Huey). Consisting of colours named earth yellow and field drab, the camouflage on their top surfaces and sides was slightly lighter than that on Esfahans, and they usually had the top side of their noses painted in black. While serials (in the range 6–4300 upwards) were applied in black on the fin, most received full service titles – in English and in Farsi – on the cabin doors. (Artwork by Tom Cooper)

During the 1970s, the Iranian Army closely followed the helicopter-related developments and thinking of the US Army. When, based on experiences from Vietnam, the Americans decided to develop hunter-killer teams consisting of light scout helicopters and dedicated armoured attack helicopters, the Iranian Army Aviation followed in fashion. One of the results was the acquisition of 214 Bell 206s, the majority of which entered service with the army and were camouflaged as shown here, in dark sand and dark earth on top surfaces and sides, and light grey on undersurfaces. In addition to use as scouts, they were primarily deployed for utility purposes. The insets show an interim variant of the IRIAA's crest (applied on many of its Bell 206s and AH-1Js during the second half of the 1980s and later on), and the service title of the IRIAA in Farsi (more commonly known as 'Havaniruz'). (Artwork by Tom Cooper)

Although their numbers frequently dwindled to fewer than 50 operational examples due to combat attrition, incidents, and requirements of periodic maintenance, the IRIAA's AH-1Js remained the most important means of close air support for army and IRGC troops throughout the war with Iraq. While still retaining their camouflage pattern in dark yellow-sand and dark earth over, and pale grey under, most began receiving standardised service titles: 'IRIAA' was usually retained on the boom, while the Farsi-version was applied below the pilot's (rear) cockpit, together with the new crest of the Havaniruz. The principal armament of AH-1Js consisted of the 20mm M197 gun and M260 (17 tubes, illustrated here) and M261 (7 tube) launchers for 3.75in (68mm) unguided rockets. Frequent clashes with Iraqi helicopters and fighter-bombers led to some experimentation with installation of AIM-9J Sidewinder missiles on adapters and rails illustrated in the inset. (Artwork by Tom Cooper)

Out of 202 AH-1J Cobras acquired by Iran in the 1970s, 65 were modified through the addition of M65 TOW sights and were thus compatible with BGM-71 TOW ATGMs. They became the primary killers of Iraqi armour during the war of 1980–1988. Despite frequent shortages of TOWs (mostly caused by problems related to the Iranian logistics, rather than true lack of rounds), the carriage of eight rounds remained standard for most of that conflict. In addition to its standard camouflage pattern, this Cobra is shown wearing an 'interim' variant of service title – applied in white, in larger letters than usual, underneath the pilot's (rear) cockpit. Curiously, this example served for most of the war without the usual fin flash. (Artwork by Tom Cooper)

APPENDIX I

ARMS ACQUISITIONS AND GROUND FORCES EQUIPMENT OF IRAN

Generally, during the second half of the twentieth century and until the end of the war with Iraq, Iranian arms acquisitions went through three distinct phases:

- 1950s-1960s: USA were the primary supplier, mostly with surplus equipment left over from the Second World War
- 1970s: major military build-up of Iran, including large-scale acquisitions from the USA, Great Britain, and the USSR
- 1980s: haphazard acquisition from more than 20 different countries, the largest of which were the Democratic People's Republic of Korea (North Korea), and the People's Republic of China.

Ironically, a third major supplier of arms for Iran during the Iran–Iraq War was Iraq – because the Iranian ground forces had captured so much equipment from the Iraqi ground forces. Combined with the fact that several Western suppliers were breaking their own arms embargoes, their transactions were shrouded in secrecy and thus remain poorly documented. As a result, this has made the issue of tracking the stocks of Iranian arms a complex issue.

Inventory of 1978–1980

The following table is based on an Iranian source listing major pieces of equipment at the start of the war. Notably, the source in question does not always use the correct designations, and thus some interpretation is necessary. For example, the BTR-60 was referred to as the 'Wheeled Russian APC', and Finnish-made Soltam mortars were designated 'Tampella' by the Iranians.[1]

Table 30: 1978 Iranian Army and Air Force Inventory according to the British Defence- and Air Attaches in Tehran, 1978[2]

Number	Equipment
707	Chieftain Mk3/3 & Mk5
145	Chieftain Mk5/3
14	Chieftain AVLB[3]
415	M47M
460	M60
250	Scorpion
600 (+)	MAZ Tank Transporter
64	M113
575	M113A1

Table 30: 1978 Iranian Army and Air Force Inventory according to the British Defence- and Air Attaches in Tehran, 1978[2]

Number	Equipment
322	M577A1
852	BTR-50PK
520	BTR-60PB
120	BMP-1
40	ZSU-23-4
1,000	ZU-23-2[4]
150	35mm Oelikon GDF[5]
82 (?)	US 40mm[6]
80	ZSU-57-2
258 (?)	Swedish 75mm AA[7]
330	105mm M101
172	130mm M-46
130	155mm M114
350	155mm M109A1B
55	203mm M115
28	M110
46	M107
906	US 81mm mortar
220	US 107mm mortar[8]
400	Tampella mortar
3,235	M20 Bazooka
1,950	RPG-7
910	M18 57mm recoilless
1,357	M40 106mm recoilless
1,000	SS.11
240	SS.12[9]
380	TOW
64	BM-21
11	HAWK (batteries not launchers)
36	Rapier
14	Tigercat
6	Seacat[10]

Table 31: Iranian Inventory, September 1980 (Iranian and US Sources)

Number	Equipment
888	Chieftain
13	Chieftain ARV
248	Scorpion
50	Ferret
472	M60A1
385	M47M
12	M48A5
180	M113
213	M113 120mm mortar carrier
44	M113 81mm mortar carrier
155	M113 with TOW
357	M577
424	M548
92	Light ammunition carriers[11]
501	Jeep with TOW
687	Dragon ATGM
937	BTR-50PK
324	BTR-60PB
896	BMP-1
14,588	RPG-7
609	M18 57mm recoilless
362	105mm M101
388	130mm M-46
102	155mm M114
400	M109A1B
48	M107
45	203mm M115
40	M110
1,004	ZU-23-2
90	ZSU-23-4
83	BM-21
107	ZSU-57-2
1,942	SA-7 'Strela 3' (probably missiles not launchers)
408	ZPU (unknown type)[12]
168	Soltam 120mm mortar
90	Soltam 81mm mortar

Most of the M113s were converted to weapons carriers, those that were not were apparently in storage.[13]

Table 32: Iranian Inventory, 1987 (DIA)[14]

Number	Equipment
350-400	Chieftain
14	Chieftain AVLB
75+	Scorpion

Table 32: Iranian Inventory, 1987 (DIA)[14]

Number	Equipment
250+	M60A1
200	M47M
50–100[15]	T-55
60–90[16]	T-62 (Chonma Ho)
20[17]	T-72
200–300	M113[18]
?	TOW ATGM
?	Dragon ATGM
?	Sagger ATGM
400	BTR-50PK
300	BTR-60PB
400	BMP-1
?	US 40mm Grenade Launcher
?	RPG-7
?	M20 Bazooka
?	M18 57mm recoilless
?	B-10 82mm recoilless
?	M40A1 106mm recoilless
175	105mm M101
225	130mm M-46
80	155mm M114
60–100	155mm GHN-45
200	M109A1B
20	M107
40–50	203mm M115
10	M110
?	107mm Type 63 MRL
?	BM-11
40–50	BM-21
200	ZPU-2[19]
200	ZPU-4
?[20]	ZU-23-2
200[21]	35mm GDF-002
?[22]	ZSU-23-4
?[23]	ZSU-57-2
?[24]	SA-7
?[25]	Rapier
?[26]	Tigercat
6[27]	SA-2
30[28]	HQ-2
?	HAWK
1–2	SCUD B SSM
5–8	PMP Pontoon Sets
65+	GSP Ferry
60+	TMM Bridge

ARMS ACQUISITIONS AND GROUND FORCES EQUIPMENT OF IRAN

Table 32: Iranian Inventory, 1987 (DIA)[14]	
Number	Equipment
?	Bailey Bridge
7	M4T6 Bridge
?	German Ribbon Bridges
10,000	1/4t to 1t Truck
12,000+	1.5t to 5t Truck
500	Over 5t Truck
900	Tank Transporters

Overview of Iranian Equipment[29]	
Heading	Explanation
Weapon	Name of the weapon. Towed artillery is prefixed by its calibre
Supplier	The name of the nation that supplied the weapons to Iran. This is usually but not always the country of manufacture. For example, Syria passed on Soviet made weapons, but the supplier is listed as Syria. If the weapons were second-hand then the supplier is the nation that used them 'first-hand'. If the weapons were new but transported via a third party the supplier is listed as the manufacturing country. For example, Bofors (Sweden) sent RBS-70 SAMs via Singapore, but the supplier is listed as Sweden. Given the highly convoluted nature of arms trades during the war, it probable that there are errors in this column
Number Delivered	The number of weapons delivered. Different sources often disagree or round their figures so this should be treated as a guideline
Start Date	Year deliveries started
End Date	Year deliveries ended
Source	The primary source this was taken from. See the section on sources for the abbreviations used
Notes	General notes. For US MAP deliveries, this has the actual name used in the MAP database, if it was present. They are capitalised as in the original report

Table 33: Main Suppliers of Arms to Iran, 1980–1987

Weapon	Supplier	Number Delivered	Start Date	End Date	Source	Notes
105mm M101	USA	250	61	64	SIPRI	Probably referring to the Howitzers delivered by MAP
105mm M101	USA	110	66	67	MAP	HOW TOWED 105MM M101A1
105mm M3	USA	?	?	?	Picture	No documentation, but there are several pictures available. Probably delivered in the 50s
106mm M40	USA	199	63	63	MAP	106 MM RECOILLESS RIFLES
160mm M40	USA	100	?	?	FMS	Exact date unknown but pre-1977
106mm M40	France	200	80	83	CIA[30]	Exact date unconfirmed
106mm M40	France	60	80	83	CIA[31]	Exact date unconfirmed
106mm M40	Greece	135	80	83	CIA[32]	Exact date unconfirmed
106mm M40	Portugal	100	80	83	CIA[33]	Exact date unconfirmed
106mm M40	Spain	200[34]	84	84	CIA[35]	
107mm Type 63	PRC	550[36]	81	90	SIPRI	Only a few pictures exist of towed mounts. Jeep mounted weapons are more prevalent.
107mm Type 63	North Korea	200	82	86	SIPRI	MFW shows only 29 being delivered in 1986
122mm M-30	Syria	90	81	81	MFW	

Table 33: Main Suppliers of Arms to Iran, 1980–1987 (continued)

122mm M-30	North Korea	?	84	84	MFW	Unknow number delivered. Given OEA says 100 were in service as of 2010, it is possible that 100 or more were delivered.
122mm Type 60	China	75	86	86	MFW	Given how similar these are to the Type-59-I they are impossible to distinguish by satellite, it is possible these may have been Type 59-I guns
130mm M-46	USSR	70/100	70	?	CIA[37]/ SIPRI	CIA shows 70, SIPRI shows 100 delivered. There are claims some were sent immediately after the start of the war[38]
130mm M-46	Libya	24	81	81	MFW	
130mm M-46	Syria	50	82	82	MFW	
130mm Type 59-1	PRC	29	86	86	MFW	
130mm Type 59-1	North Korea	480	83	88	SIPRI	MFW shows 201 delivered between 1981 and 1986
155mm GCN-45	Austria	90	85	86	MFW	One source shows 140 delivered but does not give dates, so some were probably delivered after 1986[39]
155mm M114	USA	100	63	63	MAP	155MM HOWITZERS
155mm M114	USA	2	63	64	MAP	HOW TOWED 155MM M114
155mm M114	USA	100	68	69	SIPRI	
203mm M115	USA	20	63	64	MAP	8 INCH HOWITZERS
203mm M115	USA	28	67	67	MAP	HOW TOWED 8IN M115
203mm M115	USA	50	68	69	SIPRI	Given inventory numbers in 1981 (52) this entry is probably an amalgamation of the MAP deliveries incorrectly dated
35mm GDF	Switzerland	100	75	76	SIPRI	Corroborated by CIA report[40]
35mm GDF	Switzerland	24	87	87	Fan[41]	Corroborated by CIA report 'Oerlikon AA guns'[42]
57mm M18	USA	682	?	?	JCS	Supplied before 1958
BM-11	North Korea	100	82	87	SIPRI	MFW shows 200 delivered in 1981
BM-21	USSR	70	67	68	SIPRI	A CIA report[43] shows 64 in 1971
BM-21	Libya	?	83	85	MFW	Number delivered is unknown
BMP-1	USSR	896	78	?	Hos	Possibly 937. Photographic evidence suggests that some of these were BMP-1K command versions[44]
BMP-1	Hungary	300	87	87	DIA[45]	Unconfirmed Intelligence report
BTR-50PK	USSR	852	67	71	CIA[46]	Delivery estimates range from 200 to nearly 1,000 depending on the source. Iranian sources give 937
BTR-60PB	USSR	500	67	70	CIA[47]	SIPRI only gives 300. The 1980 inventory was 324
Chieftain AVLB	UK	14	?	?	FCO	Certainly, delivered but unserviceable during most of the war, thus there are no photographs
Chieftain ARV	UK	41	72	79	SIPRI	
Chieftain MBT	UK	707	71	75	SIPRI	
Chonma Ho	North Korea	150	82	83	SIPRI	MFW shows only 60 delivered 1982. A 1986 CIA report shows 60–90 in service which may be based on delivery numbers (see above)
Dragon Launcher	USA	687	77	78	Hos	
Dragon missile	USA	9,716	77	78	SIPRI	
Ferret	UK	50	70	71	SIPRI	Served with the Gendarmerie, later passed to IRGC
HJ-7 Missile	PRC	6,500	82	88	SIPRI	Indistinguishable from Soviet Sagger
HN-5A Missile	PRC	500	86	88	SIPRI	Difficult to distinguish from SA-7

ARMS ACQUISITIONS AND GROUND FORCES EQUIPMENT OF IRAN

Table 33: Main Suppliers of Arms to Iran, 1980–1987 (continued)							
HQ-2 Launcher	North Korea[48]	30	8549	86	DIA[50]	
HQ-2 Missile	North Korea	120	85[51]	86	DIA[52]	
I-HAWK Launcher	USA	37	74	79	SIPRI	
I-HAWK Missile	USA	1,811	74	79	SIPRI	FMS shows only 1,442
Kwasong 5 Missile	North Korea	90–100	87	88	Other[53]	Scud derivative. Number of launchers unknown
M107	USA	40	73	73	SIPRI	FMS shows 46
M109	USA	440	70	77	FMS	SIPRI gives 50 delivered in 1970
M110	USA	38	73	73	SIPRI	FMS shows 42
M113	USA	64	63	63	MAP	CARR PERS ARMD M113
M113A1	USA	54	65	66	MAP	CARR PERS ARMD M113A1
M113A1	USA	400	66	78	SIPRI	Most converted to weapons carriers. Iranian 1980 inventory shows 180 APCs. FMS shows 903 pre-mid-1977 but that may include M577
M113 + TOW	Iran	155	73	?	Hos	Converted in Iran
M113 + 81mm	Iran	44	?	?	Hos	Converted in Iran, Soltam mortar
M113 + 120mm	Iran	213	?	?	Hos	Converted in Iran, Soltam mortar
M1978 SPG	North Korea	20	85	85	IIV3	
M1985 MRL	North Korea	100	87	87	SIPRI	
M18 Hellcat	USA	55	?	?	JCS	Delivered before 1958. Not used in Iran–Iraq War
M20 Armoured Car	USA	140	55	57	SIPRI	Not used during the war
M20 Bazooka	USA	3,235	?	?	FCO	
M24 Chaffee	USA	100	54	56	SIPRI	Use during the war is dubious, though there is a video capture of one apparently in use in Khorramshahr
M4 Sherman	USA	15	51	51	SIPRI	
M4 Sherman	USA	99	63	63	MAP	TANK MED M4
M4A3 Sherman	USA	11	63	63	MAP	TANK MED M4A3
M36	USA	99	?	?	JCS	Delivered before 1958
M47	USA	450	58	59	SIPRI	
M47	USA	414	63	63	MAP	TANK CBT MDM 90MM M47
M48A5	Pakistan	20	79	79	Other[54]	Only 12 in service at the start of the war
M548	USA	416	?	?	FMS	'Carrier CGO Armoured' delivered before mid-1977
M548	USA	100	78	79	TC	
M577	USA	304	78	79	TC	
M60A1	USA	460	69	70	SIPRI	
M74 ARV	USA	43	63	63	MAP	RECOV VEH FTRAC M74
PMP Bridge	USSR	7	71	71	CIA[55]	7 bridge sets
PTS-M	USSR	?	?	?	Picture	There are pictures of these in service, but no documentary evidence of their delivery
Rapier Launcher	UK	81	72	75	SIPRI	
Rapier Missile	UK	1,250	72	73	SIPRI	

Table 33: Main Suppliers of Arms to Iran, 1980–1987 (continued)							
RPG-7	USSR	1,500	70	70	IIV1	IIV1 says the Gendarmerie used them pre-war. This is corroborated by a CIA report[56]. The 1980 inventory gives significantly greater numbers (14,588) and TO&E shows use by the Army
SA-2 Launcher	Libya	6	?	?	DIA[57]	Delivery date probably circa 1985
SA-2 Missile	Libya	25–30	?	?	DIA[58]	Delivery date probably circa 1985
SA-7 Missile	USSR	2,000	76	76	SIPRI	Hos shows 1,942 still in service in 1980
SA-7 Launcher	Libya	140	87	87	DIA[59]	Unconfirmed intelligence
SA-7 Missile	Libya	2,000	87	87	DIA[60]	Unconfirmed intelligence
Sagger Missile	?	2,000	82	83	SIPRI	SIPRI shows Syria as the provider, MFW shows 2,012 missiles from Libya
Sagger Missile	North Korea	1,185	81	82	MFW	
Sagger Missile	North Korea	4,000	86	89	SIPRI	
Scorpion	UK	250	75	76	SIPRI	
Scud B Launcher	Libya	1–2	85	85	DIA[61]	Only a 'small number' of missiles delivered[62]
SS.11	USA	1,409	63	63	MAP	SS.10/11 MSLS AND SUP EQP Almost certainly only used for training during the war. No pictures are known to the author
Stinger Launcher	USA	52	87	87	DIA[63]	Unconfirmed intelligence
Stinger Missile	USA	100	87	87	DIA[64]	Unconfirmed intelligence
T-54	Libya	60	81	81	SIPRI	MFW shows 100 T-54/55 delivered between 1981 and 1982
T-54 'modernised'	Hungary	50	87	87	DIA[65]	Unconfirmed intelligence. The source document does not make it clear what is modernised about the tanks
T-55	Libya	65	81	81	SIPRI	MFW shows 100 T-54/55 delivered between 1981 and 1982
T-62	Libya	65	81	81	SIPRI	MFW shows only 30 delivered in 1983
Tigercat Launcher	UK	15	69	70	Other[66]	
Tigercat Missiles	UK	400	69	70	Other[67]	Up to 400 SAMs delivered.
TOW	USA	19,064	76	79	SIPRI	Confirmed by FMS
TOW	Israel	1,008	85	85	SIPRI	
TOW BGM-71A	USA	4,760	73	76	SIPRI	
TMM Bridge	USSR	2	70	70	CIA[68]	
ZPU-4	USSR	408	?	?	Hos	Pre-war delivery. May not all be ZPU-4, possibly some ZPU-2 or 1. They are not in the Army's order of battle so may have all been delivered to the airforce.
ZPU-4	North Korea	16	84	84	CIA[69]	Probably part of a much larger shipment
ZSU-23-4	USSR	30	71	71	CIA[70]	Both V and V1 versions were imported[71]. Given the timing these were probably V versions
ZSU-23-4	USSR	200	77	78	SIPRI	Both V and V1 versions were imported[72]. Given the timing these were probably V1 versions
ZSU-57-2	USSR	80	67	67	CIA[73]	SIPRI gives the number delivered as 100
ZU-23-2	USSR	1,000	67	70	CIA[74]	

The following weapons have been mentioned in various sources as being delivered to Iran. However, there is no photographic evidence of them and no corroboration in other sources.

ARMS ACQUISITIONS AND GROUND FORCES EQUIPMENT OF IRAN

Table 34: Weapons Systems never delivered to Iran
75mm M116 (USA)
75mm M20 (USA)
85mm D-44 (USSR)
85mm M1939 AA Gun
122mm Type-60 (PRC; probably confused with the 130mm Type 59-I which looks very similar)
122mm Type-83 (PRC; proper designation 122mm Type 54-I, index PL83; probably a confusion with the 100mm Type-54 that – probably – was delivered)
122mm Type-83 (PRC; an Iranian source mentions the import of such MRLS, but it appears very few were actually acquired, and then for development purposes only)
BTR-152 (USSR)
EE-9 Mk III (Brazil, via Libya; pictures of captured Iraqi EE-9 Mk IV are common. The Mk III has a distinctive turret but no pictures of this have been found to date)
M8 armoured car (USA; there are photographs of the M20 scout car but none of the turreted M8)
PT-76 (USSR; the confusion arises because the AFV repair plant built by the Soviets for the Iranians could repair PT-76 tanks;[75] however, none were purchased)
Type-59 MBT (PRC); *CIA Handbook of Major Foreign Weapon Systems Exported to The Third World: 1981–86*, which list all recipients does not list Iran
Type 69-II (*PRC; CIA Handbook of Major Foreign Weapon Systems Exported to The Third World: 1981–86*, which lists all recipients does not list Iran; all Type-69s operated by Iran were captured from Iraq)
SA-9 (USSR; see entry for PT-76 above)

Table 35: Iranian Equipment captured from the Iraqis

This section deals with captured equipment used by the Iranians that was not otherwise in their inventory (usually, such equipment was operated by the IRGC).

37mm Type-65 anti-aircraft gun (probably captured, probably prompting the Iranians into importing additional pieces, ammunition and spares, imports of which are poorly documented)
57mm S-60 anti-aircraft gun (some Chinese Type-69 guns were captured from the Iraqis, as they were seen in Iranian service while still wearing Iraqi camouflage colours. However, it is possible that some were also delivered from the DPRK or the PRC)
73mm SPG-9 (anti-tank rocket launcher)
82mm B10 (recoilless rifle)
105mm M18/61 howitzer (14th Imam Hossein Infantry Brigade reported having an artillery detachment of 'Yugoslav made 105mm howitzers', most likely captured from Iraq)[76]
107mm B11 (recoilless rifle)
122mm D-30 (howitzer)
152mm D-20 (there is a possibility that these guns were bought directly from China – as Type-66 – rather than being captured)
2S1 (self-propelled howitzer)
9P133 (BRDM-2 with AT-3 Sagger)
AMB-S (tracked ambulance vehicle based on the chassis of the BMP-1 IFV; there is a single picture of this vehicle in Iranian service; given how late in the war this was delivered to Iraq its unlikely many examples were captured; the picture of the vehicle does not show any red crescent markings so it may have been re-proposed by the IRGC)
BRDM-2 (armoured car)
EE-9 Mk IV (armoured car)
EE-11 (APC)
M-60 (APC, of Yugoslav design and production)
MT-LB (APC)
Type-69 (MBT)
T-72 MBT

Iranian Ground Transport Vehicles

Up to the mid-1970s, the majority of military transport vehicles in Iranian service were US-supplied. In the mid-1970s, there was a huge influx of Soviet- and East European equipment – to a degree where trucks made in the USSR formed the backbone of the Army's fleet. Due to combat losses and then the formation of the IRGC, there was not enough transport to go around for most of the war: not only the IRGC, but also the IRIAF became heavily reliant on requisitioned civilian transport vehicles – foremost the ubiquitous Toyota pickups. Another favourite of the IRGC was the Honda XL dirt bike, while they and the Army also made extensive use of so-called 'jeeps' – mostly as weapons carriers for TOWs, recoilless rifles and Type-63 MRLS.

No reliable inventories or delivery records are avaialble. Correspondingly, the researcher is reliant on visual evidence. The CIA did unearth a partial delivery list of Soviet vehicles, as detailed below.

Iranian Ground Transport Vehicles
US-made Trucks

FMS sales up to mid-1977 show that the following trucks had been bought by Iran.[77] The number of US-made trucks in service probably exceeded this amount as some may have been delivered by the Military Aid Programme (MAP)

- ¼t Trucks (i.e. jeeps): 2,212
- 2½t Trucks: 143
- 5t Trucks: 530
- Other Trucks: 5
- Commercial Trucks: 26
- Semi-trailers: 123
- Other Trailers: 527

East-European-made Trucks

Iran made extensive use of the East German IFA W50, which were used by the Army, and IRGC. The IFA was the civilian version and not the version used by the East German Army. The IRGC also used smaller numbers of the Romanian DAC trucks, though these may have all been captured from Iraq.

Israel-made Trucks

The Israelis supplied an unknown number of M325 'Nun Nun' light trucks. The available pictures show them carrying command shelters.

Jeeps

The USA supplied M38, M606 and M151 Jeeps. The Iranians made a copy of the M38 called the Keohwa M-5GA1.

The M38 and the Keohwa are similar but easily distinguished, the M38 having vertical radiator slits the Keohwa horizontal slits. The M606 has a much higher bonnet than the M38 and Keohwa. The M151 is much lower slung than the others are and has angular rear mudguards.

All the Keohwa jeeps were fitted with a split windscreen to allow a 106mm gun to be mounted, though not all jeeps actually had the gun. Besides the 106mm-armed jeeps, Keohwa jeeps and perhaps M38s were also used as carriers for the Chinese 107mm Type 62 MRL.

Many M151 jeeps were fitted with TOW missile launchers.

Land Rovers

The UK supplied ¾ ton Land Rovers to tow the Air Force's Rapier missiles before the war. During the war, the Spanish Santana Land Rover was supplied to Iran to be assembled in kit form[78], the first vehicles arriving in late 1982 or early 1983. In 1986, the UK signed a deal to sell 3,000 Land Rovers to Iran.[79] These were ostensibly civilian but were almost certainly used at the front.

Soviet 4WD-Vehicles

The Soviets supplied both GAZ-69 and UAZ-469 to the Iranian Army before the war. Further examples were captured from Iraq during the conflict.

Toyota Landcruisers

The Landcruiser was the IRGC's ride of choice and was used in very large numbers. Many were used as weapons carriers carrying 107mm Type 63 MRLs or 14.5mm ZPU-2 AA guns. At least one example was modified to carry a TOW missile. There was a chemical decontamination vehicle, though it is unclear how common this was.

Iranian Infantry Weapons: Small Arms

At the start of the war the Army was equipped with German-designed G3 Rifles and MG3 machine guns. These and their ammunition were produced in Iran. Production was insufficient to meet the needs of the newly formed IRGC so large numbers of Soviet-designed AK assault weapons were imported. These were supplemented by Soviet-designed MGs: PKN, RPD and RPK. Photographic evidence suggests that machine guns appeared to be in short supply.

As the war progressed, some army units were equipped with Soviet style small arms and home-produced weapons found their way to the IRGC. This sometimes resulted in units with mixed armament.

Sniper Rifles

The only widely used sniper rifle appears to have been the Soviet SVD. It is possible these were Chinese copies (Type 79) or captured from the Iraqis. They appear to have been issued only to the IRGC.

Medium and Heavy Machine Guns

Tripod-mounted rifle-calibre machineguns appear to have been quite rarely used by the Iranians. This is not surprising given the shortage of LMGs in the rifle units. Heavy MGs are relatively common with the Browning M2 .50 Cal and the 12.7mm DshK types being seen.

RPG-7 and Type-69

Shortly before the war, RPGs were supplied in large numbers to the Army, though it is unclear how widely distributed they were before the start of hostilities. During the war, they were distributed to IRGC units too and were ubiquitous throughout the armed forces.

There were three types of RPG in service
- The Soviet model RPG-7
- The Chinese made Type-69
- An Iranian made copy

For the most part the Iranians used the basic PG-7V rocket, though there are a small number of pictures of the improved PG-7VM in service. Iran also made its own ammunition called the Nader, with West German assisiance

M20 Bazooka

The Bazooka was the standard Iranian shoulder fired AT weapon in the 1950s and 1960s until it was replaced by the DM22 rifle grenade. As it was an old weapon and as RPGs were plentiful pictures of it in use are rare.

Rifle Grenades and Grenade Launchers

By far the most common rifle grenade in service was the Iranian-manufactured copy of the German DM22 anti-tank grenade. This was fired from the G3 rifle. The Iranians developed the SA100 rifle fragmentation grenade during the war, though only one picture of it in service is known to the author. A small number of US supplied M79 40mm grenade launchers were used by the IRGC.

Mortars

Excluding the enigmatic 37mm 'Marsh Mortar', the Iranians used three different calibres of mortars in the war: 60mm, 81mm and 120mm. It is possible they used captured Iraqi 82mm mortars but so far, no photographic evidence has been found.

60mm Mortars

The majority of 60mm mortars in use appear to be Yugoslavian copies of the US M2 60mm. Nearly all pictures of mortars with sights fitted show the Yugoslavian sight. Its possible new Yugoslavian sights were fitted to old M2 mortars. Also widely used were 60mm Tampella mortars licence produced by Soltam. Mortars captured from the Iraqis were used, including the Chinese Type 63.

81mm Mortars

The only 81mm mortar in service was the Soltam 81mm.[80] The Iranians did get the 81mm M1 from the USA in the 1950s but these were almost certainly out of service when the war started.

120mm Mortars

The majority of 120mm mortars in service were the Soltam-produced Tampella 120 Krh 62A-H. The 120mm M43 was used by the IRGC. These may have been delivered by the Chinese (making it a Type 55) or captured from the Iraqis.

APPENDIX II
ORGANISATION OF THE IRANIAN ARMY

Introduction

The Iranian Army was reorganised in 1971. That organisation served almost unchanged until the end of the war. However, firstly due to the effects of the revolution and latterly due to casualties, the Army was almost constantly understrength for the duration of the war.

At the start of the war the Iranian armed forces on the ground were mostly Army units supported by a smattering of IRGC militia. As the war progressed IRGC units came to the fore and the Army was relegated to a less important role. Army units were allocated to IRGC formations to provide much needed heavy support.

This section contains order of battle information for the entire Army at the start and in the middle of the war. It also contains detailed organisations of frontline troops. Sources for some of the units, such as the divisional reconnaissance squadrons/battalions is scanty, so must be thought of as provisional.

Order of Battle 1981

In August 1981 the CIA recorded the Iranian Order of Battle[1] as follows.

The strengths in this order of battle were compiled entirely by satellite imagery. Thus, it probably slightly underestimates unit strengths as, for example, if vehicles were in workshops and not parked in the open, they would not be counted.

The original documents counted 'tanks' and it is not clear if Scorpions were included in this total or not. It also did not further define what is counted as an APC and so this may or may not include support versions such as mortar carriers.

The document is geographically based. However, the geographical distribution of units may not reflect the military organisation. One example of this are the tank battalions of the infantry divisions. The tanks were not part of the infantry brigades per TO&E and were actually divisional units. The astute reader will notice that divisional artillery battalions are almost always co-located with a tank or infantry brigade. While it is not unreasonable to assume that the artillery battalion is usually allocated to support that brigade, this does not indicate that the battalion is organisationally part of the brigade.

The strengths given in the table were equipment holdings. However, after the revolution the Iranian Army was not in good shape and the Iranians struggled to get their units into the field. For example, at the time that the source document was published, US analysts estimated that the 1st Brigade of the 16th Armoured

Table 36: Iranian Army Pre-War Order of Battle			
Unit	Location of Barracks[2]	Battalions	Strength
16th Armoured Division	Qazvin		
1st Tank Brigade	Qazvin	2 tank battalions, 1 mechanised battalion	82 tanks, 64 APC
2nd Tank Brigade	Hamadan	2 tank battalions, 1 mechanised battalion	36 tanks, 40 APC
3rd Tank Brigade	Zanjan	2 tank battalions, 2 mechanised battalion	66 tanks, 92 APC
Artillery Battalion	Qazvin	1 artillery battalion	16 M109A1
Artillery Battalion	Hamadan	1 artillery battalion	18 M109A1
Artillery Battalion	Zanjan	1 artillery battalion	10 M109A1
81st Armoured Division	Kermanshah		
1st Tank Brigade	Zahab	2 tank battalions, 1 mechanised battalion	79 tanks, 60 APC
2nd Tank Brigade	Shahabad	2 tank battalions, 3 mechanised battalions	53 tanks, 136 APC
3rd Tank Brigade	Hajjiiabad	2 tank battalions, 1 mechanised battalion	92 tanks, 28 APC
Artillery Battalion	Zahab	1 artillery battalion	17 M109A1
Artillery Battalion	Shahabad	1 artillery battalion	12 M109A1
Artillery Battalion	Hajjiiabad	1 artillery battalion	17 M109A1
Artillery Battalion	Shahabad	1 artillery battalion	10 105mm
88th Armoured Division	Zahedan		
1st Tank Brigade	Zahedan	1 tank battalion, 2 mechanised battalions	29 tanks, 20 APC
Artillery Battalion	Zahedan	1 artillery battalion	10 M109A1

ORGANISATION OF THE IRANIAN ARMY

Table 36: Iranian Army Pre-War Order of Battle			
Unit	Location of Barracks[2]	Battalions	Strength
92nd Armoured Division	Ahvaz		
1st Tank Brigade	Ahvaz	2 tank battalions, 3 mechanised battalions	96 tanks, 53 APC
2nd Tank Brigade	Dezful	2 tank battalions, 1 mechanised battalion	82 tanks, 30 APC
3rd Tank Brigade	Hamidiyeh	2 tank battalions, 2 mechanised battalions	92 tanks, 98 APC
3 Artillery Battalions	Ahvaz	3 artillery battalions	60 M109A1
Artillery Battalion	Dezful	1 artillery battalion	13 M109A1
37th Armoured Brigade (Independent)	Shiraz	3 tank battalions, 1 mechanised battalion	89 Tanks, 71 APCs
1st Infantry Division[3]	Tehran		
Tank Brigade	Tehran	2 tank battalions, 1 mechanised battalion	98 tanks, 26 APC
2 Infantry Brigades	Tehran	3 infantry battalions	trucks and jeeps
Artillery Battalion	Tehran	1 artillery battalion	12 105mm
Artillery Battalion	Tehran	1 artillery battalion	18 130mm M-46
Artillery Battalion	Tehran	1 artillery battalion	17 155mm
Artillery Battery	Tehran	1 artillery battery	4 203mm towed
2nd Infantry Division	Tehran		
Tank Brigade	Tehran	1 tank battalion, 1 mechanised battalion	36 tanks, 44 APC
Artillery Battalion	Tehran	1 artillery battalion	18 M109A1
28th Infantry Division	Sanandaj		
1st Infantry Brigade	Sanandaj	3 infantry battalions	trucks and jeeps
2nd Infantry Brigade	Saqqez	1 infantry battalion	trucks and jeeps
3rd Infantry Brigade	Marand	2 infantry battalions	trucks and jeeps
Tank Battalion	Saqqez	1 tank battalion	27 tanks
Artillery Battalion	Sanandaj	1 artillery battalion	10 105mm
Artillery Battalion	Saqqez	1 artillery battalion	17 105mm
Artillery Battalion	Saqqez	1 artillery battalion	11 155mm
64th Infantry Division	Rezaiyeh		
1st Infantry Brigade	Khaneh	2 infantry battalions, 1 tank company	trucks, jeep & 15 tanks
2nd Infantry Brigade	Shalpur	3 infantry battalions	trucks and jeeps
3rd Infantry Brigade	Mahabad	2 infantry battalions, 1 tank battalion	trucks, jeeps & 24 tanks
2 Tank Battalions	Qushchi	2 tank battalions	43 tanks (combined)
Artillery Battalion	Khaneh	1 artillery battalion	18 105mm
Artillery Battalion	Shalpur	1 artillery battalion	18 105mm
Artillery Battalion	Mahabad	1 artillery battalion	15 155mm
Artillery Battalion	Qushchi	1 artillery battalion	18 105mm
77th Infantry Division	Mashad		
1st Infantry Brigade	Bojnurd	2 infantry battalions	trucks and jeeps
2nd Infantry Brigade	Quchan	3 infantry battalions	trucks and jeeps
3rd Infantry Brigade	Mashad	2 infantry battalions, 1 tank battalion	trucks, jeeps & 49 tanks
1 Tank Battalions	Torbat	1 tank battalion	49 tanks
Artillery Battalion	Bojnurd	1 artillery battalion	15 105mm
Artillery Battalion	Quchan	1 artillery battalion	18 105mm
Artillery Battalion	Mashad	1 artillery battalion	18 105mm
Artillery Battalion	Bojnurd	1 artillery battalion	16 155mm

Table 36: Iranian Army Pre-War Order of Battle			
Unit	Location of Barracks[2]	Battalions	Strength
84th Infantry Brigade (Independent)	Korramabad	3 infantry battalions	trucks, jeep & 48 tanks
Artillery Battalion	Korramabad	1 artillery battalion	14 105mm
23rd Special Forces Brigade	Tehran	5 SF battalions	
55th Airborne Brigade	Tehran	5 infantry battalions	trucks and jeeps
11th Artillery Group	Maraghah		
Artillery Battalion	Maraghah	1 artillery battalion	12 175mm SP
Artillery Battalion	Maraghah	1 artillery battalion	12 203mm SP
Artillery Battalion	Maraghah	1 artillery battalion	12 203mm towed
Artillery Battalion	Maraghah	1 artillery battalion	18 M109A1
Artillery Battery	Maraghah	1 artillery battery	6 130mm M-46
MRL Battalion	Maraghah	1 MRL battalion	12 BM-21
22nd Artillery Group	Shahreza		
Artillery Battalion	Shahreza	1 artillery battalion	12 175mm SP
Artillery Battalion	Shahreza	1 artillery battalion	12 203mm SP
Artillery Battalion	Shahreza	1 artillery battalion	18 130mm M-46
Artillery Battalion	Shahreza	1 artillery battalion	18 130mm M-46
MRL Battalion	Shahreza	1 MRL battalion	12 BM-21
33rd Artillery Group	Tehran		
Artillery Battalion	Tehran	1 artillery battalion	12 175mm SP
Artillery Battalion	Tehran	1 artillery battalion	18 130mm M-46
Artillery Battalion	Tehran	1 artillery battalion	9 130mm M-46
MRL Battalion	Tehran	1 MRL battalion	12 BM-21
44th Artillery Group	Esfahan		
Artillery Battalion	Esfahan	1 artillery battalion	12 203mm SP
Artillery Battalion	Esfahan	1 artillery battalion	14 130mm M-46
MRL Battalion	Esfahan	1 MRL battalion	12 BM-21
55th Artillery Group	Esfahan		
Artillery Battalion	Esfahan	1 artillery battalion	12 M109A1
Artillery Battalion	Esfahan	1 artillery battalion	14 130mm M-46
MRL Battalion	Esfahan	1 MRL battalion	12 BM-21
Artillery Training Regiment[4]	Esfahan		
Artillery Battalion	Esfahan	1 artillery battalion	11 105mm
Artillery Battalion	Esfahan	1 artillery battalion	18 105mm
Artillery Battalion	Esfahan	1 artillery battalion	13 155mm

Division had only 27 tanks and 19 APCs in the field, or about one third of its strength. This is unsurprising as the Army suffered from mass desertion after the revolution, with a figure of 60 percent cited[5]. An Iranian source estimates manpower was at 45 percent of TO&E levels, heavy equipment at 60 percent and light equipment 'less than that'.[6] Although heavy and light are not clearly defined, it appears that heavy refers to tanks and light to APCs. CIA intelligence indicates that Army strength declined from 280,000 men before the revolution to 150,000 shortly after. By 1983 strength had increased to circa 235,000 men.[7]

There was no corps-level command in the Iranian Army. During the war Army units served together with IRGC units in to 'Forces' or 'Bases' which in effect acted as higher-level HQs.

Artillery Order of Battle November 1980

Taken from Iranian sources,[8] unlike the US-derived Order of Battle, it has battalion designations. Divisions are shown in geographical order, north to south. An artillery battalion (-) has two batteries only. The third will have been attached to another unit.

US sources note that units were still mobilising in November. What is given below are all of the artillery units at the front in November 1980. The artillery order of battle looks mostly complete as artillery units had been somewhat less effected by the revolution than the tanks and infantry.[9]

64th Infantry Division
- 304th, 306th & 308th Battalions – 105mm M101
- 385th Battalion – 155mm M114
- 380th AA Battalion – 23mm ZU-23-2
- 331st Battalion[10] attached from 11th Artillery Group – 130mm M-46

28th Infantry Division
- 310th, 391st & 393rd Battalions – 105mm M101
- 358th Battalion – 155mm M114
- 329th Battalion – 23mm ZU-23-2
- 349th Battalion (-) – 130mm M-46
- 1 Battery from an unknown battalion attached from 77th Division – 105mm M101
- Unknown battalion attached from 44th Artillery Group – 105mm M101
- Unknown battery attached from 55th Airborne Brigade – 120mm mortar

81st Armoured Division
- 317th, 340th & 373rd Battalions – M109A1
- 316th AA Battalion (-) – mixed ZSU-57-2 & 23mm ZU-23-2
- Elements attached from the 44th Artillery Group
  - 311th Battalion (-) – M109A1
  - 1 Battery 332nd Battalion – 130mm M-46
  - 1 Battery 374th Battalion – BM-21
  - 339th AA Battalion (-) – 23mm ZU-23-2
  - 1 Battery 351st AA Battalion – 23mm ZU-23-2
- 386th Battalion attached from 11th Artillery Group – M107
- 1 Battery 350th Battalion attached from 21st Infantry Division – M109A1

84th Infantry Brigade
- 303rd Battalion – 105mm M101
- 1 Battery 372nd Battalion attached from 33rd Artillery Group – BM-21
- Elements attached from the 44th Artillery Group
  - 332nd Battalion (-) – 130mm M-46
  - 1 Battery 389th Battalion – 203mm M115
  - 1 Battery 311th Battalion – M109A1
  - 1 Battery 339th AA Battalion & 1 Battery 351st AA Battalion –23mm ZU-23-2
- Elements attached from the 81st Armoured Division
  - 396th Battalion – M109A1
  - 1 Battery 316th AA Battalion (-) – mixed ZSU-57-2 & 23mm ZU-23-2
- Elements attached from the 55th Artillery Group
  - 399th Battalion (-) – 130mm M-46
  - 1 Battery 376th Battalion – BM-21

21st Infantry Division
- 327th Battalion (-) – 105mm M101
- 313th Battalion – 155mm M114
- 350th Battalion (-) – M109A1
- 397th Battalion – 203mm M115
- 347th Battalion – 130mm M-46
- 353rd & 395th AA Battalions – 23mm ZU-23-2
- 305th Artillery Battalion attached from 22nd Artillery Group – 130mm M-46
- Elements attached from 55th Artillery Group
  - 323rd Artillery Battalion – M109A1
  - 376th Battalion (-) – BM-21
  - 1 Battery 399th Battalion – 130mm M-46
  - 1 Battery 361st AA Battalion – ZSU-23-4
  - 1 Battery 334th AA Battalion – ZSU-57-2
- Elements attached from 33rd Artillery Group
  - 342nd Artillery Battalion – 130mm M-46
  - 1 Battery 388th Battalion – M107

92nd Armoured Division
- 312th, 318th & 320th Battalion – M109A1
- 330th Battalion – 2 Batteries with M109A1, 1 Battery with 130mm M-46
- 337th AA Battalion – ZSU-23-4
- 366th AA Battalion – mixed ZSU-57-2 & 23mm ZU-23-2
- Elements attached from 22nd Artillery Group
  - 387th Battalion (-) – M107
  - 1 Battery 369th Battalion – BM-21

16th Armoured Division
- 321st, 382nd & 394th Battalions – M109A1
- 363rd AA Battalion – ZSU-23-4
- 375th Battalion – ZSU-57-2

33rd Artillery Group (supporting both 16th and 92nd Armoured Divisions)
- 343rd Battalion (-) – 130mm M-46
- 388th Battalion (-) – M107
- 1 Battery 372nd Battalion – BM-21

22nd Artillery Group (Abadan-Khorramshahr group)
- 341st & 333rd Battalion (-) – 130mm M-46
- 1 Battery 387th Artillery – M107
- 1 Battery 369th Battalion – BM-21
- 322nd AA Battalion – 23mm ZU-23-3
- 1 Battery 368th Battalion attached from 77th Infantry Division – 105mm M101
- 1 Battery 343rd Battalion attached from the 33rd Artillery Group – 130mm M-46
- 389th Battalion (-) attached from the 44th Artillery Group – 203mm M115
- 1 Battery 362nd Battalion attached from 11th Artillery Group – BM-21
- Marine Artillery Battalion attached from the Marine Brigade – 105mm M101
- 1 Battery 353rd AA Battalion attached from 21st Infantry Division – 23mm ZU-23-2

1986 Order of Battle

The following OOB was published by the Defence Intelligence Agency (DIA) in 1986.[11] It was presumably mostly reliant on satellite imagery, though all the source information is redacted in the publicly available document. A question mark in any column indicates that the unit designation was unknown to the Americans. In the equipment column towed artillery is noted by its calibre. SP artillery is noted by its equipment designation.

- The Iranians were trying to create fourth brigades in some divisions. As can be seen below most were incomplete at the time the list was compiled.

Table 37: Iranian Army Order of Battle in Early 1986			
Division	Brigade	Battalions[12]	Equipment
Infantry Divisions			
21	1	113, 130, 131, 140 Infantry	
21	2	141, 144, 150, 169 Infantry	
21	3	171, 174, 804 Infantry	
21	4	243, 250 Tank 133 Mechanised	Chieftain BMP
21	Artillery	313, 397 Artillery 347 Artillery[13] 397 Artillery[14] 395 AA	155mm 130mm 203mm 23mm
21	Support	545 Medical 546 Repair & Maintenance	
28	1	116, 155, 187 Infantry	
28	2	107, 120, 127 Infantry	
28	3	118, 120, 130 Infantry	
28	Artillery	350 Artillery 310, 391, 393 Artillery 329 AA	155mm 105mm 23mm
28	Armour[15]	225, 229 Tank 613 Tank	M47M T-55
28	Divisional Troops	203 Reconnaissance 417 Combat Engineer 464 Signal 534 Repair & Maintenance 537 Supply & Transport 28 Admin Company	Scorpion
30[16]	1	166, 190 Infantry	
30	2	189, 801, 805 Infantry	
30	3	806 Infantry, 631 Support[17]	
58	1	?	
58	2	?	
58	3	?	
64	1	169, 173, 198 Infantry	
64	2	109, 117, 132 Infantry	
64	3	115, 167, 195 Infantry	
64	4	822 Infantry	
64	Artillery	304, 306, 308 Artillery 385 Artillery 300 AA	105mm 155mm 23mm
64	Armour	245, 275 Tank 614 Tank	M47M (Not given)
64	Divisional Troops	230 Reconnaissance 407 Combat Engineer 103 Infantry (division reserve) 482 Signal 510 Medical 587 Repair & Maintemance 508 Supply & Transport	Scorpion
77	1	136, 163, 178 Infantry	
77	2	122, 129, 153 Infantry	

ORGANISATION OF THE IRANIAN ARMY

Table 37: Iranian Army Order of Battle in Early 1986			
Division	Brigade	Battalions[12]	Equipment
77	3	110, 134, 148 Infantry	
77	4	No units identified as assigned	
77	Artillery	315, 368, 383 Artillery 370 Artillery 398 AA	105mm 155mm 23mm
77	Armour	246, 247, 291[18]	M47M
77	Divisional Troops	214 Reconnaissance 415 Combat Engineer 466 Signal Provisional Training Battalion 569 Medical 590 Repair & Maintenance 591 Supply & Transport 543 Logistics	Scorpion
84	1	122, 139 Infantry	
84	?[19]	182, 802 Infantry	
84	Div Artillery	303 Artillery 354 AA	105mm 23mm
84	Armour	244 Tank	M47M & Chieftain
84	Div Trps	219 Reconnaissance[20] 436 Combat Engineer 593 Support	
Independent Brigades			
-	40 Infantry	807, 809 Infantry 199 Mechanised	(Not given)

-	55 Airborne	101, 126, 135, 146, 158 Airborne
		352 Mortar
		275 Reconnaissance
		444 Combat Engineer Company
		596 Support
		    Admin Company
		    Medical Company
		    Repair & Maintenance Company
		    Supply & Transport Company
		    Aerial Delivery Company
			120mm mortar
			106mm M40[21]

-	37 Armoured	237 Tank 230 Tank 239 Tank 213 Reconnaissance	M47M Chonma Ho & T-62 Chieftain Scorpion
Armoured Divisions			
16	1	105, 176 Mechanised 201 Tank	BTR-50 & BTR-60 Chieftain
16	2	114, 125 Mechanised 251 Tank	BTR-50 & BTR-60 Chieftain
16	3	124 Mechanised 224, 227 Tank	BMP Chieftain
16	Divisional Artillery	302, 321, 355, 394 Artillery 375 AA	M109 ZSU-57-2
16	Armour[22]	220, 254	Chieftain

Table 37: Iranian Army Order of Battle in Early 1986			
Division	Brigade	Battalions[12]	Equipment
16	Divisional Troops	221, 234, 252 Reconnaissance 496 Combat Engineer 475 Signals 501 Medical 502 Repair & Maintenance 503 Supply and Transport	Scorpion
81	1	123, 195 Mechanised 222 Tank	BMP M60A1
81	2	184 Mechanised 285, 290 Tank	BTR-50 & BTR-60 M60A1
81	3	119, 143 Mechanised 211 Tank	BTR-50 & BTR-60 M60A1
81	4	811, 812 Mechanised 610 Tank	(Not given)
81	Divisional Artillery[23]	317 Artillery 340, 373, 396 Artillery 316 AA	M109 & 130mm M109 ZSU-57-2
81	Armour[24]	210 Tank 215, 217 Tank	(Not given) M60A1
81	Divisional Troops	265 Recce 434 Combat Engineer 495 Signals 81 MP Company 504 Medical 505 Repair & Maintenance 506 Supply & Transport	Scorpion
88	1	196, 197 Mechanised 255 Tank	BTR-60 & M113 M60A1
88	2	157 Mechanised	BTR-60 & M113
88	3	(No info given)	
88	Divisional Artillery	300? ? ?	M109 130mm 23mm
88	Divisional Troops	212 Reconnaissance	Scorpion
92	1	121 Mechanised 165 Mechanised 264 Tank	BMP BTR-50 & BTR-60 Chieftain
92	2	105 Mechanised 207, 256 Tank	BTR-60 & BMP Chieftain
92	3	100, 145 Mechanised 231 Tank 293 Tank	BMP M60A1 Chieftain
92	4	(no info given)	
92	Divisional Artillery	312, 316, 320, 330 Artillery 336 Artillery 349 Artillery 366 AA	M109 105mm 130mm ZSU-57-2
92	Armour	232, 261 Tank	Chieftain

ORGANISATION OF THE IRANIAN ARMY

Table 37: Iranian Army Order of Battle in Early 1986			
Division	Brigade	Battalions[12]	Equipment
92	Divisional Troops	151 Fortress 221, 263 Reconnaissance 429 Combat Engineer 479 Signals 507 Medical 508 Repair & Maintenance 509 Supply & Transport	Scorpion
Special Forces Division			
23	1	137, 154, 172 Special Forces	
23	2	101, 172, 192 Special Forces	
23	3	(No info given)	
23	Divisional Troops	'Malek Oshitor'[25] 23 Psy Ops Company 23 Support Company 23 Signal Platoon 23 Guerrilla Ops School	
Artillery Groups			
11	-	331 Artillery 381 Artillery 386 Artillery 390 Artillery 392 Artillery 362 MRL 319, 328 AA	130mm M109 M107 M110 203mm 'Katusha'[26] 23mm
22	-	305, 389 Artillery 333, 341 Artillery 387 Artillery 369 MRL 314, 322, 332 AA	203mm 130mm M107 BM-21 23mm
33	-	342, 343 Artillery 388 Artillery 397 Artillery 372 MRL 325, 353 AA	130mm M107 203mm/M110[27] BM-21 23mm
44	-	301 Artillery 302 Artillery 309 Artillery 311 Artillery 332 Artillery 374 MRL 339, 351 AA 363, 371 AA	105mm & 130mm 105mm 203mm 155mm 130mm BM-21 23mm ZSU-23-4
55[28]	-	323 Artillery 399 Artillery 324 AA 307, 365 AA ?, ? AA 363, 376 MRL	M109 130mm ZSU-57-2 ZSU-23-4 23mm BM-21
Army Engineer & Signals Units			
-	411 Engineer Group	409, 436 Combat Engineer 414 Bridging	
-	404 Signals Group	(No info given)	

351

Table 37: Iranian Army Order of Battle in Early 1986

Division	Brigade	Battalions[12]	Equipment
-	412 Signals Group	(No info given)	
-	Other Battalions	401, 411, 431 Bridging 419 Engineer 402 Electronic Warfare Company	
Training Units			
Infantry Training Centre	-	191 Infantry 301 AT Missile Platoon 314 Mortar	SS.11 ATGM 120mm Tampella
Armour Training Centre	-	597 Mechanised[29]	M113, BTR-50 & BTR-60
Artillery and Missile Training Centre	44 Artillery Group	(No info given)	
Artillery and Missile Training Centre	45 Artillery Group	(No info given)	

Unit Designations[30]

Divisions in the Army had individual numbers, for example the 16th Armoured Division. In order to abbreviate units' names, the Iranians used code letters, thus the 16th Armoured Division had the code L-16. 'L' was the code for a division and 'T' the code for a brigade. Thus T-2 L-16 was the 2nd Brigade of the 16th Armoured Division. To avoid confusion the type of division was appended to the end of the designation, so for example T-1 L-77 Infantry. If the brigade was not the same type as the parent division, then that was explicitly stated, for example: T-4 armoured L-21 Infantry.[31]

The brigades within a division were numbered consecutively with the brigades of the same type as the parent division named first. So, the T-1, T-2, T-3 brigades of the L-21 Infantry would be infantry brigades and the T-4 would be the armoured brigade.

The artillery groups also used a 'T' designation, so T-44 was the 44th Artillery Group.

Battalions usually had individual three-digit numbers. The first digit indicated the type of battalion.

Table 38: Battalion numbering scheme

Number	Type
1xx	Infantry & Mechanised Infantry
2xx	Armoured, tanks and armoured cavalry (reconnaissance)
3xx	Artillery
4xx	Engineers and Signals
5xx	Maintenance and Medical
6xx	Late war tank
8xx	Late war infantry

The ranges 1xx to 5xx are pre-war designations continued into war time. The 8xx range was allocated to infantry battalions formed later in the war, possibly because the Iranians ran out of numbers in the 1xx range. US intelligence identified some tank battalions in the 6xx range.[32] The reason for this is unclear as the Iranians did not raise more than 100 tank battalions during the war.

Special Forces battalions were numbered with a single digit starting from 1.

As there could be confusion as to the exact type of unit the battalion designations usually specified it, for example: 281 Armoured Cavalry; 320 155mm SP Artillery or 429 Armoured Engineers. The artillery battalions' designations always mention their equipment type. Tank battalions' designations sometimes mention the equipment type, though this only seems to be the case if the units had M60 tanks, probably because the large majority of tank battalions in armoured units used the Chieftain. An example is the 231 Tank M60.

Companies were numbered consecutively from 1. Only 'line' companies such as tank and infantry companies were numbered. HQs and support companies were just designated by their name.

So, 2 Company, 100 Mechanised Infantry, T-3, L-92 was the second mechanised infantry company, 100th Mechanised Infantry Battalion of the third brigade of the 92nd Armoured Division.

Organisation

According to Iranian sources units were organised as shown in Table 39.[33]

ORGANISATION OF THE IRANIAN ARMY

Table 39: Organisation of Iranian Army Formations

Unit	Brigades	Number of Battalions	Infantry or Mechanised Infantry Companies	Tank Companies	Reconnaissance Troops	Field Artillery Batteries	AA Batteries	Engineering & Signals Companies
Infantry Division	4	12	36	8	4	17[34]	4	8
Armoured Division	3	9	15	18	5	12	3	6[35]
Infantry Brigade (Independent)	1	2	6	2	-	2	2	4
Airborne Battalion	-	1	4	-	-	1 Artillery & 1 Mortar	-	2
Special Forces Battalion	-	1	3	-	-	-	-	-
Infantry Battalion	-	1	2	-	-	-	-	-
Artillery Group	-	5	-	-	-	20	5	-
Combat Engineer Battalion	-	1	-	-	-	-	-	2

All columns show the overall divisional totals.

Infantry Divisions

The Iranian Army was reorganised in 1971[36] and the basic structure of an infantry division became three infantry brigades each of infantry battalions each; a divisional engineer battalion, a divisional signals battalion, a divisional reconnaissance 'squadron'[37] and the divisional artillery. As can be seen above the Iranians then set about adding armour to the organisation by adding two divisional tank battalions, though it seems some infantry brigades also received M47M tanks. This process was not fully completed before the war started.

The intention appears to have been to raise another infantry brigade to bring the total to four. In October 1980 the 21st Infantry Division had four infantry brigades, two tank battalions (with about 30 tanks each) and six artillery battalions[38]. However, most divisions were still forming their fourth brigade in early 1986.

Armoured Divisions

When the armoured divisions were reorganised in 1971, they consisted of three brigades of two tank and one mechanised battalion or two mechanised and one tank battalion. As can be seen from the order of battle section by the time of the war all tank brigades had two tank battalions and a variable number of mechanised battalions, up to three. The division also had a divisional engineer battalion, a divisional signals battalion, a divisional reconnaissance 'squadron' and the divisional artillery.

37th Armoured Brigade

This was a training unit before the war thus has a mix of Chieftain, M60 and M47s.[39] The 239th Armoured Battalion had M60 and M47M,[40] the 237th Armoured Battalion likely had Chieftains though this is not confirmed. The unit also had the 177th Mechanised Battalion.[41]

Infantry Battalions

Each infantry battalion had three infantry companies and a support company.[42] The support company had 120mm Soltam mortars and TOW missiles on jeeps. Numbers are unclear but the pre-war inventory was sufficient for four to six mortars and six or more TOW.

An infantry company had three infantry platoons and a support platoon. The support platoon had two 106mm M40 recoilless guns on jeeps and three 81mm Soltam mortars.

US sources say that Iranian Army organisation was 'based on' US ROAD organisations.[43] No sources have been seen that indicate how closely the organisation was followed. A US ROAD infantry battalion had

- CHQ – 13 officers and men
- 3 Infantry Platoons – 44 men
- HQ – 3 men
- 3 squads of 10 men
- Weapons squad of 11 men[44]

A squad of 11 men had two 'automatic rifles', two grenade launchers and six rifles. The weapons squad has two Light MGs and two 90mm recoilless rifles. The total staffing for a company was 181 men.

As the Iranians had no 'automatic rifle' or 90mm guns these would have been missing from their organisation. It is likely that the Dragon missile replaced the 90mm in at least some infantry battalions and there were certainly enough missile launchers purchased to be able to do this. The RPG-7 almost certainly replaced the grenade launcher, though there are plenty of pictures showing the DM22 rifle grenade still in use during the war and one source shows 57mm recoilless rifles still in service.[45]

The US ROAD organisation did not have the company-level support platoon, so this was a distinctive Iranian addition.

Tank Battalions[46]

A full strength a tank company in an armoured division was 35 Officers, 309 NCOs[47] and 177 men.

An Iranian tank battalion in an armoured division was a very large organisation consisting of three tank companies, a reconnaissance company and a mortar battery. There were 53 tanks in the battalion which implies the US model of 17 per company with two at BHQ. The reconnaissance company had eight Scorpions and the mortar battery had four M113s with 120mm Soltam mortars. There were also two APCs in the organisation though their allocation is unclear.

The tank in the armoured divisions deployed at the start of the war was usually the Chieftain, though some battalions had the M60.

Although the author does not have a detailed breakdown for a tank battalion in an infantry division, the Iranians had insufficient Scorpions and M113 mortar carriers in service to equip those units with either type of vehicle, thus it is likely they only had tanks. Table 39 above indicates that each battalion had four companies rather than the three found in the battalions in the tank divisions.

Mechanised Infantry Battalions[48]

A full-strength mechanised infantry battalion with two BTR-50 companies and one BTR-60 company had 39 Officers, 300 NCOs and 584 men.

The TO&E for a mechanised battalion had: 803 G3 Rifles, 57 RPG, nine 81mm mortars, 14 wheeled APCs (i.e. BTR-60), 33 tracked APCs, eight jeeps with M40A1 106mm recoilless guns, six TOW mounted on M113 and four M113 120mm mortar carriers. Given the paucity of M113 81mm carriers in the inventory at the start of the war it is unlikely that the 81mm mortars were mounted in M113.

Thus, it seems likely that there were three infantry companies one in BTR-60 and two BTR-50. In addition, there was a support company with four M113 carriers with 120mm mortars, six M113 with TOW and eight jeeps with 106mm recoilless guns. The 81mm mortars were almost certainly company-level weapons with three per company, which reflects the organisation of a non-mechanised infantry company. It is likely each company had a pair of Dragon anti-tank missiles which reflects US practice.

As the first BMPs were not delivered to the Iranian Army until mid-1978,[49] it seems few if any battalions received them before the war. The 133rd Mechanised Battalion which was part of the newly forming 21st Infantry Division had BMPs (as well as BTR60s).[50] The CIA noted two mechanised infantry battalions of the 88th Armoured Division had them by September 1980 (as well as both BTR-50s and -60s)[51] and three battalions of the 81st Armoured Division with BMP (as well as BTR-50s) in November 1980.[52] Thus, there was a concerted effort to re-equip units before committing them to combat.

All the basic M113 APCs were in storage until March 1981 and so these were probably never used as an APC in the war before that time.[53]

Divisional Reconnaissance Squadrons

The organisation of a reconnaissance squadron is unclear from Iranian sources, though it is confirmed that they used M113 carrying TOW.[54] US sources confirm they were equipped with Scorpion.

The most likely answer is that the reconnaissance squadrons were tank-only units, at around company strength (17 tanks) probably with the standard US organisation of three troops of five tanks and two at HQ, with a M113 mortar and M113 TOW platoon attached. There is some evidence to support this as the Shah in 1966 asked the US government for 130 light tanks or armoured cars for seven armoured cavalry squadrons, which is 18.5 per squadron. If we allow for some training vehicles then 17 per squadron does not look unreasonable.[55] A pre-revolution video shows a group of five Scorpions parked in a row, and no APCs.[56]

Artillery and Anti-Aircraft

It is not clear if a division had a higher-level HQ for its artillery or if the battalions assigned were independent. Although the garrison arrangements hint that a battalion was assigned to support each manoeuvre brigade, the battalions were organisationally grouped at divisional level.

Infantry divisions had three M101 105mm towed howitzer battalions and a 155mm M114 towed howitzer battalion. Each division had an AA battalion of four batteries equipped with ZU-23-2 AA guns.

The armoured divisions had three or four battalions of M109A1 155mm self-propelled guns. They had at least one battalion of AA guns with three batteries equipped with ZSU-23-4, ZSU-57-2 or a mix of ZSU-57-2 and towed ZU-23-2 guns.

Non-divisional artillery groups had a mix of guns and always included a BM-21 battalion (see Table 37).

All artillery battalions had three batteries of guns. Guns of 155mm and smaller were deployed in batteries of six guns. 175mm guns, 203mm howitzers and the BM-21 rocket launchers were deployed in batteries of four guns or launchers. The HQ element of a battalion was reported as three APCs. In one case BTR-50s were reported but examination of photographs indicates M577s were more likely.[57] Pictures indicate that M548 tracks were used for ammunition supply.

The exact size of an AA battalion is unclear. Photographic evidence shows the Gaz-69 pickup used as the tractor for the ZU-23-2.[58]

Engineer Battalions

The engineering company of a tank division was organised with three companies of engineers, a plant company, a bridging company and a supply company. Later in the war a boat company was added.[59]

For the most part details of equipment are unavailable, however the bridging unit is known to have had a PMP pontoon bridge set.[60] The plant company consisted of construction equipment such as bulldozers and diggers.

The 414th Engineer Battalion was the only Army-level bridging unit. It had four PMP bridge sets, 10 GSP ferries and 10 BMK boats.[61]

151st Fortress Battalion

This battalion was unique in the pre-war Iranian army. It defended the border with Iraq in a series of strong points. Rather surprisingly it survived the initial border battles, but was likely to have reverted to a more conventional organisation later in the war.

The battalion had 1,300 men and manned 32 outposts and two 'forts' along the Iran–Iraq border.[62] The forts were at Shalamcheh and Koshk and acted as local HQs. Each outpost held 14 men, two 106mm M40A1 recoilless guns and two immobile tanks. At the

HQ at Shalamcheh the battalion had eight Chieftains from the 37th Armoured Brigade.[63]

One source gives the battalion 120 106mm recoilless guns. This leaves about 50 such guns not assigned to the forts, which may have been used as a mobile reserve. Even if the number is erroneous, it would have taken 64 guns to equip all the forts and outposts.

Photographic evidence shows that the majority of tanks were Shermans, M36 tank destroyers or in one case an M24 Chaffee.[64]

Combat Organisation

The Iranian Army had a reasonably flexible combat organisation. During the war battalions frequently formed combat teams. This involved attachment of another company to a battalion either as a swap or as reinforcement. For example, a mechanised infantry company was often attached to a tank battalion to make a combat team. The team maintained the designation of the largest battalion. So, the 201st Combat Team would have been based on the 201st Tank Battalion.

Brigades often received reinforcements and were then referred to as combat taskforces. It was standard practice to attach a divisional slice of the divisional support elements to each brigade: an artillery battalion in direct support, an engineer company and a signals company.

The lowest level at which Army and IRGC units were interchanged was brigade level. At the start of the war IRGC units were usually attached to Army brigades. As the IRGC became more politically and militarily powerful as the war progressed it was usual for Army battalions to be attached to IRGC brigades and divisions.

Iranian artillery followed US doctrine. Each manoeuvre brigade usually had an artillery battalion in direct support. Additional artillery was in general support at divisional level.

Mobilisation and Strength

The Iranian Army was chronically understrength for the entire war. At the start it was hurt by swingeing manpower reductions after the revolution (as described above). As the war progressed the IRGC became politically dominant and nearly all imported weapons were supplied to them.

Due to the manpower issues the Army was very slow to mobilise.[65] US satellites tracked the mobilisation and often recorded small units leaving barracks, sometimes a company at time. Even as late as mid-1981 units were still mobilising.

At the start of the war the 121 Mechanised Infantry Battalion had the following proportions of its manpower and equipment:
- Officers: 38 percent
- NCOs: 31 percent
- Men: 42 percent
- G3 Rifles: 90 percent
- RPG-7: 29 percent
- 81mm mortars: 100 percent
- BTR-60: 43 percent
- BTR-50: 73 percent
- 120mm mortars: 100 percent but only 25 percent of the M113s to carry them
- Jeep with 106mm M40: 50 percent
- M113 with TOW: 83 percent

At the start of the war the position of the 232 Tank Battalion was as follows:
- Officers: 35 percent
- NCOs: 59 percent
- Men: 33 percent
- Chieftain Tank: 61 percent
- Scorpion: 25 percent
- Command APC: 0 percent
- 120mm mortars: 25 percent but there was no M113 available to carry the single mortar

On 21 June 1981 the units participating in Operation Allah Akbar had the personnel strengths as shown in Table 40.[66]

Table 40: Personnel Strengths in Operation Allah Akbar

Unit	Actual Strength	TO&E Strength	% Strength
16 Armoured Division	10,981	14,661	74.9%
21 Infantry Division	14,637	16,989	86.2%
77 Infantry Division	3,536	2,601	135.9%
92 Armoured Division	19,300	15,904	121.4%
55 Airborne Brigade	2,044	3,339	61.2%
84 Infantry Brigade	3,095	3,100	99.8%
55 Artillery Group	1,209	1,985	60.9%

As can be seen some units are overstrength and others considerably understrength.[67] However, the bald numbers hide other weaknesses and the source notes that units were short of officers. The individual return for the 3 Brigade, 92 Armoured Division notes it at 70 percent strength for both men and equipment despite the fact that the 92 Armoured Division is listed as overstrength.[68] Even worse, the second brigade was listed at 40 percent strength.

Bald divisional strength figure includes the whole division. However, the casualties preponderantly fall on the teeth arms; tanks and especially the infantry. As such, the percentage of frontline strength available would have been lower than the table suggests,[69] and, for example, the 261 and 293 Tank Battalions were at 50 percent strength.

APPENDIX III
ORGANISATION OF THE ISLAMIC REVOLUTIONARY GUARDS CORPS (IRGC)[1]

Origins

The IRGC was formed on 5 May 1979 with the mission of preserving the revolution. It was used to consolidate several revolutionary paramilitary forces that supported the ayatollahs. It was a paramilitary rather than properly military organisation. Before the war the constitution of Iran still entrusted the territorial defence of the country to the Army.

Organisation

The organisation of the IRGC evolved throughout the war.[2] The IRGC started life by co-opting the popular militias that had sprung up at the start of the war and after Operation Thamen al-Aimah in September 1981 the IRGC recruited 15 battalions in this way. This increase in recruitment convinced the IRGC leadership a further level of command was needed and so brigade HQs were formed.

For a short period battalions were just added to the existing brigades, until some brigade HQs were commanding as many as 18 battalions. This was obviously unwieldy so after the completion of Operation Muharram in late-1982/early-1983 the IRGC started to form divisions on a standard pattern with three brigades, each of three battalions, which in turn had three companies. This organisation remained until the end of the war.

Manpower is further discussed below but at this point it is worth noting that IRGC battalions were small, with between 250 and 350 men. Table 41 shows the organisation of the 17th Division Ali bin Abi Talib in March 1983.[3]

Table 41: 17th Division Ali bin Abi Talib

Brigade	Battalion Name	Number of Companies	Manpower
1	Holy Spirt	3	395
1	Seved al-Shohada	3	320
1	Iman Reza	3	318
2	Ali bin Ali Talib	3	311
2	Musa bin Jafar	3	310
2	Karbala	3	315
3	Battalion of the Prophet	3	?
3	Vali Asr	?	?
3	Independent Company Jondallah	1	?
3	Independent groups of Iman Hussein	?	?

Table 42 shows the organisation of the 14th Division Iman Hussein in January 1987.[4]

Table 42: 14th Division Iman Hussein

Battalion Name	Manpower
Musa bin Jafar	330
Imam Hussein	250
Abolfazl	240
Imam Reza	220
Amir	210
Maleek	160
Zahra	200
Abolfazl[5]	240

The second Abolfazl battalion is noted as having three companies of 80 men each. The Zahra battalion is noted as having two companies of 90 men each and a cadre company, presumably of 20 men. The division also had a tank unit with 10 tanks. The entire division is noted as having:
- At least four 60mm mortars
- At least two 81mm mortars
- Four 120mm mortars
- Eight 'Katusha' – all probably Type 63 'Mini Katusha'
- At least six 106mm M40 recoilless guns
- An unknown number of Sagger launchers, but there were only 15 missiles available
- One 105mm howitzer
- One 130mm gun
- At least five Toyota trucks
- At least one 'Mio' truck
- 20 boats

Although some small artillery and tank units were raised, IRGC units were very much light infantry forces. The large majority of men were armed with an AK-47 or G3 rifle. RPGs were plentiful with around one in five men so armed. Even light machine guns were in very restricted supply with perhaps one in 20 men so armed.[6]

The 8th Najaf Division had the following heavy weapons for Val Fajr 8 in February 1986. These are the totals for the entire division:
- Two B-10 82mm recoilless guns
- Four M40A1 106mm recoilless guns
- Two 'RPG 11'[7]
- Two DshK 12.7mm heavy machine guns
- One Type 63 107mm rocket launcher
- 10 60mm mortars

- Three 81mm mortars
- Three 82mm mortars
- Three 120mm mortars
- Five Sagger launchers
- Four 'Sahand' launchers[8]
- Three TOW launchers

The division was supported by the Lashkar Artillery Unit which had:
- One 130mm piece
- One 122mm piece
- Two 105mm pieces

The division had a tank unit that was of 'company' strength, thought the equipment is unspecified. There was also a combat engineering 'unit' of unspecified strength'

IRGC Order of Battle

At the end of the war the following divisions were in the IRGC order of battle:
- 7th Valiasr Division
- 8th Najaf Ashraf Division
- 14th Imam Hossein Division
- 17th Ali ibn Abi Taleb Division
- 25th Karbala Division
- 27th Mohammad Rasulullah Division
- 31st Ashura Division
- 33rd Al-Mahdi Division
- 41st Tharallah Division

Unit Strength

In manpower terms IRGC units were much weaker than the equivalent Army units. They tended to be the size, or a little bigger than the next smallest Army unit. So, for example, an IRGC division was the size of a reinforced Army brigade; IRGC brigades were usually the size of a reinforced Army battalion; and the battalions were only a little bigger than an Army company. Only in mid-1982 did IRGC brigades start to approach the size of Army brigades in terms of staffing. However, this size increase was short lived and IRGC brigades returned to their smaller size once the IRGC started to organise divisions.

Given the rather ad hoc nature of the IRGC's mobilisation there appears to be no standard organisation and so unit strength varies between brigades and divisions. In the very early part of the war one of the first forming IRGC battalions, Muslim Bin Aqil, had a strength of 250 men.[9]

For Operation Undeniable Victory in 1982 the IRGC brigades had the following strengths:[10]
- 3rd Iman Hussein Brigade – 9 battalions
- 7th Vali-e-Asr Brigade – 9 battalions
- 8th Najaf Ashraf Brigade – 8 battalions
- 17th Ali ibn Abi Taleb Brigade – 6 battalions
- 25th Karbala Brigade – an unknown number of battalions
- 27th Mohammad Rasulollah Brigade – 9 battalions
- 33rd Al-Mahdi Brigade – 6 battalions
- 35th Iman Sajjad Brigade – 11 battalions
- 41st Tharallah Brigade – 6 battalions
- 46th Fajr Brigade – 5 battalions

The IRGC battalions were noted as having 282 men each.[11] For comparison, an Army battalion had over 900 men, making the IRGC battalions just over the strength of an Army company, and the IRGC brigades equivalent to Army battalion strength.

For Operation Ramadan in 1982, Fatah 'Base' had three IRGC brigades:[12,13]
- 14th Iman Hussein Brigade – 18 battalions
- 17th Ali Banabi Brigade – 13 battalions
- 25th Karbala Brigade – 17 battalions

IRGC Armoured Units

All captured Iraqi equipment was passed on to the IRGC, including tanks. Iran captured substantial amounts of Iraqi equipment during the offensives in 1981 which allowed the formation of several IRGC armoured units.

Armoured Brigades

An IRGC armoured brigade consisted of an HQ company and two armoured battalions. The armoured battalions in theory had 30 vehicles apiece. A battalion could have either tanks or APCs (including BMPs).[14] This gives a total of 60 vehicles, which is a very small brigade. A full-strength Army battalion had about the same number of AFVs.

The brigade HQ did not have any armoured vehicles and was essentially an administrative unit. There were no battalion HQs either, with the unit intended to be broken into penny packets, probably companies, and used to directly support the IRGC's infantry.

The APC units did not have integral infantry and were designed to transport existing IRGC infantry units. Given the dearth of IRGC heavy weapons they were almost certainly also used for fire support. This is supported by the common pictures seen of otherwise unarmed BTR-50s with DshK machine guns welded to the front hull.

Battalions within the brigades were named rather than numbered. For example, the 20th Ramazan IRGC Tank Brigade had two battalions: Meghdad (30 tanks) and Salman (20 tanks).

Divisional Battalions

A number of the IRGC divisions formed an armoured battalion which was 10 tanks strong (actually company strength). The 8th, 14th and 41st divisions are confirmed as having tank units.[15] It is likely the others did too.

IRGC Artillery Units

The IRGC created four non-divisional artillery 'groups' which are sometimes referred to as 'battalions'.[16] In common with other IRGC units they were smaller than their Army counterparts, being battery sized or slightly larger.
- The 61st Muhurram Group was created in 1982
- The 15th Khordad Group was probably created in 1983
- The 63rd Khatam al-Anbiya Group was formed in 1984
- The 64th Al-Hadid Group was formed in 1985

For the most part details of the units' organisations are lacking. At the end of 1986 the 63rd group had two batteries of three guns. Unfortunately, the source does not give the type of guns used but photographic evidence suggests that the IRGC were mainly equipped with 130mm Type 59-I. At the start of 1987 a battery of three BM-11 'Katusha' were added.[17]

IRGC Anti-Tank Battalions

In the middle of the war IRGC infantry divisions formed Anti-Tank Battalions (the 41st Division formed theirs in 1984[18]). Details are lacking but given the usual IRGC policy of overstating their unit sizes these were probably company strength. The units were holding formations for whatever AT weapons the divisions were issued with and which could include almost every type of recoilless gun or ATGM in the Iranian inventory. It is likely all the AT weapons were with the AT battalion.

APPENDIX IV
IRAQI WEAPONS DELIVERIES

Introduction

This appendix addresses arms supplies to Iraq from the 1950s up to the end of the war in 1988. Iraq sourced items from all over the world and in the 50s their main suppliers were the UK and USA.[1] After General Abd Al-Karim Kassem came to power in 1958 the Iraqis turned to the USSR as their main supplier. There was a small pause in Soviet arms supplies between 1963 and 1964 after the coup that overthrew General Kassem and put the Ba'athists in charge. However, once Colonel Abd as-Salem Muhammad Aref was formally in power, deliveries restarted. There was yet another brief pause in supplies between mid-1975 and mid-1976 due to Iraqi ties with President Sadat in Egypt who the Soviets were trying to politically isolate, though supplies resumed when the Soviets realised that the embargo was not having the desired effect and was driving a wedge between Iraq and Moscow. Deliveries from the Soviet Union then ran smoothly until early 1980 when the Iraqis were against the Soviet intervention in Afghanistan and voted for the UN resolution condemning the Soviet actions. Predictably the USSR responded by cutting off arms supplies which were not resumed until 1982. During this time Iraq purchased arms from France and Brazil as well as other smaller nations. The Iraqis also started negotiations with the Chinese, leading to China becoming one of the largest arms suppliers to Iraq in the latter part of the war.

Iraq had a modest arms industry in place at the start of the war, eventually producing small arms, RPGs and artillery ammunition. They progressed to the modification of existing vehicles such as mounting the Chinese 107mm Type 63 on the Soviet MT-LB, although it is not clear how many of these conversions saw action in the war.

There is no publicly available source from Iraq covering their purchases and inventory. The interested scholar is forced to rely on Western and Iranian intelligence information and reports from defence attaches, all cross referenced with the available photographs. Many reports show weapons systems in service with the Iraqi Army for which no other corroborating evidence can be found, such as the French AMX-30 MBT. Similarly, estimates of numbers of weapons delivered can vary wildly.

Inventory as of mid-1980

The following inventory was gathered by the British Defence Attaché in Iraq in the mid-1980.[2] It is supplemented by data from the 1977 report which covers weapons of smaller calibres and some older equipment that was not reported in 1980.[3] Entries followed by a * are from the 1977 report. The attaché's reports lament the lack of access to the Iraqi Army and all the equipment totals are clearly labelled as estimates. Some entries are not supported by any other evidence and these have been shaded in the table.

Table 43: British Defence Attaché's Report, 1977 and 1980	
System	Estimated Quantity
12.7mm AAMG*[4]	300
14.5mm ZPU-4*	218
20mm AA (USSR)*[5]	100
23mm ZU-23-2*	245[6]
30mm Vz.53[7]	316
37mm AA*[8]	300
40mm AA*[9]	160
57mm S-60 (from Hungary)*	180
57mm ZIS-2*	36
60mm Yugoslav mortar	350
75mm mortar[10]	36
76mm ZIS-3*	28
82mm SPG-82*	500
82mm B10*	128
82mm mortar (inc. Yugoslav)[11]	650
85mm D44*	150
87mm 25pdr*	36
90mm M1 AA*	16
94mm 3.7" AA Gun*	78
100mm 'a/tk launcher'[12]	72
100mm BS3	140
100mm KS-19 AA	81
106mm M40A1 (from Spain)	400
107mm B11	200
120mm Mortar[13]	250
122mm A19	40
122mm D-30	60
122mm M-30	130
122mm D-74	180
130mm 'Coastal Gun'	'Some'
130mm M-46	375
145mm 5.5" Gun	18
152mm D1	75
152mm ML-20	50

359

Table 43: British Defence Attaché's Report, 1977 and 1980	
System	Estimated Quantity
180mm S23	8
200mm 'Rocket Launcher' (Spain)	300
203mm Mortar[14]	13
2S1	60
2S3	30
AMX-30	100
ASU-57	6
AT-1 Snapper & AT-3 Sagger Missiles	3,250
BM-13-16	20
BMD-200 MRL	100
BMP-1	600
'BRDM'[15]	150
BRDM-2	650
BRDM-2 plus Sagger	130
BTR-40*	140
BTR-50*	125[16]
BTR-60*	294[17]
BTR-152*	450[18]
Cobra Missiles	700
EE-9 & EE-11	204
FUG-70 (PZSH)	180
FROG Rockets	48
HOT Missiles	500
JSU-152	54
K61 Tracked Amphibian	45
M3 Panhard	220
M24 Chaffee*	30
M113*	112
MILAN Missiles	1,400
OT-62*	496[19]
OT-64	540[20]
PT-76	110
RPG-2*	900
RPG-7*	2,500
SA-2 Launcher	80
SA-2 Missile	270
SA-3 Launcher	78
SA-3 Missile	800
SA-6 Launcher	105
SA-6 Missile	950
SA-7 Launcher	300
SA-7 Missile	3,000
SA-9 Launcher	34
SA-9 Missile	120
Saracen	250

Table 43: British Defence Attaché's Report, 1977 and 1980	
System	Estimated Quantity
SCUD missiles	48
SU-100	120
T-34/85	180[21]
T-54/55	1,000
T-62	1,400
T-72	100+
Tank Transporters	1,200
'TOBAZ'[22]	113
VCR-TH & ERC-90[23]	430
ZSU-23-4	32
ZSU-57-2	64

The 1980 report notes that the 25-pdr, 5.5" Gun and 3.7" AA Gun were no longer in service, though Iranian sources mention the 5.5" gun was in service at the start of the war and US sources show 25-pdrs and divisional artillery in some infantry divisions.

Inventory as of early 1981

The following is taken from US intelligence sources.[24] Again, some entries are not supported by any other evidence and these have been shaded.

Table 44: US Intelligence sources, 1981	
System	Estimated Quantity
23mm ZU-23-2	245
2S1	126
2S3	54
37mm M1939	325
40mm Bofors	160
57mm S-60	800
57mm ZiS-2	36
76mm ZiS-3	40–60
82mm B-10	250
85mm D-44	170
94mm (3.7") Mountain Gun	78
100mm BS-3	126
100mm KS-19	288
105mm M56	36
105mm OTO Melara	40
106mm M40 on Land Rover	300
107mm B-11	200
12.7mm AAMG[25]	300
122mm A-19	40–66
122mm D-30	126
122mm D-74	60
122mm M-30	135
130mm KS-30	160
130mm M-46	400

IRAQI WEAPONS DELIVERIES

Table 44: US Intelligence sources, 1981	
System	Estimated Quantity
14.5mm ZPU-2	500
14.5mm ZPU-4	640
150mm (5.5") Gun	18
152mm D-1	36–50
152mm D-20	75
152mm ML-20	96
180mm S-23	9
203mm B-4	13
Abbot	6
AML M-3	200
AML-60 & 90	145
ASU-57	6
AT-3 Sagger (Manpack)	2,300[26]
BM-13-16	54
BM-21	36
BMD-20	6
BMP-1	620[27]
BRDM-1 & 2[28]	750
BRDM-1 Snapper	20
BRDM-2 Sagger	220
BTR-152	132
BTR-40	140
BTR-50 & OT-62	600
BTR-60 & OT-64	780
Cobra ATGM launcher	160
EE-11	20
EE-9	200

Table 44: US Intelligence sources, 1981	
System	Estimated Quantity
Ferret Mk 2/3	66
FROG-7 (Luna M)	24
FUG-70 (PZSH)	175
Gaz-69 Snapper	108
HOT ATGM[29]	100
JSU-152	52
M113 & M113A1	150
M-60 APC	150
Milan ATGM	100
Praga M53/59	414
PT-76	105
RPG-2	1,000
RPG-7	2,000
Saracen	250
Scud	11–12
SPG-82	500
SU-100	100
T-34/85	50
T-55 & T-55	1,400
T-62	1,300
T-72 Ural	155
ZSU-23-4	125
ZSU-57-2	60

The report also notes 'some' Centurion and M24 tanks in storage.

Inventory as of mid-1986

In 1986 the British defence attaché estimated the strength of the Iraqi Army, as noted in Table 45.[30] It is interesting to note the discrepancies between the 1986 report and the 1980 report.

Table 45: British Defence Attaché's Estimate, 1986				
System	Pre-war	Estimated losses	Deliveries (After June 82)	Inventory mid-1986
AA Gun Towed	3,117	200–250	1,130	Approx. 4,000
AA Gun SP	599	15–20	18	597–602
SA-9	50	0	0	50
Towed artillery 100mm+	1,205	400–450	1,500	2,450–2,500
SP artillery 100mm+	186	0	200	386
MRL 100mm+	96	Unknown	50	Less than 150
'Armoured Vehicles'	1,335	250–300	210	1,245–1,298
PT-76	100	10–15	0	85–90
T-54/55/62	2,700	1,200–1,300	750	2,150–2,250
T-72	155	Unknown	660	Approx. 815
Type 63 APC	0	Unknown	375	375
Type 69[31]	0	Unknown	665	665

MIDDLE EAST@WAR SERIES SPECIAL #1: THE IRAN-IRAQ WAR

Table 46: Weapons Deliveries	
Heading	Explanation
Weapon	Name of the weapon. Towed artillery is prefixed by its calibre
Supplier	The name of the nation that supplied the weapons to Iraq
Number Delivered	The number of weapons delivered. Different sources often disagree or round their figures so this should be treated as a guideline
Start Date	Year deliveries started
End Date	Year deliveries ended
Source	The primary source this was taken from. See the section on sources for the abbreviations used
Notes	General notes. For US MAP deliveries, this has the actual name used in the MAP database, if it was present. They are capitalised as in the original report

Weapon	Supplier	Number Delivered	Start Date	End Date	Source	Notes
14.5mm ZPU-1, 2 & 4	USSR	218[32]	?	?	Pic	Many of each type delivered. Satellites observed ZPU-2 as early as 1972[33]
23mm ZU-23-2	USSR	?	67	?	ECME	
23mm ZU-23-2	USSR	79	?	?	IWMD	Delivered sometime between 1983 and 1986. NiK83 shows 49 guns shipped in 1983
30mm Vz.53	Czechoslovakia	334	68	70	CAE	
37mm M1939	USSR	66	59	59	Bloc	ECME gives 1958 as delivery date
37mm Type 65	China	50	82	82	CIA[34]	Listed as 'probable' 37mm guns. It is possible that the guns may have been Type 55 instead but there are pictures of the Type 65 in use in Iraq during the war
57mm S-60	Hungary	118	?	?	IWMD	Delivered sometime between 1983 and 1986
57mm Type 59	China	683	?	?	IWMD	57mm S60 copy. Delivered sometime between 1983 and 1986. One source shows 128 delivered in 1982[35]
60mm Brandt mortar	France	?	?	?	Pic	Picture was taken in 1974
60mm M57	Yugoslavia	?	?	?	MII	Picture taken in 1981 confirms presence in Iraq
60mm M70 mortar	Yugoslavia	?	?	?	MII	Picture confirms presence in Iraq. This mortar was copied and built by Iraq as the Al Jaleel command mortar. It is unknown if the Iraqi copies served during the war
60mm Type 63	China	?	?	?	MII	No pictures of use during the Iran–Iraq war but give the large influx of Chinese weapons the author considers it highly likely they were used
73mm SPG-9	USSR	?	?	?	Pic	
81mm m/937	Portugal	?	80	83	IIBW	Described as 81mm mortar in the reference document. The m/937 is the Portuguese version of the French 81mm Brandt of Second World War vintage and in the author's, opinion is the most likely mortar exported
82mm B-10	USSR	?	67	?	ECME	
82mm M69A	Yugoslavia	?	?	?	MII	Picture confirms presence in Iraq. The British defence attaché notes it was in service as of 1977[36]
82mm BM-37M mortar	USSR	?	66	?	ECME	Type not specified in ECME but Janes identifies it as an 'M37M'[37]
82mm Type 67 mortar	China	?	75[38]	?	MII	No pictures of use during the Iran–Iraq War but given the large influx of Chinese weapons the author considers it highly likely they were used
82mm Vz.52	Czechoslovakia	100	72	72	CAE	Use in Iran–Iraq War not confirmed

IRAQI WEAPONS DELIVERIES

Weapon	Supplier	Number Delivered	Start Date	End Date	Source	Notes
85mm D-44	USSR	14	60	?	ECME / Bloc	MSH confirms use in the Iran–Iraq War. The British Defence attaché notes 150 in service in 1977[39]
87mm 25-pdr	UK	84	?	?	MILI	MSH confirms use in Iran–Iraq War
100mm BS3	USSR	?	58	?	ECME	
100mm BS3	USSR	100	73	76	RAND	
100mm KS19	USSR	?	60	?	ECME	Probably not used in Iran–Iraq War
100mm MT12	USSR	100	71	75	SIPRI	
100mm Type 71	China	?	?	?	MII	No pictures of use during the Iran–Iraq War but anecdotally it was delivered during the war[40]
105mm M56	Yugoslavia	?	?	?	MSH	Listed as 'Howitzer Yugoslavian (105mm)'. Delivered before April 1981 (MSH), It is possible the 36 '105mm Howitzers' listed as delivered sometime between 1983 and 1986 by IWMD are the M56
105mm M101	USA	?	?	?	MSH	Source designates them, American 105mm, delivery before 1967[41]
105mm Pack Howitzer	Portugal/UK	54+	80	83	IIBW	OTO Melara. Described as 105mm Howitzers in the source document. It is possible, but unlikely, these were 105mm M101. The UK also delivered and unknown number of 105mm Howitzers in the same period[42]
106mm M40	USA	108	63	63	MAP	Original description: 106 MM RECOILLESS RIFLES. Probably Jeep mounted
107mm 4.2" mortar	UK	16	?	?	NILI	Delivered before 1953. MSH notes them as participating in the Iran–Iraq War, though uses the incorrect calibre '4.1'
107mm M30 mortar	USA	93	63	63	MAP	Original description: 107 MM 4.2 INCH MORTARS. Possibly still in service in the Iran–Iraq War, MSH notes the use of a 'American Mortar 120mm'. As there was no US 120mm Mortar available at that time it is likely this is the M30
107mm Type 63	China	100	84	88	SIPRI	MFW shows an unknow number imported between 1981 and 1986. One CI source shows 'over 700' as being exported
114mm 4.5" gun	UK	8	?	?	MILI	Delivered before 1953. Guns may have been used in the Iran–Iraq War but MSH shows not ammo expenditure in April 1981, so if they were used, they were not used for long
120mm AM50	France	?	?	?	MSH	Delivery before April 1981
120mm M1943 mortar	USSR	100	67	70	SIPRI	Delivery confirmed by ECME. MII indicates that the Type 55 Chinese copy was in Iraq too
120mm M75 mortar	Yugoslavia	?	?	?	MII	Not confirmed as in use during the Iran–Iraq War. MSH does not show any in use in April 1981
120mm SL	Spain	?	?	?	MII	MSH notes the use of a 'Spanish 120mm Mortar' in 1981
122mm A19	USSR	40[43]	67	?	ECME	
122mm D-30	Egypt	210	85	89	SIPRI	MFW only shows 36 on order as of the end of 1986 with none delivered before that
122mm D-30	USSR	84	81	86	MFW	SIPRI shows much higher numbers at 572
122mm D-30	Poland	20	81	81	MFW	
122mm M-30	USSR	250	58	62	SIPRI	ECME gives a 1961 delivery date. MSH shows they were used in the Iran–Iraq War
122mm Type 60	China	102	81	81	MFW	These are almost indistinguishable from the Type 59-I even very close up so these might actually be Type 59-I
130mm M-46	USSR	?	67	?	ECME	

Weapon	Supplier	Number Delivered	Start Date	End Date	Source	Notes
130mm M-46	Romania	400	81	81	MFW	Not shown in SIPRI
130mm M-46	USSR	52	81	83	MFW	
130mm M-46	Egypt	96	81	83	SIPRI	MFW does not show any delivered, with 36 being on order at the end of 1986
130mm Type 59-I	China	720	82	88	RAND	MFW shows 254 delivered between 1982 and 1985 with a possible extra 196 from North Korea. The number delivered in 1981 is listed as unknown, it could possibly be 102 that were mistakenly identified as 122mm Type 60. CI says up to 1,000 were delivered
145mm (5.5") Gun	UK	8	53	?	NISI	Use in the Iran–Iraq War confirmed by MSH
152mm 2A36	USSR	180	86	88	SIPRI	
152mm D-20	USSR	50	76	76	SIPRI	
152mm D-20	USSR	16	?	?	IWMD	Delivered between 1983 and 1986. Nik87 indicates 4 were delivered in 1983
152mm ML-20	USSR	20	59	59	Bloc	Described as '152mm Gun Howitzers' in the original document
152mm ML-20	USSR	?	67	?	ECME	
152mm ML-20	USSR	11	83	83	MFW	
152mm Type 66	China	207	81	83	MFW	
152mm Type 83	China	165	85	86	MFW	Shown as 152mm M1984 in source documents[44]
152mm Type 83	China	50	88	89	SIRRI	Probably delivered after the end of the Iran–Iraq War
155mm FH-70	S. Arabia	12	86	86	RAND	
155mm G-5	South Africa	100	85	88	SIPRI	MFW weapons shows an unknown number delivered in 1985 and 54 delivered in 1986. It shows an outstanding order of 46 guns
155mm GCN-45	Austria	200	81	86	SIPRI	MFW agrees with the numbers but give delivery dates as 1984 and 1985
155mm M114	USA	?	?	?	MSH	Described as a 'American (155mm) Howitzer, delivery before 1967'.[45] The Iraqis may have used the Yugoslavian M65 howitzer (which is a clone of the M114) as the source documents notes a 'Yugoslavian Howitzer (155mm)'
155mm M114	Jordan	30	81	81	RAND	Seller unconfirmed, may have been captured from Iran
160mm M160	USSR	20	59	59	Bloc	These may have been M1943 or a mix of both types. MSH notes they were in use during the Iran–Iraq War
160mm M1943	USSR	?	?	?	Pic	20 may have been delivered in 1959
180mm S23	USSR	8[46]	?	?	MSH	Delivered before mid-1980
203mm M115	USA	18	56	56	SIPRI	
240mm M-240	USSR	25	81	81	SIPRI	
2S1	USSR	50	80	80	SIPRI	
2S1	USSR	49	86	86	MFW	Including 7 from Bulgaria. SAD87 notes 42 SPGs were delivered in 1987 but does not distinguish type
2S3	USSR	50	80	80	SIPRI	
2S3	USSR	18	84	84	MFW	SAD87 notes 42 SPGs were delivered in 1987 but does not distinguish type

IRAQI WEAPONS DELIVERIES

Weapon	Supplier	Number Delivered	Start Date	End Date	Source	Notes
2P27 (BRDM Snapper)	USSR	28	61	?	CIA[47]/ECME	Described in the CIA source document as: anti-tank missile vehicles with three missiles per vehicle. The 9P27 is the only AT vehicle to match that description. ECME only describes the vehicles as BRDM and does not mention missiles. No documented use in Iran–Iraq War but given the Iraqis kept the Cobra missiles of the same era it is not impossible
9P133 (BRDM Sagger)	USSR	100	73	82	SIPRI	One document from 1990 shows 108 vehicles in service implying there must have been additional deliveries[48]
Al-Nasirah (RPG7)	Iraq	?	87?	?	Web[49]	RPG-7 clone. 1987 is the earliest in-service date the author has been able to track down but production may have started earlier. CAE indicates production started in the early 1980s. Sometimes spelled Al-Nassira
AML-60 & AML-90	France	158	67	72	SIPRI	Delivery data does not distinguish between the two types. Photographic evidence suggests that the AML-90 was more prevalent on the front lines
AMX-10	France	100	81	82	SIPRI	AMX-10P, AMX-10VLA & AMX-10VFA. Used with 155mm GCT Batteries. IWMB indicates the last deliveries were in 1983. MFW shows only 10 deliveries in 1985 (between 1981 and 1986) though that might be only pure APC versions and not the specialist artillery versions
AMX-GCT	France	85	83	85	SIPRI	MFW shows 76 delivered between 1982 and 1986 with a further 9 on order
AMX Roland	France	13	85	85	SIPRI	RAND notes that 105 were delivered between 1982 and 1988 with 'at least' 30 by 1983. IWMD notes that only one 'Roland 1' was delivered between 1983 and 1986
APR-40 122mm MRL	Romania	34	81	86	MFW	
Armbrust	Germany	?	?	?	Web[50]	'Very small numbers' in use before 1991, so it is possible they were delivered during the Iran–Iraq War
ASTROS-2	Brazil	67	84	88	SIPRI	Also 13 AV-UCF fire control radar. MFW shows an unknown number of systems imported in 1981 and 1982 then 36 imported between 1983 and 1986. KVK shows 200 delivered in 1987
AT-2 (3M11) Swatter missiles	USSR	250	73	76	SIPRI	Used on Mi-25D gunships
AT-3 (9M14M) Sagger missiles	USSR	20,000	73	89	SIPRI	MFW does not show any transfers between 1981 and 1986. One source shows 144 launchers in service in 1990 which probably holds true for 1988 too[51]
AT-4 (9M111) Spigot missiles	USSR	3,000	86	89	SIPRI	Used on BMP-2, given the reservations about BMP-2 delivery dates the dates of missile delivery are also suspect. WMW does not show any being delivered to Iraq in 1986
AT-5 (9M113) Spandrel missiles	USSR	?	86	86	MFW	Unknown number delivered, probably for BMP-2
BM-13-16	USSR	20[52]	61	?	ECME	Use in Iran–Iraq War confirmed by MSH
BM-14-16	USSR	?	?	?	Pic	Use during the Iran–Iraq War unlikely
BM-21 Grad	USSR	100	79	80	SIPRI	
BM-21 Grad	USSR	90	81	86	MFW	SIPRI shows 560 delivered, but given the relative preponderance of pictures between the BM-21 and APR-40 the SIPRI figure is almost certainly in error
BM-21 Grad	Egypt	80	86	?	KVK	
BMD-1	USSR	25	81	81	SIPRI	

Weapon	Supplier	Number Delivered	Start Date	End Date	Source	Notes
BMD-1	USSR	118	83	85	MFW	Most delivered in 1983
BMD-1	Czechoslovakia	48	85	85	MFW	
BMP-1	USSR	200	74	75	SIPRI	
BMP-1	USSR	452	82	86	MFW	
BMP-1	Czechoslovakia	289	83	86	MFW	
BMP-2	USSR	200	87	89	SIPRI	SAD87 notes 91 BMP delivered in 1987 but does not indicate if they were BMP-1 or 2. It is unclear if BMP-2s were deployed during the war. The British defence attaché notes their appearance in 1989
BRDM-1	USSR	?	?	?	Pic	
BRDM-2	USSR	250	67	73	SIPRI	Photographic evidence indicates that some of the BRDM supplied were Rkh chemical reconnaissance versions
BRDM-2	USSR	326	82	86	MFW	
BRDM-2	USSR	62	87	87	SAD87	
BTR-50	USSR	250	69	73	SIPRI	Included some BTR-50PU command versions
BTR-50 with 30mm M53	Iraq	?	?	?	Pic	Numerous conversions made. Possibly used during the Iran–Iraq War
BTR-60PB	USSR	250	69	73	SIPRI	Iraq also brough BTR-60PU-12 command versions probably as AA and SAM command vehicles. It is unclear if they are included in the 250 total or not
BTR-60PB	USSR	192	81	86	MFW	Includes some BTR-60PU-12 command versions. IWMD notes that between 1983 and 1986, 97 BTR-60PB were delivered and 8 BTR-60PU
BTR-60PB	USSR	63	87	87	SAD87	Just listed as BTR, BTR-60 is the most likely type
BTR-152	USSR	200	60	64	SIPRI	No evidence these were used during the war. Bloc indicates that 20 'APCs' were delivered in early 1959. MASS shows 290 delivered sometime between 1955 and 1961. ECME shows 1961 as the delivery date
Centurion Mk5/1	UK	55	56	57	SIPRI	Given as a gift to Jordan after the 1973 war, not used in the Iran–Iraq War
Chieftain Mk 5	Iran	114	82	?	*53	114 Chieftains were captured by Iraq in 1980 and by mid-1982 agreement had been made with the UK government to refurbish them. However, one source indicates the spares were never supplied.[54] 29 Chieftain ARVs were sold to Iraq from the UK which were then cannibalised for spares to refurbish captured Chieftains in advance of the UK refurbishment deal[55]
Chieftain Mk 5	Jordan	50	84	84	RAND	Delivery is noted as unconfirmed
Cymbeline radar	UK	20	76	77	Web[56]	A further contract was signed in 1988 but those radar were delivered after the war; operators being trained in 1990[57]
EE-9	Brazil	400	79	85	SIPRI	Mk IV version. MFW shows 576 delivered in 1981–1985
EE-11 M3	Brazil	100	80	80	SIPRI	
EE-11 M3	Brazil	104	81	84	MFW	
Ferret	UK	25	53	55	SIPRI	No evidence these were used during the war
FROG-7 (Luna M) TEL	USSR	24	78	79	SIPRI	Obviously, some missiles must have been delivered at the same time but these are not enumerated
FROG-7 (Luna M) rockets	Egypt	40	82	82	MFW	

IRAQI WEAPONS DELIVERIES

Weapon	Supplier	Number Delivered	Start Date	End Date	Source	Notes
FROG-7 (Luna M) rockets	USSR	15	86	86	MFW	
HN-5A missiles	China	1,000	86	87	SIPRI	
HOT missiles	France	3,650	77	82	SIPRI	MFW shows no deliveries in 1981 or 1982
HOT missiles	France	410	83	83	MFW	
ISU-152	USSR	54[58]	?	?	Pic	Pictorial evidence shows a destroyed machine in 2003 or later. No evidence is available as to whether they took part in the war
JVBT-55KS	Czechoslovakia	30	73	74	CAE	ARV
JVBT-55KS	Czechoslovakia	44	81	82	CAE	ARV
K-61 (GPT)	USSR	?	61	?	ECME	
Land Rover + 106mm M40A1 RCL	Spain	?	80	83	IIBW	Pictures show them mounted on Santana Land Rovers
Long Track radar (P40)	USSR	10	80	84	SIPRI	
M3 VTT	France	200	70	84	SIPRI	
M24 Chafee	USA	40	56	58	SIPRI	No evidence these were still in service during the war
M24 Chafee	USA	36	63	63	MAP	
M-53/59	Yugoslavia	?	?	?	Pic	At some point in time the twin 30mm guns were removed from the wheeled Praga chassis and mounted on BTR-50 or OT-62 chassis
M-60	Yugoslavia	?	?	?	Pic	
M109A1	Jordan	100	81	83	RAND	Seller is noted as unconfirmed. Some may have been captured from Iran
M113	USA	150	63[59]	?	Web[60]	May well have also included M577. Use in Iran–Iraq War uncertain, though there is a well know picture of an M577 in Iraqi service
MILAN missiles	France	4,450	75	79	SIPRI	The British Defence Attaché notes the first Milan were brough in 1976 and the first 20 were in the inventory as of 1977[61]
MILAN missiles	France	2,242	81	86	MFW	A document from 1990 shows 108 Milan launchers in use at that time which should approximate to the number available at the end of the Iran–Iraq War[62]
MTU-20	USSR	?	?	?	Pic	
MT-55KS AVLB	Czechoslovakia	8	70	70	CAE	
MT-LB	USSR	750	83	90	SIPRI	IWMD notes 196 delivered from Bulgaria and 59 from the USSR between 1983 and 1986
MT-LB + ZU-23-2	Iraq	?	?	?	Pic	Numerous conversions, served during the war.
MT-LB + Type 63 107mm	Iraq	?	?	?	Pic	Numerous conversions, served during the war
MT-LB SNAR 10	USSR	?	?	?	Pic	Ground Surveillance Radar. Not confirmed as serving during the war
MT-LBu (ARCV-2)	USSR	15	?	?	IWMD	Delivered sometime between 1983 and 1986. Mix of sub-types unknown
OT-62	Czechoslovakia	615	69	72	CAE	36 were OT-62R3MT command versions. Satellite intelligence shows some equipped with recoilless guns in the 1970s, presumably 82mm T21.[63] The author has seen no pictures of the recoilless armed version in service in the Iran–Iraq War

Weapon	Supplier	Number Delivered	Start Date	End Date	Source	Notes
OT-62A	Czechoslovakia	70	71	71	CAE	Ambulance version
OT-64C	Czechoslovakia	173	69	74	CAE	Includes 13 OT-64/R2 command versions and 18 armed with 23mm NS-23 aircraft cannons
P-27	Czechoslovakia	100	72	72	CAE	Czech version of the RPG-2. Use in the Iran–Iraq war not known but likely give the limited numbers of AT weapons available
PT-76	USSR	45	68	70	SIPRI	
PT-76	Egypt	30	82	83	MFW	
PT-76 + 57mm S60	USSR	2+	?	?	Pic	At least two converted. Not confirmed as serving during the war
PSZH (FUG)	Hungary	200	81	81	SIPRI	
RASIT	France	42	83	?	KVK	Ground Surveillance Radar (GSR)
Resistance 40	Iran	4+	?	?	Pic	80mm MRL on a Gaz-66 chassis. At least four were at Camp Taji when it was taken by the Americans in 2003. One was seen at the Baghdad Arms Fair in 1989, so it is possible they were deployed during the Iran–Iraq War
Roland missile	France	2,260	81	90	SIPRI	KVK shows 300 delivered in 1983
Roland Shelter (MAN)	France	100	82	85	SIPRI	IWMD notes that only 22 were delivered between 1983 and 1986 KVK indicates 113 were delivered starting in 1981
RPG-2	USSR	900[64]	60	?	ECME	Although the author has not seen pictures of use in Iran–Iraq War, one US source indicates the rockets were in use[65]
RPG-7	USSR	2,500[66]	67	?	ECME	
RPG-7	Switzerland	5,000[67]	80	83	IIBW	
SA-2 Site	USSR	?	?	?	[68]	First satellite image of SA-2 launch site was taken in 1974. No missiles were deployed at that point
SA-2 launcher	USSR	42	?	?	IWMD	Delivered sometime between 1983 and 1986
SA-2 missile	USSR	76	?	?	IWMD	Delivered sometime between 1983 and 1986
SA-3 (S-125M) launcher	USSR	30	72	73	SIPRI	CIA reported first site under construction in 1973[69]
SA-3 (S-125M) launcher	USSR	17	?	?	IWMD	17 launchers and 6 missile transport trucks delivered between 1983 and 1986
SA-3 (S-125M) launcher	USSR	8	87	87	SAD87	
SA-3 (V-601) missiles	USSR	1,100	72	73	SIPRI	
SA-6 (2K12) launcher	USSR	20–25	77	85	SIPRI	KVK shows 52 delivered starting in 1979 IWMD notes 6 delivered between 1983 and 1986
SA-6 (2K12) launcher	USSR	1	87	87	SAD87	KVK shows 40 systems delivered in 1987
SA-6 (9M9) missile	USSR	1,200	77	86	SIPRI	KVK shows 520 delivered starting in 1979 IWMD notes 240 delivered between 1983 and 1986
SA-8 (9K33) launcher	USSR	50–80	82	85	SIPRI	KVK shows 39 delivered starting in 1982. IWMD notes 12 delivered between 1983 and 1986, plus 6 resupply vehicles
SA-8 (9K33) launcher	USSR	1	87	87	SAD87	
SA-8 (9M33) missiles	USSR	1,500	82	85	SIPRI	KVK shows 432 delivered starting in 1982
SA-9 (Strela 1) launcher	USSR	50	?	?	[70]	Delivery before the start of the war. Presumably a number of missiles were delivered at the same time

IRAQI WEAPONS DELIVERIES

Weapon	Supplier	Number Delivered	Start Date	End Date	Source	Notes
SA-9 (Strela 1) launcher	USSR	>20	82	?	KVK	
SA-9 (Strela 1) missiles	USSR	2,500	82	85	SIPRI	KVK gives a total of 240 missiles
SA-13 (Strela 10) launcher	USSR	30	85	85	SIPRI	IWMD notes 12 delivered between 1983 and 1986
SA-13 (9M331) missiles	USSR	1,500	85	86	SIPRI	
SA-14 (Strela 3)	USSR	500	87	88	SIPRI	Unclear if this is missiles or launchers. No pictures available to the author but in 2003 one was fired at an Airbus in Iraq. The SA-14 used was likely from Saddam's weapons stockpile[71]
SCUD B TEL (9P117)	USSR	12	75	75	SIPRI	KVK shows 9 delivered
SCUD B (R-17) missile	USSR	40	82	84	SIPRI	MFW shows 45 delivered between 1984 and 1986. KVK shows 350 delivered in 1983
SCUD B (R-17) missile						
SPR-1	USSR	?	?	?	Pic	Proximity fuse jammer
SU-100	USSR	250	59	63	SIPRI	MASS shows 120 delivered between 55 and 61. MSN confirms use in the Iran–Iraq War
T-34/85	USSR	125	59	65	SIPRI	MASS shows 260 between 55 and 61. ECME shows 1960 as first delivery date. These tanks started the war in storage but were later taken out to be used as artillery[72]
T-54	USSR	300	59	68	SIPRI	Bloc indicates 20 were delivered by early 1959
T-55	USSR	?	66	?	ECME	Including 'command version'. KMT-5 and PT-55 mine clearing gear was delivered at the same time as well as bulldozer attachments
T-55	USSR	700	74	75	SIPRI	
T-55	Many	1,049	81	86	MFW	Sources differ on the origin of these tanks. MFW gives the following numbers but SIPRI also indicates deliveries from DDR USSR, 66, 1982–1983 North Yemen, 43, 1981 Egypt, 200, 1982–1984 Romania, 50, 1982 Poland, 690, 1981–1985
T-55 with 57mm S-60	Iraq	3+	?	?	Pic	This Iraqi conversion was certainly completed during the war as there is a photo of one captured by the Iranians. Pictures of at least three vehicles exist
T-55 with 160mm mortar	Iraq	10+	?	?	Pic	10 captured at Camp Taji in 2003. One exhibited in Bagdad in mid-1989.[73] It possible but not confirmed they were used in the Iran–Iraq War
T-62	USSR	2,850	74	89	SIPRI	MFW shows only 121 tanks delivered between 1981 and 1986 (actually all delivered 1981–1982)
T-72 Ural	USSR	50	79	79	SIPRI	SIPRI identifies these as B models, however the T-72B was not in production in 1979. Photographic evidence indicates these were the Ural model
T-72M	USSR	925	81	87	MFW / SAD87	260 tanks delivered in 86 were T-72M1. SAD87 indicates 287 were delivered in 1987. SIPRI shows deliveries continuing to 1990, so there may have been deliveries in 1988
T-72M1	Czechoslovakia	90	86	87	CAE	
TOW missile	Iran	?	?	?	Web[74]	Use of 'small units' of captured weapons

Weapon	Supplier	Number Delivered	Start Date	End Date	Source	Notes
Type 54-I	China	11	84	86	MFW	Probably converted to 120mm mortar carriers
Type 69-II	China	1,500	83	87	SIPRI	MFW notes 2,000 delivered between 1981 and 1985. CI shows 2,500 to 2,860 delivered including Type 69-IIA command tanks. A British report shows 665 delivered between mid-1982 and mid-1986[75]
Type 653 ARV	China	25	86	87	SIPRI	CI shows around 280 vehicles delivered
UAZ-469 + Cobra ATGM	Iraq	25+[76]	?	?	Pic	Several made and used from the start of the Iran–Iraq War. One source indicates that the missiles were brought in the mid-1960s.[77] British Defence Attaché's Report 1980: FCO 8/3715 indicates 700 missiles were in service in 1980
UR-67 Mineclearer	USSR	?	?	?	Pic	It is possible that these were the four BTR-50 delivered in 1986 (MFW)
YW531C (Type 63C)	China	1,077	83	86	MFW	SPRI shows deliveries continuing until 1988 Numbers delivered depend on source SIPRI and some CI sources show 650 Other CI sources show 450 The British show 375[78] MFW shows the highest number of deliveries but this is close to what CI sources show for combined 531 and 701 deliveries so it may be a combined total Some YW-351 82mm mortar carriers were delivered which may or may not be included in these totals. CI shows them being delivered during the war
YW-701	China	144	?	?	IWMD	Delivered sometime between 1983 and 1986. CI shows they were ordered in 1981 so delivery is likely to have started in 1983. CI shows 600 YW-701 were ordered
VCR-TH	France	100	79	81	SIPRI	
ZSU-23-4	USSR	200	73	76	SIPRI	
ZSU-23-4	USSR	18	?	?	[79]	Delivered sometime between mid-1982 and mid-1986
ZSU-57-2	USSR	100	71	73	SIPRI	

Soft Transport

Delivery data for trucks is fragmentary at best. The CIA has a list of transport delivered up to 1970[80], after that the historian is reliant on photographs. Trucks known to be in service are listed below, though this is probably not a comprehensive list.

CIA List to 1970
- Gaz-63
- Zil-151
- KrAZ-219
- Gaz-69
- KrAZ-214
- MAZ-502V
- ZiL-485 Amphibian
- Csepel D-346
- Csepel D-344
- SPK-5 recovery vehicle

US Vehicles Supplied Under MAP
Unfortunately, the source database does not give the exact types. The number in brackets is the number supplied. It is not known how many, if any, survived in service until the Iran–Iraq War.

- 5 Ton Wrecker (24)
- M939[81] 5 Ton Cargo (24)
- M35[82] 2½ Ton Cargo (1,146)
- ¾ Ton Cargo (572)
- ¼ Ton Cargo (i.e. Jeep) (730)

Vehicles Identified from Photographs
- IFA W50 (civilian version)
- Unimog U1300
- Gaz-69
- UAZ-469
- Ural-375
- ZiL-157
- ATS-59
- ATS-59G
- AT-T
- PTS-M amphibian
- GSP Ferry
- KrAZ with PMP Bridge

Vehicles from Other Sources
- Land Rover 3/4t[83]
- SBAT111S[84]
- TATRA 138 AV-8 Crane[85]
- TATRA 148[86]
- TATRA 805[87]
- TATRA 813 tank transporter[88]

Small Arms

Small arms deliveries are not well documented. However, the CIA has a list of deliveries before 1970 (ECME) and The US Army has an intelligence document from 2004 showing the small arms in Iraq.[89] Between the two we can see the armament of the Iraqi infantry has remained consistent over a period of 30 years which gives us a clear indication of the weapons in use during the Iran–Iraq War.

The standard assault rifle was the AKM (or one of its foreign derivatives) or the AK-47. Folding stock versions were used as well as solid stock versions. The Iraqis locally-produced a version of the Yugoslavian Zastava M70, called the Tabuk. Production started in 1980.[90]

The light machine guns used were the Soviet RPK and RPD, or their foreign copies. From 1980 Iraq produced the Al Quds MG which was a copy of the Yugoslav Zastava M72.[91] The standard medium machine guns were the PKM and Type 67-2.[92]

The infantry made use of the Yugoslav M60 rifle grenade which was fired from the Yugoslav Zastava M70 or the Iraqi Tabuk. There was an Iraqi produced version of the grenade designated 'VAZ'[93] which probably entered production in 1980 with the Tabuk rifle. HE, HEAT and smoke grenades were issued.

There were some SVD sniper rifles, or foreign copies, in service. More common was the Tabuk sniper rifle based on the Zastava M76.[94]

Grenades in use were the Soviet F1, RG-42, RGD-5, RGO-78 and the Chinese Type 86P. Some RKG-3 anti-tank grenades were still in the inventory.

Notes on Sources used in this Appendix

Researching the Iran–Iraq War can be a daunting task with many sources being of variable quality. Those primarily consulted for this appendix are listed below, with commentary where appropriate:

SIPRI arms transfer data base. The most easily accessible arms transfer database but it has some errors and is not fully comprehensive.

Rachel Schmidt, Global Arms Exports to Iraq, 1960–1990 (RAND, 1990). Ostensibly the data in this document is compiled from the SIPRI database. However, there are entries in the RAND document that do not appear in the current online version of the SIPRI database.

CIA, *Handbook of Major Foreign Weapons Systems Exported to the Third World, Volume II, Ground Forces Equipment* (MFW). Based on intelligence information.

CIA, *Iraq: Major Weapon Deliveries and their Impact of Force Capabilities* (IMWD), February 1987. This report covers January 1983 to 31 December 1986. Numbers tend to be lower than those indicated by SIPRI. The CIA data probably came from satellite pictures so it seems reasonable that these counts could be affected by periods of poor weather. However, many of the numbers are very much lower than what is reported in SIPRI.

CIA, *Exports of Communist Military Equipment to The Less Developed Countries* (ECME): A Catalogue of Prices (1970). Useful as it includes 'minor' items such as small arms and transport. Unfortunately, it does not give numbers, but confirms a given piece of equipment was delivered starting from a given date.

Mortars in Iraq (MII). Part of a document produced for US forces in 2004. There is no guarantee that the mortars were in service during the Iran–Iraq War, so unless otherwise stated all information must be treated as unconfirmed.

Iran–Iraq: Buying Weapons for War (IIBW): CIA. Useful as it has details of deliveries from 'minor' European nations.

Martin Smisek, *Czechoslovak Arms Exports* (CAE). A preview of a very detailed and well researched account of Czech exports to Iraq with information exclusively sources from Czech archives. This is assuredly much more accurate than US intelligence of SIPRI and has been used in preference to other sources. This research is currently being published by Helion and Company in the Middle East @War series as a multi-part mini-series.

Williamson Murray and Kevin M. Woods, *The Iran–Iraq War: A Military and Strategic History* (MSH). Table 5.1 was apparently taken from an original Iraqi document and deals with ammunition expenditure for the Iraqi Army, so giving an insight into the weapons in the inventory.

CIA, *National Intelligence Survey Iraq* (NISI), Section 81 Ground Forces (1953). Useful as it contains a listing of weapons in service at that time, some of which were still serving during the Iran–Iraq War.

Reza Jahanfar and Fahimeh Karami. *Khaterat Va Khatarat* (KVK). An Iranian book on air defence that presumably takes its data from Iranian intelligence sources.

Several Chinese internet (CI) sources were consulted. These were all secondary sources so their provenance cannot be confirmed. They are reasonably consistent but not do not always agree on the numbers of weapons delivered:

- *In the 1980s, My Country Exported 3,000 tanks to* Iraq, and in the Gulf War lost them all at once, https://www.163.com/dy/article/G2DHTFBH0515DICI.html;
- How many weapons did China export during the Iran–Iraq War? Veteran workers: work overtime day and night in the factory, https://www.sohu.com/a/285972523_100185094;
- China's Diplomatic Wisdom in Uniting Small Countries, Time is Silent, https://zhuanlan.zhihu.com/p/165451878;
- In those years, the complete set of weapons and equipment imported by Iran and Iran from my country, https://new.qq.com/omn/20200922/20200922A0DB4900.html
- Inventory of the Six Major Nations who bought Chinese weapons in the 1980s, https://zhuanlan.zhihu.com/p/164874072

APPENDIX V
IRAQI ORGANISATION

ORDER OF BATTLE IN 1980

The Iraqi Army started the war with 12 divisions plus a large number of independent brigades and battalions. There were five infantry divisions, sometimes called mountain divisions as they operated in the mountainous north of the county, five armoured divisions and two mechanised divisions.

The Iraqi order of battle presented here is an amalgamation of many sources nearly all of which are based on foreign intelligence.[1] Unfortunately, sources do not always agree and being intelligence-based they probably contain errors. Major discrepancies are dealt with in the endnotes. Where a unit is without a number the number was not given in the source documents. Unfortunately, there are no details of the corps-level, non-divisional, supporting units.

At lower levels Iraqi organisation was fairly inflexible. However, divisional composition was flexible. Divisions swapped subordinate units to other divisions and often took command of one or more of the numerous independent brigades and battalions. This flexibility may well account for the discrepancies between US and Iranian intelligence estimates for the Iraqi order of battle.

All Iraqi divisions had a name and a number. The name of the division appears in brackets after the number.

All battalions in infantry brigades are numbered 1st through 3rd, they are omitted here for the sake of brevity.

1st Corps

- **2nd (Khalid) Infantry Division**
  - 2nd, 4th & 36th Infantry Brigades
  - 3rd & 4th Independent Infantry Battalions[2]
  - 8th Tank Battalion[3]
  - Divisional Artillery
    ◊ 4th Field Artillery Battalion (122mm[4])
    ◊ 47th Field Artillery Battalion (25-pounder)
    ◊ 37th & 53rd Field Artillery Battalions[5]
    ◊ 27th AA Battalion (30mm)
    ◊ 28th AA Battalion[6]
    ◊ 5th, 13th & 18th Mortar Batteries
  - 2nd Commando Battalion (12 platoons)[7]
  - 2nd (Ibn As) Reconnaissance Battalion (BRDM[8])
  - 2nd Engineer Battalion
  - 13th, 16th and one Unknown Field Engineer Company
  - 2nd Signals Battalion
  - 2nd Chemical Company

- **4th (Qaqaa) Infantry Division**
  - 5th, 18th & 29th Infantry Brigades[9]
  - 1st & 2nd Independent Infantry Battalions[10]
  - 4th Tank Battalion
  - Divisional Artillery
    ◊ 2nd & 9th Mountain Artillery Battalions (25pdr)
    ◊ 22nd Mountain Artillery Battalion[11]
    ◊ 18th and 98th Field Artillery Battalions (attached)
    ◊ 24th & 45th AA Battalions[12] (37mm)
    ◊ 40th & 62nd AA Battalions
    ◊ 6th, 8th & 12th Mortar Batteries (4.2" mortar[13])
  - 4th Commando Battalion (14 platoons)
  - 4th (Al Haritha) Reconnaissance Battalion
  - 174th AT Battalion[14] (attached)
  - 4th Engineer Battalion
    ◊ 1st & 4th Field Engineer Companies
    ◊ 26th Field Workshop
  - 4th Signals Battalion
  - 4th Chemical Company

- **7th (Mansour) Infantry Division**
  - 19th, 38th & 39th Infantry Brigades[15]
  - 9th Tank Battalion[16]
  - Divisional Artillery
    ◊ 10th, 64th, 80th, 82nd, 94th, 57th & 126th Artillery Battalions[17]
    ◊ 165th AA Battalion[18]
    ◊ 14th. 19th & 22nd Mortar Batteries
    ◊ 3rd AT Battalion
  - 7th Commando Battalion (12 platoons)
  - 7th (Ibn Waqas) Reconnaissance Battalion
  - 7th Flamethrower Company
  - 7th Engineer Battalion
    ◊ 8th, 25th, 26th and 27th Field Engineer Companies
  - 7th Signals Battalion
  - 7th Chemical Company

- **8th (Muthanna) Infantry Division**
  - 3rd, 22nd & 23rd Infantry Brigades[19]
  - 2nd Tank Battalion[20]
  - Divisional Artillery
    ◊ 6th, 16th, 48th, 66th and 83rd Artillery Battalions[21]
    ◊ 4th, 15th & 44th Mortar Batteries
    ◊ 5th AT Battalion
  - 8th Commando Battalion (12 platoons)
  - 8th (Abnjrah) Reconnaissance Battalion[22]
  - 16th Defence Battalion
  - 8th Engineer Battalion
    ◊ 14th, 23rd and 24th Field Engineer Companies.
  - 8th Signals Battalion
  - 8th Chemical Company

372

IRAQI ORGANISATION

- **11th (Miqdad) Infantry Division**
  - 44th, 45th & 48th Infantry Brigades[23]
  - 12th Tank Battalion[24]
  - Al Qaqa Tank Battalion
  - Divisional Artillery
    ◊ 6th, 65th and 120th Artillery Battalions[25]
  - 11th Commando Battalion (6 platoons)
  - 11th (Hatin) Reconnaissance Battalion
  - 11th Engineer Battalion
  - 11th Signals Battalion

- **12th (Nauman) Armoured Division**[26]
  - 37th Armoured Brigade
    ◊ 12th, 15th and 19th Tank Battalions
    ◊ 11th Mechanised Battalion
  - 50th Armoured Brigade
    ◊ 23rd, 24th and 25th Tank Battalions
    ◊ 12th Mechanised Battalion
  - 46th Mechanised Infantry Brigade
    ◊ 1st to 3rd Mechanised Battalions
    ◊ 20th Tank Battalion
  - Divisional Artillery
    ◊ 103rd, 104th and 108th Field Artillery Battalions
    ◊ AA Battalion
  - Commando Battalion (9 platoons)
  - Osama Reconnaissance Battalion
  - 12th Engineer Battalion
  - 12th Signals Battalion
  - 12th Chemical Company

2nd Corps

- **3rd (Saladin) Armoured Division**[27]
  - 6th Armoured Brigade
    ◊ Khalid, Yarmouk and Miqdad Tank Battalions[28]
    ◊ 1st Mechanised Battalion
  - 12th Armoured Brigade
    ◊ Al Mu'tasim, Quadisiyah and Quitalba
    ◊ 3rd Mechanised Battalion
  - 8th Mechanised Infantry Brigade
    ◊ 1st to 3rd Mechanised Brigades
    ◊ 3rd Tank Battalion
  - Divisional Artillery[29]
    ◊ 15th Field Artillery Battalion (130mm)
    ◊ 20th, 21st, 62nd and 110th Field Artillery Battalions (122mm, one or two of which were 2S1. There may have also been a 2S3 battalion[30])
    ◊ 35th AA Battalion (37mm)[31]
    ◊ 71st, 72nd & 73rd SP AA Batteries[32]
  - 3rd Commando Battalion (9 platoons)
  - 3rd (Saleh Al Din) Reconnaissance Battalion
    ◊ Anti-Tank Battalion[33]
    ◊ Independent Anti-Tank Company[34]
  - 3rd Engineer Battalion
    ◊ 6th, 9th & 17th Field Engineer Companies
  - Bridging Battalion (attached)[35]
  - 3rd Signals Battalion
  - 3rd Chemical Company

- **6th (Saad) Armoured Division**[36]
  - 16th Armoured Brigade
    ◊ Al-Mahlab, Hudhayfah and Al Rafdin Tank Battalions
    ◊ 4th Mechanised Brigade
  - 30th Armoured Brigade
    ◊ Tariq, Muthanna and Sharhbil Tank Battalions
    ◊ 5th Mechanised Brigade
  - 25th Mechanised Brigade
    ◊ 1st to 3rd Mechanised Battalions
    ◊ 6th Tank Battalion
  - Divisional Artillery[37]
    ◊ 12th Field Artillery Battalion (122mm)
    ◊ 16th & 52nd Field Artillery Battalions (130mm)
    ◊ 25th Artillery Battalion (SU-100)
    ◊ 33rd Field Artillery Battalion (145mm (5.5" Gun))
    ◊ 42nd AA Battalion (30mm)[38]
    ◊ 175th SAM Battalion
  - 6th (Walid) Reconnaissance Battalion[39]
  - 6th Anti-Tank Battalion
  - 2nd and 15th Defence Battalions[40]
  - 6th Engineer Battalion
    ◊ 12th, 15th & 20th Field Engineer Companies
    ◊ 6th, 22nd & 23rd Workshop Companies
  - 6th Signals Battalion
  - 6th Chemical Company

- **10th (Nasr) Armoured Division**
  - 17th Armoured Brigade
    ◊ 14th (Tamuz), 30th (Tamuz)[41] and Hamad Shahab[42] Tank Battalions
    ◊ 6th Mechanised Battalion
  - 42nd Armoured Brigade[43]
    ◊ Jaffa, Saddam and Al Baath Tank Battalions
    ◊ 9th Mechanised Battalion
  - 24th Mechanised Infantry Brigade
    ◊ 1st to 3rd Mechanised Battalions
    ◊ 1st (Hazirah) Tank Battalion
  - 90th Infantry Brigade (attached)[44]
  - Divisional Artillery
    ◊ 16th, 39th, 49th & 51st Field Artillery Battalions[45]
    ◊ 103rd AA Battalion[46]
    ◊ ? Independent AA Batteries[47]
    ◊ 179th SAM Battalion[48]
  - 10th Commando Battalion (? Platoons)
  - 10th (Nasr) Reconnaissance Battalion
  - ? Defence Battalion[49]
  - 39th Anti-Tank Battalion[50]
  - ? Independent ATGM Companies
  - 10th Engineer Battalion
    ◊ 9th & two unidentified Field Engineer Companies
  - 10th Signals Battalion
  - 10th Chemical Company

3rd Corps

- **1st (Abu Obeida) Mechanised Division**[51]
  - 1st Mechanised Brigades (T-54/55 & BTR-60)
    ◊ 1st to 3rd Mechanised Battalions
    ◊ 1st Tank Battalion[52]

- 27th Mechanised Brigade (T-54/55 & BTR-60)
  - 1st to 3rd Mechanised Battalions
  - 8th Tank Battalion
- 34th Armoured Brigade (T-54/55)
  - Andalusia, Cordoba & Ashbil Tank Battalions[53]
  - 8th Mechanised Brigade
- Divisional Artillery[54]
  - 1st, 8th and 28th Field Artillery Battalions (122mm)[55]
  - 23rd Field Artillery Battalion (130mm)[56]
  - 143rd AA Battalion[57]
  - 1st (Qadsi) Commando Battalion (10 Platoons)
  - 1st (Quds) Reconnaissance Battalion (AML and Panhard M3)
  - 4th Anti-Tank Battalion (85mm)
  - 1st Engineer Battalion
  - 2nd, 7th and 11th Field Engineer Companies
- 1st Signals Battalion
- 1st Chemical Company
- 20th Services Battalion

- 5th (Muhammad Qasim) Mechanised Division[58]
  - 15th Mechanised Brigade (OT-64)
    - 1st to 3rd Mechanised Battalions
    - 5th Tank Battalion[59]
  - 20th Mechanised Brigade
    - 1st to 3rd Mechanised Battalions
    - 10th Tank Battalion[60]
  - 26th Armoured Brigade
    - Ali, Hussein and Hassan[61] Tank Battalions
    - 7th Mechanised Battalion
  - Divisional Artillery[62]
    - 7th, 12th 36th and 40th Field Artillery Battalions (122mm)
    - 106th Field Artillery Battalions (130mm)
    - 29th AA Battalion[63]
    - 185th SAM Battalion (SA-6)[64]
  - 5th Commando Battalion (? Platoons)
  - 5th (Hanin[65]) Reconnaissance Battalion
  - 2nd Anti-Tank Battalion (85mm)
  - 5th Engineer Battalion
    - 7th, 10th and 11th Field Engineer Companies
  - 5th Signals Battalion
  - 5th Chemical Company

- 9th (Osama) Armoured Division
  - 14th Mechanised Brigade
    - 1st to 3rd Mechanised Battalions
    - 12th (Nebuchadnezzar) Tank Battalion
  - 35th Armoured Brigade[66]
    - Al Badr, Alkandi and Diryasin Tank Battalions
    - 13th Mechanised Battalion
  - 43rd Armoured Brigade
    - Haifa, Gaza and Hawlah[67] Tank Battalions
    - 10th Mechanised Battalion
  - Divisional Artillery
    - 30th Field Artillery Battalion (122mm)[68]
    - ? Field Artillery Battalion (130mm)
    - ? Field Artillery Battalion (115mm)[69]
    - 116th Field Artillery Battalion (?mm)

  - 2nd AA Battalion[70]
    - 128th & 180th SAM Battalions
  - 9th (Dhiqar) Reconnaissance Battalion
  - 9th Engineer Battalion
  - 9th Signals Battalion

GHQ Reserve

- 31st Special Forces Brigade
  - 1st & 2nd Parachute Battalions
  - 3rd Commando Battalion
  - 77th Field Artillery Battalion (105mm OTO Melara)
  - 15th Mortar Battery (120mm AM50 mortar)
  - ? Light AA Battery
  - ? AT Company

- 32nd Special Forces Brigade
  - 4th, 5th & 6th Commando Battalions
  - 78th Field Artillery Battalion (105mm OTO Melara)
  - 17th Mortar Battery (120mm AM50 mortar)
  - ? Light AA Battery
  - ? AT Company
  - ? Engineer Company

- 33rd Special Forces Brigade[71]
  - 3 Commando Battalions[72]
  - ? Field Artillery Battalion (105mm OTO Melara)
  - ? Mortar Battery (120mm AM50 mortar)

- 7th Marine Brigade[73]
  - 3 Marine Battalions
  - 89th Artillery Battalion[74]
  - 44th Mortar Battery[75]
  - ? Light AA Battery

- 10 Reserve Infantry Brigades (low readiness)
  - 90th to 99th
    - 6 Reserve Infantry Battalions each

- 3 Training Brigades
  - 7th, 9th and 11th
    - 3 Training Battalions each

- 6 SAM Brigades[76]
  - 145th SAM Brigade
    - 5 SA-2 Batteries
  - 146th SAM Brigade
    - ?
  - 147th SAM Brigade
    - ?
  - 148th SAM Brigade
    - ? SA-6 Batteries
  - 149th SAM Brigade
    - ?
  - 195th SAM Brigade
    - 10 SA-3 Batteries[77]

- 3 Missile Brigades
  - 223rd (?) & 224th (Scud)
    - 225th (FROG)

- 8 Independent Infantry Battalions[78]
  - 2nd Coastal Defence
  - 194th and 324th to 329th Infantry

- 1 Independent Marine Battalion
- 9 Independent Tank Battalions
- 1 Independent Reconnaissance Battalion
- 13 Independent Artillery Battalions
- 24 (Airforce) AA Battalions

- 201st AT (missile) Battalion
  - 6 AT companies

C in C Reserve

- Republican Guard Brigade[79]
  - Tank Battalion (T-72 Ural)
  - Republican Guard Infantry Battalion
  - Special Forces Battalion
  - Artillery Battalion
  - MRL Battalion (BM-21)

- 10th Armoured Brigade[80]
  - 14th Ramadan, Al Wehda & Al Mansour Tank Battalions (T-72)
  - 2nd Mechanised Infantry Battalion

Ministry of the Interior
- 19 Border Guard Brigades
  - 1st, 3rd to 11th and 101st to 109th
    ◊ 4 Battalions each
- 28 Independent Border Guard Battalions

Unit Numbering Conventions

Iraqi corps were numbered initially from 1 to 3 at the start of the war but ranging from 1 to 7 by 1988. There was also the 1st Special Corps which was not the same as the 1st Corps.

Divisions are numbered in the order in which they were raised starting with the first and proceeding in strict numerical order into the 1950s, the exception being that there was no 13th division. All divisions were also given names and it is notable that veterans more frequently mention the division's name rather than its number.

Brigades were also numbered in sequence irrespective of their type; however, the sequence is not complete. Border Guard brigades, not belonging to the Army, appear to overlap the Army's numbers

Battalions were numbered but the numbering convention depended upon the type:
- Tank, AT, AA, special forces and artillery battalions were numbered in a running sequence independent of their parent formation
- Divisional battalions (and independent companies), such as commandos, Reconnaissance, engineer and signals took their number from the parent division
- Infantry and mechanised infantry were numbered sequentially 1–3 in their brigades. Thus, both the battalion and brigade numbers are required to uniquely identify the unit, for example the 2nd Battalion, 15th Mechanised Brigade. The exceptions were the mechanised brigades that were part of armoured brigades which had their own numeric sequence independent of the parent formation. As this includes the 1st through 3rd battalions, they must also reference their parent brigade in order to be unequivocally identified.

Some smaller units also had names. It seems that all tank battalions were named and at least some reconnaissance battalions had names too. Some commando companies appear to have had names and it appears that at least some engineer companies were also named.

Within battalion's, most companies were numbered 1st, 2nd, 3rd etc.[81] Numbering restarted at 1 for each battalion. HQ companies and support companies were designated as such, and not numbered. Some small units had their own numbering sequence independent of the parent battalion; SAM batteries, mortar batteries that were part of the divisional artillery and field engineers that were part of the divisional engineer battalion are examples of this.

ORGANISATIONS

Armoured and Mechanised Divisions

Armoured and mechanised divisions had a conventional organisation. A glance at the order of battle above shows that divisions fairly closely followed the outline organisation shown below but the artillery and AA allocation was a little more variable.

At the start of the war an armoured division was organised as follows.[82] This organisation only shows 'teeth' arms and not supporting formations:
- DHQ
- 2 Armoured Brigades
  - 3 Armoured Battalions
  - 1 Mechanised Battalion
- 1 Mechanised Brigade
  - 1 Armoured Battalion
  - 3 Mechanised Battalions
- Division Artillery
  - 3 to 4 Artillery Battalions
- Divisional Anti-Aircraft
  - 1 AA Battalion
  - 0–1 SAM Battalion
- Anti-Tank Battalion
- Reconnaissance Battalion
- Commando Company or Battalion
- Engineer Battalion
- Signal Battalion
- Chemical Defence Company

A mechanised division was similar but had two mechanised brigades and one armoured brigade. US sources only show the AT battalion in mechanised divisions not in the tank divisions.[83] US sources also show an independent tank battalion at divisional level for both the armoured and mechanised divisions.

By the end of the war an armoured division was organised as follows:[84]
- DHQ
- 2 Armoured Brigades
  - 3 Armoured Battalions
  - 1 Mechanised Battalion
- 1 Mechanised Brigade
  - 1 Armoured Battalion
  - 3 Mechanised Battalions
- 1 Commando Brigade (some units only have a single battalion)

- 3 Commando Battalions
- Division Artillery
  - 3 to 4 Artillery Battalions
- Divisional Anti-Aircraft
  - 1 SP AA battery
  - 1 SAM battery
  - 1 Towed AA Battalion
- Anti-Tank Battalion
- Reconnaissance Battalion
- Commando Brigade or Battalion
- Engineer Battalion
- Chemical Defence Company

In 1986 the British estimated an armoured brigade to consist of 2,400 men and mechanised brigade to consist of 3,000 men.[85]

Infantry Divisions

Infantry divisions were sometimes referred to as mountain divisions as at the start of the war they were all deployed in the mountainous north of the country. At the start of the war an infantry division was organised as follows:[86]

- DHQ
- 3 Infantry Brigades
  - 3 Infantry Battalions
- Divisional Artillery
  - 3–5 Artillery Battalions
- Tank Battalion
- Reconnaissance Battalion
- Commando Battalion
- 1–2 AA Battalions
- Engineer Battalion
- Signal Battalion
- AT Battalion
- Chemical Defence Company

In 1981 the Americans estimated an infantry brigade to consist of 3,500 men.[87]

By the end of the war the organisation was largely unchanged, though some divisions had a commando brigade rather than a battalion.[88]

Reserve Infantry Brigade

There is very little information available on the reserve brigades:
- Brigade HQ
- 6 Infantry Battalions
- Command Company
- Chemical Company

Tank Battalion

Sources vary considerably concerning the number of tanks in a battalion, with the average reported as 44–45 tanks. Towards the end of the war the number was reduced to 31–35 tanks. However, structure was consistent throughout the war, each battalion had three companies and a reconnaissance platoon.

At the start of the war a tank battalion was organised as follows:
- BHQ
- Reconnaissance Platoon – 6 BRDM-2
- 3 Tank Companies
  - 4 Platoons – 3 tanks

There were 45 tanks and five APCs in a battalion. That implies a CHQ had two tanks and an APC while the BHQ had three tanks and two APCs. One Iraqi veteran's report give the battalion 44 tanks which implies a BHQ of two tanks.[89] According to some veterans some battalions had AML-90 or EE-9 armoured cars instead of the BRDM-2. However, the BRDM-2 was the most common car used.[90]

A 1986 British report gives the following strength for a tank battalion, depending on its parent formation:[91]
- In an armoured brigade: 31 tanks
- In a mechanised brigade in a mechanised division: 40 tanks
- In a mechanised brigade of an armoured division: 31 tanks
- In a tank battalion in an infantry division: 51 tanks
- In an independent tank battalion: 51 tanks

However, a 1987 US report shows all tank battalions with 48 tanks.[92]

By the end of the war organisation was as follows – presumably for the tank battalion in an armoured brigade:
- BHQ – 3 tanks & 4 APCs
- Reconnaissance Platoon – 6 BRDM-2
- 3 Tank Companies
  - HQ – 2 tanks and 1 APC
  - 3 Platoons – 3 tanks

Tanks in infantry divisions were T-55, those in armoured and mechanised divisions T-62. Initially the T-72 was supplied only to the Republican Guard but later it served in the armoured divisions too. The Type 69 served in mechanised and armoured divisions. APCs were BTR-50 or OT-62.

Mechanised Battalion

Sources are reasonably consistent concerning the strength of a mechanised battalion, showing 47–48 APCs. Towards the end of the war at least some battalions were fielded at reduced strength with 35 APCs.

At the start of the war a mechanised battalion was organised as follows:[93]
- BHQ – 2 APC
- HQ Company
  - Reconnaissance Platoon – 4 BRDM-2
  - Signals Platoon
  - Maintenance Platoon
- 3 Mechanised Companies
  - HQ – 1 APC, 2 snipers
  - 3 Mechanised Platoons
    ◊ PHQ – 1 APC, 60mm mortar, 1 SA-7
    ◊ 3 Squads – 1 APC, 1 LMG, 1 RPG-7, 1 rifle grenade
  - MG Section – 1 APC, 2 tripod MG
  - Mortar Section – 2 82mm mortars in trucks
- Support Company
  - Mortar Battery – 4 120mm mortar towed by trucks
  - AA Platoon – 3 ZPU-4. Transported by trucks
  - Engineer Platoon – 3 APC

APCs could be any BTR50, BTR-60, OT-62, OT-64 or BMP-1. BMP battalions often used MT-LB or other APCs as command vehicles and for their engineers.

A 1986 British report gives the following strengths for mechanised battalion:[94]
- With BMP: 42 APCs
- Without BMP: 47 APCs

A 1987 US report shows all battalions with 48 APCs.[95]

In 1987 at least some battalions were fielded at reduced strength.[96] The companies had 11 APCs with each platoon having three APCs. The engineering APCs were removed although it is not clear if the engineer platoon was removed or was remounted in trucks.

A US source indicates there may have been a platoon of four BRDM-2 with Sagger with the support company of mechanised battalions.

Infantry Battalion

Infantry battalions were sometimes called mountain battalions. The organisation given below is for a regular battalion.[97] Reserve battalions were not equipped to the same level although they were apparently re-equipped before being committed to the front. The border guards were also more lightly equipped, at least at the start of the war, though details of their organisation are lacking.[98]

- BHQ
- 4 Infantry Companies
  - CHQ
    - MG Section – 2 tripod MG
    - Sniper Section – 2 snipers
    - Radio Section – 4 men
  - 3 Platoons
    - PHQ
  - Mortar squad – 1 60mm mortar
    - 3 Squads – 10 men, 1 RPG-7, 1 rifle grenade, 1 LMG, 7 rifles
- Support Company
  - 8 recoilless rifles
  - 8 82mm mortars
  - 3 12.7mm or 14.5mm HMG
  - Engineer Platoon

The overall strength of a battalion was approximately 700 men. Each infantry company had 120 men. Recoilless guns could be 82mm B10, 107mm B11 or 106mm M40, the latter being the least likely. Later in the war the SPG-9 was available. Mortars were the 82mm M37M or 82mm M75. Later in the war the Chinese 82mm became available. Given the heterogeneous nature of the weapons in the support company it is likely the weapons were attached to the infantry companies as needed.

Popular Army Battalion

The Popular Army was a militia commanded by the Iraqi Ba'ath Party. They were not administratively part of the regular armed forces, though units were sent to the front to fight. Details of the weapons held are scanty but the formations only had light small arms. It is not clear to what extent, if any, they were re-armed before being committed to the front. A regional battalion was organised as follows:

- BHQ
- 6 Infantry Companies
  - CHQ
  - 6 Platoons – 25 men

Artillery Battalion

Artillery battalions followed standard international practice and were formed into batteries of six guns.

An artillery battalion at the start of the war was organised as follows, it was fundamentally unchanged by the end of the war:

- BHQ
- 3 Batteries – 6 guns, 12–13 2½t trucks and 1 ½t truck

A battalion had eight RPG-7s and 83 assorted vehicles.

US intelligence indicates one battalion supported each brigade in a division with the other battalions being used for general support.[99] Although artillery doctrine was nominally based on British practices, lack of technical expertise meant that the Iraqis often relied on unobserved fires targeted at terrain features and they were unable to mass the fire of multiple battalions. Iraqi artillery was often kept well back from the front line which meant that it was unable to fire deep behind Iranian lines. Their use of artillery did improve as the war progressed but was not judged to be as effective as, for example, US artillery.

Gun tractors were usually trucks, though there were a number of ATS-59, ATS-59G and AT-T tracked tractors in service.

The Iraqis had Corps and GHQ artillery battalions. They were organised with 18 guns, as per divisional battalions. Further details are lacking.

Reconnaissance Battalion

Reconnaissance battalions were organised differently at the start of the war depending on the parent formation. By the end of the war they all had 18 armoured cars.

At the start of the war the reconnaissance battalion for an infantry division was organised as shown below:

- BHQ
- Maintenance Platoon
- Signals Platoon
- 3 Reconnaissance Companies
  - CHQ
  - 3 Reconnaissance Platoons

US intelligence gave overall battalion strength as 650 men.[100]

The reconnaissance battalion in a mechanised or armoured division was organised in the following fashion:

- BHQ
- 1 Air Reconnaissance company
- 3 Reconnaissance Companies
  - 4 Reconnaissance Platoons – 6 BRDM-2
- 1 Support Company

A 1981 US report gave the 1st Reconnaissance Battalion of the 1st Mechanised division of a strength of 24 AML and 24 M3 APC, implying only two reconnaissance companies rather than three in that formation.[101]

A 1986 British report gave the strength of a reconnaissance battalion as 42 'APCs' and six tanks.[102] It is not clear what the mix of BRDMs and 'real' APCs was, though the strength closely matches the end of war battalion given below, except that no tanks were present in the end of war battalion.

A 1987 US report gives a reconnaissance battalion 30 BRDMs and six tanks.[103]

By the end of the war the battalions were organised somewhat differently:

- BHQ
- 2 Reconnaissance Companies
  - 3 Reconnaissance Platoons – 6 BRDM-2
- 1 Service Company
- 1 Maintenance Company

Reconnaissance companies also had five APCs each: BTR-50, OT-62, M3 VTT or M-60.

During the war the Iraqis formed corps-level reconnaissance battalions, presumably along the same organisational lines. These were likely to have heavier armoured cars than the BRDMs in the divisional battalions. Also, during the war, the Iraqis formed brigade reconnaissance units with six BRDMs each.

Commando Battalion

All Iraqi divisions had a divisional command battalion, at the end of the war some had commando brigades of three battalions. The commandos were light infantry, without the heavy support weapons of standard regular infantry battalion but with a heavier allocation of squad and platoon weapons. The role of the commando battalions was to lead assaults and counterattacks.

A commando battalion at the start of the war had:
- BHQ
- 3 Commando Companies

Each company had: four 60mm mortars, six RPG-7s, 12 LMGs (probably PKM). 12 'automatic rifles' (probably RPD), and six radios. There were eight officers, 12 NCOs and 132 men. US intelligence give a battalion an overall strength of 550 men.[104] Although this was the nominal organisation it is clear from the Iraqi order of battle that the actual number of companies was quite variable. At the end of the war the company had three 60mm mortars and nine RPG-7s. Numbers of MGs were not specified.

Anti-Tank Battalion

Infantry and mechanised divisions each had an anti-tank battalion. AT battalions were not combat formations and their weapons were allocated to the manoeuvre brigades in the division.

A divisional AT battalion at the start of the war consisted of:
- BHQ
- 106mm Recoilless Company
- Milan ATGM Company
- Sagger ATGM Company
- 85mm D-44 towed AT Gun Company (not all battalions)

Unfortunately, equipment levels are not specified by the source. Working from inventory levels there were probably nine or 10 Milan launchers in the battalion, and a similar number of Sagger launchers. There were enough 106mm guns and 85mm D-44s in the inventory to allow for similar numbers, but there may have been more.

The sole GHQ ATGM Battalion at the start of the war had six companies. The majority of these had BRDM with Sagger. It is unclear as to whether the Cobra missiles carried by UAZ-469 were part of this formation. One source indicates there were around 40 BRDM-2 with Sagger in the formation.

During the war the 202nd Battalion was formed with six companies, probably each with 16 VTH HOT. The seventh company was formed with TOW missiles carried by jeeps, captured from Iran[105]

One source mentions GHQ AT Gun battalions without giving any further details.[106] Given there were over 200 100mm AT guns in the Iraqi inventory and they otherwise do not appear in the order of battle it seems probable such battalions existed.

Anti-Aircraft Battalion

All divisions had at least one AA battalion with many having several more. An early war AA battalion was reported by US intelligence to have 54 guns. That is probably three large batteries of 18 guns each

The late war AA battalion in an infantry division had:
- BHQ
- 3 AA Batteries – 6 AA guns

The AA guns could have been of any of the available types, 57mm, 37mm, 30mm, 23mm or 14.5mm. 57mm gun batteries would have been equipped with the appropriate fire control radar.

Armoured and mechanised divisions had battalions similar to the infantry divisions. Mechanised and armoured divisions also had sperate AA batteries, one each with nine ZSU, nine 30mm on BTR-50, nine 23mm on MT-LB or nine SA-9 (Strela 2).

Iraqi doctrine was to keep the heavier guns (57mm) and SAMs (SA-6 and SA-9) to the rear of their positions to defend the HQ elements and artillery. The lighter guns accompanied the forward troops.

Surface to Air Missile (SAM) Battalion

At the start of the war many divisions had an SA-6 (2K12) battalion. This was organised in the same way as a Soviet SA-6 unit with:[107]
- HQ – Long Track (P-40) and Thin Skin (PRV-9) radar
- 5 SAM Batteries – four SA-6 (2K12) SAM launcher and one Straight Flush (1S91) radar

As the war progressed these battalions were removed from divisions and placed under corps control.

Combat Engineer Battalion

All Iraqi divisions had engineer battalions of three companies. The companies were usually attached one each to the manoeuvre brigades.

At the start of the war a combat engineer battalions consisted of:
- BHQ
- 3 Combat Engineer Companies
- Engineer Park Company
  - Heavy Equipment Platoon
  - Bridge Platoon – MTU-20 AVLB
  - Telecommunications Equipment Platoon
  - Maintenance Platoon

This was largely unchanged at the end of the war. The bridge platoon was not present in the infantry divisions. Engineer platoons had trucks rather than APCs. An Iraqi corps also had an engineer battalion which was likely organised in a similar manner to the divisional battalion. A corps also has a bridging battalion with PMP bridging and GSP ferries.

Location Battalion

Location battalions were used to locate enemy artillery batteries. It is not clear if such units were available at the start of the war but by the end there was one available to each corps.
- BHQ – 1 Medium truck and trailer
- 3 Locating Batteries
  - HQ – 1 medium truck and trailer
  - Sound Ranging Platoon – 1 truck with sound ranging equipment and 3 Land Rovers
  - Radar Reconnaissance Platoon – 3 radars
  - Flash ranging platoon – 2–3 flash ranging sets
  - Liaison Section – 4 men
  - Survey Section – 1 UAZ-469
  - Meteorological Section – 2 trucks

The type of radar used is not specified. It is likely that they were usually M3 APCs with RASIT ground surveillance radar (GSR) but could have been SNAR-10 GSR or towed Cymbeline Counter Mortar Radar (CMR).

Mortar Battery

In many sources these are referred to as 'light artillery' batteries but they were inevitably equipped with mortars. Each battery had 12 120mm mortars, with the exception of those in the special forces brigades which had six 120mm mortars. The batteries were usually attached directly to a manoeuvre brigade. Independent 160mm or 240mm mortar batteries were found at Corps or GHQ level.

Chemical Company

Every Iraqi division had a chemical company. The decontamination platoons were usually attached one each to the manoeuvre battalions.

A chemical company had:
- CHQ
- Chemical Reconnaissance platoon
- 3 decontamination platoons

By the end of the war the number of decontamination platoons had been reduced to two.

Unit Strengths

In 1987, towards the end of the war, US Intelligence estimated the average strength of various units compared their estimated full strength. As the figures are averages that implies some units were better off and some units were fighting at reduced strength under the average.

Table 47: US estimates of Iraqi unit strengths, 1987

Unit	Authorised strength	Average actual strength	Percentage
Infantry Division	21,000	15,775	75%
Mechanised Division	19,000	14,725	78%
Armoured Division	18,500	14,300	77%
Infantry Brigade	3,500	2,700	77%
Mechanised Brigade	3,000	2,300	77%
Armoured Brigade	2,400	1,850	77%
Special Forces Brigade	3,000	2,300	77%
Commando Brigade	3,000	2,300	77%

It can be clearly seen that the US analysts took a percentage strength estimate and then calculated the actual strength from the authorised strength. However, it clearly illustrates the point that many Iraqi formations were fighting at reduced strength.

These figures are misleading, however. The majority of casualties fall on the frontline forces of tanks and infantry. If a whole formation is at 77 percent strength it implies that the sub-units on the front line are at considerably less strength and conversely the rear area sub-units are at correspondingly higher strength. Second World War experience demonstrated that the infantry suffered the most.[108] The fact that armoured formations and infantry formations in the table above have the same percentage casualty rates should raise questions about the validity of these estimates.

Expansion of the Iraqi Army During the War

At the start of the war the Iraqi Army was 250,000 men strong and by 1988 it had grown to around 800,000 men.[109] Some new units were created but he Iraqis often chose to bring reserve infantry units up to strength and to reconfigure border guard infantry units as regular infantry units. This gave the Iraqis a great many new or refurbished infantry units which were then dug-in along the front line to support Iraq's defensive strategy. The main place where the Iraqis created new units was in a large expansion of the Republican Guard.

The movement of many refurbished infantry units to the front required the formation of many new divisional and corps HQs to effectively control them.

Outline Iraqi Order of Battle 1988

The following shows the outline of the Order of Battle for the Iraqi Army at the end of the war. Corps are ordered north to south; divisions are in numerical order.[110]

5th Corps
- 23rd, 33rd, 38th and 45th Infantry Divisions

1st Corps
- 10th Armoured Division
- 4th, 7th, 24th, 27th, 29th, 34th, 36th, 39th, 40th, 43rd, 44th, 46th and 48th Infantry Divisions

2nd Corps
- 10th and 17th Armoured Divisions
- 1st Mechanised Division
- 16th, 19th, 21st, 22nd, 28th and 41st Infantry Divisions

1st Special Corps
- 1st, 2nd and 3rd Special Divisions
- 10th Special Commando Brigade
- 54th Armoured Brigade

4th Corps
- 20th, 29th Infantry Divisions

6th Corps
- 25th, 31st, 32nd, 35th Infantry Divisions

3rd Corps
- 3rd and 6th Armoured Divisions
- 1st Mechanised Division
- 8th, 11th, 19th, 30th and 42nd Infantry Divisions

7th Corps
- 15th, 26th, 37th Infantry Division

Republican Guard (RG)[111]
- Bagdad Force
  - 4th, 5th, 6th and 7th RG Infantry Brigades
- Medina Force
  - 2nd and 10th RG Armoured Brigades
  - 14th RG Infantry Brigade
- Hammurabi Force
  - 8th and 17th RG Armoured Brigades
  - 15th Special Forces Brigade
  - 3rd, 16th and 28th RG Infantry Brigades
- Nebuchadnezzar Force
  - 11th and 12th RG Commando Brigades
  - 19th, 20th and 22nd RG Infantry Brigades

Al Faw Force
- 9th RG Armoured Brigade
- 18th and 29th RG Mechanised Brigades
- 27th and 28th RG Infantry Brigades
- Adnan Force

- 11th, 12th, 21st and 31st RG Infantry Brigades

Missile Forces[112]
- 223rd Brigade – 6 Al-Hussien SSM Launchers
- 224th Brigade – 10 Scud and Al-Hussien SSM Launchers
- 225th Brigade – Frog-7 (Luna M) and ASTROS MRL

Iraqi Divisions Created After the Start of the War

Iraq created many divisional HQs during the war. For the most part they took command of existing reserve formations that had been brought up to full strength and equipment, though some brigades were newly created.[113]

Table 48: Iraqi Divisions Created After the Start of the War

Division	Name	Date	Initial Brigades	Subsequent Brigades[114]
1st Special	-	1986	1st, 2nd and 3rd Special	
2nd Special	-	1986	3rd, 4th and 5th Special	
3rd Special	-	1986	7th, 8th and 9th Special	
14th Infantry	?	1981	60th Armoured[115] 18th and 96th Infantry[116]	1986: 422nd, 426th and 805th Infantry
15th Infantry	Farooq	1981	44th, 104th and 802nd Infantry[117]	
16th Infantry	Zulfiqar	1982	99th, 505th and 606th Infantry 64th Tank Battalion	
17th Armoured[118]	Abbas	1982	59th, 70th and 80th Armoured 99th Infantry	80th Brigade subsequently moved to another division
18th Infantry	Tariq Ibn Ziyad	1982	58th Armoured 95th, 702nd and 704th Infantry	
19th Infantry	Qutaiba	1982	421st and 601st Infantry	2nd Formation: 110th, 113th, 419th and 503rd Infantry 3rd Formation: 82nd, 108th and 427th Infantry
20th Infantry	Mesopotamia	1982	44th, 420th, 435th and 501st Infantry	
21st Infantry	Muslim Ibn Aqil	1983	90th, 603rd, 706th and 801st Infantry[119] 47th Tank Battalion (T-55)	Added 603rd, 706th and 801st
22nd Infantry	Great Badr	1983	93rd, 425th and 706th Infantry	
23rd Infantry	Shaibani	1983	33rd, 98th, 437th and 604th Infantry[120]	
24th Infantry	Mu'tasim	1983	81st, 97th and 411th Infantry	
25th Infantry	Hudhayfah	1983	87th, 103rd and 428th Infantry	
26th Infantry	Omar Ibn Yasser Force	1983	111th + ?	
27th Infantry	Al-Siddiq	1983	72nd, 199th and 806th Infantry	
28th Infantry	Hassan	1984	78th, 412th and 417th Infantry	
29th Infantry	Sharhabeel	1984	83rd, 84th and 703rd Infantry	1985: added 117th Infantry
30th Infantry	Abdullah Ibn Rawahah	1984	55th, 101st and 120th Infantry	
31st Infantry	Hussein	1984	49th, 79th and 605th Infantry	
32nd Infantry	Ibn Ghazwan	1984	86th + ? Infantry[121]	
33rd Infantry	Badr	1984	433rd, 438th, 603rd and 703rd Infantry[122]	
34th Infantry	Al-Harith	1985	76th, 424th and 504th Infantry	
35th Infantry	Musa Ibn Nussair	1985	115th, 118th, 429th and 707th Infantry	
36th Infantry	Al-Amin	1985	?	
37th Infantry	Ajnadin	1985	7th, 91st and 452nd Infantry	

IRAQI ORGANISATION

Division	Name	Date	Initial Brigades	Subsequent Brigades[114]
38th Infantry	Omar Ibn Abdul Aziz	1985	846th, 847th and 848th Infantry 49th Tank Battalion	
39th Infantry	Tabuk	1985	92nd, 434th and 443rd Infantry	
40th Infantry	Al-Mughira	1986	76th, 82nd and 98th Infantry	
41st Infantry	?	1986	444th + ? Infantry	
42nd Infantry	Fotouh	1986	?	
43rd Infantry	?	1986	?	
44th Infantry	Mustafa	1986	121st, 438th and 702nd Infantry	
45th Infantry	Talha	1986	119th, 121st and 446th Infantry	
46th Infantry	Al-Zubayrben	1986	87th, 88th and 426th Infantry	
47th Infantry	?	1987	?	
48th Infantry	?	1987	802nd, 803rd and 807th Infantry	

The 49th to 57th Divisions were formed in late 1987 to 1988 but saw little or no combat. The 58th and 59th Divisions were forming in 1988 but formation was cancelled by the end of the war.

In addition to the divisions the 65th, 66th and 68th Special Forces Brigades were raised in 1982 when the 31st, 32nd and 33rd Special Forces Brigades were disbanded.

COLOUR SECTION 5

Although generally assessed as at least 'Soviet influenced', the olive-green field dress of Iraqi Army officers rather resembled that of British Army officers from the 1970s. It included the highly popular Burberry pullover, and a black beret. This officer is shown studying a captured FN FAL assault rifle. (Artwork by Renato Dalmaso)

COLOUR SECTION 5

Many Iraqi Army Commandos went into the war with Iran wearing uniforms patterned after the US BDU design, though often combined with plain green trousers – and nearly always topped with the 'balaclava' woollen cap. Camouflage fatigues of other designs, and 'Chicom' webbing entered widespread service later during the conflict: only their orange berets – identifying them as members of special purpose units – remained in widespread use. (Artwork by Renato Dalmaso)

MIDDLE EAST@WAR SERIES SPECIAL #1: THE IRAN-IRAQ WAR

Typical for the Iraqi Army tank-crewmen, this soldier is shown wearing the field dress in olive-green overall with a canvas belt, locally-made leather boots, and the black padded Soviet tanker's helmet – the typcial fatigues of the Iraqi armoured and mechanised vehicle crews of the 1980s. (Artwork by Renato Dalmaso)

COLOUR SECTION 5

The general appearance of the Iranian Army troops of the 1980s was very similar to that of the US Army troops of the late 1960s and early 1970s: the M1 helmet (without camouflage) was usually worn with one of many uniform models manufactured locally – all bleached by the sun and sand. Troops generally wore no unit or national insignia, and – at least early on – next to no webbing. His armament consisted of the German-designed MG 3 light machine gun, locally manufactured as the MGA3. (Artwork by Renato Dalmaso)

MIDDLE EAST@WAR SERIES SPECIAL #1: THE IRAN-IRAQ WAR

British-trained and equipped before the war, operators of the Iranian Special Boat Service initially wore camouflage fatigues with US Woodland pattern and a black beret. Gradually, most Western equipment was replaced by whatever local versions of US uniforms and boots were available; even their FN FAL assault rifles were replaced by omnipresent AK-47/AKMs. (Artwork by Renato Dalmaso)

COLOUR SECTION 5

Combat divers of the IRGC were deployed in constantly growing numbers ever since Operation Khyber, in 1984, but never before in such numbers as during Val Fajr-8, when they led all the major assaults and also attempted to storm the main port of the Iraqi Navy in Um Qasr. They wore a mix of black and camouflaged diving suits, but otherwise only a minimum of equipment and armament. On the contrary, combat divers of the Navy and the IRGC naval service wore blue diving suits, with most of equipment – including breathing apparatus of British origin – in front. (Artwork by Renato Dalmaso)

MIDDLE EAST@WAR SERIES SPECIAL #1: THE IRAN-IRAQ WAR

Operated by about a dozen squadrons, over 150 MiG-21F-13/FL/PFM/MF/bis and MiG-21UM formed the backbone of the Iraqi fighter-fleet during the war with Iran. Relatively easy to maintain and fly, they proved highly popular, even if underequipped and short ranged, and flew more than 50 percent of all combat sorties undertaken by the IrAF during the conflict. As well as the older MiG-21FL/PFMs that served in Syria during the October 1973 War with Iraq, the mass of Iraqi '21s' wore different variants of this standardised camouflage pattern during the 1980s. Usually, this consisted of beige (BS381C/388) and olive drab (BS381C/298) on upper surfaces and sides, and light admiralty grey (BS381C/697) on undersurfaces: this MiG-21bis belonged to a batch delivered between 1982 and 1984, on which light stone (BS381C/361) was used instead of beige. The family was compatible with a wide range of air-to-air and air-to-ground ordnance: shown are R-13M (AA-2 Atoll; on inboard pylon) and R-60MK (AA-8 Aphid) air-to-air missiles. (Artwork by Tom Cooper)

Another warhorse of the IrAF during the war with Iraq was the Sukhoi Su-20/22 family, nearly 150 of which were acquired between 1975 and 1985 and operated by half a dozen squadrons. The survivability of this big and powerful fighter-bomber, and its compatibility with a wide array of ordnance made it highly popular, which is why some top IrAF commanders favoured it over any other available types – including Mirages – and dozens of pilots flying Su-20/22s were highly decorated. However, losses were extensive: more than 70 were shot down in the eight years of war. Iraqi Sukhois wore very different camouflage patterns, usually consisting of chocolate brown and dark green on upper surfaces and sides, and light admiralty grey (BS381C/697) on undersurfaces. Many had two sets of national markings applied on the fuselage, and this Su-22M-3K was decorated by a symbol of excellence (a shield with the inscription *Iraq* in Arabic and English). It is shown armed with four FAB-500M-62 bombs. (Artwork by Tom Cooper)

Between April 1981 and June 1988, Iraq acquired a total of 86 Dassault Mirage F.1EQ single-seaters, and 15 Mirage F.1BQ two-seaters. Thanks to their advanced navigation and weapons control systems, the four units operating them deployed them for day-time CAS, interdiction, tactical bombing, strategic bombing, naval strikes, and air defence. Most of the fleet wore the standardised camouflage pattern in *Brun Café* (dark sand, FS30475) and *Khaki* (FS36134) on top surfaces and sides, and light blue grey (FS35189) on undersurfaces. This Mirage F.1EQ-4 is shown with some of the most-frequently deployed weaponry, including (from left to right) the Matra Super 530F air-to-air missile, Remora ECM-pod, two SAMP Type-21 general purpose bombs (under the wing), a Matra R.550 Magic Mk.I air-to-air missile (wingtip), BLG-66 Belouga CBU, and the South-African CBU.470. Shown under the centreline is the giant, *Irakien* drop tank of 2,200-litre capacity. (Artwork by Tom Cooper)

COLOUR SECTION 5

Between 1967 and 1978, Iran acquired a total of 224 McDonnell Douglas F-4D, F-4E, and RF-4E Phantom IIs and they formed the backbone of its fighter-bomber and reconnaissance fleets during the war with Iraq. All Iranian Phantom IIs wore a camouflage pattern standardised as 'Asia Minor', and consisting of tan (FS30400), brown (FS30140), and dark green (FS34079) on upper surfaces and sides, and light grey (FS36622) on undersurfaces. The F-4 family was compatible with a wide range of conventional bombs, a small selection of those most widely deployed by the IRIAF is illustrated here, including (from left to right): US-made Mk.82 general purpose bomb (with Mk.12 Snakeye retarding fins), British-made Hunting BL755 CBU, US-made M117s (on a triple-ejector rack under the inboard underwing pylon), SUU-30/A, CBU-57A/B, and CBU-59s. (Artwork by Tom Cooper)

Iran acquired 141 Northrop F-5E and 28 F-5F Tiger IIs as a stopgap measure until either the General Dynamics F-16 or McDonnell Douglas F/A-18 would have been ready, and as advanced trainers. Eventually, this plan was never realised, and thus the type found itself serving as the primary close-support platform of the IRIAF during the war with Iraq, for which it proved underequipped. The air force entered the conflict with about 128 intact F-5Es and 26 F-5Fs, but attrition was heavy – especially during the Battle of Khuzestan in October and November 1980 – decreasing the number of available airframes to fewer than 80 just two years later. This example is illustrated together with some of the weapons it deployed, including (from left to right): Mk.82, CBU-59, CBU-57/B and BL755, and one of 1,066 AIM-9P Sidewinders acquired for this type in 1976. (Artwork by Tom Cooper)

Out of 80 Grumman F-14A Tomcats ordered by Iran, 79 had been delivered and 76 were intact at the time of the Iraqi invasion. Organised into four squadrons, they formed the backbone of the Iranian air defences. Described as 'non-operational' by both the West and Iraq, they caused heavy losses to the Iraqi air force during the first three years of the war. Attrition of men and material, and deployment of ever more advanced interceptors by the IrAF, eventually limited them to flying CAPs over Khark, during the latter stages of the war. The entire Iranian F-14 fleet wore a unique camouflage pattern TO 1-1-4, consisting of tan (FS30400), brown (FS30140), and dark green (FS34079) on upper surfaces and sides, and grey (FS36622) on undersides. This example is shown with standard weapons configuration for the middle phases of the war, consisting of (from bottom towards top) AIM-54A Phoenix, AIM-7E-2 Sparrow, and AIM-9J/P Sidewinder air-to-air missiles. (Artwork by Tom Cooper)

BIBLIOGRAPHY

As will probably be obvious to the reader, this book is the product of many years of research by a group of authors drawing upon a wide range of conventional printed sources, digital publications, websites, forums and social media sites in addition to many interviews. Whilst every effort has been made to faithfully record sources, it has not always been possible to record the precise time and date of access to these resources, or even the exact location of some of these. In some instances, those resources may no longer exist or may have moved. Every effort has been made to verify and update the information presented in this bibliography, and the further references included within the endnotes, however it has become apparent that some of the links no longer work. Nevertheless these have been retained here and annotated as (dead link) for the sake of completeness.

Books

Alibabaie, G.R., *A History of the Iranian Air Force* (in Farsi) (Tehran: Ashian, 2002)

Al-Marashi, Ibrahim & Sammy Salama. *Iraq's Armed Forces: An Analytical History* (London: Routledge, 2009)

Buchan, James. *Days of God: The Revolution in Iran and its Consequences* (London: John Murray, 2013)

Bulloch, John & Harvey Morris, *The Gulf War: Origin, History and Consequences of Islam at War* (London: Methuen Publishers, 1989)

Connell, Michael, *Iranian Operational Decision Making: Case Studies from the Iran-Iraq War* (Alexandria VA: CNA Analysis & Solutions, 2013)

Cooper, T., & Milos Sipos, *Iraqi Mirages: The Dassault Mirage Family in Service with the Iraqi Air Force, 1981–1988* (Warwick: Helion & Co., 2019)

Cooper, Tom & Farzad Bishop, *Iran-Iraq War in the Air 1980–1988.* (Atglen: Schiffer Military History, 2000)

Cooper, Tom, et al, *IRIAF 2010* (Houston: Harpia Publishing, 2010)

Cordesman, Anthony H., & Abraham R. Wagner, *The Lessons of Modern War: Volume II: The Iran-Iraq War* (Boulder, San Francisco: Westview Press, 1990/London: Mansell Publishing Ltd, 1990)

Cordesman, Anthony H., *The Iran-Iraq War and Western Security 1984–1987* (London: Jane's Publishing Company Ltd, 1987)

De Lestapis, Jacques (ed.), *Military Powers Encyclopedia, League of Arab States; Irak, Jordan, Lebanon, Syria, PLO, Iran, Israel* (Paris: Society I³C, 1989)

Dunston, Simon. *Chieftain Main Battle Tank 1965–2003* (Oxford: Osprey Publishing, 2003)

Dupuy, Colonel Trovor N., *Elusive Victory: The Arab-Israeli Wars 1947–1974* (London: Macdonald and Jane's Publishers, 1978).

Farrokh, Dr Kaveh, *Iran at War 1500–1980* (Oxford: Osprey Publishing, 2011)

Foss, Christopher (ed), *Jane's Armour and Artillery, 1996–1997* (Coulsdon: Jane's Information Group, 1996)

Foss, Christopher (ed), *Jane's Armour and Artillery, 2007–2008* (Coulsdon: Jane's Information Group, 2007)

Goldsack, Paul (ed.), *Jane's World Railways 1980–1981* (Coulsdon: Jane's Information Group, 1980)

Hiro, Dilip, *The Longest War: The Iran-Iraq Military Conflict* (London: Paladin Grafton Books, 1989)

International Institute for Strategic Studies, *The Military Balance 1980–1982* (London: 1980–1982)

Khazraji, General (General Staff) Nizar Abdul Karim Faisal Al, *Al Harb Al Iraqiya- Al Iraniya) 1980–1988 Muthakerat Muqatel (The Iraq-Iran War1980–1988. Memoirs of a Fighter)* (Doha, Qatar: Arab Centre for Research & Policy Studies, 2014)

Khoury, Dina Rizk, *Iraq in Wartime: Soldiering, Martyrdom and Remembrance* (Cambridge: Cambridge University Press, 2013)

Makki Khamas (Makki) General Aladdin Hussein, *Maarik Al Tahrir Al Kubra Al Iraqiya 1988 (The Great Iraqi Battles of Liberation 1988)* (Amman, Jordan: Academiuoon Publishing Company, 2014)

Malovany, Colonel Pesach, *Milhamot Bavel ha-Hadasha (The Wars of Modern Babylon)* (Tel Aviv: Ma'arachot, 2010)

Malovany, Colonel Pesach, *Wars of Modern Babylon* (Lexington KY: The University Press of Kentucky, 2017)

Middle East Watch, *Genocide in Iraq: The Anfal Campaign Against the Kurds* (Washington: Human Rights Watch, 1993)

Murray, Williamson & Kevin M. Woods, *The Iran-Iraq War: A Military and Strategic History* (Cambridge: Cambridge University Press, 2014)

National Training Center, *The Iraqi Army: Organization and Tactics* (Boulder, Colorado: Paladin Press, 1991)

Nejad, Parviz Mosalla (ed.), Shalamcheh (Shalamcheh: Sarir Publication, 2006). Downloaded from website Shalamcheh Author: *The Hub of Resistance Literature & History* (sajed.ir/upload%5Ctopic%5Cebook-Shalamcheh.pdf)

Nixon, John, *Debriefing the President: The Interrogation of Saddam Hussein* (London: Random House, 2017)

O'Ballance, Edgar, *The Gulf War* (London: Brassey's Defence Publishers, 1988)

Pelletiere, Stephen C., et al, *Iraq Power and U.S. Security in the Middle East* (Carlisle Barracks, PA: Strategic Studies Institute, US Army War College, 1990)

Pelletiere, Stephen C., *The Iran-Iraq War: Chaos in a Vacuum* (Westport CT and London: Praeger, 1992)

Pollack, Kenneth M., *Arabs at War. Military Effectiveness 1948–1991* (Lincoln & London: University of Nebraska Press, 2002)

Pollack, Kenneth M., *The Persian Puzzle* (New York: Random House, 2004)

Razoux, Pierre (translated by Nicholas Elliott), *The Iran-Iraq War* (London: The Belnap Press of Harvard University Press, 2015)

Rottman, Gordon L. *The Rocket Propelled Grenade* (Oxford: Osprey Publishing, 2010)

Sadik, Brig.Gen. Ahmad & Tom Cooper, *Iraqi Fighters, 1953–2003: Camouflage & Markings* (Houston: Harpia Publishing, 2008)

Scales, Brigadier-General Robert H. (Director Desert Storm Study Project), *Certain Victory: The United States Army in the Gulf War* (Washington DC: Office of the Chief-of-Staff, United States Army, 1993)

Schmidt, Rachel, *Global Arms Exports to Iraq, 1960–1990* (Santa Monica: California, RAND, 1991)

Stockholm International Peace Research Institute (SIPRI), *Yearbooks 1980–1989. World Armaments and Disarmament* (Oxford: Oxford University Press, 1980–1989)

Taghvaee, Babak, *Desert Warriors: Iranian Army Aviation at War* (Solihull: Helion & Company, 2016)

US Arms Control and Disarmament Agency, *World Military Expenditures and Arms Transfers 1972–1982* (Washington DC: 1984)

Ward, Steven R., *Immortal: A Military History of Iran and its Armed Forces* (Washington DC: Georgetown University Press, 2009)

Woods, Kevin M., et al, *Project 1946* (Alexandria: Virginia, Institute for Defense Analyses, 2008)

Woods, Kevin M., et al, *Saddam's Generals: Perspectives of the Iran-Iraq War* (Alexandria, Va: Institute for Defense Analysis, 2010)

Woods, Kevin M., et al, *Saddam's War: An Iraqi Military Perspective of The Iran-Iraq War* (Washington DC: United States Dept. of Defence (McNair Papers), 2009)

Woods, Kevin M., *The Mother of all Battles: Saddam Hussein's strategic plan for the Persian Gulf War* (Annapolis: US Naval Institute Press, 2008)

Zabih, Sepehr, *The Iranian Military in Revolution and War* (London: Routledge, 1988). New version published 2011 (under author Sepehr Zabir) as part of Routledge Library Editions: Iran, (Abingdon: Routledge, 2011)

Articles, Essays, Monographs, Papers, Theses

Abramowitz, Jeff, et al, 'Iraq: the military build-up', *IDF Journal*, Vol. III No. 2 (Spring 1986)

Aldridge, Colonel B., British Defence Attaché, Baghdad, A Review of the Military Situation in Iraq Over the Period April 1986 to April 1987 (21 May, 1987). Kindly provided by the Foreign Office under the Freedom of Information Act

Ali, Javed, 'Chemical Weapons and the Iran-Iraq War: A Case Study in Noncompliance', *The Nonproliferation Review* (Spring 2001)

Atkeson, Major General Edward B., 'Iraq's Arsenal: Tool of Ambition', *Army* (March 1991), pp.22–30

Banks, Tony, 'The changing war for Kurdistan', *Jane's Defence Weekly* 12 August 1989 p.249

Beuttel, H.W., 'Iranian casualties in the Iran-Iraq War: A re-appraisal. Parts 1 & 2', TNDM, Vol. 2 No. 3 (December 1997) and Vol. 2 No. 4 (December 1998)

Boyne, Sean, 'Saddam's shield: The role of the Special Republican Guard', *Jane's Intelligence Review* (January 1999) pp.29–32

Bruce, James, 'No sign of counter-attack by Iraqis', *Jane's Defence Weekly* (21 February 1987), p.265

Childs, Nick, 'The Gulf War: Iraq under pressure' *Jane's Defence Weekly* (9 May 1987) pp.899–901

Cooper, T., & Fontanellaz, A., 'La bataille de Susangerd: Duel de chars dans le Golfe', *Batailles & Blindes Magazine*, No. 57 (2014)

Cooper, T., Sadik, A., & Bishop, F., 'La Guerre Iran-Irak: Les combats aériens Volume 1', *Avions*, Hors Serie 22 (2007)

Cooper, T., Sadik, A., & Bishop, F., 'La Guerre Iran-Irak: Les combats aériens Volume 2', *Avions*, Hors Serie 23 (2007)

Cooper, Tom, & Bishop, Farzad, 'Fire in the Hills: Iraq and Iran in Conflict', *Air Enthusiast,* Issue 104 (March/April 2003), pp.14–24

Cooper, Tom, 'La Guerre des Villes: Baghdad contre Téhéran', *Air Combat*, No. 8 (2014)

Davis, Major Mark J. *Iranians' Operational Warfighting Ability: An Historical Assessment and View to the Future* (School of Advanced Military Studies, United States Army and Command General Staff College, Fort Leavenworth, Kansas, 1992)

Eccles, Colonel R.G. (British Defence Attaché, Iraq) Review of the Iraq military situation August 1983-April 1986, April 27, 1986. These were kindly provided by the British Foreign Office under the Freedom of Information Act

Eshel, Lieutenant Colonel David, 'Fighting Under Desert Conditions', *Armor* Vol 99 No 6, (November-December 1990)

Forouzan, Adar, 'Iranian Tank Commander', *Military History* (Herndon, VA.) Apr 2004. Vol. 21, Issue 1 pp.44–46 (In Iran-heritage.org/interestgroups/war-iraqiran-news2.htm)

Furlong, D.M., 'Iran A power to be reckoned with', *International Defence Review* (June 1973)

Grau, Lieutenant Colonel Lester W. and Lieutenant Jason Failvene, 'Mountain Combat: Hard to move, hard to shoot, even harder to communicate,' *Journal of Military Studies* September 2008

Griffin, Lieutenant Colonel Gary B., 'The Iraqi Way of War: An operational assessment' (Fort Leavenworth, Kansas: School of Advanced Military Studies, United States Army Command and General Staff College, 1990)

Heyman, Charles, 'Advance of the Intelligent Battlefield: The current world market for anti-personnel mines', *Jane's Defence Weekly* (1997)

Jupa, Richard and James Dingeman, *'The Republican Guards: Loyal, Aggressive, Able', Army*, (March 1991) pp.54–62

Lamont, Lieutenant Colonel R.W., 'A Tale of Two Cities – Hue and Khorramshahr', *Armor*, Vol. 108 No. 3 (MayJune 1999)

Lortz, Michael G. 'Willing to Face Death: A history of Kurdish Military Forces. The Peshmerga-From the Ottoman Empire to Present Day Iraq' (Electronic thesis from Florida State University 28 October 2005. Web site 'Willing to Face Death' citeseerx.ist.psu.edu/viewdoc/download?doc=10.1.1.661.6369&rep=rep)

McLaurin, R.D., 'Military Operations in the Gulf War: The Battle of Khorramshahr' (Aberdeen Proving Ground, Maryland: US Army Human Engineering Laboratory, 1982). Cached copy (www.dtic.mil/dtic/tr/fulltext/u2/b067661.pdf.)

No author, 'Disarming Khomeinei, Special Report', *NLA Quarterly*, Autumn 1988

No author, 'Growing indications of another Basra offensive', *Jane's Defence Weekly* (10 October 1987)

No author, 'How Saddam kept deadly gas secret', *Independent* (3 July 1998)

No author, 'Iran masses troops for major offensive in Gulf', *Jane's Defence Weekly* (28 November 1987)

No author, 'Iran needs '$15–25b to rebuild forces', claim, *Jane's Defence Weekly*, (4 February 1989)

No author, 'Iran tries to remould revolutionary guards', *Jane's Defence Weekly*, (1 October 1988)

No author, 'Iran's assault in Iraq-A morale booster?' *Jane's Defence Weekly* (25 June 1988)

No author, 'Iran's men of influence', *Jane's Defence Weekly* (30 June 1990)

No author, 'Iraq in successful attack on occupied territory', *Jane's Defence Weekly*, 2 July 1988

No author, 'Iraq's southern successes', *Jane's Defence Weekly*, 23 July 1988

No author, 'Kirkuk oilfield raid-damage disputed', *Jane's Defence Weekly*, 18 October 1987

No author, 'Kurdish villages razed in punitive Iraqi campaign', *Jane's Defence Weekly*, 10 October 1987

No author, 'Mobilisation problem for Iranian leaders', *Jane's Defence Weekly* (2 April 1988)

No author, 'Mujahideen strength growing in Iran', *Jane's Defence Weekly*, 28 December 1986

No author, 'NLA and the struggle against Tehran', *Jane's Defence Weekly*, 20 February 1988

No author, 'NLA Chief of Staff Describes Operation 'Shining Sun'', *NLA Quarterly*, Spring 1988

No author, 'Operation 'Shining Sun', *NLA Quarterly*, Spring 1988

No author, 'Special Report', *NLA Quarterly*, Autumn 1988

No author, 'The international arms industry: Final casualty of the Gulf War', *Jane's Defence Weekly* (30 July 1988)

No author, Scott, Aziz, 'PKK opens second front', *International Defense Review* 7/1991 pp.702–703

O'Ballance, Colonel Edgar, 'Iran vs Iraq: Quantity vs Quality?' *Defence Attaché* No 1/1987, pp.25–31

Perkins, Major General K., 'Death of an Army: A short analysis of the Imperial Iranian armed forces', *The RUSI Journal* (June 1980)

Philipps, Richard, 'Tactical Defensive Doctrine of the Iraqi Ground Forces', *Jane's Soviet Intelligence Review* (March 1991) pp.116–119

Samuel, Annie Tracy. *Perceptions and Narratives of Security: The Iranian Revolutionary Guards Corps and the Iran-Iraq War.* Discussion Paper 2012-06 (Belfer Center for Science and International Affairs, John F.Kennedy School of Government, Harvard University, Cambridge, Mass 2012)

Tucker, A.R., 'Armored Warfare in the Gulf', *Armed Forces* (May 1988), pp.223–226

Warford, Captain James M., 'The Tanks of Babylon: Main Battle Tanks Of The Iraqi Army', *Armor*, Vol 99 No 6 (November-December 1990)

Various periodicals published by the Iranian and Iraqi Ministries of Defence, 1980s, 1990s and 2000s

Documents
CIA

CIA-DOC_ 0000072254.pdf: Iraq's Chemical Warfare Program: More Self-Reliant, More Deadly. August 1990.

CIA-DOC_00010797.pdf: Impact and Implications of Chemical Weapons Use in the Iran-Iraq War. 20 March 1988.

CIA-RDP86T01017R000202020001-4: After Al Faw: Implications and Options for Iraq and Iran. 12 March 1986.

CIA-RDP86T01017R000302670001-2: Iran's Improving Ground Forces. 10 July 1986.

CIA-RDP86T01017R00050539001-8: Soviet Military Forces Opposite Iran and In Afghanistan. 18 November 1986.

CIA-RDP86T01017R000808180001-5: The Iran-Iraq War; Impact of the Wet Season. 2 December 1986.

CIA-RDP89S01450R000200230001-0: Iran's Ground Forces: Morale and Manpower Problems. April 1988.

CIA-RDP89S01450R000600600001-5: Iran-Iraq: A Comparison of Two War-Weary economies. November 1988.

CIA-RDP90G01353R001200090002-2: An Evaluation of DI Reporting on Iran's Acceptance of a Cease-Fire in the Iran-Iraq War. 17 August 1988.

CIA-RDP90R00961R000300060001-1: Is Iraq Losing the War? April 1986.

CIA-RDP90T00114R000700800002-2: Iran's Preparations for the Next Offensive. 15 December 1987.

CIA-RDP90T01298R000300670001-8: The Iraqi Chemical Weapons Program in Perspective. 1985.

RDP90T00784R000100300010-1 British Chieftain Tank. Leningrad Tank Testing Area.

Conflict Record Research Center (CRRC)

SH-ADGC-D-000-731: Transcript from three Audio Files of a Meeting of the General Command of the Armed Forces. March 24 1988.

SH-AFGC-D-000-686: Orders of the President and Commander-in-Chief of the Armed Forces. February-December 1984.

SH-GMD-D-000-530: General Military Intelligence Directorate (GMID) Correspondence Regarding Reports on the Movements of Troops during the Iran-Iraq War. Apr 1988

SH-GMD-D-000-842: General Military Intelligence Directorate Report Assessing Political, Military and Economic Conditions in Iran. (Probably July 1980).

SH-GMID-D-000-266: General Military Intelligence Directorate Correspondence about Iranian Military Sites and Plans during the Iraq-Iran War. 1987–1988.

SH-GMID-D-000-301: Reports from General Directorate of Military Intelligence regarding the Iraq and Iran War. 1982–1987.

SH-GMID-D-000-302: Iran-Iraq Military Activity Report 1981.

SH-GMID-D-000-337: Reports by the General Military Intelligence Directorate regarding movements of Iranian Divisions and current military operations on the border. 1988

SH-GMID-D-000–529: Comprehensive Study of Al-Khomeini Guards during the Iranian-Iraqi War in 1988. October 1988.

SH-GMID-D-000–531: General Military Intelligence Directorate (GMID) Intelligence Reports about Iranian Force Movements during the Iran-Iraq War. April–May 1982

SH-GMID-D-001–369: Correspondence between the GMID, the Ministry of Defence, and the Ministry of Interior regarding Iranian military movements and the distribution of Iranian troops. 1985.

SH-IDGS-D-000–854: Reports by the General Security Intelligence Directorate to the Deputy Directorate regarding a study presented by the American Military Attache in Baghdad detailing Iranian military capabilities and Iranian anti-armour weapons purchases. Dec-86 to Mar-88.

SH-MISC-D-000–827: Saddam and Senior Iraqi Officials Discussing the Conflict with Iran, Iraqi Targets and Plans, a recent Attack on the Osirak Reactor, and Various Foreign Countries (1 October 1980).

SH-MISC-D-001–350: The Passing of Two Years of War: Iran-Iraq, Political Office of the Islamic Revolution Pasdaran Corps.

SH-MISC-D-001–3740: Report on the Al-Sulaymaniyah Security Governate from 1985–1988 including An-Anfal.

SH-PDWN-D-000–730: Transcript of an Armed Forces General Command meeting regarding the Iran-Iraq War, al-Fao, and military and diplomatic aspects of the war. May 26, 1988.

SH-PDWN-D-001–021: Transcripts of Meetings Between Saddam and Senior Iraqi Officials Discussing Military Tactics During the War with Iran, Including the Use of Napalm and Cluster Bombs, Tank Maneuvering and Attacking Oil Refineries (meeting on 6 October 1980).

SH-SHTP-A-000–788: Saddam Discussing the Iraqi Stance Toward respecting International Law. Circa June-July 1988.

SH–SHTP-A-000–835: Saddam and His Advisors Discussing Iraq's Decision to Go to War with Iran September 16, 1980.

SH-SHTP-A-001–045: Saddam and High Ranking Officers Discussing Plans to Attack Kurdish 'Saboteurs' in Northern Iraq and the Possibiity of Using Special Ammunition (Weapons). (Undated but circa 1985).

SH-SHTP-D-000–538: Transcript of a Meeting between Saddam and his Commanding Officers at the Armed Forces General Command Regarding the Iraq-Iran War. June 27 1988.

SH-SHTP-D-000–856: Transcript of a Meeting between Saddam Hussein and the Armed Forces General Command (22 November 1980).

SH-SPPC-D-000–229: Handwritten letter from Saddam Hussein to the Chief-of-Staff advising him in war issues. June 5 1988.

SP-PDWN-D-000–552: Documents from the Presidential Diwan regarding arms agreements signed between Iraq and the Soviet Union in 1981 and 1983.

Defense Intelligence Agency

DDB-1100–342–86: Ground Forces Intelligence Study Iran (May 1986).

DDB-1100–343–85: Ground Forces Intelligence Study Iraq (November 1985).

DDB-1100-IZ-81: Ground Order of Battle Iraq (March 1981).

DDB-2680–103–88 Part II: Military Intelligence Summary: Volume III, Part II Middle East and North Africa (Persian Gulf) (cut-off date 1 July 1987).

Foreign Broadcast Interception Service (FBIS)

FBIS-NES-93–074 Saddam Address on al-Faw Anniversary (April 19, 1993)

UK National Archives

BT 241/2929: Iran Military Supplies
FCO 8/2793: Sale of Chieftain Tanks from the United Kingdom to Iraq 1976
FCO 8/2845: UK Defence Sales to Iraq
FCO 8/3020: Report of Defence Attaché's, Baghdad, September 1979
FCO 8/3023: Sale of Chieftain Tanks from UK to Iraq 1977
FCO 8/3107: British Defence Attaché's Annual Report – Iran
FCO 8/3124: Arms Sales to Iran 1978
FCO 8/3135: Sale of Shir Iran Main Battle Tanks to Iran
FCO 8/3624: Supply of Military Equipment to Iran
FCO 8/3715: Defence Attache's Annual Report on Iraq 1980
FCO 8/3841: Head of Defence Sales Visits to the Gulf
FCO 8/4146: Defence Sales to Iraq: Tanks
FCO 8/4156: UK Defence Attache's Annual Report 1981
FCO 8/4162: Sale of Barmine and Ranger to Iraq
FCO 8/4164: Sale of Tanks to Iraq
FCO 8/3020: Report of Defence Attaché's, Baghdad September 1979
WO341/204: Report on Shir I (FV 4030)

US Army Intelligence and Security Command

Untitled and undated history of Iran-Iraq War from September 1980 to the spring of 1983. Released under NGIA FOIA request NGA #20130255F and US Army Intelligence and Security Command request FOIA#2456F-12 on 19 November 2013. Declassified 19 March 2013.

Websites

(http) iiarmy.topcities.com/army/ground/iigf.html. February 6, 2003
(www) harvardmun.org/wp-content/uploads/2012/01/JCCIran1.pdf
(www) iran-e-azad.org/English/nla/etl.html
(www) Ironsides8m.com/army/ir.htm~army
Ahwaz Climate, world-climates.com
AllRefer Country Study and Country guide, Iran. (http) (allrefer.com/country-guide-study/iran/iran155.html). Iran- The Revolutionary Period and Supreme defence Council of Iran
AllRefer.com, Country Study and Country guide (allrefer.com/country-guide-study), Iran (http) (allrefer.com/country-guide-study/iran/iran155.html)
Anfal: The Iraqi State's Genocide against the Kurds, The Center of Halabja against Anfalization and genocide of the Kurds (CHAK), February 2007 www.wadinet.de/news/dokus/Anfal_CHAK.pdf
CIA FOIA (https) cia.gov/library/reading room/home
CIA National Intelligence Dailies from web sites (www.) foia.cia.gov/browse_docs.asp
Cipher Machines website, www.ciphermachines.com

Climatological Normals of Abadan, www.hko.gov.hk/wxinfo/climat/world/eng/asia/westasia/abadan_e.htm
Country Study and Country guide, Iran, allrefer.com
Freemeteo website, www.freemeteo.com. Weather history, Kuwait and Diyarkabir. Daily archive
Genocide in Iraq. hrw.org/reports/1993/iraqanfal/ANFAL.htm
Imposed War web site (www) sarjed.ir or (http) English. tebyan,net
Iranian Army, iiarmy.topcities.com
Iraqi Armed Forces Forum web site (www: http) Iraqmilitary.org
kuwait pages:kuwait wars (http): kuwaitpages.blogspot.com/2007/08/kuwait-wars.html
Weather History, Kuwait and Diyarkabir, harvardmun.org
Web site (www) gulflink.osd.mil/declassified/cia/19961102/110296_93663-72538_01.text
World Climate: www. world-climates.com/city-climate-ahwaz-iran-asia/
www.harvardmun.org/wp-content/uploads/2012/01/JCCIran1.pdf
www.iiarmy.topcities.com/army/ground/iigf.html (6 February 2003)

NOTES

PART I

Chapter 1

1. During the Battle of Qadisiyya (or Qadisiyyah or Qadeisiyya) in November 636, the Arabs defeated a Sassanid Persian army, marking the beginning of the end of Persian rule in Iraq and of the Persian Empire. Hiro, p.44.
2. Cordesman et al, pp.2–3.
3. See H.W. Beuttel's articles in the TNDM newsletter.
4. *Lessons*, pp.2–3; *Jane's Defence Weekly*, 'The international arms industry: Final casualty of the Gulf War', 30 July 1988.
5. The background to the Gulf War is sketched out in O'Ballance, *The Gulf War*, pp.12–19, hereafter O'Ballance. *Lessons*, pp.10–39. There are numerous works which provide greater detail.
6. Conflict Record Research Center (CRRC) SH –SHTP-A-000-835. See also Al-Marashi and Salama, *Iraq's Armed Forces*, hereafter Marashi & Salama, pp.121–122; Cooper & Bishop, *Iran-Iraq War in the Air*, pp.61–63, hereafter Cooper & Bishop; Farrokh, *Iran at War*, pp.313–317, hereafter Farrokh; Pollack, *Arabs at War*, pp.176–182, herafter Pollack, *Arabs*; Ward, *Immortal: A Military History of Iran and its Armed Forces*, p.203, hereafter Ward. UK Defence Attache's Annual Report 1981, UK National Archives (UK NA) FCO 8/4156. Strictly, the Iraqi leader should be referred to as Hussein, but the West's more common use of his personal name will be retained in this narrative.
7. Cooper & Bishop, p.62; Farrokh, pp.313–317.
8. *Lessons*, pp.54, 91.
9. Op cit, p.22.
10. Saddam was a civilian, despite his military titles. He was also chairman of the supreme decision-making body, the Revolutionary Command Council (RCC).
11. Khomeini is also transliterated as Khomeyni.
12. Murray & Woods, *The Iran-Iraq War*, pp.38–39, 44, hereafter Murray & Woods.
13. Op cit, p.44.
14. Similar views shaped his decision to invade Kuwait in 1990.
15. CRRC SH-GMD-D-000-842.
16. The town would become infamous due to the American treatment of prisoners in the jail.
17. For the Iraqi Army and the decision to go to war, see Woods et al, *Project 1946*, pp.48–49, hereafter *Project 1946*. This is qualified by Woods et al, *Saddam's War: An Iraqi Military Perspective of The Iran-Iraq War*, pp.27–29, hereafter *Saddam's War*, and *Saddam's Generals: Perspectives of the Iran-Iraq War*, pp.55, 115–116, hereafter *Saddam's Generals*; Murray & Woods, p.47.
18. Comment by Lieutenant General Aladdin Hussein Makki Khamas and in UKNA FCO 8/4156. See also Murray & Woods, p.64 f/n 52.
19. *Saddam's Generals*, pp.53, 113.
20. This suggestion was first made by US journalist R. Halloran, 'British in 1950, Helped Map Iraqi Invasion of Iran', in the *New York Times*, 16 October 1980. Farrokh, p.347; O'Ballance, p.48.
21. For planning, see Malovany *Milhamot Bavel ha-Hadasha*, *The Wars of Modern Babylon*, pp.109–112, 116–117, hereafter Malovany; *Saddam's Generals*, pp.128–130; *Saddam's War*, pp.54–55, 113, 115–116.
22. *Saddam's Generals*, pp.52, 56–57.
23. All weather data is based upon the Kuwait weather forecast, Weather History, daily archive in the Freemeteo website and Kuwait archive for the period 1980–1988.
24. Based upon websites Climatological Normals of Abadan and Ahwaz Climate Climate of Ahwaz Iran/world climate.

Chapter 2

1. For the Iraqi Republic Army before 1980, see Al-Marashi & Salama, pp.107–128; Pollack, *Arabs*, pp.156–182; Murray & Woods, pp.52–66.
2. Pollack, *Arabs*, pp.167–176; Dupuy, *Elusive Victory*, pp.467–469, 533–535.
3. Details of military equipment performance and sales based upon DIA DDB-1100-IZ-81, pp.xxix-xxiii; Christopher Foss, *Jane's Armour and Artillery*, various editions, hereafter Foss; and Jacques de Lestapis, *Military Powers Encyclopedia*, hereafter Lestapis. See also Murray and Woods, Table 5.1. Following the 1972 Friendship and Cooperation Treaty with Moscow, 1,600 Soviet tanks were delivered. In addition, Iraq retained some of the 135 M-30 122mm howitzers and 60 A-19 122mm guns it had received earlier, the former in mountain divisions. British-made 25-pdr (87mm) gun-howitzers and 5.5in (139.7mm) howitzers inherited from the British were held in store and would be used in small numbers during the Iran-Iraq War. The Iraqis also retained, and would use a small number of Soviet SU-100 armoured self-propelled assault guns.
4. DIA DDB-1100-IZ-81, pp.89, 75. Also SIPRI Trade Register 1980.
5. Interviews with IRIA veterans, including former NCOs of the 88th and 92nd Armoured Division.
6. The ERC-TH were delivered from 1981. Contrary to many reports, Paris did not supply Iraq with AMX-30 tanks.
7. SIPRI claims 100 EE-11 Urutu wheeled APC were also supplied, but they appear to have arrived later.
8. IDF Journal, Volume III No.2 (spring 1986). Jeff Abramowitz, Jacqueline Hahn, Jerry Cheslow (based on IDF Intelligence Branch briefings), *Iraq: the military build-up*. It is possible that Baghdad augmented 'commercial' acquisitions with Soviet MAZ 537G.
9. *Lessons*, p.57; Military Balance 1980. For the Iraqi Army, see also DIA DDB-1100-IZ-81. This estimated (p.6) Iraqi strength in September 1980 at 350,000, with 6,000 AFV and 1,200 guns.
10. Marashi & Salama, p.156; Pollack, *Arabs*, p.182; *Saddam's Generals*, p.129 f/n 137. The order of battle information is based upon UK NA FCO 8/3715 Defence Attache's Annual Report on Iraq, dated 26 June 1980, amended with information from Pesach Malovany.
11. DIA DDB-1100-343-85, p.21.
12. Op cit, pp.39–40.
13. Marashi & Salama, pp.125–126; Pollack, *Arabs*, p.182; CRRC SH-MISC-D-000-827, p.13.
14. Murray & Woods, pp.57–59, 65–66.
15. DDB-1100-343-85, pp.28–29.
16. Murray & Woods, p.65. The RPG-7 was the primary short-range anti-armour weapon of the Iran-Iraq War and is described by the Soviets as a hand-held, anti-tank grenade, but the Western description of Rocket Propelled Grenade is more accurate. It has an effective range with its 93mm diameter, 2.6kg HEAT warhead, of 200 metres and a maximum range of 920 metres. It is also deadly against infantry, fortifications and even helicopters. See Rottman, *The Rocket Propelled Grenade*, hereafter Rottman.
17. Al-Marashi & Salama, pp.127–130.
18. See Perkins' article in the RUSI Journal, but also see Cooper & Bishop, pp.44–45; Farrokh, pp.317–318; Murray & Woods, pp.72–78; Ward, pp.203–205; Zabih, *The Iranian Military in Revolution and War*, pp.4–14, hereafter Zabih. Furlong's 1973 article 'Iran: A power to be reckoned with'.
19. For the IRIA, see Farrokh, pp.320–322; *Lessons*, p.57; Military Balance 1980; Ward pp.193–197, 201–210; Zabih, pp.31–34. Website www.Ironsides8m.com/army/ir.htm~army and AllRefer.com, Country Study and Country guide (allrefer.com/country-guide-study), Iran http:allrefer.com/country-guide-study/iran/iran155.html); 'Iran, The Revolutionary Period'; website iiarmy.topcities.com /army/ ground/iigf.html.

20 Iran accounted for a third of total US arms sales between 1972 and 1977. Pollack, The Persian Puzzle, p.109, hereafter Pollack, Persians.
21 Ward, p.196, estimates up to 30 percent of the Imperial Iranian Army were gunners.
22 Details of the Chieftain programmes from UK NA FCO 8 series. Specifically 3124, 3135, 3624, 4164, as well as BT 241/2929 and WO341/204.
23 BT 241/2929. In 2014, the United Kingdom Ministry of Defence was ordered by an international tribunal to pay Iran £390 million for its failure to complete the FV 4030 programme.
24 Production of the Shir Iran began only in March 1979, with the first tanks completed by the end of the year; they were sold to Jordan as the Khalid, in November of the same year.
25 The Iranians also produced the RPG-7 under licence as Sageg. Rottman, p.38.
26 Tom Cooper, 'La Guerre des Villes: Bagdad contre Téhéran', Air Combat magazine, No.8/2014.
27 Murray & Woods, p.78 f/n 115.
28 For the impact of the revolution upon the IRIA, see Farrokh pp.119–120, 338; Marashi & Salama, p.131; Murray & Woods, pp.81–82; Ward, pp.211–225, 228–230, 238–240, 244–245; Zabih, pp.141–163.
29 Farrokh, pp.335–336; Ward, pp.231–234; Zabih, p.237.
30 Website iiarmy.topcities.com/ army/ground/iigf.html.
31 DIA DDB-2680-103-88, pp.28–29, and DDB-1100-342-86, p.59.
32 For the hostage crisis, see Farrokh, pp.339–341; Pollack, Persians, pp.153–180; Ward, pp.236–237.
33 For the status of Iranian forces, see Buchan, Days of God, p.341, hereafter Buchan; Cooper & Bishop, pp.50–51; Farrokh, pp.329–330, 335–336, 338–339, 348, 453 f/n 34; Pollack, Persians, p.186. CRRC SH-GMD-D-000-842.
34 Farrokh, pp.334–335. Another transliteration is Sipah-i Pasdaran-i Inqilab-i Islami. Annie Tracy Samuel, discussion paper 'Perceptions and Narratives of Security', p.1 f/n 1, hereafter Samuel.
35 Samuel, p.2.
36 Op cit, p.4 f/n 13. DIA DDB-1100-342-86, p.46.
37 Samuel, p.2; Ward, pp.226–228. CRRC SH-GMD-D-000-842.
38 Murray & Woods, pp.79, 81–83.

Chapter 3
1 CRRC SH-GMD-D-000-842. See also Hiro, p.49.
2 Lessons, p.41.
3 CRRC SH-GMD-D-000-842.
4 Even the following year, the Iranian section had only six.
5 For the GMID, see Marashi & Salama, pp.146–147; Saddam's Generals, pp.20, 89.
6 For the border fighting, see Cooper & Bishop, pp.63–68; Farrokh, pp.344–345; Malovany, pp.181–182, 124–125; Murray & Woods, pp.91–92; CRRC SH-SHTP-A-000-835 and US Army Intelligence and Security Command history, pp.4–2 to 4–5, hereafter US AISC.
7 See Cooper & Bishop, pp.63–68.
8 Parviz Mosalla Nejad (ed.), Shalamcheh, pp.9–10, hereafter Nejad.
9 See Murray & Woods, p.93.
10 US AISC, pp.4–2, 4–5.
11 Op cit, pp.4–9.
12 Cooper & Bishop, p.67; Nejad, p.10.
13 Even then, the IRGC ignored his orders, see Farrokh, p.349; Ward p.247.
14 CRRC SH -SHTP-A-000-835. This is the CRRC heading, but Murray & Woods, p.49 f/n 137, state the document is entitled 'Meeting Between Saddam Hussein, the National Command and the Revolutionary Command Council Discussing the Iran-Iraq War, 16 September 1980'.
15 For the Iraqi decision to go to war, see Murray & Woods, pp.48–50, 93–98.
16 Murray & Woods, pp.114.
17 Farrokh, pp.344–345.
18 Farrokh, pp.349–350; Ward, p.244; US AISC, pp.4–5.
19 Ward, p.251.
20 US AISC, pp.4–6.
21 Op cit, p.244.
22 Cooper & Bishop, pp.77–81; Project 1946, pp.47–48.
23 Sadik, interview, March 2005.
24 Cooper et al article, La Guerre Iran-Irak, Volume 1, hereafter Guerre Vol.1.
25 Cooper & Bishop, pp.72–75; La Guerre, pp.42–44; Malovany, pp.125–129; Murray & Woods, pp.100–108; US AISC, pp.4–5.
26 These figures are based upon the order of battle and AISC data. Sources quoting larger figures assume the whole Iraqi Army was deployed in the invasion.
27 J. Wagner, 'Iraq', in Gabriel, Fighting Armies, p.68.
28 See comments by Murray & Woods, pp.108 and f/n 80, 114, 124, 131.
29 Griffin, The Iraqi Way of War, p.18, hereafter Griffin.
30 Op cit, pp.20–21.
31 Saddam's Generals, pp.128–130.
32 Murray & Woods, pp.116 f/n 97, 118.
33 Op cit, p.113.
34 SIPRI data suggests Iran received 23,800 TOW missiles before the revolution. Saddam was so impressed by the obvious superiority of these weapons over the Soviet missiles used by his helicopters that in January 1981 he asked his staff to seek TOW missiles and launchers from the Saudis and Jordanians. Murray & Woods, p.154.
35 For the air war, see Cooper & Bishop and the same authors' article 'Fire in the Hills'. This passage benefits from information provided by both authors.
36 Buchan, p.339; Pollack, Arabs, p.193.
37 Murray & Woods, p.117.
38 O'Ballance, p.41.
39 Murray & Woods, pp.116, 125.
40 Farrokh, p.350.
41 Ward, p.251. US AISC, pp.4–9, 4–11, 4–45 to 4–47.
42 Zabih, p.134 f/n 30.
43 US AISC, pp.4–9.

Chapter 4
1 For the Arab uprising in Khuzestan 1979–1980, see Farrokh, p.337; O'Ballance, p.21; Ward, p.233; Zabih, p.15. The Iranian governor at the time was Admiral Ahmad Madani, who would later flee to France.
2 Saddam's Generals, pp.30, 32. Others were Brigadier General Hisham al-Fakhri, General Nizar al-Khazraji and Brigadier General Taha Shakarji.
3 UK NA FCO 8/4156.
4 Operations of 1st Mechanised and 10th Armoured Divisions are described in the section on the Central and Northern Fronts. Information on 10th Armoured Brigade from General Makki.
5 For the invasion and northern axis, see Cooper & Bishop, pp.90–91; Farrokh, pp.352–354; Lessons, pp.87, 95–96; Malovany, pp.137–139; O'Ballance, pp.35–36, 38, 40–41; Pollack, Arabs, pp.186–193. CRRC SH-PDWN-D-001-021. US AISC, pp.4–23, 4–27.
6 Unknown author, 'Iranian Army Captain H Ebrahimi-Saeed' (in Farsi), Balatajan.ir, 2016. This and following accounts of the first few days of action by the 283rd Armoured Cavalry Battalion of the 92nd Armoured Division are all based on the same article.
7 Buchan, p.338.
8 For the sunken vehicles, see O'Ballance, pp.40–41; Hiro, pp.44–45.
9 Murray & Woods, p.110, quoting CRRC SH-MISC-D-001-350.
10 CRRC SH-SHTP-D-000-856.
11 For 5th Mechanised Division's advance on Ahwaz, see Hiro, p41; Lessons, p.87; O'Ballance, pp.35–37. AISC, pp.4–23, 4–27; Imposed War website.
12 The Iraqis received 45 GSP by 1970, ordered another 200 second-hand units in 1983 and received them the following year. Iraqi armoured and mechanised units also had Soviet MTU-20, Czech MT-55KS and East German BLG-60 Armoured Vehicle-Launched Bridges (AVLB). For Iraqi Army water-crossing, see The National Training Center, The Iraqi Army: Organization and Tactics, p.150, hereafter NTC Iraqi Army.
13 Saddam's Generals, pp.9, 160.
14 Information from Tom Cooper.
15 For initial operations along the northern bank, see Nejad, pp.10–16; US AISC, pp.4–23; Imposed War website.
16 Murray & Woods, p120.
17 Cooper & Bishop, p.85.
18 See Malovany and McLaurin in his monograph, The Battle of Khorramshahr, hereafter McLaurin, for excellent sketch maps.
19 For Khorramshahr, see Cooper & Bishop, pp.96, 102–103; Farrokh, p.354; Hiro, pp.41, 43–44; Lessons, pp.92–94; Malovany, pp.140–141, 145–148; Marashi & Salama, p.157; McLaurin, pp.27–32; Murray & Woods, pp.113, 120–22, 124; Nejad, pp.15–19; O'Ballance, pp.37–38, 40; Project 1946, pp.68–69; Ward, pp.251–252. Lieutenant Colonel R.W. Lamont, 'A Tale of Two Cities Hue and Khorramshahr', Armor magazine; US AISC, pp.4–28, 4–29, 4–33, Figure 4-10; CRRC SH-MISC-D-000-827 and SH-

NOTES

SHTP-D-000-856, DIA DDB-1100-343-85, pp.55–56, and DDB-2680-103-88, p.19; Imposed War website.
20 CRRC SH-MISC-D-000-827, p.15.
21 Marashi & Salama, p.157; DIA DDB-1100-343-85, p.33.
22 Whether or not the 25-pdrs were sent to this front is unclear. The Iraqis used 25-pdrs and even former British 5.5in (139.7mm) gun-howitzers, and during the week 19–25 April 1981, these guns fired 806 and 354 rounds respectively. Murray & Woods, Table 5.1.
23 US AISC, pp.4–28, 6–19.
24 Based upon DIA DDB-1100-342-86 and the Imposed War website.
25 Murray & Woods, p.121.
26 The DIA stated 5,000 Iraqis were killed. DDB-1100-343-85, p.56. Jahanara, who would be killed in later fighting, had organised a brave and sustained defence at great cost; one figure quotes 7,000 Iranian casualties; Ward, p.252.
27 The first Abadan Pasdaran unit was the Tarigholgods Battalion, which later expanded into the Fathol-Mobin Brigade and then the 30th Beit-ol-Moghaddas Division. Zabih, p.156.
28 Davis, *Iranians' Operational Warfighting Ability*, p.7, hereafter, Davis.
29 The Iraqis had six Hooks, capable of carrying a 12-tonne load, and they were used to move jeep-type vehicles and light trucks, as well as supplies, across both the Karun and the Karkheh. Information from Farzin Bishop.
30 For Abadan, see Buchan, p.339; Cooper & Bishop, pp.98, 100; Farrokh, p.360; Hiro, p.43; *Lessons*, pp.94–95; Malovany, pp.148–150; McLaurin, p.31; Murray & Woods, pp.123, 153; O'Ballance, pp.37, 39–40; *Saddam's Generals*, pp.130–131; US AISC, pp.4–28, 4–29, 4–33; CRRC SH-PDWN-D-001-021; DIA DDB-1100-343-85, pp.55–56; Imposed War website.
31 Murray & Woods, p.120.
32 US AISC, pp.4–33, 4–34.
33 Op cit, pp.4–27.
34 DIA DDB-2680-103-88, p.19.
35 *Project 1946*, p.53.
36 Griffin, p.19.
37 Griffin, p.18; Murray & Woods, pp.126, 128–129.
38 McLaurin, p.27; Ward, p.248.
39 Murray & Woods, pp.123, 153.
40 US AISC, pp.4–34, 5–30, 5–32, 5–33.
41 Op cit, p.5–33; US DIA DDB-1100-342-86, pp.24–25.
42 For Iraqi logistics, see US AISC, pp.4–43 to 4–45, 5–35.
43 DIA DDB-1100-IZ-81, p.xxi.
44 CRRC SH-MISC-D-000-827, p.35.
45 O'Ballance, p.51; Murray & Woods, p.155; Pelletiere, *The Iran-Iraq War*, p.44, hereafter Pelletiere. SIPRI yearbooks.
46 See Atkeson's article' Iraq's Arsenal: Tool of Ambition'.
47 DIA DDB-1100-343-85, p.45.
48 Op cit, p.62.
49 The 180mm battery was attached to II Corps, but the Iraqi Army had only 1,400 rounds for it. CRRC SH-SHTP-D-000-856, pp.27, 44.
50 DIA DDB-1100-343-85, pp.8–9. Saddam was especially critical of IrAF reconnaissance efforts. Murray & Woods, p.119 and f/n 109.
51 Based upon DIA DDB-1100-343-85, pp.58–59, Figure 21.
52 US AISC, pp.4–34.
53 Cooper & Bishop, p.94. US AISC, pp.4–34, 4–47, Fig 4-12. Imposed War website.
54 DIA DDB-2680-103-88, p.5, DDB-1100-342-86, pp.14, 22, Figures 12 and 15. The 3rd Area Support Command was transferred from Tehran.
55 DIA DDB-1100-342-86, p.35.
56 Farrokh, p.322; O'Ballance, pp.51, 65; Zabih, p.147. All Refer Country Study and Country guide website: Iran The Revolutionary Period.
57 Davis, p.7, quoting Ye Gromov, 'Principal Iranian Communication Routes and Ground Transportation', *Zarubezhnoye Voyennoye*, No.11 (November 1987), pp.40, 43.
58 For the Iranian rail system, see Davis, *Iranian ... Ability*, p.67; Goldsack, *Jane's World Railways 1980–1981*, pp.290–291, 484; DIA DDB-1100-IZ-81, DDB-1100-342-86, pp.23–25, DDB-2680-103-88, p.14. The DIA calculated Iran had 4,061km of track.
59 The DIA claimed there were 424 locomotives, 4,730 enclosed freight wagons (boxcars), 1,488 open wagons (flatcars) and 2,347 tank wagons for liquids.
60 For the road system, see DIA DDB-2680-103-88, p.14, and DDB-1100-343-85, pp.23–25.
61 Truck strength, DIA DDB-2680-103-88, pp.12–13.
62 Davis, p.7; Ward, p.263.
63 USAIC, pp.5–32.
64 Op cit, pp.5–32.
65 DIA DDB-1100-IZ-81, p.xxx.
66 DDB-1100-343-85, p.6.
67 This description of Iraqi communications is based upon DIA DDB-1100-343-85, pp.41, 45, DDB-2680-103-88, p.19, and DDB-1100-IZ-81 pp.xxix-xxx; US AISC, pp.5–34, 5–35.
68 DIA DDB-1100-343-85, p.41.

Chapter 5

1 For Hoveyzeh/Nassr, see Buchan, pp.341, 458 f/n 15; Cooper & Bishop, pp.113–114, 135 n. 183; Farrokh, pp.357–358; Hiro, p.49; *Lessons*, pp.112–114; Malovany, pp.162–166; Murray & Woods, pp.143–416, 149–150; Pollack, Arabs, pp.193–195; *Saddam's Generals*, pp.132–133; O'Ballance, pp.60–63; Pollack, p.194; Ward, pp.253–254. US AISC, pp.4–37, 4–39, 4–43, 4–44, 4–45, Fig. 4–14, 5–9, Figs 5–5, 5–6. This incorrectly identifies the defenders as 6th Armoured Division, as does Pollack, but provides much useful information; Imposed War website. I would like to express my gratitude to General Makki for reviewing this chapter and making corrections as well as numerous helpful comments. This and all later accounts also benefit from both sides' communiqués published in the *Baghdad Times* and *Tehran Times* and/or broadcast and published in the BBC's 'Summary of World Broadcasts' or the US FSIB.
2 US AISC, p.4–37.
3 Cooper & Bishop, p.113.
4 US AISC, p.4–37.
5 DIA DDB-1100-343-85, p.42.
6 Shukur had two battalions of T-72s which Iraq received from July 1979. A combination of maintaining Iraqi prestige and a shortage of spares would restrict the battlefield use of the T-72 until 1982. DIA DDB-1100-IZ-81, p.xx, DDB-1100-343-85, p.62. Details of Shukur's counterattack from General Makki based upon Shukur's memoirs.
7 Cooper & Bishop, p.113.
8 A T-72 carries 39 rounds, while a T-55 has 43. Foss, *Armour and Artillery 2007–2008*, pp.105, 126.
9 For tank gun performance, see Foss, *Armour and Artillery 2000–2001*, pp.93, 124–125.
10 Foss, *Armour and Artillery 2007–2008*, p.104; US AISC, pp.4–43.
11 Cooper & Bishop, p.114.
12 The Iraqis had been interested in Chieftains since September 1976, but the British informed Baghdad their production facilities were fully committed to meeting the Iranian order. By February 1981, the Iraqis had probably captured 100–150 Chieftains, and asked the British to refurbish them. Most were transferred for this to western Iraq near the Jordanian border, with a few being left at Camp Taji, here they were discovered by American forces in 2003, but as the Chieftain needed special ammunition and had a poor automotive system, most of the tanks were given to Jordan. UK NA FCO 8/2793, 2845, 3023, 4164.
13 Cooper & Bishop, p.114; *Lessons*, p.114. US AISC, pp.4–44.
14 Information from General Makki.
15 O'Ballance, p.63; Pollack, pp.194–195.
16 Cooper & Bishop, p.114; *Lessons*, p.112; O'Ballance, p.64; Pollack, p.194. Imposed War website.
17 Cooper & Bishop, p.113; Ward, pp.246–247; Samuel, p.3 and p.3 f/n 8. DIA DDB-1100-342-86, p.2.
18 Murray & Woods, pp.70–71; *Saddam's Generals*, pp.20–21. The author would like to thank Mr Ralph Simpson of the Cipher Machines website (ciphermachines.com) and Mr Paul Reuvers of the Crypto Museum for help on cryptographic matters.
19 Farrokh, p.358; Hiro, p.50.
20 For Iman Ali and follow-on operations, see Buchan, p.339; Farrokh, p.358; *Lessons*, p.115; *Saddam's Generals*, pp.120–121. This claims the defenders were 26th Armoured Brigade, but this was with 5th Mechanised Division near Abadan. US AISC, pp.5–17, 5–20, Figs 5-8, 5-11.
21 The difficulties of holding ground in tank against infantry combat are illustrated in the 2014 Brad Pitt movie 'Fury'.
22 DIA DDB-1100-342-86, Appendix B, p.74.
23 Cooper & Bishop, p.126; Farrokh, pp.360–361; *Lessons*, pp.114, 117–118, 420; O'Ballance, p.65; Ward, pp.254–255.
24 Ward, pp.245, 247.

25 O'Ballance, p.65; Ward, p.255; US AISC, pp.5–15, 5–17. Website AllRefer.com, Country Study and Country Guide, Iran.
26 Davis, p.27.
27 Murray & Woods, p.81.
28 Based upon CRRC SH-GMID-D-000-529 and DIA DDB-1100-342-86. IRIA companies had about 140–150 men and battalions up to 600.
29 Malovany, pp.168–169; Murray & Woods, p.172.
30 *Lessons*, pp.117, 122; O'Ballance, pp.64–65; Pollack, p.195. US AISC, pp.5–2.
31 For the Iranian forces, see Ward, p.253; DIA DDB-1100-342-86, pp.5, 46; DDB-2680-103-88, p.5.
32 US AISC, pp.5–33.
33 Op cit, pp.5–1, 5–20.
34 *Saddam's Generals*, p.120.
35 Op cit, pp.120–121, and information from General Makki.
36 US AISC, pp.5–34.
37 Hiro, p.89. Hiro estimated Popular Army strength at 500,000, but this is an exaggeration.
38 *Lessons*, p.426; Marashi & Salama, pp.154–155; *Project 1946*, p.59.
39 DIA DDB-1100-343-85, pp.32, 59–60, 66.
40 *Project 1946*, p.69.
41 Murray & Woods, p.149.
42 Op cit, pp.172–173.
43 For Samene-al-Aeme, see Cooper & Bishop, p.127; Farrokh, pp.361–362; Hiro, pp.52–53; *Lessons*, pp.117, 123–124; Malovany, pp.180–181; Murray & Woods, p.173; O'Ballance, pp.66–67; Pelletiere, p.41; Pollack, p.195. US AISC, pp.5–9, 5–15, 5–20, 5–29, Figs 5-7, 5–11, 5–12. A.R. Tucker's article 'Armored Warfare in the Gulf and Armies of the Gulf War'. Samene-al-Aeme was the Shi'ites' eighth Imam, also written Samen-ol-A'emeh, Samenol A'emeh, Thamil ul' Aimma or Thamen-ol-A'emeh.
44 Cooper-Bishop, p.86.
45 Buchan, p.351; Davis, p.23; A.H. Cordesman, *The Iran-Iraq War and Western Security 1984–1987: Strategic Implications and Policy Options* (London: Jane's, 1987), p.61.
46 DIA DDB-1100-343-85, pp.52, 62.
47 O'Ballance, p.68.
48 It is unclear who made this order, either Ni'ami or Saddam, probably the former. Murray & Woods, p.173.
49 Reports that the brigade lost a third of its tanks are exaggerated, the DIA concluding that from 1981–1985 only 25–50 T-72 were destroyed, mostly by ATGM and 15–18 captured, of which one was reportedly used as a target during evaluations of the missile. The Soviets tested captured TOW, and in October 1981 passed on detailed reports through the Iraqi Military Attaché in Moscow, to GMID. CRRC SH-GMID-D-001-084; DIA DDB-1100-343-85, pp.52, 62.
50 Cooper & Bishop, pp.127–128; *Lessons*, p.125; O'Ballance, p.68. Website AllRefer.com, Country Study and Country Guide, Iran Joint Crisis: Supreme Defense Council of Iran, 1980. Harvard Model United Nations 2012. Copy on website www.harvardmun.org/wp-content/uploads/2012/01/JCCIran1.pdf.
51 Ward, p.255; DIA DDB-1100-342-86, Appendix B, p.72.
52 Based on information from General Makki.

Chapter 6

1 For Iraqi road-building operations, see NTC Iraqi Army, p.149.
2 Tarigh al-Qods is also written Tariq al-Quds and Tarigh ol-Qods. An alternative translation is *The Path to Jerusalem*. Some sources suggest it was also called Karbala 1.
3 For Tarigh al-Qods, see Cooper & Bishop, p.130; *Lessons*, pp.125–126, 144 n.14; Malovany, pp.185–186; Murray & Woods, p.174 & f/n 16, p.175; O'Ballance, pp.68–69; Pollack, pp.195–196; Ward, pp.255–256; US AISC, pp.5–29, 5–36, Fig. 5-11; Imposed War website. Brigadier General Rashid's article in website www.netiran.com/Htdocs/Clippings/FPolitics/960615X XFP01.html.ee; also O'Ballance's article 'Iran vs Iraq: Quantity vs Quality?'. Information from Mr Tom Cooper based on the memoirs of Brigadier General Massoed Bakhtiari.
4 Murray & Woods, p.175.
5 US AISC, pp.5–29.
6 Op cit, pp.5–36.
7 Iranian figures from Imposed War website.
8 O'Ballance, p.78.
9 O'Ballance article 'Iran vs Iraq: Quantity vs Quality?'.
10 CRRC SH-MISC-D-000-827, pp.47–48. By late April, the 130mm guns could fire only two or three rounds a day. Murray & Woods, Table 5.1.
11 CRRC SH-MISC-D-000-827, p.38; SH-SHTP-D-000-856, pp.18, 20. Data in Murray & Woods, Table 5.1, indicates that by April 1981, Yugoslavia had delivered to Iraq up to 100 towed artillery pieces; M48 76mm mountain guns, M56 105mm and M65 155mm howitzers.
12 The factory began production in 1984.
13 For arms sales to both sides, see Foss, various years; De Lestapis, pp.109–112; SIPRI year books; IISS Military Balance; US AISC, p.535.
14 See Bani-Sadr's comments upon Iran's self-imposed isolation from the international community in Murray & Woods, p.97.
15 Pelletiere, p.74.
16 O'Ballance, p.103; Pelletiere, p.45. However, the actual price may have been under $230 million. See CRRC SP-PDWN-D-000-552; DIA DDB-2680-103-88.
17 UK NA FCO 8/2845, 8/3841, 8/4156, 8/4162, 8/4164. The Iraqis sought 320–420 new tanks with Cobham armour, 21 ARVs and up to 30 AVLB, together with 500 FH-70 towed 155mm howitzers. The British prevaricated because they did not want Soviet intelligence to inspect the latest Western armour. This prevarication, the high prices demanded by London and the slow delivery of parts to refurbish the captured tanks caused the Iraqis to lose interest, and in December 1981 the exasperated Director of Armour, General Salah Askar, allegedly told the British: 'We don't want your stupid tanks.' *Saddam's Generals*, pp.132–133.
18 SH-GMID-D-001-020, quoted in Murray & Woods, Table 5.1.
19 Murray & Woods, pp.153, 156–157.
20 Schmidt and US Arms Control and Disarmament Agency study on World Military Expenditures and Arms Transfers.
21 DIA DDB-1100-342-86, p.39.
22 Murray & Woods, pp.162–163; Ward, p.256.
23 For comments on Iranian operations, see US AISC, pp.5–30 to 5–33, 5–36.

Chapter 7

1 US AISC, pp.5–30, 5–34, 5–33, 5–36.
2 DIA DDB-1100-343-85, pp.6, 12.
3 For Iranian military problems, see US AISC, pp.5–30 to 5–33. Website AllRefer.com, Country Study and Country Guide, Iran.
4 DIA DDB-1100-342-86, p.35.
5 This is covered in subsequent chapters of this book.
6 For this operation, see *Lessons*, pp.128–129; Malovany, pp.190–191; O'Ballance, p.78; US AISC, pp.6–1, 6–3.
7 Information from General Makki.
8 *Lessons*, p.142; O'Ballance, pp.89–90.
9 The operation, also written Bait-al-Mugaddas and Beit olMoqaddass, is sometimes referred to by another Islamic name for Jerusalem, Quds or Holy Quds.
10 These were NVS-700 Night Vision Goggles, an export version of the AN/PVS-4 with Gen 2 Image Intensifiers.
11 Cooper & Bishop, p.130. Bizarrely, Shirazi would tell a ceremony at Ahwaz on 25 May that 'It was the first operation in which we had no intelligence reports on the enemy.'
12 For Beit-ol-Mogaddas, see Buchan, pp.352–353; Cooper & Bishop, pp.130, 132–134, 136; Hills, p.14; Farrokh, pp.362, 365–367; Hiro, pp.55, 59–60, 62, 63–64; *Lessons*, pp.129, 135–140, 142, 147; Malovany, pp.199–207; Marashi & Salama, p.146; Murray & Woods, pp.63 f/ n48, 175–176,184–185 & f/n 46; Nejad, pp.19–21; O'Ballance, pp.79, 82–85, 89; Pelletiere, p.42; Pollack, pp.198–199. Ward, pp.257–258; *Saddam's Generals*, pp.16, 31–33, 35, 36, 39, 114; *Project 1946*, p.56; US AISC, pp.6–1, 6–3, 6–7, 6–10, Fig. 6-1; SH-GMID-D-000-531.See also O'Ballance article 'Iran vs Iraq'. Summary of World Broadcasts; Foreign Broadcast Information Service. Website Imposed War; Michael Connell on Iranian operational decision-making on website www.dtic.mil/dtic/tr/fulltext/u2/a585872.pdf. I would especially like to thank General Makki for his help and comments.
13 *Saddam's Generals*, pp.34–35.
14 DIA DDB-1100-343-85, pp.31–32, 55.
15 Murray & Woods, p.181 f/n 39.
16 For Iraqi defences, see Murray & Woods, pp.180–181; DIA DDB-1100-343-85, pp.57–58.
17 The Bar Lev Line observation points were some 30km from the Lateral Road, the jump-off point for Israeli armoured counterattacks, which were thwarted by anti-armour missiles carried by the Egyptian infantry.

18 O'Ballance, pp.84–85.
19 DIA DDB-1100-343-85, pp.50–51.
20 Murray & Woods, pp.70–71. The intelligence appreciations shown in SH-GMID-D-000-531 clearly are based upon this source. Once again, I would like to thank Mr Ralph Simpson and Mr Reuvers for their advice. The price of KGB support was the delivery of a damaged Iranian F-4 Phantom.
21 Information from General Makki.
22 The 102nd, 104th, 109th, 113th and 117th Brigades were all former police formations. Information from Pesach Malovany.
23 Murray & Woods, pp.180–183. The Iraqis call this action the Fourth Battle of Khafajiah.
24 *Saddam's Generals*, pp.33, 35.
25 The Shah received Bailey Bridges from Britain, seven M4T6 pontoon bridges from the United States and ribbon bridges from Germany. In addition, US intelligence estimated he received from the USSR five to eight PMP, 65–70 GSP and 60–65 TMM. DIA DDB-2680-103-88, Part II, pp.12–13.
26 US AISC, pp.6–28.
27 A contemporary Iraqi broadcast said there was a sandstorm.
28 Cooper & Bishop, pp.132–133, 136.
29 During the offensive, IRIAA transport helicopters moved 3,561 troops, mostly reinforcements for the front line, and 101 tonnes of supplies, mostly ammunition.
30 *Saddam's Generals*, p.114.
31 Some sources suggest that part of this force inadvertently penetrated a kilometre into Iraq.
32 See Cooper & Bishop, p.134. The 3rd Brigade was reported by 18 May to be attached to 92nd Division with an M47 tank battalion. SH-GMID-D-000-531.
33 O'Ballance, p.84.
34 US AISC, pp.6–10. Information from General Makki.
35 Iranian broadcast of 17 May.
36 Murray & Woods, p.178. See also Cooper & Bishop, p.133; O'Ballance, p.84, says the garrison had three divisions and three brigades.
37 *Lessons*, p.138. O'Ballance, p.84.
38 The Iranians claimed to have taken 19,000 prisoners at Khorramshahr, but US AISC, pp.6–10, probably based upon COMINT and satellite images, puts the figure at 12,000.
39 Entry on Khorammashahr on answers.com website. The figure is surprising, given that most women, girls and boys had been evacuated in 1980.
40 Buchan, p.353.
41 *Lessons*, p.142.
42 Not divisions, as in O'Ballance, p.106.
43 US AISC, pp.6–28.
44 Op cit, pp.6–29.
45 Op cit, pp.6–28. This last statement is at odds with comments from other sources about the growing effectiveness of Iranian air defence assets, notably the Grail missiles. The IRIAA lost only four helicopters in this campaign and expended 39 TOW. Cooper & Bishop, p.134.
46 Cooper & Bishop, pp.133–134.
47 *Lessons*, p.140; Murray & Woods, p.185; US AISC, pp.6–10, 6–28. Hiro, p.60, says the IrAF was reduced to 100 serviceable combat aircraft.
48 US AISC, pp.6–27, 6–28, 6–29.
49 For the military purge, see Marashi & Salama, p.146; Murray & Woods, p.184 & f/n.
50 *Saddam's Generals*, pp.33, 35–36; *Project 1946*, p.56.
51 *Saddam's Generals*, p.36.
52 Marashi & Salama, p.146.

Chapter 8

1 Based upon Michael Connell's study *Iranian Operational Decision Making*, pp.6–9 (hereafter 'Connell'); Dilip Hiro, *The Longest War*, pp.86–87 (hereafter 'Hiro'), and Edgar O'Ballance, *The Gulf War*, pp.95–96 (hereafter 'O'Ballance').
2 The Badr Brigades have continued to exist in one form or another as a Shi'a militia, even after Hakim was assassinated by a car bomb three months after returning to Iraq in 2003. At the time of writing, they are engaging the forces of the notorious terrorist movement 'Islamic State'.
3 Hiro, pp.86–87.
4 Woods et al, *Project 1946*, p.78 (hereafter '*Project 1946*'). The US Army Intelligence and Security Command History of the Iran-Iraq War from September 1980 to the Spring of 1983 (hereafter US AISC) gives the geographic co-ordinates as 30-52N/48-00E to 30-43N/47-47E. For the defences, see Buchan, *Days of God*, p.355 (hereafter Buchan); Cordesman et al, *The Lessons of Modern War Vol II*, p.149 (hereafter '*Lessons*'); Hiro, pp.180–181; Nejad, *Shalamcheh*, pp.24, 28–29 (hereafter 'Nejad'); Pollack, *Arabs at War*, pp.203–204 (hereafter 'Pollack'); US AISC, pp.6–15 & '*Abandoned fortifications of the Iran-Iraq War*', Virtualglobetrotting website.
5 For these defences, see National Training Center, *The Iraqi Army: Organization and Tactics*, pp.150, 153–154 (hereafter NTC).
6 Nejad, pp.22–23.
7 AISC, pp.6–15; Williamson Murray and Kevin M. Woods, *The Iran-Iraq War*, p.193 (hereafter Murray et al), claim 90,000. About a third of the Iranian troops were IRIA.
8 For Operation Ramadan Mubarak, see Connell, pp.10–21; Tom Cooper & Farzad Bishop, *Iran-Iraq War in the Air*, p.138 (hereafter Cooper & Bishop); Hiro, p.87; *Lessons*, pp.150–151; Kaveh Farrokh, *Iran at War*, pp.370–371 (hereafter Farrokh); Pesach Malovany, *Milhamot Bavel ha-Hadasha* (*The Wars of Modern Babylon*), pp.216–225 (hereafter Malovany); Murray & Woods, pp.192–196; Nejad, pp.22–29; O'Ballance, pp.93–98; Stephen C. Pelletiere, *The Iran-Iraq War*, pp.63–64 (hereafter Pelletiere); Pollack, pp.204–205; Steven R. Ward, *Immortal*, pp.259–260 (hereafter 'Ward'); Stepher Zabih, *The Iranian Military*, p.181 (hereafter 'Zabih'); AISC, pp.61–12, 6–15, 6–19, Fig. 6–10, 6–17. Even if frequently drawing wrong conclusions about the reasons, O'Ballance and Pollack have the most detailed accounts, while we would like to acknowledge our deep gratitude for assistance and advice of General Makki.
9 Cooper & Bishop, p.137. The Israelis supplied US$100 million worth of aircraft spares between May 1980 and June 1981, but curtailed supplies about the time the Iranian offensive began.
10 All weather data is based upon the Kuwait weather forecast, Weather History, daily archive in Freemeteo website, Kuwait archive for the period 1980–1988.
11 Sa'adi Tumma would become Deputy Chief-of-Staff for Training and Doctrine, in the spring of 1984.
12 Woods et al, *Saddam's Generals*, pp.124–125 (hereafter Woods, *Generals*). We are again very grateful to General Makki for additional background information.
13 Murray & Woods, p.185.
14 Pollack, p.208.
15 DIA Document DDB-1100-343-85, pp.61, 65–67.
16 *Lessons*, p.149; AISC, p.6–12. Murray & Woods (p.193) claim 70,000 men.
17 Buchan, p.352.
18 Farrokh, pp.368–369.
19 Iranian police had used tear gas during the defence of Khorramshahr, in October–November 1980.
20 N Rassi, a former Chieftain tank commander, then company commander of the IRIA, interview, February 2003.
21 Simon Dunstan, *Chieftain Main Battle Tank*, p.6.
22 Adar Forouzan to Ed McCaul, Military History magazine, Vol.21/No.1 (Herndon, Va., April 2004), pp.44ff, in Buchan, pp.356–357.
23 Brigadier General Sadik recalled that Khairallah once nearly caused a collision with one of the IrAF's fighter-bombers while 'touring' the battlefield near Basrah in one of the helicopters he flew on his own (Sadik, interview, March 2005).
24 For the air war, see Cooper & Bishop, and the same authors' article '*Fire in the Hills*' (hereafter 'Cooper & Bishop, *Hills*') and Cooper & Smisek, *Iraqi Mirages*.
25 Cooper & Bishop, p.133; Cooper & Bishiop, *Hills*, p.20; AISC, p.6–15. The obsolete Swatter used five VHF radio channels, but Spiral had a radio-command link guidance.
26 Tawfik was a Sandhurst graduate and was actually a year senior to Makki, who graduated from Sandhurst a year later. Before assuming command of 8th Infantry Division, he had been commandant of the Iraqi Military Collage. He would later be commander of II Corps for a while, before becoming the first President of the Military Academy (information from General Makki).
27 For the disbandment of the 9th Armoured Division and its aftermath, see Murray & Woods, p.63 & Woods, *Generals*, pp.16, 31–32, 39.
28 Higher casualties were estimated by Pelletiere at 27,000, and *Lessons*, at 20,000–30,000.
29 Ward, p.260.

30 Rassi noted he left the army after seeing a Pasadaran commander launching an attack before any artillery preparation, with the result that his troops were smashed by enemy artillery while approaching Iraqi positions (interview, February 2003).
31 Ward, p.260.
32 Farrokh, pp.367–368.
33 AISC, p.6–29.
34 Cooper & Bishop, p.138 & DIA DDB-110-343-85, p.50.
35 Cordesman, pp.442–444 & *Project 1946*, p.53.
36 Nejad, pp.28–29.
37 General Nizar Abdulkareem Faysal al-Khazraji, *al-Harb al-Iraqiya – al-Iraniya: Muthekerat Muqatel (Iran-Iraq War 1980–1988 – Memoirs of a Combatant)*, Beirut: Arab Centre for Research and Policies, date unclear, pp.281–282 – kindly forwarded by General Makki.

Chapter 9

1 *Jane's Defence Weekly*, March 24, 1984, Iran discusses war aims amid major new assaults.
2 This is covered in later chapters of this book, detailing the Northern and Central Fronts; Pelletiere pp.79–80.
3 Anthony H. Cordesman, *The Iran-Iraq War*, p.61 (hereafter, Cordesman). After the war to drive out the pro-Shia inhabitants, the Iraqis drained a substantial portion of the marshes by diverting water, damming tributaries and building embankments along the banks of the Tigris. By 2002, only a third remained, but with the fall of Saddam efforts are now being made to restore the marshes and turn them into a nature reserve.
4 After the war deeper drilling discovered further reserves and the new field was estimated to have 23–25 billion barrels and by the beginning of the twenty-first century the state-owned Southern Oil Company was producing 50,000 barrels/day just from the developed part of the Majnoon field.
5 Other estimates put the number of production and exploration rigs in Majnoon at 52. The Nahr Umr field was discovered in 1949 and was estimated at 6 billion barrels of oil but had been regarded as too small to develop but drilling by Petrobras showed the field was much larger than originally estimated.
6 Farrokh p.375 & Ward pp.259–260. Khyber is also written as Khaibar, Kheybar and Khybar – and was originally an oasis north of Medina through which the Prophet travelled before his return to Mecca.
7 The passages on the Pasdaran are based upon CRRC SH-GMID-D-000-529, and Iranian accounts of Khyber. Buchan p.351; Ward pp.246–247.
8 Married clerics appear to have brought their families to towns near their encampments.
9 For a study of the problem for Iranian troops during the war see Tavana's article on the disease during the war.
10 For the Basiji see Ward pp.246–247; Woods, *Generals* p.35; Edgar O'Ballance article *Iran vs Iraq*; DIA DDB-1100-342-86 p.46); for the rest, Zabih p.220. Pals Battalions were raised from men from local communities or in similar employment. The traditions of one such battalion, the Artists' Rifles, were retained to form the Special Air Service.
11 Cordesman p.63.
12 For Operation 'Khyber' see Buchan pp.359–360; Cooper & Bishop pp.165–168; Cordesman pp.61–63; Farrokh pp.377–379; Hiro pp.103–105; Lessons pp.179–183; Malovany pp.259–272; Ibrahim Al-Marashi & Sammy Salam, *Iraq's Armed Forces* p.158, hereafter Marashi & Salama; Murray & Woods pp.228–230; O'Ballance pp.143–148; Pelletiere pp.82, 87–92; Ward pp.264–265; Woods, *Generals* pp.126–128; Zabih pp.186–188. We would also like to express my particular thanks to General Makki for additional information.
13 DIA DDB-1100-342-86 p.25. Post-war Pasdaran accounts claim that the bridge itself was the final objective, which is inaccurate. Jalali was IRIAA commander from 25 June 1983 until 23 October 1985, and then became Defence Minister. After the war he would command the Pasdaran Air Force and later become a defence advisor.
14 O'Ballance p.144 & DIA DDB-1100-342-86, p.25.
15 CRRC SH-AFGC-D-000-686; Makki in Woods, *Generals* p.127 (however, on p.73 he was described as 'one of the dumbest generals in the army' by Republican Guard commander General Ra'ad al-Hamdani). Rashid was a Saddam loyalist who spent many years in jail in post-Saddam Iraq and died in 2014 near Tikrit.
16 The 426th Infantry Brigade took no part in the battle. For details, see SH-GMID-D-000-30 & Woods, *Project 1946*, p.78.
17 Woods, *Generals*, pp.126–127.
18 CRRC SH-AFGC-D-000-686 & Woods, *Project 1946*, p.94.
19 Cordesman p.62 & Lessons, p.181.
20 Hiro p.104.
21 Woods, *Generals* pp.126–127; CRRC SH-AFGC-D-000-686; DIA DDB-1100-343-85 p.13. The Iraqi name was Quiadet Amaliyat Sharq-Dijilah or 'East of Tigris Command' but ETOH will be used to avoid confusing the reader. Commando brigades (Alwiyat al-Maqhaweer), numbered from 60 upwards, were assault troop units used as reaction and sometimes as raiding forces. Special forces brigades (Alwiyat al-Quwat al-Khassah) were trained to operate behind enemy lines, although rarely did so.
22 Cooper & Bishop pp.167–168.
23 *Sunday Times*, 18 March 1984; *Jane's Defence Quarterly*, 25 January 1984; Buchan (p.356) reported the conversation with Pasdaran veteran in 1999.
24 DIA DDB-1100-342-86 p.25.
25 Major Mark J. Davis, *Iranians' Operational Warfighting Ability*, p.11 (hereafter Davis) & DIA DDB-1100-342-86, p.42.
26 Cooper & Bishop, p.167.
27 Cooper & Bishop, p.168.
28 Cooper & Bishop, p.168; Woods, *Generals* pp.127–128 & correspondence with General Makki.
29 Davis pp.18–19 & Sadiq, interview, March 2006.
30 DDB-1100-343-85, p.67, Figure 26.
31 *Review of the Iraq military situation August 1983–April 1986* by Defence Attaché Colonel R.G.Eccles dated 27 April 1986 (hereafter Eccles Report 1986); DIA DDB-1100-342-86 p.44 & DDB-1100-343-85 p.67.
32 Ward pp.264–265.
33 Farrokh pp.377–379 quoting *Sunday Times* 29 April 1984.
34 Colonel Edgar O'Ballance, 'Iran vs Iraq: Quantity vs Quality?' *Defence Attache* No 1/1987 pp.25–31.
35 CRRC SH-GMID-D-000-529 & Cordesman, p.64.

Chapter 10

1 For this operation see Cooper & Bishop p.180; Farrokh p.379; Malovany p.282; O'Ballance pp.160–164; DIA DDB-1100-343-85 pp.68–70 & Woods, *Project 1946* pp.98–99.
2 DIA DDB-1100-342-86 pp.42, 44.
3 Badr was the Prophet's first victory over the 'infidels'.
4 DIA DDB-1100-342-86 p.36. Other sources put the strength at between 100,000 and 300,000. After the war Major General Hassani-Sa'di would become Vice Chairman of the Joint Armed Forces Staff.
5 Both weapons actually use 105mm calibre ammunition, the US Army describing the M40 as '106mm' to avoid confusion in ammunition supply. One US intelligence report suggested that each Pasdaran squad had three RPG-7 DIA DDB-1100-342-86 p.41).
6 US intelligence observed several 81st Armoured Division M60 MBTs 'with snorkels' in the vicinity of the marshes, although there are no reports of them being used.
7 Pelletiere p.95; Murray & Woods pp.246–247 (quoting an after-action report of 21–22 April 1985 from CRRC SH-GMID-D-001-369); O'Ballance, *The Battle for the Hawizah Marshes*, Asian Defence Journal, June 1985; CRRC SH-GMID-D-000-216. US intelligence correctly noted that the ETOH headquarters was transferred to the boundary of II and IV Corps in October 1984 and remained there until February 1985 when it returned to its old location (DIA DDB-1100-343-85 p.17 & DIA DDB-2680-103-88 Part II p.14).
8 CRRC SH-GMID-D-000-216.
9 SH-GMID-D-000-216. Farrokh p.382, based upon C. Saivetz, *The Soviet Union and the Gulf in the 1980s*, (Westview Press, Boulder, Colorado, 1989) p.58.
10 *Ibid*. For Badr see Cooper & Bishop pp.179–180; Cordesman pp.73-74; Farrokh pp.379–382; Hiro pp.136–139; *Lessons* pp.201–204, 215; Malovany pp.283–290; al-Marashi & Salama pp.158, 160; O'Ballance pp.160–167; Pelletiere pp.88–90; Ward pp.265–266; O'Ballance's article, 'The Battle for the Hawizah Marshes'; SH-GMID-D-000-216 and Annual Report by British Defence Attaché, Colonel R.C. Eccles, 22 September, 1985.
11 DIA DDB-1100-343-85 p.40; SH-GMID-D-001-369; Murray & Woods 245.
12 *Lessons*, p.202. The movement of these bridges echoes the achievement of Israel's General Bren Adan during the October 1973 Arab-Israeli War in moving a bridge across the desert to the Suez Canal.
13 During the campaign the IRIAA moved 7,165 troops. Night assault missions involved six Bell 214 troop carriers and two Cobras as escorts

in the face of constant anti-helicopter patrols by Iraqi PC-7s which also dropped flares. The Iranians later claimed to have taken 3,000 prisoners.
14   Farrokh p.382.
15   In a bizarre move, on 17 March the Iraqis relieved Qadir as commander of ETOH and replaced him with Major General Sultan Hashim Ahmed, while simultaneously III Corps was given responsibility for the southern sector. In part the decision may be blamed on rivalries with Thanun and Fakhri, but it may also reflect the fact that the enemy were able to cross the Tigris and establish a bridgehead. Qader was put in charge of the Planning Directorate while his replacement and Rashid received most of the kudos for the success.
16   O'Ballance p.164.
17   Murray & Woods p.245.
18   Estimates of Iraqi casualties or 'killed' ranged from 2,000 to 14,000, the former being a contemporary Iraqi admission, and Iranian casualties from 10,000 to 50,000, see Cordesman p.63; Farrokh p.382; Hiro p.137, *Lessons* p.203; O'Ballance p.147; Ward p.266. Other information from DIA DDB-110-342-88 p.11, DIA DDB-1100-343-85 p.52 and DDB-1100-342 pp.41, 56.
19   DDB-1100-343-85 p.32.
20   Hiro p.137.
21   Cordesman p.74 quoting *Middle East Review* (World Almanac Publications, London, 1986) p.110-111.
22   Malovany, pp.290–291.
23   Malovany, pp.291–293 & Ward p.266.
24   Khoury, *Iraq in Wartime*, pp.113–114 (hereafter Khoury) & Ecccles Report Para 20.

Chapter 11
1   AISC pp.7-8.
2   Davis, pp.7-8.
3   All details on arms purchases based upon Sipri arms transfer reports. *IISS Military Balance*; *Jane's Armour and Artillery*; Lestapis. DIA DDB-1100-342-86 & DDB-2680-103-88 and assorted articles. Reports that Iran purchased North Korean and Syrian T-62s and Chinese Type-69s and that Iraq acquired T-72s from Czechoslovakia appear to be inaccurate, although the Iranians did use captured Type-69 MBTs. Similarly reports of the Soviet Union supplying Iraq with T-62s from 1972 are also inaccurate for Baghdad ceased acquiring these MBTs after 1979.
4   Farrokh, p.385.
5   US General Accounting Office report on Defense Department transfer of arms to the CIA.
6   This information comes from private sources in the defence industry.
7   DDB-1100-343-85, p.41.
8   Holthaus & Chandler, 'Myths and Lessons of Iraqi Artillery', *Field Artillery*.

Chapter 12
1   Cooper & Bishop p.196; *Lessons* pp.217–218. Malovany pp.302–303; O'Ballance p.173.
2   For Iranian planning see Connell pp.23–26; Cooper & Bishop pp.195–196; Cordesmann pp.88–89.
3   UKNA FCO 8/5005. Non-UK Defence Sales to Iraq. Davis pp.7–8; Farrokh p.385 and US General Accounting Office report on Defense Department transfer of arms to the CIA. Notably, 30 years later, oil sales not only remained crucial for the local economy: in the case of Syria, and via Kurdish-controlled northern Iraq and Turkey, they played an important role in financing the 'Islamic State'.
4   Before the war the Faw refinery was responsible or 75 percent of Iraq's oil exports. Cordesman p.263. Further details from Davis pp.26–27 (based upon James Breckenridge, *The Iran-Iraq War 1980–1988*, unpublished, p.22) & Efraim Karsh, *The Iran-Iraq War: A military analysis*, International Institute of Strategic Studies, Adelphi Paper No 220, Henry Ling, Dorchester, 1987) p.41.
5   Quoted by Connell p.24. The terminals were southeast of Faw City in the Gulf and fed from oil tanks around al-Faw. Further details from Connell p.25; Cordesman p.92; *Lessons* p.218.
6   Connell, p.25; Cordesman, p.92; *Lessons*, p.218; Tom Cooper, 'War of Cities', *Air Power* (France), No.4/January-February 2014.
7   Val Fajr is from the opening line of the 89th Surah of the Koran, and 'Dawn' is the vernacular translation, the literal translation being 'By the dawn' (Connell p.24). The Arab transliteration is Walfajir. Further details from 'Political Deputy of the General Headquarters', War Studies and Research, Battle of Faw (Val Fajr 8 Operation), hereafter *Battle of Faw*.
8   Hiro, p.170; Farrokh, pp.385–386; *Battle of Faw*.
9   Cooper & Bishop, p.196; Cooper, Sadik & Bishop article, Volume 2, p.43.
10   Connell, p.31 (quoting Hoseyn Zakariani, '*Safavi: If the Enemy Acts Foolishly, Our Response Will Be Very Strong and Crushing*', Jomhuri-ye Eslami, 22 September 2004).
11   For the failure of Iraqi intelligence see Murray & Woods pp.265–266; *Project 1946*, pp.102, 104; Woods, *Generals* pp.21–22, 93–95, 105–106, 115; and information from General Makki. However, Lieutenant General Raad Majid Rashid Al-Hamdani, who would become the Republican Guard's senior training officer, blamed Major Wafiq Al-Samarrai, the GMID Deputy Director and Head of the Iran Department. Notably, Mahmood Shukur Shahin distinguished himself while commanding the 10th Armoured Brigade in 1981, but was no trained intelligence officer and – perhaps – too much of a courtier. He knew Saddam and the Army leadership believed the enemy would attack north of the Shatt, and refused to provide his superiors with unwelcome news. Indeed, he might have sat on other reports, deciding not to use them. After the fall of Faw, he would become the scapegoat for all the intelligence- and other sorts of failures, and re-assigned the empty sinecure of Senior Secretary at the Defence Ministry. After a year 'in exile' from the frontlines he returned as a Chief-of-Staff to the I Special Corps, where remained until the end of the war. Shahin retired in 1989, but returned to serve as Director of the Iraqi Police in 1993–1995, and was then assigned the post of the Governor of the Wasit Province until his final retirement, in 1999.
12   DIA DDV-1100-343-85 p.17; DDB-2680-103-88 Part II p.14.
13   CRRC, SH-AFGC-D-000-686. Orders of the President and Commander-in-Chief of the Armed Forces, February-December 1984.
14   According to Makki, the 15th Division had been formed within the IV Corps in 1981, from the former 44th Infantry Brigade of the 11th Infantry Division. It was deployed in the north of the Faw Peninsula, opposite to Khorramshahr and Abadan. Established within the III Corps in 1983, the 26th Division held the southern part of the peninsula.
15   DIA DDV-1100-343-85 p.17; DDB-2680-103-88 Part II p.14.
16   NTC, p.153.
17   Information on Iraqi radars kindly provided by John Wise from the Carpenter Partnership.
18   For more details on Val Fajr-8 see Connell pp.27–33; Cooper & Bishop pp.197–206; Cordesman pp.92–96, 98–100; Farrokh pp.385–389; Hiro pp.167–170; *Lessons*, pp.219–224; Malovany pp.306–316, 402; Al-Marashi and Salaman pp.161–168; Murray & Woods pp.263–272; Pelletiere pp.96–102; Pollack pp.217–218; O'Ballance pp.173–179; Ward pp.274–277; Woods, *Generals* pp.180–182; Zabih pp.190–192; *Battle of Faw* (which, in best tradition of the IRGC, completely ignored the IRIA's participation), and Eccles Report 1986.
19   Faw City. Other sources claim the code word was 'Ya Zahra'.
20   O'Ballance pp.173-174.
21   Murray & Woods p.269 quoting document SH-PDWN-D-001-024. It is unclear which 155mm weapons were used. The implication is that they were towed weapons which suggests either Austrian GHN 45 or its cousin the South African G-5.
22   Cooper & Bishop p.199.
23   Sean Boyne, 'Saddam's shield: The role of the Special Republican Guard', *Jane's Intelligence Review*, January 1999, pp.29–32. During the fighting the Guards Special Forces Brigade was reported to have been decimated (p.30).
24   British Military Attaché Colonel Eccles thought the southern attack might have been a diversion which proved more successful than anticipated. He was puzzled by the delayed Iraqi reaction and wondered if it was due to them being pre-occupied by the operations around Umm al-Rasas but noted a coherent reaction had evolved by 16–18 February and said counterattack plans, based upon a three-pronged approach, were revealed on 19 February (see Eccles Report 1986 Paras 14–16).
25   Woods, *Generals*, pp.166.
26   Buchan p.368.
27   Between the New Year and 12 February 1986, the F-4E Phantom IIs of the IRIAF dropped nearly 90 tonnes of bombs on the headquarters of III and VII Corps.
28   DIA DDB-2680-103-88 p.8.
29   Connell, p.28.
30   Information kindly provided by General Makki.

31 Pelletiere, pp.96–103.
32 kuwaitpages.blogspot.com/2007/08/kuwait-wars.html.
33 Reports of the northward movement of Kuwaiti Chieftains led to press reports that they were being handed to the Iraqis. In fact, the Iraqis never deployed any Chieftains in combat.
34 Information on the Kuwaiti Air Force based on research for Hooton et al, Operation Desert Storm, Volume 1 and Volume 2 (see Bibliography for details).
35 *Project 1946*, p.106.
36 Cordesman, p.95 & *Lessons*, p.221.
37 Iraqi sources like Makki and Sadiq indicate the Faw campaign involved two IRIA divisions with a Pasdaran contribution of 10 divisions and six brigades.
38 Cooper and Bishop p.201. O'Ballance (p.176) claims the IrAF 'carpet-bombed' the bridgehead, though actually – and in addition to FROG-7s, the Iraqis deployed their Tu-16 and Tu-22 armed with massive Soviet-made bombs such as the FAB-1500M54, FAB-3000M54, FAB-6000M54 and FAB-9000M54.
39 For the use of chemical weapons in this campaign see Woods, *Generals* p.145. The Western European fashion away from beards towards trimmed moustaches during and after the First World War was driven by the same factors.
40 Khoury, pp.209–210.
41 Eccles 1986 Report Paras 17–20, 28.
42 Tucker, 1988, p.226.
43 Cooper & Bishop, pp.200–203. For additional context, and many additional details – mostly acquired only during the last 10 years – see also Cooper & Smisek, *Iraqi Mirages*.
44 According to Makki, the IrAF and the IrAAC lost only 17 aircraft and helicopters in the entire campaign.
45 According to Makki, al-Marashi & Salama's claims (pp.163–164) that III Corps' officers protested about the departure of the foul-mouthed Rashid are wrong.
46 Connell, p.28.
47 Farrokh (p.388) claims the Pasdaran had flooded the area to channel enemy armour.
48 This incident had echoes of one during the October 1973 Arab-Israeli War, when Israel's Major General Avraham Mendler, commander of 252nd Division, was killed.
49 Malovany, p.402.
50 Farrokh, p.389.
51 Connell, p.28.
52 Hiro, p.213; Ward, p.277 & 'Anniversary offensive: Gulf flare-up', *Jane's Defence Weekly*, 1 March 1986.
53 Connell, p.30 & DIA DDB-2680-103-88 p.8.
54 Connell, p.28.
55 Pollack, p.220.
56 Pollack, p.220.

Chapter 13
1 CIA-RDP86T01017R000202020001-4.
2 CIA-RDP86T01017R000202020001-4.
3 CIA-RDP90R00961R000300060001-1.
4 CIA-RDP86T01017R000808180001-5.
5 For planning see Cordesman, *The Iran-Iraq War* pp.105, 123, hereafter Cordesman; Farrokh, *Iran at War* p.392, (hereafter Farrokh); Cordsman & Wagner, The Lessons of Modern War pp.245–246, hereafter Lessons; Malovany, *Milhamot Bavel ha-Hadasha* p.345, (hereafter Malovany); O'Ballance, *The Gulf War* pp.189–190 (hereafter O'Balance); Pollack, *Arabs at War* p.221 (hereafter Pollack); Pollack, *The Persian Puzzle*, p.221, (hereafter Pollack, Puzzle); Zabih, The Iranian military in Revolution and War pp.194–195, hereafter Zabih. SH-GMID-D-000-301.
6 Bulloch & Miller p.157.
7 For the defences see Bulloch & Miller p.157; Hiro, The Longest War pp.180–181, (hereafter Hiro); Lessons p.149; National Training Center, *The Iraqi Army: Organization and Tactics* pp.150, 153–154, hereafter NTC; Pollack pp.203–204. Colonel B. Aldridge's Report para 52; US AISC p.6-15; DIA DDB-2680-103-88 p.12; Edgar O'Ballance's article 'Iran vs Iraq: Quantity vs Quality?'; Richard Philipps' article *Tactical Defensive Doctrine of the Iraqi Ground Forces*. Virtualglobetrotting web site 'Abandoned fortifications of the Iran-Iraq War.' The original version of this site, with images taken circa 1990 clearly showed the triangular strong points but they are almost obliterated in the more recent version whose images were taken some 20 years later.
8 Iraq deployed 4 million mines during the war with Iran and had some 6 million in stock. Mines were usually laid manually but the Iraqi Army also had Russian PMR-3 and Italian Valsalla minelayers, while many MLRSs had rockets which could carry anti-personnel mines. The mines were acquired from Chile, China, Egypt, Italy, Singapore and the Soviet Union.
9 During the war shell fire destroyed millions of date palms while many more were lost to post-war salination.
10 For Coalition operations against Iraqi fortifications see Robert H. Scales' *Certain Victory*, pp.200–206, 226.
11 Farrokh p.392; Pollack, Puzzle, p.221.
12 Cordesman, The Iran-Iraq War p.123, hereafter Cordesman.
13 Buchan, Days of God p.369, hereafter Buchan.
14 For Karbala-4 see Cooper & Bishop *Iran-Iraq War in the Air*, pp.231–233 (hereafter Cooper & Bishop); Cordsman pp.103, 105, 109, 122-4; Farrokh pp.392–393; Hiro p.180; Lessons pp.245–247; Malovany pp.345–349; O'Ballance pp.189–192; Pelletiere, The Iran-Iraq War p.118 (hereafter Pelletiere); Pollack p.221 passim; Ward, Immortal pp.277–278 hereafter Ward; Zabih pp.195–196, 242.
15 Cooper & Bishop p.232.
16 SH-GMID-D-000-301.
17 Brigadier General Ahmad Sadik (retired officer of the Iraqi Air Force Intelligence Department), interview with Tom Cooper, March 2005.
18 Rashid was described as 'colourful' by Nick Childs, 'The Gulf War: Iraq under pressure', *Jane's Defence Weekly*, 9 May 1987 pp.899–901, (hereafter Childs JDW).
19 'Return of 175 Iranian bodies from Iraq stirs painful memories', *al-Monitor*, 21 May 2015.
20 After the war, both Iraqi corps commanders were accused of exaggerating enemy casualties to enhance their own prestige; see General Hamdani in 'Institute for Defense Analyses Project 1946', pp.114–115 (hereafter Project 1946).
21 Murray & Woods p.293 & Buchan p.369.
22 According to Zabih p.196 the new offensive, 'Karbala-5', had its origins in an invitation by Khamenei in late 1985 to a specially convened group of retired IRIA officers to plan an offensive against Basra.
23 There was intermittent rain and fog from 19 December 1986 onwards, see Kuwait daily weather forecast provided by Freemeteo web site & Buchan p.369.
24 Cordesman, The Iran-Iraq War and Western Security p.37, (hereafter Cordesman, Security).
25 For 'Karbala-5' see Al-Marashi & Salama *Iraq's Armed Forces* pp.169–170 (hereafter Marashi & Salama); Cooper & Bishop pp.235–240. Cordsman p.125-131, 135-136. Farrokh pp.393–395; Griffin, *The Iraqi Way of War*, pp.23–25 (hereafter Griffin); Hiro p.180-185. Lessons pp.247–254, 269 f/n 101, f/n 104, f/n 114, 115, 116; Parviz Mosalla-Nejad, Shalamcheh pp.30–55 (hereafter Mosalla-Nejad); O'Ballance pp.195–198; Pelletierre pp.117–122; Pollack pp.221–224; Ward pp.278–279; Project 1946 pp.114–118 (including an interview with General Raad Hamdani); Zabih pp.196–199, 242–243; 'Imposed War Official Webite'sajed.ir (Karbala-5 entry); Colonel B. Aldridge's report Pars 52–53 & SH-GMID-D-000-266; SH-GMID-D-000-301.
26 Mosalla-Nejad p.33.
27 Mosalla-Nejad, pp.30–31.
28 While the IRGC's units generally operated a miscellany of APCs captured from the Iraqis, and some of Chinese and North Korean origin, they also deployed BTR-50s re-engined with US-made Diesels.
29 Four of the involved helicopters were used for supporting chemical decontamination operations. During Karbala-5 the IRIAA is known to have moved 5,292 troops with 108 tonnes of supplies and evacuated 5,601 injured.
30 Op-cit p.35. 'Ya-Zahra' is a Shi'a chant popular with the IRGC, calling on Mohammad's fourth daughter, Fatemeh Zahra, for strength and perseverance.
31 Iraqi artillery was organised into battalions, designated 'regiments' – each consisting of three batteries.
32 P. P., veteran of Ramadan Armoured Brigade, IRGC, interview by Tom Cooper, December 2003 & A. R., former Iranian Army NCO, interview by Tom Cooper, February 2004.

33 General Hamdani in *Project 1946* pp.114–118. The text describes him visiting the headquarters of 'V Corps' – although this was the headquarters of the 5th Mechanised Division.
34 SH-GMID-D-000-301. While some Iraqi sources remain sceptical about such reports, Iranian and other Iraqi sources cite that the two (E)C-130H Khoofash ('Bat') ELINT/SIGINT-aircraft operated by the IRIAF were capable of reading Iraqi radio communications in real time. For example, Brigadier General Sadik (interview with Tom Cooper, March 2005), stressed that this was the reason why the IrAF repeatedly attempted to intercept such aircraft – although these operated relatively deep inside the Iranian airspace. Indeed, IrAF's pilots eventually claimed two of what the Iraqis believed would have been four (E)C-130Hs during the war. However, the IRIAF actually had only two such aircraft, and both are still operational as of 2017.
35 Sadik, interview by Tom Cooper, March 2005 & SH-GMID-D-000-301.
36 A. R. noted that during Karbala-5 the IRIAA's Cobras launched 67 TOW and claimed 43 AFVs.
37 NTC p.123.
38 General Nawfal Ismail Khudayyir (Khudayyir), the 8th Inf Division commander, distinguished himself during Karbala-5 by retaking the island and was rewarded with command of 6th Armoured Division, which would take part in the 1988 Faw Peninsula offensive.
39 Cooper & Bishop p.237.
40 Aldridge *Report Para 53*.
41 *Lessons* p.251. Most accounts claim Saddam visited the front, but Malovany makes it clear it was Khairallah who kept a watching brief on III Corps.
42 Murray & Wood, *The Iran-Iraq War* p.294 (hereafter Murray & Wood), quoting memoirs of General Saadoun Hamdani & Malovany, p.354. The latter is providing a figure of 3,000, but most likely number of cases was about 1,700.
43 Mosalla-Nejad p.51.
44 According to Sadik (interview with Tom Cooper, March 2005), all sorties of IrAF's Tu-16 and Tu-22 bombers were supported by an entire 'electronic warfare package' involving a pair of Mirage F.1EQ with Caiman ECM pods, others armed with Baz-AR anti-radar missiles, and Sukhoi Su-22s armed with Soviet-made AS-8 Kyle anti-radar missiles. However, on this occasion the Mirage failed to appear due to a combination of technical snags and bad weather, leaving one of the Tu-16 formations fatally exposed. Notable is that the Baz ('Falcon')-AR (AR stood for 'anti-radar') was a custom-tailored version of the Anglo-French Martel missile with a more sophisticated, French-designed seeker head.
45 For example, Brigadier General Sadik (interview with Tom Cooper, March 2005), strongly denied the possibility of the IrAF losing more than 23 aircraft during Karbala-5 and listed most of losses in question. A cross-examination with other (including Iranian) sources confirmed nearly all of his list, while providing details of only 2–3 additional losses of IrAF's combat aircraft during this period.
46 Sadik, interview with Tom Cooper, March 2005.
47 General Makki, interview with Ted Hooton, March 2017. Contrary to certain other claims, 'Salahaddin' – Saad ad-Din Aziz – was not a Basra-born Shia but a Mosul-born Sunni. The changes of command were first reported in an Iranian communiqué of 25 February 1987, while the first public reference to Jamal commanding III Corps was an Iraqi Iraqi communiqué from 1 March 1987.
48 Childs JDW.
49 Hiro p.182.
50 Lessons p.253.
51 Al-Marashi and Salama p.169.
52 Childs JDW.
53 Al-Marashi and Salama p.169.
54 James Bruce, in Jane's Defence Weekly, 21 February 1987. Hereafter Bruce JDW.
55 Hiro p.185.
56 Pollack p.224.
57 Aldridge report Para 48.
58 After Karbala-5, the Ramadan Brigade had replaced its BTR-50s for M113s taken from the 16th Armoured Division IRIA.
59 SH-GMID-D-000-266. The Iranians were also supported by 34 helicopters, including 12 gunships which claimed almost 20 AFVs. However, the aircraft flew only 306 hours in five days.
60 For further details on Karbala-8 see Cooper & Bishop p.243; Cordsman p.139; Hiro p.185; Lessons pp.260, 292- 3; Malovany pp.360–362; Mosalla-Nejad pp.56–60; O'Ballance p.203; Zabih pp.199–200. SH-GMID-D-000-266.
61 P. P., veteran of Ramadan Armoured Brigade, IRGC, interview with Tom Cooper, December 2004.
62 P. P., veteran of Ramadan Armoured Brigade, IRGC, interview with Tom Cooper, December 2004.
63 SH-GMID-D-000-266.
64 SH-GMID-D-000-266.
65 For the changes in Iraqi strategy, see Murray & Woods, p.320. Ironically, even at the end of 1987 the CIA continued to believe the next major Iranian attack would still be on the Southern Front. CIA-RDP90T00114R000700800002-2.
66 Lessons p.254, quoting Keyhan of 29 June and repeated in FBIS of 7 July 1987. We would like to thank Mr David Isby for his help in tracking this quote.
67 'Mobilisation problem for Iranian leaders', Jane's Defence Weekly, 2 April 1988, hereafter 'JDW, Mobilisation'.
68 Cordesman pp.259–260.

Chapter 14

1 Khoury, *Iraq in Wartime*, pp.211 (hereafter Khoury).
2 Mosalla-Nejad pp.61–65.
3 General Makki, interview with Ted Hooton, November 2016.
4 Buchan p.357; Bulloch & Miller pp.148–149.
5 This paragraph is based upon Eshel's article in *Armor*.
6 This chapter is based upon DDB-1100-342-86, DDB-1100-343-85 and DDB-2680-103-88, Part II.
7 Bulloch & Morris p.247.
8 Khomeini promotes 10, *Jane's Defence Weekly*, 16 May 1987.
9 Hiro pp.195.
10 Based upon DDB-2680-103-88 Part II pp.10–11. IRIA divisions had four artillery battalions with a nominal 54 tubes.
11 CRRC SH-PDWN-D-000-730. JDW, Mobilisation.
12 No Sign of Counter-Attack by Iraqis, Jane's Defence Weekly February 21 1987.
13 Bulloch & Morris pp.244–245.
14 Buchan p.357; Bulloch & Morris pp.148–149; Khoury pp.211 & A. R., interview with Tom Cooper, February 2007.
15 See interview with Forouzan.
16 Data on the Pasdaran comes from DDB-1100-342-86 and SH-GMID-D-000-529, material in Iranian publications together with units identified in press releases.
17 Tank strengths from SH-GMID-D-000-529.
18 DDB-2680-103-88 Part II pp.10–11.
19 SH-GMID-D-000-529 & A. R., interview with Tom Cooper, February 2007.
20 'Iran tries to remould revolutionary guards', *Jane's Defence Weekly*, 1 October 1988, (hereafter JDW Revolutionary Guards). A 1986 CIA study examined the problems facing Iran's ground forces noting both strengths and weaknesses. CIA-RDP86T01017R000302670001-2.
21 DDB-2680-103-88 p.12.
22 CIA-RDP90T00114R000700800002-2.
23 DDB-2680-103-88.
24 CRRC SH-IDGS-D-000-854.
25 See Davis' article on *Iranian Operational Warfighting Ability* p.32; JDW, Mobilisation & CRRC SH-IDGS-D-000-854.
26 DDB-2680-103-88. In February 1979 the IRIAA had 820 helicopters and 44 fixed-wing aircraft (information provided by A. R. and M. T., in interviews with Tom Cooper, April 2009).
27 Bulloch & Morris p.244.
28 Aldridge report, 21 May, 1987 Para 45.
29 Bruce JDW. A barrel is 159 litres.
30 CIA-RDP89S0145000600600001-5.
31 Based upon Lessons, Table 9.6. For the economic problems see Hiro pp.109–113, 192, 194 who noted the oil price had stabilised in early 1987 to $15–18 per barrel. See also CIA-RDP89S0145000600600001-5.
32 CIA-RDP90T00114R000700800002-2.
33 CIA-RDP89S0145000600600001-5.
34 CRRC SH-APGC-D-000-731.
35 DDB-2680-103-88.

36 Lessons pp.440, 447. See also *Jane's Armour and Artillery, 1996–1997*, pp.48–49 for improved Iraqi armour and Warford's article on tanks.
37 Hiro p.195; Khoury p.95.
38 Khoury p.32 & DDB-2680-103-88 p.14. The Americans estimated about 20,000 Egyptian and Sudanese volunteers were serving in the Iraqi Army. While exact figures for the Sudanese remain unclear, Egyptian sources indicate presence of special forces, and at least a detachment of the Egyptian Air Force (EAF), including a number of instructor pilots and ground support personnel. Whether the EAF indeed deployed half a squadron of Dassault Mirage 5 fighter-bombers to Iraq, as reported by several unofficial Egyptian, and even some of Iranian and US sources, remains unclear. Finally, large numbers (some estimates go as high as 2 million) of Egyptians are known to have worked in Iraq of the 1980s, some of them in civilian organisations and services supporting the Iraqi Army.
39 Khoury pp.99–100 and information from General Makki. See also Woods, *Mother of All Battles*, p.100.
40 DDB-2680-103-88 p.30.
41 In Arabic a brigade is Liwa and brigades are Alwiya. The order of battle is based upon DIA DDB-2680-103-88. CRRC SH-PDWN-D-000-730 87. The US DIA put Iraqi Army strength at 146 infantry brigades, six special forces and 17 commando brigades. The three original Special Forces brigades, 31st, 32nd and 33rd were renumbered 65th, 66th and 68th in the mid-1980s and a flexible number of brigades were created. While they were intended to operate behind enemy lines conducting reconnaissance and precision sabotage operations, in practice by 1987 they were often used as specialist assault troops who also doubled as a reaction force. The distinction is between cat-burglars and smash-and-grab specialists.
42 DDB-2680-103-88, p.14 & JDW, Mobilisation.
43 US intelligence calculated the Iraqis had some 10 battalions of self-propelled artillery with some 180 weapons DDB-2680-103-88 p.9.
44 DDB-2680-103-88 p.16.
45 Nevertheless, Washington permitted the open sale of Bell 214STs and the MD.500 helicopters for 'agricultural use' knowing they would be used for military purposes. Furthermore, Washington did not oppose delivery of South-African made bombs based on US design for Mk.84 to the IrAF – via Saudi Arabia (Sadik, interview with Tom Cooper, March 2005). The Soviet Southern Theatre of Military Operations was estimated in 1986 to have had 26 divisions and 1,800 aircraft capable of invading Iran together with five divisions and 575 aircraft in Afghanistan CIA-RDP86T01017R00050539001-8.
46 General Makki, interview with Ted Hooton, November 2016. Rashid's predecessor, Dhiya ad-Din Jamal, became Director of Ordnance. Khazraji continued serving as Chief-of-Staff Army until August 1990, when he learned of Saddam's invasion of Kuwait on the radio, while driving to the office. Increasingly out-of-step with the regime, he was replaced by Hussein Rashid and then fled to Jordan, in 1996. According to Makki, Defence Minister Major General Abdul Jabbar Shanshall was also kept out of the loop, and Hussein Rashid apparently plotted the invasion of Kuwait behind their backs with Ayad Futayyih al-Rawi – commander of the Republican Guards Corps since 1988.
47 Marashi and Salama p.168.
48 Khoury pp.83–85, 97.
49 Aldridge report, 21 May, 1987, Para 57.
50 Aldridge report, 21 May, 1987, Para 48.
51 Aldridge report, 21 May, 1987, Paras 49, 51 & 56. In fact the eastern approaches to Baghdad are open but cultivated terrain with numerous fields, groves, villages and towns. Unsurprisingly, the IRIA developed a contingency plan for an 'all out' advance on Baghdad through exactly this area as early as of 1981. This was presented to the Joint Chiefs of Staff in Tehran at latest in May 1982 but turned down because the IRGC declared it a 'gamble' (T. L., former DIA analyst, interview to Tom Cooper, May 2002). On the other hand, and like many of his attaché colleagues, Aldridge underestimated the value of fixed defences against an enemy lacking armour and artillery. His comment on problems with deploying of CWs was accurate when referring to the FEBA. However, the Iraqis made extensive use of chemical weapons on the Iranian rear, notably during Val Fajr-8. In interviews with Tom Cooper, Sadik also pointed out that the Iraqi Army had a forward air controller assigned to every brigade since 1962.

52 Al-Marashi and Salama pp.167–168; Woods (et al) *Project 1946*, pp.111–114, 119 & Jupa and Dingeman's article 'The Republican Guards: Loyal, Aggressive, Able'.
53 *Project 1946*, pp.111–113.
54 Khoury pp.85–86, f/n 11.
55 American sources suggest these divisions were numbered respectively 1st, 2nd, 3rd and 5th while the 'Nebuchadnezzar' Division was numbered 6th. The majority of former Iraqi officers stress that they were known only by their names – except for the Special Purposes Division, which for some reason was unnamed (the last is sometimes referred to as the Special Forces Division but the Iraqi designation is retained). However – and whether under US influence or not – an increasing number of Iraqi sources are using numerical designations, too.
56 Guards units formed in 1986 were 8th, 9th, 10th Armoured; 14th, 15th Mechanised; 5th, 6th, 7th Infantry, 11th, 12th Cdo and 16th SF Bdes followed – in 1987 – by 18th Armoured; 20th, 22nd, 23rd, 24th, 25th Infantry, 21st Cdo and 26th Naval Cdo Bdes. The naval commando brigade was reportedly trained by Egyptian instructors and was assigned to the SP Division, reportedly designated 'as-Saiqa' (commandos).
57 Hussein Kamel al-Majid would fall out with Saddam and in 1995 fled to Jordan with his brother, Lieutenant Colonel Saddam Kamel al-Majid. They were persuaded to return in February 1996 but their homes were attacked by Special Forces and both were killed.
58 Khoury, pp.90–92 and Makki's comments. 'Abu Khalil' was the equivalent to 'GI Joe' or 'Tommy Atkins'. It developed from Khalil (Hebron) where the Iraqi Army distinguished itself during the 1948–1949 War with Israel. Khoury claims the correct name was Abu Tahrir but this was used only for a short period.
59 Khoury pp.98.
60 The French Army soldiers faced similar problems which contributed to the 1917 mutinies. Aldridge (in Para 59) noted that enemy action might mean soldiers staying up to 50 days in the front line. Such cases were rather rare and if, then applicable for the Central and Northern Fronts: in the south, the 31-days rule was rarely exceeded.
61 Comments by General Makki & Khoury pp.84, 88, 96–97, 71, 167–168, 176–177. Some 62,000 Iraqis were taken prisoner by Iranians during this war, of whom 40,000 were repatriated in 1990 and 16,700 by 2003 while 4,600 opted to remain in Iran. The Iraqis released 37,861 prisoners by 1990 (Khoury pp.103–110). Aldridge, in Para 58, noted that servicemen who had distinguished themselves, families of the killed, and crippled soldiers could at least acquire Brazilian-made Volkswagen Passat cars at cheap rates.
62 Khoury p.83.
63 SH-PDWN-D-000-730-87.
64 Details from Foss, *Jane's Armour and Artillery 2007–2008*, p.106 & Juppa and Dingeman article.
65 Khoury, pp.91–92 & 99.
66 Murray & Woods p.297.
67 Khoury pp.73, 99 f/n 35.
68 Ba'ath Regional Command Council 01-3212-0001-0546/0550 quoted by Khoury pp.75.
69 Khoury, pp.102–103, 177–178, 2015. Claims that they may have included Sudanese and Egyptian troops appear to be untrue.
70 Aldridge Paras 58, 59; Eccles Para 62.
71 Op cit Para 60. They appear to have been more medical isolation than prison facilities.
72 Bulloch & Morris p.237.
73 Murray & Woods p.297 f/n 36.
74 A. R., former Iranian Army NCO, interview by Tom Cooper, February 2004. Notable is that there appears to have been a minor drugs problem within the Iranian Army already during the rule of the Shah, in 1970s.
75 P. P., veteran of Ramadan Armoured Brigade, IRGC, interview by Tom Cooper, December 2005.
76 Rafiqdoust was replaced by Ali Shamkhani who had previously been the Pasdaran ground forces commander (JDW Revolutionary Guards). A year later the ministry was absorbed by the Defence Ministry.
77 Bulloch & Morris pp.243–244; JDW, Mobilisation. A CIA study of April 1988 noted that the number of volunteers had declined 10 percent per year since 1985. CIA-RDP89S01450R000200230001-0.
78 See Murray and Woods pp.297–301 for Saddam's concerns about army morale.

Chapter 15

1. Lessons p.329 & Ward pp.286–287.
2. Bulloch & Morris pp.241–243; 'Growing indications of another Basra offensive', *Jane's Defence Weekly*, 10 October 1987 & 'Iran masses troops for major offensive in Gulf', *Jane's Defence Weekly*, 28 November 1987.
3. Murray & Wood p.321.
4. For Ramadan Mubarak see Bulloch & Morris pp.241–243; Cooper & Bishop pp.266–267; Farrokh pp.405–406; Hiro pp.203–204; Al-Khazraji Muthakerat Muqatel pp.475–514 (hereafter Khazraji); Lessons pp.373–375; Makki Maarik Al Tahrir Al Kubra Al Iraqiya pp.231–286 (hereafter Makki); Malovany pp.399–423; Marashi and Salama p.171; Murray & Woods pp.319–322; Pelletiere pp.141–142; Pollack 224–225; Ward pp.292–293. FBIS-NES-93-074. See also an article in the Iraqi Armed Forces web site from 27 February–30 August 2013 by Major General Fawzi Berzinji who commanded 19th Infantry Brigade during the offensive.
5. The Raphael-TH pods were delivered to the French Air Force in late 1986 and to the IrAF early in 1988 with Mirage F.1EQ-6s. Information from Tom Cooper, August 26 2016. Based upon Sadik & Cooper, Iraqi Fighters pp.81–82, 99, 101 For the re-organisation of the IrAF see Cooper & Bishop pp.212–213. Only 19 COR pods were produced by Dassault Aviation.
6. Murray & Woods p.325.
7. FBIS-NES-93-074 Part 1, April 19, 1993.
8. For the Iraqi Navy in the invasion of Kuwait and in 1991, when Allied forces sank IrN *Nouh* and *Atika*, see Woods, Mother of all Battles pp.73–78.
9. NTC p.149.
10. Op cit p.145.
11. Woods et al, Saddam's Generals pp.22, 99–100 (hereafter, Saddam's Generals). Khudayyir had distinguished himself as 8th Infantry Division's commander during Karbala-5 and had been given the armoured division as a reward.
12. The Guards commando brigades appear to have remained in the north.
13. FBIS-NES-93-075.
14. The 'Tawakkalna ala Allah' Republican Guards Armoured Division appears to have remained as strategic reserve during this operation and the May 1988 offensive.
15. Strengths are based upon the order of battle and DDB-2680-103-88 p.14.
16. SH-GMID-D-000-529. Najaf Ashraf Division arrived early in 1988 as part of the 'reinforcement' mixed with the bluff of acting as a diversion with the necessity of reinforcing the garrison (P. P., veteran of Ramadan Armoured Brigade, IRGC, interview by Tom Cooper, December 2005).
17. Cordsman p.373.
18. Lessons p.406 f/n 34 & JDW Mobilisation.
19. It is possible that the attack on the northern bridges was made by the 200 Iraqi Navy SEALs mentioned in Saddam's Generals p.177. Account of the air strike on the southern bridge was provided by Brigadier General Ahmad Sadik, interview to Tom Cooper, October 2007.
20. Meteorological data from nearby Kuwait on Freemeteo web site. The SS-30 vehicle fired 32 127mm rockets with high explosive warheads up to 30 kilometres far.
21. Javed Ali article p.51.
22. For more details of Iraq's chemical weapons programme see CIA-DOC_00010797.pdf, CIA-DOC_ 0000072254.pdf; CIA-RDP90T01298R000300670001-8; 'How Saddam kept deadly gas secret', *The Independent*, 3 July 1998.
23. Buchan p.371; Razoux p.441 based on interview with Iraqi medical officer; Saddam's Generals p.48; Javed Ali article pp.49–51. General Makki, who has researched the 1988 offensives for his in-depth history, dismisses this claim.
24. Javed Ali article p.49. Overall sortie data for IrAF and IrAAC as provided by General Makki. Earlier Iraqi reports (see Cooper & Bishop p.266) cited a total of 318 sorties by both services. Total IrAF commitment to the operation was 12 squadrons: 6 with fighter-bombers, two with bombers, three reconnaissance and one electronic warfare. The Air Defence Command provided three fighter-interceptor squadrons.
25. NTC, p.150.
26. NTC, pp.147 & 151.
27. It appears that advanced parties of both brigades had established forward bases on Kuwait's Bubiyan Island – with Kuwait's agreement (FBIS-NES-93-074).
28. By 1993, the dismissed brigade commander became a senior military leader in the Dawah Party, possibly their army Chief-of-Staff.
29. Bulloch & Morris p.242; Lessons p.374.
30. Saddam's Generals p.49.
31. For naval operations see Saddam's Generals p.177.
32. Saddam's Generals p.16. Lieutenant General Abid Mohammed al-Kabi, former commander of the Iraqi Navy (1982–1987), interview with Ted Hooton, May 2017.
33. Hiro p.203; Bulloch & Morris p.244. Born in Qom, Shahbazi entered the staff college at the age of 22 and at the time of the revolution was a junior staff officer. He had very close links to the Pasdaran and was regarded as a Khomeini loyalist.
34. For details on 'Praying Mantis' see Cooper & Bishop pp.267–273, 278–279 f/n 430–433; Farrokh pp.406–408; Lessons pp.375–381, and Hiro p.236.

Chapter 16

1. NTC pp.151–153. Heyman article, Advance of the Intelligent Battlefield p.35; DIA Ground Forces Intelligence Study, Iran p.42. Iran acquired some 2.5 million American M-2, M-16A, M-14, M-18A1 anti-personnel and M-15, M-19 and M-21 anti-armour mines between 1969 and 1979, while China, Italy and North Korea supplied both anti-personnel and anti-armour mines.
2. They were identified by Iraqi intelligence as 7th 'Vali Asr', 9th 'Badr',10th 'Seyed o-Shohada', 17th'Ali Ibn Abu Talib', 19th 'Fajr', 21st 'Iman Reza', 27th 'Mohamad Rasoolallah', 31st 'Ashura', 32nd 'Ansar al-Hossein', 41st 'Sarallah' and 155th 'Shohada' Divisions. CRRC SH-GMID-D-000-530. In addition the 10th 'Seyed ol-Shohada' Division which participated in the Hawizah Marshes battles was also sent north.
3. This order of battle is based upon Iraqi intelligence.
4. 'On God we depend' although it has been translated as 'In God We Trust'. Afterwards it was re-designated as 'Tawakkalna ala Allah 1'.
5. For Tawakkalna ala Allah 1 see Cooper & Bishop pp.273–274; Farrokh pp.408–409; Hiro pp.206–207, 238; Lessons pp.381–383, 385–386, 407 f/n 58; Khazraji pp.515–536; Makki pp.287–330; Malovany pp.424–429; Marashi and Salama pp.171–172; Murray & Woods pp.325–327; Pelletiere pp.142–144; Pollack pp.225–227; Ward p.293.
6. Meteorological data from nearby Kuwait on Freemeteo web site.
7. For his reasoning see CRRC SH-PDWN-D-000-730.
8. Based upon the ORBAT from DIA DDB-2680-103-88 p.14.
9. See NTC pp.164–167 for Iraqi offensive and defensive chemical capabilities.
10. For the last-minute changes see Makki p.294; Murray & Woods p.326. Iranian sources claim IRIAF SIGINT was conducting real time interceptions of Iraqi Army communications.
11. For Iraqi artillery techniques see NTC pp.115–122.
12. Lessons pp.445–447.
13. Lessons, p.443.
14. For Iraqi Army tactics see NTC pp.50, 54–70.
15. Lessons p.382.
16. Francona, pp.27–28.
17. Hiro p.207; Lessons p.383.
18. Bulloch & Morris p.244; Hiro, pp.207–209.
19. JDW, Mobilisation & SH-GMID-D-000-530.
20. For these discussions see CRRC SH-PDWN-D-000-730.
21. See Chapter 4 for a description of the Iranian transport network; Murray & Woods p.320; CRRC SH-PDWN-D-000-730.
22. VI Corps had 12th Armoured, 25th, 31st, 32nd and 35th Infantry Divisions.
23. CRRC SH-PDWN-D-000-730.
24. CRRC SH-SPPC-D-000-229.
25. Mosalla-Nejad pp.62 & 67; meteorological data from nearby Kuwait on Freemeteo web site.
26. For Operation 'Beit-ol-Mogaddas 7' see Bishop & Cooper pp.274–275; Farrokh pp.409–410; Hiro pp.207–208, 238; Lessons p.386; Malovany pp.429–430; Makki pp.346–347; Mosalla-Nejad pp.61–70; Pellettiere p.144; CIA National Intelligence Dailies from website foia.cia.gov/browse_docs.asp June 18; 'Iran's assault in Iraq – A morale booster?' *Jane's Defence Weekly*, 25 June 1988 (hereafter JDW Morale Booster).
27. Rafsanjani claimed this offensive involved 50 battalions (25,000) while the Iraqis reportedly engaged 10–12 brigades (40,000). JDW Morale Booster. See also CIA National Intelligence Daily 18 June 1988. All of available

Iranian publications are curiously silent about the IRAA's involvement in this operation.
28 Mosalla-Nejad p.67.
29 JDW Morale Booster.
30 CIA National Intelligence Daily.

Chapter 17

1 For 'Tawakkalna ala Allah 2' see Cooper & Bishop p.276; Farrokh pp.410–411; Hiro pp.209–210, 238; Khazraji pp.537–560; Lessons pp.388–390, 408 f/n 81;Makki pp.331–332, 335–345, 348–376; Marashi and Salama p.172; Malovany pp.433–440; Murray & Woods pp.327–332; Pelletiere p.144; Pollack pp.227–228; Ward pp.293–294; Iraqi Offensive in Majnoon Island Area Begins at gulflink.osd.mil/declassified/cia/19961102/110296_93663-72538_01.text; CIA National Intelligence Dailies at foia.cia.gov/browse_docs.asp 18 and 22 June, and Iran-Iraq Frontline entry in web site gulflink.osd.mil.
2 Iraqi strengths based upon the order of battle and DIA DDB-2680-103-88 p.14.
3 CIA-RDP90T00114R000700800002-2.
4 Shaheed Bassim had distinguished himself in the marsh battles in which he was killed. CIA National Intelligence Dailies June 18. Murray & Woods p.327 identify the Majnoon defenders as '85th Pasdaran Brigade and the 3rd Armoured Brigade of the 23rd Pasdaran Division.' In fact the 85th 'Hejrat' Pasdaran Brigade was a mechanised unit usually of two infantry and one tank battalions but the armoured unit had been reduced to a company of 10 MBTs. The 23rd Division was the IRIA special forces formation and would not have had an armoured formation, especially in that terrain.
5 There was no time left to train attacks on the secondary objectives.
6 Meteorological data from nearby Kuwait on Freemeteo web site.
7 Ironically, the CIA noted, 'No evidence of chemical weapons use was in the battle areas. The two decontamination stations had not moved and there was no discernible activity'. CIA National Intelligence Dailies 26–27 June 1988 & CIA National Intelligence Daily 27 June 1988.
8 The CIA reported that the Iraqis stopped at 31-11N 48-10E and 31-09N 47-55E.
9 CRRC SH-SHTP-D-000-538.
10 The Iraqi figure probably includes both elements of divisions and independent brigades. CRRC SH-SHTP-D-000-538.
11 Lessons p.389.
12 Lessons pp.395–396; Atkeson, *Iraq's Arsenal: Tool of Ambition*; & 'Iran needs '$15–25b to rebuild forces', *Jane's Defence Weekly*, 4 February 1989.
13 He was the brother of the VII Corps commander General Maher Abd al-Rashid. Our thanks to General Makki for this information.
14 For the background to the war's end see Bulloch & Morris pp.237–238, 245, 248–249; Hiro pp.206, 210–211, 232–233, 241–249; Razoux pp.455–468.
15 CIA-RDP90G01353R001200090002-2 17 August 1988.
16 JDW Revolutionary Guards.

PART II

Chapter 18

1 Lortz thesis, pp.48–51.
2 Hiro, *The Longest War*, p.35 (hereafter Hiro).
3 Murray & Woods, p.332.
4 Patrick Bishop, 'The real Iraq menace now the war is over', *Daily Telegraph*, 13 September 1988.
5 Mahabad had been the heart of the Kurdish uprising and the emerging Kurdish autonomous republic established with support from the Union of Soviet Socialist Republics (USSR, also 'Soviet Union'), in December 1945. This was crushed by the Iranians within a year. It was during this period that the expression 'Peshmerga' became something like 'official'. See Lortz thesis, pp.26–30 (hereafter Lortz).
6 For Kurdish operations in Iran in 1979–1980, see Lessons, pp.26–27 & O'Ballance, pp.132–133.
7 Farrokh, *Iran at War*, p.351 (hereafter Farrokh) & Malovany, *Wars of Modern Babylon*, pp.124 & 141–142 (hereafter Malovany).
8 US Army Intelligence and Security Command history, p.4.9 (hereafter AISC).
9 Farrokh, p.349 & Ward, *Immortal*, p.247 (hereafter Ward).
10 For air support, see Cooper & Bishop, *Iran-Iraq War in the Air*, pp.83, 85–86, 89, 96–97 (hereafter Cooper & Bishop) & Farrokh, p.352.
11 Cooper & Bishop, pp.67–68, 96; Farrokh, pp.351–352; Hiro, pp.40–41; Cordesman & Wagner, *The Lessons of Modern War*, p.85 (Hereafter Lessons); Malovany, pp.116–121; Murray & Woods, *The Iran-Iraq War*, pp.111–113 (heraftar Murray & Woods); O'Ballance, *The Gulf War*, pp.33 & 35 (hereafter O'Ballance); AISC, pp.4–11; Conflict Record and Resource Center (CRRC) SH-SHTP-D-000-847. Note that some sources erroneously credit 7th Mountain Division with taking Qasr-e Shirin.
12 Cross-examination of different reports shows the 30th Armoured Brigade lost one third of its MBTs destroyed or damaged, and being left with a weak mechanised infantry battalion and its organic special forces battalion only.
13 Murray & Woods, p.116.
14 CRRC SH-PDWN-D-001-021.
15 Cooper & Bishop, pp.101–102.
16 O'Ballance, p.35; Hiro p.41.
17 For operations around Mehran see Farrokh, p.352; Hiro, p.41; Lessons, pp.85–87; Malovany, pp.121–122; Murray & Woods, p.115; O'Ballance, pp.35–36; AISC, pp.4–13; CRRC SH-MISC-D-000-827, SH-PDWN-D-001-021 and SH-SHTP-D-000-847.
18 CRRC SH-PDWN-D-001-021.
19 Information on commanding Iraqi officers from General Makki. Reports that the 4th and 7th Infantry Divisions advanced on Fakkeh and Bostan are now known to be inaccurate.
20 AISC pp.4-13 & 4-19.
21 Murray & Woods, pp.147–148.
22 Cooper & Bishop, p.112; Hiro, p.49; Lessons, p.96; Malovany, p.154; O'Ballance, pp.41–42. Notable is that many Iranian martyrs of the war with Iraq were posthumously advanced at least one, sometimes two ranks. Because there is no certainty in each case, only their last known ranks are mentioned – which are likely to be higher than while they were still alive.
23 Hiro, p.49; Malovany, p.174; O'Ballance, pp.41–42, 133–134.
24 Malovany, pp.160–170.
25 Cooper-Bishop, p.113; Lessons, p.112; Malovany, p.155; Woods et al Project 1946, pp.55–56 (heraftar Project 1946); O'Ballance, pp.60, 63–64; Pollack, p.195; Ward, pp.253–254; AISC, p.5-17.
26 Malovany, p.155.
27 Malovany, pp.155–158; AISC, p.5.2.
28 Malovany, pp.168–170; AISC, p.5-2, Figure 5.1.
29 Lessons, pp.126, 128; Malovany, pp.173–174; O'Ballance, pp.69, 78.
30 Malovany, pp.128–129.
31 Malovany, pp.168, 171; AISC, pp.5-4, Figures 5.2 & 5.3 & 5.4.

Chapter 19

1 This chapter is largely based on Malovany, pp.282 & 790; DDB-1100-342-88 & DDB-2680-103-88.
2 Divisional strengths varied from 8,000 in 58th and 64th Infantry Divisions, to 25,000 in 21st Division, or from 10,000 in 88th Division to 18,000 in 81st Division. Most armoured brigades had fewer than 90 MBTs. The artillery groups usually totalled about 3,300 personnel and included seven tube- and MLRS battalions. IRIA's support formations included the Transportation- and Engineering Commands (the latter including engineering and bridging battalions), signal groups, and a supply framework based on the 1st and 2nd Area Support Commands (Kermanshah and Dezful, respectively).
3 The GMID identified the units in question as 7th Vali Asr, 9th Badr, 10th Seyed o-Shohada, 17th Ali Ibn Abu Talib, 19th Fajr, 21st Imam Reza, 27th Mohammad Rasoolallah, 31st Ashura, 32nd Ansar al-Hossein, 41st Sarallah and 155th Seyed ol-Shohada Divisions. Some of units in question were actually 'borrowed' from the NFOHQ for operations Karbala-4/5/8. See CRRC SH-GMID-D-000-530.
4 SH-GMID-D-000-53.
5 DDB-1100-342-88; DDB-2680-103-88 & DDB-1100-343-85, p.16.
6 The corps was scheduled to be designated VIII Corps but at Saddam's suggestion the unique command was renamed I Special Corps. It was disbanded in 1989.
7 SH-SHTP-D-000-538 & special thanks to General Makki for explaining the backgrounds.
8 SH-PDWN-D-000-730.
9 DDB-1100-343-85.
10 Malovany, p.372.
11 Malovany, p.717; DDB-1100-343-85.

NOTES

12 Malovany, pp.822–824; DDB-1100-342-88; DDB-2680-103-88.
13 The Iraqi term was (Qiyadet Jahafel al-Difa' al-Watani). Khoury, *Iraq in Wartime*, pp.91–92, 99, 100–102, fn 40, 41, 43 (hereafter Khoury); Malovany, pp.827–828; Middle East Watch, *Genocide in Iraq*, Chapter 1 (herafter Watch with chapter number).
14 Khoury, p.101, p.101 fn 43 & Malovany, p.380 fn 2.
15 Ba'ath Regional Command Council, 01-2140-0003 quoted by Khoury, pp.75 & 91–92.
16 Khoury, p.100 fn 37 & Watch, Chapter 1.
17 Bulloch & Morris, *The Gulf War*, p.253 (herafter Bulloch & Morris). NLA Chief-of-Staff Describes Operation 'Shining Sun', *NLA Quarterly*, Spring, 1988.

Chapter 20

1 The fluent state of IRGC's formations during this period of war is readable in many of Iranian accounts, which variously describe the two Pasdaran formations in the Task Force Nasr as brigades or divisions. The distinction appears to have been in their support elements.
2 For a photo of an Iranian mock-up of an Iraqi strongpoint, see DDB-1100-342-88, p.21.
3 Buchan, Days of God p.352 (hereafter Buchan); Cooper & Bishop, pp.130–131; Farrokh, pp.363–364; Griffin article, p.21; Hiro, pp.55–56 &180; Lessons, pp.128–133, p.144 fn 14, 17 & 18; Malovany, pp.181–185; Murray & Woods, pp.175–177; O'Ballance, pp.78–82; Pelletiere, *The Iran-Iraq War*, p.42 (hereafter Pelletiere); Pollack, *Arabs at War*, pp.196–198 (hereafter Pollack); Ward, p.256; Project 1946, pp.74–76; AISC, pp.6-1, 6-3, 6-7; DDB-1100-343-85, p.66; Imposed War Official Web Site (http) sajed.ir; O'Ballance article, 'Iran vs Iraq: Quantity vs Quality?'.
4 Hiro, p.55; Farrokh, p.362; Project 1946, p.75.
5 O'Ballance, p.81.
6 Project 1946, p.76.
7 Murray & Woods, p.177; Pollack, p.196.
8 Farrokh, p.364 (based upon J. Miller & L. Mylroie, *Saddam Hussein and the Crisis in the Gulf*, Times Books, New York, 1990, p.114). General Makki recalls Saddam later related to this incident, too.
9 Pollack, p.196 & O'Ballance, p.29. Apparently, this was the first time the Basiji were deployed as conventional infantry on the battlefield. Until that time, they had been primarily used as labourers and porters.
10 Farrokh, p.363.
11 O'Ballance, p.82 & Buchan, p.352.
12 Farrokh, p.366; Lessons, p.137; Malovany, pp.185–186.
13 O'Ballance, pp.85–86; Lessons, p.140; Malovany, pp.198–216; AISC, pp.6-10.
14 Connell, *Iranian Operation Decision-Making*, pp.13–14 (hereafter Connell); Farrokh, p.371; Malovany, pp.216–219; O'Ballance, pp.98–99; AISC, pp.6-19 & 6-25.
15 'The Day of the Helicopter Gunship', *Baghdad Observer*, 27 October 1982. Widely accepted as 'truth' and repeated in multiple publications in the English language area of the 1980s, this claim was entirely unsubstantiated. Iraq never operated genuine Mi-24s (only the export variant Mi-25), and never received any AT-6s during the war with Iran. As far as is known 30 and more years later, no IrAAC Mi-25 has ever shot down any IRIAF F-4.
16 Connell, p.14.
17 Connell, pp.14–16; Cooper & Bishop, pp.144–145; Farrokh, pp.371–372; Hiro, p.91; Lessons, p.154; Malovany, pp.221–224; O'Ballance, pp.99–101; AISC, pp.6-25, 7-1, 7-6, Figures 6.18, 7.2.
18 AISC p.6-25 & Cooper & Bishop, p.147.
19 Why this operation not codenamed Val Fajr-1 remains unknown, but its designation continues to confuse historians.
20 Hiro, p.95; Farrokh, p.373; Lessons, pp.159–161; Malovany, pp.225–228; O'Ballance, pp.114–116; Ward, p.261; AISC, pp.7-1, 7-6, 7-7, Figure 7.2.
21 AISC, p.7-7. US intelligence concluded the Iranians lost about 100 armoured fighting vehicles, including some 20 MBTs.
22 Marashi & Salama, pp.135–136; Farrokh, p.373; Lessons, p.162; Malovany, pp.228–230; O'Ballance, p.118; AISC, p.7.7; DDB-1100-343-85, pp.67–68.
23 Cooper & Bishop, p.156; Farrokh, pp.374–375; Hiro, p.97; Lessons, pp.1678, 1703, 187 fn 17; Malovany, pp.235–238; O'Ballance, pp.119–120; Ward, p.261.
24 For Val Fajr-5 and -6, see Cooper & Bishop, p.165; Cordesman, *The Iran-Iraq War and Western Security*, p.62 (hereafter Cordesman); Farrokh, p.377; Hiro, pp.102–103; Lessons, p.179; Malovany, p.249; O'Ballance, pp.142–143 & Ward, pp.263–264.
25 Cooper & Bishop, p.165; Farrokh, p.377; Lessons, p.179; Malovany, pp.250–251; O'Ballance, p.143 & Ward, pp.263–264.
26 Cordesman, p.69; Hiro, pp.132–134; Malovany, pp.264–265, O'Ballance, pp.151–153.
27 The best sources for such tit-for-tat operations are Malovany, pp.269–270 & 278–279, but also Farrokh, pp.379–380; O'Ballance, p.160 & DDB-1100-343-85, pp.68–70 (Figure 27).
28 Malovany, pp.315–316.
29 According to Makki: a senior member of Ba'th Party, Hamadi was appointed commander of 6th Armoured Division in 1988. He died in exile in Amman in 2013.
30 Marashi & Salama pp.164 &.; Cooper & Bishop, pp.215 & 217–219; Cordesman, pp.101–103 & 118, fn 43; Farrokh pp.389–390; Hiro, pp.1712; Lessons, pp.227–228, 236, 264 fn 38; Malovany, pp.317–319; O'Ballance, pp.179–180, 185, 189; Pelletiere, pp.103–104.
31 It remains unknown who took over as commander of 17th Armoured Division during the following period.
32 Malovany, p.318.
33 Marashi & Salama, p.190.
34 Malovany, pp.326–327.
35 Pelletierre et al, Iraqi Power and US Security in the Middle East, pp.15–16 (hereafter Iraqi Power).
36 Malovany, pp.319 & 327.
37 Cordesman, p.129; Hiro, p.181; Lessons, pp.256–257; Malovany, pp.340–341; O'Ballance, p.198 & SH-GMID-D-000-301, p.26.
38 Cordesman, p.260; Hiro, p.185; O'Ballance, pp.203–204.
39 Malovany, pp.345 & 358–359; SH-GMID-D-000-530. Malovany claims the latter attack was thwarted. However, in 1988, the Iraqis had to advance *towards* the river.

Chapter 21

1 Cooper & Bishop, pp.155–156, 222–223; Cordesman, pp.137–138; Farrokh, pp.374 & 395–396; Hiro, pp.967, 102, 174, 185; Lessons, pp.166–167, 187 fn 16, 234, 259, 266 fn 59 & 259–260; Malovany, pp.234–235, 282–285, 315–317, 343 & 356–357; Marashi & Salama, p.142; O'Ballance, pp.119, 138–139, 189 & 201; Pelletiere, pp.76–77; Project 1946, pp.90–95.
2 Iraqi Major General Hamadani latter denied reports about deployment of chemical weapons during this campaign (see Project 1946). Helicopters of the IrAAF reportedly flew in 5,350 troops and 880 tons of supplies, while withdrawing 1,100 injured. Detail on Il-76s being deployed as bombers was provided by Brigadier General Sadik (IrAF, ret.), in interview to Tom Cooper, March 2005.
3 Most of this chapter is based on Cordesman, pp.98, 99, 111; Cooper & Bishop, pp.157, 206; Farrokh, p.375; Hiro, pp.102, 169, 174, 185–186, 201; Lessons, pp.161–162, 175–177, 188 fn 23, 224–225, 264 fn 26, 281–282, 292–293, 362–363 & 386–388; Malovany, pp.238–243, 247 fn 9, 308–310, 354–357; Marashi & Salama, p.170; O'Ballance, pp.139–140, 175, 180–181; Pelletiere, pp.76–78; Ward, p.261 & Review of the Military Situation in Iraq by Colonel R.G. Eccles, *British Defence Attaché*, 27 April 1986.
4 Malovany, p.242.

Chapter 22

1 Interestingly, the Iraqi intelligence identified the presence of 23rd IRIA Special Forces Division and 1st Brigade of 64th IRIA Infantry Division on this sector in January 1988. This should have been reinforced by Pasdaran 9th Basdr Infantry Division, 39th Nabi al-Akram and 65th Kilan Rasht Infantry Brigdes, 622nd Beit-ol-Moghaddas Mountain-, 89th Moharram Artillery- and a mechanised brigade from 20th Ramadan Mechanised Division. SH-GMID-D-000-337.
2 For details on these three offensives, see Farrokh, p.404; Hiro, p.199; Malovany, pp.367–368 & 430.
3 SH-PDWN-D-000-730.
4 Plagued by technical problems, this power station became operational again only in 2013.
5 For Tahrir ol-Quds see Cooper & Bishop, p.165; Malovany, p.249; O'Ballance, p.141; Hiro, p.149 & Lessons, p.179.
6 During this attack, the Iraqis noted that the Pasdaran were now splitting their divisions into 'assault' and 'follow-up' elements, a concept first used by the Imperial Germany Army in 1918 (SH-GMID-D-000-530).
7 For Val Fajr-10, see Cooper & Bishop, pp.262–263; Hiro, p.202; Farrokh, p.404; Lessons, pp.369–372, 405–406 fn 29; Malovany, pp.370–373; Marashi & Salama, p.172; Watch, Chapter 3; Project 1946, p.83 & SH-GMID-D-000-530. In Project 1946 General Hamdani confusingly refers

to these operations being in 1987. Watch also confuses Val Fajr-10, with Zafar-7 and Beit-al-Moghaddas-6.
8   Project 1946, pp.83–84; Watch, Chapter 3; Nixon, *Debriefing the President*, pp.122, 170–172 (hereafter Nixon) & Malovany, p.371. While some Iraqis have claimed that this attack was an omen of the Anfal COIN campaign, there is strong evidence it was launched as a separate decision – one reflecting the massive use of chemical weapons in most Iraqi campaigns of 1988. Khazraji latter claimed that neither he nor any other military leader was involved, but that Saddam alone took the decision, in agreement with Majid and his military production chief – Hussein Kamel. On the contrary, Saddam denied all knowledge and blamed Khazraji. In Project 1946 General Hamdani claimed that Talbani had informed Baghdad that the Kurds, on his instructions, had largely evacuated the area and optimistically claimed only '75–150' were killed. Most other Iraqi sources insist until today that either no chemical weapons were deployed by their armed forces against Halabja at all, or that this attack – or at least a part of it – was actually undertaken by the Iranians. For their part, the Iranians insist that Khomeini refused permission for development and deployment of chemical weapons because Islam prohibits those who fight for it from polluting the atmosphere – even in a 'Jihad' (Hiro, p201). The Iranian propaganda about the Halabja attack was designed to arouse public condemnation around the world – but had also the demoralising effects at home. Finally, there are notes that the Iraqi deployment of chemical weapons did play a part in their military success of 1988, but foremost as a part of 'superior tactics', rather than being the sole reason (Iraqi Power, p.36).
9   Hiro, p.202; Lessons, pp.371–372 & Malovany, p.373.
10 The Guards barely had time to unpack their kit bags before they were on the way back south to join the Faw offensive, apparently without the commando brigades, and to the bewilderment of the many Iraqi generals unaware of the planned offensive on Faw.
11 SH-GMID-D-000-530.
12 SH-SHTP-D-000-538.
13 SH-SHTP-D-000-538.
14 Hiro, pp.237–238 & 241; Lessons, p.390; Malovany, pp.425, 430–432.

Chapter 23
1   For operations in 1981 see Lessons, pp.97, 122 & O'Ballance, pp.63–64, 133–134.
2   A. R., former Iranian Army NCO, interview by Tom Cooper, February 2004.
3   Hiro, p.96; Lessons, p.166 & O'Ballance, pp.135–136 & 138–140.
4   Farrokh, p.374.
5   As of late May 1983, the only Iraqi Army unit left in Kurdish-dominated parts of northern Iraq was 502nd Infantry Brigade, deployed in the BArzan-Zakho area (see SH-PDWN-D-000-730).
6   O'Ballance, p.112 & Lortz, p.55.
7   Farrokh, p.374 & Watch, Chapter 1.
8   Hiro, pp.59, 102, 141; Marashi & Salama, pp.14 & 168; Lessons, p.167; O'Ballance, pp.135–138 & 141; Pelletiere, p.78; Watch, Chapter 1 & DDB-1100-343-85.
9   According to Hiro (p.149) this agreement had been signed in secrecy in 1978, but was made public only in 1984. It allowed each side to pursue 'subversive elements' up to 15 kilometres miles beyond the border.
10 Watch, Chapter 1.
11 Hiro, p.149 & DDB-1100-343-85.
12 Cooper & Bishop, pp.206 & 226; Cordsman, pp.82–83, 89, 98, 99, 111; Farrokh, p.374; Hiro, pp.150,169, 174; Lessons, pp.200–201, 207–208, 224–225, 257–258, 264 fn 26 & 334–335 fn 27; Malovany, pp.327–328; Marashi & Salama, p.168; O'Ballance pp.141, 167–168, 175, 180–181; Watch, Chapter 1 & SH-MISC-D-001-3740.
13 Murray & Woods, p.333.
14 Watch, Chapter 10, fn 5 & Lortz, p.40.
15 Watch, Chapter 1 & Project 1946, pp.94–95.
16 Watch, Chapter 1 & Project 1946, pp.94–95.
17 'Kirkuk oilfield raid-damage disputed', *Jane's Defence Weekly*, 18 October 1987.
18 In a broadcast on 13 June 1988 the unnamed commander of the 'Ramadan' headquarters claimed that in addition to major offensives the previous 12 months saw 496 minor operations which claimed to have destroyed or captured 170 AFVs, 1,525 soft-skinned vehicles, 87 guns and to have captured 50,000 individual and crew-served weapons. Foreign Broadcast Information Services/British Library.
19 Hiro, pp.185–186 & 191; Lessons, pp.257, 259, 292, 319–320, 370–371, 405 fn 27; Malovany, pp.354–357; O'Ballance, pp.200–201; 'Kurdish villages razed in punitive Iraqi campaign', *Jane's Defence Weekly*, 10 October 1987; Foreign Broadcast Information Services/British Library & SH-MISC-D-001-3740.
20 Sadik, interview, March 2005.
21 Khoury, p.100 fn 43.
22 Malovany, pp.822–824.
23 Lessons, pp.320 & 370–371; Watch, Chapter 1 & SH-GMID-D-000-530.
24 Watch (Chaper 1) reports deployment of guns with 25 miles (40 kilometres) range. Given the Soviet-made M-46s have had a range of 27 kilometres, it is possible that the Iraqis deployed some Austrian-made GHN-45 155mm guns.
25 Watch, Chapters 1 & 2.
26 SH-MISC-D-001-3740; Hiro, p.197; Marashi & Salama, p.170; Murray & Woods, pp.253, 310–311; Watch, Chapter 39. Majid should have personally executed up to 30 prisoners in Basra, in 1991.
27 Murray & Woods, p.332. The NDBs were reportedly concentrated into five divisional-sized commands (see Malovany, p.828).
28 Lessons, p.288; Murray & Woods, pp.254–255, 311, 332–334; O'Ballance, p.149 & SH-SHTP-A-001-045.
29 See Air 19/109 Method of Employment of the Air Arm in Iraq 1924. The commander of No 45 Squadron in Iraq during this period was Squadron Leader Arthur Harris, the wartime commander of Bomber Command and an advocate of area attack (and also known as 'Bomber Harris').
30 Watch, Chapter 2.
31 Watch, Chapter 2.
32 For operations in 1988 see Lessons, p.383; Malovany, pp.357, 370–371; Watch, Chapter 2; Foreign Broadcast Information Services/British Library & SH-MISC-D-001-3740.
33 Murray & Woods, pp.332–334 quoting SH-SHTP-A-000-788.
34 Marashi & Salama, p.172; Malovany, pp.368–373 & 440–442; Murray & Woods, pp.333–334; Khazraji, *Al Harb Al Iraqiya*, pp.581–598 (hereafter Khazraji); Khoury, pp.33, 118–121, 216; Watch, Chapters 3–7 & 10; CHAK web site & Military Campaign, pp.17–41.
35 Malovany, p.372.
36 CHAK (p.23) identifies 37 brigades including four commando/special forces but this seems unlikely.
37 Watch, Chapter 11.
38 For the aftermath of the offensives see Watch, Chapter 12 & CHAK web site (pp.5 & 75).

Chapter 24
1   SH-PDWN-D-000-730.
2   SH-SHTP-D-000-538.
3   Farrokh, pp.411–412; Hiro, p.238; Lessons, p.395; Khazraji, pp.537–561; Makki, *Maarik at-Tahrir al-Kubra al-Iraqiya*, pp.383–402 (hereafter Makki); Malovany, pp.425–440, 448 fn 1, 449 fn 3; Pelletiere, p.144; Iraqi Power, p.30; Pollack, p.228 & Ward, p.295.
4   Lessons, pp.395–396.
5   Hiro, p.246; Iraqi Power, pp.30–31; Lessons, pp.387 & 396–398; Khazraji, pp.561–580; Makki, pp.403–462; Malovaney, pp.432–438, 440; Pelletiere, pp.144–145; Pollack, pp.227–228; 'Iraq's southern successes', *Jane's Defence Weekly*, 23 July 1988. For III Corps' contribution see later in this volume.
6   Malovany, pp.438–439.
7   For the background to MeK/MKO's activities see Hiro, pp.69, 99–101, 202, 230–231 & O'Ballance, pp.89–90.
8   Bulloch & Morris, p.235.
9   Bulloch & Morris, pp.254–255.
10 Buchan, pp.370–371; Bulloch & Morris, pp.252–257; Hiro, p.202; Lessons, pp.320–321; Malovany, pp.356 & 377; 'Mujahideen strength growing in Iran', *Jane's Defence Weekly*, 28 December 1986; 'NLA and the struggle against Tehran', *Jane's Defence Weekly*, 20 February 1988; 'Operation 'Shining Sun', *NLA Quarterly*, Spring 1988 & 'Special Report', *NLA Quarterly*, Autumn 1988.
11 Farrokh, p.410; Hiro, p.209; Lessons, pp.387–388, 408 fn 73 & 75; Pollack, p.227; 'Iraq in successful attack on occupied territory', *Jane's Defence Weekly*, 2 July 1988 & 'Disarming Khomeinei', Special Report, NLA Quarterly, Autumn 1988.
12 Final Report on Operation Eternal Light, General Command of the National Liberation Army; Bulloch & Morris, pp.255–257; Farrokh, pp.413–414; Hiro, pp.246–247; Lessons, pp.398, 409 fn 103; Malovany, pp.439 & website <iran-e-azad.org/English>

13   Bulloch & Morris, p.253.

Appendix I

1   http://maarefjang.ir/uploaded/files/Books/Tarikh%20nezami_J2.pdf; Soltam was a company created by Tampella to circumvent Finnish export restrictions, thus Soltam and Tampella mortars are essentially the same weapons.
2   The FCO 8/3107 of the National Archives of Great Britain contain the Defence Attaché's reports that are including inventory numbers. Related entries are marked with 'FCO' in the tables below.
3   Noted as unserviceable in the source document. Other documents indicate there was a problem with the chromium plating on the hydraulic rams. This would explain the absence of wartime pictures of the AVLB. However, the DIA report *Ground Forces Intelligence Study – Iran* (DDB-1100-342-86), dated May 1986 indicated that the Chieftain AVLBs had been used 'recently'.
4   The air attaché report gives 360 in service with the airforce, it is not clear if these are included in the 1,000 total or additional to it.
5   The air attaché report gives 128 in service with the airforce, it is not clear if these are included in the 150 total or additional to it.
6   The US 40mm is a mystery as there are no supporting delivery documents or pictures.
7   In 1941 Iran had 46 Bofors 75mm AA guns. http://kavehfarrokh.com/military-history-1900-present/iranian-artillery-units-early-1900s-1941/ It is possible that these were still in storage in 1978, though it seems very unlikely there were ever 258 guns. There are no pictures of them during the Iran–Iraq War.
8   This seems to be in error, there is no pictorial evidence of any 107mm mortars being used by the Iranians. It may be that the attaché saw the M113 120mm mortar carrier and assumed they were the M106 with 107mm rather than local conversions. The numbers reported are very close to the actual number of M113 120mm mortar carriers.
9   Probably in service with the navy, not the army.
10 The report is clear that these are Seacat being used for land defence.
11 This is a literal translation; it is unclear to the author what vehicle the entry refers to.
12 The original table just says 14.5mm anti-aircraft gun. They were most likely ZPU-4 as there are pictures of those serving with the army.
13 CIA, *Iran Military Summary*, March 1981, CIA/FOIA/Electronic Reading Room (henceforth CIA/FOIA/ERR). The same document indicates that the M113s were removed from storage only in March 1981
14 DIA, *MIS Vol.III, Part II: Middle East and North Africa* (Persian Gulf). The data presented in this document (and thus this table) was, at least partially, compiled by analysing satellite imagery. A question mark indicates the inventory as unknown to the DIA at the time, while shaded entries indicate new equipment introduced to service since the start of the war with Iraq. 60mm, 81mm, 82mm, 120mm and 160mm mortars were all noted as being in service in unspecified numbers. It was probably impossible to determine the type of mortar from satellite imagery and so these records are likely based on other intelligence sources. It should be noted that there is no pictorial record of 82mm or 160mm mortars in use by the Iranians.
15 It is unclear whether this number includes captured tanks. The T-72 entry explicitly mentions the tanks are captured, the T-55 entry does not, so this may be a delivery number rather than an inventory. If it does include captured tanks, it presumably includes captured Type 69s which would be indistinguishable from T-55s on satellite imagery and which are not given a separate entry of their own.
16 It is unclear whether this number includes captured tanks. The T-72 entry explicitly mentions the tanks are captured, the T-62 entry does not. Additionally, the source is noted as North Korea. So, this number may refer to the number of Chonma Ho delivered and exclude captured Iraqi tanks.
17 Clearly noted as captured from Iraq.
18 Presumably this includes mortar carriers and TOW launchers as well as the APC, as they are not otherwise listed by the DIA. The M577 is also not listed so may also be included in this total.
19 Both the ZPU-2 and ZPU-4 are noted as being of North Korean origin. This would appear to be the number of deliveries rather than an inventory.
20 Pre-war inventory shown as 1,100.
21 Pre-war inventory shown as 288.
22 Pre-war inventory shown as 55.
23 Pre-war inventory shown as 80.
24 Number of launchers is unknown, but 1,500 missiles are shown in the inventory.
25 Pre-war inventory is noted as 52 launchers and 250 missiles.
26 Pre-war inventory is noted as 14 launchers and 575 missiles.
27 25–30 missiles supplied.
28 120 missiles supplied.
29 The principal source for the following tables is the SIPRI Arms Transfer Database. Although imperfect, it is by far the most extensive treatment available. Data based on documents of the US Military Aid Programme (available online) covers only the period from 1950 until the early 1960s: such entries are noted with 'MAP'. Other sources used include: Foreign Relations of the United States, 1958–1960: Near East Region, Iraq, Iran, Arabian Peninsula, Volume XII, p.237; Colonel Seyed Yaghoub Hosseini, *Military History of the Imposed War until September 31, 1369, Volume 2: Pre-War Encounters* (in Persian) (hereafter 'Hos'); Data from CIA and DIA documentation released by the CIA/FOIA/ERR are noted as 'CIA' and 'DIA'; CIA, *Handbook of Major Foreign Weapons Systems Exported to the Third World, Volume II: Ground Forces Equipment* (CIA/FOIA/ERR) (hereafter 'MFW'); US Army, The Operational Environment Assessment Iran: Iran (of lesser use because obviously based on one online publication and includes blatant inaccuracies; quoted only where no other useful sources are available), (hereafter 'OEA'); Visual evidence (photographs and videos of the equipment deployed by Iran during the war with Iraq); Data from the original printing of the present work on the Iran–Iraq War, as prepared by Hooton et al (hereafter 'IIVx'); and additional details provided by Tom Cooper based on his personal notes, are marked with 'TC'.
30 https://www.cia.gov/library/readingroom/docs/CIA-RDP85T00283R000500120005-5.pdf
31 https://www.cia.gov/library/readingroom/docs/CIA-RDP85T00283R000500120005-5.pdf
32 https://www.cia.gov/library/readingroom/docs/CIA-RDP85T00283R000500120005-5.pdf
33 https://www.cia.gov/library/readingroom/docs/CIA-RDP85T00283R000500120005-5.pdf
34 https://en.wikipedia.org/wiki/International_aid_to_combatants_in_the_Iran%E2%80%93Iraq_War gives this number. However, the sources the page reference do not specify how many were delivered, so the numbers should be considered unconfirmed.
35 https://www.cia.gov/library/readingroom/docs/CIA-RDP85T00283R000500120005-5.pdf
36 The OAE Iran report only shows 100 delivered. MFW shows an unknown number being delivered in 1985.
37 https://static.history.state.gov/frus/frus1969-76ve04/pdf/d181.pdf.
38 Kenneth R. Timmerman, *Fanning the Flames: Guns, Greed & Geopolitics in the Gulf War*, http://www.iran.org/tib/krt/fanning_index.htm
39 http://www.dasrotewien.at/seite/noricum-skandal
40 https://www.cia.gov/library/readingroom/docs/CIA-RDP80T01782R000200080001-7.pdf
41 Timmerman, *Fanning the Flames*.
42 https://www.cia.gov/library/readingroom/docs/CIA-RDP85T00283R000500120005-5.pdf
43 https://static.history.state.gov/frus/frus1969-76ve04/pdf/d181.pdf
44 https://www.facebook.com/php?fbid=210756450924775&set=p.210756450924775&type=3
45 http://www.dia.mil/FOIA/FOIA-Electronic-Reading-Room/FOIA-Reading-Room-Iran/FileId/89384/
46 https://static.history.state.gov/frus/frus1969-76ve04/pdf/d181.pdf
47 https://static.history.state.gov/frus/frus1969-76ve04/pdf/d181.pdf
48 http://webarchive.loc.gov/all/20011111192116/http://cns.miis.edu/pubs/opapers/op2/fbmsl.htm
49 Delivery date from Arms Control and Missile Proliferation in the Middle East: https://bit.ly/2RQDNaQ
50 DIA report DDB-2680-103-88, MIS Vol III, Part II Middle East and North Africa (Persian Gulf)
51 Delivery date from Arms Control and Missile Proliferation in the Middle East: https://bit.ly/2RQDNaQ
52 DIA report supplied by TC.
53 http://webarchive.loc.gov/all/20011111192116/http://cns.miis.edu/pubs/opapers/op2/fbmsl.htm
54 Evidence is anecdotal only: https://www.facebook.com/groups/296582530470388/permalink/2882953151833300/. Both SIPRI

and OEA show large deliveries (260 and 150 respectively) however the British Defence Attaché report of 1976 together with the lack of pre-war pictures of M48s, would seem to indicate these are in error. *Jane's Main Battle Tanks*, CF Foss, indicates that the Iranians were upgrading Pakistani M48A2 tanks at the time of the revolution and that these were never returned to Pakistan.

55   https://static.history.state.gov/frus/frus1969-76ve04/pdf/d181.pdf
56   https://static.history.state.gov/frus/frus1969-76ve04/pdf/d181.pdf
57   DIA report DDB-2680-103-88, MIS Vol III, Part II Middle East and North Africa (Persian Gulf)
58   DIA report DDB-2680-103-88, MIS Vol III, Part II Middle East and North Africa (Persian Gulf)
59   http://www.dia.mil/FOIA/FOIA-Electronic-Reading-Room/FOIA-Reading-Room-Iran/FileId/89381/
60   http://www.dia.mil/FOIA/FOIA-Electronic-Reading-Room/FOIA-Reading-Room-Iran/FileId/89381/
61   DIA report DDB-2680-103-88, MIS Vol III, Part II Middle East and North Africa (Persian Gulf)
62   https://en.wikipedia.org/wiki/Scud#Iran%E2%80%93Iraq_War
63   http://www.dia.mil/FOIA/FOIA-Electronic-Reading-Room/FOIA-Reading-Room-Iran/FileId/89381/
64   http://www.dia.mil/FOIA/FOIA-Electronic-Reading-Room/FOIA-Reading-Room-Iran/FileId/89381/
65   http://www.dia.mil/FOIA/FOIA-Electronic-Reading-Room/FOIA-Reading-Room-Iran/FileId/89384/
66   Arms Control and Missile Proliferation in the Middle East: https://bit.ly/2RQDNaQ
67   Arms Control and Missile Proliferation in the Middle East: https://bit.ly/2RQDNaQ
68   https://static.history.state.gov/frus/frus1969-76ve04/pdf/d181.pdf
69   https://www.cia.gov/library/readingroom/docs/CIA-RDP85T00840R000102850001-2.pdf
70   https://static.history.state.gov/frus/frus1969-76ve04/pdf/d181.pdf.
71   http://publ.lib.ru/ARCHIVES/T/"Tehnika_i_voorujenie",2005,N03.[djv-fax].zip
72   http://publ.lib.ru/ARCHIVES/T/"Tehnika_i_voorujenie",2005,N03.[djv-fax].zip
73   https://static.history.state.gov/frus/frus1969-76ve04/pdf/d181.pdf
74   https://static.history.state.gov/frus/frus1969-76ve04/pdf/d181.pdf
75   http://publ.lib.ru/ARCHIVES/T/"Tehnika_i_voorujenie",2005,N03.[djv-fax].zip
76   https://www.facebook.com/groups/161471874272371/permalink/614850692267818/
77   https://www.quora.com/What-was-the-nature-of-US-foreign-policy-toward-Iran-and-its-importance-prior-to-the-1979-Iranian-Revolution
78   https://elpais.com/diario/1982/09/11/economia/400543212_850215.html
79   https://www.nytimes.com/1986/11/25/world/iran-in-6-year-search-for-arms-finds-world-of-willing-suppliers.html
80   The designation of the Soltam mortar is unclear https://www.nmm.nl/zoeken-in-de-collectie/detail/234029/ indicates that the long barrel version of the mortar has the designation B-502. https://www.smallarmsreview.com/archive/detail.arc.entry.cfm?arcid=20417 indicates this designation was for the split barrel version and the example in the Dutch museum is clearly not split barrel, so there is some doubt about the designation. Some sources, including some editions of *Jane's Infantry Weapons* give the mortar the designation of M64, this may be the service designation, but this is unclear.

Appendix II

1   CIA RDP 81 T 00380 R 000100480001-0 Ground Force Mobilisation Iraq/Iran
2   The spelling used here is as per the original document.
3   Shortly after the revolution the 1st and 2nd Infantry Divisions were merged to make the 21st Infantry Division: http://rahrovan-artesh.ir/index.php?/topic/1068-%D8%AA%D8%A7%D8%B1%D9%8A%D8%AE%DA%86%D9%87-%D8%AA%D8%B4%D9%83%D9%8A%D9%84-%D9%84%D8%B4%D9%83%D8%B1-21-%D8%AD%D9%85%D8%B2%D9%87-%D8%AA%D8%A7-%D8%AD%D9%85%D8%B6%D9%88%D8%A8%D8%B1-%D8%AF%D8%B1-%D9%85%D9%86%D8%B7%D9%82%D9%87/ (dead link)
4   This unit is not described in Iranian sources. Given its location it may in fact be part of the 44th or 55th Artillery Groups.
5   Military history of Iran, Wikipedia, https://en.wikipedia.org/wiki/Military_history_of_Iran#Under_Khomeini_(1979_to_1989)
6   Colonel Sayed Yaqub Hosseini, *Military history of the Imposed War until 31st of September 1980 (Volume 2) Pre-war border clashes*, http://maarefjang.ir/uploaded/files/Books/Tarikh%20nezami_J2.pdf
7   Iran, Military Manpower Problems Limit Options, CIA-RDP84S00927R000100120003-8 https://www.cia.gov/readingroom/docs/CIA-RDP84S00927R000100120003-8.pdf
8   Brigadier General, Mohammad Najafi Rashed, *Artillery in Defence, Stabilising the Aggressor*, http://maarefjang.ir/uploaded/files/Books/Toopkhaneh%20jeld%201_96-10-11.pdf
9   Brigadier General Nasser Arasteh & Brigadier General Masoud Bakhtiari, *Artillery in the Sacred Defense – An analysis of the role of ground force artillery in the Army of the Islamic Republic of Iran*.
10 The number not given in original source and is taken from the 1986 DIA Order of Battle below.
11 Ground Forces Intelligence Study – Iran, DIA, (DDB-1100-342-86).
12 In a few places the numbers in the source document are unclearly printed, the numbers given are the author's best interpretation.
13 Number not given in original source. Number assumed from 1980 artillery OOB.
14 Number not given in original source. Number assumed from 1980 artillery OOB.
15 No brigade HQ is indicated. Given there are three tank battalions and three infantry brigades it is possible one tank battalion was operationally subordinate to each infantry brigade.
16 The 30th division is listed without artillery or divisional support units. It was probably still forming.
17 Given that the 6xx range was used for tank units this battalion is probably miss-identified.
18 The 291st is noted as being attached rather than an organic unit.
19 No brigade affiliation is shown in the source document.
20 No equipment mentioned in the original document.
21 Although not stated in the source document this battalion is almost certainly jeep mounted.
22 This armour is shown as directly under command of the division, not subordinate to a brigade.
23 The operational subordination of the artillery battalions is given in the source: 317 is in general support, 340 is in direct support of the third brigade, 373 in direct support of the second brigade and 396 in direct support of the first brigade. No artillery is allocated in support of the fourth brigade which suggests it is still forming.
24 It is curious that there are tank battalions that are not subordinate to the division and these battalions were not allocated to form the fourth brigade.
25 No information is given as to what type of battalion this is.
26 This is written as 'Katusha' in the source document. All other groups are noted as having '122mm MRL BM-21'. Iranian documents generally refer to the BM-21 as a Katusha, so it may be an editing error in the table. Alternatively, the unit could have North Korean BM-11 or M1985 MRL.
27 The source document does not specify whether the guns are self-propelled or towed.
28 This unit is marked 'SCH SPT' in the source document, without any further explanation. This probably stands for school support, though it is unclear what this role entails. Of the subordinate units only the 323, 399 and 324 are listed as 'Sch Sup'.
29 This number is outside the normal numbering sequence for mechanised units, so it may be erroneous.
30 'Philosophy of Naming Army Ground Forces', Military.ir Forum, http://www.military.ir/forums/topic/29917-%25d8%25ac%25d9%2586%25da%25af-%25d9%2587%25d8%25b4%25d8%25aa-%25d8%25b3%25d8%25a7%25d9%2584%25d9%2587-%25d8%25a7%25db%258c%25d8%25b1-%25d8%25a7%25d9%2586-%25d9%2588-%25d8%25b9%25d8%25b1%25d8%25a7%25d9%2582-%25d8%25a7%25d8%25b2-%25d8%25af%25d8%25b1%25db%258c%25da%2586%25d9%2587-%25d8%25a7%25db%258c-%25d8%25af%25db%258c%25da%25af%25d8%25b1/?page=5
31 The 21st Infantry Division was formed after the start of the war from the pre-war 1st and 2nd Infantry Divisions.
32 Ground Forces Intelligence Study – Iran DIA (DDB-1100-342-86).

NOTES

33 Colonel Sayed Yaqub Hosseini, *Military history of the Imposed War until 31st of September 1980 (Volume 2) Pre-war border clashes*, http://maarefjang.ir/uploaded/files/Books/Tarikh%20nezami_J2.pdf
34 Almost certainly a typo. US intel consistently shows 16 batteries.
35 Comparing this to the known organisation of the 429th Engineering Battalion it seems only the 'line' engineers are accounted for. Bridging and plant companies are not included in the total.
36 *National Intelligence Survey 33; Iran; Armed Forces* CIA-RDP01-00707R000200070042: https://www.cia.gov/readingroom/docs/CIA-RDP01-00707R000200070042-2.pdf
37 Some sources refer to this unit as a battalion.
38 *21/7/1359 Operations of Division 21 Hamzah (AS) West of Karkheh River (Dezful & Shoush region)*: http://rahrovan-artesh.ir/index.php?/topic/604-گنج-ال-اول-رد-ینی-زمی-یوری/&page=5. It seems that the fourth brigade became armoured at a later date.
39 *Iraq/Iran Military Summary* CIA-RDP80T01782R000200240001-9: https://www.cia.gov/readingroom/docs/CIA-RDP80T01782R000200240001-9.pdf
40 On 20 October 1980 the Brigade had 10 M60 and 1 M47M.
41 37th Armoured Brigade in Operation Samenallameh, Majid Saremi.
42 Qasim Karimi, *The Epic Makers of Tang Hajian. Memories 110 Infantry Battalion 3 Brigade 77 Khorasan Division*.
43 Reorganisation Objective Army Division. This was the name used for US TO&E in the 1970s and early 80s. See *Military Intelligence Summary Vol III, Pt III, Middle East and North Africa (Persian Gulf)* (DDB-2680-103-88 part II).
44 Virgil Ney, *Evolution of the U.S. Army Division 1939-1968*, https://web.archive.org/web/20210206223658/https://apps.dtic.mil/dtic/tr/fulltext/u2/697844.pdf
45 Qasim Karimi, *The epic makers of Tang Hajian. Memories 110 Infantry Battalion 3 Brigade 77 Khorasan Division*.
46 Colonel Sayed Yaqub Hosseini, *Military history of the Imposed War until 31st of September 1980 (Volume 2) Pre-war border clashes*, http://maarefjang.ir/uploaded/files/Books/Tarikh%20nezami_J2.pdf
47 The direct translation of the Persian term is 'petty officer'.
48 Colonel Sayed Yaqub Hosseini, *Military history of the Imposed War until 31st of September 1980 (Volume 2) Pre-war border clashes*, http://maarefjang.ir/uploaded/files/Books/Tarikh%20nezami_J2.pdf
49 FCO 8/3107: British Defence attaché's annual report – Iran
50 *Mechanized Infantry Battalion 133*: http://rahrovan-artesh.ir/index.php?/topic/1068-%D8%AA%D8%A7%D8%B1%D9%8A%D8%AE%DA%86%D9%87-%D8%AA%D8%B4%DA%A9%D9%84-%D9%84%D8%B4%DA%A9%D8%B1-21-%D8%AD%D9%85%D8%B2%D9%87-%D8%AA%D8%A7-%D8%AD%D8%B6%D9%88%D8%B1-%D8%AF%D8%B1-%D9%85%D9%86%D8%B7%D9%82%D9%87/ (dead link)
51 *Iraq/Iran Military Summary* CIA RDP81T00380R000100880001-6: https://www.cia.gov/readingroom/docs/CIA-RDP81T00380R000100880001-6.pdf and *Iraq/Iran Military Summary* CIA RDP80T01782R000300340001-7 https://www.cia.gov/readingroom/docs/CIA-RDP80T01782R000300340001-7.pdf
52 *Iraq/Iran Military Summary* CIA RDP81T00380R000100880001-6: https://www.cia.gov/readingroom/docs/CIA-RDP81T00380R000100880001-6.pdf and *Iraq/Iran Military Summary* CIA RDP80T01782R000300340001-7 https://www.cia.gov/readingroom/docs/CIA-RDP80T01782R000300340001-7.pdf
53 *Iraq/Iran Military Summary* CIA-RDP81T00380R000100390001-0 https://www.cia.gov/readingroom/docs/CIA-RDP81T00380R000100390001-0.pdf.
54 *The Memory of all the Martyrs, Veterans and Fighters of the 283 Battalion, Mahdi Bakhtiari*, https://twitter.com/Mahdiibakhtiari/status/1006222539545350145
55 *Foreign Relations of the United States 1964–1968, Volume XXII Iran*, http://nasser.bibalex.org/Data/USDocWeb/HTML/XXII-Iran%201964-1968/www.state.gov/www/about_state/history/vol_xxii/d.html
56 *Army out in Force in Streets of Tabriz*: https://www.britishpathe.com/video/VLVADWYUSIIPWYXA2P4XXFI6G4WAR-IRAN-ARMY-OUT-IN-FORCE-IN-STREETS-OF-TABRIZ-AFTER-SOME-SOLDIERS/query/iran
57 *Iraq/Iran Military Summary* CIA-RDP80T01782R000200260001-7: https://www.cia.gov/readingroom/docs/CIA-RDP80T01782R000200260001-7.pdf
58 *Troops Mark Armed Forces Day with Parade Through Streets of Tehran*: https://www.britishpathe.com/video/VLVAE63JNJD1GRB2PWN5ME1X2U4Q2-IRAN-TROOPS-MARK-ARMED-FORCES-DAY-WITH-PARADE-THROUGH-STREETS-OF/query/iran
59 *Martyr Hassan Tahmasebi Commander of 3rd Company 429th Battalion of 92nd Armored Division of Ahvaz, Colonel Shabrochi Shapur Shirdel*: http://mabarenoor.ir/memoirs/516-%D8%B4%D9%87%DB%8C%D8%AF-%D8%AD%D8%B3%D9%86-%D8%B7%D9%87%D9%85%D8%A7%D8%B3%D8%A8%DB%8C-%D9%81%D8%B1%D9%85%D8%A7%D9%86%D8%AF%D9%87-%DA%AF%D8%B1%D9%88%D9%87%D8%A7%D9%86-%D8%B3%D9%88%D9%85-%DA%AF%D8%AF%D8%B1%D8%A7%D9%86-429-%D9%85%D9%87%D9%86%D8%AF%D8%B3%DB%8C-%D8%AA%D8%AE%D8%B1%DB%8C-%D8%A8-%D9%84%D8%B4%DA%A9%D8%B1-92-%D8%B2%D8%B1%D9%87%DB%8C-%D8%A7%D9%87%D9%88%D8%A7%D8%B2.html
60 The role of combat engineering forces in combat operations: http://raza73.blogfa.com/post/1678
61 *Operation Jerusalem*: https://aja.ir/Portal/home/?news/65190/66445/65200/%D8%B9%D9%85%D9%84%D9%8A%D8%A7%D8%AA-%D8%A8%D9%8A%D8%AA-%D8%A7%D9%84%D9%85%D9%82%D8%AF%D8%B3 (dead link)
62 *The Fortresses that Forever Symbolises Resistance, Endurance and Courage*, http://kayhan.ir/fa/news/98765
63 *The Narration of the Only Surviving 'Fortress' of Khorramshahr from the Fall to Freedom*, https://www.fardanews.com/fa/news/525230/%D8%B1%D9%88%D8%A7%DB%8C%D8%AA-%D8%AA%D9%86%D9%87%D8%A7-%D8%A8%D8%A7%D8%B2%D9%85%D8%A7%D9%86%D8%AF%D9%87-%D8%AF%DA%98-%D8%AE%D8%B1%D9%85%D8%B4%D9%87%D8%B1-%D8%A7%D8%B2-%D8%B3%D9%82%D9%88%D8%B7-%D8%AA%D8%A7-%D8%A2%D8%B2%D8%A7%D8%AF%DB%8C
64 Editorial note: There remains some doubt as to the exact status of these older tank-types, with some anecdotal evidence that they were no longer operational and served only as decoys, albeit ones already well known as such to the Iraqis.
65 The following CIA report is typical, but the overall picture emerges when the reporting on the war is read as a whole. CIA *Iraq/Iran Military Summary*, RDP81T00380R000100880001-6 https://www.cia.gov/library/readingroom/docs/CIA-RDP81T00380R000100880001-6.pdf
66 Colonel Seyed Yaghoub Hosseini, *Operation Allah Akbar*: http://maarefjang.ir/uploaded/files/Books/Allah%20Akbar%20Operation_93-5-5.pdf
67 It is not stated in the source but it is probable that the over-strength comes from attached units that were not integral to the division.
68 A shortage of 120mm mortar ammunition and TOW missiles is also noted.
69 Bob Mackenzie, *The Rules of Infantry Combat*, http://bobmack3d.com/bob/Rules%20of%20Infantry%20Combat.htm

Appendix III

1 This is the official name of the Corps. Within Iran the organisation is almost universally referred to as the Sepah, 'the Corps'. Individual members are referred to as Pasdar, or Pasdaren in plural, which means guardians. Islamic Revolutionary Guard Corps, Wikipedia, https://en.wikipedia.org/wiki/Islamic_Revolutionary_Guard_Corps#Terminology
2 Holy Defense Documentation and Research Centre, *Investigating the Developments of the IRGC Combat Organization on the Eve of the Valfajr Operation*, https://web.archive.org/web/20181010154359/http://defamoghaddas.ir/fa/news/%D8%A8%D8%B1%D8%B1%D8%B3%DB%8C-%D8%B3%DB%8C%D8%B1-%D8%AA%D8%AD%D9%88%D9%84%D8%A7%D8%AA-%D8%B3%D8%A7%D8%B2%D9%85%D8%A7%D9%86-%D8%B1%D8%B2%D9%85-%D8%B3%D9%BE%D8%A7%D9%87-%D8%AF%D8%B1-%D8%A2%D8%B3%D8%AA%D8%A7%D9%86%D9%87-%D9%88%D8%A7%D9%84%D9%81%D8%AC%D8%B1-%D9%85%D9%82%D8%AF%D9%85%D8%A7%D8%AA%DB%8C

MIDDLE EAST@WAR SERIES SPECIAL #1: THE IRAN-IRAQ WAR

3 *17th Division of Ali ibn Abi Talib in Operation Badr, Nader Zarezadeh*, https://web.archive.org/web/20160807203338/http://www.negineiran.ir/article_4770.html

4 *A Pure Narration of the Operation of Imam Hussein's 14th Division in Karbala 5, Seyed Mohammad Ishaqi*, https://web.archive.org/web/20170715012019/http://negineiran.ir/article_5287.html

5 The reason for the duplicated battalion name is unclear from the source document.

6 Published small arms holdings for IRGC units are non-existent. These figures have been derived by the author by analysing the large number of group photos posted on the internet.

7 This is the designation used in the source document. Given the document reports in order of increasing calibre these are almost certainly 107mm B11 recoilless guns

8 This is how it is reported in the source document. The system is almost certainly an anti-tank missile as its sandwiched between the Sagger and the TOW. Sahand is the name of a volcano in Iran which provides no clues. Given there were limited types of missiles available to the Iranians the author believes these are probably Dragon missile launchers.

9 *Introduction and Formation of the 14th Division of Imam Hussein*, https://web.archive.org/web/20161118091158/http://www.lashkar14.ir/Page-7

10 'Operation Fath ol-Mobin', Wikipedia, https://en.wikipedia.org/wiki/Operation_Fath_ol-Mobin

11 Holy Defense Documentation and Research Center, *Report on the Performance of Nasr Camp in the Fatah al-Mubin, operation.* https://web.archive.org/web/20190330220432/http://defamoghaddas.ir/fa/quarterlyarticle/%DA%AF%D8%B2%D8%A7%D8%B1%D8%B4-%D8%B9%D9%85%D9%84%DA%A9%D8%B1%D8%AF-%D9%82%D8%B1%D8%A7%D8%B1%DA%AF%D8%A7%D9%87-%D9%86%D8%B5%D8%B1-%D8%AF%D8%B1-%D8%B9%D9%85%D9%84%DB%8C%D8%A7%D8%AA-%D9%81%D8%AA%D8%AD-%D8%A7%D9%84%D9%85%D8%A8%DB%8C%D9%86

12 A "base" or "camp" can be considered and ad-hoc Corps grouping of divisions and independent brigades.

13 http://defamoghaddas.ir/fa/news/عملیات-بنت-هی-متزواج (dead link)

14 Iran-Iraq War Study Group, https://www.facebook.com/groups/161471874272371/permalink/910348392718045/ . The diagrams on that page were taken from: https://web.archive.org/web/20160428045536if_/http://negineiran.ir/article_3499_8892e588d02a3a231b668af7d21bf3e4.pdf

15 *Haj Qasim and Command in the 41st Sarollah Division, Mohammad Reza Bakhtiari*, https://www.isna.ir/news/98101309348/%D8%AD%D8%A7%D8%AC-%D9%82%D8%A7%D8%B3%D9%85-%D9%88-%D9%81%D8%B1%D9%85%D8%A7%D9%86%D8%AF%D9%87%DB%8C-%D8%AF%D8%B1-%D9%84%D8%B4%DA%A9%D8%B1-%DB%B4%DB%B1-%D8%AB%D8%A7%D8%B1%D8%A7%D9%84%D9%84%D9%87

16 The was a 5th group, the 42nd Younis Group, but that was a coastal artillery 'beach' unit.

17 *The three riflemen traveled the hundred-year-old overnight, A narration of three teenage fighters of the 63rd Artillery Group of Khatam al-Anbiya, Haj Hamid Reza Sabbaghi*, https://www.javanonline.ir/fa/news/845809/%D8%A2%D9%86-3-%D8%AA%D9%81%D9%86%DA%AF%D8%AF%D8%A7%D8%B1-%D8%B1%D9%87-%D8%B5%D8%AF-%D8%B3%D8%A7%D9%84%D9%87-%D8%B1%D8%A7-%D9%8A%D9%83-%D8%B4%D8%A8%D9%87-%D8%B7%D9%8A-%D9%83%D8%B1%D8%AF%D9%86%D8%AF

18 41st Tharallah Division, Wikipedia, https://en.wikipedia.org/wiki/41st_Tharallah_Division

Appendix IV

1 Rachel Schmidt, *Global Arms Exports to Iraq, 1960–1990*, (RAND, 1990) https://www.rand.org/pubs/notes/N3248.html

2 British Defence Attaché Report 1980 – FCO 8/3715

3 British Defence Attaché Report 1977 – FCO 8/3020. The same table is repeated verbatim in the 1978 report.

4 Presumably the Soviet DshK.

5 There is no Soviet 20mm AA gun. May be a confusion with the ZU-23-2 or the ZPU-2

6 Includes 200 Czech 23mm guns.

7 Identified as 'M53' in original document.

8 Type and nation not noted but probably the Soviet 37mm M1939.

9 Noted as 50mm UK guns in the source document. As the UK never made a 50mm AA gun this is probably a typo for the 40mm Bofors, probably the WW2 vintage 40L60 version.

10 The author knows of no likely weapons that would fit this description.

11 Individual types not enumerated beyond the fact that some were Yugoslavian.

12 It is unclear to the author as to what this entry refers to. The only possible candidate is the 100mm version of the Belgian Blindicide

13 Type unspecified.

14 Probably a misidentification of the 240mm M240 mortar.

15 Presumably BRDM-1 but may include the 9P27 missile launching variant.

16 The 1980 report gives a combined total for BTR-50 and OT-62 as 820 vehicles.

17 The 1980 report gives a combined total for BTR-60 and OT-64 as 650 vehicles.

18 The 1980 report gives a combined total for the BTR-40 and BTR-152 as 885 vehicles.

19 The 1980 report gives a combined total for BTR-50 and OT-62 as 820 vehicles.

20 The 1980 report gives a combined total for BTR-60 and OT-64 as 650 vehicles.

21 In reserve.

22 Presumably a typo for TOPAS the Polish version of the OT-62.

23 There is no further evidence that any ERC-90 were delivered, however as there are no AML-90 on the list there may be some confusion as to the correct designation.

24 DIA, *Ground Order of Battle Iraq*, DDB-1100-IZ-81, March 1981.

25 Presumably DshK.

26 It is unclear if this is launchers or missiles. From the context it is likely launchers, although it is a rather large number for such.

27 Rather confusingly the source has an entry for 'Sagger on BMD' which gives a total of 650. The author presumes 'BMD' is a typo for 'BMP'. Although Iraq did use a few BMD they are not mentioned elsewhere in the document. Alternatively, SIPRI mentions delivery of BMDs to Iraq in 1981 (see below) so this figure may be a combined BMP and BMD total implying 30 BMDs in the inventory. This is remarkably close to the SIPRI total of 25.

28 Source only gives a combined total but other sources indicate the vast majority would have been BRDM-2.

29 Probably VCR/TH.

30 *Valedictory Report, Final review of the military situation in Iraq over the period August 1983 to April 1986 by the defence attaché to Her Britannic Majesty's Ambassador Baghdad*, 27/4/86: DEFE69/1709.

31 The original document shows Type 59, but that is certainly in error.

32 Defence Attaché's Report 1977: FCO 8/3020. Only ZPU-4 are mentioned.

33 *Oak Supplement Part 15 Kh-9 Mission 1204 11 October – 17 December 1972*: https://www.cia.gov/readingroom/docs/CIA-RDP78T04752A000200010008-7.pdf

34 *China-Iraq Arms Delivery Tuwwal Port Facilities, Saudi Arabia*, CIA, 1982. https://www.cia.gov/readingroom/docs/CIA-RDP90T00784R000100160008-0.pdf This is a snap shot in 1982 only.

35 *China-Iraq Arms Delivery Tuwwal Port Facilities, Saudi Arabia*, CIA, 1982. https://www.cia.gov/readingroom/docs/CIA-RDP90T00784R000100160008-0.pdf

36 Defence Attaché's report 1977: FCO 8/3020.

37 Major F Hobart, *Jane's Infantry Weapons* (1975). Although *Jane's* identifies it as an M37M the correct designation is BM-37M: https://en.wikipedia.org/wiki/82-BM-37

38 Major General Fawzi Barzanji, *The Operations of The Valiant Iraqi Army in 1974 – 1975 in Northern Iraq*, https://www.algardenia.com/terathwatareck/7196-1974-1975.html. Its possible first deliveries were a little earlier.

39 Defence Attaché's report 1977: FCO 8/3020.

40 Iraqi Armed Forces Forums, *Iraqi Army Mortars*, http://iraqimilitary.org/forums/viewtopic.php?f=6&t=364 and Major General Fawzi Barzanji, *The Battle of the East Tigris (Battle of the Crown of Battles) in March 1985*, https://www.algardenia.com/terathwatareck/6076-%20.%20%20%201985.html

41 *Persian Gulf 1975, the Continuing Debate on Arms Sales: Hearings Before the Special Subcommittee on Investigations of the Committee on International Relations, House of*

42 *Extremely Rare Iraqi 105mm L3A1 56 Pack Howitzer Chassis Plate* https://www.ebay.co.uk/itm/GULF-WAR-1-EXTREMELY-RARE-IRAQI-105mm-L3A1-56-PACK-HOWITZER-CHASSIS-PLATE-/193841799215 (Item no longer viewable)
43 *British Defence Attaché's Report 1980*: FCO 8/3715.
44 MFW shows the 'm1984' as a version of the 152mm Type 66. See http://www.china-defense.com/smf/index.php?topic=3774.0 for the link between the two systems.
45 *Persian Gulf 1975, the Continuing Debate on Arms Sales: Hearings Before the Special Subcommittee on Investigations of the Committee on International Relations, House of Representatives, Ninety-fourth Congress, First Session 1976*, https://books.google.co.uk/books?id=TzkmAAAAMAAJ&pg=PA51&lpg=PA51&#v=onepage&q&f=false
46 *British Defence Attaché's Report 1980*: FCO 8/3715.
47 CIA, *Recent Trends in Communist Economic and Military Aid to Iraq*, 1971: https://www.cia.gov/readingroom/docs/CIA-RDP85T00875R001700030031-3.pdf
48 *Iraq: UPDATE – Small Arms (Infantry Weapons) Used by the Anti-Coalition Insurgency*: https://wikileaks.cash/us-ngic-iraq-small-arms-2004.pdf
49 *Al Nasirah RPG7*: https://www.iwm.org.uk/collections/item/object/30029940
50 *Iraq: UPDATE – Small Arms (Infantry Weapons) Used by the Anti-Coalition Insurgency*: https://wikileaks.cash/us-ngic-iraq-small-arms-2004.pdf
51 *Iraq: UPDATE – Small Arms (Infantry Weapons) Used by the Anti-Coalition Insurgency*: https://wikileaks.cash/us-ngic-iraq-small-arms-2004.pdf
52 *British Defence Attaché's Report for 1980*: FCO 8/3715.
53 *Iraq: Refurbishment of Captured Chieftain Tanks*: DEFE68/650.
54 *Arming Saddam. The Supply of British Military Equipment to Iraq 1979 – 1990* https://caat.org.uk/wp-content/uploads/2020/11/1991-arming-saddam.pdf
55 Nick Dowson, *The MoD, The Arms Deal and a 30-Year-Old Bill for £400m*, https://www.independent.co.uk/news/uk/home-news/mod-arms-deal-and-30-year-old-bill-pound-400m-1952972.html
56 *UK arms sales to 'respectable' Iraq*: http://news.bbc.co.uk/1/hi/uk/7156645.stm
57 *Arming Saddam. The Supply of British Military Equipment to Iraq 1979 – 1990*, https://caat.org.uk/wp-content/uploads/2020/11/1991-arming-saddam.pdf
58 *British Defence Attaché's Report 1980*: FCO 8/3715. The author is sceptical of this number given the paucity of photographical evidence.
59 *Iraqi Armed Forces Forum, Before History Leaves Us*, http://iraqimilitary.org/forums/viewtopic.php?t=698
60 *Iraq: The Quest for US Arms*, CIA-RDP85T00287R001302340001-0 https://www.cia.gov/readingroom/docs/CIA-RDP85T00287R001302340001-0.pdf
61 *Defence Attaches Report*: FCO 8/3020.
62 *Iraq: UPDATE – Small Arms (Infantry Weapons) Used by the Anti-Coalition Insurgency*: https://wikileaks.cash/us-ngic-iraq-small-arms-2004.pdf
63 *Oak Supplement Part 15 Kh-9 Mission 1204 11 October – 17 December 1972*: https://www.cia.gov/readingroom/docs/CIA-RDP78T04752A000200010008-7.pdf
64 *British Defence Attaché's Report 1977*: FCO 8/3020. This is an inventory number so number delivered may have been higher.
65 *Iraq: UPDATE – Small Arms (Infantry Weapons) Used by the Anti-Coalition Insurgency*: https://wikileaks.cash/us-ngic-iraq-small-arms-2004.pdf
66 *British Defence Attaché's Report 1977*: FCO 8/3020.
67 How Switzerland obtained 5,000 RPGs is a mystery, the author suspects they were an intermediary.
68 *Oak Kh-9 Mission 1208-1 11-24 April 1974*: https://www.cia.gov/readingroom/docs/CIA-RDP78T04752A001500010003-8.pdf
69 *Oak Supplement Part 10 Kh-9 Mission 1205 10 March – 11 May 1973*: https://www.cia.gov/readingroom/docs/CIA-RDP78T04752A000500010010-1.pdf
70 *Valedictory Report, Final review of the military situation in Iraq over the period August 1983 to April 1986 by the defence attaché to Her Britannic Majesty's Ambassador Baghdad*, 27/4/86: DEFE69/1709
71 *2003 Baghdad DHL Attempted Shootdown Incident*, https://en.wikipedia.org/wiki/2003_Baghdad_DHL_attempted_shootdown_incident
72 Army of Iraq Facebook group: https://www.facebook.com/groups/2284947011788598/posts/3030587840557841/ at least one battalion (numbered 28th) was formed circa 1982.
73 The Bagdad Arms Fair was conceived to sell off weapons used and developed during the war: Iraqi Armed Forces Forum, Military Industrialization Exhibition 1989, http://iraqimilitary.org/forums/viewtopic.php?f=25&t=293&start=30
74 *Iraq: The Quest for US Arms* https://www.cia.gov/readingroom/docs/CIA-RDP85T00287R001302340001-0.pdf
75 *Valedictory Report, Final review of the military situation in Iraq over the period August 1983 to April 1986 by the defence attaché to Her Britannic Majesty's Ambassador Baghdad*, 27/4/86: DEFE69/1709.
76 *Iraqi Military Activity in The Kurdistan Region of Iraq: CIA 1972*: https://www.cia.gov/readingroom/docs/CIA-RDP78T05162A000300010013-4.pdf .
77 *Iraqi Armed Forces Forum, Anti-Armour Guided Missiles in the Iraqi Army*, http://iraqimilitary.org/forums/viewtopic.php?f=6&t=391
78 *Valedictory Report, Final review of the military situation in Iraq over the period August 1983 to April 1986 by the defence attaché to Her Britannic Majesty's Ambassador Baghdad*, 27/4/86: DEFE69/1709.
79 *Valedictory Report, Final review of the military situation in Iraq over the period August 1983 to April 1986 by the defence attaché to Her Britannic Majesty's Ambassador Baghdad*, 27/4/86: DEFE69/1709. Shown as "SP AAA" in the source document, but there is no candidate other than the ZSU-23-4.
80 CIA, *Exports of Communist Military Equipment to The Less Developed Countries: A Catalogue of Prices* (1970): https://www.cia.gov/readingroom/docs/CIA-RDP79S01091A000200030011-5.pdf
81 *List of Military Trucks*: https://en.wikipedia.org/wiki/List_of_military_trucks
82 *List of Military Trucks*: https://en.wikipedia.org/wiki/List_of_military_trucks
83 300 were sold in July 85. *Arming Saddam. The Supply of British Military Equipment to Iraq 1979 – 1990*: https://caat.org.uk/wp-content/uploads/2020/11/1991-arming-saddam.pdf
84 *Scania SBA111*: https://en.wikipedia.org/wiki/Scania_SBA111
85 Martin Smisek, *Czechoslovak Arms Exports*. 80 delivered between 1970 and 1971.
86 CIA, *Iran/Iraq Military Summary*, CIA-RDP80T01782R000200400001-1, https://www.cia.gov/readingroom/docs/CIA-RDP80T01782R000200400001-1.pdf
87 CIA, *Iran/Iraq Military Summary*, CIA-RDP80T01782R000200400001-1, https://www.cia.gov/readingroom/docs/CIA-RDP80T01782R000200400001-1.pdf
88 Martin Smisek, *Czechoslovak Arms Exports*. 140 delivered between 1973 and 1974.
89 *Iraq: UPDATE – Small Arms (Infantry Weapons) Used by the Anti-Coalition Insurgency*: https://wikileaks.cash/us-ngic-iraq-small-arms-2004.pdf
90 Vladimir Onokoy, *The History of the Iraqi AK Tabuk Rifle*: https://www.recoilweb.com/the-history-of-the-iraqi-tabuk-ak-rifle-156496.html
91 *Al Quds*, https://guns.fandom.com/wiki/Al_Quds
92 Iraq purchased "tens of thousands", *In Those Years, The Complete Set of Weapons and Equipment Imported by Iran and Iran from my Country*, https://new.qq.com/omn/20200922/20200922A0DB4900.html
93 *Army of Iraq* Facebook page: www.facebook.com/groups/2284947011788598/permalink/2977049545911671
94 *Tabuk Sniper Rifle*: https://en.wikipedia.org/wiki/Tabuk_Sniper_Rifle. The sniper rifle and the standard assault rifle both have the same name. The in-service date in the reference is given as 1978. Most other sources indicated production did not start until 1980.

Appendix V

1 The Order of Battle is taken from the following documents. The first two documents are the primary references: DIA, *Ground Order of Battle Iraq* DDB-1100-IZ-81, date 20 March 1981; Colonel Ahmad Ahmadi, *Iraqi Army from September 1980 to June 1983*, p.158 onwards; CIA, *Ground Force Mobilization, Iraq/Iran*, https://www.cia.gov/readingroom/docs/

MIDDLE EAST@WAR SERIES SPECIAL #1: THE IRAN-IRAQ WAR

CIA-RDP81T00380R000100480001-0.pdf; Iraqi Army Formations, Iraqi Armed Forces Forums, http://iraqimilitary.org/forums/viewtopic.php?f=6&t=388; Colonel Sayed Yaqub Hosseini, *Military history of the Imposed War until 31st of September 1980 (Volume 2) Pre-war border clashes*, http://maarefjang.ir/uploaded/files/Books/Tarikh%20nezami_J2.pdf; Malovany, *Wars of Modern Babylon*.

2. The independent battalions are only mentioned in Iranian sources. However, they are not mentioned in the same source in the table containing the list of infantry formations, so their presence must be considered as unconfirmed.
3. US sources show the tank battalion as the 2nd with the possible of attachment of the 7th Tank Battalion too.
4. Type not given but almost certainly M-30 or D-30
5. US sources show the 16th and 22nd Field Artillery Battalions with the 22nd equipped with 25-pdr.
6. Not shown in US sources.
7. US sources show 14 companies.
8. Exact type not specified.
9. US sources show the 29th as a mechanised brigade with three mechanised battalions and a tank battalion.
10. The independent battalions are only mentioned in Iranian sources. However, they are not mentioned in the same source in the table containing the list of infantry formations, so their presence must be considered as unconfirmed.
11. US sources show the 37th Battalion instead of the 22nd. It is denoted as using 25-pdr.
12. AA battalion not shown in Iranian sources only in US intelligence, however their presence is highly likely.
13. Possibly some old British 4.2" mortars were still in use but more likely US M30 107mm.
14. US sources show the 39th AT Battalion.
15. 19th Brigade is noted as 'motorised' in Iranian source documents. US sources show the 28th and 40th Brigades attached to the division and the 166th Border Guard Brigade.
16. US sources show the 7th and 9th Tank battalions.
17. US sources show the 10th, 64th, 65th and 80th Artillery Battalions. The armament of the 80th is not show the others have 122mm likely either M-30 or D-30.
18. US sources show the 58th battalion armed with 30mm instead.
19. US sources additionally show the 95th and 97th Reserve Infantry Brigades attached each with 6 reserve infantry battalions.
20. US sources show this as the 9th Tank Battalion.
21. Both the 8th and 11th divisions are listed as having a 6th Artillery Battalion. This is likely a typo in the source document. Unusually sources agree on the numbering of the artillery battalions excepting the 83rd which appears in Iranian documents but not US documents.
22. US sources only show a single company.
23. US sources show the 47th, 48th and 49th Border Guard Brigades, but this is likely in error as most other sources show the brigades as the 44th, 45th & 48th.
24. US sources only show a single divisional tank battalion. They do not give a battalion number or name.
25. US sources also show three mortar batteries
26. US sources do not show the 12th as an armoured divisions but show it previous organisation as an infantry division.
27. US sources show 93rd and 96th Reserve Infantry Brigades attached.
28. Tank battalions have both names and numbers but only rarely do sources have both pieces of information. The spelling of names should be taken as indicative only. There are multiple ways of transliterating Arabic names to English (https://en.wikipedia.org/wiki/Romanization_of_Arabic) and the source documents do not indicate which was used. Furthermore, many of the names presented have been transliterated to Persian first and then to English. To further compound the reporting issue the printing and scanning of US intelligence documents available to the author is of poor quality.
29. US sources only show 15th, 19th 20th and 21st Artillery Battalions, the 20th is shown as an SP battalion. They also show the 7th Mortar Battery.
30. CIA, *Iraq/Iran Military Summary 18-23 September 1980*: https://www.cia.gov/readingroom/document/cia-rdp80t01782r000100560001-5
31. US show in addition a 31st AA Battalion with 57mm S-60.
32. Iranian sources only show two batteries and do give numbers for them.
33. Not shown in US sources.
34. Not shown in US sources.
35. Not shown in US sources.
36. US sources show the 94th Reserve Infantry Brigade attached
37. US sources show 25th, 33rd, 50th and 52nd Artillery Battalions. 50th with 122mm, 52nd with 130mm and the 33rd Self-propelled. The 10th Mortar Battery is also shown with 120mm mortars.
38. US source also show the 41st AA Battalion equipped with 37mm.
39. US sources show the 6th and Walid battalions as two separate units.
40. Not shown in US sources. It is unclear in the Iranian source what a 'defence battalion' is.
41. Both US and Iranian sources agree the two battalions had the same name.
42. US sources denote this battalion as Al Hamad.
43. US sources show the 35th Tank Brigade, but this is likely in error as other sources agree on the 42nd.
44. Iranian sources show three battalions, US sources show six.
45. US sources only show three battalions. Only the 49th is identified. One of the unidentified battalions is labelled as self-propelled.
46. US sources show the AA Battalion as the 60th.
47. There were four total AA and AT companies. The source document does not specify how many of each type. These are not shown by US forces.
48. Not shown by US sources.
49. Not shown in US sources. Not numbered in Iranian sources.
50. Not shown by US sources.
51. US sources show 21st Infantry Brigade, 91st Reserve Infantry and 98th Reserve Infantry Brigades attached. The 98th is only shown with a single battalion. Iranian sources show the 51st Armoured Brigade attached with the 3rd, 29th and Abu Amdieh Tank Battalions plus the 5th Mechanised Brigade.
52. US sources show this as the 4th Tank Battalion.
53. As reported by Iranian sources. US sources seem uncertain about the names giving several suggestions for each battalion. There is only one overlapping name with Iranian sources: Cordoba. Unfortunately, neither source gives numbers.
54. US sources show only three battalions one of which is self-propelled. One of the towed battalions is listed as the 49th the numbers of the others are listed as unknown.
55. US sources give the 1st and 28th Battalions 152mm ML-20 and the 8th 130mm M-46.
56. Not shown by US sources.
57. US sources show the 230th AA Battalion which is equipped with 37mm AA.
58. US sources show the 92nd Reserve Infantry Battalion attached. Iranian sources show the 55th Armoured Brigade attached with 1st, 27th and Zinalqous Tank Battalions and 2nd Mechanised Battalion.
59. Not shown by Iranian sources.
60. Not shown by Iranian sources.
61. US sources show Wahdah instead of Hassan.
62. US sources show the 7th, 18th and 40th artillery battalions with the 8th having 122mm Howitzers.
63. US sources show the 17th, 25th, 29th and 39th AA Battalions with the 29th equipped with 37mm, they also show the 46th AA Battery.
64. Not shown by US sources.
65. US sources spell this Janin.
66. US sources show the 42nd and 43rd brigades but this is likely in error as most other sources show the 35th and 43rd.
67. Iranian sources do not show the Hawlah battalion.
68. US sources show the 30th and two other artillery battalions with unknown numbers. In addition, they show the 2nd Mortar Battery.
69. It is not clear what these guns are. The best candidate is the British 4.5" Gun which has a calibre of 114mm. Iraq had eight in service in 1953.
70. US sources do not show any AA or SAM battalions.
71. The 33rd Brigade was organised marine brigade according to Iranian sources (*Iraqi Army Formations*, Iraqi Armed Forces Forum, http://iraqimilitary.org/forums/viewtopic.php?f=6&t=388&start=120#p25374) Supporting units were probably similar to the 31st and 32nd.
72. Presumably had the 7th, 8th and 9th Commando Battalions.
73. Not shown by US sources There was possibly an AT and Engineer company in this unit.
74. Although not given in the source documents its likely this had 105mm OTO Melara.
75. Although not given in the source documents its likely this had 120mm AM50 mortar.

76 Iranian sources show a 125th SAM Brigade with a mixture of SA-2 and SA-3. However, no other sources mention this unit.
77 One of the batteries was numbered the 36th. From *The Lessons of the Battle – The Effort and Hardships of War – from the Eight-Year War*, Arabic Army Forum, https://arabic-military-army.yoo7.com/t7137-topic
78 US sources do not detail the independent battalions.
79 *Iraqi Army Formations*, Iraqi Armed Forces Forums, http://iraqimilitary.org/forums/viewtopic.php?f=6&t=388; US Intelligence shows this unit organised as a mechanised brigade.
80 Major General Mahmoud Shukr Shahni, *From Field Command to Intelligence Command in The War, Secret and Memories 1980 -1988*, https://ia800105.us.archive.org/18/items/awraq_jondi_iraqi/awraq_jondi_iraqi.pdf
81 *Army of Iraq*, https://www.facebook.com/groups/2284947011788598/posts/3029080257375266/?comment_id=3032883233661635&reply_comment_id=3034062086877083
82 Colonel Sayed Yaqub Hosseini, *Military history of the Imposed War until 31st of September 1980 (Volume 2) Pre-war border clashes*, http://maarefjang.ir/uploaded/files/Books/Tarikh%20nezami_J2.pdf
83 DIA, *Ground Order of Battle Iraq*, DDB-1100-IZ-81, 20 March 1981.
84 National Training Centre, *THE IRAQI ARMY Organization and Tactics, National Training Centre Handbook 100-91*, 3 January 1991. It is possible there were some changes between the end of the Iran and Iraq war and 1991, but the author judges the organisation is very likely correct.
85 *Valedictory Report, Final review of the military situation in Iraq over the period August 1983 to April 1986 by the defence attaché to Her Britannic Majesty's Ambassador Baghdad*, 27/4/86: DEFE69/1709.
86 Colonel Sayed Yaqub Hosseini, *Military history of the Imposed War until 31st of September 1980 (Volume 2) Pre-war border clashes*, http://maarefjang.ir/uploaded/files/Books/Tarikh%20nezami_J2.pdf
87 DIA, *Ground Order of Battle Iraq*, DDB-1100-IZ-81, March 1981.
88 National Training Centre, *THE IRAQI ARMY Organization and Tactics, National Training Centre Handbook 100-91*, 3 January 1991.
89 *Iraqi Army Formations*, Iraqi Army Forums, http://iraqimilitary.org/forums/viewtopic.php?f=6&t=388&start=15
90 *Army of Iraq*, https://www.facebook.com/groups/2284947011788598/permalink/2974338282849464/
91 *Valedictory Report, Final review of the military situation in Iraq over the period August 1983 to April 1986 by the defence attaché to Her Britannic Majesty's Ambassador Baghdad*, 27/4/86: DEFE69/1709.
92 DIA, *Military Intelligence Summary, Volume III Part II, Middle East and North Africa (Persian Gulf)*, DDB-2680-103-88 Part II July 1 1987.
93 Details from *Army of Iraq*, https://www.facebook.com/groups/2284947011788598/permalink/2977049545911671 used to allocate APCs to the organisation. The BMP numbers are probably BMPs only. It is very probable there were five other APCs (command and engineer) to bringing the overall total to 47.
94 *Valedictory Report, Final review of the military situation in Iraq over the period August 1983 to April 1986 by the defence attaché to Her Britannic Majesty's Ambassador Baghdad*, 27/4/86: DEFE69/1709.
95 DIA, *Military Intelligence Summary, Volume III Part II, Middle East and North Africa (Persian Gulf)*, DDB-2680-103-88 Part II July 1 1987.
96 Details from *Army of Iraq*, https://www.facebook.com/groups/2284947011788598/permalink/2977049545911671 used to allocate APCs to the organisation.
97 *Army of Iraq*, https://www.facebook.com/groups/2284947011788598/posts/3029080257375266/
98 Calculations by the author show that the inventory of heavy weapons was only sufficient to equip the regular infantry battalions and mechanised battalions.
99 DIA, Ground Order of Battle Iraq, DDB-1100-IZ-81 March 1981.
100 DIA, Ground Order of Battle Iraq, DDB-1100-IZ-81 March 1981.
101 DIA, Ground Order of Battle Iraq, DDB-1100-IZ-81 March 1981.
102 *Valedictory Report, Final review of the military situation in Iraq over the period August 1983 to April 1986 by the defence attaché to Her Britannic Majesty's Ambassador Baghdad*, 27/4/86: DEFE69/1709. The tanks may have been PT-76s, there were certainly enough in the Iraqi inventory to equip all the divisions. However, it is curious they do not appear in the early war organisation.
103 DIA, *Military Intelligence Summary, Volume III Part II, Middle East and North Africa (Persian Gulf)*, DDB-2680-103-88 Part II July 1 1987.
104 DIA, Ground Order of Battle Iraq, DDB-1100-IZ-81 March 1981.
105 *Iraqi Army Formations*, Iraqi Army Forums, http://iraqimilitary.org/forums/viewtopic.php?f=6&t=391
106 National Training Centre, *THE IRAQI ARMY Organization and Tactics, National Training Centre Handbook 100-91*, 3 January 1991.
107 National Training Centre, *THE IRAQI ARMY Organization and Tactics, National Training Centre Handbook 100-91*, 3 January 1991.
108 Bob Mackenzie, *The Rules of Infantry Combat*, http://bobmack3d.com/bob/Rules%20of%20Infantry%20Combat.htm#1a
109 Razoux, *The Iran Iraq War*. Estimates of strength vary, in 1987 the US DAI reported a strength of c 850000 men.
110 Malovany, *Wars of Modern Babylon*.
111 *Iraqi Army Formations*, Iraqi Army Forums, http://iraqimilitary.org/forums/viewtopic.php?f=6&t=388&sid=7d6efe71dc3b83b55530af35a40da4bb&start=15#p1752
112 *Iraqi Army Formations*, Iraqi Army Forums, http://iraqimilitary.org/forums/viewtopic.php?f=6&t=388&start=90#p1902
113 *Iraqi Army Formations*, Iraqi Army Forums, http://iraqimilitary.org/forums/viewtopic.php?f=6&t=388&start=30
114 These are known changes and may not be exhaustive.
115 Had two tank battalions and an infantry battalion.
116 18th Brigade was transferred from the 4th infantry division. In 1984 the 18th Brigade had Chinese Type 71 100mm mortars in its battalion mortar batteries. Major General Fawzi Al-Barzanji, *My experience leading an infantry brigade in wartime*, https://www.algardenia.com/terathwatareck/5954-2013-08-18-20-16-14.html
117 The 44th brigade was transferred from the 11th Infantry Division.
118 Formed as a replacement for the disbanded 9th Armoured Division.
119 This had changed by the end of the war to the 423rd, 430th and 706th Brigades.
120 The 33rd was converted from a special forces brigade to infantry in 1982.
121 One source shows the 32nd Infantry Brigade.
122 The 433rd Infantry Brigade was originally the 31st Special Forces Brigade. It was converted to infantry in 1982.